Information Technology and Societal Development

Andrew Targowski
Western Michigan University, USA

 **INFORMATION SCIENCE REFERENCE**

Hershey · New York

Director of Editorial Content:	Kristin Klinger
Director of Production:	Jennifer Neidig
Managing Editor:	Jamie Snavely
Assistant Managing Editor:	Carole Coulson
Typesetter:	Bonnie Walker
Cover Design:	Lisa Tosheff
Printed at:	Yurchak Printing Inc.

Published in the United States of America by
Information Science Reference (an imprint of IGI Global)
701 E. Chocolate Avenue, Suite 200
Hershey PA 17033
Tel: 717-533-8845
Fax: 717-533-8661
E-mail: cust@igi-global.com
Web site: http://www.igi-global.com

and in the United Kingdom by
Information Science Reference (an imprint of IGI Global)
3 Henrietta Street
Covent Garden
London WC2E 8LU
Tel: 44 20 7240 0856
Fax: 44 20 7379 0609
Web site: http://www.eurospanbookstore.com

Targowski, Andrzej.

Information technology and societal development / Andrew Targowski.

  p. cm.

Includes bibliographical references and index.

Summary: "This book investigates the role of information and communication in civilization's development, because it is information and communication that decide how human organization, knowledge, and wisdom are applied in decisions impacting human survival"-- Provided by publisher.

ISBN 978-1-60566-004-2 (hardcover) -- ISBN 978-1-60566-005-9 (ebook)

1. Information technology--Social aspects. 2. Communication--Social aspects. 3. Technology--Social aspects. 4. Information society. I. Title.

HM851.T375 2008

303.48'330112--dc22

                    2008010311

British Cataloguing in Publication Data
A Cataloguing in Publication record for this book is available from the British Library.

All work contributed to this book set is original material. The views expressed in this book are those of the authors, but not necessarily of the publisher.

Table of Contents

Section III
The Information Ecology of Civilization

Section IV
Modeling of Civilization

Section V
The Future of Civilization

Preface

The purpose of this book is to evaluate the questions: Is civilization developing for the benefit of humankind? What is civilization's future? To answer these questions, we must investigate the role of information and communication (under the form of information-communication technology [ICT]) in civilization's development, because it is information and communication that decide how human organization, knowledge, and wisdom are applied in decisions impacting human survival.

This book is written for a broad audience of academics, students, professionals, and those people who are interested in how information and communication and, later, information-communication technology (ICT) played a role in the development of civilization and what is its current state and future. In the 20th and 21st centuries, the ICT professionals are the main developers of civilization, which has been transforming from developing to developed or even overdeveloped in some regions. Therefore, it is very important, particularly for ICT professionals, to be aware how and why to develop certain ICT systems in order to avoid harm to individuals, society and civilization. Also users, managers/executives and politicians should be aware of the same issues in respect to their environments and in the broader context of civilization.

A concept of information has many dimensions, which are addressed in this book; however, one can state that from the users' points of view, they deal with information as the end product. But this end product is shaped by different kinds of information technology, for example, such ones as alphabet, books, newspapers, journals, files, databases, data warehouses and data retrieval and mining, with either by manual effort or recently with the help of computers. The latter is called in the U.S. "information technology" (IT) and in Europe "informatics" (automated information). Furthermore, with the intensive applications of computer networks, the Internet, e-mail and so forth have transformed our humanity to an e-communicating species. Hence the classic IT has been transformed into information-communication technology (ICT). The role of IT and ICT is specifically supporting our civilization in many positive aspects as well as also conquering civilization in many negative ways. This book analyzes these aspects and exposures mostly at the big-picture level, preferring rather synthesis than analysis to better grasp overall concepts, problems and solutions.

An interdisciplinary, holistic method is applied to investigate civilization's complexity with the help of graphic-cybernetic modeling (a tool of ICT). This allows for the inclusion of known macro-structures, large-scale processes, and their relationships to universalize their dynamics.

The reason for this approach is to conduct huge comparisons of big structures and large processes in their totality, leading to variation-finding[1] and universal rules or eventual laws. In such a way, perhaps individual ontology will be more understandable and some answers can be defined for the questions raised above. This book is based on the model of macrostructures and processes leading to their synthesis, which is shown in Figure I.

Civilization is about 6,000 years old, which in comparison to the age of the Earth, 4.5 billion years, is rather a fresh endeavor. Its solutions are very spectacular but may lead to the overpopulation and

Figure 1. The model of marcostructures and info-communication-driven processes leading to their synthesis

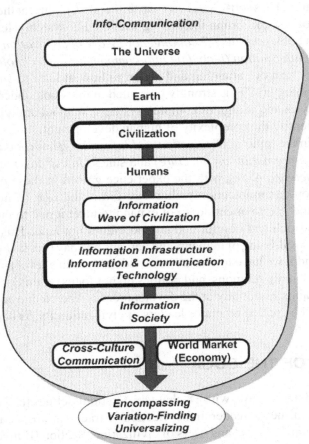

depletion of strategic resources. Therefore, we call it Civilization I, since if we do not change our life style, this civilization can fall apart in the third millennium. Perhaps future civilizations (II, III, n) may follow the patterns of the present one.

Robert Denes (former Eaton executive) suggests that my arguments remind him of *Plato's Republic* ruled by wise people, but this republic does not work in practice, since Denes believes in a free spirit in man, who successfully traveled from primitive ancestry to modernity and thinks he/she will continue on for a long time to come. I am not so optimistic and at least offer here a shift from current *"paranoia"* to future *"metanoia"* (defined by Leszek Koakowski[2]) which emphasizes human wisdom and willingness to change.

This book proposes that in order to ensure the well-being of humankind on Earth, the global civilization should transform into a universal-complementary civilization, based on dialogue, universal values, and self-sustainability, acceptable by all religion-driven (autonomous) civilizations. Otherwise, in the not-too-distant future, humans may be forced to emigrate to other planets, which due to the high cost and practical impossibility of traveling faster than the speed of light, will likely remain in the realm of science fiction. On the other hand, in the very long term, humankind must look beyond even the Solar

System, since the Sun will stop or change the radiating pattern within a few billion years, very probably destroying life on our planet.

Although Civilization I has self-organizing capabilities[3], in reality, at the beginning of the 21st century, it enters into a stage of disequilibrium interacting with the Ecosystem. Hence, the future of Civilization I is rather bleak. This book presents *the contingency theory of civilization (as a product of social development) based on the information (including info-communication technology) handling and processing approach,* which may turn our attention and action to how at least to survive on Earth. Information-communication technology (ICT) is strongly presented in this book under a form of graphic modeling, a tool of system analysis and design of complex systems. Without applying this kind of tool, it would be very difficult to identify the complexity of human development.

My involvement in the topic of *Civilization and Information* has roots in my work on the informatization of enterprises (*information architecture*) and states (*Infostrada[4]*) and *local, national and global information infrastructures.* Along with the experience gained in these projects, I noticed that overly aggressive information-communication technology limits the role of humans in civilization. When populations expand and employment does not expand to meet it due to increased productivity, the gap between informed and rich and uninformed and poor does not fade. This type of "wild" greed-driven progress threatens the well-being of humans, and perhaps one day (yet far away) we may call for the "end of progress?" To avoid it we have to elevate our wisdom to such a level as can save the Human Project. So far, the wealthy (money), religions, and politics do not focus on this issue, which is also analyzed in this book. This book aims essentially at the development of knowledge and wisdom about civilization, which eventually can be applied by major leaders of civilization for its benefits.

ORGANIZATION OF THE BOOK

The book is organized in five parts with 18 chapters. SectionI defines the basic concepts of civilization, which are applied in further considerations. Section II traces the roots and developmental issues of humans, who are the main creators and users of civilization. Section III investigates the role of information-communication processes and systems functioning in civilization, which are the dominant factors in knowledge and wisdom development and which determine the fate of civilization. Section IV applies some systemic-cybernetic techniques in modeling communication and economic processes, which are basic to civilization. Lastly, Section V investigates the future of civilization on the Earth and beyond, providing a comprehensive architecture of the Universe, which integrates material and information-communication processes.

Chapter I defines the civilization grand model based on a critique of existing approaches and the history of civilization development. This model is presented as a cybernetic model, which is dynamic and system-oriented with three major components: human entities, culture, and infrastructure. This kind of identification of components allows for the comparative investigation of civilizations' patterns of behavior, leading to the recognition of grand laws of civilization, which govern the world and planet civilizations. These two kinds of civilizations are synthesized at the level of their major components and their relations.

Chapter II investigates why a civilization rises and falls. The majority of the chapter addresses these processes. The answer is provided under a form of the generic civilization life-cycle. As a result of this investigation, a concept of wave-driven civilization life-cycle is provided and its current and future implementations are offered.

Chapter III compares current civilizations' development level and its consequences for the current state of the world affairs. Some strategies of how to cope with civilization conflicts in the 21st century are defined. Also, some challenges that humans must cope with in order to make sure civilization functions and develops competently are defined.

Chapter IV investigates the phenomenon of humans on the Earth. What kind of factors determined our evolution from animals into humans? The investigation is limited to the information-communication processes (symbol processing), which triggered the human brain. These processes are recognized as the main ones which led to human beings, the pioneers and developers of civilization.

Chapter V concentrates on wisdom as the highest unit of cognition, which determines the well-being of humans and their civilization. Some suggestions of how to combine philosophical approaches to wisdom are presented in order to be wisely in charge of civilization challenges. Eventually, a model of multi-layered existence in the advanced civilization is defined in order to explain the kind of challenges that lie in front of people for handling life in a world that communicates across cultures.

Chapter VI investigates the issue of whether humans are wise enough to rightly control civilization operations and development. After some comparative analysis of different philosophies' approaches (western and Asian mostly) to wisdom, the answer is that humans are not wise enough to meet the current civilization problems. The difficulty is in our partial approach to the investigation of theoretical knowledge, including philosophy itself. A solution under the form of the Wisdom Diamond is offered and its applications in other sciences are discussed.

Chapter VII investigates the emergence of global civilization in the 21st century and concludes that it is just a solution very convenient for big business, driven by greed. This civilization is not stoppable but should be controlled by the new civilization layer, which should be common and complementary-values-driven. This new solution is called the Universal-Complementary Civilization, which should be a product of agreement of all people who live and share the same planet, which, perhaps, can be called the Rainbow Planet. This new civilization, if developed rightly, should minimize conflicts and wars, since it should build tolerance in all of us from our childhood.

Chapter VIII develops the theory of critical total history of civilization. In order to wisely control civilization, its developers and users must understand the history of civilization. So far, it is mostly based on lengthy narratives and lost in many less important details. This theory emphasizes the critical issues of the civilization's total history and differentiates them from peripheral issues secondary for the well-being of civilization. Eventually, grand laws of western civilization are defined to provide examples of how to investigate other civilizations.

Chapter IX investigates civilization in terms of the current information wave. First, the role of information in civilization history is analyzed. The invention and application of printing (15th century) had a very strong impact on the development of intellectual, political and commercial revolutions, which led to the rise of the information wave, exemplified by the application of millions of computers and their networks embracing the globe in the 21st century. This wave is characterized in its mission, goals, and strategy as well as in ideology, which should be taken into consideration when information systems and services are designed and operated.

Chapter X defines what is information in terms of quantitative, qualitative, cognitive, computer, decision-making, and managerial perspectives. Furthermore, information images are analyzed as resource, system, mind, communication, synchronism, superhighway, power, and art. This kind of approach is important for correct design and operation of information systems, services, and infrastructure. Therefore, a case of enterprise information infrastructure is analyzed and its generic model is presented. As a result of these considerations, the informated architecture of management and a concept of how to informate the industrial enterprise are provided. The latter is important for the practice of transforming old industrial endeavors into new informated enterprises.

Chapter XI defines generic service processes and their systems within six kinds. Four criteria, which impact e-service systems' architecture, have been defined as: service business model, customer contact and level of involvement (service user interface), service provider's enterprise complexity (enterprise systems and networks), and scope of goods involved in service. Based on the nature of presented service systems, a scope of service science has been defined. Also, its developmental and innovation strategy has been defined based upon six stages of service systems developments and the three laws of service systems. In conclusion, seven recommendations are offered for the further development of service science.

Chapter XII defines the information laws, which govern our cognitive development and based on it, our functioning in civilization. Four such laws are defined. These laws should be applied in all our information-driven undertakings.

Chapter XIII investigates the birth of the electronic global village and its composition under a form of a generic architecture. Based on this approach, the architectures of several kinds of informated organizations are defined. Also, major components of contemporary civilization such as global economy, global culture, electronic culture, and eventually electronic global citizenship are also defined.

Chapter XIV traces the evolution of an information society, which has several distinctive implementations, affected by the availability of information-communication tools. Some paradigms and key indicators are defined in order to better measure the impact of such societies on civilization.

Chapter XV models a process of asymmetric communications between different civilizations. A case of interaction of American and Egyptian culture is taken to show how cross-culture communication can be analyzed in terms of quantitative indicators. As a result of this case, five rules of this kind of communication are defined.

Chapter XVI models the markets from the civilization point of view. This approach perceives the economic integration of some areas of the world along the civilization lines. The question of whether China will dominate the world market is analyzed and the answer is that the western civilization will respond with its own integration under a form of transatlantic free trade zone. This trade zone will be formed by the U.S. and the E.U. and should dominate world trade. The future of capitalism is also addressed. What kind of capitalism or other economic system must be applied in order to keep the world population within the threshold of the Ecosystem is analyzed. The answer to this question will determine the future of civilization.

Chapter XVII synthesizes the issues impacting the future of civilization. Three bombs, population (P), ecological (E) and depletion of strategic resources (R), will lead in the near future (about the year 2050) to the death triangle of Civilization I and perhaps to the next generation of civilization. Different factors and strategies are offered in order to slow down or eventually prevent the decline of Civilization I.

Chapter XVIII defines the informated architecture of the Universe. So far, the physicists investigate the Universe with their classic matter-oriented techniques, which were available in the 20th century. However, the information wave of the 21st century brings in the importance of information-communication processes which "activate" matter and its relations with the environment. This approach is offered in this chapter; however, the complexity of a new model of the Universe is still too big for our tools to solve its puzzle.

ENDNOTES

[1] Tilly, Charles. (1984) inspired me by providing the insight to these kinds of issues in his book *Big structures, large processes, huge comparisons.* New York, NY: Russell Sage Foundation.

[2] Editorial. (2004). The award of the first John w. Kluge Prize for lifetime achievement in the human sciences to Leszek Kolakowski. *Dialogue and Universalism, XIV,* 3-6.

[3] The biologists call these autopoietic systems.

[4] Targowski, A. (2007). The genesis, political, and economic sides of the Internet. In: L. Tomei (Ed.), *Integrating information & communications technologies into the classroom,* (pp.62-82). Hershey, PA: Information Science Publishing.

Acknowledgment

I am grateful to Professor Mattew Melko (Wright State University), a pioneer of the study on civilization and one of the former presidents of the International Society for the Comparative Study of Civilizations (ISCSC); to Professor Wayne M. Bledsoe (University of Missouri-Rolla), a former president of the ISCSC; to Professor Michael Pitchard, a philosopher (Western Michigan University); to Dr. Teresa Kubiak, a molecular biologists (Pfizer), and to Professor Andrzej Walczak, a physicist (Military Technical Academy in Warsaw), for reading my manuscript and providing very important comments, which led to some improvements of the presented solutions.

I am thankful to Professor Janusz Kuczynski (Warsaw University), a founder and the honorary president of the International Society for Universalism ([ISU] now for Universal Dialogue [ISUD]), for introducing me to his great philosophical ideas of dialogue and universalism. Also, I would like to thank very much John K. Hord, an accomplished researcher on civilization and Dr. Thomas Rienzo from Western Michigan University and Marie Rienzo from Michigan State University for looking through and commenting upon my manuscript, limiting its errors, and making it more understandable.

Andrew Targowski
Kalamazoo, Michigan, USA, 2008

Section I
Structures of Civilization

Chapter I
The Civilization Grand Model

INTRODUCTION

The purpose of this study is to develop a comprehensive model of generic civilizations and world civilization, applying the cybernetic technique of analysis and synthesis. Identifying the role of information-communication processes is particularly important for this quest, because these processes strongly influence the progress of civilization at the beginning of the 21st century. Three models, developed by Braudel (1993), Toynbee (1957), and Koneczny (1962), serve as both justification for this type of study and the foundations for a new model.

The spectacular progress in technology and living standards achieved by mankind at the beginning of the third millennium prompts research on the grand view of the human condition. Numerous questions need to be answered:

1. What is a civilization?
2. What types of civilizations can be recognized at the beginning of the third millennium?
3. What are the relationships between any particular civilization and the world civilization?
4. What is the role of information and communication in a civilization?
5. What types of laws rule any particular civilization and the world civilization?
6. What are the prospects of the world civilization?

Answers to these questions should help us to understand our current condition and the direction of its improvement or perhaps mankind's further well-being.

THE CIVILIZATION APPROACH TO HUMAN DEVELOPMENT

The study of human development involves several scientific disciplines such as anthropology, archaeology, geography, history, sociology, political science, economics, art and literature, and cybernetics. Each of these disciplines develops its own methods of analysis and synthesis; however, only a few attempts exist toward the formulation of grand models of human development. The scientific tendency in historiography is more toward analyzing than toward synthesizing.

One of the earliest researchers of civilization was Fukuzawa Yukichi in Japan, who defined it as follows:

Civilization comforts man physically and elevates him spiritually...Civilization advances the well-being and dignity of man, since man acquires these benefits through knowledge and virtue. Civilization can be defined as that which advances man's knowledge and virtue.

In his opinion, *"morals had remained almost unchanged throughout history, but intellect had shown marked growth and progress* (Miyaki, 2004).

These are excellent thoughts, and very important for those of us living in the 21st century to consider in our approach to "the knowledge dociety," which looks mostly for *artificial* intelligence in profit-driven data mining and robotics and neglects the moral values of *natural* intelligence.

In Western historiography, six attempts were undertaken in the last century to define a grand model of human developmental history. These undertakings generated more criticism than applause, and the Polish study is not widely known to the historical community.

The German philosopher Oswald Spengler published a study *The Decline of the West* (1932), in which he reflects the pessimistic atmosphere of Germany after World War I. Spengler maintained that history has a natural development in which every culture is a distinct organic form that grows, matures, and decays. He insisted that civilizations are independent from external influences. He predicted a phase of "Caesarism" in the future development of the Western Culture, which he believed was in its last stage.

The English historian Arnold Toynbee published his greatest work in the twelve-volume *A Study of History* (1957). He compared the history of 26 different civilizations, every one of which presumably follows a similar pattern of evolution through a cyclical pattern of growth, maturity, and decay. He believed that societies thrive best in response to challenges and that a society's most important task is to create a religion. He was less anxious than Spengler with characterizing civilizations, and more concerned with the criteria by which they are to be determined. He stressed religious and philosophical factors as guiding civilizations. Withal, he never defined "civilization" clearly. Though he saw the Western civilization to be in its decay phase, he saw hope for the future formation of one spiritually-oriented world community.

The Polish historian Feliks Koneczny wrote three books on the theory of civilizations: *On the Plurality of Civilizations* (1962), *For an Order in History* (1977), and *History Laws* (1982). His works on civilizations were never published in communistic (then Stalinist) Poland. Koneczny, who published 173 works, was an empirical theoretician who discerned (in contrast to Spengler's *a priori* model) that there is no one linear history of mankind. He perceived seven major civilizations and examined their common laws. A civilization for him is a regime of collective life. His main inquiry was to find factors differentiating civilizations. These are named Quincunx: truth, goodness, beauty, health, and prosperity. Also the Triple Law (family law, inheritance law, and property law) differentiates civilizations. Human attitudes toward the Quincunx and laws are the key to understanding the civilization process. He was against the idea of cycles of civilizations and formulated two laws of civilizations.

According to the first law, each civilization has a cause and purpose. The second law states that to endure, each civilization must harmonize interrelations among categories of existence and laws. Otherwise, a civilization may vanish. Mergers between civilizations lead to chaos, disintegration, and decay, since civilizations may have opposing attitudes toward categories of existence and the Triple Law. Toynbee, in a preface to the English edition of *On the Plurality of Civilizations*, judged highly Koneczny's contributions and called him "indomitable," because the Polish historian wrote his last works during the German occupation of Poland, when he found himself in very poor conditions.

Russian-born Pitirim Sorokin, professor at Harvard, in his *Social and Culture Dynamics* (1937), quantified all conceivable components of a culture from Greco-Roman to Western. He collected data spanning a period of 2,500 years and discovered a pattern of recurrent fluctuation between "sensate" and "ideational" value systems:

- During a sensate period, life is controlled by a materialistic worldview, and economic and scientific activities blossom, particularly during the "active" phase. During the "passive" phase, hedonistic behavior prevails, and in the final "cynical" phase the sensate mentality negates everything, including itself.
- During an ideational period, life is controlled by spirituality and moves from the "ascetic" phase to the "active" (expansionistic) phase, and finally degenerates into the "fideism" phase (a desperate effort to sustain the faith by means of official persecutions).
- Occasionally, a harmonious combination of the best elements of both types may occur. Sorokin calls these happy periods "idealistic," and they are characterized by a balance of faith, reason, and empiricism (Greece during the age of Socrates and Europe during the Renaissance are examples of this type.) Other mixed types of periods do not demonstrate this agreeable integration.
- These fluctuations of value systems are, according to Sorokin, controlled by two principles:

1. The principle of "immanent self-determination," which means that a socio-cultural system unfolds according to its inherited potentialities. Although external factors can impact the development of the system, they cannot change its fundamental nature.
2. The principle of "limits," which states that growth cannot last forever, since sooner or later it exhausts its creativity and begins to wane.

According to Richard (1996), several scholars attempted to replicate Sorokin's findings. Results were mixed, but no one recommended abandonment of his general theory. Sorokin wrote his theory about 50 years ago when he argued that we in the West had entered a sensate period, in which cynicism is the dominant theme. We had also entered a period of "transition and crisis," marked by the international conflicts, social pathology and so forth. Sorokin's approach is very useful in analyzing world events; however, it is not applied by him to define or classify civilizations. He criticizes Toynbee's classification of civilizations, which he says were "dumps of cultural phenomena mistaken for vast socio-cultural systems........vast pseudosystems of civilizations, taken out of an enormous mass of other cultural complexes without any uniform *fundamentum divisionis*, on the basis of different and somehow indefinite criteria"—a procedure both illogical and unscientific (Wilkinson, 1996). Later, Toynbee revised his list of civilizations (1961) and Sorokin agreed with the new classification. Sorokin perceived a civilization as "a cultural field where a multitude of vast and small cultural systems and congeries—partly mutually harmonious, partly neutral, partly contradictory—coexists" (Sorokin, 1950, p. 213). Sorokin was not a civilizationist and his units of study are not civilizations, but he was the founding president of the International Society for the Comparative Study of Civilizations, and he has been given considerable attention by members of the ISCSC.

Alfred Louis Kroeber, the doyen of American anthropology, was interested in (among other topics) historical synthesis at the world level, particularly in the history of civilized societies, both ancient and modern. The basis of Kroeber's point of view is the natural history of culture, with strong emphasis on: a) humanistic factors, particularly silent ones, b) classification of cultures, and c) culture as a phenomenon. His book *The Nature of Culture* (1952) is the main presentation of his ideas on these topics. In his famous work *Configurations of Culture Growth* (1944), he analyzes cultures as anthropologically complex entities but not significantly different. From the civilizationist's point of view the most interesting book is *Culture, a Critical Review of Concepts and Definitions* (1952), co-authored by him and Clyde Kluckhohn. In this book, the authors provide a very broad review of different definitions of culture and civilizations used in different countries. They define culture as "a product; is historical; includes ideas, patterns, and values; is selective; is learned, is based upon symbols, and is an abstraction from behavior and the product of behavior." In respect to civilization, the authors identify *civilization* with the objective technological and informational activities of society, but *culture* with subjective religion, philosophy, and art [1].

The French historian Fernand Braudel was a "structuralist" who perceived human development to occur in three historical structures ("measures of time"): the quasi-immobile structure (*la longue durée*), the intermediate scale of "conjectures" (rarely longer than a few generations), and the rapid time-scale of individual events. Each was applied in one of the three parts of *La Mediterranee* (1949). In his book *A History of Civilizations* (1987), he contrasts his own approach to history to the "over-simple theories" of Oswald Spengler and Arnold Toynbee. He assumes that the history of human development is the history of civilization. A student should learn history as *a whole*, as only this *whole* is a *civilization*. Civilization for him

is a process rather than a temporarily stabilized construct. It is a structure of transformational streams in a realm of daily activities of human life. He perceives one civilization as a human *continuum* or, depending upon the context, he may delimit hundreds of civilizations (e.g., "Roman civilization" or "industrial civilization"). He also, like Koneczny, developed his triple structure idea during World War II while he was a prisoner in Germany.

THE CONTEMPORARY CIVILIZATION APPROACH TO HUMAN DEVELOPMENT

Rushton Coulborn, in his book *The Origin of Civilized Societies* (1959), debates a very difficult question concerning origins of civilized societies and addresses two questions: 1) Is there a distinction between civilized and primitive societies? 2) Were civilized societies of single or multiple origin? He reserved the term "civilized" for the large societies and the term "civilization" for their high culture considered abstractly (he was a student of A.L. Kroeber). He found five of the first seven primary civilized societies in river valleys (Egyptian, Mesopotamian, Indian, Andean, Chinese societies), one on a small island (Cretan society) and another in a tropical forest (Middle American society). Among factors creating these societies, he perceived the following: warmer climate, settlement, creation of religion by the settlers, which led to the creation and integration of these societies, change of leadership during migrations from more to less dangerous locations, adaptation to water supplies, and establishment of a new religion based upon some parts of old religion or brought by newcomers with charismatic leaders (e.g., the Spaniards colonizing America). The most intriguing part of the author's method is that he applies comparisons among these civilized societies, which show some analogies and some differences. For example, he defined one distinction between civilized and primitive societies which is "*perfectly clear and is not only quantitative: civilized societies are all subject to a cyclical movement of rise and fall in the course of their development, but no similar movements occur in the development of primitive societies.*" From this author's 21st-century perspective, cyclical development is controlled by growing cognition of a given society, which learns how to survive and develop itself.

Carroll Quigley, in his *The Evolution of Civilizations* (1961), analyzes mechanisms of civilization rise and fall, claiming that a process of change is neither rigid nor single in any society, but rather that each civilization is a confused congeries of such processes in all types of human activities. Furthermore, he insists that to recognize one decisive factor in this process is not a description of reality. He also criticizes approaches to periodizations of history, offering seven stages of human development in just the millennium 950-1950 (mixture, gestation, expansion, age of conflict, universal empire, decay, and invasion), and divides each stage into seven levels (intellectual, religious outlook, social group, economic control, economic organization, political, military)—two more than Toynbee's.

Matthew Melko, in his book *The Nature of Civilizations* (1969), defines some elements of a basic model of civilizations, such as their components (outlook, aesthetics, society, economics, government, international) and their developmental stages (crystallization, transition, complete disintegration, ossification [a freezing at a crystal stage]) as well as developmental macro-phases of feudal system, state system, and imperial system, which he analyzes separately from stages. He thinks that civilizations are large and complex cultures which can control their environments. Civilizations may have different levels of cultural integration, but each of them has a basic pattern (of government, economy, war) that allows them to be distinguished from each other. Melko did not characterize any particular civilization. He

recognized the civilizations' ability to have transformations and conflicts. His strong contribution is in providing an interesting model of civilization development through three macro-phases. Later, Melko (2008) provides a very interesting question: "Are civilizations real or simply reifications?" And answers as follows: "They are reifications (visible-invisible entities) based upon cultural and transactional observations, somewhat in the sense that Europe or Indian Ocean are reifications. All have geographical reality but depend for their identity on consensus."

David Wilkinson (1987) proposes for current times to analyze only one central civilization, not several. For him, civilizations are not cultural groups but rather socio-political groups or *poly-cultures*. His civilizations are social units, larger than states, integrated by political interest. Wilkinson insists that 13 major civilizations evolved in the last 3,500 years into a central civilization, which today has transformed into a single global civilization. This process began in 1500 B.C., when Egyptian and Mesopotamian civilizations merged. Later, the central civilization was swallowing other civilizations at different phases, such as Near Eastern (1500-500 B.C.), Greco-Roman (500 B.C.-500 A.D.), Medieval (500-1500 A.D.), Western (1500-2000 A.D.), and Global (2000-present). Of course, penetration of ideas, people, goods, and so forth among civilizations takes place and influences internal dynamics of each one. However, particularly after September 11, 2001, the boundaries of different autonomous civilizations are well seen, and the civilization super-layer of the global civilization is well perceived in all paths of mainstream human development.

The International Society for Comparative Study of Civilizations (ISCSC) tried several times in the 1970s and 1980s to generate discussions on civilizations' classification, their origin and spatial and temporal boundaries. About 56 researchers offered their views on these topics in a post-conference book *The Boundaries of*

Civilizations in Space and Time, edited by Melko and Scott (1987). As a result, we read "comments to comments," with a lack of clear agreement on most issues, except for a definition of civilization as a large and complex culture (super-culture) with a history. This definition supports the Anglo-French-American view of civilization as a monolithic model.

Lee D. Snyder (1999), in his major book *Macro History-A Theoretical Approach To Comparative World History*, which appeared by the end of the 20th century, had a chance to synthesize contributions of many 20th-century historians and scientists who made sense of world history. The author argues that the largest historic framework is a "culture-system," called a culture or civilization by many. However, his basic unit of study is the Historic Cycle of 300 to 400 years, when macro- and micro-history can be analyzed within a framework of five dimensions: economic, sociopolitical, intellectual (insight, spiritual aspect, subjective side, ideas, "culture"), geographic, and expressive (art, literature, and music). Since his book is rather on world macro-history than on civilization, the author is mostly preoccupied with the timing of the historic cycle and how it is influenced by these five dimensions of culture-system. He is innovative in defining the role of an individual in a culture-system.

Felipe Fernandez-Armesto (2001) defines "a civilization" as an area or period distinguished, in the mind of the person using the term, by striking continuities in ways of life and thought and feelings. At a further level, the word "civilization" denotes a process of collective self-differentiation from a world characterized implicitly or explicitly as "barbaric" or "savage" or "primitive." Societies which have achieved such self-differentiation can be called "civilized." In recognizing a civilization, the quoted author puts strong emphasis on the criterion of geography, since civilizing, according to him, means transforming the environment for their own ends. Hence, he is fascinated with

such civilizations as Small-Islands civilizations, Atlantic civilization, and Pacific civilization.

THE WORLD-SYSTEM APPROACH TO HUMAN DEVELOPMENT

A discussion on the role of civilization in human development at the end of the 20th century looked to be saturated with *jeu le mot* which led nowhere. Immanuel Wallerstein understood this very well and offered the world-system concept as a new approach in analyzing human development. In *The Modern World-System* (1974), he offered a tool to recognize what is the most useful interpretation of what happened historically. In his interpretation, the "units of analysis" are "world-systems," which means something other than the modern nation-state, something larger than the nation-state, and something that was defined by the boundaries of an effective, ongoing division of labor. He was concerned about the special dimension of a world-system; hence, he later offered Einstein's TimeSpace concept to keep "historical systems'" issues. When he was working on this new approach, it was a time of Cold War and the rise of computer, management and political systems applications (e.g., PERT technique, analyzing only main events ("world-systems") of a given project to find a critical path to determine the success or failure of the whole project. One such "world-system" was, in the mentioned period, NATO or "capitalism," which was winning against "communism." Today we can add to them the European Union, NAFTA, the Internet, the World Trade Organization, "geopolitics" (Moczulski, 2000), and so forth. A world-system implies the hierarchical existence of a world core, semi-periphery, and periphery, which reflects the old issue of North versus South (Poverty War) or West versus East (Cold War). Of course, while this approach is a useful tool, it cannot substitute the issues of civilization dynamics, governing human development at the small-scale, grass-roots level. Wallerstein considers the accepted concepts of civilization only useful for a long-term, large-scale analysis of social change. For a short-term study, 'world-systems' are more useful units of analysis.

The world-systems analysis and synthesis became a popular approach, which is expanded by Christopher Chase-Dunn and Thomas D. Hall in their book *Rise and Demise, Comparing World-Systems* (1997). The authors' goal is to trace the transformation of "modes of accumulation" from "kin-based" (based on "normative" social cohesion) to "tributary" (where "organized coercion of labor" predominates) to "capitalist" and "socialist" world-systems.

David Wilkinson (1995) offers again a very interesting idea that "civilizations" are "world-systems," particularly his unique central civilization. To a degree he is right, but not all civilizations are "world-systems." Nowadays, we could classify only global civilization and Western civilization as world-systems, which rule the world through their critical paths.

Lauren Benton (1996) rejects the world-system concept as the "master narrative," because it is more important to understand social experience. Cultural perspective rather than the goal illuminates the structure of the whole. This position resembles the progress made in modern physics when the Bohr Solar Model (1913) of the atom was modified by the Heisenberg Uncertainty Principle, which states that we do not know both the precise location and the precise velocity of any given nuclear particle. The new Charge-cloud Model (1950s) uses indistinct and overlapping "probability clouds" to approximate the position of an electron in its orbit (defined by Niels Bohr and kept in the 1950s model). Therefore, positions taken by Wallerstein and Benton should not be exclusive but additive, as is shown in Figure 1-6 [2].

All of these maneuvers with the issues of civilizations, macro-history and world-systems are limited, because we have to investigate more components of civilization through modern system and cybernetic tools that can be applied to complex entities. For example, we have to recognize a role of technology-driven infrastructures that support human life and culture. A sign of this role is indicated in William McGaughey's book *Rhythm and Self-Consciousness: New Ideal for an Electronic Civilization* (2001), which shows that as civilization has moved from print to electronic culture, its ideals have changed from the classic "truth, beauty, and good" to an elusive element called rhythm (the energy and control of the individual and of human society), and how self-consciousness (concentrating on ourselves), enemy of rhythm, underlines the complexity of modern life. We who live today feel a strong presence of technology in our *modus operandi*; hence, technology can be considered as one of those world-systems. Neil Postman (1993) even insists that we live in *technopoly*, which surrounds culture to technology. A good sign of it is a statement that "distance is dead" (Cairncross, 1997), because geography, borders, and time zones are becoming irrelevant to the way we conduct our business and personal lives, courtesy of the information-communication revolution which allows us to travel less to achieve the same results.

There are about 200 million computers installed and 7 billion chips embedded in smart products (more than there are people on the Earth), which leads to the emergence of the global digital nervous system. Levy (1997) even perceives this trend as the birth of "collective intelligence," which develops a new world of mankind, based on cyberspace. This new world is being planned to work as the computing utility, where computing power could be as simple to tap as electricity from a socket. Sensor networks already begin to track everything from weather to inventory, stirring popular fears of governmental and corporate intrusion. The broad application of mobile devices, cellular phones, wireless devices leads to the connected individual anywhere and anytime (WiFi).

Furthermore, marrying electronics and biology promises new devices that could transform million of lives. Right now, most bio-artificial organs are meant as temporary solutions until the patient receives a human organ. Ultimately, scientists want to "grow" living tissue that will eliminate the need for a transplant. These new technologies will force us to change our approach toward how we define life, culture, and civilization. What is gained and what is lost by being digital is answered by the Krokers (1997) in their fascinating book under a very meaningful title "*Digital Delirium.*" Grossman (1995) thinks that we are even building the Electronic Republic, where democracy is being redefined by information-communication processes.

Therefore, the role of technology cannot be ignored in discussion on civilization. One of the first who understood this role very well was Lewis Mumford (1966), who in his book *Technics and Human Development*, goes back to the origins of human culture and does not accept the view that man's rise was the result of his command of tools and conquest of nature. Mumford demonstrates how tools did not and could not develop greatly without a series of more significant inventions in ritual, language, and social organization. Mumford and McLuhan (1962), both great philosophers of technology, did not live to see the information-communication revolution (late 1990s) and could not extend their findings about the role of electronic information-communication processes in civilization. The modern role of technology is marked in the world-system model of production in Figure 1-8.

THE EMERGENCE OF CIVILIZATION

Civilization had been growing gradually along with the cultural and industrial development of man as *homo sapiens* during the last 200,000 years. About 40,000-50,000 years ago, humans underwent a very important genetic mutation, when the DRD4 gene was developed that encodes the dopamine neurotransmitter. It is this neurotransmitter which is responsible for human personality traits (Ding et al., 2002). In such a way, humans became more intellectually alert and as a result developed increasing capacities for leadership and socializing. Fortunately, the climate warming that occurred around 10,000 B.C. [3] helped humans demonstrate their more developed societies, allowing them to migrate across continents and form the beginnings of infrastructure. Some time after 10,000 B.C., people became farmers, animal breeders, and pottery makers. When the Ice Age ended in about 8,000 B.C., the warmer climate was friendlier for humans and their civilizing processes. In the years between 8,000 and 6,000 B.C., sheep, pigs, cattle and other livestock were domesticated and more people were settling in the Euphrates-Tigris river valley. Around 7,500 B.C., villages were growing in nearby Anatolia.

Growing populations required more food and more productive farms, which led to the development of irrigation systems and work specialization. The latter and other kinds of non-farming tasks in 5,000 B.C. led to the rise of elites, which were living in towns and worshiped in temples. Eventually about 4,000 B.C., city-states were formed in Mesopotamia. One of these was Uruk, where several thousand people lived, with crafts, architecture and writing. These city-states were united under power-keeping dynasties and led to the creation of the Mesopotamian civilization, the first historic example. According to Toynbee (1995), there were about 26 different civilizations. Nowadays, these have eight heirs: the Chinese, Japanese, Western, Eastern ("Orthodox Christian," or "Byzantine-Russian"), Islamic, Buddhist, Hindu, and African civilizations. All these interact with the emerging global civilization.

A model of the process by which civilizations emerge is shown in Figure 1-1.

Figure 1-1. The emergence of civilization (civilizations' duration not in a scale)

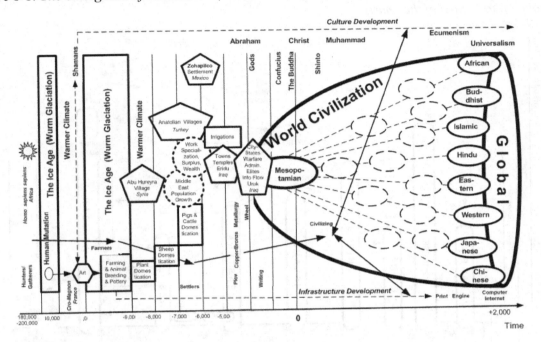

THE EMPIRICAL MODEL OF CIVILIZATION EVOLUTION

In this study of civilization, we begin with the construction of an empirical model of civilization development. Figure 1-2 illustrates this model and indicates that the world civilization has a continuous character and can be also perceived as a mosaic of *autonomous* civilizations.

There is only one world civilization, yet there are about 29 main autonomous civilizations that have been developed in the last 6,000 years. Perhaps, if one could find more autonomous civilizations or rather satellite civilizations (cultures), their number could reach 100 or even more. However, for the clarity of this synthesis, we would like to limit the number of candidates to 29 autonomous civilization-types. In this sense, Toynbee as well as Braudel were right; there is one civilization and at the same time there are many.

The world civilization as a *continuum* never dies—only evolves from one stage to another. This evolution takes place through the life cycle of *autonomous* civilizations. At the very beginning of human civilization, there were several successful formations of living entities that could be considered initial *autonomous* civilizations. They took place in different parts of the world and created about eight cases. The first autonomous civilization is the Mesopotamian civilization (including Sumerian), which emerged in the valley of the Euphrates and Tigris rivers in the Middle East, about 4,000 B.C. In the Far East, the first autonomous civilizations rose inland: Indus (Harappan) around 2,500 B.C. and Sinic around 1,500 B.C. In Africa, the initial civilization was the Egyptian in 3,100 B.C. In South America, early autonomous civilizations included the Andean civilization that emerged around 1,500 B.C. In Central America, the first autonomous civilization was the Mesoamerican civilization

Figure 1-2. The empirical model of autonomous and global civilizations development (time progresses from top to bottom of the chart)

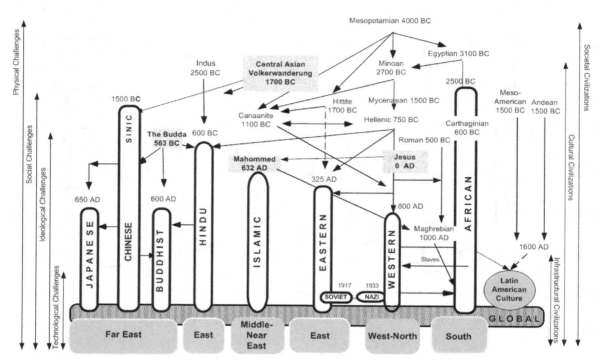

which rose around 1,500 B.C. Both civilizations fell around 1,500 A.D.

Autonomous civilizations rose in a response to physical challenges of nature (ecosystem). Humans began to organize themselves into a society which provided exchangeable and specialized services, such as food hunting, food production, house building, road construction, transportation, healthcare, and entertainment. These services and growing human communication led toward the formation of cities. These types of autonomous civilizations we will call *societal* civilizations.

In addition to the environmental challenges, the societal civilization as a whole has been threatened by its own internal structure involving power, wealth creation, beliefs enforcement, family formation, leadership, and so forth. As societal civilizations evolved into more complex entities, they were managed by cultural manipulation. This type of autonomous civilization we will name the

cultural civilization. By culture, we understand a values- and symbols-driven patterned behavior of a human entity.

Ever since religion was transformed from beliefs in magic to beliefs in poly-gods and then to a mono-god, the cultural civilization has applied religion as the main tool of cultural control. Religious and military forces were the foundations of the power apparatus that maintained the society as a governed entity. These forces civilized the society and moved it into higher levels of organization. Among cultural civilizations, one can recognize about 16 cases, such as the Egyptian civilization (3,100 B.C.), the Minoan civilization (2,700 B.C.), the Mycenaean civilization (1,500 B.C.), the Sinic civilization (1,500 B.C.), the Hellenic civilization (750 B.C.), the Canaanite civilization (1,100 B.C.), the Hindu civilization (600 B.C.), the Roman civilization (500 B.C.), the Eastern civilization (350 A.D.), the Hellenistic

(Hellenic) civilization (323 B.C.), the Buddhist civilization (600 A.D.), the Ethiopian civilization (400 A.D.), the Sub-Saharan civilization (800 A.D.), the Western civilization (800 A.D.), the Islamic civilization (632 A.D.) and the Maghrebian civilization (1,000 A.D.). The cultural civilization evolves into a civilization with challenges generated by intra- and inter-civilization issues of war and peace. These types of issues have been managed by technological means of domination. Such a civilization we will call the *infrastructural* civilization.

The *infrastructural* civilization's purpose is to expand spheres of influence by means of technology. Technology drives the development of infrastructural civilizations. The prime target of technological applications has been a war machine which supports the main values of a given civilization. By-products of military applications of technology affect the civilian part of its infrastructure. Among eight infrastructural civilizations one can recognize the Sinic civilization, the Hindu civilization, the Japanese civilization, the Western civilization, the Eastern civilization, the Buddhist civilization, the Islamic civilization, and the African civilization (Burenhult, 2003).

By the end of the 2nd millennium, infrastructural civilizations had become civilizations responsible for world or hemispheric influence and domination. Hence, the Western civilization dominates the western hemisphere, the Eastern and Hindu civilizations rule the eastern and southern sub-continents, the Islamic civilization rules the Near and Middle Eastern sub-continent and some parts of the Far Eastern continent, the Japanese civilization governs some parts of the Far Eastern continent, the Chinese civilization influences the majority of the Far Eastern continent, and the Buddhist civilization influences a small part of the Far Eastern continent

In the majority of autonomous civilizations, one can differentiate more than one culture, with the exception of the Egyptian, Hittite, and Japanese civilizations, which are mono-cultural. Figure 1-3 provides 88 examples of empirical civilization cultures. By "empirical" cultures, we would like to emphasize that their names have been created by historians during the discovery process. Of course, some names have been modified to read as they are perceived nowadays.

METHODS OF CIVILIZATION STUDY

Civilization is an info-material structure developed by humans to cope effectively with themselves, nature, and their creator. It is a vibrant "interface" which differentiates civilized humans from animals (Figure 1-3). The concept of "civilization" is applied to a wide diversity of particulars: to the level of religious ideas, to the level of customs, to the level of technology, to the level of manners, to the level of knowledge, and so forth. It can refer to the type of a city, or a relationship between men and women in family, tribe, or society. A type of a law and its application reflects civilization also.

The mission of a civilization is to improve human existence. As Toynbee (1995, p. 87) writes, "the goal of Mankind's continuous and increasing endeavors is still out of sight, we know, never the less, what it is." What changed our pre-human predecessors into human beings is the attainment of awareness and problem-solving faculties. The cost of human independent thinking, learning, and quest for freedom is a mental and moral relativity. Hence, the goal of a civilization, or in general of the world civilization, is to minimize "hate" and maximize "love"—two opposite forces driving the pulse of human relativity.

A role of civilization is shown in Figure 1-4, which reflects in a graphic model the system of the Universe. The Universe system is composed of three sub-systems: humans, nature (ecosystem), and civilization. The creator is the steerer of the Universe. Relationships among these four components are of two types. The first one contains imbedded relationships such as A, B, and D, that

Figure 1-3. The empirical classification of civilization cultures

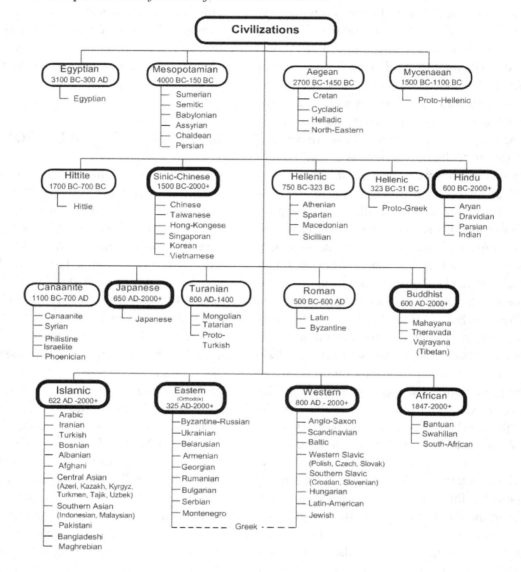

are rather beyond civilization control, with some exception for sects (e.g., New Age) that define their own gods (the southern direction of the A relation). The second type of relationships, such as F, E, and C are controlled by the civilization.

To understand the control function of a civilization, one must open the civilization structure and analyze its purpose, components, and their relationships. In civilization studies, one can recognize so far two approaches to this task. The English, French, and American single-elemental model (SEM) of the humans' interface treats equally "civilization" and "culture." The German two-elemental model (TEM) subordinates "*zivilisation*" to "*kultur.*"

Figure 1-4. The universe system

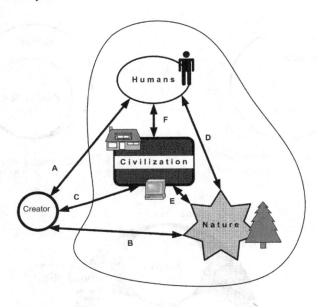

The English-French-American concept of "civilization" contains all aspects of human life: religious, political, social, economic, and cultural. The German concept of *"zivilisation"* is limited to useful things, but is nevertheless considered only a value of the second rank. The value of the first rank is *"kultur,"* which refers to religious, intellectual, and artistic achievements. The *"kultur"* controls *"zivilisation"* and develops it as a continuous motion of material-driven human development. The German concept of *"kultur"* emphasizes differences among nations that may share the same *"zivilisation."*

There is no doubt that the German model is more elaborate than the English-French-American model. However, the German model is still limited, since it does not recognize human entities that determine the whole civilizing process. A new model is needed which could integrate the contributions of these two historic models.

The new model of civilization recognizes the following elements (dimensions):

- **Human Entity** - organized humans in the pursuit of civilization; it is an existence-driven community.
- **Culture** - a value- and symbol-guided continuous process of developing patterned human behaviors, feelings, and reactions, based upon symbols, learning from it and being a product of it. Cultures do not satisfy needs; rather, they demand values and define symbols [1].
- **Infrastructure** - a technology-driven additive process of acquiring and applying material means.

The comparison of these socio-genesis models of human development is shown in Figure 1-5. In the new three-elemental model (TTEM), the German concept of *"zivilisation"* has been replaced by a concept of an "infrastructure," and the German concept of *"kultur"* has been kept intact only in reference to the infrastructure, since the English-French-American concept of civilization prevails as the developed, holistic structure of human existence. The third component—the entity—has been

Figure 1-5. The Targowski three element model (TEM)

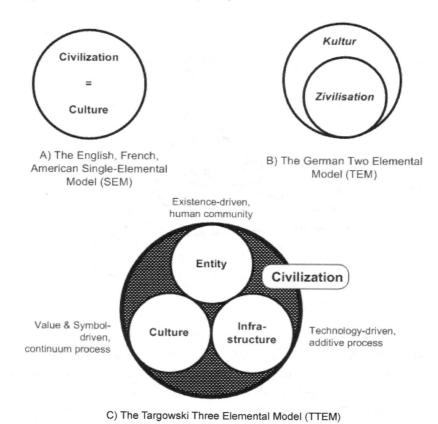

A) The English, French, American Single-Elemental Model (SEM)

B) The German Two Elemental Model (TEM)

C) The Targowski Three Elemental Model (TTEM)

included in the concept of civilization. This model is similar to the Greek model called *Paideia* that unified civilization, culture, tradition, literature, and education, and has been described by Jaeger (1945). This approach reflects to a certain degree a civilization concept as a set of wealth, power, and meaning, defined by Arnason (2003).

The 49 empirical components of civilization are categorized and shown on Figure 1-6. This list is a static model and is of course a product of knowledge that we can apply now. In the past, this list would be much shorter. A list-hierarchy of entities requires some explanation. The world civilization began when human individuals organized themselves in a family, tribe, or ethnos.

These entities created pre-historic, primitive civilization, since every human group socializes itself, since it has a purpose, responds to challenges, and applies tools. Toynbee associates the beginning of a civilization with the emergence of a society. We could add that the emerged society triggers the outburst of an autonomous civilization developed from itself and leading to the development of the world civilization.

These civilization components are self-explanatory. A dynamic model of relationships among these components is a subject of the remaining part of this study. Most of these components have been developed or added along the 6,000 years of civilization history. The most recent compo-

Figure 1-6. The components of civilization as they are perceived in 2008

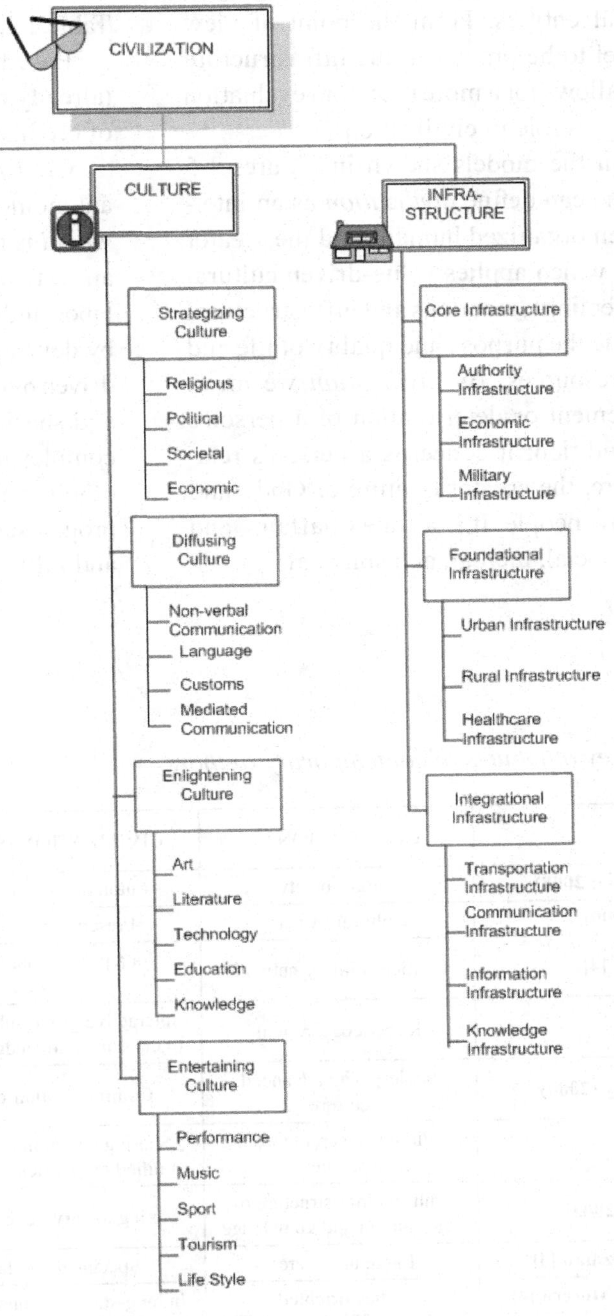

CIVILIZATION

HUMAN ENTITY
- Individual
- Family
- Band
- Tribe
- Ethnos
- Chiefdom
- Society
- People
- Proto-nation
- Nation
- State
- Empire
- Power
- Superpower
- Hegemonic power
- Political Society
- Transnational Community
- Supranational Community
- Spheric Community
- Global Society
- Global Political

CULTURE

Strategizing Culture
- Religious
- Political
- Societal
- Economic

Diffusing Culture
- Non-verbal Communication
- Language
- Customs
- Mediated Communication

Enlightening Culture
- Art
- Literature
- Technology
- Education
- Knowledge

Entertaining Culture
- Performance
- Music
- Sport
- Tourism
- Life Style

INFRA-STRUCTURE

Core Infrastructure
- Authority Infrastructure
- Economic Infrastructure
- Military Infrastructure

Foundational Infrastructure
- Urban Infrastructure
- Rural Infrastructure
- Healthcare Infrastructure

Integrational Infrastructure
- Transportation Infrastructure
- Communication Infrastructure
- Information Infrastructure
- Knowledge Infrastructure

nents are those which belong to the integrational infrastructure and those which are emerging as post-national entities. From the point of view of the model to be proposed, the infrastructure dimension allows for a more profound evaluation of technology's role in civilization.

Based on the models shown in Figures 1-5 and 1-6, one can define *civilization* as an interface between organized humans and the creator and nature, which applies value-driven cultural behaviors, feelings, reactions and infrastructural tools to guide the purpose and quality of life and to control resources. By *civilization* we mean the improvement or deterioration of a person's external condition; it concerns a person's relation to nature, the creator (Nature or God), and his/her fellow people. It is a state of affairs, and is physical, social, mental, and spiritual.

However, more components one must add to a definition of civilization as it is shown in Table 1-1.

Based on these attributes and early definitions (already cited authors), the *composite* definition of civilization is as follows:

Civilization is a large society living in an autonomous, fuzzy reification (invisible-visible) which is not a part of larger one and exists over an extended period of time. It specializes in labor and differentiates from other civilizations by developing its own advanced cultural system driven by communication, religion, wealth, power, and sharing the same knowledge system within complex urban, agricultural infrastructures, and others such as industrial, information ones. It also progresses in a cycle of rising, growing, declining and falling.

Table 1-1. Key attributes of contemporary authors

AUTHOR	CIVILIZATION IS	CIVILIZATION IS ALSO	CIVILIZATION IS ALSO
Melko (1969; 2008)	Large society	Autonomous reification	Vague boundaries
Snyder (1999)	Cultural System	Preserving integrity	Adapting
Wilkinson [4]	Politico-military network	Not a part of a larger such network	
Hord [4]	Knowledge system	Interactive group subscribing to the same knowledge system	
McCaughey (2000)	Society with advanced culture	Communication-driven	Power-driven
Blaha [4]	Minimum several thousand people	Sharing common culture & unified by political structure	In monumental architecture, cycle-driven
Bosworth (2003)	Cultural infrastructure of information and knowledge	Aiming to survive & continue	Cultural memory
Farhat-Holzman [4]	Large urban area	Specialized in labor	Wealth accumulating
Fernandez-Morera [4]	Cities-oriented	In long-standing constructions	Larger than culture
Fernandez-Armesto (2001)	Distinguished area or period	striking continuities in ways of life and thought and feelings	Self-differentiation to be civilized
Krejci (2004)	In division of labor	Urbanized & literate	Above primitive societies
Targowski	Info-material interface between humans and Creator and nature	Composed of humans, culture & infrastructure	Cycle-driven

HUMAN ENTITIES AND THEIR DYNAMICS

A human entity is a set of structured relationships among a group of humans. It can be organized under several forms, ranging from less to more flexible ones.

- **A family** – a set of parents and children or relations, living together (or not) as the members of a household, serving the needs of family.
- **A band** – a few dozen people who move continuously in the search for food. They are associated with a hunting and gathering form of subsistence economy. Bands have informal leaders who may provide guidance.
- **A tribe** – a group of (especially primitive) families or communities, linked by social, economic, religious, or blood ties, and usually having common customs, dialect, and one or more recognized but informal leaders. A tribe can be considered a segmented society devoted to horticulture or pastoralism or to highly specialized and very productive forms of hunting and gathering hunting and gathering.
- **An ethnos** – a homogeneous community at an early stage of sharing the same culture and awareness of togetherness that strives for further civilization development (e.g., Inkas).
- **A chiefdom** – an autonomous, socio-political unit comprising a number of villages or communities under the permanent control of a paramount chief with aristocratic ethos, but without formal, legal apparatus of forceful repression, and without the capacity to prevent fission.

A society is a group of people on the same territory organized to support their own existence through the exchange of specialized, civilization services. The society shares a common interest and responds to challenges. As a result, the society develops its civilization means. Along with the development of power and economic infrastructures, the society transforms into a people.

A people is a politically and economically organized society in which one can distinguish a hierarchy of subordinated levels. At the beginning of 600 B.C., the Hindu civilization's people were divided into three honorable classes: priest (*brahmana*), noble warrior (*kshatriya*), and commoner (*vaisya*), including both farmers and artisans, augmented by a fourth group, the slaves (*sudras*) consisting of non-Aryans. Around 31 B.C., the Roman civilization had people organized into two classes: patricians, who could belong to the Senate, and plebeians, or commoners. The patricians were more prosperous farmers of specified senatorial ancestry who secured privileges for themselves. Without the access to day-to-day control of the state, plebeians became clients of the patricians, who protected them in return for attendance and service. In the 16th and 17th centuries, Poland's people were divided into three strata: aristocracy (1%), szlachta (10%), and plebs (89%). France organized people in three estates: nobles, clergy, and commons. Every state or empire had its own social hierarchy, in which people at the top felt that they were in charge of a state's affairs. The remaining people were oppressed and indifferent to the state's well-being. The force of the civilizing process was coming from a very limited group of people, who were, however, very much interested in the creation of wealth and all means leading to it.

In the 19th century, just after the American Revolution (1775-1783) and French Revolution (1789-1799), the concept of a nation began to emerge. A Frenchman or an American served no longer a king but the French or American "nation" (*patrie*). In nationalist theory, the nation became an entity as the result of a pact between the sovereign people and the state. The whole

19th century is the history of rising nation-states, such as the U.S., Germany, Italy, France, Serbia, Bulgaria, and Romania. In the 20th century many more nation-states have formed, such as Poland (after 123 years of partition), Czechoslovakia (after 300 years of Austro-Hungarian rule), Hungary, and Yugoslavia.

A proto-nation is an entity usually ruled by an empire. It is an entity that may eventually evolve into a nation. Although this entity is at the stage prior to a nation, it is a result of the formation of the nation concept. An example of a proto-nation is Hungary, which self-ruled within the Austro-Hungarian Empire in the 19th century. In the modern sense, Hungary became a nation in 1919, when its state was established. Czechoslovakia passed through the same process in 1919 and Slovakia in 1995. The fall of Yugoslavia from 1995-1997 has the same roots, with Slovenia and Croatia creating nation-states. The disintegration of the USSR in 1991 led to the creation of such nation-states as Russia, Belarus, Ukraine, Armenia, Georgia, Azerbaijan, Kazakhstan, Kyrgyzstan, Turkmenistan, Tajikistan, Uzbekistan, Lithuania, Estonia, and Latvia. Proto-nations were Poland, Czechoslovakia, Hungary, Romania, Bulgaria, East Germany, and Mongolia under the rule of the Soviet Empire from 1945-1989. However, these regimes did not develop the Polish nation, or the Hungarian nation, since they were promoting the Empire's interest which was in conflict with these nations' interests. From the civilization point of view, proto-nations are *arrested mini*-civilizations. Almost 50 years of the Soviet Union's domination over Central-Eastern Europe led to misdevelopment of this sphere.

A nation is an entity which has a common language, culture, memory of historic events, and "national consciousness." It does not mean that the nation must share a common territory. This condition is applied toward a state rather than toward a nation. In this model, a state is a

category of power infrastructure. Moreover, the state creates the nation. This means that emigrants from a nation-state may claim a nationality of origin from their original nation-state, which may be thousands of miles away. They may say, for example, that they belong to the Irish nation, even while living in the U.S. and having its citizenship. This new affiliation, however, should mean that an emigrant transforms (voluntarily or involuntarily) him/herself into a member of a new nation since the emigrant is a "subject" of a new state. The combination of nation-with-state is a strong force, which, where it is present, drives the civilizing process. The World Wars in the 20th century were experiments in the civilizing process, inspired by strong nationalism, even professed superiority of one nation-race over another, as was the case of Nazi Germany. The Cold War from 1945-1989 was a case of the rivalry between the American nation and the Soviet "nation"-empire. Although the USSR was a federation of tens of proto-nations, it was all the time enforcing the development of the "Soviet" nation, even a *Homo sovieticus.* Likewise, the German Democratic Republic was also developing the "GDR" nation.

A state is an autonomous political unit, encompassing many communities within its territory and having a centralized government with power to draft men and women for war or work, levy and collect taxes, and decree and enforce laws. A state possesses the attribute of sovereignty.

An empire is a state of large size exercising political dominion over others, with or without the latter's consent.

A power is a state, which is militarily or economically strong relative to others. For example, in 2003, China was militarily strong and Japan was economically strong.

A superpower is a state, which in its military arsenal has dominating military system and is politically very influential. For example, during the Cold War, the superpowers were the U.S. and USSR which had nuclear weapon.

A hegemonic power is a state which dominates its world politically, militarily, economically, and scientifically. For example, at the beginning of the 21st century, the U.S. plays such a role in the world.

A political society is a multi-ethnic entity which evolves from a nation. A good example is the United States at the end of 20th century. During World War II, the U.S. fought as one nation-state, very proud of its heritage and values. Afterwards, along with the development of American democracy, minorities (of all types, including ethnic but mostly race and gender-oriented) evolved into strong interest groups that influenced politics (elections) and led to the transformation of the American nation into the American political society. This society emphasizes its immigrant roots and uses its services and resources for its own segmented aims in disregard of the common interest. In this type of entity, the civilization process is guided by the priority of infrastructure over culture. This society has become very productive but without a sense of how to aim for a meaningful life. The best solution for the U.S. is to sustain its one-nation model and prevent fragmentation along the lines of race and gender.

A transnational community is a regional entity, which organizes itself against the challenges of the global economy. Examples of this entity type are: the Association of the Eastern Alps, the Celtic Arc, the European Port Cities Network, Working Communities of the Pyrenees, and the Rhine Hub including the German states Nordrhein-Westfalen, Rhineland-Pfalz, Bayern, and Baden-Wurttemberg, plus Switzerland, Piedmont and Eastern France (including Burgundy, the Rhone Valley, the Cote d'Azur, and Languedoc). These centers will rival such centers in America as Montreal-Boston-Philadelphia, Pittsburgh-Detroit-Toronto-Chicago, and San Diego-Los Angeles-San Francisco. Asian regional entities are emerging around Tokyo and Osaka, Shanghai-Guangzhou-Hong Kong. Changes after the Cold War in Central and Eastern Europe are creating a regional community embracing Vienna-Budapest-Prague (somewhat a revival of the Hapsburg Empire), and in Northeastern Europe Copenhagen-Hamburg-Szczecin-Gdansk-Klaipeda-Liepaja-Riga-St.Petersburg-Helsinki. The civilization process of this entity-type is strong since it is based on voluntary cooperation and respect for each partner's achievements or potential. Priority is placed upon infrastructure development, but within a shared culture. The regional community is a very strong force in leveling disproportions of civilization developments among partners.

A supranational community is a cross-whole-national entity, which removes states' borders in a pseudo-formal sense and also in the sense of economic and political barriers. An example of this entity-type is the European Union, and perhaps even NATO, that step by step slowly expands toward a multi-national super-state with common market, common currency, single economic policy, and eventually military. This entity's civilization process leads to the development of a strong common infrastructure, which may lead to the homogenization of cultures. In a very long perspective, this development may lead to the formation of the political society. At the end of the 20th century, leaders of EU states have just become aware of it and look for solutions which could prevent the homogenization of national cultures. They would like to guide EU development by the policy of "unity in diversity." They are aware that the homogenization of cultures leads to lower cultural standards and eventual vulgarization of existence. Since the introduction of one legal language in the EU is impossible, it is therefore unfeasible to create one European nation. If this is true, the supra-national community must protect different cultures as the pre-requisite of meaningful life. However, this life's comfort depends upon commonly shared infrastructures, which sooner or later will trigger the homogenization of cultures. This is the dilemma of the current EU.

A spheric community is an entity of several nations from the same civilization. Examples of this entity are three states, the U.S., Canada, and Mexico that are united by the NAFTA (North American Free Trade Agreement) treaty. The civilization force of this entity-type lies in the area of infrastructural development.

The global society or the society of post-nations is the entity which emerges from the development of a global economy and global culture. This is an entity of stateless and post-national individuals and groups as well as organizations that promote free trade, free flow of ideas and people as a prerequisite of world peace and "happiness." This entity is a strong civilization force that leads toward the most effective civilization solutions, particularly in the area of the integrational infrastructure (the Internet, airlines, CNN), especially its leisure-time indulgence culture (Coca-Cola and Nike).

The global political society is an entity that may emerge from the global society. An example of this entity is the G-7+ group of the most developed nations that promote a common economic policy. This is an inter-civilization group of seven nations plus Russia (from three civilizations), which has been included in this Group as a reward for silent acquiescence with the inclusion of Poland, the Czech Republic, and Hungary in NATO. This entity's civilization power lies in the promotion of global standards of products and services as well as in promotion of democracy and peace. This action leads toward the modernization of world civilization and the reaction against the

westernization of the world. Both challenges are positive.

Utopia is an entity of calm and stagnation or perhaps even the beginning of civilization death. It seems at the first glance that utopia is the desired state of the world civilization; however, it may be just its end.

A civilization can be composed of one or a combination of these human entities, which in the case of the latter is a sort of human-entities configuration, as Sorokin calls it a set "made up of several wholes, halves, and quarters of divers language, state, religious, economic, territorial groups and unorganized populations" (Sorokin, 1950).

OBSERVATIONS FROM THE EMPIRICAL DEVELOPMENT OF CIVILIZATION

Observation 1: Figure 1-2 illustrates the historical development of succeeding civilizations, which emphasizes three such macrostructures: the societal, cultural, and infrastructural. This sequence indicates only the significant factors in stimulus-response processes. However, this sequence is inclusive and the next macrostructure of civilization development includes attributes of the previous macrostructure ("civilization additive memory"). This type of dynamics is shown in Figure 1-7.

Observation 2: Among driving forces of civilization development, one can recognize the following:

- Each civilization macrostructure's experience drives remaining macrostructures.
- The information-communication process is crucial in providing better information flows and communication among humans, first by

Figure 1-7. The civilization generations

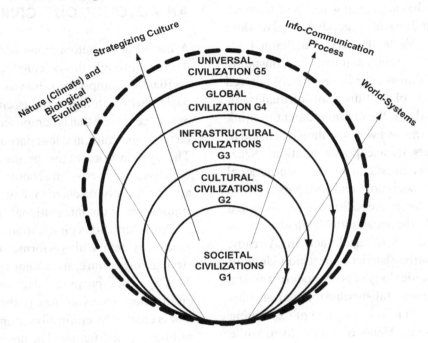

developing speech, later symbols, papyrus, books, newspapers, telephones, mass media, and the computer and its networks. These leads to higher awareness and more knowledgeable, perhaps wiser, decision-making by civilized humans.

- The world-systems are critical for historic evolution of civilization, such as "capitalism," "democratic revolutions," "industrialization," "scientific knowledge," "world wars," and world organizations like NATO, EU, GATT, WTO, NAFTA, the Internet, and so forth. These world-systems one can classify as large-scale, mid-scale, and small-scale [2].

- Each civilization macrostructure is influenced by nature and biological evolution and vice versa.

Observation 3: In the last 6,000 years, the development of vertical civilizations, such as the Mesopotamian, Egyptian, Sinic, Japanese, Islamic, and Western, took place. Around the year 2000, the first horizontal civilization (not having a sovereign center, and world-wide coverage is required to qualify) begins its existence, under a form of the global civilization. It is an infrastructural civilization, based on mediated information-communication and extended transportation networks, guided by a policy of a free flow of ideas, goods, and services, and still limited flow of people, through the global marketplace. This civilization, being mainly driven by market forces, does not satisfy many socially-minded people, hence there is a strong criticism of globalism.

Such an idealistic view of the future promotes the necessity to work on development of the universal civilization (horizontal civilization, driven by cultural behavior), taking the best from all civilizations and providing goodness and wisdom for all humans. Vaclav Havel (1996) defined this quest in the following manner: "…Constantly talking about Europe, we have entirely ignored one of the pillars of the European spiritual tradition—universalism, the commandment to think of everyone, to act as everyone should act, and to look for universally acceptable solution." Szczepanski (former president of the International Sociological Association) and Kuczynski (1991) stated that: "Today, universalism can be co-created as undoubtedly the most suitable answer to the challenges of the ideological vacuum. Already, universalism can be a barrier against individualism and egoism, the ideology of post-modernism, and all sorts of fundamentalisms and totalitarianisms. Universalism will also be capable of examining and solving the problems of nationalism, while retaining the most authentic values of national cultures." Janusz Kuczynski (1986), founder and honorary president of the International Society for Universalism, stated that: "Universalism has to advocate the solidarity of all peoples and nations which is rooted in our common human fates and in our joint struggle against the ever more numerous and greater threats, including the nuclear suicide of Mankind."

Figure 1-8 illustrates a model world-system of production at the beginning of the 21st century, as one of models which may help to understanding civilization change and continuity nowadays. This model takes into account the world-system of production, the information-communication process under a form of global, national and enterprise information infrastructures (GII, NII, EII), the global financial infrastructure and the global and national strategizing cultures. The latter concentrates on religion, political, societal, and economic cultures, putting aside diffusing, enlightening, and entertaining cultures (listed in Figure 1-6).

A DYNAMIC MODEL OF AN AUTONOMOUS CIVILIZATION

A model of an autonomous civilization can be defined through the oriented configuration of civilization components shown in Figure 1-9. The basic part of an autonomous civilization is the existence system that is composed of an entity, entertaining culture, and foundation infrastructure. This system is kept alive by the logistic system, which is composed of an economic infrastructure and a culturally-oriented management within the framework of the integrational infrastructure.

An autonomous civilization is steered by the guiding system, which is formed by a world view, strategizing culture, and authority infrastructure. This system's purpose is to stabilize a given civilization. Its extension is the power system that is created by culturally-oriented politics and military infrastructure. The power system keeps intact its own civilization as well as interacting with other civilizations.

The well-being of a civilization is proportional to the advancement of the knowledge system. The latter is composed of an enlightening culture and knowledge infrastructure, such as schools, universities, know-how centers, and libraries. This system's purpose is to generate awareness of the status of a civilization's affairs. The promotion of civilization awareness is carried out by the communication system, which is formed by a diffusing culture and communication infrastructure, such as media and their networks, telecommunication networks, and so forth. The communication system keeps its own civilization informed and interacts with other civilizations.

The civilizing process within a civilization is generated by every mentioned civilization system and exchange of their contributions, supported by the integrational infrastructure, which is composed of the communication, transportation, knowledge and information infrastructures. The last is emerging by the end of the 20th century and is known under a metaphoric term as the Information

Figure 1-8. The world-system of production (21st century) (EII-Enterprise Information Infrastructure, NII-National Information Infrastructure, IS-Information Systems, AP-Computer Applications)

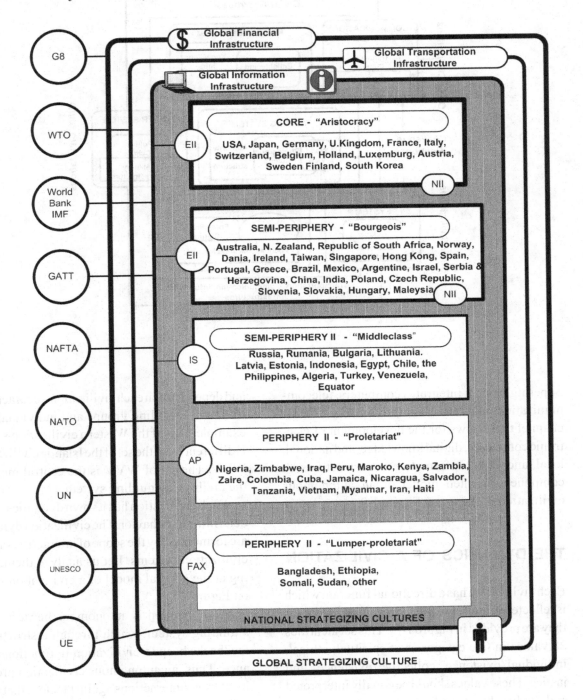

Figure 1-9. A civilization system

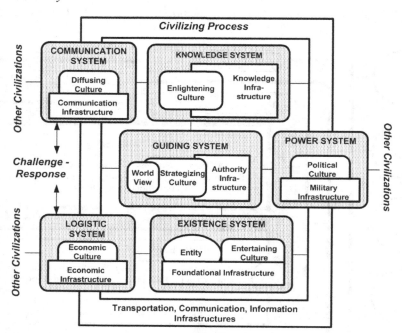

Superhighway. It integrates computers, telecommunication, and television into one multimedia channel that allows for the development of electronic commerce, digital knowledge, and national, local, and global information infrastructures. A component-oriented model of an autonomous civilization is shown on Figure 1-9.

THE DYNAMICS OF A CIVILIZATION

Each civilization has a directional function which is reflected in a set of world view values (WVV) as they are provided in Figure 1-10. This set identifies 28 values in five categories of spiritual, ethical, individual existence, collective existence, and justice. These values should be equally interpreted and applied by all (informed to certain degree) members of a given civilization. Of course, a degree of interpreting and applying them differs

and depends upon each civilization's character and tradition, including groups and individuals. For example, a set of the Western civilization's WVV is different from the set of the Islamic civilization's WVV. The set of WVV is the central means of the civilization guiding system.

Each civilization has its own dynamics, which determine its behavior. The civilization dynamics are formulated by the scope of interactions among civilization systems. Let us analyze them, looking at the general model of a civilization shown on Figure 1-11.

A civilization is autonomous because it has a guiding system, which through a structure of feedbacks keeps a civilization in functional balance. Thus, an autonomous civilization protects itself by counteractions against factors that could destroy it. An autonomous civilization tends to protect its existence through prophylactic measures against challenges coming from other

Figure 1-10. The world view values set (21st century)

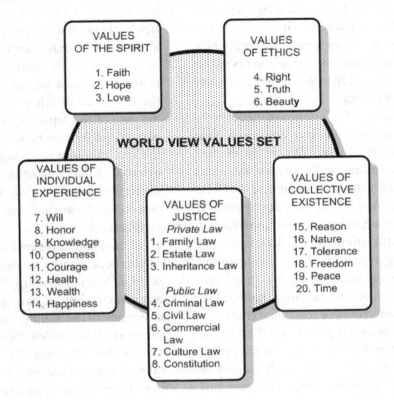

WORLD VIEW VALUES SET

VALUES OF THE SPIRIT
1. Faith
2. Hope
3. Love

VALUES OF ETHICS
4. Right
5. Truth
6. Beauty

VALUES OF INDIVIDUAL EXPERIENCE
7. Will
8. Honor
9. Knowledge
10. Openness
11. Courage
12. Health
13. Wealth
14. Happiness

VALUES OF JUSTICE
Private Law
1. Family Law
2. Estate Law
3. Inheritance Law

Public Law
4. Criminal Law
5. Civil Law
6. Commercial Law
7. Culture Law
8. Constitution

VALUES OF COLLECTIVE EXISTENCE
15. Reason
16. Nature
17. Tolerance
18. Freedom
19. Peace
20. Time

Figure 1-11. A generic civilization system

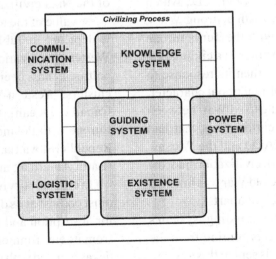

Civilizing Process

COMMU-NICATION SYSTEM

KNOWLEDGE SYSTEM

GUIDING SYSTEM

POWER SYSTEM

LOGISTIC SYSTEM

EXISTENCE SYSTEM

civilizations and through control of challenges coming from within it. There are two levels of guiding-system involvement. The first is at the level of communicating and informationally interpreting challenges and the second is at the level of registering and interpreting energy-driven challenges of existence.

The first level of civilization operations generates awareness of events and challenges by the knowledge system. The more mature and experienced a knowledge system, the more sophisticated the generated awareness is. Once awareness is passed to the guiding system, it triggers a reflection, which is communicated as a response to the stimulus. Civilizations with a weak guiding system do not generate strong enough reflections (motivations), and then inter-actions between the communication, knowledge, and power systems reflect a reactional character. This type of behavior is typical for civilizations in decline, such as the Soviet civilization after 1985; this was mostly reactional, without the ability to generate a motivational reflection. However, this civilization could fight (without any awareness of consequences). Moreover, its power system was based on the use of atomic weapons as a reaction to an external threat. Another example is the Eastern civilization in the first millennium A.D., which had a good guiding system with a strong WVV that preferred an alliance with the Turks turban rather than with the Roman miter. If a civilization has a good guiding system, then its response to challenges is of reflectional-reactional character. Such was the case during the Cold War between the Western and Eastern civilizations that had strong guiding systems (NATO and the Warsaw Pact). After 1985, the Eastern civilization had lost its guiding system, and the Cold War was finished in 1991 as the USSR had fallen apart.

The second level of the guiding system's involvement deals with threats coming from the existence system and controls sent to this system. These controls are guided by the reflectional responses of the guiding system. The quality of

the existence system depends upon the level of available resources. Every autonomous civilization begins with some level of resources; however, along with its existence this level may decline or rise. If a civilization does not have enough resources, then it begins to search for them in the territories of other civilizations. (This was the case of the Japanese civilization in the first part of the 20th century). As history indicates, the application of the power system (in the war mode) was the main solution in this quest. The stronger power system was used to determine the outcome of the war and the well-being of involved civilizations.

In the quantitative evaluation of a civilization, a cybernetic, generic model invented by a Polish scientist Marian Mazur (1966) is applied. Each autonomous civilization acts in a given resourceful environment that supplies to it external mechanical power (later called "power"), which we will call civilization power (P_c). A civilization cannot take in more power than it can process or more power than there are its needs for total power (P_t). In other words, internal power of civilization (P_{in}) cannot be greater than the civilization power and total power. Otherwise a given autonomous civilization may be destroyed, as it was in the case of the Nazi civilization (1933-1945).

A value of the total power (P_t) of civilizations is depicted in Table 1-2 on a seven-point scale. Western civilization, which is composed of ten cultures, has been divided into four cultural clusters: Western-West (Western Europe, U.S., Canada, Oceania), Western-Central (Central Europe with Poland liberated in 1989, the Czech Republic, Slovakia, and Hungary), Western-Latin (Latin America), and Western-Jewish.

In order to survive, an autonomous civilization must possess at its disposable working power (P_w) for absorption and processing of power taken in from its environment and compensating difficulties associated with it. For example, working power is needed to produce food, housing, and clothes. Without these goods and processes a civilization

Table 1-2. The total power (P) of civilizations characterized by level of energy consumption in coal equivalent - kg/capita/year in 1984

Scale Range	Energy Consumption	Civilizations
7	10,000 - 15,000	Western-West
6	7,000 - 9,999	
5	5,000 - 6,999	Western-Central
4	3,000 - 4,999	Japanese, Eastern
3	2,000 - 2,999	Western-Jewish
2	1,000 - 1,999	Islamic
1	Below 1,000	African, Buddhist, Hindu, Chinese, Western-Latin

Source: George Th. Kurian: The New Book of World Rankings, Facts on File Publications: New York, 1984, p. 226.

Table 1-3. Working power (P$_w$) of civilizations, characterized by average hours per week in manufacturing in 1984

Scale Range	Hours Per Week	Civilizations
7	35 - 39	Western-Jewish
6	40 - 42	Japanese, Western-West, Western-Central
5	43 - 44	
4	45 - 47	Western-Latin
3	48 - 49	Eastern, Buddhist, Islamic,
2	50 - 54	Chinese, African
1	55 - 60	Hindu

Source: George Th. Kurian: The New Book of World Rankings, Facts on File Publications: New York, 1984, p. 248.

could not afford idle power (P$_{id}$) such as rest, recreation, leisure, healthcare, education, and entertainment, which are needed for the support of operations. Values of working power (P$_w$) for different civilizations are shown in Table 1-3.

The idle power (P$_{id}$) of civilizations expressed in the number of cinema seats per 1,000 people is shown in Table 1-4.

Each active civilization must possess at its disposable safeguarding power (P$_s$). This power compensates for working and idle power. Otherwise working power will dissipate into idle power, limiting civilization operations. The main purpose of empires was the search for safeguarding of power that could secure their long-term existence while maintaining the luxury of idle power possessed by their elites.

Table 1-4. The Idle Power (P_{id}) of civilizations, characterized by the number of cinema seats per 1000 people in 1984

Scale Range	Number of Cinema seats	Civilizations
7	over 100	Eastern
6	60 - 99	Western-Central
5	40 - 59	Western-Jewish
4	25 - 39	Western
3	10 - 24	Buddhist, Western-Latin
2	5 - 9	Japanese, Islamic, Hindu
1	below 5	African, Chinese

Source: George Th. Kurian: The New Book of World Rankings, Facts on File Publications: New York, 1984, p. 403.

A civilization which cannot maintain its necessary level of secured resources will decline into lower stages of existence, but this decline can be arrested. A civilization could also lose its strength and pass into transition or arrest if its idle power (P_i) exceeds its working power (P_w). This is the case for the Roman (31 B.C.-476 A.D.) and Soviet (1917-1991) civilizations. These considerations [3] allow a definition of civilization secured power P_s:

$$P_s = P_w + P_{id} \qquad [1]$$

A relation of the working power to secured power we will call a coefficient of power supply:

$$r = P_w / P_s \qquad [2]$$

Hence, the working power P_w is defined as follows:

$$P_w = r \, P_s \qquad [3]$$

Inserting the expression [3] into the formula [1] we obtain a formula for secured power:

$$P_s = P_{id} / (1 - r) \qquad [4]$$

If $r = 0$, the taking in of resources from the environment does not require any work. This means that the existence of a civilization depends upon the size of its secured power which only needs to cover idle power $P_s = P_{id}$. This is the case for the Islamic civilization and its abundant oil resources at the beginning of the 21st century.

The bigger r is, the more work is needed to take in energy from the environment. This means that a civilization must take in more energy and its secured power (P_s) must be bigger.

If r approximates to 1, in other words, when the taking in of energy by a civilization requires vast work, then secured power approximates to infinity. This means that a civilization does not have idle power (P_{id}) regardless of how much secured power it is taking in from the environment. This is the case in arrested civilizations, like the Mayan, Andean, Yucatec-Mexican, Eskimo, Indian and Polynesian specimens. To a certain degree it also represents some parts of the present African civilization.

There is some surplus of power, which remains after total power covers secured power.

Figure 1-12. The distribution of the total power of a civilization, where: P_t - total power, P_{id} - idle power, P_w - working power, P_d - disposable power, P_k - coordination power, P_s - secure power

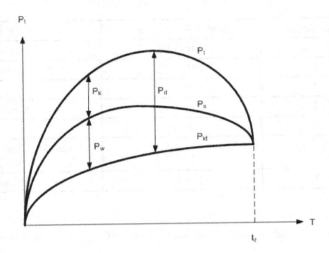

The remaining power we will call coordination power P_k:

$$P_k = P_t - P_s \qquad [5]$$

Then, the total power P_t of a civilization can be expressed as follows:

$$P_t = P_s + P_k \qquad [6]$$

or if we substitute the expression [1] for P_s then:

$$P_t = P_{id} + P_w + P_k \qquad [7]$$

The disposable power P_d of a civilization is defined as follows:

$$P_d = P_w + P_k \qquad [8]$$

All components of the total power are shown on Figure 1-12.

To survive, a civilization must produce total power no lower than its secured power ($P_t \geq P_s$), which depends upon existing civilization power (P_c). However, a civilization can reduce its secured power (P_s) by triggering changes in the environment that cause civilization power to increase. This means that a civilization may move into a territory with better resources or it may invade another civilization with such resources. This strategy explains the clashes among civilizations. To do so, a civilization must spend some power, which we called coordination power (P_k).

The more coordination power that is at the disposable of a civilization, the more changes it can invoke in the environment. Mastery of information distribution and utilization are at the heart of coordination power, and it produces a positive feedback cycle: more coordination power produces more civilization power, which in turn requires less working power and less secured power. As a result coordination power becomes bigger. This effect means that a civilization reaches its maximal coordination power and civilization power at the same time it has its minimal secured power. This is a highly desirable situation where a civilization uses its coordination power to secure the best environmental conditions, and increases its own existence timeline. In the long

Table 1-5. The Coordination Power (P$_k$) of civilizations, characterized by the number of computers per 1000 people in 1996

Scale Range	Number of Computers	Civilization
7	301 - 600	Western-West
6	201 - 300	Western-Jewish
5	101 - 200	Japanese
4	21 - 100	Western-Central
3	11 - 20	
2	2 - 10	Eastern, Chinese, Hindu, Buddhist, Western-Latin
1	below 1	African, Islamic

Source: Karen Peteska-Juliussen and Egil Juliussen, 8th Annual Computer Industry Almanac, 1996, 1997 Almanac, Information Please, p. 566.

run, mastery of information increases awareness and knowledge which results in wiser decision making about all civilization system components. Most civilizations last for many years, enduring decisions of varying quality, but information coordination provides capacities to eventually turn data into wisdom for the benefit of a given civilization. Coordination power is characterized by the number of computers per 1,000 people, as it is shown in Table 1-5.

It must be mentioned that along with increased civilization power (P$_c$), working power (P$_w$) decreases but idle power (P$_{id}$) does not decrease. The latter is defined by a civilization's status of aging and development. Therefore, even if civilization power (P$_c$) could be infinitely great, secured power (P$_s$) does not decrease to zero, but to the magnitude of idle power (P$_{id}$). It means that an autonomous civilization increasing civilization power (P$_c$) may extend its existence (determined by the crossing point of the curve (P$_t$) with the curve (P$_s$)) to a value equal to theoretical existence time (defined by the crossing point of the curve (P$_{tt}$) with the curve (P$_{id}$)) but not to infinity. One can say that

the civilization effort to improve external conditions is not the struggle to prolong its existence but rather to avoid shortening it.

In civilizations, the role of civilization power (P$_c$) involves money, machines, robots that can substitute human work, authority-commanding work force, and so forth. Civilization power can be illustrated at the level of an individual. For example, children have too little disposable power to generate working power and idle power and thus, total power; therefore, they have to rely upon their parents' power to obtain secured power. Also, at the end of human life, disposable power is small, so one can function with the help of civilization power (P$_c$) such as money, family help, and welfare until the total power (P$_t$) cannot cover idle power (P$_{id}$).

Larger coordination power (P$_k$) improves the chances a civilization has in searching, comparing, digging out, acquiring and shaping the external environment in order to increase civilization power (P$_c$). We can express this process by defining the autonomy coefficient

$$f = P_k / P_d \qquad\qquad [9]$$

which means that with a portion of its power (P_d), a civilization can focus on improvements of external conditions.

Expression [8] indicates that if ($P_w = P_d$) then ($P_k = 0$) and $f = 0$. In other words, if $P_{id} = 0$ a civilization has no flexibility and its behavior is forced. This is the case of African civilization, which was invaded by Islamic and Western civilizations that were looking for slaves.

Another extreme case takes place when working power ($P_w = 0$) is entirely substituted by civilization power (P_c). Then, secured power contains only idle power ($P_s = P_{id}$), coordination power becomes equal to disposable power ($P_k = P_d$) and the autonomy coefficient f = 1. This leads us to the following sequence of relationships: if a civilization has possibly the highest autonomy coefficient, it means that coordination power is possibly highest and it can organize the possibly highest civilization power. In effect, secured power is possibly minimal and a civilization can exist longer than without these conditions. Hence, one can draw the following rule: the bigger the coordination power is, the longer a civilization exists. Coordination power is mastery of information. This rule emphasizes the critical role played by good management techniques and effective information systems in strong Western civilization development during the 20th century.

A CHARACTER OF A CIVILIZATION

With the help of the Mazur General Cybernetic Model (1966), we can describe a character of each civilization. A civilization character can be described by its dynamism (D), developmental coefficient (G), aging coefficient (R) and dynamism coefficient (n=G/R). Based on the values of these coefficients, one can distinguish the following types of civilization character:

A - endodynamic civilization ($G \leq R$, $n \leq 1$, $D \leq 0$), characterized by accelerated development, or,

B - static civilization (G=R, n=1, D=0), characterized by development equal to aging, and/or,

C - exodynamic civilization ($G \geq R$, $n \geq 1$, $D = 0$) characterized by slow downward development.

The coefficient (n) and number (D) characterize a civilization character based upon the flow of total power (P_t) and idle power (P_{id}). In practice, there are smaller differences between civilization characters than between A and B or B and C. Therefore, we will introduce two intermediary classes of civilization character:

AB - endostatic civilization, and
BC - exostatic civilization

Since endodynamic civilizations employ slow development, their characteristics may be identified in the following manner. Slow development means that the guiding system is not intensive and therefore the existence system evolves very slowly. The slow guiding system means that reflection potential is low and awareness generated by the knowledge system is weak. Coordination power (P_k) is low and saved for the eventual increase of civilization power (P_c). This means that the guiding system tolerates challenges and delays and limits its response toward the removal of obstacles only.

The A-class civilizations control themselves toward the *status quo* policy of maintaining civilization power only. Their behavior is reactionary toward challenges. The main factor which increases the power of a member of this class of civilization is the policy of survival, leading to the constant prolongation of existence. Among such civilizations one can classify the Hindu, Buddhist, and African civilizations.

The C-class civilizations have opposite characteristics. Their fast development indicates that the guiding system is intensive and therefore their existence system undertakes fast evolution. Such civilizations have a big disposable power (P_d) and their responses to challenges are strong. Their coordination power (P_k) is also big; therefore, when civilization power (P_c) is declining and secured power (P_s) is growing, total power (P_t) is sufficient to insure that their existence is not threatened. To cover working power (P_w) and secured idle power (P_{id}), civilization power (P_c) does not to have to be increased.

The C-class civilizations orient their life toward the maintenance of big coordination power (P_k), and their responses are mostly directed toward internal challenges. The Spartan, Soviet and Nazi civilizations belong to the C-class.

Comparison of A and C classes of civilizations is provided in Table 1 - 6.

The endodynamic civilizations (A) function according to a doctrine "lasting longer brings longer satisfaction," while exodynamic civilizations (C) prefer a doctrine "living intensively brings more life." The purpose of endodynamic civilizations is to achieve a positive balance of life, while exodynamic civilizations' purpose is to increase participation in life. Static civilizations (B) aim toward a balance between current effects

and security for the future. The endodynamic civilizations make decisions based on the criterion "what is effective," while the exodynamic civilizations will based their choice according to the criterion "what is pleasant." Static civilizations prefer the criterion of "what is right" in their decision making. The extreme civilizations do not follow the rules while static civilizations look for moral behavior. The static civilizations' balance between spending and saving leads toward a predilection for order, which very often means "order for the sake of order." Endodynamic civilizations neglect the order if it becomes ineffective, while the exodynamic civilizations disregard order if it is not useful to them.

Endodynamic civilizations organize themselves around moves that increase civilization power in connection with the strategy of extending its life. Therefore, this kind of civilization behaves with reason, carefully calculating measures and looking for consequences in the future. The exodynamic civilizations seek short-term effects, behave in a less reasonable, rather negligent and unsteady manner. The static civilizations assign lasting meaning to principles. Hence they act with confidence and even when it is a doubtful strategy, they continue to believe in their principles, which sometimes look naive to outsiders. The latter is exemplified by the Western civilization's

Table 1-6. Comparison of the A and C classes of civilizations

Endodynamic Civilizations (A)	Exodynamic Civilizations (C)
Slow development	Fast development
Low-intensive guiding system	High-intensive guiding system
Small increments of reflectional potential	Big increments of reflectional potential
Rare responses	Frequent responses
Weak responses	Strong responses
Aspiration toward big civilization power	Aspiration toward big coordination power
Slow removal of obstacles	Fast removal of obstacles
Sensitivity toward changes in the external environment	Sensitivity toward changes in their own existence system
Control upon future results	Control of the current results

approach to the USSR during the Cold War from 1945 to 1991.

With respect to the information and communication infrastructure, the endodynamic civilizations consider information carefully to make decisions about their future. In static civilizations, information is collected and distributed in a limiting manner, since only such information is needed that satisfies the criterion "know only what you should know." The exodynamic civilizations prefer general and "surface" information but they communicate with great confidence and "loudly." They prefer to manipulate information in such a way as suits their purposes.

In terms of admitting successes and failures each class of civilization has its own way of coping. Endodynamic civilizations minimize their successes and exaggerate their failures, since they do not have enough coordination power and civilization power; hence, they always look for ways to increase them. Therefore, they remember what they had in deficit more than what they had in surplus. Also, fearful of competition, they do not want to share with other civilizations the sources of their successes and failures. The exodynamic civilizations, possessing large coordination power, exaggerate their successes and minimize their failures in order to gain stature in the world's opinion. Static civilizations react toward success and failure from the point of view of their lasting principles. They are terrified by big successes and failures, since these events invert their established order.

The comparison of civilization character is illustrated in Table 1-7. This comparison is very general in nature and serves only as a point of departure. The Western-Latin and Islamic civilizations are considered exodynamic since despite coordination power (low computer power), they have strong guiding systems, based either on theocratic or authoritarian principles.

In general, the exodynamic and endodynamic civilizations provide most of the contributions to culture. On the other hand, the static and endostatic civilizations provide most of the solutions in civilization infrastructures. Some endodynamic and endostatic civilizations contribute significantly in so-called philosophies of life.

A MODEL OF THE WORLD CIVILIZATION

Until now we have dealt with the modeling of civilization as it was initiated by Toynbee (1957) and Koneczny (1962). However, presently we are

Table 1-7. The comparison of civilization characters

Endodynamic (A)	Endostatic (AB)	Static (B)	Exostatic (BC)	Exodynamic (C)
Hindu	Chinese	Western-West	Western-Central Western-Jewish	Western-Latin
Buddhist		Japanese	Eastern	Islamic
African				Soviet
				Nazi

changing our point of reference from a civilization or civilizations to the world civilization as it has been perceived by Braudel (1993).

Following Braudel, we assume that the more broad and complete a perspective is, the more accurately we can infer conclusions about the fate of the world from it. In this section, we are going to expand the Braudel model. His four historical macro-structures of the world civilization are modeled into four "wheels" which strongly influence each other in the Braudel-Targowski model presented on Figure 1-13.

The four macrostructures are defined in the following manner:

A. The quasi-immobile macrostructure of 6,000 years of history of people's civilization with emphasis on the last millennium

B. The intermediary macrostructure of the history of the civilization (epochs, phases, and periods of the 19th and 20th centuries) which bind the most important events in the cause-effect chain

C. The current macrostructure of the history of civilization in which we are functioning now and which is a result of two previous structures that directly influence the future

D. The future macrostructure of the history of civilization, as a sketch of the results of the present structure of civilization. It is a history in *status nascendi*, whether probable or not, whose purpose is to warn us of wrongs or to confirm our good

The model of history macrostructures of civilization (HMoC) in Figure 1-13 illustrates the correlation between different intervals of historical time. By the logic of the arrows in the model, each macrostructure leads to another, both in selection of facts and in interpretation of the past from the point of view of the present.

No one should be surprised, therefore, that the current macrostructure of the history of the civilization implies a quasi-immobile macrostructure. For example, we have changed our opinion about

Figure 1-13. Braudel-Targowski Model of history macrostructures of the world civilization

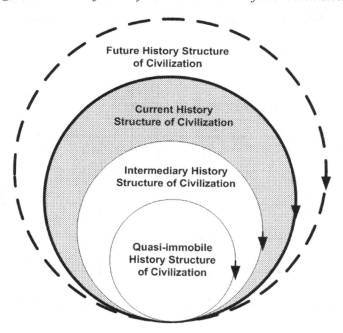

the Crusades of the 12th and 13th centuries. In the past, they were considered as expeditions to loot the pagans. Contemporarily, we believe that the Crusades had a religious character and the crusaders were genuinely interested in converting the pagans (Riley-Smith, 1995).

Therefore, the logic of the arrows should not cause doubts regarding the dependency of future structures on the previous ones. It is obvious that particular macrostructures of the history of world civilization have a dynamic character. As time goes by, especially periods measured in hundreds and thousands of years, the time scope of these four structures will modify and move foreword along with the calendar.

GRAND LAWS OF THE WORLD CIVILIZATION

The idea of laws of the world civilization history is controversial, especially after an assumption of a developmental course of history. History does not have to repeat itself according to the laws regarding the past. From studies of the fate of the world in the last 6,000 years, which are contained in this book, three rather important laws result:

The First Grand Law of the World Civilization is the Ability of Man to Develop:

People have seen themselves as entering the world with a potential of many gifts, and they hope to fulfill these gifts in the development of their own lives (Bronowski & Mazlish, 1962).

The Second Grand Law of the World Civilization is the Right of Man to Freedom and Reason. We formulate it as follows:

People constantly aim for freedom; the range of this freedom and reason depends on the level of a nation's knowledge, communication ability and knowledge of the international community.

During 6,000 years of civilization, man steadily increased his freedom, to some extent, as an achievement of knowledge about social life. In practice, man was liberated from political, economic and social discrimination by the end of the 20th century, when many dictatorships fell, including Communism and other oppressive regimes. People started to increase their freedom only in the 2nd millennium. Examples of this occurred during the Renaissance when print was widespread and during the beginning of the development of natural sciences. Moveable type and natural science gave birth to the Enlightenment, which created the American Revolution and the French Revolution. This led to democracy, in other words the rule of the people. In the process of the development of knowledge, the Industrial Revolution strengthened democracy by a gradual economic liberation of mankind. Further reinforcement of the development of knowledge is happening during the Information Revolution, which reverses the former human path toward knowledge. During this time, people do not need to seek out the information because the computer networks bring data to them wherever they are.

The Third Grand Law of the World Civilization is the Law of Conscious Historical Evolution, which we formulate in the following way:

Mankind consciously steers the development of civilization through the formulation of main ideas and values in each given epoch.

The Renaissance, the Enlightenment, and Modernism each left a permanent mark on the course of history in their particular periods, phases, and stages. Formulating those ideas or values can often happen in a sharp conflict or even in a social revolution.

The law emphasizes a sphere of conscious culture, which guides the remaining spheres of social life. This way, one pulls out of the "oppression" of the economic field which, according to Karl Marx, justly and solely directs the awareness and the action of man. More and more people in the world are convinced that consciousness comes first and that the brain or even the soul is metaphorically comparable to material subjects, which contradicts the Marxist Theory (Herman, 1988; Cook, 1991; Rotschild, 1991; Renesh, 1992).

The Fourth Grand Law of the World Civilization is the Historical Right of a Country's Success, which develops in the following way:

The historical degree of a country's success is proportioned to the level of harmony among its political, social and economic domains.

If a country lacks this harmony, sooner or later chaos will manifest itself, which will lead to collapse. The history of Poland during the last 350 years is proof of this law. Poland, however, is not the only example; another would be the breakdown of Russia, Yugoslavia, Somalia, Rwanda and Burundi. The next possible candidates for this kind of collapse would be Belarus and even Canada (Quebec) or Belgium. This law can also be applied to the present situation in the Central European states, when it is said that these states have their own prosperous economies and political systems in disarray. A lack of harmony between these two spheres, for example, could lead to a collapse of Poland for the third time.

FROM WORLD TO PLANETARY CIVILIZATION

At the beginning of the 3rd millennium, the emergence of the global civilization is taking place. This sets new standards in business communications, international travel, world products, and international behavior based upon common fashion, food, pop music, and movie "taste."

Thus, a citizen of any civilization has to cope with two civilizations' challenges: one set by his/her own civilization and one set by the global one. The global civilization should not replace an autonomous (vertical) civilization as it is perceived by many leaders of "invaded" civilizations. On the contrary, it is necessary to develop behaviors which can cope simultaneously with these two civilizations. It looks like this will be one of the biggest challenges of the 3rd millennium for all inhabitants of the Earth.

The emergence of the global civilization creates the second layer of the world civilization, above the first one represented by each autonomous civilization. The third layer of the world civilization is created by the universal civilization. Three layers of the world civilization increase the degree of civilization complexity, which is a new difficulty for all civilizations and their participants who have to formulate intelligent responses to challenges (Figure 1-14). Needless to say, all three levels of the world civilizations are inclusive. However, the universal civilization is the guiding one, which generalizes and popularizes the best of all civilizations and influences them in a feedback manner. Perhaps, in a *tres longue duree*, all the autonomous civilizations will converge into the universal-central civilization.

Another major challenge of world civilization is the accelerated development of technology that attacks the well-being of people. At first glance such technologies as robotics and computerization improve productivity and lower prices of products and services. This is, however, a short-term view. In a long-term view, this type of technology eliminates jobs and shrinks the consumer base, which in turn will weaken the strength of the economy. Its consequences may lead to social unrest and crises for the Western and Japanese civilizations or all those civilizations that copy this strategy as they modernize.

A general model of the planetary civilization as a set of vertical and horizontal civilizations is shown in Figure 1-15. The planetary civilization has been developing by "division" into *vertical* (autonomous) civilizations through the last 6,000 years. However, "some of these civilizations have been or are more dynamic than others and are

Figure 1-14. Four layers of the Pianet Civilzation

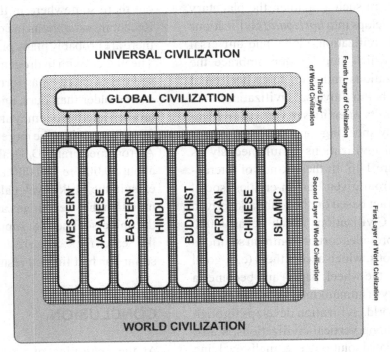

Figure 1-15. The 21st century planet civilization of the earth as a set of vertical civilizations (A-African, B-Buddhist, Ch-Chinese, E-Eastern, H-Hindu, I-Islamic, J-Japanese) and horizontal civilizations (Global and Universal)

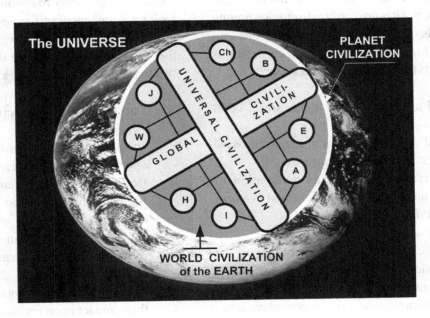

outgoing and bringing their outlook…to others" (Melko, 1987). In such a manner, the planetary civilization develops into *horizontal* civilizations such as world civilization, global and universal civilizations, which step by step embrace the vertical civilizations and even some horizontal ones (from global to universal civilization).

A human entity or entities of vertical civilizations, or strictly speaking—people—nowadays, live in several civilizations simultaneously as shown in Figure 1-16. In these kinds of interactions, people from given human entities (social organizations) act based on the foundation given by the World Civilization, which began 6,000 years ago and provides certain common solutions to all civilizations, which accept them (e.g., good vs. bad, music, the wheel, paper) and becomes a storage memory of humankind's common experience. As the world civilization develops through interactions among vertical civilizations, it also specializes in global solutions, eventually evolving into the global civilization. This civilization has an ambition to include all vertical civilizations under its wings, but due to many factors it can so far touch only certain segments of these civilizations. The same role would likely play out in the universal civilization, but it is now only a discussion among intellectuals. Consequently, nowadays one can recognize three levels of horizontal civilizations belonging to the planetary civilization:

1. World civilization (old habits since 4,000 B.C.)
2. Global civilization (as a mutation of world civilization), 20th-21st centuries
3. Universal civilization (as a mutation of world and global civilizations) yet in *status nascendi*

The full classification of civilizations of the Earth is provided in Figure 1-17. This classification includes a possible civilization created by ETI–Extraterrestrial Intelligence, which nowadays is beyond human comprehension. Is humankind alone in the universe? Or are other intelligent beings out there somewhere in the hugeness of space? Recent investigations in cosmology indicate that there are probably many planets hospitable to life. The planets with hydrogen-rich gases, water, and sources of energy may form life. Perhaps this life can be older than ours, and one can believe that an alien intelligence may attempt to communicate [4] with us and can be more advanced than we are. Astronomer Frank D. Drake (1962) guesses that about 10,000 to 100,000 advanced civilizations exist in the Milky Way galaxy alone. Opponents maintain that we humans are unique and alone in the universe. The U.S. supports the SETI project, the Search for Extraterrestrial Intelligence, which so far has had limited results.

CONCLUSION

At the beginning of the 21st century the idea of "civilization" becomes more popular as we are facing terrorism, which is de facto a war of civilizations. At the same time the concept of a "state" changes, when for the sake of *globalization* some states are ready to minimize their roles and look for a concept of self-supporting citizens and growing business in a world without borders. Both these two factors emphasize the growing role of "civilization" in world affairs.

A. Further Research Directions

- Investigation of relationships among human specializations, culture, and infrastructure (technology) developments as the determining factor in civilizations' advancement or decline
- Investigation of human entities and their dynamics in transformations within a community's ladder
- Investigation of different world-systems and their impact upon civilization development or regression

Figure 1-16. A vertical civilization among horizontal civilizations

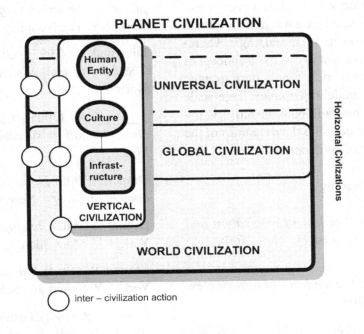

- Investigation of civilization dynamics characterized by different configurations of key indicators
- Investigation of civilization characters by application of different configurations of key indicators
- Investigation of the world civilization and its impact on international relations

B. Research Opportunities

- The research opportunities are in the interdisciplinary studies of history, political science, technology, anthropology, medicine, and others

C. Additional Ideas

- How civilization concepts impact the globalization processes in the 21st century and lead to a new kind of civilization— perhaps a global one

D. Rationale

- To understand the world dynamics in the 21st century one must understand the paths of civilization. The contemporary Western civilization is seen not only as the promoter of comprehensive globalization but also—due to the multifaceted impact of growing information, medical, electronic, and transportation technologies—as the seed-bed of anthropological mutation. Yet contrasting demographic and ecological developments in other civilizations of the world may turn the apparent trend in another direction. Human history is relatively short, since civilization is only 6,000 years old. However, it is very complex in societal, cultural, and infrastructural relations. Furthermore, different religions create different mindsets and complicate civilization issues even more. One such issue is the Civilization War in the 21st century, which is called the War on Terrorism. One can imagine what would happen if this war were called the Civilization War. In almost every community we would face a war and the human fate would be even worse and tragic. Therefore, it is important to discuss a concept of civilization and apply the modern graphic technique of modeling complex, large-scale processes. The traditional narrative is too simplistic for defining the dynamics of the current state of civilization.

E. Additional Reading

Adams, B. (1943). *The law of civilization and decay: An essay on history.* New York, NY: Knopf.

Adams, H. (1928). *The tendency of history.* New York, NY: Macmillan.

Appleby, J., Hunt, L., & Jacob, M. (1994). *Telling the truth about history.* New York, NY: Norton.

Barnes, H. (1937). *An intellectual and cultural history of the western world.* New York, NY: Reynal & Hitchcock.

Barzun, J. (2000). *From dawn to decadence.* New York, NY: HarperCollins.

Beard, C. (1957). *The economic basis of politics and related writings.* Compiled by W. Beard. New York, NY: Random House.

Berman, M. (2006). *Dark ages America: The final phase of empire.* New York, NY: Norton.

Brzezinski, Z. (2007). *Second chance: Three presidents and the crisis of American superpower.* New York, NY: Basic Books.

Bury, J. (1913). *A history of freedom of thought.* New York, NY: Holt.

Carr, E. (1967). *What is history?.* New York, NY: Knopf.

Cohen, J. (1995). *How many people can the earth support?.* New York, NY: Norton.

Condorcet, A-N. (1955). *Sketch for a historical picture of the progress of the human mind.* New York, NY: The Noonday Press.

Diamond, J. (1997). *Guns, germs, and steel: The fates of human societies.* New York, NY: Norton.

_____. (2005). *Collapse: How societies choose to fail or succeed.* New York, NY: Viking.

Draper, J. (1905). *History of the intellectual development of Europe.* New York, NY: Harper.

Drake, F. (1962). *Intelligent life in space.* New York, NY: Macmillan.

Durant, W. (1954). *The story of civilization.* New York, NY: Simon and Schuster.

Emerson, R. (1841). History. *Essays: First Series* (1841), included in *Emerson: Essays and Lectures* (pp. 235-256).

Ferguson, N. (2006). *The war of the world: Twentieth-century conflict and the descent of the west.* New York, NY: Penguin.

Fischer, D. (1970). *Historians' fallacies: Toward a logic of historical thought.* New York, NY: Harper.

Fisk, R. (2005). *The great war for civilization: The conquest of the Middle East.* New York, NY: Knopf.

Freeman, C. (2004). *The closing of the western mind: The rise of faith and the fall of reason.* New York, NY: Knopf.

Freud, S. (1961). *Civilization and its discontents (1930).* New York, NY: Norton.

Garraty, J., & Gay, P. (Eds.). (1985). *The Columbia history of the world.* New York, NY: Harper.

Garrett, L. (1994). *The coming plague: Newly emerging diseases in a world out of balance.* New York, NY: Farrar Straus and Giroux.

Greider, W. (1997). *One world, ready or not: The manic logic of global capitalism.* New York, NY: Simon & Schuster.

Hegel, G. (1952). *The philosophy of history (1837).* Chicago, IL: Great Books.

_____. (1974). *Lectures on the history of philosophy.* London: Humanities Press.

von Herder, H. (1968). *Reflections on the philosophy of the history of mankind (1784-1791).* Chicago, IL: University of Chicago.

_____. (1993). *Preparing for the twenty-first century.* New York, NY: Random House.

_____. (2002). *Wealth and democracy: A political history of the American rich.* New York, NY: Broadway.

_____. (2006). *American theocracy: The peril and politics of radical religion, oil, and borrowed money in the 21st century.* New York, NY: Viking.

Herman, A. (1997). *The idea of decline in western history.* New York, NY: Free Press.

Himmelfarb, G. (1994). *On looking into the abyss: Untimely thoughts on culture and society.* New York, NY: Knopf.

Hume, D. (1985). Of the study of history. *Essays Moral, Political, and Literary* (1741-1742); Liberty Classics, (pp. 563-568).

James, W. (1910). Great men and their environment. In *The Will to Believe and Other Popular Essays (1897),* (pp. 216-254). New York, NY: Longman.

Jaspers, K. (1953). *The origin and goal of history.* New Haven, CT: Yale University Press.

Johnson, C. (2004). *The sorrows of empire: Militarism, secrecy, and the end of the republic.* New York, NY: Holt.

_____ (2006). *Nemesis: The last days of the American Republic.* New York, NY: Holt.

Johnson, P. (1976). *A history of Christianity.* New York, NY: Touchstone.

Kennedy, P. (1987). *The rise and fall of the great powers: Economic change and military conflict from 1500 to 2000.* New York, NY: Random House.

Kroeber, A. (1944). *Configurations of culture growth.* Berkeley, CA: University of California Press.

Lecky, W. (1955). *History of European morals from Augustus to Charlemagne.* New York, NY: Braziller.

Lewis, B. (2002). *What went wrong? Western impact and Middle Eastern response.* Oxford: Oxford University Press.

von Mises, L. (1969). *Theory and history: An interpretation of social and economic evolution.* Arlington, VA: Arlington House.

Murray, C. (2003). *Human accomplishment: The pursuit of excellence in the arts and sciences, 800 BC to 1950.* New York, NY: HarperCollins.

Nietzsche, F. (1983). On the uses and disadvantages of history for life. In *Untimely Meditations (1874),* (pp. 57-123). Cambridge: Cambridge University Press.

Phillips, K. (1990). *The politics of rich and poor: Wealth and the American electorate in the Reagan aftermath.* New York, NY: Random House.

Popper, K. (1957). *The poverty of historicism.* Boston, MA: Beacon.

Russell, B. (1938). *Power: A new social analysis.* New York, NY: Norton.

Schopenhauer, A. (2005). *The world as will and idea.* Online: Kissinger Publishing.

Smith, P. (1930). *A history of modern culture*. New York, NY: Holt.

Stiglitz, J. (2002). *Globalization and its discontents*. New York, NY: Norton.

_____(2006). *Making globalization work*. New York, NY: Norton.

Tainter, J. (1988). *The collapse of complex societies*. Cambridge: Cambridge University Press.

Toynbee, A. (1948). *Civilization on trial*. Oxford: Oxford University Press.

_____ (1953). *The world and the west*. Oxford: Oxford University Press.

_____(1957). *A study of history, (1934-1961)*. Oxford: Oxford University Press.

White, A. (1995). *A history of the warfare of science with theology in Christendom*. New York, NY: Braziller.

REFERENCES

Arnason, J. (2003). *Civilization in dispute, historical questions and theoretical traditions*. Boston, MA; Leiden: Brill

Benton, L. (1996). From the world-system perspective to institutional world history: Culture and economy in global theory. *Journal of World History, 7*(2), 261-289.

Bosworth, A. (2003). The genetics of civilization: An empirical classification of civilizations based on writing systems. *Comparative Civilizations Review, 49,* 9.

Braudel, F. (1993). *A history of civilizations*. New York, NY: Penguin Books.

_____ (1992a). *The wheels of commerce*. Berkeley: University of California Press.

_____ (1992b). *The structures of everyday life*. Berkeley, CA: University of California Press.

_____(1995). The Mediterranean and the Mediterranean world in the Age of Philip II. Berkley, CA: University of California Press.

Bronowski, J., & Mazlish, B. (1962). *The western intellectual tradition*. New York, NY: Harper Perennial.

Burenhult, G. (2003). *Great civilizations*. San Francisco, CA: Fog City Press.

Caincross, F. (1997). *The death of distance*. Boston, MA: Harvard Business School Press.

Chase-Dunn, C., & Hall, T. (1997). *Rise and demise, comparing world-systems*. Boulder, CO: Westview Press.

Coulborn, R. (1959). *The origin of civilized societies*. Princeton, NJ: Princeton University Press.

Cook, B. (1991, October 21). Quality: The pioneers survey the landscape. *Industry Week*.

Christian, D. (2005). M*aps of time, an introduction to big history*. Berkley, CA: University of California Press.

Ding, Y-C., Chi, H., Grady, D., Morishima, A., Kidd, J., Kidd, K., et al. (2002). Wvidence of positive selection acting at the human dopomine receptor D4 gene locus. *Proceedings of the National Academy of Sciences, 99,* (pp. 309-314).

Fernandez-Armesto, F. (2001). *Civilizations, culture, ambition, and the transformation of nature*. New York, NY: A Touchstone Book; Simon & Schuster.

Grossman, L. (1995). *The electronic republic*. New York, NY: Viking Penguin.

Havel, V. (1996). Europe as task. *Dialogue and Universalism, 6*(5-6), 10-17.

Herman, W. (1988). *Global mind change: The promise of the last years of the twentieth century*. Indianapolis, IN: Knowledge Systems.

Huntington, S. (1996). *The clash of civilizations and the remaking of world order.* New York, NY: Simon & Schuster.

Jaeger, W. (1945). *Paideia: The ideals of Greek culture.* New York, NY: Oxford University Press.

Johnson, A., & Earle, T. (1987). *The evolution of human societies.* Stanford, CA: Stanford University Press.

Koneczny, F. (1962). *On the plurality of civilizations.* London: Wydawnictwa Towarzystwa im. Romana Dmowskiego (Publications of the Roman Dmowski Association).

_____ (1977). *For an order in history* (Polish edition only). London: Wydawnictwa Towarzystwa im. Romana Dmowskiego (Publications of the Roman Dmowski Association).

_____ (1982). *History Laws* (Polish edition only). London: Wydawnictwa Towarzystwa im. Romana Dmowskiego (Publications of the Roman Dmowski Association).

Krejci, J. (2004). *The paths of civilization, understanding the currents of history.* New York, NY: Palgrave; Macmillan.

Kroeber, A. (1944). *Configurations of culture growth.* Berkeley and Los Angeles, CA: University of California Press.

_____ (1952). *The nature of culture.* Chicago, IL: University of Chicago Press.

Kroeber, A., & Kluckhohn, C. (1952). *Culture. A critical review of concepts and definitions.* Cambridge, MA: The Museum.

Kroker, A., & Kroker, M. (1997). *Digital delirium.* New York, NY: St. Martins Press.

Kuczynski. J. (1986). Universalism as the meaning of recent history. *Dialectics and Humanism, 13*(1), 101-118.

Kurian, G. (1984). *The new book of world rankings.* New York, NY: Facts on File Publications.

Levy, P. (1997). *Collective intelligence.* New York, NY: Plenum Press.

Maynard, H., & Mehrtens, S. (1996). *The fourth wave. Business in the 21st century.* San Francisco, CA: Berrett-Koehler Publishers.

Mumford, L. (1966). *Technics and human development.* San Diego, CA: Harcourt Brace Jovanovich.

Mazur, M. (1966). *Cybernetyczna teoria ukladow samodzielnych. (Cybernetic theory of self-dependent units).* Warsaw: PWN.

McGaughey, W. (2001). *Rhythm and self-consciousness: New ideal for an electronic civilization.* Minneapolis, MN: Thistlerose Publications.

McLuhan, M. (1962). *The Gutenberg galaxy.* Toronto, ON: University of Toronto Press.

Melko, M. (1969). *The nature of civilizations.* Boston, MA: Porter Sargent Publisher.

_____ (1987). World civilization: A Faustian perception of Hellenistic phase. In: M. Melko & L. Scott (Eds.), *The boundaries of civilizations in space and time.* Lanham, MD; New York, NY; London: University Press of America.

Melko. M., & Scott, L. (Eds.). (1987). *The boundaries of civilizations in space and time.* Lanham, MD; New York, NY; London: University Press of America.

Melko, M. (2008). Melko's legacy. *The ISCSC Newsletter, 48*(1), 3.

Miyaki, M. (2004). *Civilization and time.* Poznan, Poland: The Historical Institute of the Adam Mickiewicz University.

Moczulski, L. (2000). *Geopolityka.* Warsaw: Bellona.

Postman, N. (1993). *Technopoly: The surrender of culture to technology.* New York, NY: Vintage Books.

Quigley, C. (1961). *The evolution of civilizations.* New York, NY: McMillan Co.

Renesh, J. (Ed.). (1992). New tradition in business: Spirit and leadership in the 21st century. San Francisco, CA: Berrett-Koehler Publishers.

Riley-Smith, J. (1995). Religious warriors: Reinterpreting the crusades. *The Economist, 337*(7946), 63-67.

Richard, J. (1996). Applying Sorokin's typology. In: J. Ford, M. Richard, & P. Talbutt (Eds.), *Sorokin & civilization, a centennial assessment.* New Brunswick: Transaction Publishers.

Rotschild, M. (1991, December). Call it digital Darwinism. *Upside.*

Snyder, L. (1999). *Macro-history, a theoretical approach to comparative world history.* Lewiston, NY: The Edwin Meller Press.

Sorokin, P. (1937). *Social and cultural dynamics.* New York, NY: MacMillan.

_____ (1950). *Social philosophies in an age of crisis.* Boston, MA: Beacon Press.

Spengler, O. (1939). The decline of the West, (Der untergang des abendlandes). New York, NY: Knopf.

Szczepanski, J., & Kuczynski, J. (1991). Dialogue and humanism—dialogue and universalism. *Dialogue and Humanism, 1*(1) I-VIII.

Toffler, A. (1980). *The third wave.* New York, NY: Morrow.

Toynbee, A. (1995). *A study of history.* New York, NY: Barnes & Noble.

Wilkinson, D. (1987). Central civilization. *Comparative Civilizations Review, 7,* 31-59.

Wilkinson, D. (1996). Sorokin versus Toynbee on civilization. In: J. Ford, M. Richard, & P. Talbutt (Eds.), *Sorokin & civilization, a centennial assessment.* New Brunswick: Transaction Publishers.

Wallerstein, I. (1974). *The modern world-system, vol. 1, Capitalist agriculture and the origin of the European world-economy in the sixteenth century.* New York, NY: Academic Press.

ENDNOTES

[1]   This definition is a generalization of A.L. Kroeber's (1952) approach to culture.

[2]   For some civilizations, the idea of world-systems is not clear; however, this author concurs with Wallerstein and Wilkinson's idea that this kind of approach is valid in tracing civilization development.

[3]   The current climate pattern consists of brief interglacials, or warm periods, lasting abort 10,000 years, and much longer cool periods. The most recent ice age began about 100,000 years ago, and lasted until about 10,000 years ago. For the last 10,000 years, the earth has been in a warm, interglacial phase of these cycles (Christian, 2005, p. 131).

[4]   Provided in a letter to the Author.

Chapter II
Civilization Life Cycle:
Introduction

INTRODUCTION

The purpose of this study is to define the role of civilization's critical powers in the civilization life cycle. The role of information-communication processes is particularly crucial in this quest. The terms "rise" and "fall" of civilization reflect this chronic issue in comparative civilization studies.

Spengler, in his book *The Decline of the West* (1918), argued that all cultures are subject to the same cycle of growth and decay in accordance with predetermined "historical destiny."

Toynbee in his *Study of History* (1934), compared civilizations to organisms and perceived their existence in a life cycle of four stages: genesis, growth, breakdown, and disintegration. A mechanism of "challenge-response" facing civilizations influences their abilities at self-determination and self-direction. However, according to him, all civilizations that grow eventually reach a peak, from which they begin to decline. It seems that Toynbee's civilization life cycle is too short, since his "breakdown of growth" phase is in fact a point in time and the "disintegration" phase is too pessimistic in its title, only perceiving the "universal state," often under a form of "empire," as an *ancient regime* which only wants to maintain the status quo and is doomed to fail.

But history shows that some civilizations may last a long time in relatively good shape without being in imminent danger of disintegration.

Sorokin argued in *Social and Cultural Dynamics* (1937) that three cultural mentalities, ideational (spiritual needs and goals), sensate ("wine, women, and song"), and idealistic (a balance of needs and ends) are the central organizing principles of a civilization's life cycle, and that they succeed each other always in the same order according to super-rhythms of history. According to Sorokin, Western civilization has for the last 500 years been in the sensate stage, reaching now its limit, and will soon pass to the next idealistic stage (which, according to this author, could be the universal civilization).

A discussion about a civilization's life cycle among contemporary researchers is still very interesting. Quigley (1961), in *The Evolution of Civilizations,* offered seven stages of a civilization's change: mixture, gestation, expansion, age of conflict, universal empire, decay, and invasion. Each stage is divided by Quigley into further sub-stages and characterization is provided for the levels of intellectual life, religious outlook, social grouping, economic control, economic organization, political, and military. Quigley perceived his famous book as a study not of history but of the analytical tools assisting the understanding of history. He argued that many historic books have been written about the same subject over and over without touching main issues, because the right historic tools were not applied.

Melko, in his book *The Nature of Civilizations* (1969), provides a model of a civilization life cycle's stages including crystallization (C), transition (T), complete disintegration (D), and ossification (freezing at a crystallized stage) (O). He also introduced a concept of civilization phases, including primitive (P), feudal (F), state (S), and imperial (I) culture. Based on these categorizations, Melko develops different "trees" of a civilization's paths, similar to formulas applied in organic chemistry. He emphasizes the strong role of a transition stage, which can lead to different stages, not necessarily always to the same one.

Sanderson (1995) writes that "civilizations, like symphonies, retain characteristic patterns notwithstanding fluxes of formation, disintegration, and reconstitution." This statement is approved by a discussion of 56 researchers, recorded in the book *The Boundaries of Civilizations in Space and Time* (Melko & Scott, 1987). Their main discussion was organized around the origins and terminations of civilization in 32 short papers. The discussants agreed that civilizations rise and fall but they were lost in defining generic stages and main factors causing these stages.

Snyder (1999) proposes the most striking solution how to categorize the historic cycle of culture-systems (civilizations). He distinguishes three eras: First era (3,000 B.C.-1,600 B.C.), Transition, Second era (1,200 B.C.-200 A.D.), and Transition and Third era (600 A.D.-2000 A.D.). As a parallel time division, he recognizes seven historic cycles: Proto-Formative cycle, Formative cycle, Classical cycle, Renewal cycle, Secularization cycle, Frontier cycle and Transitional cycle, each lasting 300-400 years. He divided each cycle into four distinct stages of 75 to 100 years in length: reform stage, post-revolutionary stage, consolidation stage, and disintegration stage. This correlates with the traditional Chinese theory of

the dynastic cycle, or the rise and fall of dynasties. This framework, according to Snyder, is based on his empirical study of Western European and old world culture-systems. He perceives the disintegration stage as not a negative change but one necessary for the next formative stage. He defines a culture-system or a civilization as existing if it has at least three core cycles: Classical, Renewal, and Secularization. He analyzes the culture short cycle (300-400 years) within the world long cycles, such as the Classical cycle, Renewal cycle, Secularization cycle, and the Next cycle. This is a very important association, but is limited by the author to the political sub-system (dimension) only.

Blaha (2002) quantifies Toynbee's cycle (growth, breakdown, disintegration, and social challenge) in an elegant mathematical model[1] with three main variables: the societal level (S), the rate of change (C), the acceleration of the civilization (its growth rate socially) (A), force (F), the "mass" of the civilization (m), and time (T). However, there is no way to measure these variables excepting (T). The force is measured "using simple everyday thinking" (Blaha, 2002, p. 47). The social level in his model reflects the overall feelings of the civilization's inhabitants, not necessarily their population size, energy use, material resources, production of goods, technological advancement, and so forth. Stephen Blaha, as a noted contributor to the elementary particle theory of physics, perceives history as a continuum composed of wave oscillations with their peaks and valleys. It is interesting to note that he found that the interval of time between the breakdown of a civilization (the point at which growth stops) and the beginning of the universal state (at the end of the time of troubles) is approximately T=400 years. A similar interval time has been found by Snyder (1999) and this author, who calls it a cycle of human curiosity (Chapter VIII). The model assumes that the interval time between a civilization's consecutive waves' peaks is approximately T=267 years and Blaha calls this a general feature of civilizations. He assumes that it takes four generations to go from the top to the bottom of a cycle (a rout) and another four generations to reach the top again (a rally). If one generation is 33.375 years, then the eight generations could total to 267 years. Another interesting feature of the model is the assumption of the start-up phase of civilization, which takes 133.3 years before the breakdown of the civilization. He compares his theory with various civilizations' main events and in many cases he is right but in others he is wrong, according to Mark Hall (2003).

Every model in science simplifies reality, and particularly such a complex reality as the history of civilizations. Even if his model does not identify the reality in 1:1 isomorphic relationship, the model introduces us to a new way of analyzing and synthesizing civilization. The Blaha model is designed for long-lasting examples, which is the case of the majority of old civilizations. His model is also an excellent example of application of quantitative method to social science, which leads to better understanding of reality.

What about short-lived civilizations such as the Soviet civilization and Nazi civilization, which lasted less than a century? This problem can be solved by defining what constitutes a civilization. If it is an entity guided by a special values set, then those mentioned units are civilizations in the empire phase of Toynbee's disintegration phase.

So, the quest for the answers why civilizations rise and fall, and in what more general if not generic phases and stages they do it, is still valid.

CIVILIZATION CONTINUITY AND MEMORY

The developmental process of civilizations is based on the evolution of one civilization into another (Figure 2-1). For example, Western civilization has its eventual (though not immediate) roots in the Mesopotamian civilization beginning

4,000 B.C. Since then, the latter has transformed into six civilizations and has now reached its 7th level of development. In this sense, one can state that Western civilization is the 7th generation of the Mesopotamian civilization. This empirical evolutionary process of autonomous civilizations is shown in Figure 2-1.

This process indicates that civilizations never die, because many (but not necessarily all) of their contributions are passed on to succeeding civilizations. For example, the Classical civilization is alive in spirit and in worldview today.

There are five exceptions to this rule. We call these "arrested civilizations," but they have transformed themselves into another mutation or generation. Every civilization has its own memory and roots that can be considered as its "DNA." For example the Western civilization's "DNA" recorded the experience of its previous six civilizations.

This means that the civilization process has additive character: solutions of previous civilizations, particularly in the area of infrastructures, are cultivated by the next succeeding civilization. Of course, many old solutions may be rejected through the process of progress.

UNIVERSAL LAWS OF A CIVILIZATION

Based on a model of empirical development of civilization (Figure 1-2) and discussions on this subject, one can define the following universal laws of a civilization[2].

The Civilization Challenge-Response Law (The Toynbee Law defined):

The Life Cycle of Civilizations is steered by the challenge-response capability of the human entity.

Figure 2-1. Memory and empiric process of the Western civilization development

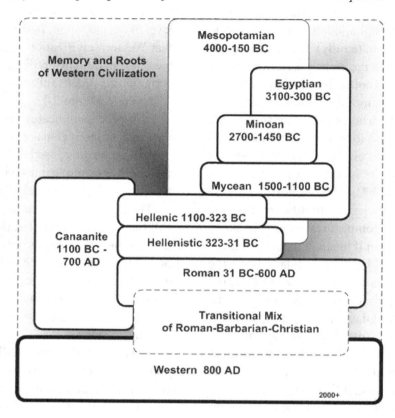

Discussion: A survey of the great myths in which the wisdom of mankind is enshrined suggests the possibility that man achieves civilization, not as a result of superior biological endowment or geographical environment, but as a response to a challenge in a situation of special difficulty which rouses him to make unprecedented efforts. The Egyptian, Chinese, Mayan, Minoan, and Indic civilizations originated from the challenge of barbaric countries. The challenges of blows indicate in the examples of the Hellenic and Western civilizations that a sudden crushing defeat motivates defeated parties to respond by setting their house in order and preparing to make a victorious response. Certain classes and races have suffered for centuries from various forms of oppression imposed upon them by other classes or races

that had mastery over them. The hordes of slaves imported to Italy from the Eastern Mediterranean during the last centuries B.C. were a "freedmen" class which proved alarmingly powerful. From this slave world came Christianity.

This law reflects natural biological evolution and the human ability to survive and develop.

The Civilization Transformation Law (The Koneczny-Targowski Law):

Transformation of a civilization takes place when the civilization in decline cannot respond to challenges and an old World Values View set is transforming into another set. This transformation is stimulated either by force of a conqueror or by the dissidents of the old guiding system in a situation when almost 100% of the silent majority is passive and the old guiding system has lost coordination power.

Discussion: The Hellenistic civilization replaced the Hellenic civilization (which rose in 750 B.C.) after the death of Alexander the Great in 323 B.C. A new WVVS (World View Values Set, discussed in respect to Figure 1-10, where the word "set" is not to be understood mathematically) was emerging from the teachings of Aristotle (384-322 B.C.), Epicurus of Samos (342-270 B.C.), and Zeno of Citium (335-263 B.C.). "Eupicureanism" promoted ways of maximizing pleasure by acting in moderation, while Zeno's "stoicism" condemned emotion and called for a stern life of devotion to virtue and duty. Hipparchus (190-120 B.C.) introduced the scientific approach to astronomy. The Roman Empire rounded out its classical borders in 31-27 B.C. by conquering the last bastion of Alexander the Great's Empire, Egypt, annexing the Hellenistic civilization into the Roman civilization with a new WVVS. At its beginning the WVVS was based on the *Pax Romana*, law, civil service (perceived as the legacy of the whole period of Roman Empire), and the rise of Latin literature. The Hellenic-Hellenistic values of truth, goodness, and beauty had been modified by the Roman values of rightness, courage, strength, comfort, pleasure, and entertainment. Socrates' (470-399 B.C.) quest for the truth had been replaced by mystic philosophies ("irrational" only in our times. In the terms of those times, they were considered highly rational, even such irrationalities as astrology and emperor-worship played the great role in then). After 313, the Roman civilization began to accept Christianity; after Constantine's conversion to Christianity (337 B.C.), a new WVVS emerged. Such values as faith, hope, and love were promoted and became a new WVVS of the new Western civilization, established (about 800 B.C.) by the powerful Charlemagne, head of the Frankish Empire. Since then, a new WVVS has been formulated, adding such values as wealth, justice, happiness, tolerance, democracy, civil rights, and health. Western civilization has been challenged in the 20th century by the Soviet and Nazi civilizations that promoted different WVVS, based among other values respectively upon collectivism and classless society or on racism. These civilizations have been eliminated by the Western civilization military and moral fight for the victory of Western WVVS.

This law reflects the power of information-communication processes, which define and communicate the world values view set.

The Civilization Knowledge Law (The Targowski Law).

A new World Values View Set emerges as a consequence of developed and acquired knowledge based on the experience of challenge-response practice. The richer the record of unpredictable challenges and successful responses, the greater the awareness generated and the higher the probability of civilization development.

Discussion: Western civilization developed strong empirical sciences enlightening their human entities in the second part of the 2nd millennium. The superior Western knowledge of technology and management helped the West to defeat the Nazi and Soviet civilizations and flourish in the second part of the 20th century. Due to its strong knowledge system, Western civilization achieved an effective awareness that helps in self-repairing its own condition.

This law reflects the power of information-communication processes, which define and communicate knowledge.

The Civilization World-System Law (The Eckhard Law).

Civilizations, empires, and wars interact in such a manner as promotes one another's growth up to a point where surplus wealth is diminished and they cannot any longer be afforded. Their loss is another civilization's and empire's gain. An empire plays the role of a world-system, which through wars expands its territory and civilization.

Discussion: This law reflects Alexander's conquest of the Persian Empire. The first 2,500 years of civilization showed no dramatic increases in population or territory, or in such signs of civilization as statesmanship, philosophy, religion, literature, fine arts, scholarship, science, music, business, and so forth. The great leap forward in all these areas occurred about 600 B.C., when the Medes and the Persians developed civilization, empire, and war into arts based on hierarchical delegation of power such as the world had not known before. The next great leap came with the Muslims in the 7th century A.D., another with the Mongols in the 13th century, and finally with the Europeans in the 16th century. In the 20th century, 95% of the earth's surface belonged to empires[3], which were spreading their civilizations (Eckhard, 1995).

The question is posed: can we have civilization without empires and wars, which develop civilization? Can the Internet be treated as an electronic empire, which promotes civilization?

GENERAL MODEL OF THE CIVILIZATION LIFE CYCLE

The transformational process of civilizations is continuous from the point of view of the world civilization. However, from the individual civilization's point of view, there is a question of what causes a civilization to grow, mature, decline, and transform into the next mutation or to disappear. The answer to this question lies in the general model of civilization life cycle, shown in Figure 2-2.

Although a civilization is not an organism, which once born must die, it rises, stabilizes, and

Figure 2-2. The general model of an autonomous civilization life-cycle

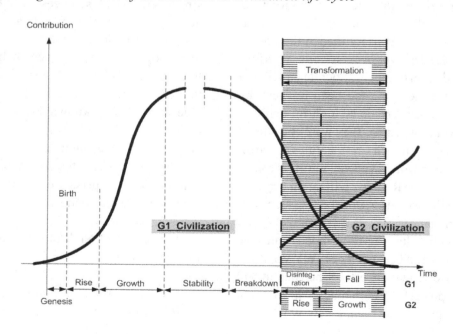

eventually dies too. Civilization is an entity and as well as a process that we observe empirically throughout history. This processes the civilization life cycle, which may take centuries or millennia to complete, or may never be concluded. The Hindu and Chinese civilizations have lasted 2,600 to 3,500 years, respectively and may function another three to five millennia or forever.

The civilization life cycle general model in Figure 2-2 indicates that a civilization may develop through the following phases:

Phase 0: The Birth of a Civilization is triggered by a creative individual, such as Caesar, Jesus Christ, the Buddha, Muhammad, Henry VIII of England, Lenin or Hitler, who have been elevated to a leadership position either by their inner mission or by external circumstances in response to such ongoing kinds of challenges as physical (from nature), social (cultural, political, economic), religious, technological, and so forth. Such a creative leader provides a consistent world view values set (WVVS) and motivates his followers to apply it. In this phase, civilization coordination power (P_k) rises and is concentrated in the hands of a few new leaders who are integrated, committed, and capable of promoting a new WVVS. In order to do so they must be knowledgeable and have idle power (P_{id}) providing free time for learning. This phase is driven mostly by information-communication processes and the Civilization Knowledge Law, the First World Civilization Grand Law—the right of man to freedom and reason—and the Third World Civilization Grand Law—the law of conscious historical evolution.

Phase 1: The Rise of a Civilization is promoted by a group of pioneers, followers of the creative leaders. For example, among these is the apostle Paul, who won converts to the new religion of Christianity, or Stalin, who played the same role in the proliferation of communism. At this phase, a civilization's coordination power (P_k) triggers the rise of the civilization's working power (P_w).

As far as Western civilization is concerned, its working power at this phase (around A.D. 800) can be measured by the number of traders and transportation workers employed (including the commercial fleet, e.g., The Netherlands and Venice's activities in the second Millennium). This phase is driven by information-communication processes, the Civilization Knowledge Law (P_{id}) in respect to WVVS dissemination, and The Challenge-Response Law in respect to the generation of working power and the Third World Civilization Grand Law—the law of conscious historical evolution (P_{id}).

Phase 2: The Growth of a Civilization is supported by a committed group of members of the new guiding system who generate coordination power and secured civilization power within the boundaries of a given environment. They expand their own microcosms of WVVS into a macrocosm of human entities, creating a nation. This occurred from the 15th to the 20th centuries for Western civilization (the English Revolution 1642-1649, the French Revolution 1773-1789 and the American Revolution 1776-1787). It also happened during the years 1922-1956 for the Soviet civilization and between 1934 and 1942 for the Nazi civilization. At this phase, the critical powers are coordination power (P_k), measured by the number of clerks employed in the state apparatus, and working power (P_w) measured by economic measurements.

This phase is driven by information-communication processes exemplified by the Ability of Man to Develop Law, the right of man to freedom and reason, and the Civilization Knowledge Law in respect to developing human opportunities, which implies free time for learning (P_{id}).

Phase 3: The Stability of a Civilization is experienced by the majority of the human entity. It may have its ups and downs, but on average steadiness characterizes this period. This is a time of *Pax Romana* from 31 B.C. to A.D. 235

in the Roman civilization or the years 1956-1976 of the Soviet civilization. During this phase, the critical factor is a co-efficient of power supply (r), which identifies the relation of working power (P_w) to secure power ($P_s = P_w + P_{id}$), $r = P_w/P_s$. If $r = 0$, taking in resources from the environment does not require any work (a case of Islamic civilization and slave-driven Western civilization, where work existed but was facilitated by slaves, contemporary "robots"). On the other hand, if r approximates 1, this means that the taking of energy by a civilization requires vast work and secure power approximates to infinity. This means that a civilization does not have idle power (P_{id}), regardless of how much secure power (P_s) it is taking from the environment. This is the case in African civilization and perhaps in Hindu civilization at the beginning of the 21st century. To calculate r, one must measure secure power (P_s) by calculating a sum of idle power (P_{id}) and working power (P_w), where the former can be measured by the number of workers per capita employed in the entertainment industry and working power can be measured by the number of employed per capita in the civilization's economy. The working power can be measured as well as by GNP or GDP per capita and idle power can be measured in monetary productivity of workers employed in the entertainment industry.

This phase is driven by information-communication processes, the ability of man to development (P_{id}), the civilization knowledge law in respect to developing secure power via new tools and media (P_s), (P_{id}), and the world-system law in respect to the generation of idle power for the elites, who can better disseminate civilization into new territories and the generation of higher productivity of working power (P_w). The stability of civilization is driven by the historical right of a country's success grand law which speaks about the harmony of a country's all major areas of existence, which requires a good coordination power (P_k). Of course, the civilization's stability is achieved if the right of man to freedom and

reason is applied (P_w) and working power is good and productive. To keep a civilization at this phase long, the Conscious Historical Evolution Grand Law must be intact (P_{id}). This case reminds the Cold War, when the both sides were developing strong awareness about their causes.

Another measuring option can be based on a civilization's index (Chapter III), which if between 0.5 and 0.75, means that a given civilization is able to produce a surplus of wealth, supporting its smooth existence.

Phase 4: The Breakdown of a Civilization begins when the leaders are losing self-determination and the majority of the population is isolated from the destructive, corrupted guiding system and drilled into passivity. These are the years 235-284 for the Roman Empire or the years 1968-1976 for the Soviet civilization, particularly in its satellites Czechoslovakia (*Prague Spring*, 1968) and Poland (KOR, 1976, see below). To survive, a civilization must produce total power ($P_t = P_s + P_k$) no lower than secure power ($P_t \geq P_s$). However, a civilization may apply its coordination power (P_k) to move to a new territory ("globalism," "europeism") through so-called "clashes of civilization." In reality, some kinds of civilizations, mostly based on dictatorships, may fail to spot their opportunities or be unsuccessful in implementing them. This happened to the Brezhnev Doctrine, when the USSR tried to defend its empire in the 1960s and 1970s and eventually failed in 1991 (triggered by the rise of the Polish Solidarity movement and the fall of communistic regime in Poland in 1989). In summary, at this phase, a civilization's total power is lower than secure power. The calculation is based on measurements of all mentioned powers (already defined in possible measurement terms) at this time. In fact, all civilization laws are applied at this phase. For example, the ability of man to development (P_{id}) implies that citizens would like to get out from under the old regime and be able to develop new opportunities (a cause of the Soviet Empire's fall). The right of man to freedom and reason supports this case, as well as remaining laws, which influence performance of total power, secure power, coordination power, and so forth (Table 2-1).

Another measuring option can be based on a civilization's index (Chapter III), which if close to 1, means that a given civilization is saturated and either will expand externally or will decline, since it is not able to produce a surplus of wealth supporting its smooth existence. At this phase, the, in Toynbee's term, "internal proletariat," shows discontent and puts a civilization in the "time of troubles."

Phase 5: The Disintegration of a Civilization takes place when masses become estranged from their leaders, who then try to cling to their position by using force as a substitute for their loss of an effective guiding system. The human entity disintegrates into five segments: a dominant minority, silent majority, outspoken dissidents, external supporters, and disconnected souls. In the Soviet civilization's Poland, this process began in 1976 when outspoken dissidents organized the official Committee for Workers' Defense (KOR—*Komitet Obrony Robotnikow*) against the dominant minority—the Communist Party apparatus. Later, in 1980, KOR facilitated the birth of Solidarity (an independent labor union), which gained supporters among the Polish emigrant community and several foreign labor unions. The rulers' response to these challenges was the introduction of the Martial State in 1981. The fifth segment was the underground literature, theater, and press that initiated an intellectual current toward a new WVVS.

To measure performance of a civilization at this phase, one must take into account coordination power (P_k), which is not able by itself to rule a civilization. In the Soviet civilization, it happened when in Poland the readership of the underground political press exceeded the readership of the official press.

This phase is driven by information-communication processes, the Civilization Transformation Law, the Civilization Knowledge Law with respect to a definition and dissemination of a new WVVS, and the World-System Law with respect to the shift of paradigm (e.g., from "communism" to "capitalism"). In fact all civilization laws are applied, causing negative performance of all types of civilization powers. At this phase, in terms of Toynbee's terminology the "external proletariat" either shows support for the "internal proletariat" or takes action (either military or ideological) against a given civilization in the time of troubles. For example, this is the case of the American (Western civilization) military intervention in Afghanistan and Iraq.

Phase 6: The Fall of a Civilization takes place when a new WVVS officially replaces the old one and a new guiding system is put in to place. The old regime fights for its survival, sometimes even gains some recognition (winning parliamentary victories between 1993 and 1995 in the post-communist countries), but its plight is widely recognized. This phase took place in Poland in 1989 when the conference at the round table between the communistic rulers and the opposition transferred the power systems into the hands of Solidarity representatives. The fall of the entire Soviet civilization took place in 1991 when Boris Yeltsin replaced Mikhail Gorbachev and the universal state of the USSR fell apart[4]. The old WVVS has been and is still replaced by a new WVVS.

It is difficult to measure a civilization's performance at this phase. One must instead to evaluate the shift of civilization paradigm in the scope of WVVS.

This phase is driven mostly by information-communication processes, the Civilization Transformation Law, the Civilization Knowledge Law with respect to WVVS dissemination, and the World-System Law with respect to the shift of paradigm (e.g., from "communism" to "capitalism").

The most dramatic and interesting part of the civilization life cycle is *the Super Phase of Transformation* from an old to a new generation of a civilization. This phase is dark-shadowed in Figure 2-2 and indicates the co-existence of four sub-phases: G1 (disintegration) versus G2 (rise) and G1 (fall) versus G2 (growth). In Western civilization this phase took place between the 5th and 15th centuries, when the Roman civilization was disintegrating and the Western civilization was emerging[5]. In the Soviet civilization, the transitional phase, beginning in the 1980s, is still taking place.

This phase is driven mostly by information-communication processes, the Civilization Transformation Law, the Civilization Knowledge Law with respect to WVVS replacement, and the World-System Law with respect to the shift of

paradigm (e.g., from "communism" to "capitalism").

To measure a civilization's performance in all its life cycle's phases can be difficult due to a lack of appropriate data. Therefore, some substitutions of ideal data can be accepted if they are reasonable. This approach is offered in Chapter III, when the civilization index is computed.

The quantification of comparisons among different civilizations can be difficult, because each kind of civilization has a different internal logic of functioning. For example, in civilizations based on authoritarian/dictatorial/totalitarian rule, coordination power consumes much more of the available resources than in civilizations based on democracy. Hence, different levels of coordination power may trigger different consequences in each civilization. For example, when working power (P_w) in communistic Poland between 1980 and 1989 was at the level of $5,000 per capita (in *ppp-purchasing power parity*) providing a quite good

Table 2-1. The application of civilization laws and critical powers in the life cycle

Grand Civilization Laws	Birth	Rise	Growth	Stability	Breakdown	Transition Disintegration	Fall
Ability of Man to Development	P_{id}	P_{id}	P_{id}	P_{id}	P_{id}	P_{id}	P_{id}
Right of Man to Freedom and Reason	P_k P_{id}		P_w P_{id}	P_w P_{id}	P_w P_{id}	P_w P_{id}	
Conscious Historical Evolution	P_{id}	P_{id}	P_{id}	P_{id}	P_{id}	P_{id}	P_{id}
Historical Right of a Country's Success	P_{id}	P_{id}	P_k	P_k P_s R	P_k P_s r P_t	P_k P_s r	P_k P_s P_t
Universal Laws of a Civilization							
Challenge-Response Law		P_w P_k	P_w		P_w P_k	P_w P_k	P_w P_k
Knowledge Law	P_k P_{id}	P_w P_k P_{id}	P_{id} P_w P_k	P_{id}	P_{id}	P_{id}	P_{id}
World-System Law				R	R	r	r

level of living, it triggered social dissatisfaction because expectations rose. Eventually, this led to the civilization transformation in 1989. In Western civilization's states such as the U.S., such a level of working power put this country in the Great Depression, more than 60 years ago (Maddison, 2001). However, the internal analysis of power dynamics in each civilization may explain its behavior and politics.

Table 2-1 illustrates the application of Grand Laws of the World Civilization (Chapter I) and Universal Laws of a Civilization and critical civilization powers in the civilization life cycle.

The process of civilization development through time becomes independent from the birth and rise phases. For example, in the Soviet civilization a later period of "Stalinism" was quite different (independent) from a beginning period, associated with "Leninism." A *longue duree* of civilizations means that they are stable and when affected by disturbances, they easily return to equilibrium. A civilization is guided by the adaptive World View Values Set, which can be called the general process of a civilization's development. A civilization is stable if it has feedback from the world civilization and can minimize or eliminate disturbances. However, if external disturbances are becoming more frequent and lasting, a civilization can be either aging or still immature. A young civilization is resistant to small disturbances; an old civilization is resistant to bigger disturbances (e.g., the Western civilization's experience with terrorism). On the other hand, an aging civilization looses resistance to bigger disturbances. The last case can be illustrated by the state of the Islamic civilization in the 21st century, which is very "energetic" but with a message which is not acceptable to all its faithful. On the other hand, these hostile activities did not terminate the Islamic civilization. Even the destruction by the Mongols of the Abbasid caliphate (Baghdad) in the 13th century or the decay of the Ottoman Empire in the 19th and 20th centuries did not terminate the Islamic civilization.

If civilizations act in the environment of the highly influential world civilization (e.g., the global civilization in the 21st century), a young civilization may not have enough time to become mature, which is the case of the African civilization. Such a civilization has problems in returning to the equilibrium and its WVVS is no longer guiding the developmental process. Those civilizations which can easily return to the equilibrium remain intact, because they have the ability of self-steering. Certainly such civilizations include the Western and Japanese civilizations.

A civilization has the ability to develop if it has differentiated components which produce inputs and outputs to other components not in full agreement to each other. Rather they are in contradiction, which pushes a civilization into motion and forward, as takes place in democracy.

In general, one can state that those civilizations last, which do not have contradictions between their beginning and later phases. In other words, it happens when those civilizations cultivate their WVVS. For example, both Soviet and Nazi civilizations experienced that type of contradiction. On the other hand, the Western civilization is still strong since it likes to look to its own roots of ideas (the birth phase; the English, American and French Revolutions and constitutional systems).

One can mention that the quantification of a state's power is a popular quest and is applied in international political studies (Taylor & Judice, 1983; Cline, 1994; Moczulski, 2000).

The quantification of the civilization life cycle cannot properly be a unique approach. It should rather be a supplement to the qualitative analysis and synthesis of civilization change and continuity.

THE WAVE MODEL OF THE WORLD CIVILIZATION LIFE CYCLE

The three wave-like models of world civilization were offered by Toffler (1980) and can be treated as world-systems, as follows:

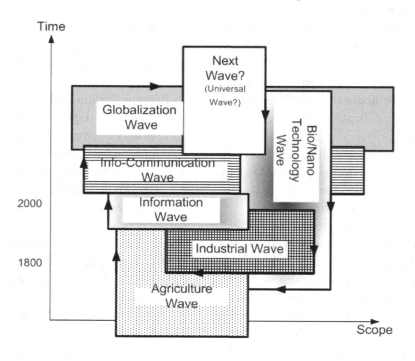

Figure 2-3. The relationship among civilization waves (The Targowski-Zacher Model)

First Wave - Agriculture (4000 B.C.-2000+): We are in disagreement and we must gather in order to survive.

Second Wave - Industrialization (1780 - 2000+): We are divided and must compete in order to rise to affluence.

Third Wave - Information (1980-2000+): We are in touch and we must cooperate in order to match global competition.

Civilization development at the beginning of the 21st century emphasizes the emergence of the next waves, defined by Targowski and Zacher[6], such as:

Fourth Wave – Info-Communication Wave (2000+): We are aware that instant communication optimizes our well-being.

Fifth Wave – Bio/Nano-Technology Wave (2000+): We want to improve our health and quality of life through the better understanding of nature's frontiers. Examples of such solutions are life-cloning or smart drugs (bio-robots) at the molecular level.

It is important to notice that succeeding civilization waves do not replace previous waves but optimize their development and operation. For example, the Industrial Wave did not replace the Agricultural Wave; it improved agriculture's productivity and profitability. The relationships among civilization waves are shown in Figure 2-3.

The wave approach towards world civilization development must take into account the different levels of countries' development. The leaders of this type of development (driven by waves of technological impact) come mostly from the Western civilization and Japanese civilization; however. The leaders and average users of the civilization

Figure 2-4. Countries in civilization transformations (The Targowski-Zacher Model)

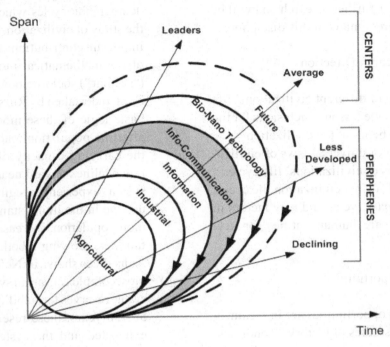

waves create civilization centers that cooperate through fast diffusion of solutions. The remaining countries form the civilization's peripheries, which either adapt the centers' solutions slowly or even reject them on grounds of inadequate address of those countries' systems of values. The former is the case of the policy "to modernize but not Americanize" a country. Malaysia and Iran are good examples of this policy. A case of the rejection of the center was the policy of the Taliban government of Afghanistan.

Of course, the Wave Model is a rather limited paradigm which mostly emphasizes one civilization component—the infrastructure. On the other hand, this model provides a very good intuitive understanding of human development during the civilization centuries (Figure 2-4).

CONCLUSION

The modeling of civilization development and modeling of history in general are intrinsically based on "models," which must simplify the reality. This is their weakness. On the other hand, this approach is widely applied in many sciences, particularly in physics, chemistry, biology, medicine, and computing. These disciplines are invasive of individual humans, and errors in modeling their processes and systems may have strong repercussions in real life. But without "modeling," these disciplines could have only slow progress. For example, the Solar model of an atom developed by Niels Bohr in 1913 had a strong impact upon later discoveries in physics. Today, the Charge-cloud model of atoms is quite different from the original model, due to progress made in physics.

One may hope that *presented* models of civilization will trigger further research and will be improved by progress made in this discipline.

A.   Further Research Directions

•   Investigation of different civilizations' life cycles to provide lesson conclusions for the current well-being of the civilization
•   Investigation of universal laws of civilizations in terms of civilizations' life cycles
•   Prediction of further civilization life cycles based upon past cycles and new factors in order to prepare human entities for new challenges

B.   Research Opportunities

•   The research opportunities are in the interdisciplinary studies of history, economics, political science, technology and others

C.   Additional Ideas

•   How do different generations of humans impact the development or regression of civilization?

D.   Rationale

•   Interpretation of history as the repeating cycles of events was first put forward in the academic world in the 19th century in historiosophy (a branch of historiography) and was soon adopted by sociology. The *Saeculum* was first identified in Roman times. Unlike the theory of social evolutionism, which views the evolution of society and human history as progressing in some new, unique direction(s), cyclical social theories argue that events and stages of society and history are repeating themselves in cycles and thus there cannot be any social progress. Note that this is not valid for the modern theories of long-term ("secular") political-demographic cycles, which can be applied for the study of civilization. Recently, the most important contributions to the development of the mathematical models of long-term ("secular") socio-demographic cycles have been undertaken by Russian scientists. The basic logic of these models is as follows: after the population reaches the ceiling of the carrying capacity of land, its growth rate declines toward near-zero values. The system experiences significant stress with decline in the living standards of the common population, increasing the severity of famines, growing rebellions, and so forth. As has been shown by Nefedov (2003; 2004), most complex agrarian systems had considerable reserves for stability, however, within 50-150 years, these reserves were usually exhausted and the system experienced a demographic collapse (a Malthusian catastrophe), when increasingly severe famines, epidemics, increasing internal warfare and other disasters led to a considerable decline of population. As a result of this collapse, free resources became available, per capita production and consumption considerably increased, the population growth resumed and a new socio-demographic (civilization?) cycle started. It has become possible to model these dynamics mathematically in a rather effective way. Note that the modern theories of political-demographic cycles do not deny the presence of trend dynamics and attempt at the study of the interaction between cyclical and trend components of historical dynamics.

E.   Additional Reading

Aristotle. (1927). Metaphysics. In: W. Ross (Ed.), *Aristotle* (pp. 105-118). New York, NY: Scribner.

Chu, C., & Lee, R. (1994). Famine, revolt, and the dynastic cycle: Population dynamics in historic China. *Journal of Population Economics, 7,* 351-378.

Debord, G. (1995). *The society of the spectacle.* Cambridge, MA: The MIT Press.

Dewey, E. (1951). The 57-year cycle in international conflict. *Cycles, 2*(1), 4-6.

_____(1952). The 142-year cycle in war. *Cycles, 3*(6), 201-204.

Ellis, M. (1997). *Unholy alliance: Religion and atrocity in our time.* Minneapolis, MN: Fortress Press.

Fukuyama, F. (1992). *The end of history and the last man.* New York, NY: Penguin Group.

Geyl, P. (1955). *Debates with historians.* London: Collins.

Gibbon, E. (1776). *The history of the decline and fall of the Roman Empire.* New York, NY: Random House.

Hegel, G. (1900). *The philosophy of history.* New York, NY: Collier.

Kant, I. (1963). Idea for a universal history from a cosmopolitan point of view. In: L. Beck (Ed.), *Kant on history* (pp. 11-26). New York, NY: Bobbs-Merrill.

Korotayev, A., & Khaltourina, D. (2006). *Introduction to social macrodynamics: Secular cycles and millennial trends in Africa.* Moscow: URSS.

Krus, D., & Blackman, H. (1980). Time scale factor as related to theories of societal change. *Psychological Reports, 46,* 95-102.

Krus, D., & Ko, H. (1983). Algorithm for autocorrelation of secular trends. Educational and psychological measurement. *Psychological Reports, 43,* 821-828.

Makridakis, S., & Wheelwright, S. (1978). *Interactive forecasting: Unvaried and multivariate methods.* San Francisco, CA: Holden-Day.

McClelland, D. (1961). *The achieving society.* Princeton: Van Nostrand.

_____(1975). *Power: The inner experience.* New York, NY: Halstead.

McGaughey, W. (2000). *Five epochs of civilization.* Minneapolis, MN: Thistlerose Publications.

Moyal, J. (1949). The distribution of wars in time. *Journal of the Royal Statistical Society, 112,* 446-458.

Nash, R. (1969). *Ideas of history.* New York, NY: Dutton.

Nefedov, S. (2003). *A theory of demographic cycles and the social evolution of oriental societies. Orient, 3,* 5-22.

_____(2004). A model of demographic cycles in traditional societies: The case of ancient china. Social evolution & history. *Orient, 3*(1), 69-80.

Popper, K. (1957). *The poverty of historicism.* London, UK: Routledge.

Postan, M. (1973). *Essays on medieval agriculture and general problems of the medieval economy.* Cambridge: Cambridge University Press.

Press, W., Teukolsky, S., Vetterling, W., & Flannery, B. (1986). *Numerical recipes: The art of scientific computing.* Cambridge: Cambridge University Press.

Richardson, L. (1960). *Statistics of deadly quarrels.* Pacific Grove, CA: Boxwood Press.

Russell, E. (1971). Christianity and militarism. *Peace Research Review, 4*(3), 1-77.

Silver, N., & Hittner, J. (1998). *Guidebook of statistical software for the social and behavioral sciences.* Boston, MA: Allyn & Bacon.

Strauss, W., & Howe, N. (1997). *An american prophecy, the fourth turning, what the cycles of history tell us about america's next rendezvous with destiny.* New York, NY: Broadway Books.

Toynbee, A. (1934). *A study of history.* Oxford, UK: Oxford University Press.

Tucker, R. (1990). *Philosophy and myth in Karl Marx* (2nd ed.). Cambridge, MA: Cambridge University Press.

Turchin, P. (2003). *Historical dynamics: Why states rise and fall.* Princeton, NJ: Princeton University Press.

_____(2006). *War and peace and war: The life cycles of imperial nations.* Upper Saddle River, NJ: Pi Press.

Turchin, P., et al. (Eds.). (2007). *History & mathematics: Historical dynamics and development of complex societies.* Moscow: KomKniga.

Usher, D. (1989). The dynastic cycle and the stationary state. *The American Economic Review, 79,* 1031-1144.

Wilkinson, D. (1980). *Deadly quarrels: Lewis F. Richardson and the statistical study of war.* Berkeley, CA: University of California Press.

Wright, Q. (1965). *A study of war* (2nd ed.). Chicago, IL: University of Chicago Press.

Vico, G. (1968). *The new science.* New York, NY: Cornell University Press.

REFERENCES

Blaha, St. (2002). *The life cycle of civilizations.* Auburn, NH: Pingree-Hill Publishing.

Cline, R. (1990). *The power of nations. A strategic assessment.* Lanham, MD: University Press of America.

Ding, Y-C., Chi, H-C., Grady, D., Morishima, A., Kidd, J., Kidd, K., et al. (2002). Evidence of positive selection acting at the human dopamine receptor D4 gene locus. *Proceedings of the National Academy of Sciences, 99,* 309-314.

Eckhard, W. (1995). A dialectical evolutionary theory of civilization, empires, and wars. In: St. K. Sanderson (Ed.), *Civilizations and world systems, studying world-historical change.* Walnut Creek, London; New Delhi: Altamira Press.

Hall, M. (2003). The rhythms of history: A universal theory of civilizations. *Human Nature Review, 3,* 38-40.

Koneczny, F. (1962). *On the plurality of civilizations.* London: Wydawnictwa Towarzystwa im. Romana Dmowskiego, (Publications of the Roman Dmowski Association).

_____(1977). *For an Order in History.* (only Polish edition), London: Wydawnictwa Towarzystwa im. Romana Dmowskiego, (Publications of the Roman Dmowski Association).

_____(1982). *History laws.* London: Wydawnictwa Towarzystwaim. Romana Dmowskiego, (Publications of the Roman Dmowski Association).

Kroeber, A. (1944). *Configurations of culture growth.* Berkeley and Los Angeles, CA: University of California Press.

Maddison, A. (2001). *The world economy. A millennial perspective.* Paris: OECD.

Maynard, H., & Mehrtens, I. (1996). *The fourth wave, business in the 21st century.* San Francisco, CA: Berrett-Koehler Publishers.

Mazur, M. (1966). *Cybernetyczna teoria ukladow samodzielnych.* (*The cybernetic theory of independent systems*). Warsaw: PWN.

Melko, M. (1969). *The nature of civilizations.* Boston, MA: Porter Sargent Publisher.

Melko. M., & Scott, L. (Eds.). (1987). *The bound-*

aries of civilizations in space and time. Lanham, MD; New York, NY; London: University Press of America.

Moczulski, L. (2000). *Geopolityka. (Geopolitics)*. Warsaw: Bellona.

Quigley, C. (1961). *The evolution of civilizations*. New York, NY: McMillan Co.

Redman, C. (1978). *The rise of civilization, from early farmers to urban society in the ancient near east*. San Francisco, CA: W. H. Freeman & Company.

Sanderson, S. (1995). *Civilizations and world systems*. Walnut Creek, London; New Delhi: Altamira Press.

Snyder, L. (1999). *Macro-history, a theoretical approach to comparative world history*. Lewiston, NY: The Edwin Mellen Press.

Sorokin, P. (1937). *Social and cultural dynamics*. New York, NY: MacMillan.

Spengler, O. (1932). *Decline of the west*. London: Allen and Unwin.

Taylor, C., & Judice, D. (1983). *World handbook of political and social indicators*. New Haven; London: Yale University Press.

Toffler, A. (1980). *The third wave*. New York, NY: Morrow.

Toynbee, A. (1934). *A study of history*. Oxford; New York: Oxford University Press.

_____(1995). *A study of history*. New York, NY: Barnes & Noble.

ENDNOTES

[1] C = dS/dt, and F = mA, where C = Change = the rate of change of the social level with time. S = Societal Level = the strength of a civilization in terms of political and social institutions, social cohesion, ability to innovate to solve social problems, capacity for technological innovation, flexibility in finding solutions, enterprise in meeting challenges. Mathematically, C is the time derivative of S.

[2] Grand models of the world civilization are defined in Chapter I.

[3] By the word "empire," this author understands a political unit having an extensive territory or comprising a number of territories or nations and ruled by a single supreme authority.

[4] M. Melko perceives the election of Boris Yeltsin as "476 A.D.," a decisive event in the termination of a civilization.

[5] Many historians call the period 1,500-present "Modern History."

[6] The models were developed by Andrew Targowski and Lech Zacher during a seminar at the Western Michigan University in March 2000.

Chapter III
The Civilization Index

INTRODUCTION

The purpose of this chapter is to define energy levels of civilizations, particularly in respect to a role of information-communication processes. Rapid changes in the world economy and social structure have brought into question traditional assumptions, prompting some intellectuals to speak of a "clash of civilizations" (Huntington, 1993; 1996) or even "the end of history" (Fukuyama, 1989; 1992). Before one can speculate about a new world order, it is necessary to develop an appropriate set of measurements to compare human societies and a terminology to describe them. The environment described as a "civilization" by Toynbee (1995) and "the world civilization" by Braudel (1993) has changed so drastically that those definitions are no longer sufficient.

The spectacular progress in technology and social life that has been achieved at the beginning of the third millennium stimulates an extensive investigation into the human condition and the world status. Questions like the following need to be answered:

1. What is the state of Western and other civilizations at the beginning of the 21st century?

2. How can it be compared to other civilizations in terms of level of development?
3. What criteria and measurements should be applied in evaluating and comparing civilizations?
4. What is the relationship between a given civilization and the world civilization?

This study falls into a category of wide-ranging comparisons of large structures and processes, in order to understand how human entities behave in a certain way because of the consequences of the civilization system's behavior as a whole (Tilly, 1984).

THE NEXT ENTITY TO MEASURE

Several attempts to measure civilizations' vitality have been undertaken. Most of these studies were conducted at the level of the development of regions over several millennia. Kroeber (1944) counted "geniuses," whom he defined as "superior individuals" whose superiority had been established by a consensus of encyclopedia and textbook authors. He counted them in seven disciplines: philosophy, science, grammar (philology), sculpture, painting, drama, and literature, through the 59 centuries from 4,000 B.C. to 1,900 A.D.

He found 5,323 geniuses; of whom 56% were from Europe, 11% from the Far East, 3% from India, 8% from the Middle East, and 22% from elsewhere (assuming 50% of it from America). Hence, one can assume that about 67% of geniuses were "generated" by the Western civilization. According to Kroeber, the Middle East provided the overwhelming majority of geniuses from 3,000 to 800 B.C. Then Europe took over the supply until 500 A.D., followed by the Far East for a few centuries. The Middle East prevailed for a few centuries, to pass the leadership to Europe since the 12th century. He stopped counting at 1,900 A.D., so "geniuses" from the U.S. in the 20th century are not included, but certainly they received the most of the Nobel Prizes.

Sorokin (1937) provided a count of historic persons, scientific discoveries and technological inventions only in the scope of "Europe" and the "rest of the world." Naroll, et al. (1971) assumed implicitly that creativeness and civilization were synonymous terms, or at least indicative of each other (Eckhard, 1995).

Taagepera (1978) measured imperial systems of Africa and Eurasia in terms of their areas in square megameters, one square megameter equaling 386,000 square miles. Until 600 B.C., empires were small. Later, when the Medes and Persians invented more effective hierarchical bureaucracy, the sizes of empires grew. There was a leap in average size after 1,600 A.D., influenced by the European trade-industry-transportation and communication revolutions. This progress of empires in the world is meaningful. In the 6th century B.C., they covered only 6% of the earth's surface; in the 20th century their coverage grew to 95%.

Several researchers measured the number of wars (battles) and number of deaths caused by them. Measurement of battles reflects the intensity of wars as a synonym of civilization. Dupuy and Dupuy (1986) recorded 4,511 battles (29% in Europe) in the last 3,500 years.

Eckhard (1995) correlated geniuses, civilizations, empires, and wars at the global and regional levels of analysis and found that the more civilized we became, the larger was the area of the earth that came under imperial control. Empires were spreading civilization over larger territories (e.g., Poland, the largest state in 16th century Europe, was civilizing the east in the 16th-17th centuries; the United Kingdom was civilizing its colonies in the second part of the second millennium A.D. He concluded that the relations between civilizations, empires, and wars is such that these three interact in such a way that "promotes" each other's growth up to a point where surplus wealth diminishes and turns into a deficit. At this point, civilizations, empires, and wars cannot be afforded anymore, and they fall, as is exemplified by the failures of the Persian, Chinese or recent Soviet empires.

In conclusion, one may notice that measuring civilizations should lead to answers why civilizations "rise" and "fall" and whether can we develop civilization without wars by reinventing our values.

THE ARCHITECTURE OF A CIVILIZATION

Civilization is an "interface" that differentiates humans from animals in dealing with nature and the creator (Big Bang or God, according to one's beliefs). In the general model on Figure 1-5c, one may recognize the following components of a civilization (Targowski, 2004a):

- Human Entity: an existence-driven community, being a member of a given civilization

- Culture: a values and symbols-driven, continuous process of developing patterned human behavior

- Infrastructure: a technology-driven, additive process of acquiring and applying material means

The history of civilization so defined[1] is as long as humanity's life in organized societies. According to accepted estimates, humans began living on Earth about 6-5 million years ago. (Burenhult, 2003). The development of more modern mankind began about 200,000-150,000 years ago, when *homo sapiens* were living in eastern Africa and anatomically resembled a modern man. From this location, *homo sapiens* began to move to southwestern Asia (100,000 years ago), Australia (50,000 years ago), Europe (40,000 years ago), New Guinea (30,000 years ago), Siberia (25,000 years ago), and North America (12,000 years ago) (Burenhult, 2003). Modern man began to be more social first as a hunter/gatherer; later, when the Ice Age ended, as a farmer and a town dweller. The oldest recorded historic civilization is about 6,000 years old (Burenhult 2003a) and is associated with the rise of Mesopotamian civilization (including both Sumerian and Semitic peoples) (4,000 B.C.). Next came the Egyptians (3,100 B.C.); then, others.

Human civilization began about 6,000 years ago, marked by the emergence of organized human entities, under a form of urbanized society. These early info-material structures, or civilizations, were created by humans as a means of coping with themselves, nature, and the creator. During the next six millennia humans developed about 26 civilizations (Toynbee, 1995). Currently, at the beginning of the 21st century, one can discern eight well-established religion-oriented civilizations (Huntington, 1993). The empirical model recognizes (in order of longest duration) the Chinese (3,500 years), Hindu (2,600), African (2,500), Eastern (2,325), Buddhist (1,400), Japanese (1,350), Western (1,200), and Islamic (1,400) civilizations.

A civilization is not a monolithic structure but is made up of many cultures and sub-cultures. The 26 recorded civilizations comprised about 88 cultures and perhaps 100-120 sub-cultures (Targowski, 2004c). The existence of so many smaller components brings into question whether it is a civilization or a culture that determines the new world order. Certainly, "culture" denotes a mode of world exchanges that is currently based on skills of communicating across cultures.

A religion-oriented civilization is an autonomous structure made up of numerous systems in support of its self-dependent existence. A general model of a civilization as shown in Figure 1-9 reflects the following components:

The "brain" of a civilization is the guiding system, composed of:

- a world view values set (WVVS) common for all members of a given civilization
- a strategizing culture
- an authority infrastructure

The existence system is composed of:

- a human entity
- an entertaining culture
- a foundational infrastructure

The knowledge system is composed of:

- an enlightening culture
- a knowledge infrastructure

The logistic system is composed of:

- a management (strategizing culture)
- an economic infrastructure

The communication system is composed of:

- a diffusing culture
- a communication infrastructure

The power system is composed of:

- politics (strategizing culture)
- a military infrastructure

The integrational infrastructure is composed of:

- a communication infrastructure
- a transportation infrastructure
- an information infrastructure (e.g., the modern "information superhighway")

A civilization is controlled by its guiding system, which identifies threats to the existence system and generates reflections that are transmitted to the knowledge system. The knowledge system creates awareness and returns the information to the guiding system, which in turn steers the existence system—closing a loop through which flow data, information, concepts, knowledge, and wisdom. This autonomous civilization interacts with other civilizations through its communication, logistic, and power systems. The entire civilizing process takes place through the channels of the integrational infrastructure. It is interesting to note the difference between a civilization and a state. The former is steered by its guiding system and the latter by its power system. The average citizen is caught between these two systems.

In a democracy, the power system is subordinated to the guiding system, whereas in other political entities the guiding system is usually subordinated to the power system.

Table 3-1. Comparison of the existence systems of civilizations

Civilization	Total Power	Working Power	Coordination Power	Idle Power	Human Entity	Total	Ranking
Western-West	7	7	7	3	5	29	1
Western-Central CeCentral	4	6	4	3	3	20	4
Western-Latin	3	4	2	3	3	15	7
Western-Jewish	7	5	6	3	6	27	2
Japanese	5	6	5	2	3	21	4
Eastern	6	6	2	6	3	23	3
Hindu	2	2	2	4	3	13	8
Chinese	2	3	2	7	3	17	6
Islamic	2	4	1	3	3	13	8
Buddhist	1	1	2	2	3	9	9
African	2	2	1	1	2	8	10

Source: The author's estimates, Kurian (1991), Hunter (2000), and Maddison (2001).

CHARACTERISTICS OF A CIVILIZATION

The comparison of contemporary civilizations will be based on the model depicted in Figure 1-9. Since Western civilization is composed of many cultures/states sharing the same WVVS but at different stages of development, it has been divided for comparison purposes into three member components:

- The Western-West, containing Western Europe (including modern Greece) and Northern America
- The Western-Central, embracing Poland, the Czech Republic, Slovakia, Hungary, Estonia, Latvia, Lithuania, Croatia, and Slovenia (Albania, Romania, and Bulgaria are Orthodox Christian, but the latter two, since 2007 are in the E.U. and perhaps in the future may inspire to be a part of this sub-civilization)
- The Western-Latin, composed of Latin America's states (Spain and Portugal are included in the Western-West sub-civiliza-tion, despite their strong involvement in Latin America)
- The Western-Jewish, which is in terms of human entities composed of a supranational community, in many countries a very well-developed Diaspora. Culture-wise it is integrated by Judaism and the politics of returning to the Biblical Land. Infrastructure-wise it is based on global networks in finance, media, music, and politics[2].

The characteristics of each civilization[3] are rated on a scale from 1 to 7 and aggregated as a concept of a civilization. The existence system[4] is characterized in Table 3-1.

The components of the existence system are measured as follows:

- total power: energy consumption in kg (of calories) per capita/year
- working power: average hours per week in manufacturing
- coordination power: number of computers per 1,000 people

Table 3-2. Comparison of flexibility of a human entity

Range	Human Entity	Civilizations	Examples
7	Spheric Community		
6	Supranational Community	Western-Jewish	
5	Transnational Community	Western-West	NATO, EU, NAFTA
4	Political Society		
3	Nation	Western-Central, Western-Latin, Japanese, Chinese, Buddhist, Hindu, Islamic, Eastern,	
2	Proto-nation	African	
1	People		North Korea

Source: The author's estimates and Barry and Honey (2000)

Table 3-3. Comparison of the communication systems of civilizations

Range	TV sets per 1000 People	Internet Users/1K Habitants	Civilizations
7	over 700	338	Western-West, Western-Jewish
6	500-699	371	Japanese
5	300-499	20, na	Eastern, Western-Central
4	100-299	na, 18	Western-Latin, Chinese
3	70-100	10, 6	Islamic, Buddhist
2	50-69	5	Hindu
1	below 49	<1	African

Source: 1997 World Development Indicators, Washington, D.C.: The World Bank, (pp. 284-286); Hundley, R., Anderson, R., Bikson, T., & Neu, C. (2003, p. 96).

Table 3-4. Comparison of the knowledge systems of civilizations

Range	University Professors per 1000 People	Expected Years of Schooling, Males In 1992	Civilizations
7	3.8	16	Western-West, Western-Jewish
6	1.7	14	Japanese
5	1.2	11	Eastern
4	0.7-0.86	12	Western-Central, Western-Latin
3	0.3-0.34	na	Buddhist-Hindu
2	0.26	na, 9	Chinese, Islamic
1	0.2	4	African

Source: George, T. (19991). Kurian: The new book of world rankings, facts on file publications: New York. World Development Report. (1998-99).
Knowledge for Development, (p. 200-201). Washington, D.C: World Bank.

- idle power: number of cinema seats per 1,000 people
- human entity: degree of flexibility (Table 3-2)

The remaining civilization systems of a general model of civilizations are compared in the following tables:

- communication systems of civilizations are compared in Table 3-3
- knowledge systems are compared in Table 3-4
- guiding systems are compared in Table 3-5

Table 3-5. Comparison of the guiding systems of civilizations

Range	Political System	Civilizations
7	Democracy	Western-West, Japanese, Hindu, Western-Jewish
6	Quasi-Democratic	Western-Latin, Western-Central
5	Authoritarian	Buddhist
4	Authoritarian-Theocratic	Islamic
3	Dictatorship	
2	Quasi-Totalitarian	Chinese
1	Chaotic or Transition	African, Eastern

Source: The author's estimates and Honey and Barry (2000).

Table 3-6. Comparison of the power systems of civilizations

Range	Military Capability and Will	Civilizations
7	Super Power	Western-West, Eastern
6	Strong Power	Chinese, Western-Jewish
5	Good Power	Japanese, West-Central
4	Terrorist Power	Islamic
3	Power	Hindu, West-Latin
2	Little Power	Buddhist
1	No power	African

Source: George Th. Kurian: The New Book of World Rankings,
Facts on File Publications: New York, 1991, and The author's estimation.

Table 3-7. Comparison of logistic systems

Range	$ GNI per capita (Gross National Income in parity purchasing power)	Civilizations
7	35,500-45,000	
6	20,001-35,000	Western-West, Japanese, Western-Jewish
5	15,001-20,000	
4	10,001-15,000	
3	5,000-10,000	Western-Central, Eastern, Islamic
2	1001-4,999	Western-Latin
1	below 1000	Chinese, Hindu, African, Buddhist

Source: 2003 World Development Report, Washington, DC: World Bank, pp. 234-235.

Table 3-8. Comparison of integrational infrastructures

Range	Degree of Advancement	Civilizations
7	Very Advanced	Western-West, Japanese, Western-Jewish
6	Advanced	
5	Very Good	
4	Good	Western-Central, Western-Latin, Islamic
3	Poor	Eastern, Chinese, Hindu
2	Very Poor	Buddhist
1	Chaotic	African

Source: The author's estimation and Hunter (2000).

- power systems are compared in Table 3-6
- logistic systems are compared in Table 3-7
- integrational infrastructures are compared in Table 3-8

THE CIVILIZATION INDEX

A summary of civilization systems is provided in the form of the Civilization Index in Table 9. The perfect Civilization Index has 77 points, since each of civilization systems has seven points at its highest level of development and is assessed by 11 criteria (5 for the Existence System) and six criteria for remaining systems (11 x 7 = 77).

A comparison of civilizations at the end of the twentieth century permits us to draw the following conclusions:

1. The Western-West civilization is at the stage of "saturation," indicating that it is either ready to expand into other civilizations or to enter into social unrest. This civilization has an almost perfect Index: CI = 91%.
2. The Western-Jewish (CI = 87%) and Japanese civilizations (CI = 75%) are very well developed and will approach the "saturation" point in the near future.
3. The African civilization is either at the beginning of the developmental process or at the stage of disastrous development. Taking into account its very short and tumultuous history, both statements may be correct (CI = 18%).
4. The remaining civilizations have a good prospect for further development or redevelopment. This is presently taking place in the case of the Western-Central civilization after the collapse of the Soviet civilization. Civilization indeces of these civilizations vary from CI = 32% to 61%.

STRATEGIES OF CIVILIZATION DEVELOPMENT

At the beginning of the 21st century, eight civilizations are well established; the one exception is the African civilization. The developmental process of these civilizations should continue in the following ways:

- development based on internal forces within a civilization
- development based on external encounters between civilizations

Table 3-9. The Civilization Index (CI)

Civilization	Existence S.	Communica-tion S.	Knowledge S.	Guiding S.	Power S.	Logistic S.	Infrastruc-ture	Total	CI as % of Potential (77)	Rank-ng
Western-West	29	7	7	7	7	6	7	70	0.91	1
Western-Jewish	27	7	7	7	6	6	7	67	0.87	2
Japanese	21	6	6	7	5	6	7	58	0.75	3
Western-Central	20	5	4	6	5	3	4	47	0.61	4
Eastern	23	5	5	1	7	3	3	47	0.61	5
Western-Latin	15	4	4	6	3	2	4	40	0.52	6
Chinese	17	4	2	2	6	1	3	35	0.45	7
Islamic	13	3	2	4	4	3	4	33	0.43	8
Hindu	13	2	3	7	3	1	3	32	0.41	9
Buddhist	9	3	3	5	2	1	2	25	0.32	10
African	8	1	1	1	1	1	1	14	0.18	11

Of course, these processes are related and reinforced by the global civilizing process.

The development process triggered by internal forces should take place primarily among civilizations with a Civilization Index below the maturity level (CI = 75%). This category encompasses all but the Western-West and Japanese civilizations. The Chinese (CI = 45%) and Hindu (CI = 41%) civilizations have 3,500 and 2,600 years of experience, respectively, and know how to respond to challenges without threat to their future existence.

The Western civilization is divided into three sub-civilizations, of which the Western-West civilization (CI = 91%) has achieved its peak. Its further prosperous existence may be prolonged if the West-West engages the development of the Western-Central (CI = 61%) and Western-Latin (CI = 52%) civilizations. The formation of the North American Free Trade Agreement (NAFTA) sphere and the inclusion of Western-Central European States in NATO and the European Union indicate that the Western civilization is pursuing such a strategy very effectively at this time.

The developmental process based on encounters between civilizations takes place both in space and in time. Encounters in space take place between adjacent civilizations. For example, the Western-Central civilization blends with the Eastern civilization due to geographic proximity. Despite the higher Civilization Index of the former, the latter has the ambition to control the Western both militarily and politically. In fact, the Eastern civilization has the most space-related contacts with the Western-Central, Chinese, Buddhist, and Islamic civilizations, all of which are developing by gains from the fallen Soviet civilization.

Encounters in time take place among all civilizations. However, the closest encounters take place among civilizations of the same or similar character. For example, history has proven that endodynamic civilizations like the Hindu, Buddhist and African ones have very close relationships. The Hindus play the same role in Africa as the Jews in Europe or America, being in charge of commerce and knowledge. One may notice the same close relations between the Western-West and the Japanese civilizations, which are both of a static character. There is a possibility that the Western-Central and Eastern civilizations (of the same exodynamic character) will collaborate closely when post-Soviet political relations are settled.

The Chinese civilization enters inter-civilization encounters in time rather than in space. This civilization challenges the Islamic and Japanese civilizations through its extensions in South Korea, Taiwan, Hong Kong, Singapore, Malaysia, and, to a certain degree, Indonesia and even the United States (where it was ready to "buy" political influence during the 1996 election). During the 1960s, the Chinese civilization established its presence in Africa as well.

The Chinese civilization expansion is counter-measured by the Japanese civilization in eastern and southern Asia, where Japan is aiming at an economic and eventually a political dominance. This space-time-oriented sphere will be witness to eventual "clashes of civilizations" as predicted by Huntington.

The Islamic civilization at the beginning of the 21st century has an exodynamic character and strong civilization and coordination powers that will guide its expansionist ambitions against primarily the Western and Eastern civilizations. Its encounter with the Eastern civilization takes place in space and its battle with the Western civilization takes place in time. These clashes will continue as long as the Islamic civilization has at its disposal income from its vast oil reserves. Its Civilization Index is 2.1 times lower than the Western civilization's index and only 1.4 times lower than the Eastern civilization's index. As a result, the Islamic civilization has no chance to win "clashes" with the Western civilization, but it has some chance to "win" against the Eastern civilization. An example of the latter is the Russians' plight in the war with the Chechens between 1994 and 1996.

The Western civilization (as the most advanced and with the United States as its superpower) wants to play the coaching role to other civilizations. Its World View Value System is based on democracy, peace through free trade, and technology-driven infrastructures that seek an optimal solution for the entire world. Its message to other civilizations is westernization and modernization. Only two civilizations, Eastern and Hindu, are ready to accept this message, either directly or indirectly. The Chinese, Buddhist, and African civilizations accept the modernization message. The Islamic civilization generally rejects the western message, although the Malaysian and Indonesian cultures accept modernization to a degree.

The African civilization is the weakest and could be a target for some civilization to absorb. At the beginning of the 21st century it looks as if no one civilization aspires to incorporate the African civilization. The problem with this civilization has for many years been addressed through the North-South debate.

Figure 3-1. Main zones of civilization clashes and collaboration (C - Clash, M - Modernization, W - Westernization)

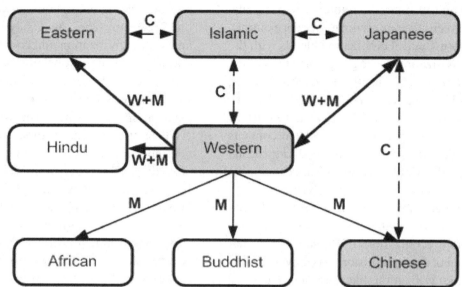

Based on the foregoing analysis, one can provide the following conclusions (Figure 3-1) about the scope and range of encounters among civilizations:

- The Clashes Zone I: Among the Islamic and Eastern, Western and Japanese Civilizations (in the area of Malaysia and Indonesia)
- The Clashes Zone II: Between the Chinese and Japanese civilizations
- The Collaboration Zone I: Among the Western, Hindu, Eastern and Japanese Civilizations
- The Collaboration Zone II: Among the Hindu, African, and Buddhist Civilizations

Encounters between Western and Eastern civilizations at the beginning of the 21st century may resemble clashes, since strong disagreements exist on the NATO expansion into parts of the world beyond the traditional area of Western Europe. This dispute, however, is influenced more by the internal politics of Russia than by any real threat from NATO. In the meantime, the Western-West civilization is providing significant financing for the transformation of the post-Soviet civilization into Eastern civilization, based on the western message.

THE CHALLENGES FOR CIVILIZATIONS AND PEOPLE

Based on the encounters between civilizations, one may offer the following prospects for the further development of the world civilization (Figure 3-2), applying such criteria as knowledge, freedom (human and civil rights, international law), modernization[5], westernization, trade, population control, ecology control, and ecumenism:

1. The modernization process is embracing all civilizations, leading to the development of an integrational infrastructure such as the global network of transportation and information exchanges (the Internet).

2. World trade is embracing all civilizations and creating stateless consortia that challenge the world's *modus operandi*.

3. The development of technological knowledge is taking place in all civilizations including African to certain degree. The development of knowledge in the social sciences is limited in the African, Chinese, and Islamic civilizations, mostly due to their authoritarian or quasi-totalitarian political systems.

4. The freedom movement is taking place in four civilizations, while the remaining civilizations are limited by their authoritarian and quasi-totalitarian political systems.

5. The westernization process is taking place in four civilizations—Western, Japanese, Eastern, and Hindu. Within the Western civilization, there is a clash between this civilization and other civilizations brought in by immigrants. It means that Western civilization is still "westernizing."

6. Ecumenism takes place only within the Western civilization, while other civilizations are afraid of converging and tend to fall into fundamentalism.

7. All the above are contributing to the emergence of the global civilization, which creates the second level of the world civilization.

8. The development of the global civilization is exerting a strong influence upon the development of each autonomous civilization as well as upon the development and spread of knowledge, freedom, modernization, and perhaps westernization.

Figure 3-2. The dynamics of the world civilization at the beginning of the 21st century (The first layer of civilization is not shown)

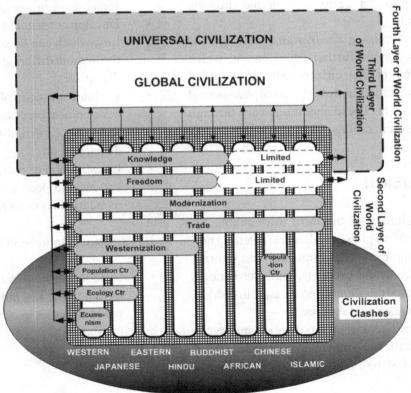

9. Control over the environment is limited to the Western-West and Japanese civilizations and this control is determining their higher quality of life.

10. Population control is limited to the Western-West, Japanese, and Chinese civilizations, and this control determines their higher quality of life. However, in the case of the Chinese civilization this influence may be felt only over a long-term perspective.

In a broad historic context, the civilization dynamics allow for the following conclusion:

1. The Western-West Civilization is in a state of saturation and must look for external expansion, which is happening under the form of globalism, europeism and pre-emptive defense doctrine, which secure the extension of its reach.

2. The Islamic civilization, having almost unlimited resources from the sales of oil, wants to change its unfavorable situation quickly.

3. The remaining civilizations have yet the space for the further development, which depends on their citizens' education, capital accumulation, and capable if not phenomenal leadership. These conditions vary through these civilizations.

CONCLUSION

At the beginning of the third millennium, the emergence of the global civilization is setting new standards in business communications, international travel, world products, and international behavior based upon a common "taste" in fashion, food, pop music, and movies.

Thus, a citizen of any civilization must cope with two challenges: that of his/her own civilization and that of the global civilization. The global civilization need not replace an autonomous civilization, as many leaders of "invaded" civilizations fear. On the contrary, it is necessary to develop behavior which can cope simultaneously with these two challenges. The emergence of the global civilization creates a second layer, superimposed upon each autonomous civilization. This second layer increases the complexity of the world civilization, creating new challenges for each individual civilization and their participants.

However, the global civilization is under strong criticism that it cannot be based only on market forces and must be regulated by the global society (Soros, 2002; 2003). Perhaps the latter may lead to the rise of the universal civilization, which will be less infrastructural and more cultural, taking the best values from all civilizations (Targowski, 2004b).

A. Further Research Directions

• Define civilization index by applying different configurations of key indicators

• Develop consistent sets of a few key indicators, which can be generalized and applied throughout different scientific and practical disciplines

• Evaluate strategies of different civilizations' development processes and eventually apply them to the current issues of civilizations' development.

• Investigation of more challenges for civilizations and people and offer some recommendations how to respond to them

B. Research Opportunities

• Include the civilization index among the most popular key indicators of national and world statistics in order to trace the state of the Earth

C. Additional Ideas

- Apply the civilization index as the measurement of the civilization's "health" and opportunity for updating human strategy in politics, science, technology, medicine, education and so forth

D. Rationale

- The civilization index makes a compelling case for rethinking what constitutes success or failure of a civilization as a supra-structure of nations and peoples with similar mindsets. Early in the 20th century, economists helped devise standards for measuring our economic progress and developing indicators to help create fiscal policy. One must now argue that it is time to make the goal of meaningful and timely measures of our civilization one of the top priorities of political, ecological, social, and technological sciences. The arrival of post-industrial society at the end of the 20th century and global society at the beginning of the 21st century have transformed traditional power, and thus methods used to measure the relative power of nations should be reassessed as well, particularly at a higher level than the nation, at the level of a civilization. Needless to say, in the present century, a war between nations may transform into a war between civilizations. The civilization index approach can be treated as some kind of quantitative approach to civilization history in a *longue-duree* cycle. Mathematical expressions of these processes help to make the implicit assumptions explicit, their consequences deduced, absurd implications deleted, and disputable statements pinpointed (Richardson, 1960; Wilkinson, 1980). Understandably, most academic historians are skeptical of this approach, limiting models to the "explanatory" capability of various philosophical ideas, which are meaningless for academic historians. At least the civilization index is not about history per se, but about the "explanatory" relations among civilizations, which are shaped by the *longue-duree* history.

E. Additional Reading

Aristotle. (1927). Metaphysics. In: W. Ross (Ed.), *Aristotle* (pp. 105-118). New York, NY: Scribner.

Bradburn, N., & Berlew, D. (1961). Need for achievement and English economic growth. *Economic Development and Cultural Change, 10,* 8-20.

Debord, G. (1995). *The society of the spectacle.* Cambridge, MA: The MIT Press.

Fukuyama, F. (1992). *The end of history and the last man.* Penguin Group.

Geyl, P. (1955). *Debates with historians.* London: Collins.

Gibbon, E. (1776). *The history of the decline and fall of the Roman empire.* New York, NY: Random House.

Hegel, G. (1900). *The philosophy of history.* New York, NY: Collier.

Kant, I. (1963). Idea for a universal history from a cosmopolitan point of view. In: L. Beck (Ed.), *Kant on history* (pp. 11-26). New York, NY: Bobbs-Merrill.

Krus, D., & Blackman, H. (1980). Time scale factor as related to theories of societal change. *Psychological Reports, 46,* 95-102.

Krus, D., & Ko, H. (1983). Algorithm for autocorrelation of secular trends. *Educational and Psychological Measurement, 43,* 821-828.

Makridakis, S., & Wheelwright, S. (1978). *Interactive forecasting: Univariate and multivariate methods.* San Francisco, CA: Holden-Day.

McClelland, D. (1961). *The achieving society.* Princeton, NJ: Van Nostrand.

_____ (1975). *Power: The inner experience.* New York, NY: Halstead.

Moyal, J. (1949). The distribution of wars in time. *Journal of the Royal Statistical Society, 112,* 446-458.

Popper, K. (1957). *The poverty of historicism.* London, UK: Routledge.

Press, W., Teukolsky, S., Vetterling, W., & Flannery, B. (1986). *Numerical recipes: The art of scientific computing.* Cambridge, MA: Cambridge University Press.

Richardson, L. (1960). *Statistics of deadly quarrels.* Pacific Grove, CA: Boxwood Press.

Russell, E. (1971). Christianity and militarism. *Peace Research Review, 4*(3), 1-77.

Silver, N., & Hittner, J. (1998). *Guidebook of statistical software for the social and behavioral sciences.* Boston, MA: Allyn & Bacon.

Spengler, O. (1920). *Der Untergang des Abendlandes (The decline of the West).* München, Germany: Beck.

Toynbee, A. (1934). *A study of history.* Oxford, UK: Oxford University Press.

Tucker, R. (1990). *Philosophy and myth in Karl Marx (*2nd ed.*).* Cambridge, MA: Cambridge University Press.

Turchin, P. (2006). *War and peace and war: The life cycles of imperial nations.* New York, NY: Pi Press.

Turchin, P., et al (Eds.). (2007). *History & mathematics: Historical dynamics and development of complex societies.* Moscow: KomKniga.

Vico, G. (1968). *The new science.* Ithaca, NY: Cornell University Press.

Wilkinson, D. (1980). *Deadly quarrels: Lewis F. Richardson and the statistical study of war.* Berkeley, CA: University of California Press.

Wright, Q. (1965). *A study of war* (2nd ed.). Chicago, IL: University of Chicago Press.

REFERENCES

Barry, T., & Honey, M. (2000). *Global focus.* New York, NY: St. Martin's Press.

Braudel, F. (1993). *A history of civilizations.* New York, NY: Penguin Books.

Burenhult, G. (2003). *People of the past.* San Francisco, CA: Fog City Press.

_____ (2003a). *Great civilizations.* San Francisco, CA: Fog City Press.

Dupuy, R., & Dupuy, T. (1986). *The encyclopedia of military history from 3,500 B.C. to the present* (2nd rev. ed.). New York, NY: Harper & Row.

Eckhard, W. (1995). A dialectical evolutionary theory of civilization, empires, and wars. In: S. Sanderson (Ed.), *Civilizations and world systems, studying world-historical change.* Walnut Creek, London; New Delhi: Altamira Press.

Fukuyama, F. (1989). The end of history. *The National Interest, 16*(3), 3-18.

Hundley, R., Anderson, R., Bikson, T., & Neu, C. (2003). *The global course of the information revolution.* Santa Monica, CA: RAND.

Hunter, L. (2000). *The environmental implications of population dynamics.* Santa Monica, CA: RAND.

Huntington, S. (1993). The clash of civilizations. *Foreign Affairs, 72*(3), 22-49.

_____ (1996). *The clash of civilizations and the remaking of world order*. New York, NY: Simon & Schuster.

Kawakubo, K. (2001). The vistas of the comparative study of civilizations. *Comparative Civilizations Review, 45,* 51-66.

Kroeber, A. (1944). *Configurations of culture growth*. Berkeley and Los Angeles, CA: University of California Press.

Kurian, G. (1991). *The new book of world rankings*. New York, NY: Facts on File Publications.

Maddison, A. (2001). *The world economy*. Paris: OECD.

Naroll, R., Fohl, B., Fried, M., Hildreth, R., & Schaefer, J. (1971). Creativity: A cross-historical pilot survey. *Journal of Cross-Cultural Psychology, 2,* 181-188.

Sorokin, P. (1937). *Social and cultural dynamics*. New York, NY: American Book.

Soros, G. (2002). *On globalization*. New York, NY: Public Affairs Press.

_____ (2003). *The bubble of American supremacy*. New York, NY: Public Affairs Press.

Taagepera, R. (1978a). Size and duration of empires: Systematics of size. *Social Science Research, 7,* 108-127.

_____ (1978b). Size and duration of empires: Growth-decline curves, 3,000 to 600 B.C. *Social Science Research, 7,* 180-196.

Targowski, A. (2004a). A dynamic model of an autonomous civilization. *Dialogue and Universalism, 14*(1-2), 77-90.

_____ (2004b). From global to universal civilization. *Dialogue and Universalism, 14*(3-4), 121-142.

_____ (2004c). A grand model of civilization. *Comparative Civilizations Review, 51*(Fall), 81-106.

Tilly, C. (1984). *Big structures, large processes, huge comparisons*. New York, NY: Russell Sage Foundation.

Toynbee, A. (1995). *A study of history*. New York, NY: Barnes & Noble.

World Development Indicators. (1997). Washington, D.C.: The World Bank, (pp. 284-286).

ENDNOTES

1. More on civilization definition is provided by Targowski (2004c).

2. Although the Jewish civilization is not based on Catholicism and Protestantism, it belongs to the Western civilization on the same premise as Greece (Hellenic), which is Orthodox, belongs to the Western civilization, because both contributed enormously to the development of the Western civilization.

3. A sequence of civilizations is provided by using a criterion from Table 9, where the sorting is given by the Civilization Index value.

4. More on this type of system in Targowski (2004a; 2004c).

5. The difference between "modernization" and "westernization" lies in applying as a modernization process "modern tools" without western values.

Section II
The Human Project

Chapter IV
(A) Liberating the Future from the Past

INTRODUCTION

The purpose of this chapter is to evaluate a role of information-communication (INFOCO) processes in human development according to the following plan:

(A) Liberating the future from the past
(B) Liberating the past from the future

The programs formulated in statements A and B above, in my view, frame the task of formulating a philosophy of life in the third millennium or, at least, in the 21st century. An examination of the relationship between the past and the future may provide an answer to the question of how we should live in the present. The turn of the 21st century is very rich in the emerging paradigms of many very fundamental fields of life. Some examples will suffice to illustrate the point: the fall of Communism makes way for a New World Order; medicine witnesses healing with the aid of gene therapy; technology sees the emergence of "cyberspace," a new dimension of civilization; in philosophy, modernism becomes transformed into progress with a human face; national econo-

mies yield to a global economy; insular societies become network societies.

In this jungle of great changes, both the average person and the professional politician, artist, or technician becomes lost and wonders "What is it all about?" "How does one conduct one's life in relation to all this?" Some are pleased with the imminent changes while others complain and curse: "You can keep your 'interesting times.'" One thing is sure, that in such "interesting times" the world is integrating, trying to make sense of itself and to avoid conflicts, and is looking at the future with hope. People are coming to the conclusions that science is not the only source of understanding truth and that the life experience of the individual is an equally meaningful source of wisdom.

In the following analysis and synthesis of programs A (liberating the future from the past) and B (liberating the past from the future), we shall outline the task of formulating a sketch of a philosophy of life for the general reader. If this work can provide a meaningful answer to the question of "how to live," then it should be able to reach every curious resident of our planet, every culture and every civilization—not, of course, as an authoritative injunction on "how to live," which could not be imposed on anyone by scientific authority, but as a set of general guidelines which each human being himself must choose to either adopt or reject.

Concurrent with the present trend to integrate, a contemporary philosophy of life should emerge from actual social processes, such as the creation of a global economy and a discussion concerning the need for the formation of an open global society. This need would seem to be particularly important because the Cold War is expected to be replaced by "clashes" among civilizations, which should be minimized. In this regard, I propose to examine and formulate the first foundations of the philosophy of communicated harmony. The basis of this process will be the analysis and synthesis of the degrees of independence and unity of the "past" and the "future." We shall look at their relationship as it regards civilization, rather than in astronomic categories of time. For it is through civilization that we understand the collective

way of people's lives, a method which embraces communal life, culture and the infrastructure. Figure 4-1 presents a general model for solving problems A and B.

THE INFOCO SYSTEM AS A MEANS FROM THE PAST

In the year 2000, mankind enters a new age of development, not because the date suggests a rarely encountered place at the end of a millennium—in our case, the end of the second and the beginning of the third—but because we have to deal with change in a paradigmatic system of communication in civilization.

The growth of humanity can be studied from many points of view, including such criteria as climatic conditions, the adoption of tools, productive method and family structures. To my mind, the most significant criterion is the evolution of the

Figure 4-1. Architecture of time ("A" Liberating the Future from the Past; "B" Liberating the Past from the Future)

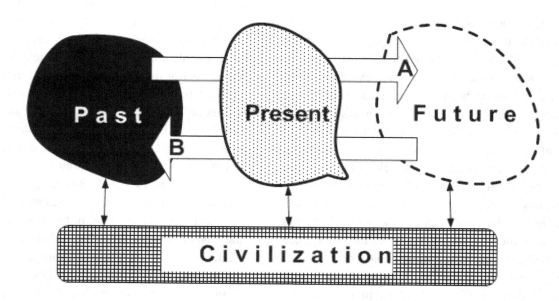

information-communication system (INFOCO), which engineered the rise of pre-historic man into taking conscious dominance of his own existence. Before we can examine the degree of the eventual "liberation of the future from the past," we must first examine the evolutionary process of man and his "liberation."

The first human, of genus *Australopithecus* (two-legged, with large brain and tools), took form around 2-4 million years ago in East and South Africa. The use of tools straightened man so that 1.6 million years ago our ancestors were already moving about in an upright position (*homo erectus*). *Homo sapiens* evolved in Africa between 130,000 and 120,000 years ago; they had probably begun to spread out into Eurasia about 100,000 years ago, or a little earlier, from that moment when a group of about 200 to 500 people left Southeast Africa (Kenya and Tanzania) and set out for Central Asia, para-social man was formed. Around 70,000 to 36,000 years ago, a stable population was organized respectively in China (68,000 years ago), Australia (50,000 ago), and Europe (36,000 ago). The European line of speaking Cro-Magnon is attributable to the curiosity of mobile man (Burenhult, 2003).

At this time, biological evolution gave birth to cultural evolution, which gave rise to the language of inter-human communication. Thus para-social man became speaking man, a milestone that can be dated around 100,000 years ago (Jones, Martin, & Pilbeam, 1992). We are thus roughly the 3,030[th] generation of speaking man—that is to say, man using the organized system INFOCO-1.

With the formation of INFOCO-1, mankind started to blossom socially and culturally. After some 94,000 years (since we began to speak as *homo verbalis*), human civilization was born at the rivers Tigris and Euphrates in the Near East with *homo tribalis* who organized a society (tribes).

The development of information and knowledge played a determining role in the development of contemporary civilization, particularly in the Western version. Christianity is nothing less than modern ideology. It is a form of emotional involvement and of information, communicated in an organized method among people, motivating its followers to a meaningful life, supported by a defined system of values, parenthetically speaking, binding Christians to our contemporary times.

Already in ancient imperial Egypt, religion was organized within an information system on papyrus, that is, a written language, system INFOCO-2. Yet writing did not make a decisive difference to social communication, since it was known only to a handful of priests, bureaucrats, and merchants. The Christian religion, on the other hand, was organized in books, hand-written and copied by monks (and available to practically no one else. Even Charlemagne struggled with being able to read and write, and eventually gave it up). The vital turn in human communication occurred with the European invention of mechanical printing by Gutenberg in 1454. (The Chinese and Koreans had mechanical printing with woodblocks for centuries before this German print. Even some of the blocks are preserved, primarily of Buddhist texts. Why did it not make a difference? Since Europe in those times was more open to innovation and science than Asia). From that point, the distribution of information among readers began to accelerate. Print type can metaphorically be called the first "computing" device, which organized and started to unite Europe and determined her primacy in the world in the first half of the second millennium. In the second half, primacy was assumed by Euro-America, situated around the Atlantic Ocean. European print gave "birth" to a new *homo libris*, as the next great leap in mankind evolution.

As illustrated in Figure 4-2, "computer arrangement," producing the printed book (INFOCO-3), initiated three interdependent revolutions in the development of Western civilization:

- The intellectual revolution, which gave rise to the exact sciences in the sixteenth century

Figure 4-2. Bifurcation of world civilization (21st century)

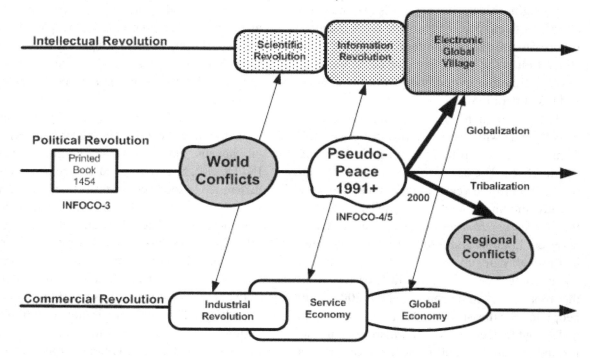

which, in turn, produced the contemporary computer around 1961 (Univac 1) and tele-communication networks in the 1990s.

- The political revolution, which led to the English Revolution in 1685-1714 which created the parliamentary monarchy, to the American Revolution (1776-1787), which gave rise to the Republican democracy; and to the French Revolution (1789-1799) which introduced the Republican system into Europe (however briefly). In the 2000th century there prevailed a period of total confrontation of democratic ideology versus militarism and totalitarianism in two World Wars and the Cold War which ended with the fall of Communism and with peace.
- The trade revolution, beginning with the formation of the first private business enterprise (The Dutch East India Trade Company, 1602, dependent on its owners' shares-stockholders), gave rise to the invention of the steam engine (1769), and to industry (the 19th and 20th centuries), the railway (1829), electric power (1866), the private automobile (1908), the airplane (1903), and modern airlines (the 1960s), and consequently led to the age of the service and global economies.

The interdependence of the above-named three revolutions is self-evident. The political revolution commissioned modern armaments from business and industry, which created a market for innovation; that is, it activated an intellectual revolution. This, in turn, influenced the course of both the political and business revolutions, an influence that has been and continues to be conveyed by information and communication. In the second half of the twentieth century, this gave way to automation and networking, thanks to computers (INFOCO-4) and their telecommunication networks (INFOCO-5).

As a result of the refining of all three revolutions, human civilization has branched out into two divisions: a billion people living in the Electronic Global Village (EGV) (Targowski, 1991) and having so-called "access to the computers," and 4.5 billion people living in manuscript-oriented conditions without such access. EGV dwellers have at their disposal highly complicated computer networks, which influence their lives in much the same revolutionary way as did spoken language sixty-thousand years ago.

What influence this will have on mankind's bio-social development, it is too early to tell; we can only speculate. As a consequence of language, people began to migrate in organized fashion, in search of greater living space and better living conditions, resulting in the rise of Asia, Europe, Australia and America. The computer network, on the other hand, produces the reverse effect. Thanks to telecommunication, man does not have to move physically from place to place. The EGV dweller can satisfy his curiosity and his search for better living options by navigating the ocean of computerized information available, for instance, on the Internet.

Does a person with the computerized system INFOCO-5 have more chance of survival than someone (*homo manuscriptus* or just *homo scriba*) from a manuscript-oriented organization? Will non-organized and noninformed tribal man perish as did *homo neanderthalensis*, which disappeared around 30,000 years ago when confronted with Cro-Magnon Man who, arriving from Asia, operated in symbolic language (Deacon, 1997) (INFOCO-1) and even created art in the form of cave murals recently uncovered in Spain and France? As it happened, Neanderthal Man who indeed, possessed a brain size of 1700 cc and yet communicated by simplistic sounds, had no subsequent influence in the development of contemporary man. Evidently, it is the INFOCO system that has deciding influence on man's greater progress and better organization.

From an optimistic viewpoint, it is *homo electronicus* (McGaughey, 2001) who has more opportunities for development (Grossman, 1995) than *homo scriba*, since the former has more advanced tools to support his/her existence.

CIVILIZATION PARADIGM SHIFTS

Now, with the passage of the year 2000, we find ourselves at the same kind of turning point as the world did 100,000 years ago, when human language arose, and 550 years ago when mechanical printing was invented in Europe. Since then, the deciding factor in human evolution has been INFOCO, whose various changes are illustrated in Table 4-1.

The change in the paradigm, during 2,000[th] from informational to network communication, is a more brutal change than the introduction of print. Certainly, writing and hand-made books were already known before the appearance of print. The significance of the printed book lies in the fact that instead of reaching only tens or hundreds of readers, information began to reach thousands and in the twentieth century, hundreds of thousands to several millions. Of course, the greatest readership has been enjoyed by popular bestsellers rather than by books offering knowledge.

Communication that utilizes computer networks universalizes information and knowledge instantly among several hundred million users. It is impossible to say at this point what result and influence this massive spread of information and knowledge will have on human development (electronic civilization?). We can surmise that man will be more aware of his limitations and possibilities.

Table 4-1. The evolution of the INFOCO system

INFOCO	Sense Organ	Humankind	Brain Size	Structure of Consciousness	Paradigm
Stimuli-Response	Nose	Hominid 10 M–6 M	500 cc	Archaic	Instinct Communication
Sound	Ear	Australopithecine 6 M.-2.5 M.	500 cc	Archaic	Sound Communication
Variety of Sounds	Ear	Homo habilis 2.5m.-1.8m.	750 cc	Archaic	Hand Communication
Intelligence (fire)	Brain	Homo erectus 1.8m.-200K	800 cc-1100 cc	Archaic Spaceless Timeless	Survival Communication
Wisdom	Brain	Homo sapiens 200K-60K	1750 cc-1350 cc	Magical 1D Timeless	Migration Communication
Language	Mouth	Homo verbalis 100K-4K BC	1350 cc	Mythical 2D Natural Tempos	Symbol Communication INFOCO-1
Civilized Language	Mouth "Feather"	Homo tribalis & Homo scirba 4K BC-1454 AD	1350 cc	Mythical 2D Organized Tempos	Social Communication Writing INFOCO-2
Print, Records	Eye	Homo libris 1452-2000	1350 cc	Mental 3D Spatial Abstract Time	Information Communication INFOCO-3
Computer Networks	Cyberspace	Homo electronicus	1350 cc-1500 cc	Integral 4D Space Free Time Free	Networked Communication INFOCO-4 INFOCO-5

THE ARCHITECTURE OF THE A.D. 2000 PARADIGM SHIFT

In the second millennium, human existence depended on man's functioning alone in the framework of large-scale laws of historical development, which, "consciously using an actually very appropriate cliché," we will call the big picture. We will refer to this way of life as the "disconnected-flat existence." After Hegel, Popper and Kuhn, we have found ourselves in a position where historical development has its own internal "spiral" dynamics and is racing toward some ultimate goals. Each spiral development is enriched with new achievements, which are the effect of the work of civilization.

As a result of the continuous development of ideas and values, man develops knowledge and awareness about him/herself, nature and civilization. Hence one can formulate after Bronowski and Mazlish (1962) the *first civilization law of man's self-fulfillment*:

People have seen themselves as entering the world with the potential of many gifts, and they hope to fulfill these gifts in the development of their own lives.

This law has absorbed the minds and work of Locke, Voltaire, Rousseau, Kant, Schopenhauer, Jefferson, Jasper, Habermas, Havel, and others. This law may be called the self-realization law.

It inspired the development of science and technology to liberate a person from his own manual effort, replacing it by mechanization, automation, and informatization. From Leonardo da Vinci through Edison, Ford, and Cray, inventors have tried to provide more free time for us that we can use for rest, entertainment, and education. This idle time provides the chance for the development of talents and dreams. In the 21st century, in some countries, it is apparent how the value of possessions is being transformed into the value of the quality of life. Intuitively, this law was applied in the movement for civil rights in the 1960s and for human rights in the 1970s and also in science and art. It would be interesting to trace this law through the historic roots of civilization.

An example of a big-picture law is the *second civilization law of man's quest for freedom* that formulates the right of man to freedom and knowledge (reason). We formulate it as follows:

People constantly aim for freedom; the range of this freedom depends on the level of the nation's knowledge and communication ability and the knowledge of the international community.

In the last 6,000 years of civilization, mankind has constantly been increasing its freedom as a result of its development of knowledge about socialization. This freedom has been enlarging ever since the Renaissance (15th century), when print was applied to disseminate information and, later, knowledge. In practice, man has been liberated from political, economic, and social discrimination only at the end of the 20th century and only in democratic states. This process is not yet finished and historians could show how this Grand Law has been emerging through civilization's history in order eventually to guide contemporary activists.

The *third civilization law of its evolution* is the law of conscious historical evolution, which we formulate in the following way:

Mankind consciously steers the development of civilization through the formulation and implementation of main ideas and values of a given epoch.

The Renaissance, Enlightenment, and Modernism impacted their times in very recognized ways. This law emphasizes the meaning of cultural consciousness, which among educated people guides economic development and not vice versa. The Enlightenment epoch created the American and French Revolutions that opened the door for the Industrial Revolution, and so on. People observe that their chosen values decide more about their fate than economic conditions. It would be an interesting task for historians to trace the historic trends in business and find out why pure competition is being replaced by a mix of cooperation and competition. Is this emerging trend based upon this law, or on a stronger emotion of greed, or the art of survival?

The *fourth civilization law of country's status* reflects the historical process which decides about country's success or failure, which develops in the following way:

The degree of a country's historical success is proportional to the level of harmony among political, social and economic domains.

In the 21st century, the world is in transition to a "New World Order." Many countries, particularly those transforming from Communism towards democracy, experience a lack of the harmony mentioned in this law. The cases of Poland (in the last 350 years), Russia (1905-1917 and 1991-2000), Yugoslavia (1988-2000), Somalia, Rwanda, Burundi, Belarus, and even Canada and Belgium demonstrate this law. Historians could again trace the application of this law through civilization's history, providing a very meaningful contribution to political science.

Mankind is entering the third millennium in communication with almost the entire world,

Figure 4-3. The paradigm shift of existence

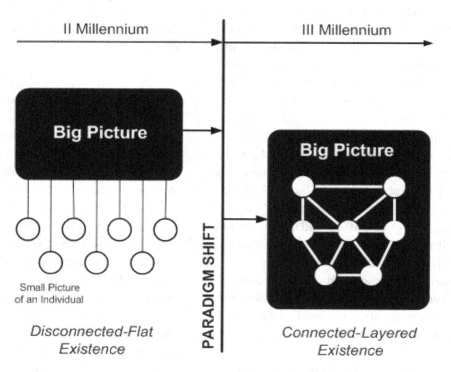

thanks to computer networks and to increasingly accessible realms of information and knowledge. Thus, man becomes better informed and realizes that he is not alone. In itself, the act of communicating with other people from another part of the globe forces people to act locally and think globally. In other words, the big picture works its way into the way of thinking of an individual who no longer considers himself alone against dominant ideas of the age. The individual becomes a part *of* rather than apart *from* the big picture. We can call this way of life a connected-layered existence.

Changes in the architecture of existence in the second and third millennia are shown in Figure 4-3.

THE CONNECTED-LAYERED EXISTENCE

Mankind is entering the third millennium forming an awareness of a four-dimensional space. This space can be described thus:

1. A space of life principles formulated in layers of big picture and small picture
2. A cultural space defined in layers of integrated native, national culture, adapted, national culture (e.g., after immigration), and an emerging global culture
3. A communication space defined in layers of integrated local, national, and global information infrastructures
4. Cyberspace, which makes it possible to do business by electronic means, for example,

Figure 4-4. Connected-layered existence

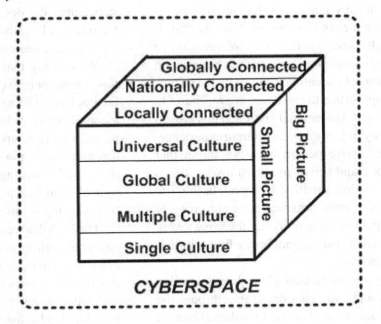

A model of a connected-layered existence is shown on Figure 4-4.

The connected-layered way of existence breaks from the previous isolated, "island" way of life in the ocean of billions of people. This form of existence increases the degree of complication in life and demands a good education as well as computer and information skills. This new existence may seem, at first glance, schizophrenic, but hopefully with better education it will be embraced. People lacking this new type of knowledge, but relying on skills of the past, will find themselves outside the system of the future. In other words, the new system of existence liberates a person from the past in his/her quest for the future.

electronic commerce, digital banking, digital libraries, and so forth

THE HARMONIC DEVELOPMENT OF EXISTENCE

A system of living in a four-dimensional space gives humanity, for the first time, a relatively effective opportunity to take advantage of consensus within a group in which this agreement makes sense. The process of seeking agreement is a process of minimizing conflicts among people, a recipe, as it were, for living in peace and equanimity. This does not mean that all conflicts will be entirely eliminated. This new opportunity for man has been put forth clearly by Jurgen Habermas in his philosophy of communication. Such a philosophy does not replace such a philosophy of rationalism as was introduced by the Enlightenment, but serves as a complement to it. Basing life exclusively on a rational foundation can be misleading, since many areas of life are excluded from man's rational judgment.

Opponents of the rational-action method argue that man usually places greater importance on defining for means than on establishing "rational" ends. It is true that the so-called quantitative methods of optimizing decisions put pressure on the technique of allocating means with the unspoken assumption that the goals are appropriate. On the other hand, the rational approach has proven itself worthy in many areas of human experience. Therefore, a wise person does not forget that what is good and serves to enrich his/her life is worth putting into practice. However, basing life solely on a rational criterion does not properly reflect actual human activity. By the same token, achieving consensus cannot be the first criterion of human activity.

Human communication alone does not lead to knowledge and truth. They do not arise through the process of agreement but are formulated through the process of rational discovery in the framework of accepted inner logic. Basing existence exclusively on communal group understanding was exploited efficiently under Communist and Nazi totalitarianism. Whatever the Politburo agreed to among themselves became the "accepted truth" for the entire society. This led to a decline in rationalism and a regression in humanism: bad became "good" and nonsense became "wisdom." As a result of rational activity, mankind achieved, by the end of the second millennium, a reasonably good standard of living, particularly in Western civilization. This does not mean, however, that even in this civilization, man is satisfied and content. There is, of course, no utopia, no place in the world where every human being is satisfied with his/her existence.

The enrichment of rational human methods involving a communicated search for consensus within a group can lead to a new standard of activity, particularly when the technique of communication is used by people open to dialogue and the search for truth. In fact, without an openly communicated attitude, it is difficult to believe that computer networks alone can ensure universal agreement. What counts is human development rather than the development of communication techniques. The latter should not be the main goal but should rather act as a catalyst.

We can say that the growth of communication among people (C) over rational, individualized activity (R) must lead, sooner or later, to a consensus of "I know that I don't know," and to set in motion rational activities, calculated to discover new knowledge and truth. Otherwise, the aim of achieving consensus, taken as an end in itself, can lead to a vicious circle, a case of a "dog chasing its own tail."

The high degree of affluence in the developed countries, reinforced by the connected-layered existence, enlarges the field of new opportunities for the enterprising individual. These new opportunities and technologies empower (P) the individual in his quest for the future. An empowered individual, however, confronts a new complexity and the need for new knowledge (K) and qualifications. The lust for knowledge, after all, is never sated, and new challenges demand either new knowledge or its realization. A new equation of connected-layered existence (E_{cl}) in the third millennium can be expressed as follows:

$$E_{cl} \rightarrow R(K) \ U \ C$$
$$\text{where: } P \geq K$$
$$\text{and } C_1 \rightarrow C_2 \rightarrow C_n \rightarrow R_n$$

Obviously, man's main motivation in rational activity and communication is the need for self-preservation. This motivation is embedded in the human subconscious and its instinctive activity. The philosophy of rationalism is solved by the left side of the brain while the philosophy of communication (influenced by emotions and aesthetics) is employed by the right one. From here it is but one step to presenting a model of both sides of brain and their role in thinking and behaving (Figure 4-5).

Figure 4-5. The harmonic development of existence

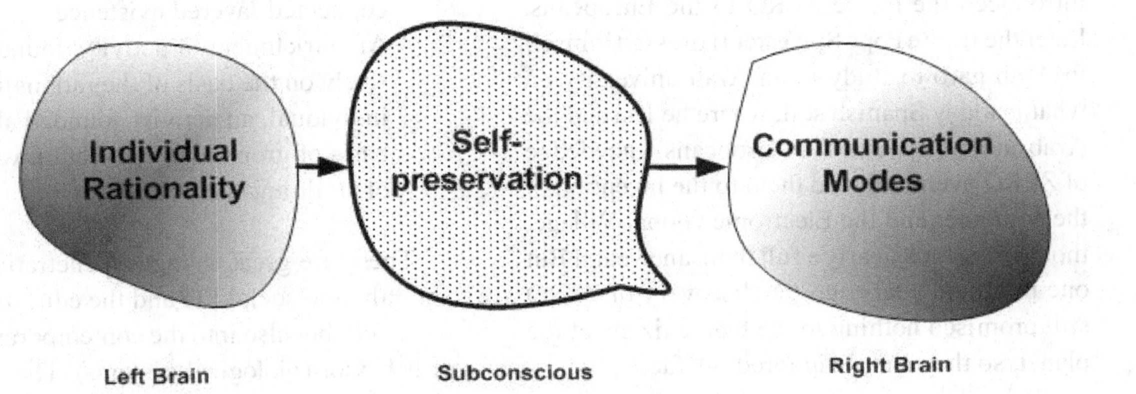

Individual Rationality → Self-preservation → Communication Modes

Left Brain — Subconscious — Right Brain

CONCLUSION:
THE "FUTURELESS" PAST

Question "A" concerning the liberation of the future from the past is, of course, a provocative inquiry that one should make on the occasion of the turn of the millennium. Is it suitable to pose such a question at every centenary turn? Should we seek a permanent solution to this problem notwithstanding the anniversary which is about to take place?

Let us examine the achievements that have accompanied previous turns of the millennium. Certainly, the turn of the year one of the first millennium is a great turning point. We accept it (erroneously) as the year of Christ's birth. Of course, only some few Christians of the time "liberated the future from the past." Indeed, the process of that liberation took them more than three centuries when, in 337 A.D., Christianity became the official religion of Rome.

In 1000 A.D. when the first millennium ended and the second began, question "A" would not have been a relevant issue. Quite the opposite, in fact, since peoples' eyes were fixed firmly on the "past." Yet even this centenary did not go overlooked. Christians were awaiting the "Second Coming" of Christ to Earth, and the Jews, the arrival of Messiah, who would take the world under his command. It did not happen, of course, and both Christians and Jews are still awaiting their respective great events. With today's hindsight, however, we can describe the turn of the second millennium as a gradual formation of Europe. Critical to this formation were the roles played by Emperor Otto III and Pope Sylvester II, who contributed to the rise of the Eastern peripheries of Europe (Poland) at a time when there already existed a western periphery, as well as a center in the form of the Holy Roman Empire. It happened only a half a century later in 1054 A.D., with the schism of the Christian church, which marks the birth of the so-called "East" and "West." This example demonstrates that history does not "wait" for turning-point dates and is capable of identifying itself in other years through phenomenal events.

Again, observing with today's hindsight, we can confirm that something great did indeed occur at the turn of the second millennium. A

Benedictine monk named Gerbert d'Aurillac introduced the figure ZERO to the Europeans. Later the future Pope Sylvester II dressed himself in Arab garb to study in an Arab university on what is today Spanish soil, where he learned the Arab number system. The Europeans' knowledge of ZERO eventually led them to the invention of the computer and the Electronic Global Village, though this took nearly a full thousand years! But one thousand years ago the discovery of ZERO still promised nothing to the then citizens of the planet, so they simply ignored the fact.

Perhaps the present turn of the century allows me to pose question "A." The nineteenth century began, practically speaking, in 1789 A.D. and ended in 1914. Nothing like the revolutions of those years occurred either in 1800/1801 A.D. or in 1900/1901 A.D. In politics, the nineteenth century found an application for the rules of "liberating the future from the past." Thus, in education, there was a strong emphasis on the past, that is, the Age of Enlightenment. Similarly, the 20ᵗʰ century ended for all practical purposes in 1991 with the fall of the Soviet Union, an event that spurred a full "liberation of the future from the past" and a change in the paradigmatic world order.

At this point, we come to the crux of the matter, which Thomas Kuhn already formulated a long time ago, that every paradigmatic change encourages and even compels us to "liberate the future from the past." If we confirm that indeed there is such a change at the turn of the third millennium, then the principle of "liberating the future from the past" should be applied.

In the preceding analysis of the transformation of civilization at the end of the first millennium, we have established that there occurred a somewhat time-eroded change in the system of human existence, and we can see this clearly. Due to the strong influence of computer networks, Internet and otherwise, the formation of a new system, INFOCO-5, is now taking place. This demands of men and women with aspirations the following changes for an eventual improved way of life:

1. A passage from a disconnected-flat to a connected-layered existence
2. An enrichment of activity, founded exclusively on the basis of the rationalism of the individual, an activity founded also on the basis of group communication with a goal of attaining consensus

These are great changes, penetrating deeply not only into social life and the educational system itself, but also into the contemporary system of behavior (biological systems). The system of human behavior has, for several hundred generations, been founded on the "disconnected-flat" existence of the individual, storm-tossed by great events independent of the individual himself. This system has indeed become a component of human nature. Those who wish to split with this system and pass over to a harmonious development of their own existence must "liberate the future from the past."

These people will start and, indeed are already starting, the transformation of *homo scriba* into *homo electronicus*. Those, on the other hand, who either choose not to, or are not prepared to, adopt the new paradigm of the third millennium, must inevitably meet with, in Toffler's words, "future shock." These people, *homo manuscriptus* will live on the peripheries of the electronic civilization. And in the long term, the electronics enthusiast will be able to ask about them: "Are they not condemned to perish?", as was, for example, *homo neandertalensis* about 30,000 years ago in what is now present-day Eurasia, despite his brain size of 1700 cc. The Neanderthal was destroyed by invaders from Asia armed with a superior INFOCO system in the form of a developed language. Then, on the other hand, the electronics pessimist could say of electronic man that his world will be so complicated that he will be easy to destroy, and therefore it is the hominids of preceding generations who have a better chance of survival—especially if we keep in mind that

Figure 4-6.

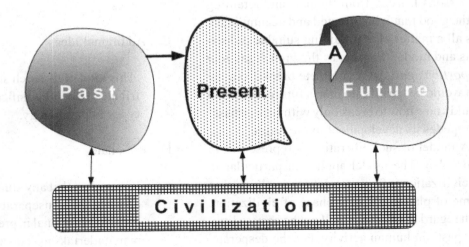

the best chance of surviving an atomic explosion is held by the most primitive of beings, such as the cockroach.

In order to function effectively, *homo electronicus* must be well-educated, since his world is four-dimensional and multi-layered with a wide range of complications. Among the many virtues of being well-educated is the attainment of a high awareness regarding existence.

Translating this into a language of interpersonal or even international relations, we can say that such a person can allow himself the luxury of "liberating the future from the past." Take for example French-German and German-Polish relations. In spite of their rather grim past, these nations, considered among the best educated, can manage to forgive each other such aggressions and crimes as were perpetrated during two World Wars. Some educated people feel that even Communist or Nazi totalitarianisms must at one time have had their place. Their ignominious defeat

is a successful if costly lesson for humankind, which has rejected this form of solution in its further development. The idea of militarism, for example, so deeply rooted in the German nation has had, after World War II, no chance of revival. Similar cases involve American-Japanese relations as well as those between South Korea and Japan. These nations are beginning to look at the "future" less and less with a complex about the "past." This represents a major triumph of "communicated humanism."

On the other hand, the low education level in the countries of the former Yugoslavia led, at the end of the twentieth century, to genocide. The similarly low education level (especially in the social sciences) in Russia is the reason that this country is adjusting with some difficulty to its non-imperial status with its neighbors.

In conclusion, we can say that the paradigmatic change in civilization at the turn of the millennium lets us propose a "liberation of the future from the past," while at the same time adopting the lessons learned from the past and retaining all the good that it has created and accumulated. It is all a matter of maintaining suitable proportions and moderation, or, as the French say *tout proportions gardes*. A complete break from the past would be harmful to man's future. Mankind should know how to break only with such a "past" as impedes its development in the future.

A model of such liberation is represented in Figure 4-6. The model applies in particular to the civilization infrastructure, especially during a time of planning a new phase of civilization. With regard to culture, it will not be easy to limit the "past" in human activity. For the desperate, whose existence is one continuous chain of hardships and indeed of tragedies, a "pastless future" is a great hope for the better.

A. Further Research Directions

- Investigation of a communication role in the confrontation of the Neanderthals and Cro-Magnon people in Europe 40,000 years ago, which was won by speaking people over using simple sounds ones
- Investigation of the INFOCO-3 system (print) versus the INFOCO-4 (computers) and INFOCO-5 (networks) systems in civilization development, particularly at the level of intellectual contributions
- Investigation of the transformation from the disconnected-flat to connected-layered existence in the 21st century and its impact on human life and performance

B. Research Opportunities

- Explain whether "*Future Shock*" (as hypothesized by Alvin Toffler) is caused (among other factors) by the transformation from the small to big-picture worldview and the poor application of this view in individual lives.

C. Additional Ideas

- This kind of research should strongly contribute to a new classification of personality types in psychology.

D. Rationale

- It is evident that any study of contemporary civilization is inseparable from history. In order to be rational in present and future human undertakings one must learn from the past. History is mostly about war, conflicts, which are the usual means of destroying one civilization and beginning another one. We rarely study the peaceful periods and learn how to apply their lessons, which would be much worthier objects of study than wars (study works of M. Melko, [1990] and Melko & Hord [1984]). Even worthier is to study how humans evolved within civilization, due to their rising intellectual capacity. From a modern perspective, past human decisions sometimes seem questionable. However we forget that those decisions were driven by human minds, which reflected human intellectual capacity at that time. This capacity evolves continuously and fortunately is growing and able to solve more complex problems. Therefore, the study of INFOCO systems' evolutions gives us a profound perspective on the human potential in solving civilization's problems. It is important how we are going to shape education, policy, and society in general, knowing what kind of INFOCO systems we have to our disposal. Particularly new for the evolution of humankind is the transformation of single-culture-oriented to multi-culture-oriented individuals, who want to be involved in the global civilization, or its successors.

E.   Additional Reading

Bell, D. (1980). *Sociological journeys: Essays 1960-1980*. London: Heinemann.

Bernal, J. (1989). *The social function of science (1939-1989)*. Berlin: Akademie-Verlag.

Brzezinski, Z. (1976). *Between the two ages: America in the technetronic era*. New York, NY: Penguin.

Burling, R. (2005). *The talking ape, how language evolved*. New York, NY: Oxford University Press.

Carter, J., & Muir, P. (1967). *Printing and the mind of man*. London: Cassel.

Chappell, W. (1980). *A short history of the printed word*. Boston, MA: Nonpareil Books.

Feather, J. (1986). *A dictionary of book history*. New York, NY: Oxford University Press.

Finlayson, C., Pacheco, F., Rodriguez-Vidal, J., et al. (2006). Late survival of neanderthals at the southern most extreme of Europe. *Nature, 443*, 850-853.

Gravina, B., Mellars, P., & Ramsey, C. (2005). Radiocarbon dating of interstratified neanderthal and early modern human occupations at the Chatelperronian type-site. *Nature, 438*, 51-56.

http://www.talkorigins.org/faqs/homs/lagarvelho.html. Retrieved March 10, 2007.

http://www.guardian.co.uk/science/story/0,,1871842,00.html. Retrieved March 10, 2007.

http://johnhawks.net/weblog/reviews/neandertals/gorhams. Retrieved March 10, 2007.

http://www.dhamurian.org.au/anthropology/neanderthal1.html.Retrieved March 10, 2007.

Kuhn, S., & Stiner, M. (2006). What's a mother to do? The division of labor among neandertals and modern humans in Eurasia. *Current Anthropology, 47*(6), 953-980.

McGaughey, W. (2000). *Five epochs of civilization*. Minneapolis, MN: Thistlerose Publications.

_____ (2001). *Rhythms and self-consciousness. new ideals for an electronic civilization*. Minneapolis, MN: Thistlerose Publications.

McMurtrie, D. (1943). *The book: The story of printing & bookmaking*. New York, NY: Oxford University Press.

Melko, M., & Hord, J. (1984). *Peace in the western world*. Jefferson, NC: McFarland.

Melko, M. (1990). *Peace in our time*. New York, NY: Paragon House.

Mellars, P. (2006). A new radiocarbon revolution and the dispersal of modern humans in Eurasia. *Nature, 439*, 931-935.

Porat, M.-U. (1976). *The information economy*. Unpublished Doctoral dissertation. Stanford University.

Richta, R. (Ed.). (1969). *Civilization at the crossroads*. New York, NY: ME Sharp.

Shannon, C., & Weaver, W. (1949). *The mathematical theory of communication*. Urbana, IL: University of Illinois Press.

Steinberg, S. (1996). *Five hundred years of printing*. London and Newcastle: The British Library and Oak Knoll Press.

Wade, N. (2006, December 5). Neanderthal women joined men in the hunt. *The New York Times*.

Wiener, N. (1948). *Cybernetics*. Cambridge, MA: MIT Press.

Veneris, Y. (1984). *The informational revolution. Cybernetics and urban modeling*. Unpublished doctoral thesis. University of Newcastle upon Tyne, UK.

(1990). Modeling the transition from the industrial to the informational revolution. *Environment and Planning, 22*(3), 399-416

REFERENCES

Bronowski, J., & Mazlish, B. (1962). *The western intellectual tradition.* New York, NY: Harper Perennial.

Deacon, T. (1997). *The symbolic species.* New York, NY: W.W. Norton Co.

Grossman, L. (1995). *The electronic republic.* New York, NY: Viking.

Grumley, J. (1989). *History and totality: Radical historicism from Hegel to Foucault.* London, New York: Routledge.

Habermas, J. (1984). *The theory of communicative action.* Boston, MA: Beacon Press.

_____ (1998). *On the pragmatics of communication.* Cambridge, MA: MIT Press.

_____ (2001). *On the pragmatics of social interaction.* Cambridge, MA: MIT Press.

Hegel, G. (1944). *The philosophy of history.* New York, NY: Willey Book Co.

_____ (1955). *Hegel's lectures on the history of philosophy.* New York, NY: Humanities Press.

_____ (1975). *Lectures on the philosophy of world history.* New York, NY: Cambridge University Press.

Jones, S., R. Marin & D. Pilbeam, M. (1992). *The Cambridge encyclopedia of human evolution.* New York, NY: Cambridge University Press.

Kuhn, T. (1962). *The structure of scientific revolutions.* Chicago, IL: University of Chicago Press.

McGaughey, W. (2001). *Rhythm and self-consciousness: New ideal for an electronic civilization.* Minneapolis: Thistlerose Publications.

Taagepera, R. (1978). Size and duration of empires: Systematics of size. *Social Science Research, 7,* 108-127.

--------------------(1978a). Size and duration of empires: Growth-decline curves, 3,000 to 600 B.C. *Social Science Research, 7,* 180-196.

Targowski, A. (1991). Strategies and architecture of the electronic global village. *The Information Society, 7*(3), 187-202.

Targowski, A. (2000). *Enterprise Information Infrastructure.* Boston, MA: Pearson Publishing.

_____ (2003). *Electronic enterprise, strategy and architecture.* Harrisburg, PA: Idea Group Publishing.

_____ (2004). From global to universal civilization. *Dialogue and Universalism, XIV*(3-4), 121-142.

Chapter V
(B) Liberating the Past from the Future

INTRODUCTION

The purpose of this chapter is to define intrinsic values of information-communication processes in human development.

The development of civilization depends upon the accumulation of wisdom, knowledge and cultural and infrastructural gain. Man is prouder of his heritage than of that which he can eventually achieve in the future. The future is often the threat of the imminent unknown, something that can destroy our stability, qualifications and position within society. On the other hand, the "future" is also the hope of the desperate for a better life.

THE ACCUMULATION PRINCIPLE

The development of man's existence is directed by his wisdom, expressed in values by which he is prepared to shape his life. Figure 5-1 illustrates a pyramid of values formed on the basis of accumulation. Each era has created its own store of values in response to the corresponding needs of civilization. If we enter the 21st century with such values as love, truth, hope, autonomy, responsibility, creativity, self-fulfillment and wisdom, it does not mean that we are rejecting the values of the previous era. Has not the value of

tolerance from the age of Enlightenment already been adopted? We can say that this value has been applied perhaps more intensely in our own time than when it was first formulated. Likewise, justice, a value formulated under ancient Judaism, is applied today with even greater firmness. Of course, not all values retained from the "past" are taken uncritically today. For example, the cult of Nationalism, formulated under Romanticism (the 18th and 19th centuries) is diminishing in value in our era of the Electronic Global Village and emerging global civilization. This example may be seen, ultimately, as an exception to the rule, yet only in Western civilization. In general, each succeeding generation can interpret old values better than the last, not only accumulating them, but bestowing on them new qualities.

Similarly, the development of knowledge occurs by accumulation (Figure 5-1), with great scientific discoveries serving as a corrective. We do not discard books containing outdated knowledge from the libraries, nor, even less, do we burn them. In this regard, we build even bigger libraries which, in the Electronic Global Village, we transform with digital knowledge, to fit onto a computer disk no bigger than a dime. We can find room on such a disk for both discoveries and solutions by **astronomers**: Copernicus, Galileo, Brahmagupta, Kepler, Lagrange; **mathemati-**

Figure 5-1. The values pyramid developed by accumulation (The Kawczak-Targowski Model, numbers identify centuries)

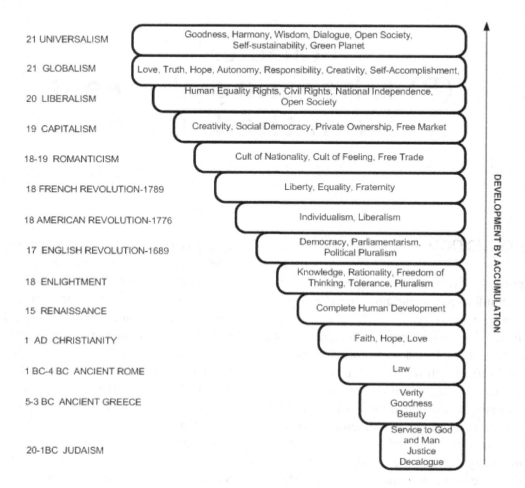

cians: Euclid, Pythagoras, Archimedes, Leibniz, Gauss, Bernoulli; **physicists**: Newton, Ampere, Bohr, Celsius, Doppler, Einstein, Fahrenheit, Faraday, Fermi, Heisenberg, Hertz, Kelvin, Kirchhoff, Maxwell, Oppenheimer, Planck, Roentgen, Rutherford, Volta, Cavendish, Galvani, Gibbs; **chemists**: Mendeleev, Nobel, Curie-Sklodowska, Pauling; **biologists**: Darwin, Fleming, Freud, Galen, Hippocrates, Jung, Pasteur, Pavlov, Salk, Warburg, Watson; **computer scientists**: Babbage, Boole, Hollerith, Pascal, Turing, Von Neumann, Cray, Wozniak; **technicians**: Newcomen, Savery, Coulomb, Jacquard, Henry, Colt, Bell, Edison, Marconi, the Wrights, Ford, Monroe, Sikorsky, Crey and many, many others. Although the achievements of these pioneers of science and technology have, in the meantime, been perfected or superseded, they nevertheless determine the immortal achievements of man from the "past."

One of the measures by which we judge a university is the extent of its bibliographic store. Harvard, for example, recognized as one of the world's best universities, has also the biggest library, comprising 12 million volumes. In other words, the measure of Harvard's greatness is its relationship to the past.

The development of culture is the development through the past which we either embrace with the greatest enthusiasm or transform with the greatest passion. Great **musical works** composed by such geniuses as Bach, Beethoven, Mozart, Brahms, Debussy, Chopin, Liszt, Dvorak, Tchaikovsky, Sibelius, Verdi, Puccini, and Gershwin are immortal. We sit in a concert hall absorbed and fascinated by the greatness of this eternally beautiful music, which allows us to forget not only about the often stressful present, but also the threatening, uncertain future.

This is equally true of **literature**. Works by Shakespeare, Dickens, Conrad, Shaw, Andersen, Balzac, Dumas, Hugo, Moliere, Zola, Goethe, Mann, Neruda, Borges, Tolstoy, Dostoyevsky, Gogol, Sienkiewicz, Pasternak, Singer, Twain, Huxley, J. D. Salinger, Hemingway or Tagore are, to my mind, a constant source of meditation on our destiny. Although these works deal with the past, it is in them that we seek the solutions to the challenges and struggles of good and evil, love and hate, faith and betrayal, and life and death. Sometimes the answer to these questions is richer when it comes from a study of the "past." The best example of this is the contemporary Italian writer, philosopher and journalist Umberto Eco who for example looks for solutions to present-day dilemmas in a medieval monastery, *The Name of the Rose*. In this novel, the narrator, a young monk, employs logic to solve a murder, and although the murderer is unmasked, the quest for knowledge leads to a dead end.

In **painting**, where a work can be created very quickly—in, as it were, an act of creative ecstasy—there occurs a certain negation of the past, since it seems that its scope has been fulfilled and there is no need for further protest and manifestos. The works of past great masters such as Vermeer, Rembrandt, Raphael, Velazquez, Goya, El Greco, and Leonardo da Vinci are (always) immortal. We look at them and admire the genius of a man who could raise himself to such heights of beauty. In the 19th century, painters began to discard the burden of patronage, which had often obligated them to paint family portraits of their sponsors. They left the studio and became awestruck with the beauty of nature in sun-drenched France. The result was the birth of the Impressionist movement with works by artists such as Degas, Manet, Monet, Van Gogh, Gauguin, Renoir and others. A further avalanche of protests, initiated by Picasso ("anti-da Vinci") and Dali, rejected past achievements and led to the avant-garde movement in art, which presented a total breach with the "past." Many avant-garde works of the twentieth century, being both beautiful and captivating for a moment, have quickly receded into the past, if they did not contain some sort of genius-driven art. In any case, the development of avant-garde art in the 20th century, having set itself the unrealistic goal of defining a "future" in utopian form, has became so inert and static that it would seem to herald the death of civilization itself. Since this is not the "future" we want, let us therefore return to the past as well as to the present, which instantly becomes the past. The avant-garde movement is directed at finding new rules of art and new forms of presenting them. This approach is based on the premise of perfecting method, so spectacular in 20th century technique. This is not such a bad thing, since to do otherwise would be to promote stagnation, or a "living death."

The infrastructure of settlements, that is, villages, towns and cities, was not built suddenly as an entity, but developed over centuries and millennia: a new street next to an old street, a new house next to an old one, and so forth. The older the "house," the greater the care we bestow on it, often even attaching to it the status of treasure, be it a national settlement or one of world historical value, recognized by experts from UNESCO. Of course there are exceptions to the rules of accumulation—cities such as Brasilia or Chandigarh, which arose from a single one-time event, a spontaneous act of creation, by a political-architectural union such as Kubitschek-Niemeyer and Nehru-Le Corbusier, respectively.

Such an act represented a brutal wish to cut with the past and build at once a modern city, ideal and immediately embedded in the "future." These experiments were not fully successful, since these towns have not developed according to the will of their residents (Brasilia is a city of bureaucrats) but from the top down, directed by city planners. Lately, the opinion prevails among urbanists that the development of a city should reflect the development of the individual. That is, it should be non-schematic, "polymorphous" rather than "linear," almost a network-island, the way Los Angeles, for example, has developed spontaneously and adapted to its own needs. It is, in other words, a historical development and thus based on honoring the achievements of the "past."

THE WISDOM PRINCIPLE

The search for wisdom is as old as *homo sapiens*, that is, thinking man. After medicine, meteorology, and astronomy (as observational studies of events), the first abstractive science created by man was philosophy which, translated from Greek, means the love of wisdom. The development of **philosophy** has been marvelous from the earliest times of Socrates, Plato and Aristotle, through the times of Descartes, Spinoza, Locke, Hume, Walter, Rousseau, Kant, Hegel, Comte, Mill, Marx, Husserl, Spencer, Kierkegaard, Brentano, Nietzsche, Pierce, Bergson, Russell, Whitehead, Carnap, Wittgenstein, Heidegger, Sartre, and in our own time, Levi-Strauss, Popper, Kuhn, Foucault, Derrida, Habermas, and others. Together with these men, billions of people are searching

for the sources of wisdom, yet the capacity for wisdom remains beyond our grasp. Wisdom means, after all, understanding the essence of existence and its rules, the better to adapt oneself to a civilized life. Wisdom is also the capacity to distinguish fact from fiction, truth from falsehood, good from evil, and beauty from ugliness. In a wise approach to solving problems, man establishes a broad context of time and space. A wise person solves his problems through the prism of a central viewpoint whose values he holds dear. Such wisdom reveals itself gradually and manifests itself in thought and action. Each of us must have his own approach to wisdom, which is why wisdom is so hard to understand, to assimilate and especially, to put into practice.

To achieve wisdom, man must have at his command the achievements of all civilization and his own existence, and therefore, according the principle of harmony, bring together two areas of existence: his own and that of civilization. Accepting what is good and rejecting what is bad, he must then file his own choices in his long-term memory, or in a computer, since one cannot create wisdom, as it were, from nothing or from the mere fact of existence.

Thus it is necessary to harmonize the rules of existence with those of civilization, or, plainly put, Hegelian philosophy with existentialism—that is, to formulate a bio-social system. To this purpose, we will introduce the concept of the harmonized laws of existence and cognition, as illustrated in Figure 5-2.

If the terms of human existence derive from man himself, human activity is directed primarily by the *law of transience*, which no one has ever broken. (There is a proverb supposedly taken from the Persians. A Persian king once told a sculptor to create a monumental inscription that would be valid forever. So he did. The inscription read: "and this too shall pass.") Nothing acts forever: Everything has a beginning and an inevitable end. Human existence begins and ends. The *law of repetition* follows from the law of transience.

Figure 5-2. Model of harmonized laws of existence and cognition

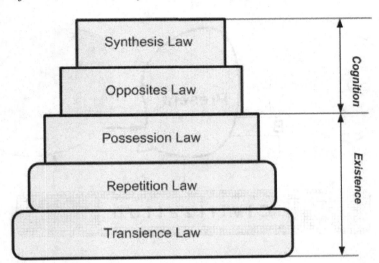

Each person must begin anew, learning and experiencing life independently, regardless of the wealth of humanity's accumulated knowledge and wisdom. Thus, at any given moment, one person is learning "this" while another is learning "that." Because the *law of possession* works atavistically (that is, as a regression to animal-like characteristics), both of the aforementioned people will defend the knowledge which they have acquired and not that which is right. At this point we can "insert" Hegel's *law of opposites*, that is, the attempt of one to defeat the other. If the *Law of Possession* were not valid, and, for instance, the Law of Right (the ability to accept only what is "real" or "valuable") were to gain acceptance, then the *Law of Opposites* would also be invalid because it would be redundant and it would not be necessary to apply it at the next step. The *Law of Synthesis* follows from the *law of opposites*.

From the view-point of "liberating the past from the future" the wisdom hierarchy illustrates the fact that existence is deeply embedded in the past. The *Laws of Transience, of Repetition* and *of Possession*, are precisely laws that derive from the past, since they derive from evolution, that is, from records in the genetic memory. In the context of the future, the agent of acquired culture enters into the game only at the level of the last two laws. This future does not emerge of itself but from the current level of knowledge and information which result from the collective memory of civilization, which is, from present and past conditions. This claim is illustrated by the example of *science fiction*. Images of the future, often the most fantastic ones, are indeed the result of civilization's current store of knowledge as well as the author's interpretation of it.

CONCLUSION: THE "FRUITLESS" PAST

In synthesizing whether it is possible to "liberate the past from the future," we draw the conclusion that, yes, indeed it is. This is because man accumulates his achievements, perfects his wisdom and raises his awareness, thanks to the continual survival of symbols of language and

Figure 5-3. The architecture of time in a mode of "B" liberating the past from the future

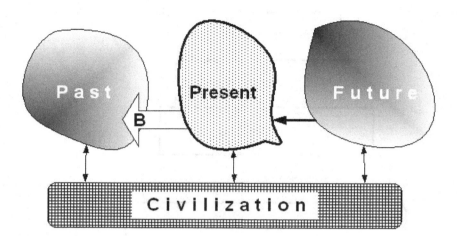

the modernization of past results. Thus we can propose a model, in Figure 5-3, which reflects the confirmation of this thesis. Adapting the words of Heine, "where books are burned, there thoughts are burned," we can generalize that "where the past is not valued, there no hope exists for the future." From here, the next step is an incantation of "*vivat passé.*" Those who are aware of what the "future" can be for about 12 or 20 billion people would prefer even to "halt" the "present" in order to prevent the future from being a "final happening."

The mere flow of time, by the same token, gives nothing. Only when you provide conditions for remembering and understanding does the "past" acquire meaning.

A. Further Research Directions

•   Verify values of the global civilization and explain their impact on the success of the globalization processes.

•   Verify values of potential universal civilization and explain their application feasibility and their impact on the betterment of the human race.

•   Investigate the harmony of existence-oriented and cognition-oriented laws and their impact on wisdom application among humans as the key factor leading to a successful life and human existence.

B. Research Opportunities

•   The research opportunity is in interdisciplinary study; including philosophy, psychology, cognition science, ecology, and anthropology.

C. Additional Ideas

•   The civilized world is driven by ideas, even if common people are not aware of it in their daily activities. Very often, even politicians are not aware of this fact. They are so engaged in tactical and operational activities and in enjoying power that it is enough for them. On the other hand in a very *long-term* cycle, the world is developing and complying with the hierarchy of values, which so far have the tendency of constant improvement of human status within civilization. Therefore, the key solution to the majority of civilization conflicts lies in the realm of conflicting values. The study of civilization's evolution in terms of values should bring us closer to civilizations' and individuals' wisdom. It is an important focus, since philosophy neglects to a degree (in a sense to convey its findings to the public) the issue of wisdom, which, however, is not only the most critical cognitive process, but that which determines mankind's success or failure in all facets of human activities.

D. Rationale

- The current status of world civilization indicates that at least the most advanced civilizations (religion-oriented) are in conflicts either internal or external. These conflicts can be eventually solved or minimized if mankind will find enough motivation and ability to apply wisdom in evaluating their values and driven by them actions; in other words, to make better choices in decision-making on life. It means that understanding and applying of "harmonizing values and wisdom" is the key leading to better future of civilization.

E. Additional Reading

Aronica, R., & Ramdoo, M. (2006). *The world is flat? A critical analysis of Thomas L. Friedman's New York times bestseller*. Tampa, FL: Meghan-Kiffer Press.

Barzilai, G. (2003). *Communities and law: Politics and cultures of legal identities*. Ann Arbor, MI: University of Michigan Press.

Bhargava, V. (2006). *Global issues for global citizens*. Washington, D.C.: The World Bank.

Collier, P., & Hoeffler, A. (2004). *The challenge of reducing the global incidence of civil war*. Oxford, UK: Oxford University Press.

Diamond, J. (2005). *Collapse: How societies choose to fail or succeed*. New York, NY: Penguin Group.

Florini, A. (2000). *The third force*. Tokyo: JCIE.

Flynn, N. (1999). *Miracle to meltdown in Asia*. Oxford, UK: Oxford University Press.

Friedman, T. (2006). *The world is flat*. New York, NY: Farrar, Straus and Giroux.

Hamburg, D. (2002). *No more killing fields: Preventing deadly conflict*. Lanham, MD: Rowman & Littlefield.

Human Security Centre. (2005). *Human security report 2005*. Oxford, UK: Oxford University Press.

Lomborg, B. (Ed.). (2004). *Global crisis, global solutions*. Cambridge, UK: Cambridge University Press.

KOF Index of globalization. Retrieved October 20, 2007, from http://globalization.kof.ethz.ch/static/pdf/method_2007.pdf.

MacGillivray. A. (2006). *A brief history of globalization: The untold story of our incredible shrinking planet*. New York, NY: Carroll & Graf.

Raskin, P., & Banuri, T., *et al.* (2002). *The great transition: the promise and the lure of the times ahead*. Boston, MA: Tellus Institute.

Richard, J-F. (2002). *High noon: Twenty global problems, twenty years to solve them*. New York, NY: Basic Books.

Saul, J. (2005). *The collapse of globalism and the reinvention of the world.* Woodstock and New York, NY: The OVERLOOK PRESS.

Sachs, J. (2005). *The end of poverty: Economic possibilities for our time.* New York, NY: Penguin Books.

Sedere, U. (2000). *Globalization and low income economies—reforming education: the crisis of vision.* Parkland, FL: Universal Publishers.

Steger, M. (2003). *Globalization: A very short introduction.* New York, NY: Oxford University Press.

Stiglitz, J. (2002). *Globalization and its discontents.* New York, NY: W.W. Norton & Company.

_____(2006). *Making globalization work.* New York, NY: W.W. Norton & Company.

Wolf. M. (2004). *Why globalization works.* New Haven, CT: Yale University Press.

World Bank. (2007). *Global economic prospects, managing the next wave of globalization.* Washington, D.C.: The World Bank.

World Bank. (2007). *Development and the next generation.* Washington, D.C.: The World Bank.

REFERENCES

Burenhult, G. (2003). *People of the past.* San Francisco, CA: Fog City Press.

Celinski, M., & Kawczak, A. (2000). Values in the 21st century, as a compass of man. In: A. Targowski and A. Ajnenkiel (Eds.), *Losy Polski i Świata (The faith of Poland and the world)* (pp. 377-403). Warsaw: Bellona.

Foucault, M. (2000). *Power.* New York, NY: New Press.

Hegel, G. (1974). *The essential writings.* New York, NY: Harper & Row.

Heidegger, M. (1966). *Discourse on thinking.* New York, NY: Harper & Row.

Kierkegaard, S. (2000). *The essential Kierkegaard.* Princeton, NJ: Princeton University Press.

Popper, K. (1966). *The open society and its enemies.* Princeton, NJ: Princeton University Press.

Sartre, J. (1947). *The age of reason.* New York, NY: Modern Library.

Tatarkiewicz, W. (2004). *Historia filozofii (History of philosophy).* Warsaw: PWN.

Chapter VI
Will Wisdom Save the Human Project?

INTRODUCTION

The purpose of this chapter is to investigate whether we humans are wise enough to save our civilization from threats of internal conflicts and natural (even cosmic) disasters. Humans have gained wisdom through life experience and philosophical investigations for the last 2,600 years. In this investigation, we would like to find out whether philosophy can be helpful in finding the wisest strategic solution, which would sustain civilization forever. If the current state of philosophy cannot do it, it will be necessary to offer a new philosophy which could undertake this task, particularly in these times when other social sciences are aware of our civilization crisis and have influenced the formation of many research foundations and centers which aim at the more harmonious development of civilization.

FROM MYTHS TO WISDOM OF CIVILIZATION

Western Philosophy as a Source of Survival Wisdom

The more humans populate the Earth, and the more we are civilized, the more we threaten civiliza-tion, since more complex artificial systems are developed that affect the natural ecosystems. The 21st century will be particularly critical; the global population will reach 8 billion people, which is estimated as the threshold of the ecosystem, with no more carrying capacity (Millennium Ecosystem Assessment, 2005).

Civilization is about 6,000 years old and during this long time, life on Earth has appeared safe, except to some religions which predicted the end of the world. For many religious people, doomsday scenarios were metaphors rather than possible events. From the very beginning, humans were very interested in how the world and people were formed (*cosmogony*) and always saw in it God's hand.

For the last 2,600 years, one can observe the systematic development of philosophy, the discipline associated with "love of wisdom." The synthesis of the development of human wisdom is illustrated Figure 6-1, which indicates that humans first learned life skills then spent 1,200 years looking for eternal happiness (6th century B.C.-6th century A.D.). During the Middle Ages, they found that there is no contradiction between faith and reason, and the latter should drive the search for knowledge and wisdom on Earth.

Based on such a foundation, humans began 500 years ago searching for knowledge about

Figure 6-1. The development of wisdom and exemplification based upon western philosophy (numbers in boxes identify centuries)

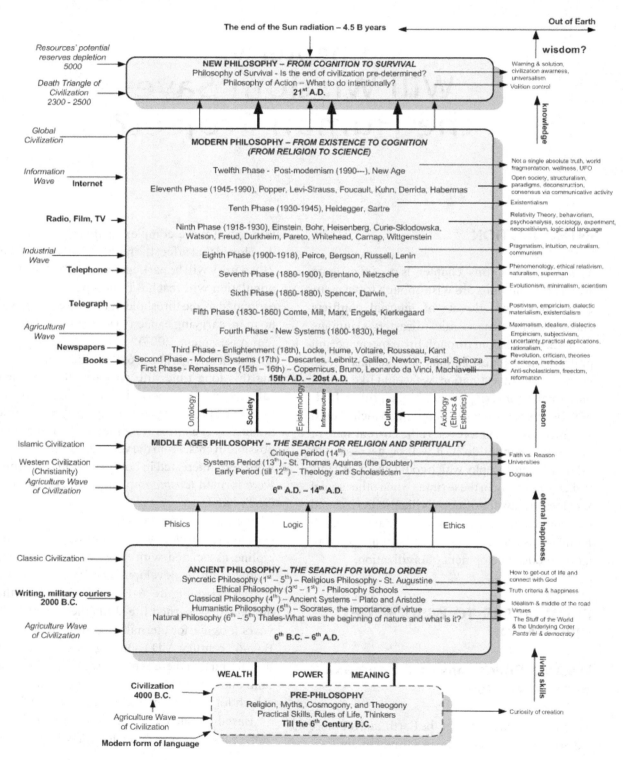

the world and life, offering rules and laws which promote wise choices and actions. In this period, philosophers defined many approaches toward knowledge and wisdom, some emphasizing cognition (Descartes, Hume, Kant, Darwin, Pierce, Einstein, Whitehead, and Carnap), some looking for better existence (Kierkegaard, Heidegger, and Sartre).

Thousands of intellectuals participated in this great cerebral movement, discovering laws of nature and civilization, mostly having in mind how to act wisely. On the other hand, the more knowledge humans discover, the more we are lost in its details, sometimes losing from the horizon the art of wisdom, which is a different unit of cognition than "knowledge."

For example, philosophy in the 20th and 21st centuries has entered a period of looking more for objective methods and information of world perception than for wise and committed solutions that are expected by the societies involved in local and global conflicts and crisis. The philosophy of action tries only bashfully to attack the question, how to live day by day wisely. Furthermore, the philosophy of social universalism offers ideas of how to be wise and good, which should limit social and state confrontations. This latter philosophy observes the dramatic challenges of the contemporary world, which in the 20th century was able to kill 200 million people and in the 21st century threatens to kill more in civilization wars with all kinds of bombs. Skolimowski (1981) even claims that current philosophy is detached from life, socially unconcerned, mute about individual responsibility, politically indifferent, and mostly oriented toward language rather than toward quality of life.

Maxwell (2005) states that nowadays knowledge instead of wisdom is at the center of academic inquiry, and this cannot solve the problems of wars, global warming, poverty and so forth. He thinks that we need a revolution in science and humanities to move from knowledge to wisdom, when the first aim of education should be to learn how to acquire wisdom. Since scientific and technological progress have massively increased our power to act in the absence of wisdom, we need wiser institutions, wiser customs, wiser social relations, and a wiser world.

Brown (2005) wants to transform our attitude from eco-phenomenology to eco-logos, based on wisdom, which should include everyday experiences in developing dwellings. Servomaa (2005) claims that the essence of beauty of nature should lead toward wisdom. Because in order to achieve wisdom, first we need to love beauty, which can contradict the rush for greedy gains and egoistic pleasures that, in reality, destroys wisdom. Only by cultivating wisdom can we recognize the difference between the false myths and the true, which is necessary to see our society functioning well (Stawinski, 2005).

The same argument motivates Hubert (2005), who argues for replacing mythos by logos to pursue the quest for wisdom. According to him "love for wisdom" as a mission of philosophy is not understood, much less practiced, by a meaningful portion of the world's population. He says also that from "love for wisdom" we need to move to building a wise civilization, which nowadays, is full of myths. To do so we need compassion as the focal point of any future philosophy in order to minimize the current apathy in our ailing planet (Krieglstein, 2005). Krieglstein claims that knowledge cannot be built on domination and exploitation, but on cooperation and partnership, hence logos should be in synchronicity with some life's myths.

Stawarska (2005) concurs with this view, adding that the self has strong impact upon supposedly "dispassionate" scientists. Unfortunately, one of those myths is perhaps the "new" conservative wisdom, which according to Havers (2005) teaches "calculated action and hedonism." It rejects Liberalism (successfully experienced in the U.S.), returning to the 19th century concepts of "Nietzsche's order and power" and de facto rejecting modernity. Eventually, "love for wisdom" should perhaps be seen as the quest for "wonder" by "asking and asking" (Stark, 2005), which means not necessarily "curiosity" by rather "transformation of existential conditions." Seeberg (2005) supports this approach, since he thinks that philosophy has the mission of mediating between reason and wisdom by making explicit the limits of scientific explanations. For example, he differentiates knowledge of the nature from knowledge of one's individual life. This quest concurs with Kant's idea of right relations between myth and logos and not replacing the former by the latter and hence leaving a narrow door for teaching wisdom.

Sugiharto (2005), coming from the Islamic civilization, criticizes Western civilization's Logo-centrism (Logical Positivism), which eventually leads to self-destruction, since it is without substance and promotes wisdom as seeing through brute facts and impersonal physical objects in the absence of soul, which is seen as something alien, an anomaly. He thinks that philosophy can accomplish its mission if it will bring back the breadth, the depth and the ambiguity of concrete human soul into its discourse. He understands wisdom as an ability to come to terms with uncertainty and insecurity, an ability to see through the "absence" (soul).

Harman (2005) argues that when philosophy began shifting the focus from reality to abstracts, the university lost its influence on life. Demenchonok (2005) thinks that wisdom can come from transforming from multiculturalism to dialogue of cultures, breaking isolation and developing some universal-transcultural solutions that are accepted by engaged parties. Kuczynski (2005) asks a very important question: "Can we cultivate logos-oriented wisdom and neglect irrational mythos?" My answer is that in the past this would not have been a good program; but nowadays we do not have such luxury of choice anymore and we should rather ask "Can our wisdom save the Human Project from overdeveloped civilization?"

Otherwise our situation will be driven by the creed "feel better and live shorter."

As a result of this kind of poor condition of mankind's wisdom, there is a trend of developing political and social philosophies which try to address issues of a good state and society, particularly with the application of reinvented pragmatism.

In conclusion, one can state that nowadays philosophy responsible for "wisdom" is more involved in tactical issues than strategic ones. Even the philosophy of post-modernism questions the whole of accumulated knowledge and wisdom. In this philosophy, objectivism is replaced by subjectivism, which leads toward comfortable relativism, which accepts every solution a given person or organization finds satisfactory. On the other hand, post-modernistic deconstruction (promoted by Jacques Derrida, 1982) may perhaps have applications if we accept that everything *panta rei* and some old and no longer appropriate solutions must be re-engineered and adapted to new challenges.

If contemporary western philosophy escapes from taking on the world systems of wisdom, that cannot be said about other social sciences, which clearly perceive the strategic challenges of civilization.

Non-Western Philosophies as a Source of Survival Wisdom

Among current non-western philosophies one may include those of India, China, Japan, and Islam. Their characteristics are provided in Table 6-1.

In general, non-western philosophies provide more wisdom on civilization development than the western one. Their main message is to develop civilization slower, in a more harmonious relationship with nature and community. If civilization enters a stage of open crisis, perhaps the Chinese Model of the authoritarian government and flexible economy can be adapted by the world civilization to better ensure its recovery and survival.

Table 6-1. Characteristics of non-western philosophies

PHILOSOPHY	TIME CONCEPT	CIVILIZATION DEVELOPMENT CONCEPT	MAIN INTEREST	LEADING PARADIGM	HELP OF WISDOM IN RESCUING CIVILIZATION
INDIAN	Cyclical Reincarnation *Samsara*	Local Involvement, *Nirvana* via Enlightenment	Truth , Reality, *Nirvana*	No violence	Scaling down large-scale undertakings
CHINESE	Circular	Steady and controlled	Morality, Social order, Family	Middle of the road	Political authority and economic flexibility
JAPANESE	Circular	Advances humanity	Zen Nature *Shinto*	Harmony	Crush and change
ISLAMIC	Linear	Development should strengthen community ties and faith	Faith	Submission	Strong critique of Western civilization

Social Awareness as a Source of Wisdom of Civilization

Social sciences, such as sociology, political science ecology and others perceive that civilization in the 21st century is at a crossroads. In religion there is a common belief that civilization is predetermined ("destiny") and in science that it is unpredictable and uncontrollable.

Table 6-2 summarizes the awareness of different scientific communities and their plans of coping with declining civilization.

The presented summary of programs is not complete, but illustrates quite well the human effort in understanding problems of civilization. In the intellectual sense, these programs characterize profound knowledge and care about the well-being of civilization. In the practical sense, these programs are segmented, dispersed, and implemented according to availability of financial support, mostly provided by private donors.

The implementation of these programs is long-term, not synchronized with a short-term political cycle lasting between 4 and 8 years. Hence, these programs are not high priorities of politicians, whose survival is assured by short-term undertakings. For them, "civilization" is an abstract term that has nothing to do with daily life and its challenges, particularly in developed countries where the life is still good.

The politics of rescuing civilization will become more active when civilization enters a very serious crisis, but then it will perhaps be too late to avoid catastrophe.

TOWARDS ECO-PHILOSOPHY

Civilization in its adaptation to nature and technology achieves steadily more complex solutions and passes from one conflict and crisis to another. These crises may be classified in the following manner[1]:

- Current crisis – as a result of world political dynamism

Table 6-2. Characteristics of awareness of needs for humankind survival action

SCENERIO/ MODEL	YEARS	CHARACTERISTICS	TAKEN ACTION	IMPACT	FURTHER ACTIVITIES
Doomsday Predictions by the Druids, the Teutons, the Hindus, the Hebrews the Cosmologists	For millennia Cosmic Catastrophism	Sins and penalty The Universe dynamics	In prayers None, due to a lack of tools	Awareness Some research is launched (NASA)	No solutions Wait and see
Accelerating Crises Oswald Spengler's "The Decline of the West"	1918-22	All cultures grow and decline, prevention of wars	His view influenced the Nazis	Wide spread Warning	Debated in social sciences' research
Club of Rome Models Aurelio Peccei and Dennis Meadows et al, Erwin Laszlo	1969-1972	"The Chasm Ahead" "Limits to Growth" "Mankind at the Turning Point" "Goals for Mankind" Economic well-being, social justice, ecological stability	Resources saving and recycling policies	Good but limited in time and scope	Credits in further research and publications, and in social new behavior
World Order Models Saul Mendlovitz Jagdish Bhagwati Ali Mazuri and others	1974-1977	World Law Fund "Economics and World Order" "Africa and World Affairs" Alienation and identity crisis	Creation of research centers publishing recommendations for future actions	Intellectualization of the issues	Credits in further research & publications influencing the Third World's policies and awareness
Sustainable Development World Bank	1980s+ 2000	Many foundations and NGO centers Millennium Development Goals by 2015	Awareness and projects Policies	Intellectualizations and practice Financing	Networking among leaders Project implementations
United Nations	2000 2001	Millennium Development Goals Global Agenda for Dialog among Civilizations	Millennium Declaration Resolution adapted by General Assembly	Focus on critical issues of education, poverty and health in the Third World Supports interactions among people from different civilizations	On-going program On-going program
Non-governmental foundations on the future of the World and Humanity	1960+	Many reports on the future of humanity	Gradual implementation of segmented solutions	Mostly Intellectual	On-going programs
Dialog and Universalism J. Kuczyński et al Universal-Complementary Civilization, A. Targowski	1980s 2004	Conflict minimalization by wise and good people Common Civilization for the common Planet	In the academic circles	Support of Philosophy of Action and Philosophy of Survival	In planning

- Short-term crisis – the "death Triangle of Civilization" composed of the Population, Ecological and Strategic Resources Depletion Bombs in years 2050-2500
- Mid-term crisis – depletion of resources' potential reserves in years 5,000+
- Long-term crisis – the end of Sun radiation within about 4.5 billion years

Minimizing these crises is a task for politicians, citizens, and scientists. As we have already noticed, it is a huge task, sometimes looking unfeasible. On the other hand, the world needs a new injection of wisdom at the level of schools, universities, work, and social and family life. This kind of wisdom should be developed by an eco-philosophy with the mission to support the survival (sustainability) of civilization, oriented towards defining solutions for these predicaments. For example, in France, the youth have an examination in philosophy during their baccalaureate examinations. The French triggered the Enlightenment, which gave reason priority over faith, and nowadays they want to keep the Human Project alive. Why not follow them?

A leading philosopher of our times, Jurgen Habermas, thinks that the Modernization Project since the Enlightenment should be kept alive with the application of communicative action and critical theory of society (Habermas, 1984). In other words, this great philosopher has a tactical solution for our civilization problems. His philosophy is very helpful in wisely solving current conflicts and to some degree should help to soften short-term crises. He claims that "modernity" is a *project* rather than a historical period, and that this project is not yet completed. This project is a cultural movement (or perhaps rather "civilization" one) undertaken in response to particular problems thrown up by the process of modernization ("industrialization") and since it is not finished it cannot be called a post-modern movement. Why is the project "unfinished?" Because, according to Habermas, the problems it addresses have not yet been solved. He also argues that alternatives to modernity and modernization are worse. One of such bad alternative is anti-modernity.

In the strategic sense, one may raise the question whether the Modernization Project can save the Human Project.

From that kind of perspective, our life takes place on a floating cake of ice, which sooner rather than later will melt, and before we reach the shore. Does it make sense to study the world, or it is wiser to concentrate on an existence driven by a strategy of *carpe diem*?

In such a case, how should we look at social life, when the maximization of existence (measured as fun and immediate satisfaction) can threaten the social order? If existence is most important, and the social order should be maintained at an acceptable level, the growing role of religion should be emphasized, since it can mitigate the human tendency towards wrong actions.

What is a derivative of such human wisdom at the level of a nation and even family? Are patriotism and family loyalty wise? Should scientific projects aimed at colonizing the universe be moved out of the realm of science fiction?

If we can believe that all potential reserves of strategic resources will last only another 3,000 years if the current pace of the civilization development is maintained, then the strategic resource vision for the Human Project is as pessimistic as one based on the dying Sun. How should humans behave, knowing their declining chances of civilization survival?

Should we pretend that there is no such issue or should we begin working on a new wisdom? What should be our social wisdom, arguing for improving democracy or improving chances of survival, which can require more authoritarian governance? The latter can support more scientific research leading to synthetic energy and materials and less reproductive humans.

Finally, how can we prevent the short-term crisis caused by the Population and Ecological Bombs within 50 years? The Population Bomb

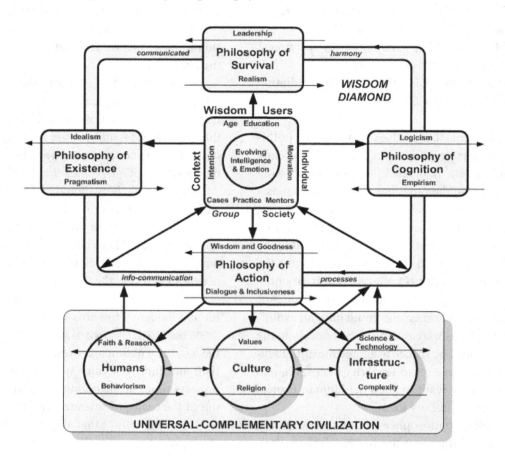

Figure 6-2. The development and application of the Wisdom Diamond in universal-complementary civilization within the framework of eco-philosphy

is very probable, since nothing almost is done to stop it and furthermore, the growth of population is recommended by the churches and poverty is tolerated, which is one of the main sources of population growth.

Philosophy of survival should support philosophy of action—how to act today and think about tomorrow. Does our actual life make sense if it does not have the physical chance to continue civilization as we know it today? However, if life makes sense, what sense does it make? Do we humans, who discovered knowledge, have a chance to survive its premises and apply them for our benefit?

Hence, the challenge for civilization is to manage the Modernization Project in such a manner as to sustain the Human Project forever. This challenge can be softened by the development and application of the Wisdom Diamond of civilization in the framework of meta-philosophy (eco-philosophy) as it is depicted in Figure 6-2. The idea of this philosophy is based on the following premises:

1. Eco-philosophy is life- & nature-oriented, seeking wisdom in respect to "How to live" and "What is it all about," which are different

Figure 6-3. The development and application of the Wisdom Diamond in enterprise civilization within the framework of new management

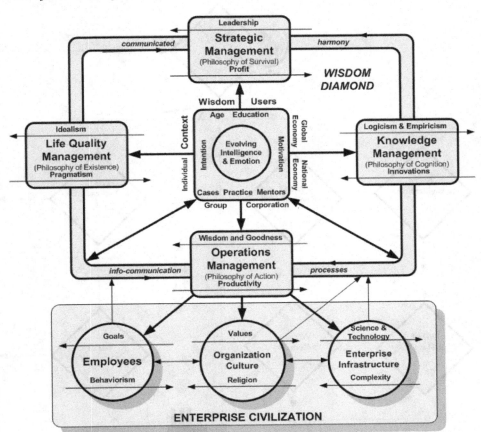

issues from the question "How to do things" (Skolimowski, 1981).

2. Eco-philosophy is comprehensive and global (Skolimowski, 1981) and communicating harmony. The development of philosophy has been based on formulation of many if not too many important or interesting ideas, but there have not been among them relationships, since each philosopher promotes usually only his or her own philosophy. Many philosophical ideas and solutions are not contradictory and therefore their wisdom should be harmonized and communicated better, aiming at betterment of humans in

accord with the idea of the Wisdom Diamond.

3. Eco-philosophy is concerned with the wisdom of civilization survival. In the situation of many civilization threats, one must develop a philosophy of survival, which should direct other philosophies of existence, cognition, or action toward the harmonized communicated wisdom of Universal-Complementary civilization[2].

The premises of a new philosophy should force philosophers to the great task of validation of actual human wisdom and elaborate new wisdom for humans and our civilization. Whether they

Figure 6-4. The hierarchy of Wisdom Diamond (WD) of major components of the world civilization

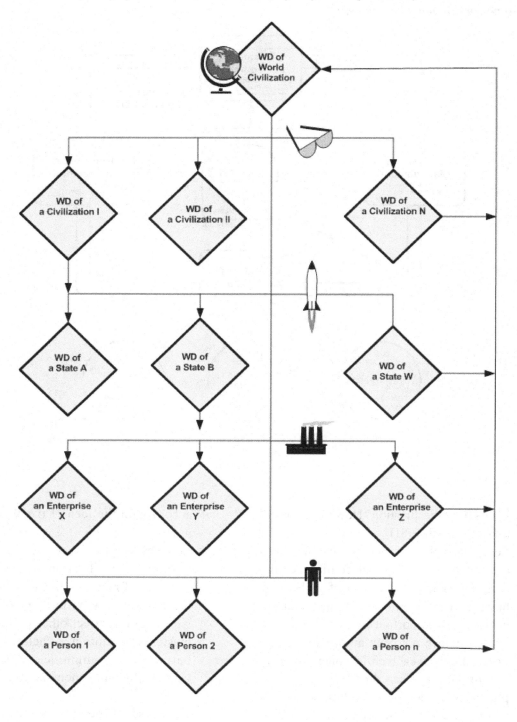

will do it remains to be seen. Time will show whether they will continue the wisdom business as usual with a stoic piece of mind, asserting that civilization has already passed through many crises and will pass through others. Of course, the development of a meta-philosophy will not stop civilization catastrophes but it is a condition *sine qua non* to introduce civilization wisdom into schools and colleges' curricula and later into political programs in a more effective manner than is done today.

THE WISDOM DIAMOND

The application of the Wisdom Diamond (WD) should take place at all levels of the social ladder. Hence, its application at the level of an enterprise is illustrated in Figure 6-3. As illustrated in the model, business practice applies two elements of the WD: strategic management and operation management. At the end of the 20th century, knowledge management is mounting along with applications of data warehouses and data mining to define rules and laws of a given business.

On the other hand, management of quality of life is lacking in the current practice of enterprise management. To the quality of life controlled at the enterprise level one may add the quality of offered products and services and their impact on the customers' quality of life. It can be perceived in the framework of a given enterprise, region, nation or the globe. To these sets of issues, one may add among many other things the following: a) the application of hostile technologies towards humans and nature, and b) the applications of technologies which increase work productivity enormously and reduce employment. To avoid these kinds of consequences, it is necessary to define a new theory of management with a close relationship with a new meta-philosophy.

The application of the WD should take place at all levels of civilization hierarchy, as shown in Figure 6-4. It is important to notice that all levels of the WD should be harmonized among themselves in order to minimize civilization conflicts and crises. The enemies of this idea may say that the "wisdom" it leads toward is totalitarian. The author does not think this way, asserting that true wisdom will avoid the trap of totalitarianism.

CONCLUSION

The rescuing of civilization from future catastrophe is the great task for everyone, organizations, politicians, and even philosophers, who should work on a new meta-philosophy in agreement with the Wisdom Diamond. If this task is unfeasible, then what kind of wisdom should we apply in the temporary current civilization? This question is directed to philosophers who are in charge of wisdom in our societies. Perhaps, our knowledge, wisdom and intelligence are not yet able to solve the civilization dilemmas. While we are becoming more knowledgeable, we are not necessarily getting wiser. Therefore, is religion the only remaining hope for humans? Do we have another hope?

A. Further Research Directions

- Investigate why western philosophy is not strongly involved in research on wisdom and its impact on the human action in all facets of civilization.
- Investigate philosophies other than western and explore whether wisdom has some impact on human activities in other civilizations.
- Investigate how the Wisdom Diamond (philosophical) can be applied in other scientific and practical disciplines, and what can be expected from its applications.

B. Research Opportunities

•   The research opportunity is in reaching for wisdom as the highest cognitive process, which is so far neglected and limited to knowledge.

C. Additional Ideas

•   The purpose of the Human Project is perhaps a test of humanity and whether we can be wise enough to continue our civilization development or whether we are not wise enough to survive, mostly as victims of our inability to be wise and good. This project could also estimate our chances for survival or extinction.

D. Rationale

•   The only hope for mankind's survival is in human wisdom, which is the ability to generate and chose the right concepts/solutions. This ability varies among civilizations. In some it is a subject of great concern; in others it is neglected and left to divine interventions. Surprisingly, western philosophy has only in the last 20 years undertaken some empirical study of wisdom, and therefore cannot yet be a bastion of knowledge about the wisdom which can be learned and popularized in a society. The presented wisdom diamond can be applicable in many theoretical and practical disciplines, and therefore it can be considered one of the most modern tools of wisdom, worth investigation and application in all facets of knowledge and practice of civilization. At least it is important to find out whether the Human Project can be successful or will fail because we are not wise enough. Then, what kind of the future we should expect and how should we plan for it?

E. Additional Reading

Alexander, B. (1993). *How great generals win.* New York, NY: W.W. Norton & Co.

Ayres, A. (1987). *The wit and wisdom of mark twain.* New York, NY: Harper & Row, Publishers.

Bellah, R., Madsen, R., Sullivan, W., Swidler, A., & Tipton, S. (1991). *The good society.* New York, NY: Alfred. A. Knopf.

Benet's Reader's Encyclopedia. (1987). New York, NY: Harper & Row, Publishers.

von Clausewitz, K. (1968). *On war.* Harmondsworth, UK: Penguin Books.

Descartes, R. (1999). *Discourse on method and related writings.* Translated by D. Clark. New York, NY: Penguin Books.

Erikson, H., & Erikson, J. (1997). *The life cycle completed.* New York, NY: W.W. Norton & Company.

Friedman, T. (2005). *The world is flat.* New York, NY: Farrar, Straus and Giroux.

Goldfarb, J. (1991). *The cynical society.* Chicago, IL: The Chicago University Press.

Goleman, D. (1995). *Emotional intelligence.* New York, NY: Putman Books.

Gribbin, J. (2004). *The scientists.* New York, NY: Random House.

Guderian, H. (1952). *Panzer leader.* New York, NY: E. P. Dutton.

Huey, J. (1998, December 7). Sam Walton, discounting dynamo. *Time,* pp. 196-197.

Huntington, S. (1996). *The clash of civilizations and the remaking of world order.* New York, NY: Simon & Schuster.

Johnson, P. (1988). *Intellectuals.* New York, NY: Harper & Row.

Keamey, A. (2005). *Global index. Foreign Affairs Policy*. Retrieved March 2, 2007, from www. atkearney.com.

Klee, R. (1997). *Introduction to the philosophy of science*. New York, NY: Oxford University Press.

Kidner, D. (1985). *The wisdom of proverbs, job & Ecclesiastes*. Downers Grove, IL: InterVarsity Press.

Kurian, T. (1984). *The new book of world rankings*. New York, NY: Facts on File Publications.

Lynn, R., & Vanhanen, T. (2002). *IQ and the wealth of nations*. Westport, CT: Praeger Publishers.

Liddell, H., & Sir Basil, H. (1928). *Great captains unveiled*. Boston, MA: Little Brown.

Ninkowitch, F. (1999). *The Wilsonian century*. Chicago, IL: The University of Chicago Press.

Noonan, P. (1998, April 13). Ronald Reagan. *Time*, pp. 176-179.

Maxwell, N. (2005). A revolution for science and the humanities: From knowledge to wisdom. *Dialogue and Universalism, XV*(1-2), 29-58.

Neisser, U. (1996). *Intelligence: Knowns and unknowns*. Washington, D.C.: American Psychological Association.

Oxford Dictionary of Quotations. (1980). Oxford: Oxford University Press.

Lock, S., Last, J., & Dunea, G. (Eds.). (2001). *Oxford illustrated companion to medicine*. Oxford: Oxford University Press.

Payne, T. (1997). *Encyclopedia of great writers*. New York, NY: Barnes and Noble.

Sartre, J-P. (1968). *Search for a method*. Translated by H. Barnes. New York, NY: Vintage Books.

Seldes, G. (1985). *The great thoughts*. New York, NY: Ballantine Books.

Schlesinger, A., Jr. (1998, April 13). Franklin Delano Roosevelt. *Time*, pp. 198-105.

Sternberg, R. (1990). *Wisdom, its nature, origins, and development*. New York, NY: Cambridge University Press.

(2003). *Wisdom, intelligence, and creativity synthesized*. New York, NY: Cambridge University Press.

Tzu, S. (1983). *The art of war*. New York, NY: Delacorte.\

REFERENCES

Bahm, J. (1979). *The philosopher's world model*. Westport, CT: Greenwood Press.

Bhagwati, J. (1972). *Economics and world order from the 1970s to the 1990s*. New York, NY: The Free Press.

Brown, C. (2005). Overcoming boundaries of wisdom: From eco-phenomenology to eco-logos. *Dialogue and Universalism, XV*(1-2), 9-18.

Lodge, H. (1975). *The new American ideology*. New York, NY: Alfred A. Knopf.

Christian, D. (2004). *Maps of time, an introduction to big history*. Berkeley, CA: University of California Press.

Delacampagne, C. (1999). *A history of philosophy in the twentieth century*. Baltimore and London: The John Hopkins University Press.

Demenchonok, E. (2005). Intercultural and African-Caribbean philosophy. *Dialogue and Universalism, XV*(1-2), 181-202.

Dewey, J. (1931). *Philosophy and civilization*. New York, NY: Minton.

Millennium Ecosystem Assessment. (2005). *Ecosystem and human well-being*. Washington, D.C.: Island Press.

Habermas, J.(1984). *The theory of communicative action* (vol. 1). London: Heinemann

_(1985). Modernity-an incomplete project. In: H. Foster (Ed.), *Postmodern culture*. London: Pluto

Harman, G. (2005). Some pre-conditions of universal philosophical dialogue. *Dialogue and Universalism, XV*(1-2), 165-180.

Havers, G. (2005). Political philosophy and the love of wisdom. *Dialogue and Universalism, XV*(1-2), 121-132.

Harre, R. (2000). *One thousand years of philosophy*. Oxford, UK: Blackwell Publishers.

Hicks, S. (2005). Wisdom: Systemic research and university education. *Dialogue and Universalism, XV*(1-2), 7-8.

Hubert, J. (2005). Replacing mythos by logos. *Dialogue and Universalism, XV*(1-2), 93-104.

Krieglstein, W. (2005). Compassion: The focal point of any future philosophy. *Dialogue and Universalism, XV*(1-2), 105-120.

Kuczynski. J.(1986). Universalism as the meaning of recent history. *Dialectics and Humanism, 13*(1), 101-118.

_(2005). Editorial. *Dialogue and Universalism, XV*(1-2), 5-6.

Kuhn, S. (1970). *The structure of scientific revolutions*. Chicago, IL: The University of Chicago Press.

(1977). *The essential tension*. Chicago, IL: The University of Chicago Press.

Laszlo, E. (1972). *The introduction to systems philosophy*. New York, NY: Gordon and Breach.

(1973). *The systems view of the world order*. New York, NY: George Braziller.

(1973).*The world system*. New York, NY: George Braziller.

(1974). *A Strategy for the future: A systems approach to world order*. New York, NY: George Braziller.

(1977). *Goals for mankind: A report to the club of Rome on the new horizons of the global community*. New York, NY: E.P. Dutton.

Matias, M. (2003). Why universalism. *Dialogue and Universalism, XIII*(7-8), 15-16.

Mazuri, A. (1976). *A federation of world cultures: An African perspective*. New York, NY: The Free Press.

Maxwell, N. (2005). A revolution of science and the humanities: From knowledge to wisdom. *Dialogue and Universalism, XV*(1-2), 29-58.

Meadows, D., Meadows, D., Randers, J., Behrens, W., III. (1972). *The limits to growth*. Washington, D.C.: Potomac Associates.

Mendlovitz, S. (1974). *On the creation of a just world order*. New York, NY: The Free Press.

Mesarovic, M. (1975). *Mankind at the turning point. The second report to the club of Rome*. New York, NY: E.P. Dutton.

Moya, C. (1990). *The philosophy of action. An introduction*. Cambridge. UK: Polity Press.

Pecci, A. (1969). *The chasm ahead*. New York, NY: Macmillan.

Sedwick, P. (2001). *Descrates to Derrida, an introduction to European philosophy*. Oxford, UK: Blackwell Publishers Ltd.

Seeberg, U. (2005). Philosophy: The narrow door to the teaching of wisdom. *Dialogue and Universalism, XV*(1-2), 141-156.

Servomaa, S. (2005). Nature of beauty—beauty of nature. *Dialogue and Universalism, XV*(1-2), 19-28.

Schafer, P. (2005). After Darwin: Myth, reason, and imagination. *Dialogue and Universalism, XV*(1-2), 79-92.

Skolimowski, H. (1981). *Eco-philosophy. Designing new tactics for living.* Salem, NH: Marion Boyers.

(1984). *The theater of mind.* Wheaton, IL: The Theosophical Publishing House.

Solomon, C., & Higgins, K. (1996). *A short history of philosophy.* New York, NY and Oxford, UK: Oxford University Press.

Stark, H. (2005). Philosophy as wonder. *Dialogue and Universalism, XV*(1-2), 133-140.

Stawarska, B. (2005). Philosopher and dispassionate scientist. *Dialogue and Universalism, XV*(1-2), 59-70.

Stawinski, A. (2005). Truth in myth and science. *Dialogue and Universalism, XV*(1-2), 71-78.

Sugiharto, I. (2005). Logos without substance: Wisdom as seeing through the absence. *Dialogue and Universalism, XV*(1-2), 157-164.

Szczepanski, J., & Kuczynski, J. (1991). Dialogue and Humanism—dialogue and universalism. *Dialogue and Humanism, 1*(1), I-VIII.

Targowski, A. (2003). A grand model of civilization. *Dialogue and Universalism, XIII*(9-10), 71-96.

(2004a). A dynamic model of an autonomous civilization. *Dialogue and Universalism, XIV*(1-2), 77-90.

(2004b). From global to universal civilization. *Dialogue and Universalism, XIV*(3-4), 121-142.

(2004c). The civilization index. *Dialogue and Universalism, XIV*(10-12), 271-286.

(2005a). Universal-complementary civilization as a solution to present-day catastrophic international conflicts. *Dialogue and Universalism, XIV*(17-8), 73-100.

(2005b). The future of civilization. *Dialogue and Universalism, XV*(11-12), 87-110.

Tatarkiewicz, W. (2004). *Historia filozofii (History of philosophy).* Warszawa: PWN

Tinbergen, J. (1976). *Reshaping the international order.* New York, NY: E.P. Dutton.

ENDNOTES

[1] More on these topics is provided in Chapter XVII.

[2] About this civilization we write in Chapter VII.

Chapter VII
From Global to Universal–Complementary Civilization

INTRODUCTION

The purpose of this chapter is to define processes triggering the emergence of global civilization at the beginning of the 21st century. In addition, a proof is provided that the fourth wave of globalization leads towards the emergence of global civilization as one of facets of world civilization, including a proposal of the direction in which one must lead the further development of world civilization.

The further purpose of this section is to define the sources of crisis affecting civilization and to define a solution by developing the concept of universal-complementary civilization. The study is based on the critical theory of civilization, which not only analyzes "how it is" but also provides some solutions "how it should be." A graphic modeling of civilizations will be applied to move from scenario-driven considerations to system-driven synthesis of components and their relationships. First to be analyzed will be symptoms of the civilization crisis in general. Later, the question is posed: Can Western and global civilizations solve this crisis? Eventually a new solution is offered under the term "universal-complementary civilization," as a foundation for all kinds of particular and common (global) civilizations. The life cycle of this new civiliza-tion is defined and the strategy how to begin its implementation will be suggested.

THE FOUR WAVES OF GLOBALIZATION

The first wave of globalization took place in the 16th and 17th centuries, when the Atlantic Europeans (from Spain, Portugal, England, France, and the Netherlands) migrated to new colonies in America and Asia at the rate of tens of thousands per year. For example, out of a maximum home population of 1.9 million, half a million Dutch emigrants moved to Asia (Indonesia mainly) between 1600 and 1700 (Parry, 1966). The "Little Ice Age" in Europe and the growth of population, as well as progress in the construction of long-distance sailing ships and firepower, triggered this wave. Raudens (1999) argues that this colonizing con-quest caused nineteenth- and twentieth-century European imperialism directly and perhaps did much to cause industrialization as well.

The second wave of modern globalization took place from 1870 to 1914 due to advances in trans-portation, reduced trade barriers and migration of 10% of the global population to less densely populated countries (from Europe to America, from India to Sri Lanka and Africa, from China to Burma, Thailand, the Philippines, Vietnam, and Singapore, and so forth). Protectionism and ineffective economic policies led to an increased gap between globalizers and the rest of the world. Two World Wars and the Great Depression stopped the global economic integration as too far-reaching for the post-war and post-crisis times.

The third wave of globalization took place from 1950 to 1980. Its goal was to integrate economically the richest countries: Europe, North America, and Japan. Policies of trade liberalization were developed within frameworks of the General Agreement on Tariffs and Trade (GATT) and the Organization of Economic Co-operation and Development (OECD). Exports from developing countries were limited to commodities and such specialized products as art.

The current and fourth wave of globalization takes place on the threshold of the third millen-

nium, and is the most extensive. The World is shrinking fast and coming together as a global civilization, which shapes our lives and changes politics, work, and families.

THE ENABLING FACTORS OF THE FOURTH-WAVE GLOBALIZATION

Preconditions of Fourth Wave of Modern Globalization

A. Technological advances in transportation and communications technologies

These technologies provide the infrastructure for globalized operations. Table 7-1 illustrates the decreased costs of transportation in the last 160 years (1830-1990); Table 7-2 shows how the

Table 7-1. Transport costs, 1830-1990

| Year | Ocean Transport | | Average Air Transportation Revenue per Passenger Mile (in 1990 US$) |
	Wheat, Percent of Production Cost Spent for Transportation	Ocean Freight 1920 = 100	
1830	79		
1850	76		
1880	41		
1910	27.5		
1920		100	
1930		65	0.68
1940		67	0.46
1950		38	0.30
1960		28	0.24
1970		29	0.16
1980		25	0.10
1990		30	0.11

Sources: Baldwin and Martin (1999), World Economic Outlook, May 1997, Table 11.

Table 7-2. Communication and computer costs, 1960-2000

Year	Cost of a 3-minute Telephone Call, New York to London (in 2000 US$)	Price of Computers and Peripheral Equipment Relative to GDP Deflator (2000=1000)
1960	60.42	1,869,004
1970	41.61	199,983
1980	6.32	27,938
1990	4.37	7,275
2000	0.40	1,000

Sources: World Economic Outlook, May 1997, Table 11, updated to 2000; U.S. Commerce Department, Bureau of Economic Analysis and Masson (2001).

costs of communication and computers declined in the last 40 years (1960-2000). During the first and second waves of globalization, technology provided incredible productivity in making and moving things. In the third wave, technology is driving the productivity of information itself.

B. Information-communication Technology (ICT)

ICT triggers a shift in the postindustrial society's *modus operandi*, which is based on new key features (Bell, 1981):

(1) The shift from a goods-producing to a service economy,
(2) The increasing reliance on theoretical knowledge, and
(3) The creation of a new "intellectual technology" based on computers and other smart machines.

Manuel Castells (1996) observes that "what has changed is not the kind of activities humankind is engaged in, but its technological ability to use as a direct productive force what distinguishes our species as a biological oddity: its superior capacity to process symbols." The ICT does not replace agriculture and industry but instead optimizes them. It leads towards the informatization of the global society, which by connecting all of us makes us the Global Open Society (Anderson, 2004). (The "Open Society," according to Karl Popper (1971) and George Soros (2003), is based on the recognition that people have divergent views and interests and that nobody is in possession of the ultimate truth. Therefore, people must be given the greatest degree of freedom to pursue their interests as they see fit, provided that these interests can be reconciled with those of others. The Open Society is based upon the postulate of radical fallibility and reflexivity.)

An emerging global digital consciousness (GDC), a symbiosis of humans and machines, provides cognition and external memory systems that support the global civilization and vice versa. Hence, the GDC is composed of

- infosphere (computerized information-communication systems composed of databases, applications, and networks)
- cyberspace (the Internet and Web applications)
- mediasphere (radio, TV, cable)
- mindsphere (global ideas generated by previous global spheres) (Arquilla and Ronfeld (1999) call it *noosphere*, a term coined from the Greek word for "mind").

The Globalization Index, which breaks globalization down into its most important components, indicates that the "most wired" countries in the world are beneficiaries of globalization. The Globalization Index tracks the movements of money in terms of investments and business transactions in the era of "electronic capitalism" (Bledsoe, 2001).

C. Manufacturing Outsourcing

In the 1980s, the developed countries began to outsource manufacturing to countries with cheap labor. As a result, poor countries broke into global markets of manufacturing goods and services. Their export of manufactured goods and services rose from 25% of total export in 1980 to more than 80% by 1998. The most successful countries in this trend are Brazil, China, Hungary, India, and Mexico, with 20 others following up. With 3 billion people, they reached a level of growth 5% higher than developed countries. The rest of the developing world trades less at the beginning of the 21st century then it did in 1980, which means that 2 billion people are marginalized, with some countries even showing negative growth. In more successful developing countries, the poverty level decreases. The total number of *poor* people in rural China alone was reduced from 250 to 34 million from 1980 to 1999 (Stern, 2002).

D. Lowering Tax Barriers

The reduction in average tariffs is highest in South Asia, from 65% in the early 1980s to about 30% in 2002. In the same period, Latin America, East Asia and the Pacific lowered tariffs from 30 percent to 15 percent, Europe and Central Asia from 15% to 10%, the most industrialized economies from 8% to 5%. Only Sub-Saharan Africa, the Middle East and North Africa lowered tariffs by small percentages, maintaining them at roughly the 20% to 25% levels that existed in 1998 (World Bank, 2001). Countries like Ethiopia and Uganda liberalized trade significantly. Average tariffs in rich countries are low, but they maintain barriers in exactly the areas where developing countries have comparative advantage, agriculture and labor-intensive manufacturing. The cost of protection by rich countries and paid by poor countries is at the level of $100 billion per year, which is twice the size of aid from the northern to the southern hemisphere (Stern, 2002).

GLOBALIZATION BENEFITS

A. Higher Economic Growth

Almost every product or service market in the major economies of the world civilization has foreign competitors. Increased foreign competition is in itself a reason for a business to globalize—in order to gain the size and skills to compete more effectively (Yip, 1995). The globalizers are mainly Americans, Europeans, Japanese and Chinese. The more globalized developing countries increased their per capita growth rate from 1% in the 1960s, to 3% in the 1970s, 4% in the 1980s, and 5% in the 1990s. The less globalized developing countries experienced negative growth, minus 2%, in the 1990s. Rich countries saw a positive 2% growth during the 1990s (Dollar & Kraay, 2001).

B. Poverty Reduction

The globalization impact on poverty reduction is well illustrated by the cases of Uganda, India, Vietnam and China in 1992-1998. These countries were able to reduce poverty by 6% to 10% annually. The number of people living on less than $1 per day declined between 1960 and 2000, from 1.4 to 1.2 billion (Stern et al., 2002).

Table 7-3. Infant mortality, life expectancy, and adult illiteracy (selected countries and regions, 1960-1999)

Country, Region	1960	1999
China		
Infant mortality rate (per 1,000 live births)	132	30
Life expectancy at birth (years)	36	70
Adult illiteracy rate (%)		17
India		
Infant mortality rate (per 1,000 live births)	151	70
Life expectancy at birth (years)	43	64
Adult illiteracy rate (%)	76	48
Ghana		
Infant mortality rate (per 1,000 live births)	131	57
Life expectancy at birth (years)	45	58
Adult illiteracy rate (%)		30
Latin America and Caribbean		
Infant mortality rate (per 1,000 live births)	82	31
Life expectancy at birth (years)		69
Adult illiteracy rate (%)		13
United States		
Infant mortality rate (per 1,000 live births)	26	7
Life expectancy at birth (years)	70	77
Adult illiteracy rate (%)	2	<5

Source: World Development Indicators and World Development Reports (various issues), World Bank

C. Life Quality Improved

The quality of life measured by infant mortality, life expectancy, and adult illiteracy has improved significantly from 1960-1999, as shown in Table 7-3.

GLOBALIZATION PROBLEM-CAUSING FACTORS

A. Inequality

The fast pace of the third globalization wave causes widespread anxiety, because it leads to inequalities within and among countries, including developed countries. The latter, by outsourcing their production and services, trigger labor layoffs in their workforce. These trends can be viewed as civilization aid provided by developed countries for developing countries at the cost of their own labor. In the long term, the outsourcing strategy may reduce the number of consumers in developed countries, who will not be able to buy even the less expensive products and services from developing countries. It may have an impact on the research and university communities in developed countries, because they will have fewer industries waiting for innovations and fewer students to educate for jobs, which no longer exist in their own countries. There is an opinion that income inequality growth in some countries, such as the U.S., India, China, and Poland, is caused by the impact of technological change on workers' skills rather than by globalization. On other hand, one cannot neglect the fact that in India, China, and

Table 7-4. Paths of human wealth development vs. the digital divide

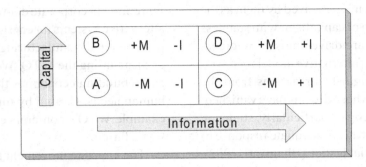

Poland such income inequality is possible only because globalization causes more demand on these countries' labor.

B. Digital Divide

ICT acts as both a greater lever of opportunity and an amplifier of inequality. Table 7-4 illustrates four paths of human wealth development and their impact on the "digital divide."

Option A describes a case of individuals who have neither money nor information and eventually no opportunities to improve their conditions.

Option B reflects "old money" which has been or is being made in a traditional manner. It is exemplified by an uninformed individual or company, who over time will lose to those who have better information.

Option C depicts a person or company with little or no money but with access to better information that may improve its financial situation. This option is exemplified by college students and some early dotcom start-ups.

Option D illustrates a case of people or companies having both money and information, so their economic/social position will grow. It is exemplified by computer/software entrepreneurs who by the end of the 20th century became the richest people in the world.

Digital Divide is illustrated in a well-known title, *Jihad vs. McWorld,* by Ben Barber (1996), who draws a line not between the political right and left but between two opposed tendencies, tribalism and globalism, each with its own vision of the world's future.

C. Volatility

The openness of national financial markets to global capital markets brings volatility of economic activities at all levels of the World Economy. The financial crisis in the 1990s was a good example of that kind of volatility, which was based on overvalued exchange rates and unsustainable fiscal positions. The lesson from that crisis is that free flow of capital requires appropriate intergovernmental regulations to correct the markets' failures.

D. Antiglobalization

Since the fall of the Berlin Wall in 1989, the deaths of fascism, socialism and communism are heavily advertised. If there is an idea that unites much leftist economic thought today, it is that globalization is the root of many evils. Many people from many international communities organize themselves against corporate power and corporate control. Globalization is perceived by them as the worldwide extension of capitalism, with stateless corporations which are driven mostly by greed. The disappearance of alternative models of development provoked anguished reactions from the old anti-capitalists, whose dreams have vanished. For many young people, particularly students, capitalism cannot create an adequate response to the challenges of social justice (Bhagwati, 2002). They also do not remember or do not know that centrally planned economies (in Eastern Europe and China) worsened rather than improved unequal access to resources. David Korten (2001) in his book *When Corporations Rule the World* provides an anti-globalist's vision of the better world—of disarmament, tolerance, gender equality, less consumption, global trust-busting, debt write-offs, the transformation of international financial institutions into democratic, cooperative institutions, voluntary executive salary caps, grassroots democracy, and so forth. He offers a vision of a market economy composed primarily though not exclusively of family enterprises, small-scale co-ops, worker-owned firms, and neighborhood and municipal corporations. He also argues that we should create societies that give a higher value to nurturing love than making money. These ideas are reminiscent of the "Small is Beautiful" (Schumacher, 1975) conception. It is easy to define noble aims, but achieving those aims in a very complex civilization is a monumental task. How do we accomplish such a transformation, through another Bolshevik Revolution?

The culmination of a three-year project by the International Forum on Globalization, whose members included Ralph Nader, David Korten, Lori Wallach, Jerry Mander, and John Cavanagh (2002), presented a sober critique of globalization as well as practical, thoughtful alternatives. The authors assert ten core requirements for democratic societies, including equality, basic human rights, local decision making, and ecological sustainability. They demonstrate how globalization undermines each. Offering specific strategies for reining in corporate domination, they address alternative systems for energy, agriculture, transportation, and manufacturing, ideas for weakening or dismantling the WTO, World Bank, and IMF, and rebuilding economies that are responsive to human needs. Caused by this type of issues, for example WTO's conference in Cancun in 2003 was a fiasco.

The opposite movement to anti-globalization is the globalizing right, which promotes Adam Smith's free market forces on the basis that these will provide greater peace and prosperity for all. They speak for minimal tariffs and economic stability ("Peace through Trade") assisted by business-friendly international institutions such as WTO, IMF, World Bank, and so forth.

E. International Institutions in Question

The belief that international institutions such as the IMF can facilitate smooth globalization is challenged by Nobel Prize laureate Joseph Stiglitz (2002) (J. Stiglitz was a chief economist for the World Bank, chairman of President Clinton's Council of Economic Advisers, and cooperated with the IMF in 1993-2000), who states that the IMF is a last resort for desperate situations. Furthermore, its remedies have failed often, even more often than they worked. IMF structural adjustment policies—the policies designed to help a country adjust to crises as well as to more persistent imbalances—led to hunger and riots in many countries. Even if the policies worked, they worked rather for those who are better off, sending those at the bottom to even greater poverty. The IMF thinks that to achieve long-term stability of a given country, some pain is necessary. Stiglitz agrees that some pain may be necessary, but the level of pain in developing countries created in the process of globalization guided by the IMF and international economic organizations has been far greater than necessary.

There is some hypocrisy in the argument that developing countries should open markets for goods from developed countries that keep their own markets protected. This type of policy makes the rich richer and the poor more impoverished—and more angry. This approach takes place, for example, in agriculture, when WTO wants the developing countries to open their markets for products subsidized by developed countries. The developing countries resist this policy because it would destroy their unsubsidized agriculture. Hence, the free global market becomes an illusion[3].

The optimal solution, as viewed by Stiglitz, is to see cooperation between government and markets to minimize their limitations and failures. This cooperation should be led not only by financially-oriented mind-sets but also by socially-oriented actions.

F. Culture Invasion

Globalization causes concerns among developing countries that it threatens their power, culture and the environment. The rest of the world, including Western Europe and Japan, is afraid that American culture will dominate them. The developing countries are too small to compete with Hollywood movies, fast food chains (McDonalds) and so forth. They are also too weak to debate the legal issues governing the global economy and environmental issues. So they suffer from global warming while developed countries generate most of the carbon dioxide (CO_2).

G. Rising Chaos

Higher business profits are a primary driver of globalization, and they can be achieved by lowering taxes. Lower taxes result in the decline of the state apparatus, which in developing nations leaves room for warlords, mafias and gangs. It is reminiscent of the Middle Ages, when after the fall of the Roman Empire, roads deteriorated, cities depopulated and taxes were collected by warlords. The Middle Ages ended when the rise of capitalism on a national scale led to powerful states with sovereignty over particular territories and people (generally accepted to be marked by the Treaty of Westphalia in 1648). Now that capitalism is operating globally, states are eroding and a new medievalism is emerging, marked by multiple and overlapping sovereignties and identities (EU, NAFTA, FTAA and so forth). This occurs particularly in the developing world, where gangs rule some areas of such mega-cities as Rio de Janeiro, Mexico City, and Baghdad and states were never strong in the first place (Rapley, 2006).

The issue of *standardization* or *homogenization* should be guided by the differentiation and harmonization rules, allowing for different solutions at national levels and universal solutions, when they are applied at the global level. The application of these rules will keep civilization active and developing.

WHY GLOBAL CIVILIZATION?

The fourth wave of globalization leads towards the emergence of Global Civilization because it meets the general criteria of civilization (Targowski, 2004). For example its:

- Human entity as the Global Society is composed of certain segments of the societies of eight autonomous civilization (Western, Eastern, Islamic, Japanese, Chinese, Buddhist, Hindu, and African), which apply global culture and infrastructures
- Culture has global character, which means that certain more or less identical patterns of behavior are practiced (*de facto* by certain segments of those societies only) in those autonomous civilizations, for example, such behaviors as the English language, profes-

Figure 7-1. The emerging global civilization as a new layer of the world civilization

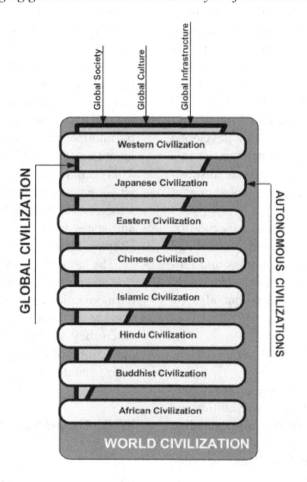

sional and student dress code, music, movies, food, drinks

- Global Infrastructure; composed of
- Information (1) (the Internet and Global Area Networks),
- Material (2) (transportation, finance, and business) is reaching every autonomous civilization and integrating them into an emerging global society and global economy
- Global Infrastructure of Regulations (3), including many international organizations

(for-profit and non-profit, official and unofficial) such as the U.N., UNESCO, GATT, WTO, WB, IMF, and NATO, This last kind of infrastructure plays paradoxical roles, promoting justice and enhancing inequality, triggering world conflicts and instability. For example, globalization triggers the anti-globalization movement putting the emphasis upon local forces and potential, which de facto can be called "GLOCAL" (GLObal-loCAL), since their uniqueness is a product

Figure 7-2. The solar medal of global civilization in the 21st century

of global forces. Among anti-global forces, one that is becoming very violent is global terrorism, which can destroy huge parts of any civilization. In response, civilization develops security systems, which protect global order against global chaos. Hence, the global infrastructure at the same time creates both order and chaos!

However, global civilization is not another autonomous civilization, which could be called *vertical*. It is in fact a world civilization, which *horizontally* penetrates autonomous civilizations as shown in Figure 7-1. Some critics may say that the reach of global civilization in the least developed autonomous civilizations is yet very modest (such as the presence of a small number of users of the Internet or telephones). On the other hand this reach is observable and known in those civilizations, whose elites are active users of global civilization.

GLOBAL CIVILIZATION IN THE 21ST CENTURY

At the end of the second millennium, two civilizations; Western-West and Japanese, were at the level of saturation. This pushed them to external expansion, leading to the creation of the global economy. From the end of World War II until 1973, the United States experienced sustained economic growth. But at the beginning of the 21st century, the U.S., with a saturated national economy, looks to assure sustainable growth by exercising competitive advantage through lowering costs with the help of outsourcing strategies around the globe. Outsourcing provides growth of the American national economy without the creation of new jobs. This process is copied by other states of the Western-West Civilization. Of course, the reaction of victims of globalization is strong and loud. It looks like workers of the Western-West civilization are not satisfied by the rise of global civilization, but stateless consortia and some developing countries are.

Almost every product or service market in the major economies of the world civilization has foreign competitors. Increased foreign competition is in itself a reason for a business to globalize—in order to gain the size and skills to compete more effectively (Yip, 1995). The global competitors are mainly Americans, Europeans, Japanese and Chinese.

The global economy is only possible because it is supported by global infrastructures, global communication (the Internet, Global Area Networks); global transportation, global finance activities, global scientific knowledge creation and dissemination, global management practices, even global peacekeeping (with less success). The Solar Model of global civilization is shown in Figure 7-2. The global civilization is controlled by an invisible and informal network composed of global financiers and banks, stateless corporations, outsourcing CEOs (receiving fat bonuses for better performing stocks), G7, IMF, WB, WTO. The evolution of this civilization is driven by the following process of wealth formation with the help of technology.

From an Invisible Hand to an Invisible Wire and an Invisible Power

The global economy influences the rise of global culture. But this is presently characterized by a lack of the organized global society[4]; therefore, this new type of culture does not remind cultures of nation-states. National societies regulate their economies according to their cultures' practice and expectations through the political process. If there is a lack of an organized global society, then there is no social pressure to regulate the global economy (Soros, 2002), since the global "greed" society prefers a lack of such control, except for promoting low tariffs.

The dynamics of global civilization are not limited to economic rivalries and financial operations only. These dynamics are more complex: religious and sectarian forces for global harmony and conflict have become pervasive and they are intensified on the Web. The accelerated migration of peoples and the speeding of e-communications, especially by means of the Internet, have led to the globalization of religion. This process has generated contradictory responses: some communities are confrontational, insisting on their monopoly of truth and access to salvation, whereas others are more adaptive.

Global culture develops in order to support a global flow of ideas, capital, goods, services, and people. It interconnects different national cultures by common patterns of behavior. English becomes the main language; the specifically Western dress code mixes with international food as the norms in global activities of business, politics, science, entertainment, and art. Global communication culture is based mostly on the Internet and "CNN" definitions of culture. Global business transactions and political dialogues are supported by Western civilization's patterns of behavior, encoded in policies of the World Trade Organization, IMF, the World Bank, the United Nations, and EU. In general, global culture interconnects national cultures to conduct global civilization's activities. However, because of the lack of a global society (or pseudo-"global government"), global culture is very weak at regulating the global economy and infrastructures.

The integrated global production system creates a job crisis that affects every citizen of the Western and Japanese civilizations. Just a few corporations, thanks to their control of earth-spanning technologies (through the global civilization infrastructure—"Electronic Global Village"), control a global commercial culture and conquer traditional societies. Their strategies and products/services can penetrate any village or neighborhood, which may lead to a "clash of civilizations." On the one hand, globalization creates the Electronic Global Village. On the other, it divides the planet in the grip of global digital divide, where there are one billion people with a "computer password" and five+ billion without it. "The Irish are coming" not only to the U.S. When *Digicel*, an Irish mobile phone operator decided to invest heavily in Haiti in 2005, it raised eyebrows. How on earth did *Digicel's* maverick owner…hope to make money in such a poor country? *Digicel* signed up new customers so fast that the company had to rewrite its business plan after the first week. After just 15 months it has signed up 1.7m customers.

Fortunately, John Nashbitt (1995) discovered the Global Paradox, which says, that

The bigger the world economy is, the more powerful are its smallest players.

He explains his paradox by providing examples of two trends: a) the world is integrating economically, and b) its component parts are becoming more numerous and smaller and more important. These trends lead to the growing global economy and also to the shrinking of its parts, by promoting smaller entrepreneurs. As a result, human potential is growing faster than any other segment of society. This trend triggers an evolutionary shift in consciousness from ego-centrism to geo-centrism (Russell, 1995). The latter also means that we are more aware of the shortcomings of global civilization, which brings the most profit-oriented benefits to stateless corporations.

GLOBALIZATION REPERCUSSIONS

The enhancement of less developed autonomous civilizations can be done by creating a world-system, identified by the metaphor of the Internet, dialogue and universalism.

The gap between the Western and African civilizations in economic terms can be estimated as 20:1 at the beginning of the 21st century (Maddison, 2001) In the year 1000, the rich countries of today were poorer than Asia and Africa. For example, Chinese shipping technology was better than Portuguese shipping technology in the 15th century. But by the end of the 17th century, European technological superiority in shipping and armaments was evident. This progress was caused by the development of universities when scientific knowledge begun to flourish particularly since the 15th century), progress in printing (information-communication processes), and communication among geniuses (Copernicus, Galileo, Descartes, Pascal, Leibnitz, Newton, and others), who lived sufficiently close to engage in dialogue among themselves. The transfer of knowledge from Europe to overseas was most successful in the case of the British who by 1776 had established nine universities for just 2.5 million people in North America. Based on this foundation, the U.S. blossomed later as the economic and technological leader of the world.

In general, one can say that the world civilization process through economic means was driven by (Maddison, 2001):

a) Conquest (imperial wars) or settlement in relatively empty and biologically rich areas
b) International trade and capital movements
c) Technological and institutional innovations

The civilization process in the third millennium should replace the conquest and settlement factor by:

d) Education and knowledge dissemination in underdeveloped and developing areas

129

e) Dialogue-mastering in all civilizations by communicating universal-complementary values within an open society ready for improvements[5]

f) Developing nations' need to engage in the global civilization (read: global economy specifically) on their own terms and not on the terms set by multilateral institutions and transnational corporations (TNC) (Bledsoe, 2001)

Because knowledge and dialogue "do not have" saturation points, strategies d) and e) can be mastered in all vertical and horizontal civilizations.

The further harmonic development of world civilization requires better knowledge and skills in conducting information-communication processes and systems supporting dialogue and understanding of world civilization and its role in influencing all civilizations, particularly global civilization, which so far is developing rapidly, driven mostly by greed. One can expect that this kind of "greed" will be replaced by more acceptable criteria of global civilization, which is a noble task for the generations to come. On the other hand, the global civilization at this moment cannot be stopped, unless the oil crisis slows down or even stops the world civilization. The French rejection of the European Constitution (in May 2005) has shown that they do not want to "Europeize" (read also "globalize") too far by creating a world without countries.

SYMPTOMS OF CATASTROPHIC INTERNATIONAL CONFLICT IN THE 21ST CENTURY

The events of the first years of the 21st century suggest the following conclusions:

- The world of 2005 is very different from that of 1945 or even of 1991 (the fall of communism).

- The civilization security threats we face reach far beyond states waging aggressive wars.
- They involve interdependence of human security as much as state security and civilization security.
- We need fundamental and far-reaching changes to both our policies and our institutions at the world civilization level, if we are to exercise that responsibility and effectively ensure the survival of humankind.

It was with a strong sense of the force of these statements that, in the context of this year's 60th anniversary of the U.N., Kofi Annan appointed in 2004 his High Level Panel on Threats, Challenges and Change to report to him on the security threats facing the world in the 21st century and how to better respond to them. We should do the same at the level of academia, which is responsible for the minds of the future generations.

The threats can be classified into the following categories:

1. Natural environmental deterioration and a lack of ability to prevent natural catastrophes (nobody envisaged a disaster on the cataclysmic scale of the Indian Ocean tsunami in 2004, which took the lives of 300,000 people)[1]

2. Poverty and disease (malaria, tuberculosis, HIV/AIDS) deterioration, which lead to internal and international conflicts

3. Terrorism, wars between and within states, weapons proliferation, and organized crime are still big and growing sources of conflicts[2]

4. Conflicts between religions leading to the war of civilizations

5. Population growth leading to ecological and resource-oriented conflicts

It is not just the events of a given year that motivate us to a fundamental rethinking of our world civilization's security priorities and performance. We can look at the events of the last ten years or more to agree that this is the time to think about the future of mankind, because (Evans, 2005; and the author):

- The loss of confidence in the existence and vitality of the rules governing the use of force, including in particular the assertion of a much more wide-ranging right than has ever previously been acknowledged to use violence in the name of self-defense

- The absence of any apparent institutional capacity or willingness to deal with the problem of failed, failing and fragile states, a recurring element in explaining the resonance and reality of most classes of contemporary security threats

- The long history of failure through the 1990s to get it right on humanitarian intervention, from the lamentable inaction in response to the Rwandan genocide in 1994, to the action in Kosovo in 1999, defensible in principle but unsupported by the Security Council

- The resurgence of unilateralist sentiment and behavior, culminating in the invasion of Iraq in 2003

- The lack of support by key countries for international treaty regimes and multilateral institutions. The manifest dysfunctions of intergovernmental organizations like the Human Rights Commission and the Economic and Social Council (ECOSOC) of the United Nations, and in many ways the U.N. Secretariat itself

- The lack of progress in promoting self-supporting economic and life styles, and so forth

The answer to these threats as provided by the U.N. Panel is limited to several administrative solutions[3]

- The creation of a brand-new institution, a peace-building commission, to address very specifically the generic problem of failed, failing, and fragile states under stress, particularly but not only in the context of post-conflict peace-building. The idea is to create the new structure as a subsidiary organ of the Security Council, which would bring together the relevant UN organs and agencies, relevant major donors, including the World Bank, the International Monetary Fund, relevant regional organizations,

Table 7-5. Advantages and disadvantages of global civilization

ENABLING FACTORS	GLOBALIZATION BENEFITS	PROBLEM CAUSING FACTORS
Advances in transportation and communication	Higher economic growth	Digital divide
Manufacturing and IT outsourcing	Poverty reduction	Inequality
Lowering tax barriers	Life quality improvement	Volatility
Media support	Widely heard advocacy	Anti-globalization movement
Creation of WTO	State and corporate problems resolution	International institutions in question
Quick wealth creation	Investment allocation according to comparative advantage	Culture invasion

and relevant bilateral donors, to address in a systematic, coherent, focused, sustained way the full range of policy responses to state fragility and failure with which we are now so familiar.

- The creation of a new deputy secretary-general's office in charge of the combination of peacekeeping, political affairs, peace operations, and the operation of the peace-building commission,

- The definition of five criteria for evaluation when military force can be used in international conflicts

These recommendations serve the short-term duties of the U.N. well; however, they do not address the long-term solutions for the world civilization's well-being.

IS GLOBAL CIVILIZATION THE ANSWER FOR THE WORLD CIVILIZATION'S PROGRESS?

The current third wave of globalization takes place on the threshold of the third millennium and is the most extensive to date. Globalization refers to a multidimensional set of social processes that create, multiply, stretch, and intensify worldwide social interdependencies and exchanges while at the same time fostering in people a growing awareness of deepening connections between the local and distant (Steger, 2003). The World is shrinking fast and comes together as a global civilization, which shapes our lives and changes politics, work, and families.

Table 7-5 depicts advantages and disadvantages of global civilization. More discussion on this topic is provided in Targowski (2004b).

A model of global civilization is shown in Figure 7-2. This model indicates that the global civilization is driven by market forces only, which in many opinions are driven by stateless corporations' greed and unregulated policies, since their strategies and operations are very difficult to regulate by international organizations. In other words, the global civilization is getting out of social control and while it can be stopped, it cannot be the only solution for the world civilization's progress and survival.

The notion of "globalization" and its universality is perceived by many as a Western value only. According to United Nations statistics, most of the people in the world do not have running water, most are illiterate, most have less than a high school education, and many are malnourished. Similarly, the "Silicon Valleys" of the "Third World," in places such as Bangalore, are sensationally displayed as further evidence of this globalism, when just a few blocks away from the Internet cafes and computer shops in Bangalore (which themselves occupy only a few blocks), rural India in all its traditional manifestations resumes its predominance. Thus, with the exception of the Group of Eight industrialized countries (G8)—all of which except one are Western—the majority of people on this globe do not truly and meaningfully benefit from, nor form a crucial part of, that globalization.

Most revealing is that nearly 95% of the world, according to publicly available statistics, does not have telephones, while only 2.5% has Internet access, perhaps the most touted symbol of globalization. Even in the United States only about 60% of all homes have computers, and of those, about 60%-65% have Internet access. It is thus a serious misrepresentation to suggest that everyone in Asia lives and thinks in western ways because a small, elite class of people dresses in western-style suits, speaks English, plays the stock market, reads the Asian World Street Journal, lives in high rises, eats at McDonald's, and watches Michael Jordan play. In reality, they represent a minuscule number of the world's population, the upper crust of a very small elite. The people who make up the world's majority are not a part of that globalization celebrated by the West.

In other words, globalization is a perspective invented for, a condition experienced by, and a situation largely in the interests of, a small even if widely dispersed elite; it is thus, arguably, a euphemism to enhance G7 economic and cultural hegemonism (Aung-Thwin, 2001).

The world's elite have led the march toward globalism, but millions of people see themselves as losers when national barriers fall. The supranational enterprises may also exhibit economic disparity and no transparency, which are regarded by many as inevitable consequences of internationalism. On one page of a business newspaper there may be a story about the CEO of a supranational enterprise earning $25 million. On the next page there may be a story about the same enterprise laying off 8,000 workers. For many people, this is unacceptable. It strengthens their belief that the elite takes care of itself and is totally unconcerned with what happens to the rest of the people. Anger is provoked further when, after thousands of layoffs, the plant is moved to another nation. The rise of large, cross-border regions in Europe, in North America, and in Asia has exactly the same consequence. These regions do attract enterprises and undoubtedly contribute to a higher standard of living, but they operate according to the rule of the market and without a political framework (Moller, 1991). Globalism has produced three dangerous reactions: nationalism, illiberal solutions, and populism (Annan, 1998).

ARE WESTERN CIVILIZATION'S ACCOMPLISHMENTS THE ANSWER FOR THE WORLD CIVILIZATION'S PROGRESS?

It looks as if each generation predicts the end of Western civilization. One of the most popular "forecasters" who dramatized this topic was Oswald Spengler (1991), who in "The Decline of the West (1918-22)" said that Western culture had been dying since Napoleon. He added that the way

cultures die is by deteriorating into urbanized, machine-dominated civilizations, rent by warring states and anarchic democracies, until a Caesar rises to dominate them all. He also said that Germans will never bring forth another Goethe, but a Caesar. The statement gave him some acceptance by the Nazis but he never was its member.

As late as 1969, Matthew Melko observed that all those systems, whether proposed by Spengler, Toynbee, Sorokin, or Kroeber, that involved the conception of a number of exclusive, durable, mortal macro-cultures have met considerable interest, which derives, no doubt, from a feeling that our own civilization might be facing the possibility of coming to an end, of 'dying' if you will, as others apparently have in the past.

Pitrim Sorokin (1941), younger than Spengler, also predicted that Western culture and society have already passed their zenith; at the present time they are in the last stage of decline. He wrote that the crisis was extraordinary because it was marked by an extraordinary explosion of wars, revolutions, anarchy, and bloodshed, by social, moral, economic, political, and intellectual chaos, by a resurgence of revolting cruelty and animalism and a temporary destruction of the great and small values of mankind, and by misery and suffering on the part of millions. His main argument was that the present trouble represents the disintegration of the sensate phase of Western culture and society, which emerged at the end of the twelfth century and gradually replaced the declining ideational form of medieval culture. However, he perceived that Western civilization had exhausted its creative abilities and therefore was declining.

Needless to say, both authors wrote those opinions under the strong influence of either World War I (Spengler) or World War II (Sorokin). During the Cold War, the Soviet propaganda spoke a lot about "the death of capitalism," but those who lived under communism used to say "how beautiful that death must be." The present author, from the following generation (World War II-The

Cold War) has the same opinion about the state of Western-West civilization's well-being, but the diagnosis is based rather upon its saturated capabilities and external expansionism's risk, which triggered the war of civilizations (which begun in 2001 in New York and later was intensified in 2004 in Iraq), than on the belief that this civilization "exhausted creative abilities" as suggested by Sorokin. In fact, in the following 60+ years it has shown great creativity, for example, inventing the Information Wave, leading to knowledge development and management and optimizing control over info-material-energy products and structures.

Melko (1990) suggests that the West is in an interstate system, or perhaps already in an imperial phase with the United States as the conquering (hegemonic at least) power. This would mean, sooner or later, a loss of vitality and economic stagnation. Such a condition is in fact seen at the beginning of the 21st century, under the form of a so-called "growing" jobless economy.

Western civilization is about 1,200 years old and is an example of spectacular development. Its driving forces are the spread of civil and human rights, the development of capitalistic trade and industry, advances in science and technology, impressive life styles, and a proliferation of democracy in the last 200 years. A decisive percentage of the most outstanding people of world civilization have lived in this civilization in the last 6,000 years, which proves that those people have had good conditions for personal growth and support for achievements. It also shows that such great talents contributed to the development of Western civilization. However, one can assume that Western civilization in the 21st century is at its peak, since many problems facing this civilization may contribute to its possible decline.

Western civilization is mainly characterized by Christianity (excluding Orthodoxy) but also by the development level, which varies among Christian countries. Hence, one can recognize three sub-civilizations: Western-West ("Euro-North American"), West-Central (Central Europe), and West-Latin (Latin America), and Western-Jewish. Western-West civilization is the leader in democracy, science and technology, and military power, which qualify its "legitimacy" to guide the world. On the other hand, this civilization has a lot of problems which challenge that leadership. Some problems are common to North America and Western Europe; some are different. Among common problems one can recognize the following:

1. The de-ideologization of political parties' programs, since in an advanced democracy a party is a tool to fix current problems, neglecting at the same time the long-term issues. This leads to the merging of left and right into a center platform and pseudo-pragmatic decision-making, glorifying anti-intellectualism. (However, historians of the United States would say this is not a problem; it is a solution. Indeed, it was the re-ideologization of the political parties in the 1850s that led to the American civil war [Potter 1976].)

2. The vulgarization of culture through the promotion of strong consumerism and hedonism. The race for fun very often uses alcohol and narcotics unscrupulously, which leads towards sexual debauchery and family crises and divorces, such that one-third of all children cope with one or two different parents.

3. The secularization of social life, since people in prosperous times do not press around religion. The Catholic as well as Protestant churches lose parishioners, which is also caused by immoral behavior of many priests and huge compensations paid by the Roman Catholic Church. Into that "free space" enter many fundamentalist sects of religious movements. As Arnold Toynbee (1995) observed, the civilization processes

of rising and falling are closely correlated with the dynamics of religion.

4. Automation and informatization at any price lead toward structured unemployment, wherein rises a group of very well paid workers, a group of temporary workers, employed depending on demand, and a group of unemployed ones. This process takes place in times when population rises and the number of new workers grows and their appetite for food, goods, and services increases also.

5. The allocation of production and some services to countries with lower wages (costs) heads towards the gradual decline of the middle class and their purchasing power, thus to an increasing inability to buy the goods and services coming from those countries. The main beneficiaries of this process are chief executive officers (CEOs), who obtain "winning lottery tickets" in the form of multimillion-dollar bonuses tied to the rise of stock prices. However, the remaining cost of the social safety net is covered by the whole society, which also pays for higher costs of education, since federal and state budgets shrink. The number of students in engineering and computer studies also declines, since these kinds of jobs are exported overseas. In such a manner developed nations transform into developing ones, since they give away the complexity of thinking which is embedded in design and manufacturing. Of course, this is a long process, which cannot be observed by "the naked eye."

Among problems facing the Western-West-U.S. civilization one can recognize the following:

1. The conviction of the right-of-center political parties that "the sky is the only limit" for business; therefore, capitalism should be deregulated, giving more freedom to the business owners.

2. The attitude of some politicians that if a worker loses his/her job due to outsourcing (mostly overseas), he/she should adapt by learning new skills. If he/she is still unable to find a new job, it is his/her fault. Needless to say, new jobs are mostly available in service, where pay is low and in fact does not require special skills.

3. The political class is convinced that the global economy limits the welfare state. The state's priority is to facilitate economic growth, which in fact is jobless, since capital goes to off-shore economies. The welfare of citizens (workers) is the second priority in this case. In this age of "the end of history," when communism has fallen and we return to the ideals of the American and French Revolutions, the sketched situation with mistreated citizens may unfortunately lead to a new "Bolshevik Revolution."

4. The confrontation with other civilizations and particularly with the Islamic civilization is limited to the so-called "war on terrorism," while "terrorism" is only a weapon of the weak. In the time of the Cold War (1945-1991), the war was not with atomic weapons, but democracy confronted totalitarianism at all levels.

Among problems facing the Western-West-European civilization one can recognize the following:

1. The dilemma is whether to tolerate so-called European scleroses at the expense of the better care of citizens, or to accept the American model in which business has advantages over labor.

2. How far should we secularize the state's social policies, while prognoses indicate that in the future the number of Muslims living in Europe will be greater than the number of Christians, who created Europe?

Figure 7-3. The relationships among "particular" civilizations (G-Globalization, Tb-Tribalization, D-Democratization, M-Moderization, T-Terrorism, W-Westernization)

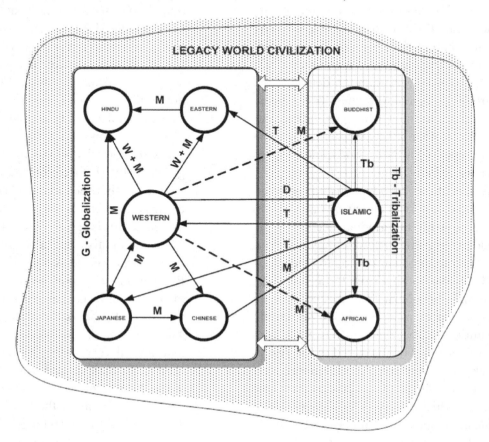

3.   How far should Western Europe be opened to Central and Eastern Europeans who will be a new market for expansion, while on the other hand limiting those new members' share in decisions on the operation and future of the European Union?

4.   How far should Europe identify with the U.S., or, alternatively, indicate independence from it, while at the same time hoping that the U.S. will still provide the military umbrella over Europe?

The comparison of the developmental level via the so-called Civilization Index of Western civilization with other civilizations shows that (Chapter III):

A.   The Western-West civilization is in a state of saturation and must look for external expansion. This is happening under the forms of globalism, Europeism and pre-emptive defense doctrine, which secure the globalization of its value systems.

B.   The Islamic civilization, having almost un-limited resources from the sale of oil, wants to change its present unfavorable situation quickly but does not know how.

C.   The remaining civilizations have space for further development, which depends on their citizens' education, on capital accumulation, and on capable if not phenomenal leadership. These conditions vary through those civilizations.

To prove the first conclusion, let us look at the relationships among "particular" civilizations of the Legacy World Civilization (of the past) mostly observing the roles played by Western and Islamic civilizations as depicted in Figure 7-3.

At the beginning of the 21st century, one can recognize six kinds of inter-civilization relationships: D-Democratization, M-Modernization, T-Terrorization, W-Westernization, G-Globalization, and T-Tribalization. Modernization is mostly associated with infrastructure improvements, using Western technologies but not necessarily its values, as is practiced by Malaysia. A model in Figure 7-3 shows that Western civilization generates most of these relationships. Democratization is disguised Westernization, strongly opposed by Islamic civilization by the means of terrorism.

Militant Islam has given up on contemporary Muslim society, its socio-political movements, the spontaneous religiosity of the masses, and mainstream Islamic organizations, in favor of violence (Al.-Azm, 2004). This violent strategy is aimed at two targets. The first target is the Western civilization, whose values are not acceptable for fundamentalist Muslims. The second target is the crisis of internal Islamic structures, which would like to modernize but cannot do it since they are too weak and the status quo is maintained forcibly by authoritarian regimes.

The conflict between globalizing and tribalizing civilizations defines a New World Order (NWO) after the Cold War. A NWO in the 2000s is a de facto war of civilizations, driven by a conflict in values, which usually is the most intensive and merciless confrontation. Furthermore, it is a much less predictable war than the Cold War; and it is a war in which no one is looking at the common issues facing the whole human civilization.

The U.S., choosing its growing reliance on foreign oil (importing 56% nowadays) in the 1970s, changed their military priorities and converted the Persian Gulf into World War IV's principal theater of operations (Podhoretz, 2007). From the outset, dominance was and is the driving force behind U.S. actions in World War IV—not preventing the spread of weapons of mass destruction, not stemming the spread of terror, certainly not liberating peoples or advancing the cause of women's rights. World War IV becomes the centerpiece of the Bush presidency, although the administration calls it "the global war on terror" (Bacevich, 2005). This is a war for resources conducted under the form of a war for values.

The presented issues, problems, and dilemmas of Western civilization's lifestyle show that this civilization has profound difficulties (regardless of the validity of the "Decline..." issue) in guiding itself and the world. This civilization's goals and strategy cannot be a sure solution for the future of world civilization, despite the fact that it has been a leader in knowledge creation during the last 500 years. Perhaps another 500 or 1,000 years will be needed to move from knowledge to wisdom, which means the right choices during the right time.

THE "DEATH TRIANGLE" OF WORLD CIVILIZATION I

The synthesis of civilization threats illustrates a model of The "Death Triangle" of Civilization I, shown in Figure 17-2. This event is driven by the Population Bomb (Bomb P) dropping around 2050, Ecological Bomb (Bomb E) dropping about 2050, and Resources Bomb (Bomb R) to be plunged about 2300-2500. The most dangerous is the Bomb P, which initiates the remaining bombs. The Bomb P's power is strengthened by ten biological and cultural threats, mentioned in the model (Chapter XVII). Although the danger of each threat is not critical for civilization, the combined dangers of all ten threats and the Bomb P may put civilization in deep crisis.

The year 2050 is the assumed beginning of the "Bomb P" activities, since about that time population will reach 9 billion. This number touches the lower limit of the ecosystem's maximum capacity, which is 9 to 12 billion people[4]. Even a total of 36.4 billion people in 2300, assuming smaller reproduction per family, will exceed three times the capacity of the ecosystem (U.N., 2003).

Worldwide, population growth will be by another New York City every six weeks. At the time of the Industrial Revolution, the population of the world was about one billion. Now we grow by one billion every dozen years. Globally, more than 840 million people suffer from malnutrition,

with 7 million children under the age of five dying from malnutrition each year (World Bank, 2001). If population demands require continued cutting of the planet's tropical forest, nearly 20% of all wildlife species could disappear within only the next few hundred years.

Such a big population on the Earth will trigger the blast of the Bomb E, which even nowadays is perceived in the less-developed countries. Its impact is strengthened by the removal of rain forest, climate change, aggressive urbanization, land desertification, and other human actions against environmental quality.

Consequently, the more productive industries will produce more goods for growing populations, causing the depletion of strategic resources in 2300-2500. It is worth noticing, however, that the

Figure 7-4. Dynamics of wars for values and resources and its consequences

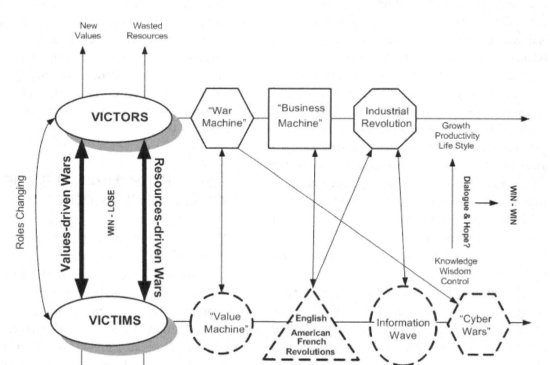

high quality level of life in developed countries is possible because 80% of the global population does not participate in the resources-rich way of life. For this reason, 20% of global population may enjoy easy access to natural resources. Of course, man is capable of substituting some man-made resources for natural ones.

The presented model indicates that Civilization I can be saved if population declines or can be transported to other planets. The first solution is feasible if the United Nations and organized religion will agree on solutions and people will follow their recommendations. The second solution requires huge funds and new discoveries, which would allow for travel faster than the speed of light. If the first solution is possible, the second is less probable at this time.

As examples of the possible R Bomb explosion, present reserves of oil will last 40 years[5] and gas, 51 years[6], if new reserves are not discovered and other forms of energy will not be widely applied in practice. Nevertheless, all potential reserves of strategic resources in the Earth should perhaps last another 3,000 years, which means that around the year 5,000, the Civilization I should end its existence.

FROM WAR & PEACE TO VALUES & DIALOGUE

The world civilization is 6,000 years old and has developed so far through a series of conflicts and wars. One can estimate that in that time about 10,000 wars have taken place[7]. Melko (1990) argues that war is not harmful to a civilization and is sometimes helpful; it encourages economic development and provides national unity. He is right; Figure 7-4 defines a model of wars, which are mostly waged for acquiring resources or imposing values. Even in times of "World Peace"[8], in 1945-1988, about 14 million people were killed in regional conflicts and wars (Melko, 1990). Their by-products are *victors* and *victims*, who develop appropriate civilization solutions.

The former specialized in creating a "War Machine," "Business Machines," Industrial Revolution, and so forth. These advances led to economic growth, productivity and richer life styles. On the other hand, the latter developed a "Value Machine," socio-political revolutions, and the Information Wave (with a so-called "Cyber War" (in cyberspace), which improve humans' knowledge, wisdom, and control over the info-material-energy-oriented processes and systems. In these solutions lies the hope that people can transform themselves from smart and bad to wise and good.

So far, a "War Machine" is being transformed into "Cyber Wars," where "zombie" armies, computer-compromised and subverted by hackers, churn out spam and malicious code in relentless raids on the PCs of home users and the commercial world's information-technology systems. It takes six to 15 seconds for a software-driven attack to find and infect an unprotected computer connected to the Internet. The good guys are fighting back through better blocking of spam, the river on which many automated attacks travel. If in 2000 there were 21,756 incidents, each of which can involve thousands of sites, then in 2003 there were 137,529 such attacks[9]. Who is going to win these machine wars? Most likely, the battle will be getting bigger and more ominous for some time (Claburn, 2005).

Interestingly, victims are more creative in new cultural solutions than victors, because they usually are oppressed and would like to change their situation. For example, a proposal for the U.N. to organize a session on "Dialogue among Civilizations" in 2001 came form such countries as Afghanistan, Azerbaijan, Egypt, Indonesia, Iran, Japan, Kuwait, Kyrgyzstan, Lebanon, Singapore, Slovakia, Tajikistan, Turkmenistan and the United States. Only Japan (in economic sense) and the U.S. can be classified as civilization victors among these 14 states.

So, finally, one can state that to replace a paradigm of war and peace that controls and terrifies the world civilization by one involving less conflict, it is necessary to address the issues of values and dialogue, which decide about human behavior and decision making on our conduct toward other men.

UNIVERSAL CIVILIZATION AS A SOLUTION TO THE WORLD CIVILIZATION'S PROGRESS AND SURVIVAL

Since the early 15th century in Europe, the flame and chalice have symbolized a commitment to religious freedom under the form of Unitarian Universalism, now a worldwide movement which teaches "religious pluralism." The growth of modern universalism was the product, in part, of the rise of consensual marriages in northwestern Europe and the existence of private property in England in the 17th century. The belief that all men should be free and each man is entitled to equal respect has come to prevail since the American and French Revolutions. The belief in universal freedom implies that everybody is free and equal, regardless of other pseudo-rational and in fact relative claims.

The critiques of such values define it as a "Parochial Universalism" of *Pax Americana*, declaring the ideals of democracy and human rights as universal doctrines. Aung-Thwin (2001) argues:

These parochial values of the superpower are indeed universal since they are 'confirmed' by the victims when they confess their 'sin' of having once worshiped false gods (like Communism) and, in return, receive absolution (and material aid). In today's context, the parochial universalism of the most materially developed countries in the world is similarly 'confirmed' by the eagerness with which 'the other' (people living in 'Third World'

countries) demonstrate their desire for the same kinds of conditions found in the former – good roads, decently paying jobs, sanitary conditions, higher standards of living (and of course, TV sets, cars, cell-phones).

Detractors of discursive universalism[10] seem to imagine that there is another alternative in which all differences would be honored without being rationally defended. But this will mean either honoring those differences that are not liked or entering a dialogue to find mutually acceptable norms. The latter is the morally and practically superior approach in solving civilization conflicts, rather than engaging in relativistic arguments.

Sir Vidiadhar S. Naipaul one of the greatest living writers in English and a Nobel Laureate, chose[11] as a title for a presentation "Our Universal Civilization," and took indirect but effective aim at cultural relativists. If any person is qualified to judge cultures, Naipaul is. He was born in Trinidad in 1932, the grandson of Hindu immigrants from India, lives in England and has probed the Muslim, Latin and African worlds. "In spite of my ancestry, and Trinidad background ...," he said, "an equally important part of me...was part of a larger civilization." That larger civilization flowered in Europe, was transplanted to America and has since spread, transcending other cultures. It is under siege in academia and in such currently popular trashy books as *The Conquest of Paradise*. "The universal civilization," said Naipaul, "has been a long time in the making. It wasn't always universal; it wasn't always as attractive as it is today. The expansion of Europe gave it for at least three centuries a racial taint which still causes pain. In Trinidad I grew up in the last days of that kind of racialism. And that, perhaps, has given me a greater appreciation of the immense changes that have taken place since the end of the (Second World) War, the extraordinary attempt of this civilization to accommodate the rest of the world, and all the currents of that world's thought."

Figure 7-5. The scenarios of western civilization development (A-African, B-Buddhist, Ch-Chinese, E-Eastern, H-Hindu, I-Islamic, J-Japanese, W-Western)

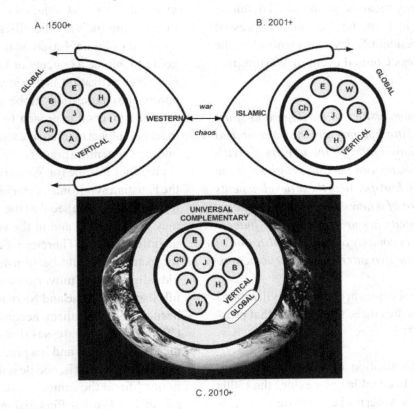

He concludes: "...other, more rigid systems in the end blow away."

A strong sentiment for the universal civilization was expressed by the former French President Jacques Chirac, who said at the Monterrey International Conference on Financing for Development (03-22-2002) that:

The world war against terrorism could be won by fighting poverty. What can be done against terrorism can surely be done against poverty, in the name of a more human, manageable globalization.

Chirac pointed out that:

There are more than 2 billion people in the world who live in dire poverty. People are still dying of cholera, tuberculosis and malaria. And HIV/AIDS is ravaging entire populations—a terrible human tragedy and an obstacle to development. Let us form a coalition to build together a universal civilization where there is a place for everyone, where everyone is respected, where everyone has a chance [03-22-2002].

Unfortunately, the French President perhaps speaks for the Western civilization, which for some people may mean hegemonism. Therefore, let us take a look at the statement expressed by Turkish President Suleyman Demirel at the Turkish Business Council event in Washington, D.C. in 1999:

With its splendor, historical heritage and spirit of tolerance, Istanbul has always contributed greatly to the blossoming of the universal civilization. The Balkans are making progress in the integration with Europe. All of these developments herald the dawn of a new era of peace, cooperation and prosperity in our wider region. Indeed, globalization of economy and universalization of law have become two interrelated phenomenon.

What is the short-term future of civilization? Figure 7-5 identifies three scenarios of that prospect, as follows:

A. The westernization of world civilization, which has been taking place since the 1500s when Euro-America began to develop. Despite its accomplishments, the accelerated growth of Western civilization if applied in all civilizations will lead to the fast depletion of strategic resources and wars for them (World War IV)

B. The terrorization of world civilization, which has been taking place since September, 11, 2001 in order to convey the Islamic message. Of course, the Islamization of world civilization, despite its noble premises, will not be accepted by people from other civilizations.

C. The universalization of world civilization, which is the only chance to protect civilization and humankind against approaching decline and death. This option is controversial, but if carefully defined, planned and implemented, it is feasible.

Since all humankind lives on the same small planet Earth, it should rather look for some *common* interests and solutions (option C) rather than having individual civilizations insisting on splendid isolation. Based on this premise, we are going to pursue a concept of Universal-Complementary civilization, at the time when civilization approaches a question "to be or not be."

The universal approach to cultural development is a subject of intensive scholarly discussions and experiments in practice. Spengler was right in saying that Europe (or Western civilization) has the Faustian syndrome of eternity and individuality. Nowadays, we see that the world civilization may not last long, and in the very long term has no infinite future. Therefore, European behavior, for example, should be transformed from individualism toward universalism as a fight against nihilism (Nietzsche and Nazism), based on hope, heritage, and pluralism, according to Kuczynski (1998; 1999). He assesses that universalism also means integration and is a process which leads to a certain order that is, needless to say, very needed in our life on the same, small, "too much used" planet. Kuczynski offers dialogue as a tool which breaks with orthodoxy and perceives a counterpartner's view leading to the universal society, which agrees on major issues and generates good synergies (Hubert, 2000).

The call for survival of humankind in our times begins with Russell and Einstein's Manifest[12] which asks us "to remember about our humanity, otherwise we will be lost." The Nobel laureate and co-inventor of the atomic bomb, Jozef Rotblat, said that "the search for a free world without wars has one goal only—survival[13]. The Rome Club in the 1960s and 1970s published alerts on civilization decline, which were heard to some degree and pushed us towards saving and recycling. Pope John Paul II thought that the revival of humans should go through ecumenism (religious integration), which in practice is not even accepted among all Christians. Another great Pole, Leszek Kolakowski (1995), argues for a radical transformation of human mentality via a so-called *metanoia* (a biblical term). He asks for the domestication of Earth (we had domesticated animals at the beginning of civilization). After 6,000 years, it is apparently time to perceive the Earth as our home. *Metanoia* means spiritual change, based on repentance that we were doing something wrong in the past and no longer want to be identified with it.

How to do it? Kuczynski (1998) offers five methods: *visionary disposition, collaboration, truthfulness, learning* and *affection*. However, he adds that although these are soft methods, they are to be seriously treated in cynical public debates. More serious address should be given to the development of Universal civilization.

The world needs, very soon, a strategic transformation into a new structure, which at this time means Universal civilization (UC), a pan-human civilization. This new structure does not mean the unification of human behavior, as was the practice in the Soviet Union, including unification of appearance as it was practiced in China before pseudo-capitalism has been introduced

after 1991. UC means that humankind is one and the Earth is one and we should at least accept and practice a few common solutions in order to maintain our planet-home. In order to implement UC, humans must accept *metanoia* as a way of shifting to a better civilization. It also means that political correctness may disturb this process, but very often this kind of debate exemplifies short-sightedness. This lack of truthfulness is a great problem of our times.

THE ARCHITECTURE OF UNIVERSAL-COMPLEMENTARY CIVILIZATION

The development of Universal civilization is based on the following six rules:

1. Humankind is one despite different races, and all people are equal.
2. The cultural diversity (or pluralism of particular civilizations) must be preserved to ensure creative and adaptive progress.

Table 7-6. The common universal – complementary values of universal civilization

Civilization	Contributed Values
AFRICAN	Ancestral Connection
BUDDHIST	Morality
EASTERN	Self-sacrifice
HINDU	Moderation
ISLAMIC	Reward and Penalty
JAPANESE	Cooperation and Nature Cult
CHINESE	Authority Cult
WESTERN	Freedom and Technology
GLOBAL	Free Flow of Ideas, Goods, Services and People according to *Pax Orbis*
UNIVERSAL	Wisdom, Goodness, Access, Dialogue, Agreement (on main principles), Forgiveness upon Condition, Human and Civil Rights, International Law, Green and Self-sustainable Planet

3. All cultures may practice their own values, but as one mankind they must share some common universal-complementary values (CU-CV) in order to minimize conflicts and wars ideology driven.

4. The civilization infrastructures of particular civilizations have the tendency to converge and become universal (house, road, electricity, currency, book, computer, the Internet, car, train, airplane, and so forth).

5. Global civilization is unavoidable; however, it should be steered by the global society governed by a political framework, steered by *Pax Orbis*, not by *Pax Consortiarum et Elitis.*

6. All the inhabitants of Earth must accept *metanoia* as a way of surviving in good shape on one planet where dialogue is the preferred communication method among conflicting parties.

7. Universalism, if incorporated in civilization, promotes a philosophy of action, a unifying approach to all civilizations, based on respectful, rational dialogue driven by justice, and it generates optimism for wise and good living (Matias, 2003).

To practice *metanoia* is easy to say, since it is a noble claim, but how to do it is another question. One can criticize past and present behavior and all kinds of socio-political frameworks, but what would be better solutions? Hence, a concrete model of Universal civilization is presented as the target for today's civilization improvements.

An example of the CU-CV is shown in Table 7-6. It is necessary to mention that it is a set of

Figure 7-6 . A model of universal civilization

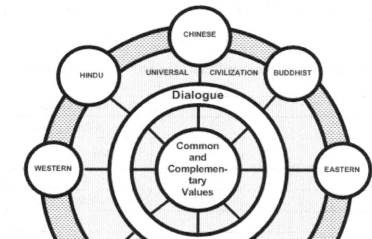

proposed values constructed by this author, and they should be subject to a strong debate (dialogue) among representatives of all civilizations. This set of common values means that each civilization is very proud of each given value as a very important one for the wise and good socio-political order on the planet and wants other civilizations to practice that value.

A choice of universally-agreed values is controversial. For example, Western civilization is very proud of practicing *democracy* at least for the last 200 years (in the U.S. and 100 years in France, perhaps longer in England). So far, there is no better system developed. On the other hand, representatives of non-Western civilization think that "perhaps the most destructive aspect of democratization is that it invariably means decentralization, which, in most non-western contexts today, encourages social and political anarchy. In countries such as Burma, anarchy is feared far more than tyranny, so that if there exists a genuine desire to promote freedom from that fear, issues important to Burmese society should be addressed, not assumptions concerning the universalism of western values" (Aung-Thwin, 2001).

Hence, to avoid that kind of unfortunate confrontation, perhaps instead of *democracy*, Western civilization would like to promote *freedom*, which sooner or later should lead to better political solutions. There is even a question for Western civilization: How long can *liberal democracy* be accepted as a way of being successful in the Fourth World War, which is a war for strategic resources?

Figure 7-7. The general model of the universal-complementary civilization life cycle

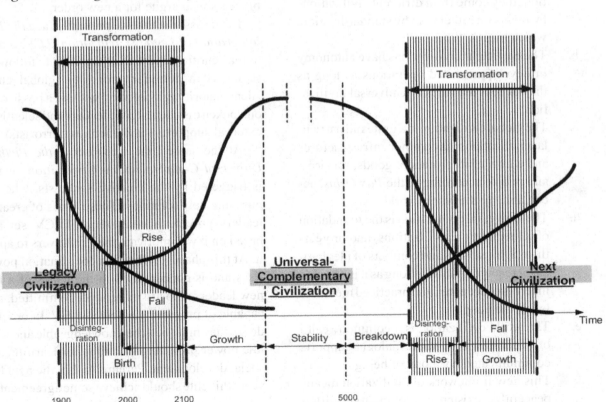

The presented set of CU-CV is not planned as a top-down strategy which could mean the elitist approach, even if that could offer better solutions, and perhaps it could. The offered approach is based on the bottom-up strategy, taking into account practiced values by existing particular civilizations. Furthermore, those civilizations paid high prices through centuries to be able to apply these values and they are proud of it; even more, they are ready to go to war and die for them. If the whole of mankind would accept them, perhaps wars and conflicts could be minimized and wisdom and goodness would prevail. At least this hope is perceived from the present perspective of other existing solutions.

A model of Universal civilization is depicted in Figure 7-6. This model indicates the following *modus operandi*:

a. The set of common, universal-complementary values is the nucleus of world civilization; they come from different civilizations by inclusion rather than by standardization, which means "*let it be.*"
b. The particular civilizations have autonomy in development and operations as long as they accept the rules of Universal civilization.
c. The global civilization integrates all particular civilizations via common infrastructures and a flow of information, goods, services, and people according to the *Pax Orbis*, acceptable by the whole world.
d. The Universal civilization is the foundation of all remaining civilizations, and protects them against wars and conflicts of ideological or resource nature as long as it is possible in terms of accepted and practiced metanoia by all the people.
e. The world civilization is a commonwealth of all civilizations, where dialogue supports communicated harmony of being.
f. This new framework of civilization means peaceful co-existence of common and differ-

ent values and a switch from a framework: ONE and MANY to a framework: ONE - COMMON - MANY, where "one" means "singularity" defined as a single mankind living on the Planet.

THE STRATEGY OF IMPLEMENTING THE UNIVERSAL-COMPLEMENTARY CIVILIZATION

The strategy of implementing the universal-complementary civilization (UCC) should follow the strategies of development of other civilizations as based on the model of civilization life-cycle in Figure 7-7. Those strategies are self-defining, along with the societal experiences during long centuries and millennia. From today's perspectives, we can observe that a new civilization rises when an old civilization falls, and at the beginning it is necessary to have an elite of civilization pioneers who argue for a new order.

Let us assume that we presently face *the Disintegration* of *Legacy Civilization (LC)* because human entities tend to disintegrate into following segments; a dominant minority (global elite), silent majority (global poor, without a password), outspoken dissidents (civic leaders and scientists), external supporters and enemies (terrorists).

At the same time we observe *the Birth of Universal-Complementary Civilization,* which is triggered by the creative scientists, who are pursuing new solutions. These types of creative leaders provide a consistent CU-CV set and based on it will motivate their followers to apply it. At this phase, civilization coordination power rises and is concentrated in the hands of a few new leaders who are integrated, committed, and capable of promoting a new CU-CV. In order to do so, they must both be knowledgeable and have idle power providing free time for learning and social development. Perhaps within the next five years this elite should achieve some agreement on the concept of UC and pass to the *Rising Phase* of UCC. If well managed, this phase may take a few years only, optimistically speaking.

The most dramatic and interesting part of the universal-complementary civilization life cycle is *the Super Phase of Transformation* from an old to a new generation of civilization. This phase is dark-shadowed in Figure 7 and indicates the co-existence of four phases: LC's *disintegration* versus UC's *rise* and LC's *fall* versus UC's growth. In Western civilization, this phase took place between the 5th and 15th centuries, when the Roman civilization was disintegrating and the Western civilization was emerging. In the Soviet civilization, the transitional phase is still taking place, having begun in the 1980s.

The *Rise Phase* of UC is promoted by a group of pioneers, followers of the creative leaders. (For example, among them in Western civilization was the apostle Paul, who won converts to the new religion of Christianity, or Stalin in Soviet civilization, who played the same role in the proliferation of communism.) At this time, it is difficult to name these pioneers, but one may suggest their background in United Nations initiatives[14], such as:

1. Accepting the concept of universal-complementary civilization
2. Accepting common parts of main textbooks on UCC and implementing courses or parts of courses on those principles at all levels of education
3. Accepting the CU-CV set in all political international and internal dealings, inserting necessary statements into international charters
4. Accepting certain insertions on the UCC rules into institutional and business organizations' charters and national constitutions
5. Selecting pilot cases to test UCC's solutions

6. Other appropriate actions, defined through gradual elaboration of UCC

This *phase* may take about 100 years, the whole 21st century, which may be much different from the tragic 20th. It is premature to define what will come later. However, let us hope that UC may last till the year 5,000, when all potential reserves of strategies resources will be depleted. Perhaps, if UC is successful, then the ominous lack of resources can be fixed through more knowledgeable and wiser human undertakings.

CONCLUSION

1. The history of humanity based on mutual negation should be stopped and replaced by Universal-Complementary Civilization.
2. The Universal-Complementary civilization embraces the major premises of contemporary socio-political critical theory and practice, such as multi-culturalism (diversification) and limited integrationalism, which leads to a better order of living on the same planet Earth.
3. The implementation of Universal-Complementary civilization is possible if people accept *metanoia* and their elites, pioneers, and politicians work toward a common goal.
4. If the UCC concept is rejected then we have to look for another civilization, another comprehensive solution, which the author does not perceive at this moment.

A. Further Research Directions

*   Investigate the emergence of the global civilization and its impact on other civilizations in the 21st century.
*   Investigate why the global civilization is not a permanent solution for a world free of major conflicts.

- Investigate which set of complementary values of different civilizations can be considered the optimal one.

B. Research Opportunities

- The research opportunity is in treating the Universal-Complementary civilization as one which is defined and pursued for development beyond religion.

C. Additional Ideas

- The Universal-Complementary civilization is a prerequisite for developing the Rainbow Planet, accepting diversity of values and societal solutions, while promoting an effective dialogue toward universal cooperation and peace.

D. Rationale

- It seems apparent that humankind in the 21st century is transforming from vertical civilizations (religion-oriented) to a horizontal-global one which is under strong criticism. This civilization cannot solve such issues as climate change, avian flu, financial instability, and terrorism, waves of migrants and refugees, water scarcities, disappearing fisheries, stark and seemingly intractable poverty. All of these examples of global issues require conflict-free cooperation among nations. Thus, the global civilization is not only not solving existing societal problems, but is also creating new ones. Therefore, another kind of civilization should be planned if humans are wise and able to predict the barriers of further civilization development. This kind of civilization is drafted in this chapter. It is called the Universal-Complementary civilization because it is double-layered. The first layer contains common values, which reflect each civilization's best ones and as a set are acceptable by all civilizations, because a single world should have one value set that is acceptable by all civilizations. On the other hand, it is impossible to abandon a given civilization's historic pattern of behavior. This means that each civilization should have a double "personality;" a set of values some of them common and some individual. These kinds of values should be a subject of education, beginning at the level of kindergarten in schools. At this time, this strategy is perhaps a unique one, which can in the long term lead to world-wide agreement on key issues of common civilization. If this strategy is wrong, another strategy for human survival by cooperation should be investigated.

E. Additional Reading

Aung-Thwin, M. (1987). *The origin of modern Burma*. Honolulu, HI: University of Hawaii Press.

Aronica, R., & Ramdoo, M. (2006). *The world is flat?: A critical analysis of Thomas L. Friedman's New York Times bestseller*. Tampa, FL: Meghan-Kiffer Press.

Barzilai, G. (2003). *Communities and law: Politics and cultures of legal identities*. Ann Arbor, MI: University of Michigan Press.

Bhargava, V. (2006). *Global issues for global citizens*. Washington, D.C.: The World Bank.

Diamond, J. (2005). *Collapse: How societies choose to fail or succeed*. New York, NY: Penguin Group.

Florini, A. (2000). *The third force*. Tokyo: JCIE.

Flynn, N. (1999). *Miracle to meltdown in Asia*. Oxford, UK: Oxford University Press.

Friedman, T. (2006). *The world is flat*. New York, NY: Farrar, Straus and Giroux.

Hamburg, D. (2002). *No more killing fields: Preventing deadly conflict*. Lanham, MD: Rowman & Littlefield.

Human Security Centre. (2005). *Human security report 2005*. Oxford, UK: Oxford University Press.

Lomborg, B. (Ed.). (2004). *Global crisis, global solutions*. Cambridge, UK: Cambridge University Press.

Korney, A. (2006). *The global top 20*. New York, NY: The Carnegie Endowment for International Peace.

Kuczynski, J. (1998). *Ogrodnicy swiata, wprowadzenie do uniwersalizmu (The gardeners of the world, introduction to universalism, part 1)*. Warsaw, Poland: Dialogue Library.

_____(1999). *Mlodosc Europy i Wiecznosc Polski (The youth of Europe and eternity of Poland, introduction to universalism, part 2)*. Warsaw, Poland: Dialogue Library.

MacGillivray, A. (2006). *A brief history of globalization: The untold story of our incredible shrinking planet*. New York, NY: Carroll & Graf.

Mathias, M. (2003). Why universalism?. *Dialogue and Universalism, XIII*(7-8), 15-16.

Moller, J. (1991). *Technology and culture in a European context*. Copenhagen: Nyt Nordisk Forlag.

OECD producer support estimate by country. (2000). Paris: OECD

OECD development aid at a glance by region. (2000). Paris: OECD

Raskin, P., & Banuri, T. (2002). *The great transition: The promise and the lure of the times ahead*. Boston, MA: Tellus Institute.

Richard, J-F. (2002). *High noon: Twenty global problems, twenty years to solve them*. New York, NY: Basic Books.

Sachs, J. (2005). *The end of poverty: Economic possibilities for our time*. New York, NY: Penguin Books.

Saul, J. (2005). *The collapse of globalism and the reinvention of the world*. Woodstock and New York, NY: THE OVERLOOK PRESS.

Sedere, U. (2000). *Globalization and low income economies—reforming education: The crisis of vision*. Parkland, FL: Universal Publishers.

Steger, M. (2003). *Globalization: A very short introduction*. New York, NY: Oxford University Press.

Stiglitz, J. (2002*). Globalization and its discontents*. New York, NY: W.W. Norton & Company.

_____(2006). *Making globalization work*. New York, NY: W.W. Norton & Company.

Wolf, M. (2004). *Why globalization works*. New Haven, CT: Yale University Press.

World Bank. (2007). *Global economic prospects, managing the next wave of globalization*. Washington, D.C.: The World Bank.

World Bank. (2007). *Development and the next generation*. Washington, D.C.: The World Bank.

Spengler, O. (1991). *The decline of the West*. New York, NY: Oxford University Press.

REFERENCES

Al-Azm, S. (2004). Islam, terrorism and the West today. *Die Welt des Islams, 15*, 114-128.

Anderson, W. (2004). *All connected now, the life in the first global civilization*. Boulder, CO: Westview Press.

Annan, K. (1998). A secretary-general of the United Nations, New York, These remarks are taken from a speech at Harvard University, September 17. New York: U.N.

Arquilla, J., & Ronfeld, D. (1999). *The emergence of noonpolitik*. Santa Monica, CA: RAND.

Aung-Thwin, M. (2001). *Myth & history in historiography of early Burma: Paradigms, primary sources, & prejudices*. Athens, OH: Ohio University Press.

Bacevich, A. (2005). The real World War IV. *The Wilson Quarterly, XXIX*(1), 36-61.

Baldwin, R., & Martin, P. (1999). Two waves of globalization: Superficial similarities, fundamental differences. *NBER Working Paper*.

Barber, B. (1996). *Jihad vs. McWorld: How globalism and tribalism are reshaping the world*. New York, NY: Ballantine.

Barnet, R., & Cavanagh, J. (1994). *Global dreams*. New York, NY: Simon & Schuster.

Bell, D. (1981). The social framework of the information society. In: T. Forrester (Ed.), *The microelectronic revolution* (pp. 500-549). Cambridge, MA: MIT Press.

Bhagwati, J. (2002). Coping with antiglobalization: A trilogy of discontents. *Foreign Affairs, 81*(1), 2-7.

Bledsoe, W. (2001). Globalization and comparative civilizations: Looking backward to see the future. *Comparative Civilizations Review, 45*(Fall), 13-31.

Bradley, S., Hausman, J., & Nolan, R. (1993). *Globalization, technology, competition*. Boston, MA: Harvard Business School Press.

Castells, M. (1996). *The information age: Economy, society and culture (vol. 1): The rise of the network society*. Oxford: Blackwell.

Cavanagh, J., & Mander, J. (2004). *Alternatives to economic globalization: A better world is possible*. San Francisco, CA: Berret-Koehler Publishers.

Claburn, T. (2005, January 15). Machine wars. *Information Week,* p. 54.

Dollar, D., & Kraay, A. (2001). *Growth is good for the poor*. Washington, D.C.: World Bank Policy Research Paper No. 2587.

Evans, G. (2005). After the tsunami: Prospects for collective security reform in 2005. Keynote Address of the President of the International Crisis Group and Member of the UN Secretary-General's High Level Panel on Threats, Challenges and Change, Institute of Southeast Asian Studies (ISEAS) Regional Outlook Singapore, 6 January 2005.

Featherstone, M. (1990). *Global culture*. Newbury Park, CA: Sage Publications.

Harman, W. (1988). *Global mind*. New York, NY: Warner Books.

Havel, V. (1996). Europe as task. *Dialogue and Universalism, VI*(5-6), 10-17.

Hubert, J. (2000). *Społeczeństwo synergetyczne (The synergetic society)*. Krakow: Universitas.

King, A., & Schneider, B. (1991). *The first global revolution*. New York, NY: Pantheon Books.

Kolakowski, L. (1995). Introductory remarks. *Dialogue and Universalism, V*(1), 9.

Kotarbinski, T. (1955). *Traktat o dobrej robocie (Treatise on a good job)*. Warsaw: PWN.

Kuczynski. J. (1986). Universalism as the meaning of recent history. *Dialectics and Humanism, I*(13), 101-118.

Kuczynski, J. (1998). *Ogrodnicy świata, wprowadzenie do uniwersalizmu, part I, (The gardeners of the world, introduction to universalism)* (p. 163). Warsaw: Dialogue Library, Warsaw University.

Kuczynski, J. (1999). *Młodość Europy i wieczność Polski, (The youth of Europe and eternity of Poland, introduction to universalism, part II)*. Warsaw: Dialogue Library, Warsaw University.

Korten, D. (2001). *When corporations rule the world*. Bloomfield, CT: Kumarian Press.

Laffin, J. (1995). *Brassey's dictionary of battles*. New York, NY: Barnes & Noble

Maddison, A. (2001). *The World economy. a millennial perspective*. Paris: OECD.

Masson, P. (2001). *Globalization: Facts and figures*. Washington, D.C.: IMF Policy Discussion Paper no.01/4.

Matias, M. (2003). Why universalism?. *Dialogue and Universalism, XIII*(7-8), 15-16.

Melko, M. (1969). *The nature of civilizations*. Boston, MA: Porter Sargent.

_____(1990). *Peace in our time*. New York, NY: Paragon House.

Moller, J. (1991). *Technology and culture in a European context*. Copenhagen: Nyt Nordisk Forlag.

Moran, R., & Riesenberger, J. (1994). *The global challenge*. London: McGraw-Hill Book Co.

Naipaul, V. (1995). *A way in the world*. New York, NY: Vintage.

Nashbitt, J. (1995). *Global paradox*. New York, NY: Avon Books.

Parry, J. (1966). *The Spanish seaborne empire*. London: Hutchison.

Peale, N. (2002). *The power of positive thinking*. Philadelphia, PA: Running Press.

Podhoretz, N. (2007). *World War IV: The long struggle against islamofascism*. New York, NY: Doubleday.

Popper, K. (1971). *The open society and its enemies*. Princeton, NJ: Princeton University Press.

Potter, D. (976). T*he impending crisis 1848-186*. New York, NY: Harper & Row.

Rapley, J. (2006). The new Middle Ages. *Foreign Affairs, 85*(3), 95-104.

Raudens, G. (1999). *Empires, Europe and globalization 1492-1788*. Phoenix Mill, UK: Sutton Publishing.

Russell, P. (1995). *The global brain awakens*. Palo Alto, CA: Global Brain, Inc.

Schumacher, E. (1975). *Small is beautiful*. New York, NY: Harper & Row.

Sorokin, P. (1941). *The crisis of our times*. New York, NY: E.P. Dutton & Co., Inc.

Soros, G. (2002). *On globalization*. New York, NY: Public Affairs Press.

_____(2003). *The bubble of American supremacy*. New York, NY: Public Affairs.

Spengler, O. (1991). *The decline of the West*. New York, NY: Oxford University Press.

Steger, M. (2003). *Globalization, a very short introduction*. New York, NY: Oxford.

Stern, N. (2002). *Globalization, growth, and poverty*. Washington, D.C. and New York, NY: World Bank, Oxford University Press.

Stiglitz, J. (2002). *Globalization and its discontents*. New York, NY: W.W Norton & Company.

Targowski, A. (1991). Computing in a totalitarian state: Poland's way to an informed society. *The Journal of Information Management, Information Executive, 4*(3), 10-16.

_____(2004a). A dynamic model of an autonomous civilization. *Dialogue and Universalism, XIV*(1-2), 77-90.

_____(2004b). From global to universal civilization. *Dialogue and Universalism, XIV*(3-4), 121-142.

_____(2004c). A grand model of civilization. *Comparative Civilizations Review, 51*(Fall), 81-106.

_____(2005). From the Cold War to Internet cathedral. *International Journal of Information and Communication Technology Education, 1*(2), 87-98.

Toynbee, A. (1995). A study of civilization. New York, NY: Barnes & Noble.

World Bank. (2001). *Globalization, growth and poverty: Facts, fears, and an agenda for action.* Research Paper Draft.

United Nations. (2003). *World population in 2300.* New York, NY: U.N.: ESA/WP.187.

U.S. Commerce Department, Bureau of Economic Analysis. (1997). *World Economic Outlook.*

Wallerstein, I. (1974). *The modern world-system (vol. 1): Capitalist agriculture and the origin of the European world-economy in the sixteenth century.* New York, NY: Academic Press.

Yip, G. (1995). *Total global strategy.* Englewood Cliffs, NJ: Prentice Hall.

ENDNOTES

[1] The Indian Ocean tsunami disaster has not been the world's deadliest—there have been worse even in recent memory, with the Tangshan earthquake killing an estimated 600,000 Chinese in 1976 and cyclone-driven floods killing some half a million Bangladeshis in 1970. But it is accurately described as the world's first truly global catastrophe. Cheap travel and mass tourism meant thousands of lives lost from many more countries than even the ten immediately affected; modern communications, technically advanced and unconstrained by national boundaries, meant instant saturation coverage around the world (in spectacular contrast to the almost complete non-coverage of the catastrophe in China thirty years ago); and the scale and intensity of the reaction has been a moving demonstration that when people and their governments are confronted in a way they can immediately understand by human suffering, they do care, deeply, and will respond accordingly.

[2] In 2005, there were about 50 states in which some sort of conflict is taking place, which means that every fourth state in the world is in crisis or a kind of crisis (International Crisis Group—www.icg.org).

[3] In fact the U.N. Panel defined 101 detailed recommendations for those three major threat issues.

[4] People are an integral part of the ecosystem. The ecosystem is a collection of the environment, plants, animals, microorganisms, and dead matter, which cohabit as a functional system. The ecosystem secures food and water for animals and people, regulates floods, droughts, land degradation, and plagues, and supports services in the scope of soil formation, food recycling, recreation, spiritual instances, religion, and so forth.

[5] World total oil proved reserves are 1,292.5 billion barrels and world total oil consumption per day is about 90 million barrels (Time Almanac, 2007, p. 553 and Organization of Petroleum Exporting Countries). Hence, proved oil reserves will last 1,292.5 bbl: (90 mbl/day x 365 days) = 39.35 years.

[6] World gas proved reserves are 6,183 trillion cubic feet and annual consumption in 2007-2030 is estimated 120 trillion cubic feet (Energy Information Administration

Report#: DOE/EIA-0484, 2007). Hence, the gas reserves will last 6,183: 120 = 51 years.

7　Laffin (1995) lists 7,000 battles from around the world in the last 3,500 years, hence, this author assumes that in the preceding 2,500 years of civilization at least another 3,000 took place.

8　It was also a period of the Cold War, but "Cold" means only that it was not a "Hot" war of military confrontations on battlefields.

9　The CERT Coordination Center, part of Carnegie Mellon University's Software Engineering Institute.

10　Discursive universalism refers to a system of political decisions based on some tradeoff of consensus decision making and representative democracy.

11　In delivering the Annual Walter Wriston lecture at the Manhattan Institute in March, 1991.

12　The Manifest was against the use of the A Bomb.

13　J. Rotblat, "Remember about your humanity," a Nobel Lecture, December, 10, 1995, Oslo.

14　The U.N. has some experience in this area, proclaiming the year 2001 "The Year of Dialogue among Civilizations." Arguing for progress of developing nations, dialogue via informatic civilization, promotion of human rights, tolerance, freedom, international law, and cultural diversification, facilitation of people's contacts by governments, minimization of the so-called "gap" between more and less developed countries. These are good ideas but very difficult to monitor its implementation.

Chapter VIII
Theory of Critical Total History of Civilization

INTRODUCTION

The purpose of this chapter is to define information-based tools for the study of the human story in order to *"informate"* traditional historic findings. By *"informate"* one may understand a gain of additional information above that found by traditional processing of historical information, by applying modern cybernetic techniques that allow for the modeling and understanding of complexity.

After literature, history is the most universal discipline of knowledge, passionately held (in their own particular versions) by millions of people on Earth. History makes us curious, perhaps because in it resides the puzzle of human existence, its successes and failures. We want to know the past because we want to learn "lessons of history" (Howard, 1991). Hence, history is popular and rich in its public role and its scientific methods are even the subject of philosophical debates.

It is still debated, as Hegel (1956) stated, whether history is not chance but is rather a rational process operating according to laws of evolution and embodying the spirit of freedom. The 19th century's positivism stipulated two roles for historians: to be disinterested observers and to find, in the records of the past, laws of human behavior. The 20th century's tremendous progress in research and technology has influenced historians to consider history as a pure science with the emphasis on large-scale forces or structures instead of individuals (Breisach, 1983).

As we move into the 21st century, new trends in the evolution of civilization, *informatization* and *globalization,* guide our awareness. These trends emphasize the application of information engineering skills and offer an expanded picture of human undertakings. The emerging world's history of civilization in the making is no longer "sequential" and "slow" but now "instant" and "fast." To understand such a dynamic civilization and take a pro-active role in it, one must develop new skills and new approaches to its study. Perhaps one should take examples from other sciences, for example, physics and chemistry, where modeling is applied in order to discover some common observations, rules, and laws. Of course, models do not completely reflect reality, but they are useful tools in grasping its essence and suggesting further investigations and quests for truth.

Of course, a new method of historical investigation, such as is presented here, must take into account concepts that have been formulated in the past. But because some tools were not widely applicable in that era, they were not introduced to historians' practice. One must mention here the work of Fernand Braudel (1993) of the French historical school of the *Annales*, in the second part of the 20th century. The founder of this school proposed a structural approach toward the Universal Total History of civilization. In his numerous books, the author sought the driving forces ("wheels") of civilization; however, his contribution focused at the level of analysis rather than synthesis.

A similar approach has been presented by the English historian Arnold Toynbee (1995), who over the course of 52 years (1920-72) investigated civilization's processes and described them in several volumes. At the end of his life, he abandoned the civilization approach, since he was convinced that religion rather than civilization had exerted a stronger influence upon human life (Breisach, 1983).

In the past, several historians have undertaken efforts to investigate a total history or so-called World History, but the applied narrative method did not allow for grasping the essence of large-scale historical processes and structures. In this respect, one may mention the German historian Leopold von Ranke, who in the 19th century published fifty-four volumes filled with historical and political writings. The author declared his intention not to pass judgment on the past but simply to report how it actually was (Breisach, 1983).

A similar effort was made by the American historians Will and Ariel Durant (1963), who published 10,000 pages in eleven volumes of *The Story of Civilization*. If those superhuman efforts of registering the past are not to be wasted, this approach should be continued in the next wave of historic investigations, which may lead toward the formulation of a grand synthesis of total history.

Snyder (1999) made an attempt to develop a theory of Macro-History by defining the Historic Cycle (300-400 years) of a culture-system, which has five sub-systems (dimensions): economic, socio-political, intellectual (insight, spiritual aspect, subjective side, ideas, "culture"), geographic, and expressive (art, literature, and music). The Historical Cycle is the basic unit of his analysis, providing a lens to see how a civilization is influenced by these five dimensions of a culture system. He is innovative in defining a role of an individual in a culture system.

This chapter offers an architectural (graphic) modeling of civilization's evolution in order to develop a big-picture grasp of *critical* major trends, bifurcations, "turning points," and consequences of *a total history* of the world, referred to as "CTH." The architectural-normative method of CTH is defined to study events in terms of historic macro-structures, mini-structures, and micro-structures. This method is a good example of the interdisciplinary approach among historians, political scientists, scientists, and informaticians.

Charles Tilly is a late historian who promoted a similar approach, based on big structures, large processes, and huge comparisons. For example, he writes that differentiation is a progressive master process of social change because it leads to advancement. Examples of such processes can be industrialization, urbanization, coercion, capital formation, proletarianization, immigration of people from alien cultures, state-making, and bureaucratization. He also thinks that the historically grounded treatment of large processes and structures is a sure path to knowledge. Furthermore, Tilly argues that individual instances cannot be replaced by big structures; rather, one should analyze how they interact among themselves. He provides a classification of ways of seeing history and its instances through: individualization, encompassment, variation-finding, and universalization, which are included in a model in Figure 8-1 on the following page.

In this process of searching for critical processes[1] and structures, the author[2] published (co-edited and contributed to) *The Fate of Poland and the World* (2000), an interdisciplinary history book with fourteen co-authors, including some prominent Polish historians. In this book on Poland's Universal Total History, the authors have taken a public role to make the reader more aware of critical processes and events. This book is a prototype for the method presented in this chapter.

If this method is accepted by the community of historians, it will mean that progress in perhaps history science (?) can be achieved faster through interdisciplinary collaboration. To skeptics about the presented approach, it is worthy of note that history and informatics are preoccupied with the same task: processing of information.

THE PURPOSE AND SUBJECT OF CIVILIZATION HISTORY

The mission of historical studies, as of the majority of the social sciences, is the investigation of the causes and effects of change and the continuation of civilization processes in a linkage with the present and future. The author thinks that in general the mission of history is the reflection of historical processes and the factors that influence them in an indirect manner from the scientific and public-role points of view.

The author's personal experience in political activities indicates that, besides history's role as a scientific study, it should exercise a public role as well. One may use the example of the biological sciences, which are developed in laboratories and clinics and publish their results in scientific journals. Their final products are new treatment methods and medicines applied in healthcare, discussions of which are also found in popular publications and TV programs, made understandable for the common person. The common person's health is the destination of those sophisticated sciences.

The same can be said about the destination of the study of history. Historical studies should also produce "medications" under the form of a critical synthesis that should help the public to better understand and control their own lives.

According to this author, the subject of his-

torical studies is the evolution of civilization, which can be understood as the method humans employ to cope with nature in harmony with its creator. Civilization contains human entities, culture and infrastructure[3], which, according to Braudel (1993), act in quasi-immobile, intermediary, current, and future structures. Even though the individual represents a very small part of this framework, the fate of an individual is as important as the fate of a structure.

In traditional historic research, the method of analysis and narration, based upon written sources, strict evidence, archives, and seminars dominates. In "informated" historic research, the search for the most important historic regularities should dominate the method of synthesis based on graphic-normative modeling[5]. Such an approach should help in properly grasping main observations, rules, and laws. Critical questions about their causes and effects should direct this research.

A model of the scope of historical studies is depicted in Figure 8-1 and the classification of civilization's components has been shown in Figure 1-5 (see Chapter I).

WHY CRITICAL TOTAL HISTORY (CTH) OF CIVILIZATION?

According to the presented classification of civilization components, one may recognize the following views (Figure 8-2):

- 20 entity views
- 19 culture views
- 10 infrastructure views

The investigation of relations (r) among these views leads toward the definition of the complexity of history, which can be expressed in the form of the following formula:

Figure 8-1. The scope of historic studies

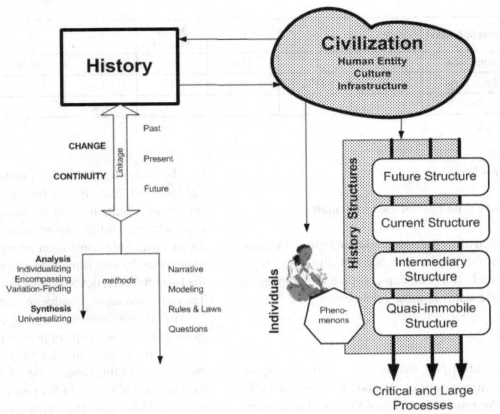

Figure 8-2. Civilization views

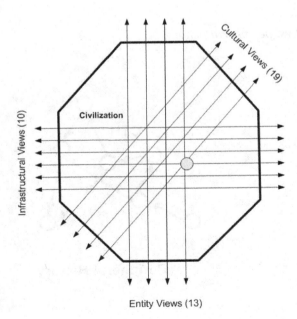

Table 8-1. The civilization total complexity

Civilization Level	e	r	S	Views Number	E	R	S
Intra-View	7	21	128	49	343	1029	6272
Inter-View	49	1176	∞	1	49	1176	∞
Total				50	392	2205	∞

$r = (e - 1)e : 2$

where e = number of views (elements)

Each of civilization's relations can be in many states, but taking into account only two states (ON and OFF) one can compute the number of historic states of those relations:

$s = 2^e$

Based on these two formulae one can compute the complexity of civilization's history in Table 8-1. We assume that each of 49 views has on average seven elements and the capital letters E, R, S are totals for the total civilization history.

The data from Table 8-1 indicate that to investigate the total civilization history one must review an infinite number of states (in trillions) even without taking into account their dynamics in time. This conclusion proves that efforts undertaken by von Ranke, Toynbee, Braudel, or the Durants could not be completed successfully. They pursued an impossible mission.

The same problem faces management studies, particularly in the scope of project management, which is much less complex than the history of civilization. In this case, in the 1960s the critical path method (CPM or PERT) was introduced to practice. This method turns management's attention mostly toward a path of activities and events that are critical for the whole project[4].

Figure 8-3. Critical vs. peripheral history

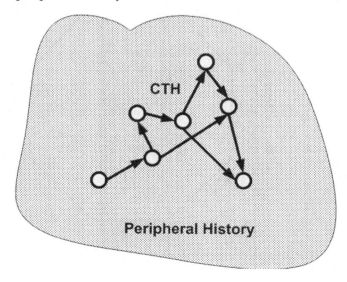

Applying management studies' contributions one may offer the following division of civilization's total history (for the world civilization and particular civilizations as well) (Figure 8-3):

- Critical total history,
- Peripheral history.

If we do not introduce this type of division, then civilization synthesis is almost impossible. The Critical Total History of civilization should focus on selected critical processes and bifurcations that determine the success or failure of civilization's evolution. The case of CTH for the Barbaric Period of the 20th century (1914-1945) is presented in Figure 8-4. In this 41-year period, we distinguished five critical processes and their cause and effects.

THE CHARACTERISTICS OF CRITICAL TOTAL HISTORY OF CIVILIZATION

The characteristics of Critical Total History in contrast to traditional history are provided in Table 8-2.

The main tools of the proposed architectural-normative method (ANM) that can be applied in investigations of CTH are as follows:

- A progressive-processive-phenomonological approach toward historic structures
- A periodization system of historic structures' dynamics
- Graphic models identifying relationships among structures' processes and events

Figure 8-4. The CTH of world wars of the 20th century

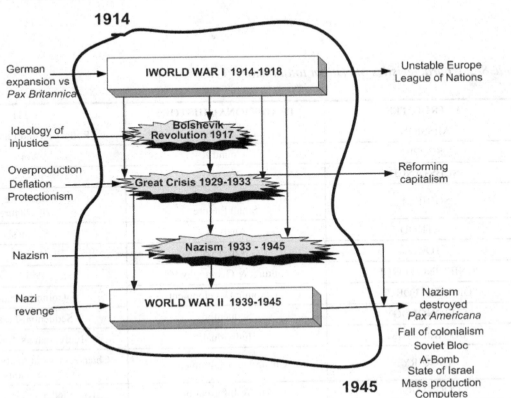

- Generalization under the form of observations, rules, and laws, when it is necessary and makes sense

Each intellectual model created by humans is a simplification of reality, particularly its historic interpretation, because civilization's history does not pass from "one point to another one" but rather flows continuously with "overlaps" or takes place in parallel processes and events. Nevertheless, the modeling approach allows for a relatively quick understanding of historic structures and their systemic dynamics in a context of cause and effect. For example, Bohr's model of an atom, which was defined in 1913, was simple; but it led to further progress toward a better understanding of matter and the Cloud-charge Model defined in the 1950s. Without this model, physics would have progressed much less rapidly, and the Pacific theater of WWII could have lasted far beyond 1945.

One may mention that Immanuel Wallerstein understood this very well and offered the world-system concept as a new approach in analyzing human development. In *The Modern World-System* (1976), he offered a system tool helping to recognize what is the most useful interpretation of what happened historically. His concept is limited to a "system," but the approach presented here has a broader context because it is a critical process, both event and system-driven.

THE STRUCTURES OF CRITICAL TOTAL HISTORY OF CIVILIZATION

Our modeling is based on abstract generalizations of historic structures as follows:

- Historic macrostructures
- Historic ministructures
- Historic microstructures

Table 8-2. Characteristics of critical total history (CTH)

ATTRIBUTES	TRADITIONAL HISTORY	CTH
MISSION	Recording	Reflection and Public Role
SCOPE	Country	World
SUBSTANCE	Event	Process
SUBJECT	Component Small Picture	Structure Big Picture
METHOD	Analysis	Synthesis
TOOL	Narrative	Model
UNIFYING FORCE	Culture & Geography [6]	Politics
DRIVING FORCE	Economic Development	Communication
CHRONOLOGY	Sequential	Sequential-Parallel
EQUILIBRIUM	Individual	Individual vs. Structure
INQUIRY	Change vs. Continuation	Change vs. Continuation & Grand Questions
COGNITION	Data & Information	Knowledge (Rules & Laws)

The dynamics of these structures are illustrated in Figure 8-5. Each structure influences other structures, as illustrated by arrows in the model. As time passes, particularly in the long term of centuries and millennia, the scopes of these four hypothesized macrostructures will change and go forward.

At the level of macrostructures one may discern three successive examples in Western-West civilization during the past millennium, with a fourth still approaching (Braudel, 1993):

I.   Quasi-immobile structure (e.g., 1000-1800)
II.   Intermediary structure (e.g., 1800-1900)
III. Current structure (e.g., 1900-2100)
IV.   Future structure (e.g., 2100+)

At the level of ministructures one may discern a nested hierarchy in Western-West civilization including for example:

A. **Epoch (e.g., Modernism 1780-1990+)**

1.   Period (e.g., World Wars 1914-1945)
      At the level of microstructures one may discern for example:

- Phase (e.g., The Bolshevik Revolution 1917-1991),
- Stage (e.g., "Thawing" and Confrontation 1956-1964)
- Interphase - a result of interactions between phases (e.g., the Cold War (1945-1991)
- *Detente* Stage (1972-80)
- Ideological Confrontation Stage (1981-1991)

By an *epoch* one may understand a long-term segment in which a civilization's dynamics are guided by the same values[7]. By a *period* one may understand an epoch's time segment in which a civilization's dynamics are subordinated to the same political aims. By a *phase* one may perceive a period's time segment in which a civilization's dynamics are ruled by the same political paradigm. In turn, by a *stage* one may define a phase's time segment, when a civilization's dynamics are ruled by the same political "shade." In this classification the hierarchy of historic structures has five levels. In between levels, there may take place interactions under the form of an inter-epoch, inter-period, inter-phase, or inter-stage.

For example, the time 1848-1861 in American history, when the country was coming apart over

Figure 8-5. The macrostructures of civilzation's history

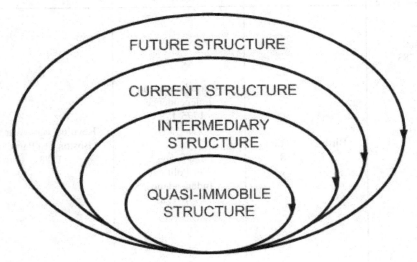

Table 8-3. A framework of mini- and microstructures in American history 1000-1788

Epoch (long-term segment)	Period (determined by political aims)	Phase (ruled by the same political paradigm)	Interphase (transitional interaction)	Stage (ruled by same political shade)
Agriculture Wave 8,000 B.C.-	Asian Migration to America 30,000-13,000 B.C. Viking Voyages 1,000-1,015 A.D. ---------------- Growth of Local Tribes 1000 - 1500 A.D	Early Medieval European Expansion 900-1,100 A.D.	European Crusades in the East 1095-1291 ------------------- Age of European Exploration & Renaissance 1400-1600 -------------------- 	
		Growth of Feudal Europe 1000s-1400s		
Pre-colonial 1000-1607	Discovering a New World 1492-1607	Clash of Cultures Indian vs. European in a New World 1500s-1800s	New Monarchies Merchant Capitalism 1460s-1700s	Wars with Indians in a New World 1490s-1800s
Globalization Wave I Colonial 1607-1783	Exploring North America 1607-1772	Settling & Colonizing 1607-1667 Jamestown-1607 Mayflower-1620 Boston-1630 Maryland-1632 Connecticut-1639 Massachusetts-1692 Virginia-1707 New Netherlands-1614 New Amsterdam-1625 New Sweden-1638	Anglo-Dutch Naval War 1664-1667 ------------------- Revolutionary Approach 1762-1774	Harvard College-1636 New York 1665-
		Colonial Affairs 1668-1776		
	Birth of a Nation 1773-1788	War of American Independence 1775-1783 Final Struggle For Political Independence 1776-1783	Revolutionary War "Boston Tea Party" 1773	First Continental Congress-1774
				Battles of Lexington and Concord-1775
				Second Continental Congress 1775-1776
				Declaration of Independence-1776
				Constitution 1787-1788
				Bill of Rights-1789

Table 8-4. A framework of mini and microstructures in American history 1778-1991

Epoch (long-term segment)	Period (determined by political aims)	Phase (ruled by the same political paradigm)	Interphase (transitional interaction)	Stage (ruled by same political shade)
Globalization Wave II Founding a Nation 1788-1900	Testing a Union 1788-1865	The Young Republic 1789-1861	Agricultural Wave 1607-	First President G. Washington 1789-1797
				Federalists 1789-1801
				Jeffersonians 1801-1829 (Louisiana Purchase 1803) (Lewis & Clark 1804-1806) (War with Britain 1812-1815)
			Innovation Wave 1830s- "Yankee Ingenuity" ------------------------- Continental Expansion 1835-1910s ------------------------- Industrial Wave 1840s- ------------------------- Civil War 1861-1865	Jacksonian Democracy 1829-1848 (War with Mexico 1846-1848 Westward)
				Slavery and Southern States Issues 1848-1861
				"Robber Barons" 1840s-1900s
				Monopolistic Capitalism 1860s-
			Spanish-American War Approach 1895-	First Gilded Age 1865-1900s

Table 8-5. A framework of mini and microstructures in American history 1901-1991

Epoch (long-term segment)	Period (determined by political aims)	Phase (ruled by the same political paradigm)	Interphase (transitional interaction)	Stage (ruled by same political shade)
Globalization Wave III Building a Superpower 1898-	Expanding Resources 1898-1945	Imperial Dreams 1898-1914 War against Spain in Cuba and Philippines-1898 Annexation of Hawaii 1898 and Panama Canal-1903 Intervention in Nicaragua-1912-1925 Mexico-1914,	World War I 1914-1919 Parity with England, Germany & France -------------------- World War II 1941-1945 (Entering the War in 1941) Dominance over Europe & Japan -------------------- Cold War 1945-1991 Information Wave 1980s- -------------------- Fall of Communism 1991	Regulated Capitalism 1910s- (income taxes & Federal Reserve Board)
				Fordism 1907- assembly lines Labor Movement Full Speed Ahead
				All Jazzed Up 1919-1929
		Economic Instability 1914-1941		Depression 1929-1933
				New Deal 1933-1941
				War Effort 1941-1945
	Emerging as a World Power 1946-1991	Age of Affluence 1945-1960		Korean War 1950-1953
		Long Strange Trip 1960-1969		Vietnam War 1959-1975
		Out of Gas 1970-1980		Civil Rights 1960s
				Oil Crisis 1974- Liberal Capitalism
		Masters of the Universe 1980-1988 (Reagan Era)		Second Gilded Age 1981-2000s

Table 8-6. A framework of mini and microstructures in American history 1991-2008

Epoch (long-term segment)	Period (determined by political aims)	Phase (ruled by the same political paradigm)	Interphase (transitional interaction)	Stage (ruled by same political shade)
Globalization Wave IV Building a Superpower 1991- "Flattening World"	Emerging as a Sole Remaining Superpower 1991	New World Order 1991-2001 Globalization of the U.S Economy 1990s-	Information Wave 1980s- ------------------ War of Civilizations New York 2001-	"Persian Gulf War" 1990-1991
				War in Afghanistan 2001-
				War with Iraq 2003-
				Managerial Capitalism 1980s-
				Off-shore Outsourcing 1980s-

slavery and, more immediately, over the ability of the Southern states acting as a group to have a veto over national policy, is also a "phase" of the Testing of a Union (1788-1865) period, while the following period would be the Forging of a Nation (1866-1900). The Civil War (1861-1865) would be the "interphase" between these two times.

Tables 8-3, 8-4, 8-5, and 8-6 illustrate a framework for the recognition of the mini- and microstructures in American history. This framework is limited to critical structures only. It is not a complete table of all the structures in American history.

The presented model of American history allows for the following observations:

Why was America discovered in the 15th century?

1. Human curiosity, geographical explorations, and scientific theories defined in the Renaissance led to a new world view and modernity, which motivated sailors to open new routes to the Indies and (by accident) across the Atlantic to the Americas.

2. The growth of new monarchies (Portuguese, Spanish, British, and French, the first modern bureaucratic states) in the 15th and 16th centuries helped to grow merchant capitalism and supported geographical explorations, eventually leading to the discovery of America and acquisition of new resources and wealth.

Why did the U.S become the only superpower within 220 years (1788-2008)?

1. The international impact is the critical factor in the attainment of hegemonic power by the U.S. in the 21st century:

   Proof:

   - The Globalization Wave I (geographical discoveries) brought Europeans to a New World, who colonized it and led to the birth of a nation (1774-1788).
   - The Globalization Wave II (Immigration Wave) populated the vast country and strengthened its continental destiny (Into the West 1840s-1910s) and Yankee ingenuity (Innovation Wave).
   - The war with Spain, the annexation of Hawaii and the Panama Canal, occupation of Nicaragua, intervention in Mexico (19th-20th centuries), and winning World Wars I and II as well as the Cold War, gave the U.S. self-confidence and a powerful ability to guide the world.
   - The Globalization Wave IV (after winning the Cold War), spectacular victory in the Persian Gulf War and very active engagement in the War of Civilizations guides the internal and external politics of the U.S from the sole superpower position.

2. The ability to generate progressive political advances [republicanism and democracy (Constitution), social equality (Bill of Rights, Civil and Human Rights, achieved after some struggle and even Civil War] and American scientific-technological leadership (innovation: Industrial Wave, Innovation Wave, Information Wave), and business leadership (evolutionary, large-scale market economy, best business schools in the world) are the second most critical factors in attaining hegemonic power in the 21st century.

3. The 220 years of dramatic events stretching from 1776—the War for Independence, creation of the Republic, continental expansion, industrialization, two victorious World Wars, victory over communism, computerization—to the War of Civilizations gave the American citizens a sense of

Figure 8-6. Three kinds of capitalism at the beginning of the 21st century

shared pioneering, successful experience, and pride of unity and achievements.

In summary, one can say that the critical ability to gain from international relations, progressive ideas, and a sense of unity led through a short 220 years to the hegemonic position of the U.S. in the 21st century. However, that this has worked in the past does not guarantee it will work in the future.

The historic American capacity of the state to engage successfully in international issues contradicts the lack of interest in this kind of issue shown by the majority of citizens, who would prefer international isolation to an active role in the world. Perhaps this contradiction has something to do with the current level of American politics, which is seen by many Americans and foreigners as disastrous (antagonization of Islamic states and talking at others from a military position, avoiding dialogue in conflicts).

American politics at the beginning of the 21st century is led by business ideas of offshore outsourcing of all possible jobs, low taxes for the rich and wars in Afghanistan and Iraq, which de facto satisfy the greed of big business. For example, Scheve and Slaughter (2007) argue that wages are falling and protectionism is rising, despite the fact that globalization annually brings $500 billion of additional income to the U.S economy. However, in 2005, 96% of the labor force suffered declines in mean real money earnings (Scheve & Slaughter, 2007). Only the best educated people (Ph.D., M.B.A., J.D., M.D— 3.4% of the labor force in 2005) experienced any growth in mean money earnings between 2000 and 2005 (Scheve & Slaughter, 2007). This means that 0.6% of the labor force (executives) takes the largest part of the globalization gains.

This is a part of the emergence of *managerial capitalism* in the U.S., which strongly promotes offshore outsourcing (cheap labor force) and *per se* supports the rise of *authoritarian capitalism*

in China and Russia under the umbrella of *global capitalism*. All three kinds of new capitalism support each other as shown in Figure 8-6. Liberal democracy, led by the U.S., may have emerged triumphant from the great struggles of the twentieth century. But the post-Cold War rise of economically successful and non-democratic China and Russia may represent a viable alternative path to modernity that leaves liberal democracy's ultimate victory and future dominance in doubt (Gat, 2007). *Managerial capitalism,* by supporting *authoritarian capitalism,* is weakening liberal democracy's world trend. It reminds one of Lenin's famous saying that "Capitalists will compete to sell you the rope with which you will hang them." *Managerial capitalism* creates such problems as the growing gap between rich and middle-class Americans, and the country's current fiscal and foreign trade deficits.

According to Frieden (2007), "some have enjoyed enormous benefits from globalization but there can be serious costs to certain regions, industries, and entire countries. It is not enough to reword the winners of globalization; we need to address the concerns of the losers too. What may be good for the entire economy may not be good for everyone in those economies." The same author reminds that the world economy was well integrated in 1860-1914 but soon the world entered depression and two world wars because "this decline was due to an ineffective response by political systems to the new economic challenges."

This downward spiral of a new American capitalism very probably may lead to protectionism and failure of global capitalism and reversing a process of "flattening" the world. For the first time in American history, the impact of international trade yields negative results as far as the American economy is concerned, as well as the World economy of the majority of the labor force. It resembles the period of "Robber Barons" (1840s-1900s), whose "free" business rides were curtailed in the 1910s by regulated capitalism (*Progressivism*). It is a question in the 21st century: Can the U.S. repair itself and return to *regulated capitalism*? How much damage will be done to the domestic industries and labor force until the greed-driven executives will be looking for solutions that are optimal in the long term for their citizens?

What about progressive ideas, as the product of Yankee ingenuity? One answer is offered by Christopher Hill (2007) in the very prestigious periodical *Issues in Science and Technology*, published by the National Academy of Sciences, National Academy of Engineers, Institute of Medicine, and The University of Texas in Dallas. He suggests that Americans live now in a post-scientific society which does not need many scientists and engineers. This is because it will be "cheaper" to do basic research abroad, particularly since young Americans express a declining interest in mathematics, science, and engineering. Americans should rather concentrate on innovating organizational, social, art and business processes, taking examples from Google and eBay innovators. Is this the future of American progressive ideas? In fact, this is rather a surrender of complex new thinking to offshore researchers on behalf of the fun society idea, which many in our young generation would certainly like.

These bad examples of international activism and innovation ideas mean that the U.S. in the 21st century is at the stage of self-poisoning. Whether it will overcome this syndrome is a question for the future history of America and the world. Another question is whether the political system can reform managerial capitalism soon enough to stop the country's march into drastic economic decline and unrest, like used to be in the 1930s.

GRAND MODELS OF THE CIVILIZATION CTH

As a rule, each generation thinks that it lives in the critical time of the whole civilization. For example, let us examine our own generation's time. Figure 8-7 depicts the CTH Grand Model of "Big and Mini Bangs." This model shows that according to the state of our knowledge one can distinguish seven Big and Mini Bangs of civilization. Three are obvious Big ones: they concern the beginnings of Earth and of mankind and one that will mark the end of the planet. The remaining four Mini-Bangs have been happening in the current and future historic macrostructures: Atomic Bomb (1945), Population Bomb (2050), Ecology Bomb (2050), and the depletion of strategic Resources Bomb (2300). The association of the last three Mini-Bangs may suggest that the years of 2050-2300 will be very critical for humankind and therefore we can call this time the Death Triangle of Mankind (or Civilization I). This case is how the Future CTH may play a vocal role in guiding the development of civilization.

The next CTH Grand Model, Info-Energy, is shown in Figure 8-8 and is organized according to two criteria: energy and information. Based upon its synthesis one may notice several following observations about the development of civilization:

- Four inventions, print, the steam (internal combustion) engine, the computer, and the Internet have decided the direction of civilization's development in the last 500 years. Print liberated thinking, and as a result, the internal combustion engine was built, which gave more time for humans to spend on education. Consequently, they designed the computer, which helps in improved control of processes and utilization of resources. Thus, each step toward the development of the Internet has revolutionized communication among humans.

Figure 8-7. The big & mini bang model of CTH of civilization

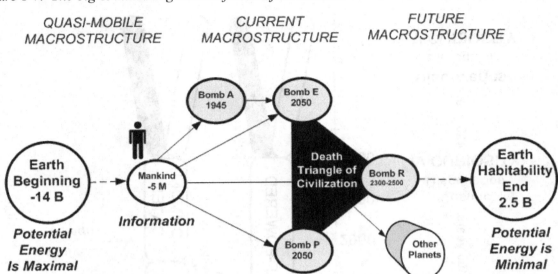

- Every 400 years, a great curiosity occurs which leads toward discoveries of lands, inventions, and cosmic and life science-oriented undertakings. In shorter segments of time a civilization's development passes through two phases, design and analysis, alternately as it is shown in Figure 8-8.

Based on this model, a historian in his public role may enrich our knowledge and awareness about more derivative observations, which may be priceless indicators for curious people on how to act today and in the future. One may mention that Snyder (1999) found that culture systems evolve in 300-400-year historic cycles, but he perceived the political factor (dynastic cycle) as the main cause of this duration.

The subsequent CTH Grand Model of Autonomous Civilization's Development, shown in Figure 1-2, is designed with the Toynbee approach, which states that the development of societal, cultural and infrastructural civilizations occurred in response to the challenges of nature, social life, beliefs, and technology. This model facilitates opinion on the so-called "clashes of civilizations" mentioned by Huntington (1993) and allows for the measurement of those "clashes" by the civilization index (see Chapter III).

The CTH Grand Model of Regional Initiatives, depicted in Figure 8-9, allows for the investigation of *critical* processes and events that decide which region of the world leads the others in civilization's transformations. Finding that type of critical solution may help achieve better equilibrium in the world. In such a manner, historic research may be applied in the planning of international policies.

The Future History Model of CTH illustrated in Figure 8-10 identifies the current state of civilization, which in addition to the "Death Triangle of Mankind" possibility indicates the bifurcation between the developed states (Electronic Global Village) and those developing states that prefer the *status quo* (Tribalism-INFOCO-3, pre-electronic)). Among the former, one may perceive another bifurcation among states which promote techno-globalism (e.g., the United States) and

Figure 8-8. The info-energy model of CTH of civilization

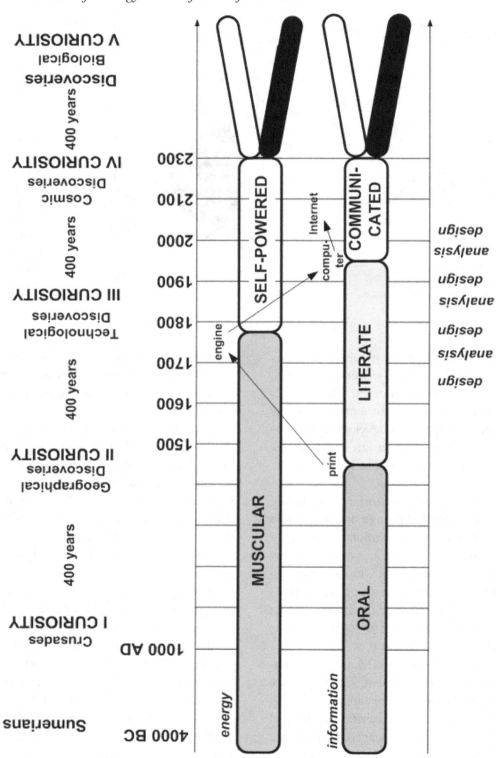

Figure 8-8 The Info-Energy Model of CTH of Civilization

Figure 8-9. The CTH grand model of regional initiatives

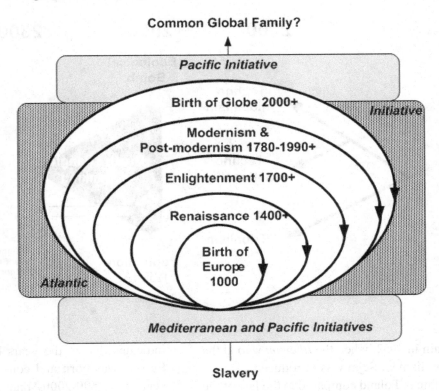

states which promote techno-nationalism (e.g., South Korea).

A more careful investigation of those bifurcations in the historic context may influence the development of international economic policies. Countries which primarily promote open market policies will be interested in how to cope with countries that promote the concept of the "fortress nation," and vice versa.

MODELS OF THE STATE CTH OF CIVILIZATION

This section will particularly use the recent history of Poland as an example. One can ask: Why Poland? Poland's 1,000-year-long history is full

of events and interesting contradicting process. The Solidarity movement in the 1980s put Poland on the world map again. In the 18th and 20th centuries, Poland was the sick man of Europe, and Winston Churchill said that when "Poland is sick then Europe is sick." The Poles always ask: Why did the Polish state, which was the largest state in 16th-century Europe, suddenly disappear from the map at the end of the 18th century? In view of this fact, one may ask the next question: Was the fate of Poland convergent with the fate of the World?

These are questions about which the CTH should seek answers. The model of Poland's CTH periods is shown on Figure 8-11. The graph shows that Poland's strength begins to wane in 1572 when the election of kings was introduced,

Figure 8-10. The future history model of CTH

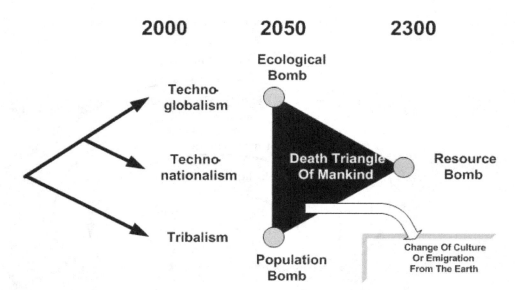

then again in 1652, when the *liberum veto* at the Polish parliament Sejm was introduced.

The fate of Poland compared to the fate of the world is illustrated in Figure 8-12, when at the moment of significant civilization bifurcations Poland was moving away from the West toward the East. As a result, Poland's political fate in 1023 years (966-1989) was 25% divergent from the Western world (in which Poland had belonged since 966) and its economic fate was 50% divergent from the West's (Targowski et al., 2000).

According to *The Fate of Poland and the World* (2000), Poland's fate can be characterized by its key success and failure factors (pseudo-rules), as represented in Table 8-6.

MODELS OF THE WORLD CTH OF CIVILIZATION

The idea of civilization's bifurcation can be applied to illustrate the dynamics of the history of Western civilization. The CTH model of Western civilization is shown in Figure 8-13. This model

indicates that in the years between 1000-1500 Europe was born and consolidated, and in the years from 1500-2000 Atlantic Europe had divided its resources and prevailed. History's bifurcation was decided by the emergence of new monarchies in England, France, Spain and Germany (in such individual princely states as Prussia), where monarchies ruled absolutely.

This polity paved the way for the ideas of the Reformation, Enlightenment (education), Democracy, and Industrialization. Those countries which were in a state of anarchy (Poland) or practiced undifferentiated absolute monarchies (Russia, Prussia) have been left behind because later in the 20th century they practiced "red" (communism) and "black" (Nazism) totalitarianism.

The formal application of CTH rules or principles is illustrated through the example of the Cold War Model in Figure 8-14. This model depicts the critical processes and leaders for the years 1945-91.

Based on this model one can offer the following rules:

Figure 8-11. Poland's model of CTH periods (The Samsonowicz-Targowski Model)

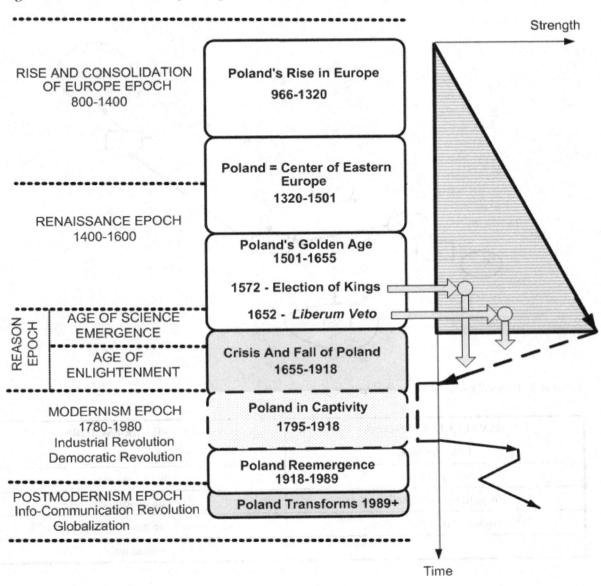

Figure 8-12. Grand civilization biofurcations and Poland

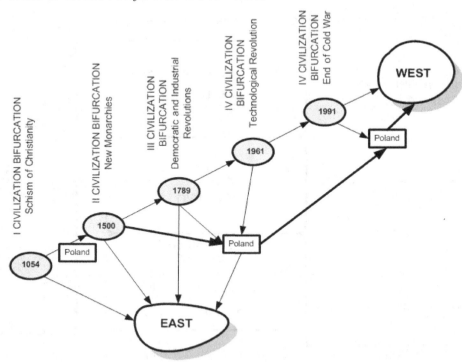

Table 8-6. Poland's key success and failure factors

KEY SUCCESS FACTORS	KEY FAILURE FACTORS
Long statehood	Privileges for few
Strong tradition	Weak leaders
Strong Religion (Catholicism)	Low education
Meaningful cultural center	Excessive self-sacrifice ("blind patriotism")
	Wasted time

- *Totalitarian Rule: A totalitarian regime is based on extended control and falsified information and coercion.*
- *Totalitarian Failure Rule: A totalitarian regime as a closed system evolves into a chaotic structure and cannot succeed in the long term.*
- *Affluence Rule: A person achieves affluence through enterprising, his/her own motivation, and the ability of the society to self-organize.*
- *Non-Aggression Rule: The best tool to minimize international aggression is the ability to communicate cross-culturally and understand others.*

Based upon the models of Western civilization, the Grand Laws of Western civilization CTH will be formulated.

Figure 8-13. Western civilization bifurcations and Poland

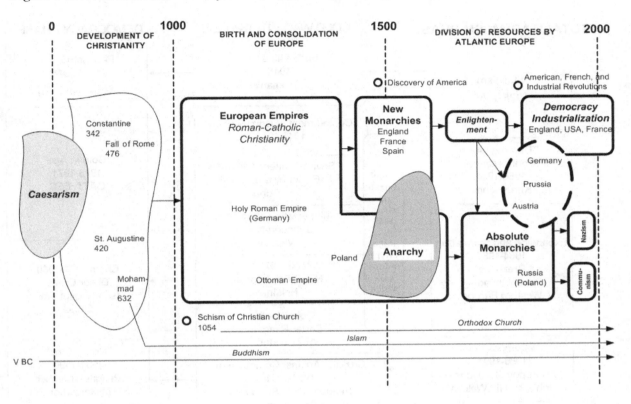

THE GRAND LAWS OF WESTERN CIVILIZATION CTH

In traditional historical research the search for rules and laws is avoided, because it is assumed that it is not appropriate to make generalizations about the past. Such past rules may not apply to the present and future. Tilly (1984) argues that the search for universal historical laws cannot be left to political scientists, sociologists and other social scientists; it is a task for historians. It is possible to define false rules and laws, or one can state that proposed regularities were correct in the past only and do not have to be correct in the future or even in present times. Such an approach is obligatory in science. For example, in physics, there is a strong tendency to define a universal theory, but with the understanding that such a theory has been

evolving and will continue to evolve according to the state of scientific knowledge.

In management there is no intention to develop a universal theory, but a contingency theory for a given period may be offered. Otherwise, if a historical investigation is not completed with conclusions or attempts to define rules or even laws, then such a work is not a strong contribution to scientific knowledge, since it contains merely data and information.

Taking into account the above comments, and based on the CTH Models of Western civilization, one can offer the following four Grand Laws of CTH[8]:

Law I: People have seen themselves as entering the world with a potential of many gifts, and they

Figure 8-14. Cold War model of CTH

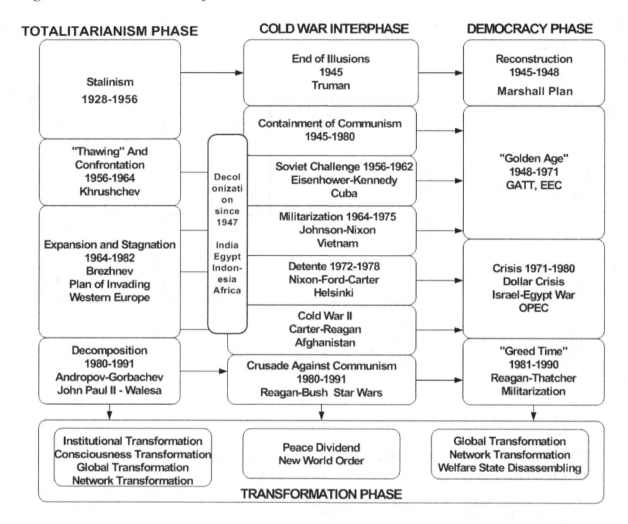

hope to fulfill these gifts in the development of their own lives (Bronowski & Mazlish, 1962).

Law II: People constantly aim for freedom; the range of this freedom depends on the level of the entity's knowledge and communication ability and the knowledge of the international community.

Law III: Mankind consciously steers the development of civilization through the formulation and

implementation of the main ideas and values of a given epoch.

Law IV: The degree of a country's historical success is proportional to a level of harmony among political, social, and economic domains.

Of course there are many other laws of civilization, but these seem to be the most *critical* laws that are used to guide the development of civilization. The question for historians is whether these laws are universal for all civilizations.

Figure 8-15. A model of the book

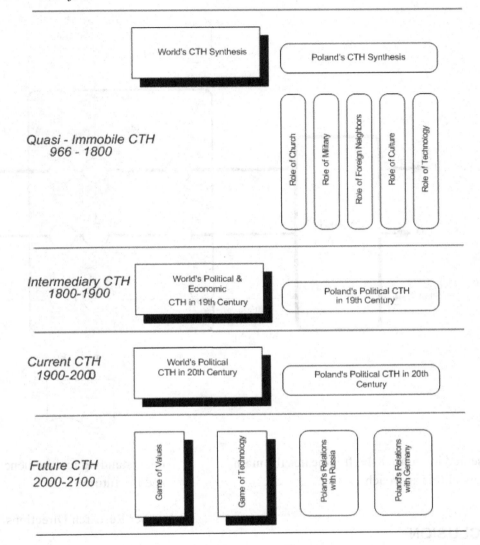

A. Targowski et al (2000). *The Fare of Poland and the World. 2000. Warsaw: Beliona.*

HOW TO INVESTIGATE CTH OF CIVILIZATION

The Fate of Poland and the World (2000), is a prototype for the CTH approach. Because the book was written by 15 authors, it was not easy to apply all CTH rules to its first written expression. But the main author hopes that in the subsequent editions, Poland's CTH will gradually be better formulated. The 1,000 years of Poland's CTH have been written according to the rules of historical macrostructures and in the context of the world's CTH. The book's model is shown in Figure 8-15.

The generic *informated* model of CTH that can be applied in the majority of historic writings

Figure 8-16. The CTH generic model

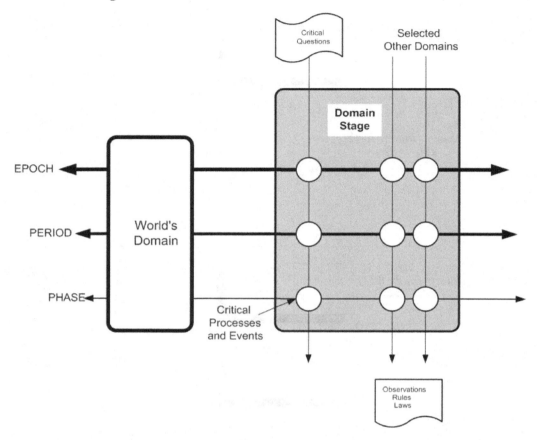

is presented in Figure 8-16. It indicates the main elements of this approach.

CONCLUSION

1. The emergence of the CTH method is the result of the Information Wave's impact upon the development of scientific methods in the 21st century.

2. The effects of that impact are to *informate* the study of history and to present its results in a more "user friendly" manner.

3. The purpose of CTH is to grasp the *critical* historical processes and events in order to better understand their influence upon civilization and to play a public role in understanding and influencing the present and the future.

A. Further Research Directions

- Investigate how classic narration of history can be transformed into a model of historical events in order to define more general rules or observations which can be applied in other comparative periods of human history.

- Investigate how huge volumes of historical narration can be synthesized by applying graphic models and paying attention to key factors.

- Investigate major historic events by applying graphic modeling and comparing the conclusions achieved by the old and new methods.

B. Research Opportunities

- Application of graphic modeling of historical events should lead to a better definition of learned lessons from the past for the current and future generations.

C. Additional Ideas

- The Critical Theory of History of Civilization should lead to better awareness of historical, current and future challenges, since it focuses on the most important issues, rules, and observations. The study should provide examples of how a new approach can change the traditional approach and what should be the right conclusion and its consequence for human action.

D. Rationale

- The history of civilization is huge and very important for human actions, since one can expect that a proper appreciation of the lessons of history should lead to fewer errors when making decisions about the well-being of humans in the future. In order to learn such lessons, history should be easily understood by common readers and by leaders. Unfortunately, histories written by professional historians are so long and full of detail that the reader is soon lost and cannot learn any lesson from the past. The historical narrative is usually sequential, from "January to December" and "from Monday to Sunday," full of footnotes but modest in conclusions, particularly at the level of defined laws, rules, or even distinctive observations. This kind of thinking is usually left to a reader. Therefore, if history is to be useful not only for the historian or intellectual (as it was in the 19th century) but for the public also, as medicine is intended to be useful not only for physicians but primarily for patients, then it should concentrate on key events/issues and include a definition of laws (if possible), rules (if applicable), or, at least, observations, well itemized and prioritized. The graphic approach to modeling complexities of history is an application of information technology which may facilitate the task of modernizing historical narratives. It is not true that the modeling approach simplifies history by generalizing too much. This happens in every science which applies models. The constant progress in science gradually improves early models. History should follow the paths of other sciences for the sake of better service for a wide and curious public, perhaps ready to learn from the past successes and failures of human journeys.

E. Additional Reading

Aristotle. (1927). Metaphysics. In: W. Ross (Ed.), *Aristotle* (pp. 105-118). New York, NY: Scribner.

Debord, G. (1995). *The society of the spectacle.* Cambridge, MA: The MIT Press.

Fukuyama, F. (1992). *The end of history and the last man.* New York, NY: Penguin Group.

Garraghan, G. (1946). *A guide to historical method.* New York, NY: Fordham University Press.

Geyl, P. (1955). *Debates with historians.* London: Collins.

Gibbon, E. (1993). *The history of the decline and fall of the roman empire.* New York, NY: Random House.

Gottschalk, L. (1950). *Understanding history: A primer of historical method.* New York, NY: Alfred A. Knopf.

Hegel, G. (1997). *Lectures on the philosophy of history (org. 1837).* Upper Saddle River, NJ: Prentice-Hall.

_____ (1967). *Philosophy of right.* New York, NY: Oxford University Press.

Howell, M., & Prevenier, W. (2001). *From reliable sources: An introduction to historical methods.* Ithaca, NY: Cornell University Press.

Kant, I. (1986). Idea for a universal history from a cosmopolitan point of view. In: E. Behler (Ed.), *Philosophical writings.* New York, NY: Continuum.

Krus, D., & Blackman, H. (1980). Time scale factor as related to theories of societal change. *Psychological Reports, 46,* 95-102.

Krus, D., & Ko, H. (1983). Algorithm for autocorrelation of secular trends. *Educational and Psychological Measurement, 43,* 821-828.

Makridakis, S., & Wheelwright, S. (1978). *Interactive forecasting: Univariate and multivariate methods.* San Francisco, CA: Holden-Day.

McClelland, D. (1961). *The achieving society.* Princeton, NJ: Van Nostrand.

_____(1975). *Power: The inner experience.* New York, NY: Halstead.

McGaughey, W. (2000). *Five epochs of civilization.* Minneapolis, MN: Thistlerose Publications.

McCullagh, B. (1984). *Justifying historical descriptions.* New York, NY: Cambridge University Press.

Mink. L. (1987). Narrative form as a cognitive instrument. In: B. Fay (Ed.), *Historical understanding.* Ithaca, NY: Cornell University Press.

Moyal, J. (1949). The distribution of wars in time. *Journal of the Royal Statistical Society, 112,* 446-458.

Ollier, Ed. (2007). *Cassell's illustrated universal history.* London: Cassell, Petter, Galpin & Co.

Popper, K. (1957). *The poverty of historicism.* London, UK: Routledge.

Press, W., Teukolsky, S., Vetterling, W., & Flannery, B. (1986). *Numerical recipes: The art of scientific computing.* Cambridge: Cambridge University Press.

Ranajit, G. (2002). *History at the limit of world-history.* New York, NY: Columbia University Press.

Richardson, L. (1960). *Statistics of deadly quarrels.* Pacific Grove, CA: Boxwood Press.

Russell, E. (1971). Christianity and militarism. *Peace Research Review, 4*(3), 1-77.

Silver, N., & Hittner, J. (1998). *Guidebook of statistical software for the social and behavioral sciences.* Boston, MA: Allyn & Bacon.

Shafer, R. (1974). *A Guide to historical method.* Homewood, IL: The Dorsey Press.

Spengler, O. (1920). *Der Untergang des Abendlandes (The decline of the West).* Munchen: Beck.

Tucker, R. (1990). *Philosophy and myth in Karl Marx.* Cambridge, MA: Cambridge University Press.

Turchin, P. (2006). *War and peace and war: The life cycles of imperial nations.* New York, NY: Pi Press.

Turchin, P. (Ed.). (2007). *History & mathematics: Historical dynamics and development of complex societies.* Moscow: KomKniga.

Vico, G. (1968). *The new science.* New York, NY: Cornell University Press.

Weber, G. (1859). *Outlines of universal history: From the creation of the world to the present time.* London: Hickling, Swan and Brewer.

Wilkinson, D. (1980). *Deadly quarrels: Lewis F. Richardson and the statistical study of war.* Berkeley, CA: University of California Press.

Wright, Q. (1965). *A study of war.* Chicago, IL: University of Chicago Press.

White, H. (1975). *Metahistory: The historical imagination in nineteenth-century Europe*. Baltimore, MD: Johns Hopkins University Press.

REFERENCES

Baron, S. (1986). The contemporary relevance of history. New York, NY: Columbia University Press.

Best, St. (1995). *The politics of historical vision*. New York, NY: The Guilford Press.

Braudel, F. (1993). *A history of civilization*. New York, NY: Penguin Books.

Breisach, E. (1983). *Historiography, ancient, medieval & modern*. Chicago, IL: University of Chicago Press.

Bronowski, J., & Mazlish, B. (1962). *The western intellectual tradition*. New York, NY: Harper Perennial.

Bock, K. (1980). *Human nature and history*. New York, NY: Columbia University Press.

Burckhardt, J. (1979). *Reflections on history*. Indianapolis, IN: Liberty Fund.

Burckhardt, J. (1999). *Judgments on history and historians*. Indianapolis, IN: Liberty Fund.

Cameron, R. (1993). A *concise economic history of the world*. New York, NY: Oxford University Press.

Carr, E. (1961). *What is history?*. New York, NY: Vintage Books.

Certeau, M. (1988). *The writing of history*. New York, NY: Columbia University Press.

Collingwood, R. (1946). *The idea of history*. Oxford: Oxford University Press.

Durant, W., & Durant, A. (1963). *The story of civilization*. New York, NY: Simon & Schuster.

Foner, E. (2002). *Who owns history?*. New York, NY: Hill and Wang

Frieden, J. (2007). Will global capitalism fall again?. *Alumni Quarterly Colloquy, Summer*(15). The Graduate School of Arts and Sciences, Harvard University.

Gat, A. (2007). The return of authoritarian great powers. *Foreign Affairs, 86*(4), 59-70.

Hegel, G. (1956). *The philosophy of history (org. 1837)*. New York, NY: Dover Publications, Inc.

Hill, C. (2007). The post-scientific society. *ISSUES in Science and Technology, XXIV*(1), 78-84.

Howard, M. (1991). *Lessons of history*. New Haven and London: Yale University Press.

Huntington, S. (1993). The clash of civilizations. *Foreign Affairs, 72*(3), 22-49.

Knauer, K. (Ed.). (2007). *America: An illustrated history*. New York, NY: TIME Books.

Maddison, A. (2001). *The world economy, a millennial perspective*. Paris: OECD.

von Radke, L. (1935). *Weltgeschichte (World history)*. Hamburg: Hoffman Und Campe.

Raudzens, G. (1999). *Empires, Europe and globalization 1492-1788*. Phoenix Mill, UK: Sutton Publishing.

Scheve, K., & Slaughter, M. (2007). A new deal for globalization. *Foreign Affairs, 86*(4), 34-48.

Schlesinger, A., Jr. (Ed.). (1993). *The almanac of American history*. New York, NY: Barnes & Noble.

Snyder, L. (1999). *Macro-history, a theoretical approach to comparative world history*. Lewiston, NY: The Edwin Meller Press.

Targowski, A. (1982). *Red fascism*. Lawrence, VA: Brunswick Publishing Company.

_____ (1991). Chwilowy koniec historii

(*The momentary end of history*). Warsaw: Nowe Wydawnictwo Polskie.

_____(Ed). (1993). Obrona Polski. (*Defense of Poland*). Warsaw: Bellona.

_____(1995a). Dogonic czas. (*In pursuit of time*). Warsaw: Bellona.

_____(Ed.). (1995b). Wizja Polski. (*Vision of Poland*). Warsaw: Cinderella Books.

_____& Ajnenkiel, A. (Eds.). (2000). Losy Polski i swiata 2000, (*The fate of Poland and the world 2000*). Warsaw: Bellona.

Tilly, C. (1984). *Big structures, large processes, huge comparisons*. New York, NY: Russell Sage.

Section III
The Information
Ecology of Civilization

Chapter IX
The Information Wave of Civilization

INTRODUCTION

This chapter will attempt to analyze the cumulative evolution of labor, intellect (information & knowledge), and politics. In pursuit of this aim, it will analyze the role of information throughout civilization history. Whereas historians reveal the myriad dimensions of social order that remained uncontrollable in the past, modern analysts consciously initiate designs that are not a product of chance—but do so in webs of dispute, ambivalence, and fuzziness of language. There are questions concerning the relevance of history (Henry Ford's famous aphorism was that history is "bunk") and the objectivity of information (to the postmodernist philosophers, there is no such thing). These cast doubt on the use of historical data for predicting the future, and also suggest its limitations.

In this section, we shall analyze the architectural relationships between intellect, politics, and labor in a historical context, in order to understand the relationships, rules, and eventually laws that govern civilization development. Through such a structural understanding of the past, it may be possible to better predict the future of civilization. Even though this may not be optimal, it is at the very least a satisfactory place and role for historians and our institutions.

The architectural approach to a history of civilization is a new layer over quantitative history based on statistical data. In an architectural history of civilization, we seek a "big picture" of "civilization ages and revolutions" to develop some criteria-oriented views of the world and its future predictability. To understand how crises and conflicts of civilization have been driven by technology in recent centuries, such analysis must be undertaken with some optimism about human proactive adaptation, survival, and development. This approach to civilization development should allow humans eventually to "reinvent the future" in a continuous manner. In due course, we should be able to predict the "rate of change" and provide "civilization-bridging solutions" based on original thinking.

In the last several centuries, civilization has been driven by its infrastructures (such as bureaucracy, electrical power, vehicle engines). Therefore, we shall look more at the role of information infrastructure, which secures the vitality of the information ecology. The information ecology (environment) is a holistic, human-centered management of information to control development and operations of info-materiel-energy-oriented processes. The first who applied this term are Bruce W. Hasenyager (1996) and Thomas H.

Davenport (1997), who emphasize people over machines in the role of handling information.

INFORMATION AND CIVILIZATION HISTORY

The history of our Universe has evolved through 13.5 billion years from its beginning. About 4.6 billion years ago, the Earth was formed and shortly afterward started to cool. About 3.8 to 3.5 billion years ago, surface conditions allowed the permanent establishment of life on this planet. The earliest possible signs of life date to roughly 3.85 billion years ago, but establishment are usually held to be marked by the coming of the stromatolites, structures of rock and algae still found in such odd places as Hamelin Pool on the western coast of Australia. Hominids had diverged from apes some ten to six million years ago (*instinct*-driven information-communication); the first humans (two-legged, with large brain and tools and *sound*-driven information-communication), took form around 6-2.5 million years ago in Southeast Africa. *Homo verbalis,* who used language, appeared about 60,000 years ago. This time can mark the beginning of first information-communication systems.

Physicists are obsessed with finding the complete theory of everything, explaining how, why, and where the world was developed (in fact limiting "everything" to the unification of the two present basic approaches to physics, quantum mechanics and general relativity), and information specialists should contribute to this quest too. If not, the complete theory will remain incomplete. Hawking (1988) has accused philosophers of not keeping up with the advance of scientific theories. The same accusation is true for physicists who limit their complete theory to energy only because energy itself is steered by communication and information (however, their true nature is still a puzzle) and vice-versa.

The Death Triangle of Civilization perhaps will be triggered by the Population-Bang IV and Ecology-Bang V in about 2050, and Resources-Bang VI will give problems around 2300-2500. By the year 5,000 A.D., all potential reserves of strategic resources will likely be depleted and it will be the end of the Civilization I, marking the End-Bang VI. Continuing this pessimistic prediction, one event is sure, that within about 4.5 billion years the Sun will stop serving us, and it will be the Final-Bang VII of civilization, as it is illustrated in Figure 9-1.

Man has survived longer than stronger animals because he has had an important advantage: a brain that can process information and communication as more than simple stimulus and response. With a brain, mankind has been able to learn, communicate, and develop a structure of consciousness. At first, probably the *eyes* and *nose* was the most important organ for the archaic, nomadic hunters. Then, about 200,000 years ago, the human information system began "upgrading" human consciousness through emotions and rituals and the *ear* became the most important organ for those hunters. Their ears developed an appreciation for music and dance. That was the first advanced pattern of human cultural behavior.

About 10,000 years ago, consciousness became mythical and two-dimensional, with some appreciation for the natural tempo of events. Mankind started farming, dreaming of a better social order for its members, and creating myth through symbolic imagination and language-driven communication. At this time, the mouth became the most important organ. Around 5,000 B.C., the Egyptian calendar, regulated by the Sun and Moon into 360 days (12 months of 30 days each), became the first organized information system (IS) device that supported man's survival and development. About 2,000 years later, the Sumerians developed writing and organizational patterns for "civilized" cities. About 2,500 B.C., the structure of consciousness became mental and three-dimensional, with a sense of abstract time,

Figure 9-1. Big bangs through the history of time

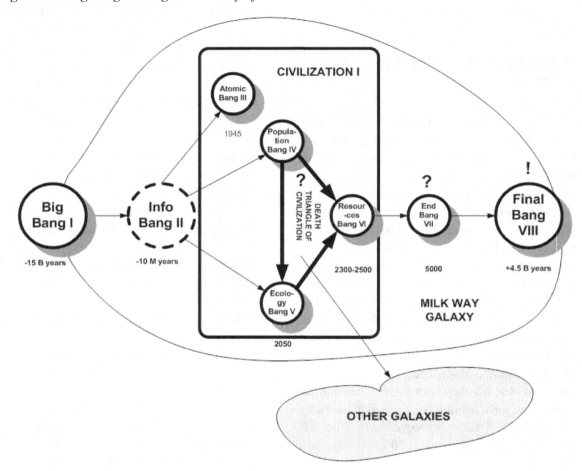

cultural curiosity for science and art, dogma, rules, and laws. The first knowledge centers appeared in Egypt, where written literature lamented on the meaning of life. Egyptians wrote these thoughts on papyri and collected them into the famous Library in Alexandria. The manufacture of objects and the production of food (bread, beer) took place. Thus, the eye again became the most important organ for the awakened man with volition and reflection about himself and the world (Simpson, 1991).

For extended periods of time, the evolution of the Earth was understood as being regulated by a relationship between nature's internal forces such as gravity, quantum mechanics, time, and general relativity. Today, the problem of life on Earth has become a puzzle based upon relationships (information-communication) among people and their level of *cognition*, and reflecting it through *information-knowledge* systems. The first approach is about the physical basis of life, the second one is largely social. There is a lack of a "bridge" between these two realms, which we can call *neural electro-chemical mechanics*.

The tool in achieving this role is *knowledge*, disseminated first by books and now by computers and their networks. Mediated communication has a long story. The invention of the printing press by Johann Gutenberg in 1454 boosted the spread of knowledge. This has become the most significant invention to separate to separate the written from the spoken word. Printing soon became a means of disseminating and intensifying intellectual endeavors. Before Gutenberg, each volume was handwritten, often by monks. In the 15th century, a book was as costly and as rare as jewels.

Before the printing press, scientists would take long trips merely to familiarize themselves with the content of a certain book. The enlightened ruler Charles IV of Luxembourg collected 114 volumes, while the French king Charles V, amassed as many as 900. Then, printing houses began to print hundreds of books. By the year 1500, within 50 years of invention of the German press[1], 30,000 reasonably priced books were in circulation. The satire of Erasmus of Rotterdam appeared during his lifetime in 27 editions. Print was steering thoughts and ideas in millions of people, inspiring them to speed, simplify and strengthen the work of the mind.

The printed alphabet in book form, which was the first "computer terminal," became an absorber and transformer of civilization. New media such as letters and printed books altered the relation between our senses and changed the mental (information processing) process. The print-made split between logic and emotion had become a trauma, which has affected Western civilization ever since (McLuhan, 1962). It created government regulations but it also inspired individualism and opposition to ideology, science, and art. Science and technology began to develop at an accelerated pace. Airplanes, cars, telegraphs, telephones, typewriters, phonographs, movies, radios, televisions, weapons, computers, automation, and telecommunications modernized human life and its story. Human consciousness has become integral and free of the constraint of a need for personal contact, allowing us to enjoy learning, loving, wholeness, and wisdom for the community and ourselves. The consciousness-driven intellect system has now become the most crucial organ, developing a meta-sense. We are

better at understanding than at explaining the purpose and rules of our existence through education and research.

American physicist John Wheeler has formulated the Theory of the Participatory Universe (Wheeler, Buckley, Peat, 1997). In this theory, observers are central to the nature of physical reality and matter is ultimately relegated to the mind. Wheeler sees the Universe as a gigantic "information processing" system with a yet undetermined output, and he has coined the phrase "IT from BIT," meaning every "thing"—a particle, a field of force, or even space-time itself—all is ultimately manifested to us through "bits" of information. John Wheeler has expressed this new approach in particularly graphic terms:

We had this old idea, that there was a universe out there, and here is man, the observer, safely protected from the universe by a six-inch slab of plate glass. Now we learn from the quantum world that even to observe so miniscule an object as an electron we have to shatter that plate glass; we have to reach in there ... So the old word observer simply has to be crossed off the books, and we must put in the new word participator. In this way we've come to realize that the universe is a participatory universe.

The curriculum of the human story, driven by science, technology and informations-communication, is illustrated in Figure 9-2. This model tries to establish some relationships between the political, labor, and intellectual perspectives of the modern history of civilization. This period begins with the Renaissance, so-called for a rebirth of learning following the supposed darkness of the medieval period. Modern times started in 1453 when Constantinople fell to the Ottoman Turks. Many scholars who fled from the Byzantine Empire were fleeing westward for safety. By happenstance, this coincided with the development of printing in Europe (1454), allowing the new ideas to spread rapidly. This boosted the questioning

Figure 9-2. The civilization of the human project-driven by science, technology, and info-communication (bold-faced titles)

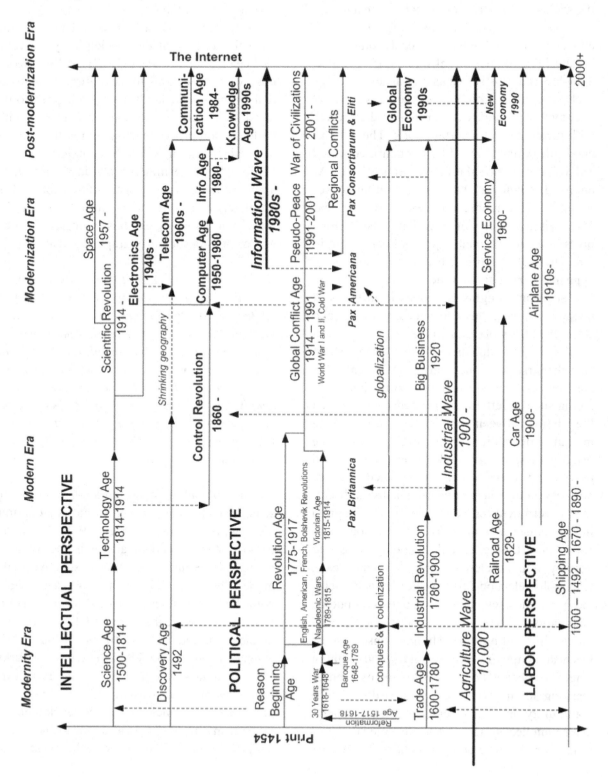

of established ideas regarding religion, art, and science. When scholarship began to develop independently of the church, the human rather than the divine in life and art was emphasized. The well rounded, informed individual (e.g., Leonardo da Vinci) become the ideal. Certain "ages" which influenced the role of information (and vice-versa) will be characterized as follows. Some "Ages" and "Eras" may overlap, since they are not exclusive.

The Modernity Era (1454-1814)

In this era, the transition took place from the Middle Ages to early modernization, which set up the spirit for further acceleration in civilization development. It is important to notice that people born in the 10th to 15th centuries had at their births a life expectancy of 24, provided that they were not among the roughly one in five infants who did not even survive being born (Maddison, 2001). Nowadays in Europe, these figures include a 77-year life expectancy and 7% infant mortality (World Development Report, 2003). This advance was achieved due to the development of the technology of power (beginning about 1000), supporting the organized monopoly of violence pursued by secular and papal governments, as well as administrative innovations sparked by the spread of literacy (by printing), professional competence and bureaucratic routine based on statistics (Levin, 2001). This era led to the creation of the modern states of France (1461), Spain (1479), and England (1485), with institutions based on Europe's ocean transports and favorable to merchant capitalism. The latter also led to the European conquest and colonization of the Far East and America, which can be considered as the first wave of globalization, whose needs triggered the Industrial Revolution (Raudzens, 1999).

The Reason Beginning Age (1558-1775) surveys the turbulent centuries of religious strife and scientific progress from the accession of Elizabeth I of England to the Age of Ideology, and began

the American War for Independence (1775). The Age is also called the Enlightenment of Europe. Here, the first heroes were the publishers, printers, and booksellers who fed the inky stream through which knowledge flowed from mind to mind and from generation to generation. The sciences advanced in logical progression through modern history, mathematics and physics in the 17th century to chemistry in the 18th century, biology in the 19th century, and psychology in the 20th century. The first electronic computers were developed during World War II and applied in reading coded messages, then improved in the next decade for scientific computations. It means that The Age of Reason continues ever since to nowadays and beyond.

The Science Age (1500-1800) begins with the strong improvements in maritime technology in ship design, navigation by compass, the sandglass for measuring time at sea, reliable chronometers, and nautical almanacs. By the end of the 18th century, ships could carry ten times the cargo of a 14th-century Venetian galley. Until the 15th century, European progress in many fields was dependent on transfers of technology from Asia (China) or the Arab world (mathematics), but by the end of the 17th century the technological leadership of Europe in shipping and armaments was apparent. The rise of universities and of such scientists as Copernicus, Erasmus, Bacon, Galileo, Hobbes, Descartes, Petty, Pascal (mechanical, sequential calculator), Leibniz (mechanical, parallel calculator), Huygens, Halley, and Newton led to the creation of intellectual societies. In public life there were improvements in banking, finance, accounting, fiscal management, and corporate governance. The first modern information system for bookkeeping, the double-entry principles of debit-credit, was developed by Leonardo da Vinci's friend Luca Pacioli in the 1480s, later published in (Pacioli, 1494) in Venice to support a growing interstate trade. The system he published included most of the accounting cycle as we know it today. He described the use of journals and ledgers, and warned that a person should not go to sleep at night until the debits equaled the credits! His ledger had accounts for assets (including receivables and inventories), liabilities, capital, income, and expenses—the account categories that are reported on an organization's balance sheet and income statement, respectively. He demonstrated year-end closing entries and proposed that a trial balance be used to prove a balanced ledger. Also, his treatise touches on a wide range of related topics from accounting ethics to cost accounting.

The Revolution Age (1685-1917). The English (1688), American (1775), French Revolutions (1789), and Bolsheviks (1917) were triggered in the Modern Era to expand popular control in society, though, particularly in 17th-century England, the recognized "populace" was still quite a limited group. They were based on an ideology of social progress in the scope of government, ownership, national independence, civil rights, justice for and freedom of an individual, religion, and so forth. These were possible due to contributions provided by the French and American philosophers exercising political and social *knowledge*, which by power of reason contested the status quo of royal absolutism. For the first time in humankind's history, *information* led to a dramatic shift in the well-being of people, who now could be referred to as an *informed citizenry*. Needless to say, the Post Office was created in North America in 1772 to support the delivery of information among citizens. In the American Revolution, 13 of Britain's North American colonies broke away from rule by the mother-country. The third revolution was the French Revolution, which overturned the dictatorship of the French kings and put forward the ideals of "Liberty, Equality, and Fraternity" though the revolutionaries did not keep to them. But ideals remained influential throughout the next century and beyond. The movement of ideas and belief which had been dominant until this time,

the Enlightenment, with its emphasis on reason and natural law, gave place in the social ferment to the Romantic Movement in the arts which favored emotions before reason, and free and individual expression. Romanticism popularized the ideals of the French revolution. The fourth revolution was the Bolsheviks Revolution, which declared the peoples' right to "self-determination." This revolution in fact was the counter-French Revolution, claiming rights for "oppressed." All these revolutions gave the intellectual and practical input to emerging political ideologies.

The Modern Era (1814-1914)
("Mindset" established by the Modernity Era)
During the tumultuous 100 years 1814-1914, Europe spread the Industrial Revolution, which was triggered by invention of the steam engine (1782), the railroad, a factory system, and such new technologies as the telegraph, telephone, and energy based on oil and electricity. It was a "new" age, relatively peaceful with the exceptions of the final consolidations of most of the European nations and small local wars of positioning among colonial powers. The mechanization of human effort led to more free time, which was consumed by growing education and engineering and more leisurely life styles. Eventually, it led to strong scientific progress in the next century. Roads eliminated wilderness and electricity lit homes and minds. The first mechanical *computer* was developed by Charles Babbage in 1832, although it was premature and useful only in simplistic calculations.

The Modern Era of Western civilization in the 19th century glorified rationality. Western societies became modern just as soon as they had succeeded in producing a bourgeoisie that was both numerous and competent enough to become the predominant element in society (Toynbee, 1954). In this era an industrial urban working class arose. A split between rich and poor began to play a significant role in the development of social dynamics. Later, in the 21st century, a similar split in the Information Wave would produce the information-rich and information-poor (*Digital Divide*).

The Control Revolution began in the 19th century, since the factory system was experiencing astonishing increases in capacity but also delays in production and transportation. Therefore, *information-communication technology* was applied to eliminate the bottleneck situations (Shapiro, 1999). Among such technologies one can mention the telegraph (1830s), punch cards (1850s), typewriter (1860s), transatlantic cable (1866), telephone (1876), cash registers (1892), adding machines (1890s), motion pictures (1894), wireless telegraphy (1895), and radio (1905). This revolution provided the foundation for the development of television (1925), computers (1950s), and their networks (1960s), and the Internet (1990s), which triggered the Information Wave.

The Modernization Era (1914-1990s)
(Wide applications of the Modern Era's solutions)
Vast technological innovations of the 19th century were applied on a large scale. It occurred when businesses and institutions invested in capital equipment to compete effectively in productivity, innovations, profitability, and market share. Germany wanted to replace *Pax Britannica* by *Pax Germanica* twice in the 20th century, waging two world wars (1914-1918 and 1939-1945), which killed at least 30 million people in Europe alone. These wars gave a strong boost to civilization development at least in technology and infrastructure. In terms of values, the period was a tragic regression.

The Electronics Age (1940s-). Two major developments occurred, triggered independently during the late 1940s. One was the development of the programmable electronic computer (ENIAC) in the U.S. in 1946. The second was the invention of the transistor in 1947. Subsequent improvements in solid-state physics led to the present-day silicon

chip with its large-scale integrated circuits. A whole variety of products incorporating microprocessors are now widely available. There are chip-controlled automatic machine tools for industry and many types of new office equipment, such as sophisticated photocopiers, which have computer chips inside. Among better known microprocessor-based consumer goods one can mention electronic calculators, digital watches, electronic toys, TV games, larger consumer durables like TV itself, washing machines, music centers, and video-cassette recorders containing computer chips. There are chip-based thermometers and weighing machines, chip-controlled warehouses, multi-story car parks, even an "electronic waiter" for direct-dialing one's order to a restaurant's kitchen. Computer chips have already invaded the supermarkets in the form of "point-of-sale" terminals and the Universal Product Code. They have invaded labor-intensive banks (Electronic Fund Transfer), people's homes (home computers), and the family car (electronic ignition, timing, and dashboard navigation instrumentation). There are even plans to invade the female bra—a chip will predict a woman's "safe" and "unsafe" periods by monitoring temperature variations from its strategic position inside the bra.

The Computer Age (1950s-1980s). In the 1950s, the first commercially available computers (Univac I and IBM 650, 701, 7000) were applied in data processing and scientific computing. Within the next three decades, mainframe computers got some new competition in the form of so-called minicomputers (PDP 8-1963) and microcomputers (Apple II-1977 and IBM PC-1981), each of which became an instant success in computing by the general public. When the World Wide Web was born in 1990 (designed by Tim Bernes-Lee at the CERN, the high-energy physics laboratory in Geneva, Switzerland), the Internet became more useful for public computing, which took off after the very user-friendly browsers MOSAIC and

Netscape (designed by Marc Anderseen and Eric Bina) were developed by the end of the 1990s. The investment in information technology reached about 3 trillion dollars in the 1990s, radically improving productivity in offices and shop-floors. However, at this age, most users learned "how to compute" rather than "what to compute" and were struggling to apply "DOS" or "Windows" to operate those computers.

The Information Age (1980s-). In the 1980s-1990s, information technology created an appetite for user-friendly computers and a need for customized, relevant information and information services. At the corporate level in the 2000s, a Management Information System (MIS) is expanding into an Executive Information System (EIS), and legacy applications are reengineered into Enterprise-wide Systems, integrating business, engineering, operations and inter-company information systems. E-commerce is taking off in the 2000s, along with e-banking and telecommuting to work. Logging into a computer no longer poses any great challenge for most users. Rather, the challenge that is replacing "how to compute?" is the challenge of "what to compute?" Users and managers want to get the right information at the right time, so as to be informed members rather than merely "clients" or "victims" of the surrounding information infrastructure. Such users look for competitive advantages, benefits, or negative impacts upon underlined processes or issues.

The Knowledge Age (1990s-). In the classic economy, the sources of wealth included land, labor, and capital. For 200 years, manufacturing facilities have brought prosperity to firms and their shareholders. Now, another engine of wealth is at work. It is science, technology, creativity, innovations, skills, and information, and it can be summarized in one word: knowledge. Knowledge creates an awareness based on scientific facts, rules, laws, coherent inferences, and well-defined methods. Knowledge provides a point of reference, a standard for our way of analyzing data, information, and concepts. Knowledge serves as a filter for making wise choices. In industries and services, most companies triumph by developing, redefining, appreciating, and rediscovering knowledge. Knowledge is a unifying process of civilization and has a global dimension.

There is a great pool of knowledge within our civilization that can be utilized. There are about 2,000 world-class research centers, 3.5 million scientists and engineers worldwide, about 1,000 world-class universities, about 4 million teachers (Kurian, 1984) and 1,000 multinational corporations, including about 100 stateless corporations. This knowledge pool is filled with a large number of international contributors, offering unexpected solutions to problems (e.g., a biological chip inserted into a fish to monitor its freshness). Contemporary knowledge is migratory and does not know or accept borders.

Why has the knowledge pool expanded? This is answered by the Computer Age and Information Age. Here, data is pre-processed into information in such a manner that new concepts, theories, and solutions can be formulated much more easily than in the past. Even the automation of inference can be offered through computer-based expert systems. These systems are based on scientific facts and rules (knowledge). New products such as smart cars with embedded knowledge are easier to drive and last longer.

The computer-supported creation of knowledge is needed by civilization in order to optimize and prolong its existence.

The Telecommunication Age (1960s). On May 24, 1844, Samuel Morse sent his first public message over a telegraph line between Washington and Baltimore, and through that simple act, ushered in the Telecommunication Age. Barely ten years later, telegraphy was available as a service to the general public. In those days, however, telegraph lines did not cross national borders. Because each country used a different system, messages had to be transcribed, translated and handed over at frontiers, then re-transmitted over the telegraph network of the neighboring country. Following the patenting of the telephone in 1876 and the subsequent expansion of telephony, the International Telegraph Union began in 1885 to draw up international legislation governing telephony.

In 1957, Sputnik-1 was launched by the Soviets, beginning the Space Age. In 1963, the first geostationary communications satellite (Syncom-1) was put into orbit following the suggestion, made by the writer Arthur C. Clarke in 1945, that satellites could be used for the transmission of information. Ever since, thousands of satellites have been launched and we now share the global economy, global shocks, global tragedies, global responses, and global parties that have transformed us into the Electronic Global Village. Whole clusters of people that have been neglected can be included in the mainstream of civilization. This, no doubt, is a positive and promising side of telecommunications. When AT&T was deregulated in 1984, telecommunication services began to be less expensive and more affordable. This led to the formation of many telecom companies and inventions, including e-mail and fax (1980) and mobile phones (1990), and of course the unlimited use of the Internet via either fiber optic or wireless lines. As a result of it, "distance is dead" (Cairncross, 1997) within network nations and net-citizens.

The Communication Age (1984). In this age all users are connected by computer networks and are "power users," since they have great opportunities for contacts and businesses. They can maximize individual choices; create more cooperation and win-win outcomes in human interactions. Some authors think that in the future an amalgam of ad hoc partnership with people combining their experiences to govern themselves as equals will be developed. They even predict that these private partnerships will eventually replace the nation-

state (Mann, 1998). The author thinks that this may happen, but questions the rationality of such a move. The more impressive side of this age is that persons begin sending information literally at the speed of light. The content of such information transfers may or may not be more enriched, but its delivery is revolutionary. Consequently, the lead time of decision-making and action becomes instant, at the same time removing intermediaries, and makes the "distance" shorter.

The Internet (1972-). The development of a universal telecommunication network is of great importance for politics and civilization. The Internet is a product of the Cold War, when in 1972 it reached its first phase of development, connecting 15 centers within the pilot system of the ARPANET (Figure 9-3). At the same time, behind the Iron Curtain, the concept of the INFOSTRADA was launched, a spin on the Italian word *La Strada*, meaning highway. The Polish INFOSTRADA was planned to transform the Polish uninformed into an informed society within the Communistic regime. Already in 1973, three nodes Gdansk–Warsaw–Katowice had been interconnected via Singer ten computers within a "packet switching" network[2]. However, while ARPANET was designed to connect the super-computers of scientific centers, INFOSTRADA was planned to support a flow of economic-social information among main organizations and citizens. Within a short period of time, the Communistic authority determined that INFOSTRADA would lead to an uncontrollable flow of information, and so closed the project and ostracized its leaders, including the author.

Of course, the INFOSTRADA project was not unknown to the American intelligence community, since it was widely publicized in the Polish press. At that time, a young congressman, Albert Gore, a member of the Congressional Intelligence Committee, was informed about the Polish project. When he became the American vice-president, he admitted in the December 1995 issue of WIRED

Figure 9-3. Relationships among civilization perspectives in respect to the Internet development

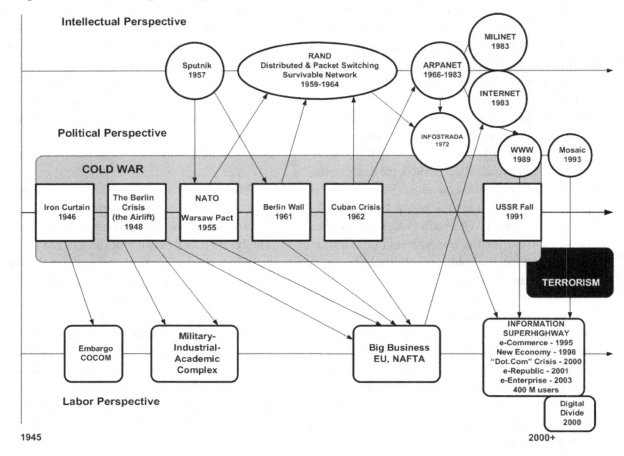

magazine that his idea of the Information Super-highway was "stolen" from "somewhere" (Hellman, 1995). This idea soon became the leading concept for the development of all sorts of information infrastructures, triggering the emergence of the so-called New Economy both in the U.S. and in the "new" global world.

The Internet, at the global scale, supports the free flow of information-communication and is positive for the spread of democracy and negative for political or theocratic dictatorships. These types of dictatorships filter the information-communication flow on their servers. Such attempts are reminiscent of the Pony Express's strategy of introducing faster horses in response to the emergence of the telegraph. (It did not work.) Of course, the Internet also enables the dissemination of criminal information-communications, including those among terrorists. The issue of practical application of Internet ethics is a hot topic among many societies. For example, in Russia, e-commerce cannot be applied due to dishonest practices among all involved parties, including organized crime.

Figure 9-3 illustrates the relationships among intellectual, political and labor revolutions. This model proves how these relationships are important for each type of revolution development.

Figure 9-4. The Internet cathedral

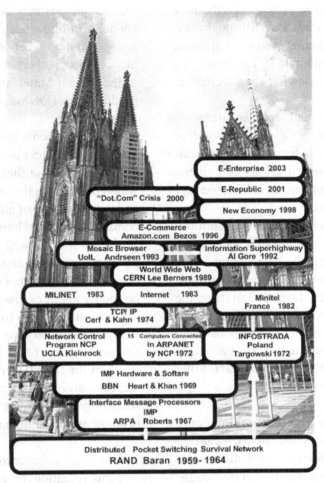

The civilization consequences of the Internet are important, since the use of the Internet requires access to a computer and an Internet Service Provider (ISP), which can only be afforded by people with resources. Hence, the digital divide issue takes place not only in underdeveloped countries but in developed ones too. Nowadays, there are 1 billion people in the world with a password to a computer net and five billion deprived, without such a password. This leads towards a bifurcation of civilization and all of the negative consequences and externalities of yet another set of haves and have-nots. One can say that the Internet accelerates the development of developed nations and relatively slows down the development of underdeveloped nations, notwithstanding that many civilization positives such as education and training can be accelerated by the Internet in those less favored nations.

Systems of the Internet's type are the outcomes of many peoples' effort, similar to a multi-century construction of a cathedral as every new builder adds a new brick and says: "I built the cathedral" (Hughes, 1998, p. 274). The Internet cathedral is shown in Figure 9-4.

New Economy. After World War II, the introduction of innovations through mass production and consumption has changed industrial production and marketing systems. In the new economy innovations are introduced through mass customization and marketing systems that create demand rather than respond to it. This emerging new economy has the following characteristics:

1. Intangible products and services – are "soft" rather than "hard." They are composed of information, knowledge, copyrights, relationships, telecommunications, computers, software, entertainment, securities, security systems, and so forth.
2. Networking and communicating – Communication is the foundation of a society, but more than that, it is the basic factor in the evolution of mankind. Mediated communication networks have developed an economic sector that is transforming other sectors to be more viable, flexible, and responsive.
3. Global reach – Businesses are becoming increasingly global. Yet nations and trading blocks seem to be polarizing.

Three-quarters of the American workforce are now employed in service-related fields, including those services mostly oriented toward information creation and handling. For example, *Wired* magazine, the mouthpiece of the Information Revolution, is located in the middle of an old-fashioned downtown city, and in one year turns 8 million pounds of dried tree pulp (this is enough to fill 48 railway cars) and 330,000 pounds of brightly colored ink into hard copies of the magazine.

The advantages of a new economy speak to those individuals and organizations, which are able to leverage capabilities of new information-communication technologies to transform businesses and invent business practices, not merrily rearrange old ones. A new economy brings also new problems, particularly in the sphere of employment and pay. Three-quarters of the American workforce is now employed in service but a substantial portion of these are in low-paying, dead-end jobs. "Competitiveness" is the tune of this new economy without borders, and the winning strategies involve "downsizing" and "outsourcing" of both production and services (desk help and other). About one-third of the jobs in the United States are at risk to the growing productivity of low-wage workers in China, India, Mexico, Indonesia, Russia and elsewhere, who are electronically connected with management and distribution centers in developed countries.

One can argue that the capitalistic journey, which began with the commodification of goods and the ownership of property, is ending with the commodification of human time and experience. In the future, we will purchase enlightenment and play, grooming and grace, and everything in between. The business of business, therefore, is no longer about exchanging property but rather about buying access to one's very existence in small commercial time segments. In the Age of Communication (Access), Rifkin (2000) asks, "will any time be left for relationships of a noncommercial nature?" And "Can civilization survive when only the commercial sphere remains as the primary arbiter of human life?"

The Postmodernization Era (1990-).
Modernization of civilization, particularly of Western civilization in the 20th century, led through three World Wars (I, II, Cold War) and the Great Depression, which required enormous progress in technology and infrastructure. Eventually, at least Western civilization has been modernized and some other particular civilizations have been partially or fully "westernized," according to their will and resources. Modernization was led by such values as rationality, authority, technology, and science, which are characteristic for the Industrial Wave. As a result, Western civilization achieved a point of saturation (Targowski, 2004) and expanded both externally (Afghanistan, Iraq) and internally by rejection of over-reaching westernization and proclaiming post-modernism. The latter is seen as a product of the Information

Wave, which creates new values and life styles with greater tolerance for ethics, cultural and sexual diversity, and individual choices concerning the kind of life one wants to lead (Inglehart, 1997). Habermas (1984; 1987) also is not satisfied with modernization's effects and thinks that it is an unfinished project. Although Western-oriented industrialization is responsible for packed highways and banal TV sitcoms, it has also been the root of an extended life span and an increased focus on the well-being of humans. The transformation from modernization to post-modernization means shifts, from maximizing economic growth to maximizing subjective well-being, from achievement motivation to post-materialism, and from rational-legal authority to a de-emphasis of both legal and religious authority (Inglehart, 1997).

These shifts are results of huge improvements caused by the influence of Western civilization, which can afford such advances of life sense. Certainly, other developing civilizations still look for the maximization of economic growth. Perhaps even the mainstream of Western civilization, whose middle class is in decline at the dawn of the 21st century due to offshore outsourcing of jobs, may not like new values. Needless to say, these new values are mostly liked by better off and better *informed* citizens, who may count for 5%-10% of Western population, certainly coming from the elite and academic circles. Furthermore, the de-emphasis of legal and religious authority values is caused by the fact that people possess better *knowledge*, which opens their eyes to some sorts of manipulations by those authorities.

THE CONTROL REVOLUTION IN THE 19TH AND 20TH CENTURIES

To say that the advanced, industrial world is rapidly becoming an information society may already be a cliché. In the United States, Canada, Western Europe, and Japan, the majority of the labor force now works in the information sector and wealth comes increasingly from information goods such as computers, software, telecommunication services. For the economies of developed countries, the processing and handling of information has begun to overshadow the processing of matter and energy.

Until the Information Wave, the processing of information ran literally at a human pace within a bureaucratic system. Since the purpose of the Industrial Wave was to speed up society's entire materiel-processing factory system, it was necessary in order to do so to apply an effective control system, either manual or mechanized by office and punch-card machines.

The Information Society, as Beniger (1986) concluded, is not so much the result of any recent social change as of increases which began more than a century ago in the speed of materiel and energy processing. Microprocessors and information-communication technologies, contrary to currently fashionable opinion, are not new forces only recently unleashed upon an unprepared society. They are merely the latest installment in the continuing development of the Control Revolution. This explains why the first examples of information technology, such as Babbage's Analytical Engine (1832), the telegraph (1844), the typewriter (1860s), the transatlantic cable for a telegraph (1866), the telephone (1876), wireless telegraphy (1895), and the magnetic tape recording (1899) were developed beginning with the first signs of a control crisis in the middle 19th century.

The transformation of an economic system from extraction and agriculture (Agricultural Wave) into production, distribution and consumption (Industrial Wave) was achieved through the advancements in control systems. They were needed since the speed and volume of demanded goods exceeded the current capacity of the existing infrastructure. The signs of this crisis are presented in Table 9-1.

It is interesting to mention that one of the richest men of this era was the industrialist Andrew

Table 9-1. Signs of a control crisis in the industrial wave in the 19th century

Economic Sector	Symptoms of Control Crisis	Solutions
PRODUCTION	Slow flow of parts	Improved a factory layout to minimize bottlenecks Cost control Bureaucracy-office workers specialization in data-oriented routines
DISTRIBUTION	Slow wholesalers	Hierarchy of professional managers
TRANSPORTATION	Delayed trains and unsafe travel	Telegraph-oriented communication for a centralized traffic control. Formalized procedures and statistics of operations
CONSUMPTION	Demand greater than supply	Market research Weekly trade papers Advertising agencies

Carnegie (1835-1919), who began his professional career as an information man: operating a telegraph and fixing traffic problems of the Pennsylvania Railroad Co. He was doing his work so well that he was noticed by his boss, who later lent him seed money to open a small business, which eventually led to the development of the U.S. Steel Co., the foundation of the American Industrial Wave.

The following examples of applied information technologies in the 19th century have been the solutions to improve the transition from the Agricultural Wave to the Industrial Wave, particularly developed within Western civilization[3].

The factory system required one or more control systems. Among the earliest information control systems one can mention:

- Pre-programmed, open-loop controllers in the Jacquard loom (1801)
- Integration of production within a *factory system* (1820s-1830s)
- Modern accounting techniques (1850s-1860s)
- Professional managers (1870s)
- Bureaucracy (Weber's term created in 1890s)

Mass-produced goods demanded similar innovations in information-driven control of distribution and transportation:

- Baltimore – Washington D.C. railroad linked by telegraph (1860s)
- Department store, chain store, and wholesale jobber (1860s)
- Monitoring of inventory movement "stock turn" (1870)
- Mail order house (1870)
- Punch-card machines (1884, Hollerith)
- Commercialization of telephone (1880s)
- Long-distance telephone (1890s)

The distribution and sale of mass-produced products required inventions in controlling the marketplace through mass-communication of marketing materiel:

- Powered printing of 2,500 pages per hour (1829, Germany)
- Montgomery Ward mailed throughout the continent a 540-page catalog listing about 24,000 products (1887)
- Sears and Roebuck's mailed catalog reached 1 million copies in 1904

The Control Revolution intensified through the 20th century, when such "soft" sciences of economy and management contributed with new methods of optimal decision-making aiming at the state level as well as at the organization units of the defense and private sectors:

- "Scientific management" (1911, Taylor)
- Modern assembly line (1914, Ford)
- Statistical quality control (1929)
- Central planning (1920s, Soviet Union)
- Fiscal policies (1920s, Keynes, in England)
- *R.U.R Rossum's Universal Robots, (Thinking Robot)* a play written in 1921 by Carl Capek, in Czechoslovakia
- National income accounts (1933, in the U.S.)
- Econometrics (1930s, Frisch, in Norway)
- Input-output analysis (1936, Leontief, in the U.S.)
- Linear programming (1930s, Koopmans in the U.S. and Bogdanowicz in the USSR)
- Statistical decision theory (1930, Shewart, in the U.S.)
- Operations research (World War II, McNamara, in the U.S.)
- General system theory (1945-1951, Bertalanfy, in the U.S.)
- Cybernetics (1949, Wiener, in the U.S.)
- System analysis (1955, Hitch, in the U.S.)
- System engineering (1960s, US-TRM)
- Production information control system (1960s, US-IBM)
- Project management by PERT (1961, Bendix, in the U.S.)
- Management by objectives (1970s, in the U.S.)
- Management information systems (1970s, in the U.S.)
- Infostrada (1972, in Poland)
- Information superhighway (1980s, in the U.S.)
- Computer integrated manufacturing (1980s, in the U.S.)
- Information warfare systems (1991, in the U.S.)
- Telecity (1990s, in the U.S.)
- America On Line (1990s, in the U.S.)
- Enterprise Resource Planning (1990s, in the U.S. and Germany)
- Balance scorecard (1990s, in the U.S.)
- Global positioning system (1990s, in the U.S.)
- Enterprise information systems (2000s, in the U.S.)
- Mobile interactive travel navigation systems (2000s, in the U.S.)

To support the application of these control techniques, the following information technologies were developed:

- Radio (1906, in the U.S.)
- Television (1923, in the U.S.)
- Nielsen's audiometer monitoring of broadcast audience (1935, in the U.S.)
- Gallup poll (1935, in the U.S.)
- Digital processing of signals (1935, Atanasoff, in the U.S.)
- Binary digits (BIT 0,1) (1937, Shannon, in the U.S.)
- Turing machine (1937, Turing, in Great Britain)
- Relay computer (1938, Bell-Stiblitz, in the U.S.)
- Digital computer (1941, Zuse, in Germany)
- MARK I – relay computer (1944, Aiken, in the U.S.)
- ENIAC – electronic computer (1946, Eckert, Mauchley, Goldstein, in the U.S.)
- UNIVAC I – first commercial computer (1951, in the U.S.)
- IBM 1400 – popular family of computers in data processing (1960s, in the U.S.)

- IBM 360 – popular family of computers family in management information systems (1960s-70s, in the U.S.
- Supercomputers to control scientific computations (weather, defense) (1970s, in the U.S.)
- LAN-Alohanet computer network (1971, in the U.S.)
- Artificial intelligence-driven smart systems (1975, in the U.S.)
- Microcomputer Apple II (1977, Wozniak and Jobs, in the U.S.)
- Most popular personal computer (1981, IBM, in the U.S.)
- Information warfare, precision-targeting (1991, in the U.S.)
- Computer servers (1992, in the U.S.)
- Rapidly expanding telecommunication services (1990s, in the U.S.)
- The booming Internet (1990s, World)

From the mid 1950s, it became apparent that energy and material-based industries were backward and waning in industrial nations. In the United States, for example, while the labor force grew by 21% between 1965 and 1974, textile employment rose by only 6% and employment in iron and steel actually dropped 10%. Similar patterns were evident in Western Europe, Czechoslovakia, Poland, Hungary and Japan. As these old-fashioned industries began to be transferred to so-called "new emerging markets" where labor was cheaper and technology less advanced, the social influence of Western civilization also began to die out and a set of dynamic new, information-based industries took a leading role in the marketplace (Toffler, 1980).

As the economy, based on the Industrial Wave, languished, the industries and regions based on the Information Wave thrived. In the United States, the shift from the Second to the Third Wave took place sometime in the middle 1950s. Old regions like the Merrimack Valley in New England sank into the status of "depressed area" while places like "Route 128" outside of Boston or "Silicon Valley" in California zoomed into prominence. Their suburban homes filled with specialists in solid-state physics, systems engineering, artificial intelligence, and polymer chemistry. The backbone industry of the Third Wave is the electronics and computer industry, with about $500 billion annual sales in the 1990s, which makes it the world's fourth largest industry, after auto, steel, and chemicals.

THE LIMITS OF GROWTH AND THE DECLINE OF THE INDUSTRIAL WAVE

The negative impact of the Industrial Wave on civilization was the subject of assessment by The Club of Rome, which asked MIT scientists to make a report on this issue. A team led by future nobel laureate Dennis L. Meadows published a book called *The Limits to Growth*, which was a best-seller with 9 million copies sold in 29 languages. The book created a furor. The combination of the computer simulations, MIT, and The Club of Rome pronouncing upon humanity's future had an irresistible dramatic appeal. The book was interpreted as a prediction of doom, but if it was a prediction at all, it was not about a preordained future. It was about a choice. It contained a warning, to be sure, but also a message of promise. Here are three summary conclusions:

1. If the present growth trend in world population, industrialization, pollution, food production, and resource depletion continues unchanged, the limits to growth on this planet will be reached sometime within the next 100 years. The most probable result will be a sudden and uncontrollable decline in both population and industrial capacity.
2. It is possible to alter these growth trends and to establish a condition of ecological and economic stability far into the future.

200

The state of global equilibrium could be designed so that the basic material needs of each person on Earth are satisfied and each person has an equal opportunity to realize his or her individual potential.

3. If the world's people decide to strive for this second outcome rather than the first, the sooner they begin working to attain it, the greater will be their chances of success.

Exactly 20 years later, the same authors published a book called *Beyond the Limits*, in which they stated that the human world is already beyond its limits. The present way of doing things is unsustainable. The future, to be viable at all, must be one of drawing back, drawing down, and healing. Poverty cannot be ended by indefinite materiel growth (interpreted as the Industrial Wave); it will have to be addressed while the material economy contracts. The authors stated:

- Human use of many essential resources and generation of many kinds of pollution have already surpassed rates that are physically sustainable. Without significant reductions in materiel and energy flows, there will be in the coming decades an uncontrolled decline in per capita food output, energy use, and industrial pollution.
- This decline is not inevitable. To avoid it two changes are necessary. The first is a comprehensive revision of policies and practices that perpetuate growth in materiel consumption and in pollution. The second is a rapid, drastic increase in the efficiency with which materials and energy are used.
- A sustainable society is still technically and economically possible. It would be much more desirable than a society that tries to solve its problems by constant expansion. The transition to a sustainable society requires a careful balance between long-term and short-term goals and an emphasis on sufficiency, equity, and quality of life rather than on quantity of output. It requires more than productivity and more than technology; it requires maturity, compassion, and wisdom.

This is a conditional warning, not a dire prediction. It offers a living choice, not a death sentence. The idea of limits, sustainability, equity, and efficiency are not barriers, obstacles, and threats. They are guides to a new world. Sustainability, not better weapons or struggle for power or materiel accumulation is the ultimate challenge to the energy and creativity of the human race.

In the 20 years since the publication of *Limits of Growth*, many people, politicians, and business executives have understood the message. The consumption of energy and materiel per capita is declining and the issue of efficiency is discussed daily in business and government in some countries, particularly in Scandinavia. This message contributes to the decline of the Industrial Wave and the search for a new social control system. As we will see later, the Information Wave is a partial and optimistic answer to this quest.

THE RISE OF THE INFORMATION WAVE

Most of the writing on civilization waves was done by Alvin Toffler (1980) who recognized the three waves, First Wave (Agricultural Wave), Second Wave (Industrial Wave) and the Third Wave (Information Wave). However, there are more waves of development of humankind, possibly five in total (Figure 9-5):

0. Settlers' Wave (9,000 B.C. - 7,000 B.C.)
I. Agricultural Wave (7,000 B.C. ff.)
II. Industrial Wave (1814 A.D. ff.)
III. Information Wave (1980 A.D. ff.)
IV. Globalization Wave (1990 A.D. ff.)

Figure 9-5. Civilization waves before the 2000s

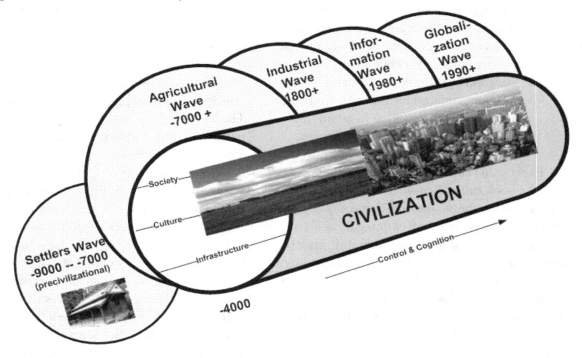

The Zero Wave, the Settlers' Wave, transformed hunters and farmers into settlers, who organized the first villages in the Middle East and stabilized their lives around animal domestication and food production. After 5,000 years of wealth accumulation, this led to the rise of the first civilization about 4,000 B.C. It is interesting to notice that after 9,000 years (7,000 B.C. to 2,000 A.D.), mankind is again on the move, becoming a "global hunter" for profit or jobs, while the Fourth Wave, globalization, takes off in the 1990s through the global infrastructures of information-communication and transportation.

The First Wave – the Agricultural Wave – began about 7,000 B.C. and will remain active as long as food is needed, which means that it will be active as long as humankind exists. The Second Wave, the Industrial Wave, is about 200 years old. It minimized human physical effort

through mechanization and released free time for education, which led to the Scientific Revolution and the invention of aircraft and computers. The latter is leading to the Third Wave, the Information Wave, and its magic tool, the Internet. The airplane and Internet increase human global mobility, which triggers the Fourth Wave, the Globalization Wave.

The civilization waves are shown in Figure 9-4. Each wave has its own set of civilization tools, which primarily support control processes by elites over their clients. The main control solutions for each wave are shown in this figure. It is important to notice that none of these waves replaces the wave that precedes it. For example, information cannot replace food, steel or plastic; it can only improve their creation and utilization.

Individual civilization waves are not displaced, except that the Settlers' Wave was de facto pre-civilized. Perhaps each new wave takes the leadership in civilization development and intercepts the best talent to work for it. Furthermore, each wave perpetuates other waves, as is shown on a model in Figure 9-5. Current job trends, which focus on such things as the outsourcing of computing to India, contradict earlier assessments that the millennial American workforce would be heavily focused in computing. In the 2000s, it is even possible to outsource computer programming to India, thousands of miles away from a company's headquarters.

As the Industrial Wave declines and the Control Revolution rises, the Information Wave rises as well. Much of the concept of the Information Wave as the Information Society draws from the theory of *post-industrialism* advanced by Daniel Bell (1976). Bell's concept of post-industrial society has five dimensions:

1. There is a shift from a goods-producing economy to a service-producing one.
2. There is an increase in size and influence of the classes of professional workers.
3. The post-industrial society is organized around theoretical knowledge.
4. A critical aim is the management of technological growth.
5. There is an emphasis on the development of methods of intellectual technology.

Figure 9-6. The convergence of multimedia in the infohighway

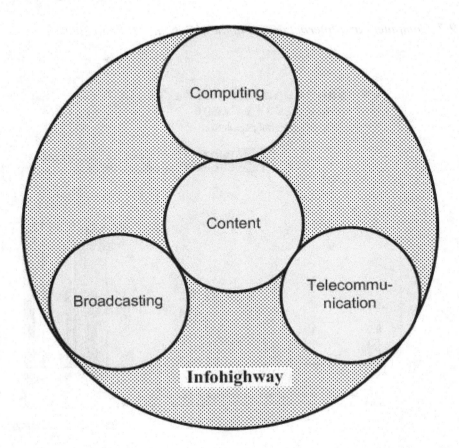

Intelligent technology under the form of global computer networks dramatically expands the power of the brain into hyper-intelligence. With appropriate control programming, a network becomes a sensitive device, not only as a physical but also as an economic, social, and political one.

The spending on information-communication technology (ICT, a core of "intellectual technology") in the U.S. in the scope of equipment was in a range of $845 billion in 1997, growing at an average rate of 12.3% a year, which can be approximated for the year 2000 to be $1 trillion[4]. If one includes information management (on the application side), it could be up to $2 trillion, which is about 16% of GDP, equal to current spending on healthcare (World Bank, 2007)!

A new approach to transmitting information (in a general sense) is represented by the concept of the information superhighway (infohighway)[5], which is emerging from the convergence of the following media (Figure 9-6):

- *Content* (entertainment, publishing, education, e-commerce, travel, marketing, information systems, etc.)
- *Computing* (computers, software, services of information systems, end-user computing, etc.)
- *Telecommunication* (telephony, cable, satellite, wireless as information-communication services)
- *Broadcasting* (television, radio).

The infohighway certainly is no longer merely a cute aphorism. It has become an important tool in many of our professional lives. The speed and

Figure 9-7. Computers and Internet access in the U.S. home: 1984 to 2000

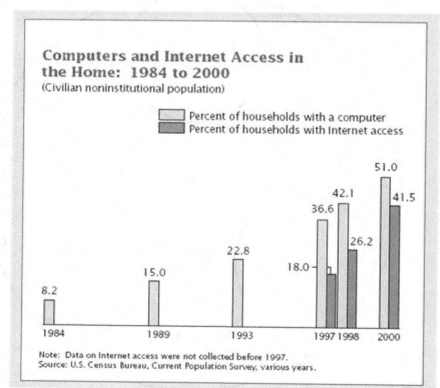

immediacy with which it can deliver valuable *information* and images is mind-boggling. Suddenly, e-commerce is no longer just an oblique concept, but rather the accepted way that we all shall be doing business in the not-so-distant future.

In August 2000, 54 million households in the U.S., or 51%, had one or more computers at home, with 41% having access to the Internet, as is shown in Figure 9-7. These figures mean that more than 100 million people in the U.S. use the Internet at home in the second part of the year 2000.

The Information Wave in Western-West civilization is becoming a mature endeavor. It has impact on work transformation, where *information (symbolic) workers* (1990: 45% of jobs in the U.S.) passed the number of *in-person service workers* (1990: 35% of jobs in the U.S.) and *routine production/service workers* (1990: 25% of jobs in the U.S.) (Reich, 1992).

The formal education of information (symbolic) workers entails refining four basic skills: abstraction, systemic thinking, experimentation, and collaboration. In the Information Wave, more people are involved in information and communication than in mining, agriculture, culture and manufacturing combined. Unlike finite industrial resources such as oil, ore, and iron, there is an inexhaustible supply of knowledge, concepts and ideas as people gain their education.

The Information Wave impacts people and organizations in almost every country and also provides the information infrastructure for the development of global civilization, where "distance" is dead since communication among remote corners of the world is instant for business or private exchanges. This trend triggered the new economy, whose products/services are "soft" and delivered immediately anywhere and anytime.

Figure 9-8. The role of control in the evolution of civilization waves

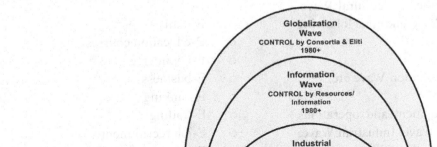

A new economy brings also new problems, particularly in the sphere of employment and pay. Three-quarters of the American workforce is now employed in service but a substantial portion of these are in low-paying, dead-end jobs.

THE MISSION, GOALS, STRATEGY, AND ARCHITECTURE OF THE INFORMATION WAVE

The 19th century eliminated wilderness through railroads. The 20th century developed science and technology that improved the well-being of many and pushed the planet to its limit resources-wise. The 21st century perhaps will implement the Information Wave across all particular civilizations to improve knowledge-based critical decisions about social life in the situation of limited resources.

The *mission* of the Information Wave is:

To knowledgeably and wisely *control* development and operations of the Agricultural Wave, Industrial Wave, Global Wave, and other following ones (Figure 9-8).

The *goals* of the Information Wave are:

1. To *optimize* development and operations of the Agricultural Wave, Industrial Wave, Global Wave, and the other following ones in order to minimize the use of resources and ecology and to increase a citizen's choices and its quality of life.
2. To sustain the development of human *cognition* in order to make conscious and wise decisions about: the sense of human possibility, life, education, health, politics, defense, business, entertainment and leisure time.

The *strategy* of the Information Wave is:

To develop and apply information-communication technology in *control systems* in a rational and human manner.

These aims should be applied at all levels of civilization, including national and local governments, schools and colleges, business and other organizations, homes, and individuals.

The general architecture and control role of the Information Wave, shown in Figure 9-9, is composed of the following metaphoric elements:

*   *Info-factories*, which generate information and seek new information, among them the following:

    o   Virtual enterprises
    o   Virtual schools and colleges
    o   Virtual communities
    o   Online governments
    o   Electronic republic

*   *Info-malls*, which provide the following services:

    o   E-mail
    o   E-education courses
    o   E-commerce
    o   E-business
    o   E-banking
    o   E-trading
    o   E-job recruitment
    o   E-information services (news, weather, sports)
    o   E-research
    o   E-publishing
    o   E-entertainment
    o   E-telephony

*   *Info-highways*, which transmit information content through information-communication services, such as:

    o   LAN – Local Area Networks
    o   MAN – Metropolitan Area Networks

- o WAN – Wide Area Networks
- o GAN – Global Area Networks
- o VAN – Value Area Networks
- o The Internet
- o TV and radio broadcasting

- *Cyberspace*, which is a digital information-based space, that is, a dispersed, infinite constellation of

- o digital files
- o databases
- o home pages
- o bulletin boards
- o directories
- o menus

where humans with a password interactively navigate in order to create, update, exchange, and retrieve information.

- *Cybernauts* (netizens), who are informed tele-computer users with a password to access billions of information tidbits and do everything online from shopping and learning to working and resting. Cybernauts can be "electronic immigrants" who telecommute to work over great distances.

The Information Wave is not just a matter of technology and economics. It involves morality, culture and ideas as well as institutions and political structure. It implies, in short, a true transformation of human affairs (Toffler & Toffler, 1994).

Figure 9-9. The general architecture and control role of the information wave

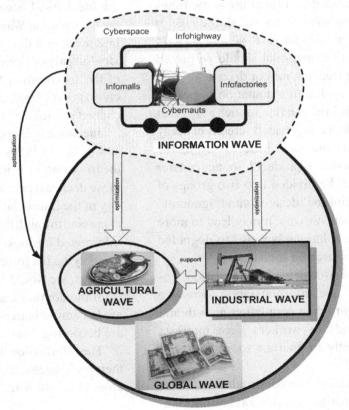

On the other hand, the unwise application of the Information Wave may be harmful for humans. Let us pose the following questions for civilization decision-makers:

1. Is it wise to automate everything that is possible or is it better to leave some critical functions of technological systems for decision-making by wise, ethical and good people? For example, on October 31, 1994 a French-Italian airplane ART-72 in icy weather suddenly spiraled into the ground killing all 68 aboard. The airplane was on autopilot, which could not recognize the effects of the freezing weather on airplane control, and to maintain a smooth flight moved the flaps of the aircraft into such a position that a crash was inevitable. A human pilot could recognize that the aircraft is "fighting" the bad weather and would select the rough ride over the "smooth" one. The FAA concluded that there are some times when automation is not worth the risk. It set up a new rule for ATR-42 and ATR-74 planes that the autopilot should be turned off during freezing rain or drizzle.

2. Is it wise to design automation, robotization, and informatization in such a way that their operators only watch screens of many instruments but have little to say in the development of a product? Sooner or later society will be divided into two groups of people: "thinking" designers and "ignorant" users of such systems. It may lead to more productive solutions but also to degraded people, a bifurcated society.

3. Should the world apply automation, robotization, and informatization to reduce employment when population growth and the demands of workers have interests often directly in contrast to strategies of efficiency?

4. Should business and public administration apply automation, robotization, and informatization to promote endless economic growth while the reserves of strategic resources are depleting and sooner or later civilization as we know it will literally run out of gas?

There are plenty of such questions which face civilization now. Most of the time, they are neglected, sometimes with catastrophic results. The potential of the Information Wave is in optimization of economic performance as well as, and even more in, wise control at the level of civilization.

THE IDEOLOGY OF THE INFORMATION WAVE

The Information Wave is an ongoing process of political (ideological), economic, social, and technical configurations and relations. The definitions and descriptions of the Information Wave are ideological because ideology inspires what the Information Wave is and how it is understood, practiced, and designed. It is the concept of the ideological position of a practitioner and designer of the Information Wave that conceptualizes a civilization's aims, structures, relationships, and characteristics.

Ideologies are people's maps for reality (Slack, 1987). In the 1980s and 1990s, the ideology of the Information Wave (as it was already called in those decades) became dominant over the ideology of the Industrial Wave. This dominance was expressed through the power of media, education, informated business, and institutions. However, by applying the Information Wave's systems and services, we would like to become emancipated from the domination of any ideology. Since we are becoming better informed and educated, we are becoming freer of an ideology's influence.

The Information Wave ideologists can describe their preferences as a choice within the following areas (Mowshowitz, 1981):

A. *Information tools* can be selected from a palette of languages, databases, knowledge bases, model management software, system software, utility software, and dialogue management techniques, to design an information system as a filter or as a source of solutions.

B. *Stimulation* of the Information Wave developers and operators as well as users can be defined in regulated directions and protections as information policies about: information privacy, censorship, properties, trade, crime, and national and international interest.

C. *Positions* taken by systems designers and operators that will influence the Information Wave ideology can be as follows:

a. *Technicism* – using the computer as an instrument of progress, where success or failure depends on the system design and implementation, with social and political consequences being ignored.

b. *Progressive individualism* – humanizing the system with computers to achieve desirable change.

c. *Elitism* – informing and rescuing the society as the mission of the computer specialist; with sophisticated social engineering as the method of steering social change in the growing complexity of social issues.

d. *Pluralism* – representing interest groups affected by computer use with "fair information practices" together with a combination of legal, regulatory, and security measures to protect consumers and users.

e. *Radical criticism* – protesting the philosophy that computers should be allowed to have their own logic of independence and that mega-computer systems should be developed to operate automatically without human control.

f. *Devolutionism* – gaining power over design but losing control over use.

g. *Computer surveillance* – producing technocratic benefits.

A combination of these choices made by Information Wave developers and operators as well as users will generate social awareness of implemented solutions. This awareness can be analyzed in the terms presented by Mowshowitz's article "On Approaches to the Study of Social Issues in Computing" (Mowshowitz, 1981):

I. *Biases* that will be influenced by the choice of information tools, for example, a technical bias advocates the belief that "technology can solve a problem," while a non-technical bias supports the view that a "problem can be solved through managerial action such as leadership or improved market strategy."

II. *Beliefs* are usually affected by the choice of stimulation. For example, computers can be seen as a strength for the planning of a business or as a threat to an individual's privacy and autonomy.

III. *Expectations* are the result of a position taken by the Information Wave developers and operators as well as users and are determined by: the information culture (a way of using information) in the scope of values (human and civil rights vs. totalitarian information slavery; creativity and electronic friendships vs. alienation); symbols (credit cards create a nearly cashless society, computer screens equate to a paperless society); competence standards (a lack of computer skills equates to illiteracy); knowledge centers (data, knowledge, wisdom bases); know-how (individual computer skills, social skills that control the information transformations), and futurology ("Star Wars").

The relationships among the Information Wave's choices of developers, operators, and users, and social awareness are shown on Figure 9-10, the Ideology Cycle of the Information Wave.

Let us examine some of these attributes. In respect to the choice of *information tools*, Marvin (1987) traced the history of information and found that all societies have had information exchange as a central element in their social make-up. What have changed are the forms of energy in which information is captured and exchanged. The application of mediated-digital information instead of analog information is the main shift in the way industrial society is transformed into the informative society (information-based).

In the area of a choice of stimulation to protect free speech, the U.S. Congress rejected any content censorship in the Internet, and rejected any special policy on it. In Somalia in 1993, the U.S. changed its policy, becoming a peace-keeper rather than a war-maker. This change was caused by televised images of war, when a warlord who could not be caught by America, the number one world power, imprisoned an American pilot. Apparently, information tools changed the power mechanism and policy.

As far as a choice of a *position* is concerned, some ideas of the early ideologists-theorists of the Information Wave, such as Daniel Bell (1973), Edwin Parker (1976), and Marc Porat (1977) claimed that information replaces industrial goods as the principal commodity and becomes an economic engine of the Information Wave. In an assumption taken from the *technicism* position, they observed the trend of a declining percentage of jobs in manufacturing and a rising percentage of jobs in the service-information sector. This does not mean that society has slowed down the consumption of goods and has begun to consume information instead. In reality, society consumes an even bigger variety of goods in the Information Wave.

From the *computer surveillance position*, Alvin Toffler (1980) optimistically predicts that the new information technology will lead to a new society, a "Third Wave" society which will be characterized by local control and broader democracy. Young (1987) argues that Toffler's prediction is naive since the new information technology was created by a given power system, which will be reproduced again by its own tools. On the other hand, information tools which were new to Soviet society created the collapse of the Soviet Union in 1991, by using the openness (*glasnost*) position.

A future driven by information tools is perceived in popular literature to be one with increased democracy, social enlightenment, and individual freedom. From the *elitism position*, Quatroop (1987) warns society that these consequences will not occur. He claims that because information technology is dominated by private capital, the trend is already leaning toward the continued erosion of the public sphere in the creation of hierarchical social relations. In effect, the future will lead us toward social passivity, manipulated leisure time, and a decrease in individual autonomy. However, one can argue that it is up to the individual to decide whether to exercise these possibilities in an intellectual or a manual way. The new telematic technology empowers the individual, allowing him to choose between more options anytime and anywhere in the synchronism of events.

In terms of *biases*, there are some claims that information-communication technology (ICT) influences the mechanism of any power. Electronic mail with special information can reach almost everyone everywhere, whether it is the president of the United States, the CEO of the Apple Corporation, or a student at Western Michigan University.

As an example of some beliefs, there exists a statement that the progress of social computing from the level of an individual to upper levels of the societal strata indicates that these new information tools can change the mechanism of power from within. It is a widely recognized fact that mass media have become the fourth power (or "fourth

Figure 9-10. The ideology cycle of the information wave

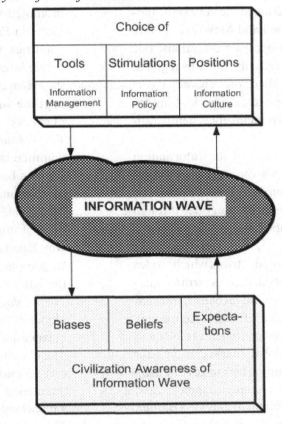

estate" building on the three estates of the French ancient regime) of modern societies.

A case of *expectations* is exemplified by the communications revolution in the 1990s that led to the broader access to information and knowledge on a global scale. In the 1990s, both sides of a military conflict watched war scenes through CNN (e.g., the Persian Gulf conflict in 1991, the Somali conflict in 1993, the Haiti conflict in 1993, the recent invasion of Iraq).

The international perspective of the Information Wave can be stressed by a metaphor: Jihad versus McWorld. To Barber (1992), there are two possible political futures—tribalism and globalism. The first is a re-tribalization of large swaths of mankind by war and bloodshed, a threatened Lebanonization of national states in which culture is pitted against culture, people against people, tribe against tribe—a Jihad in the name of a hundred narrowly conceived faiths against every kind of interdependence, artificial social cooperation, and civic mutuality. The second is borne by the onrush of economic and ecological forces that demand integration and uniformity. MTV, Macintosh, and McDonald's will press nations into one commercially homogenous global network: one McWorld tied together by technology, ecology, communications, and commerce, mesmerized through fast music, fast computers, and fast food.

The planet is falling precipitately apart and coming reluctantly together at the very same moment. The forces of Jihad and McWorld operate with equal strength in opposite directions, one driven by parochial hatreds, the other by a global market. Yet they may share one characteristic: neither offers much hope to citizens looking for practical ways to govern themselves democratically.

The following doctrines of the Information Wave (as a result of the awareness of activists) promote the globalization of civilization progress, though they are not necessarily integrated through a common implementation:

- *The Global Economy* doctrine, which erodes national sovereignty and gives birth to stateless consortia, international banks, transnational lobbies (like OPEC and Greenpeace), and world news services (such as CNN and the BBC). The global market argues for global peace, a common language (English), common currency, common standards, and common cosmopolitan behavior (Barber, 1992). It leads towards global civilization, which is open, competitive, and dynamic, based on the new Eeconomy: open, networked, information-based organization, flexible and virtual.
- *The techno-globalism doctrine*, which promotes the free trade of goods with no government policy of supporting national high-tech industries, attempting to avoid "market failure." This includes among the Western civilization nations the U.S., Canada, Western and Central Europe, Australia, and New Zealand. (Some nations practice the *Techno-Nationalism Doctrine*, supported by a governmental policy to protect the national markets.)
- *The information-communication technology doctrine*, which postulates the integration and sharing of information at the speed of light. The application of satellites leads to a borderless world. Global culture is promoted through telematic conduits; MS Excel in English is more popular in some countries than software in the country's native language. This machine program is the management of a solution and perception anytime and anywhere in the synchronism of events.
- *The resource doctrine*, which enforces a commercial and peaceful exchange of resources because some nations like Japan, Switzerland, or Korea have almost nothing they need. (Japan and Korea are in drastic need of imported food and energy. This is why Japan started the "Great Pacific War.") It promotes the interdependence of nations though the globalization of economy.
- *The ecological doctrine*, which promotes global collaboration to keep the planet in balance and prevent ecological catastrophe. The climate, water, soil, diversity of planet and animal life, and our living space are threatened. Mitigating the crisis will require a planetary perspective (Gore, 1993).
- *The political doctrine*, which promotes the New World Order, based on an open, volatile, multi-polar world, which has been developing since the end of the Cold War in 1991 and is now being challenged by the Iraq war twelve years later.

Post-Cold War tribalism (nationalism, fundamentalism, and racism) generated about thirty wars in 1991. Some small nations (like Tamils, Catalans, Quebecois, Kurds, Serbs, Zulus, Basques, Croats, Bessarabians, Ossetians, and Abkhazians) would like to seal their own borders and protect themselves from modernity. The Jihad strategy of "struggle" is a very popular one in the revolt against the status quo and Western civilization (as demonstrated by the events of September 11, 2001). Among these tribes, there are about 5 billion people without a "password" to a computer and its networks.

McWorld, according to Barber (1992), promotes "free trade," "free press," and "free love." McWorld does not look attractive to the Jihad part of the world, which, however, promotes solidarity among tribe members. Jihad is also attractive for many people alienated in McWorld.

Both ideologies are perhaps anti-democratic, since manipulation is very probable in such circumstances. The former is steering toward corporate-managed efficiency in the stateless globe; the latter is geared toward the *fuhrerprinzip*, in which a leader is governing for the sake of all pariahs[6]. At first glance, McWorld looks better than Jihad; however, it does require a careful check-and-balance mechanism. Through its telematic (computers + telecommunications + television) networks, it may lead to small regional entities, self-managed from the bottom up, with access to the global market and some sort of government run by a small state or group of states. This solution should satisfy the Greenpeace slogan—"think globally, act locally," as well as the statements "work apart and together" and "small is beautiful." There is nothing wrong with promoting managed efficiency, but it must be aimed at the policy of keeping the Earth in balance, rather than allowing it to promote corporate, stateless, short-term profit and thus support the apparent collapse of the planet's healthy life.

From the *progressive individualist position*, it can be assumed that the educated world will not follow the Jihad strategy; rather, it is McWorld, with its humane strategy that will prevail. In the process of building McWorld, we shall probably follow the history of the Industrial Revolution, which has prevailed through the last 200 years despite protests by the Mexican and Bolshevik revolutions. In effect, both revolutions ended up in the industrial world, driven by profit rather than by "social justice." Perhaps the better-educated citizens of McWorld, the members of universal civilization who are aware of the planet's possible collapse, may find some feasible solutions. At the very least, humans should strive to find it. New tools, particularly of the Information Wave, may bring in some positive results.

CONCLUSION

1. The Information Wave is a great civilization leap in accelerating the development of knowledge and tools for eventual better control of life on the Earth.
2. The Information Wave requires a motivated engagement of the societies to apply new information-communication tools in a wise and good manner.

A. Further Research Directions

- Investigate how the Information Wave optimizes the Agricultural Wave.
- Investigate how the Information Wave optimizes the Industrial Wave.
- Investigate a concept of New Economy, driven by information and its impact on the rise of the global civilization and society in the 21st century and the future.

B. Research Opportunities

- The research opportunity is in the integrated evaluation of relationships between information, economy and society within a whole civilization.

C. Additional Ideas

- The Information Wave does not replace other civilization waves; it only optimizes them. We should provide more examples and explain the mechanism better.

D. Rationale

- Alvin Toffler's book *The Third Wave* (the subject of which was later called by other writers the Information Wave), published in 1980, used a historical perspective to argue that the transition from an industrial society (the Second Wave, later called the Industrial Wave) to an information society (the Third Wave) can best be understood by looking back in time to the transition from the agricultural society (the First Wave, later called the Agricultural Wave) to the industrial society. This book was pioneering, but some futurists soon predicted that the Third Wave or the Information Wave will replace others, and that, for example, all Americans should know how to program computers. It did not happen, because we cannot replace bread by newspapers or cars by telephones. It is apparent that the Information Wave is intellectually supporting (including software and hardware) other waves by providing better control and cognition. The Information Wave is always about other waves. Without it the Information Wave has no right to exist.

- It is a wave which empowers humans in their cognition and controls the civilization processes and systems. Therefore, it is important to promote the role of the Information Wave in civilization, and in it all facets of human activities. The Information Wave makes humans more human. Even more, due to its information potential, perhaps humans can create a new civilization (A., & H. Toffler, 1994).

E.   Additional Reading

Arquila, J., & Ronfeld, D. (1999). *The emergence of noopolitik. Toward an American information strategy.* Santa Monica, CA: RAND.

Anderson, R., Bikson, T., Law, A., & Mitchell, B. (1995). *Universal access to e-mail: Feasibility and societal implications.* Santa Monica, CA: RAND.

(2000). *The global course of the information revolution: Technology trends.* Proceedings of an International Conference. Santa Monica, CA: RAND.

Arquila, J., & Ronfeld, D. (2001). *Networks and netwars. The future of terror, crime, and militancy.* Santa Monica, CA: RAND.

Arunachalam, V. (1999). *Bridging the digital divide: The Indian story.* Presented at the RAND Conference on the Global Course of the Information Revolution: Political, Economic, and Social Consequences. Washington, D.C., November 16-18.

Cairncross, F. (1997). *The death of distance.* Boston, MA: Harvard Business School Press.

Drucker, P. (1989). *The new realities.* New York, NY: Harper & Row.

_____(1993). *Post-capitalistic society.* New York, NY: HarperCollins.

Fan, M., Stallaert. J., & Whinston, A. (2002). *Electronic commerce and the revolution in financial markets.* Cincinnati, OH: Thomson Learning.

Friedman, T. (1999). *The lexus and the olive tree.* New York, NY: Farrar, Straus and Giroux.

Fukuyama, F. (1995). *Trust: The social virtues and the creation of prosperity.* New York, NY: Simon & Schuster.

Goodman, S., Burkhart, G., Foster, W., Press, L., Tan, Z., & Woodard, J. (1998). *The global diffusion of the Internet project: An initial inductive study.* Fairfax, VA: The MOSAIC Group.

Harrison, L., & Huntington, S. (Eds.). (2000). *Culture matters: How values shape human progress.* New York, NY: Basic Books.

Hundley R., Anderson, R., Bikson, T., Neu, C. (2003). *The global course of the information revolution.* Santa Monica, CA: RAND.

Kelly, K. (1998). *New rules for the new economy.* New York, NY: Viking.

Kotkin, J. (2000). *The new geography: How the digital revolution is reshaping the American landscape.* New York, NY: Random House.

Lee Kuan Yew. (2000). *From the third world to first. The Singapore's story: 1965-2000.* New York, NY: HarperCollins.

Lawrence, L. (2001). *The future of ideas: The fate of the commons in a connected world.* New York, NY: Random House.

Mann, C., & Kierkegaard, J. (2006). *Accelerating the globalization of America. The role for information technology.* Washington, D.C.: Institute for International Economics.

Mitchell, W. (2000). *E-topia. Urban life, JIM-but not as we know it.* Cambridge, MA: The MIT Press.

Nye, J., S., Jr. (2002). Information technology and democratic governance. In: E. Kamarck & J. Nye, Jr. (Eds.), *Governance.com: Democracy in the Information Age.* Washington, D.C.: Brookings Institution Press.

Ohmae, K. (1995). *The end of the nation state.* New York, NY: The Free Press.

Pacioli, L. (1494). *Summa de arithmetica, geometrica, proportioni et proportionalita* Venice.

Peet, J. (2000). Shoping around the web. *The Economist, 362*(8258), p. Survey.

Porter, M. (1998). Clusters and the new economics of competition. *Harvard Business Review, November-December,* 77-90.

Randive, V. (1999). *The power of now.* New York, NY: McGraw-Hill.

Reich, R. (1991). *The work of nations.* New York, NY: Alfred A. Knopf.

Shapiro, C., & Varian, H. (1999). *Information rules: A strategic guide to the network economy.* Boston, MA: Harvard Business School Press.

Silberglitt, R., Anton, P., Howell, D., Wong, A., Gassman, N., Jackson, B., *et al* (2006). *The global technology revolution 2020.* Santa Monica, CA: RAND.

Siegele, L. (2002, January 21). Survey: The real-time economy. *The Economist.*

Spar, D. (2001). *Ruling the waves: Cycles of discovery, chaos, and wealth from the compass to the Internet.* New York, NY: Harcourt, Inc.

Tapscott, D., & Caston, A. (1993). *Paradigm shift. The new promise of information technology.* New York, NY: McGraw-Hill, Inc.

Toffler, A., & Toffler, H. (1994). *Creating new civilization.* Atlanta, GA: Turner Publishing, Inc.

Wilson, E. (2003). *The information revolution in developing countries.* Boston, MA: MIT Press.

Wolcott, P., Goodman, S., & Burhart, G. (1997). *The information technology capability of nations: A framework for analysis.* Stanford, CA: Center for International Security and Arms Control. Stanford University Press.

REFERENCES

Baran, P. (1964). *On Distributed Communications.* Santa Monica, CA: The RAND Corp. August.

_____ (1964). *On distributed communications* (vol. v), *History, alternative approaches, and comparisons.* Santa Monica, CA: The Rand Corporation.

_____ (2002). The beginning of packet switching—some underlying concepts: The Franklin Institute and Drexel University seminar on the evolution of packet switching and the Internet. *IEEE Communications Magazine, July,* 2-9.

Barber, B. (1992). Jihad vs. McWorld. *The Atlantic Monthly, March,* 53-63.

Bell, D. (1976). *The coming of post-industrial society.* New York, NY: Basic Books.

Beniger, J. (1986). *The control revolution.* Cambridge, MA: Harvard University Press.

Davenport, T. (1997). *Information ecology.* New York, NY: Oxford Press.

Gore, A. (1993). *Earth in the balance.* New York, NY: A Plume Books.

Habermas, J. (1984). *The theory of communication action* (vol. 1). Boston, MA: Beacon Press.

_____ (1987). *The philosophy of discourse of modernity.* Cambridge, MA: MIT Press.

Hasenyager, B. (1996). *Managing the information ecology.* Westport, CT: Quorum Books.

Hellman, J. (1995). The making of the president 2000. *WIRED, December*(1995), 218.

Hawking, St. W. (1988). *A brief history of time.* Toronto: Bantam Books.

Hughes, T. (1998). *Rescuing prometheus.* New York, NY: Pantheon Books.

Inglehart, R. (1997). *Modernization and post-modernization.* Princeton, NJ: Princeton University Press.

Kurian, G. (1984). *The new book of world rankings.* New York, NY: Facts On File Publications.

Levin, D. (2001). *At the dawn of modernity.* Berkeley, CA: University of California Press.

Maddison, A. (2001). *The world economy. A Millennial Perspective.* Paris: OECD

Mann, J. (1998). *Tomorrow's global community.* Philadelphia, PA: Bainbridge Books.

Marvin, C. (1987). Information and history. In: J. Slack & F. Fejes (Eds.), *The ideology of the information wave.* Norwood, NJ: Ablex Publishing Corp.

McLuhan, M. (1962). *The Gutenberg galaxy.* Toronto: University of Toronto Press.

Meadows, D., Meadows, D., Randers, J., & Behrens, W., III. (1972). *Limits to growth.* New York, NY: Signet.

Meadows, D., & Meadows, D. (1992). *Beyond the limits.* Post Mills, VT: Chelsea Green Publishing Co.

Mowshowitz, A. (1981). On approaches to the study of social issues in computing. *Communications of the ACM, 24*(3), 146.

Parker, E. (1976). Social implications of computer/telecoms systems. *Telecommunications Policy, 1*(December), 3-20.

Porat, M. (1977). *The information economy.* Washington, D.C.: U.S. Office of Telecommunications.

Quatroop, L. (1987). The information wave: Ideal and reality. In: J. Slack & F. Fejes (Eds.), *The ideology of the Information Wave.* Norwood, NJ: Ablex Publishing Corp.

Raudzens, G. (1999). *Empires, Europe and globalization 1492-1788.* Thrupp, UK: Sutton Publishing.

Rifkin, J. (2000). *The age of access: The new culture of hypercapitalism, where all of life is a paid-for experience.* New York, NY: Tarcher/Putnam.

Reich, R. (1992). *The work of nations.* New York, NY: Vintage Books.

Shapiro, A. (1999). *The control revolution.* New York, NY: A Century Foundation Book.

Simpson, G. (1991). *Montreux MetaResort brochure.* Reno, NV: Wellness Development Ltd.

Slack, J. (1987). The information wave as ideology: An introduction. In: J. Slack & F. Fejes (Eds.), *The ideology of the information wave*. Norwood, NJ: Ablex Publishing Corp.

Tapscott, D. (1995). *The digital economy*. New York, NY: McGraw-Hill.

Targowski, A. (1991). Computing in a totalitarian state: Poland's way to an informed society. *The Journal of Information Management, Information Executive, 4*(3), 10-16.

_____(2001). *Informatyka bez zludzen* (*Informatics without illusions*) (In Polish). Torun, Poland: Adam Marszalek.

_____(2007). The genesis, political, and economic side of the Internet. In: L. Tomei (Ed.), *Integrating information & communications technologies into the classroom*. Hershey, PA: Information Science Publishing.

Toffler, A. (1980). *The third wave*. New York, NY: William Morrow.

Toffler, A., & Toffler, H. (1994). *Creating a new civilization*. Atlanta, GA: Turner Publishing.

Toynbee, A. (1955). *A Study of history*. New York, NY: Barns & Noble.

Wheeler, J., Buckley, P., & Peat, F. (1979). *A question of physics*. London: Routledge and Kegan Paul.

World Bank (2007). *World development Indicators*. Washington, D.C.: World Bank.

World Bank. (2007). *The little data book on information and communication technology*. Washington, D.C.: World Bank

Young, T. (1987). Information, ideology and political reality. In: J. Slack & F. Fejes (Eds.), *The ideology of the information wave*. Norwood, NJ: Ablex Publishing Corp.

World Development Report 2003. Washington, D.C.: World Bank.

ENDNOTES

[1] One must mention that woodblock printing of written characters was known in China by 350 A.D. Ceramic movable type was in use in China about 1, 040 A.D. The Koreans invented printing in the 5th century; however, it was not applied widely and remained unknown for others outside of Korea.

[2] Andrew Targowski learned about the technical solutions of the ARPANET from Dr. L. Roberts during the Diebold Research Program Conference in Madrid in June 1971. The INFOSTRADA project besides of the Polish funds also was sponsored by $1 million from the Singer Corporation, which wanted to apply tested solutions in its business in the U.S.

[3] The 19th century lists of these inventions were compiled from Beniger (1986).

[4] The U.S. Bureau of the Census.

[5] or INFOSTRADA in Poland-1972.

[6] Hitler's basic principle was the concentration of power in a single leader the *fuhrer*, himself. His politics were partly aimed at the proletariat, but that was among others and his principle was not based on them.

Chapter X
Information and Organization

INTRODUCTION

The purpose of this chapter is to define *information*, mainly in terms of cognition units, and also to find out its other perspectives and images. Once we understand information, it becomes possible to define its role in an organization, particularly at the level of information systems. The issue of how more complex information systems may advance an organization to higher levels of structure (configuration) will be investigated. Modern complex organization is still very recent, about 50 years old, but can already be perceived to have some evolutionary phases. Finally, the transformation from the industrial to the informated model of an enterprise is described and both models are compared, with some conclusions about meaning for civilization's well-being.

PERSPECTIVES OF INFORMATION

The Quantitative Perspective of Information

This is one of the oldest perspectives on information meaning. From a quantitative perspective, *information* is the successful selection of signs or words that form a given list, rejecting all "semantic meaning" as a subjective factor [1]. Hartley (1928) showed that a message of N signs chosen from an "alphabet" or a code book of S signs has S^N possibilities, and that the "quantity of information" is most reasonably defined as a logarithmic equation:

$$H = N \log S \qquad [1]$$

Since Hartley's time, this definition of information as a selection of symbols has been generally accepted, although widely interpreted. As a result, Hartley's theory crystallized into an exact mathematical definition, provided by Shannon (1948). According to him, the probability p of event α is:

$$I = - \log_2 p(\alpha) \qquad [2]$$

This approach is not useful in business decision-making. Let us assume, for example, that a message: "the distance from Kalamazoo to Chicago α =150 miles" has p=1 and therefore I = 0, since $\log_2 1 = 0$ (because $2^0 = 1$). In other words, from the quantitative perspective, this message contains no information. However, for the individual using his personal car for a business purpose, this message contains information that can be measured monetarily: if for each mile driven the individual receives compensation of $0.40, those 150 miles mean $60 in information value for him/her.

An increase in information yields a resultant reduction of chaos or entropy. Entropy, in statistical thermodynamics (Second Law), is a function of the probability of the states of the particles that form a gas. In the quantitative communication theory, entropy means how much information one must introduce into a given information-oriented system to make it informationally organized and at the same time reduce its chaos. The relationship between information and entropy is expressed most objectively by the Shannon-Weaver formula (1949):

$$H_{(\alpha)} = - \Sigma \, p(\alpha) \, \log_2 (\alpha) \ (\text{BIT}) \ (\text{Binary digIT}) \qquad [3]$$

In a descriptive thermodynamic sense, entropy is referred to as a "measure of disorder." Information introduced to a given system eliminates that disorder and is therefore said to be "like" negative entropy or order. Starr (1971) demonstrates the idea

of entropy using the following example: suppose that eight different commands can be transmitted from the bridge of a ship to the engine room. If each of those commands is equally likely, then the probability of any of these being sent is p=1/8. Knowing p, entropy H can be determined:

$$H = 8[1/8 \, \log_2 (1/8)] = \log_2 8 = 3 \qquad [4]$$

This result indicates that eight different orders coded into a binary format (as shown below) can be transmitted via a 3-bit-wide channel of communication:

The entropy function is widely used in communication networks in coding for the assessment of channel capacity and code efficiency. However, from the human communication point of view, this perspective has limited applications, because it does not provide any human-oriented meaning to the "bits and probabilities." This approach has a technical significance concerning how to design a technical communication channel. Finally, the entropy function lacks the semantic meaning of information, which can drive human communication.

Table 10-1. Eight messages in a binary coded format

Order Number	Binary Form
0	000
1	001
2	010
3	011
4	100
5	101
6	110
7	111

The Qualitative Perspective of Information

It is obvious that without quality, information loses its usefulness. This idea is reflected in a well-known phrase often used in information processing: "garbage in, garbage out." The emphasis on the quality aspects of information and their importance in organizations is apparent in two streams of research on:

- Message flow (e.g., Monge, Edwards, & Kirstel, 1978; Roberts & O'Reilly; 1978) Decision-making (e.g., Cyert & March; 1963; O'Reilly, Chatman, & Anderson, 1978)
- One can argue that literature addressing message flow can add context and realism to decision-making. Likewise, decision-making literature can help make the outcome variables of message flow more concrete and measurable.

In order to communicate (message flow) or make decisions (decision science) successfully, information must possess eight qualitative attributes (Targowski, 1990a):

- Relevance (R)
- Timeliness (T)
- Exclusiveness (E)
- Format (F)
- Accessibility (D)
- Accuracy (A)
- Verifiability (V)
- Price (P)

Each attribute can be measured on a scale from 1 to 5, in which the highest rating corresponds to the greatest influence of the attribute on the communicated decision-making process. A set of all the attributes creates the information quality space (IQS), which is depicted in Figure 10-1.

The IQS is the sum total of all the attributes' values. The ideal IQS_i has 8 x 5 = 40 points. If

Figure 10-1. The ideal information quality space (R-Relevance, T-Timeliness, E-Exclusiveness, F-Format, D-Accessibility, A-Accuracy, V-Verifiability, P-Price

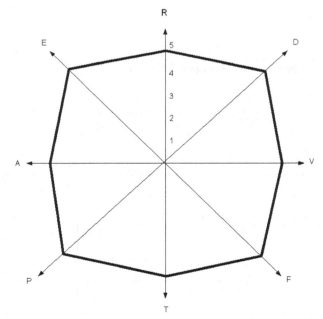

one person's $IQS_1 = 8$ and another person's $IQS_2 = 16$, then the probability of communication success (cs) between them is:

$$P(cs) = IQS_1 : IQS_2 = 8 : 16 = 0.5 \qquad [5]$$

The potential of decision-making (dm) by the first person is:

$$PT(cs)_1 = IQS_1 : IQS_i = 8 : 40 = 0.2 \qquad [6]$$

And by the second person is

$$PT(cs)_2 = IQS_2 : IQS_i = 16 : 40 = 0.4 \qquad [7]$$

Through the interpretation of message transmission and decision-making values, we are able to obtain the holistic measurement of the feasibility of decision-making driven by information F(dm) in the organizational environment:

$$F(dm)_1 = P(cs) \times PT(dm) \qquad [8]$$

$$F(dm)_1 = P(cs) \times PT(dm)_1 = 0.5 \times 0.2 = 0.1 \qquad [9]$$

$$F(dm)_2 = P(cs) \times PT(dm)_2 = 0.5 \times 0.4 = 0.2 \qquad [10]$$

The proposed qualitative assessment of information provides the following rules:

- Rule 1: The larger the information quality space is, the better communication and decision-making potential a given individual has, since a given IQS approaches the ideal IQS.
- Rule 2: The smaller the difference is between the information quality spaces of communication agents, the greater the probability of communication success these agents have, since P(cs) approaches 1.
- Rule 3: The higher probabilities of communication success and higher potentialities

of decision-making will lead to the higher feasibility of decision-making, since F(dm) approaches 1.

These rules imply that a decision maker either has quality information available [P(dm)] to make choices or will obtain information through successful communication [P(cs)]. The proposed indicators can be integrated into a "theory of choice" and a "theory of search" (Cyert & March, 1963). Some research from the pre-Information Wave period indicates that decision makers prefer to look for inexpensive and easily accessible information[2]. Let us hope that the Internet potential (paid or free information) will improve decision makers' quests for better quality information in the 21st century.

The Cognitive Perspective of Information

In order to describe the central role of information in civilization development, the theory of information ecology creates a model that views the existing body of accumulated human information as a distinct set of "entities" apart from the minds of information users. This body of information is called a cognition reservoir (CR), as is shown in Figure 10-2. The recognition of the CR permits researchers and users to assign descriptive characteristics to cognition units (among others, information), and treat it as though it were an independent entity of civilization. Information ecology considers the interaction between users and the CR to be the most significant factor shaping human civilization.

The cognition reservoir contains a semantic cross-section of cognition (decreased chaos) with cognition units of data, information, concept, knowledge, and wisdom. These units are created by humans' science and practice (culture in general) and have been stored and retrieved by different kinds of technology, such as writing,

Figure 10-2. Cognition reservoir of civilization

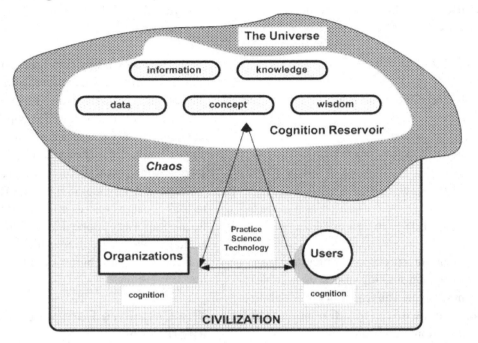

papyrus, books, print, libraries, and computers, which lead to the rise of communication information sciences and management.

The information-communication process conveys meaning through five kinds of cognition:

- **Datum (D)**

  A measuring unit of cognition that describes transactions between natural, artificial or other semantic system. In business, data can measure performance characteristics of production, distribution, transportation, construction, or service. For example, the Dow Jones Stock Index (at the New York Stock Exchange) stood at 10,000 points on February 15, 2005.

- **Information (I)**

  A comparative unit of cognition that identifies, specifies, and defines a change between the previous and the present state of natural, artificial, or semantic system. Businesses often compare performance characteristics in two or more periods. For example, if the Dow Jones Stock Index stood at 11,000 points on February 14, 2005. The change is -1,000 or 9% in comparison to the previous day February 13, 2005.

- **Concept (C)**

  A perceptive unit of cognition that generates thoughts or ideas that create our intuition and intention that give us a sense of direction. For example, due to the market's strong change, should an investor sell, buy, or hold his/her stocks?

- **Knowledge (K)**

  A reasoning unit of cognition that creates awareness based on scientific data (e.g., Census Bureau research), rules, coherent inferences, laws, established patterns, methods and their systems. Knowledge is, essentially, old data remembered in an established framework and being used to evaluate new data. It provides a point of reference, a standard for analyzing data, information and concepts. Knowledge can be categorized in many ways, for example:

o   Domain knowledge (Kd)
o   Societal knowledge (Ks)
o   Personal knowledge (Kp)
o   Moral knowledge (Km)

Once again, elaborating on the previous examples, an investor will apply his/her adviser's financial knowledge (Kd) to find out which concept he/she should apply to a market decision. He/she can also apply the remaining kinds of knowledge to evaluate each concept option.

•   **Wisdom (W)**
A pragmatic unit of cognition that generates volition—a chosen way of acting and communicating. Wisdom is a process of choosing among available concept options, based on knowledge, practice, morale, or intuition, or on all of them. Concluding our example, an investor may choose the "hold" concept option to wait and see what will be the Federal Reserve Bank's decision on interest rates.

The cognition units that compose the cognition reservoir can be structured from simplest to most complex in the semantic ladder, shown in Figure 10-3. Events that occur at the existence level are communicated as data and inserted into the semantic ladder of a person, discipline or orga-

Figure 10-3. Semantic ladder

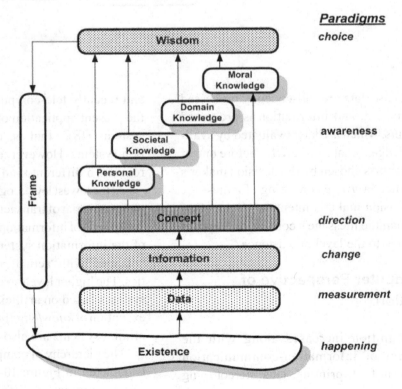

Figure 10-4. The hierarchy of computer cognition-oriented systems

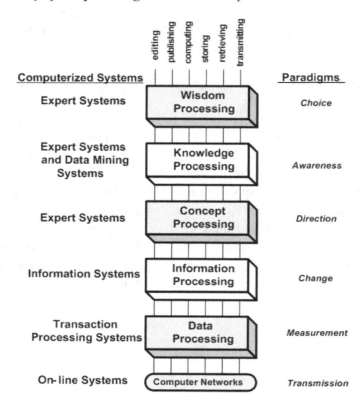

nization. These data are subsequently processed into information, and information is processed into concepts, which are later evaluated by available knowledge—that is, filtered—before one of those concepts is chosen by the decision maker's wisdom. Then, a *frame* consisting of a message and the decision maker's intentions (very often different than the message's content) is returned as a feedback to the level of existence.

The Computer Perspective of Information

Human cognition increases along with the development of information-communication technology, at first: printing, later stereotyping and recently tele-computing. Tele-computing is the present application of the label "information systems (IS)," that is, computerized information systems. However, every level of cognition requires a different kind of IS.

At the lowest level, cognition is *data processing* under a format of transaction processing systems. At the level of information, supporting systems are of the information system kind, which compare "planned" with "actual" performance characteristics. The higher levels of cognition require expert systems based on artificial intelligence, with the exception of *knowledge processing*, in which data mining systems are also of great value.

The hierarchy of computer cognition systems is depicted in Figure 10-4. Every kind of these systems requires a different architecture, skills

Figure 10-5. The cognition units-driven generic phases of problem solving (Ca-Concept A, Cb-Concept B, Cc-Concept C)

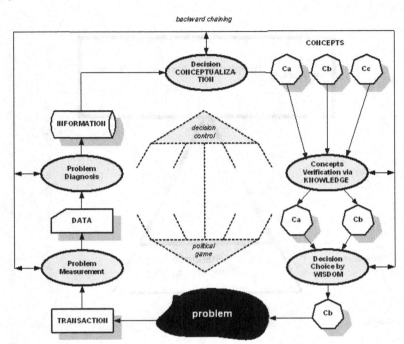

to build, timeline, and budget. It is similar to the situation in construction, in which residential houses need different know-how than public buildings, and so forth.

The Decision-Making Perspective of Information

The cognitive perspective of information can be useful in understanding how decisions are made. A decision is an act of wisdom in choosing the right course of action at the right time. To reach the cognition level of wisdom, one must pass through four semantic levels, each one specializing in a specific cognitive unit processing.

A number of frameworks have been offered to define the phases of decision-making. Perhaps the best known of these is Simon's (1965) "intelligence-design-choice of decision" triad. Ackoff (1978) perceives the decision-making process as

a function of problem solving. Mintzberg, Raisinghani and Theoret (1976) add that the decision-making process is subordinated to political game and decision control in a given circumstances.

The information-oriented approach to decision-making in problem solving is presented in Figure 9-5, in which the following five phases are recognized:

1. *The Problem Measurement Phase* – identifies a problem based upon transactions which are processed into organized data, indicating problem symptoms and implicit stimuli for action.
2. *The Problem Diagnosis Phase* – involves comparisons of different but relevant sets of data, which leads to the production of information on a change in a given state of a problem's affairs.

Figure 10-6. The hierarchy of message formats-driven by media choice

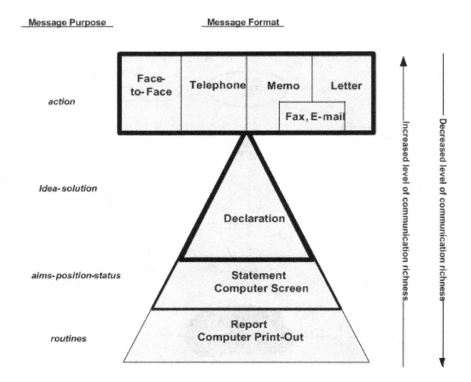

3. *The Decision Conceptualization Phase* – defines concepts of actions, triggered by the change diagnosed in phase two. The automation of this phase is very difficult; however, knowledge engineering proposes some techniques of discovering new facts. One cannot exclude the possibility that one day a new concept will be generated by the computer.

4. *The Concepts Verification by Knowledge Phase* – screens solutions by knowledge of the planned concepts and eliminates those that are unfeasible. The scientific facts, rules, and laws of a given domain of knowledge are applied in this verification. This phase creates awareness for a decision maker about consequences of possible courses of action.

A data-mining technique can useful in this phase.

5. *The Decision Choice Phase* – chooses wisely a given decision concept from many evaluated by knowledge in the previous phase. Wisdom applied at this phase is a result of accumulated (recorded in a human or computer memory) experiences coming from analysis of existence (the ontological aspect of being) or the study of knowledge (the epistemological aspect of being).

The phases of a problem-solving cycle are guided by the decision support routine—the operating system which plans the cycle (schedules, conceptualizes strategies, commits resources to the cycle, etc.) and switches the decision maker from one phase to another. The implementation

Figure 10-7. Information as a resource

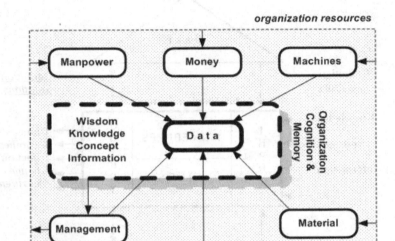

of the selected decision depends on the power game and on consensus among the persons affected by it.

The decision-making cycle incorporates a backward path in the events that feedback indicates the need to correct, clarify or repeat the previous phase. It also is implied that the cycle is applicable only to rational decisions, as Simon defined bounded rationality, where formal rules are applied.

The Managerial Perspective of Information

The premise of this perspective is that management is looking for explicit information to make rational decisions, therefore is ready to process the desired kind of information in certain manners to achieve this goal. Managers and executives apply a variety of media to process and communicate information in a correct manner. The hierarchy of professional message formats-driven by applied media is modeled in Figure 10-6.

Computer print-outs and reports describing routines are located at the lowest level in the hierarchy. These types of messages are processed by the heavily computerized information systems. At the next level one finds aims/positions/status-oriented messages which are described by statements on computer screens. These kinds of messages can be processed by computerized information systems with a friendly graphic-user interface (GUI). The third level of the hierarchy contains declarations describing ideas/solutions such as "read my lips, no more taxes," or "freedom everywhere." It is at this level where the meaning of

Figure 10-8. Information as an information source

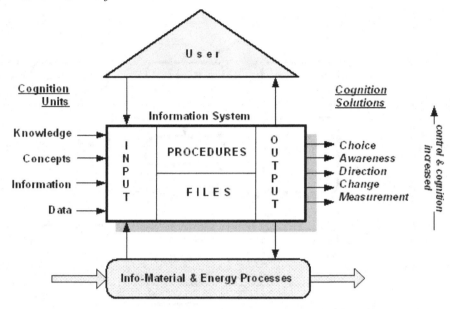

the message is of greatest importance but is very difficult to automate. At the top of the pyramid are action-oriented messages such as face-to-face communication, telephone and fax, memoranda, and letters. This type of message format is the richest in content and it will soon be a luxury to practice some of them.

The hierarchy of message formats driven by applied media reflects a concept of information richness, defined by Daft and Lengel (1986) as the potential of the information to carrying capacity of data. In this study, richness is defined as the ability to communicate a message in the most meaningful and effective manner[3].

THE IMAGES OF INFORMATION

The Image of Information as a Resource

The wide applications of computers since the 1960s first in data processing and later in complex enterprise-wide applications turned our attention toward the reliability of data files and databases. The latter approach led toward better integration of information about all resources of an enterprise, such as manpower, money, machines, material, management, market (6M) and eventually data as a new resource.

Data is a meta-resource which measures the values of 6M other resources. These data are organized in information systems that are processed by computers or manually. As a result, information, concept, knowledge, and wisdom are generated to influence or direct further *control* and *cognition* in a given action/circumstances. It is interesting to notice that without the 6M, "data" has no meaning and is useless in such a case.

Figure 10-7 depicts the role of data-information as an organization's reservoir of cognition and memory. Data-information properly gathered and processed can become a product, which can be packaged, sent and sold as a "soft commodity." Commercial databases are one such product. Another example is computer software, such as

MS Office, which is de facto organized information and sold as a product.

An early definition of the information society was based on the fact that information is an economic resource, skillfully managed by control or profit seekers.

The Image of Information as a System

Information is usually perceived as a system which integrates and controls other systems of an enterprise, such as business, engineering, production, and logistics, as a single dynamic complex system. At the end of the 20th century, a set of such enterprise information systems is managed by a chief information officer, who in general oversees the new business function of *information management.*

Figure 10-8 illustrates the architecture of an information system controlling underlying information-material and energy processes. An information system has the goal of controlling subordinated processes to produce solutions outside the system.

Among inputs can be transactions, data, information, concepts, and knowledge, and among outputs one can expect process measurements, change, awareness, choices based on wisdom leading to better decisions and cognition about those processes and their circumstances.

The way IS are designed and programmed determines information quality, which is characterized by information relevance, timeliness, exclusiveness, accessibility, accuracy, price and format.

Needless to say, IS are a main tool of civilization, beginning with language, writing, papyrus, books, accounting, publishing, and now moving into computers, networks, and artificial intelligence. Each new information tool brings a change or even a shift of civilization. Therefore, each new version of this kind of system should be carefully analyzed for its possible support or dangerous impact.

The Image of Information as a Mind

Information is the main factor in civilization development, which is associated with a human brain's ability to process information. In fact, this is what differentiates us from animals. Civilization is full of puzzles on how humans evolved due to their brain potential. For example, the Neanderthals had brains 20% bigger than ours, but they did not survive till nowadays, since they, despite larger memories, had some problems in processing new facts. Therefore, a human brain still has huge complexity which is not yet fully known in its dynamics.

The image of information as a mind, which controls a brain, can be seen as analog versus digital information processing, as modeled (with of course reduced complexity) in Figure 10-9. An analog signal guides the performance of specific electrochemical processes that are triggered within the brain structure. But these processes carry information and have a particular meaning. In other words, they may also play the part of active information for other neural processes. In this way, a series of interlocking levels of meaning, information, and electrochemical processes result.

A formative mental process manifests itself not only as an electromechanical procedure, but also as a more subtle action within the brain. Signals in a brain can be categorized as either analog or digital. An analog signal flows between bio-devices (sensors, receptors, memories, conductors, and transducers) within the cognitive and life processes (transduction-motor, behavior, communication, decision-making, and info-steering) as neural signals. This signal is a neural current in a single fiber or a bundle of redundant fibers, which has a magnitude related to the magnitudes of some set of primary sensory-nerve stimulation. In analog information processing, message representation and information reflection is continuous. According to Powers (1973), analog processing produces perceptions of intensity (light, heat, mechanical deformations), sensations (taste, temperatures, and smells), and configuration of kinesthetic reactions. In contrast, more advanced levels of human behavior are based on semantic reaction, which is controlled digitally through routines stored in memories. According to the same author, the following levels of control, such as: a) perception of change (e.g., rising or falling tone of a voice), b) control of sequence, c) control of relationships among events, d) control of strategy, e) control of principles, f) control of systems—are all based on digital signal processing.

The functional architecture of a human brain and mind (Figure 10-9) defines the brain as a system of bio-devices and hybrid operational

Figure 10-9. Information as a mind

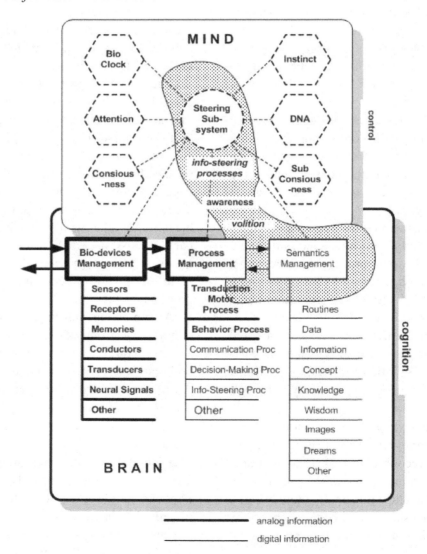

Figure 10-10. Information as human communication

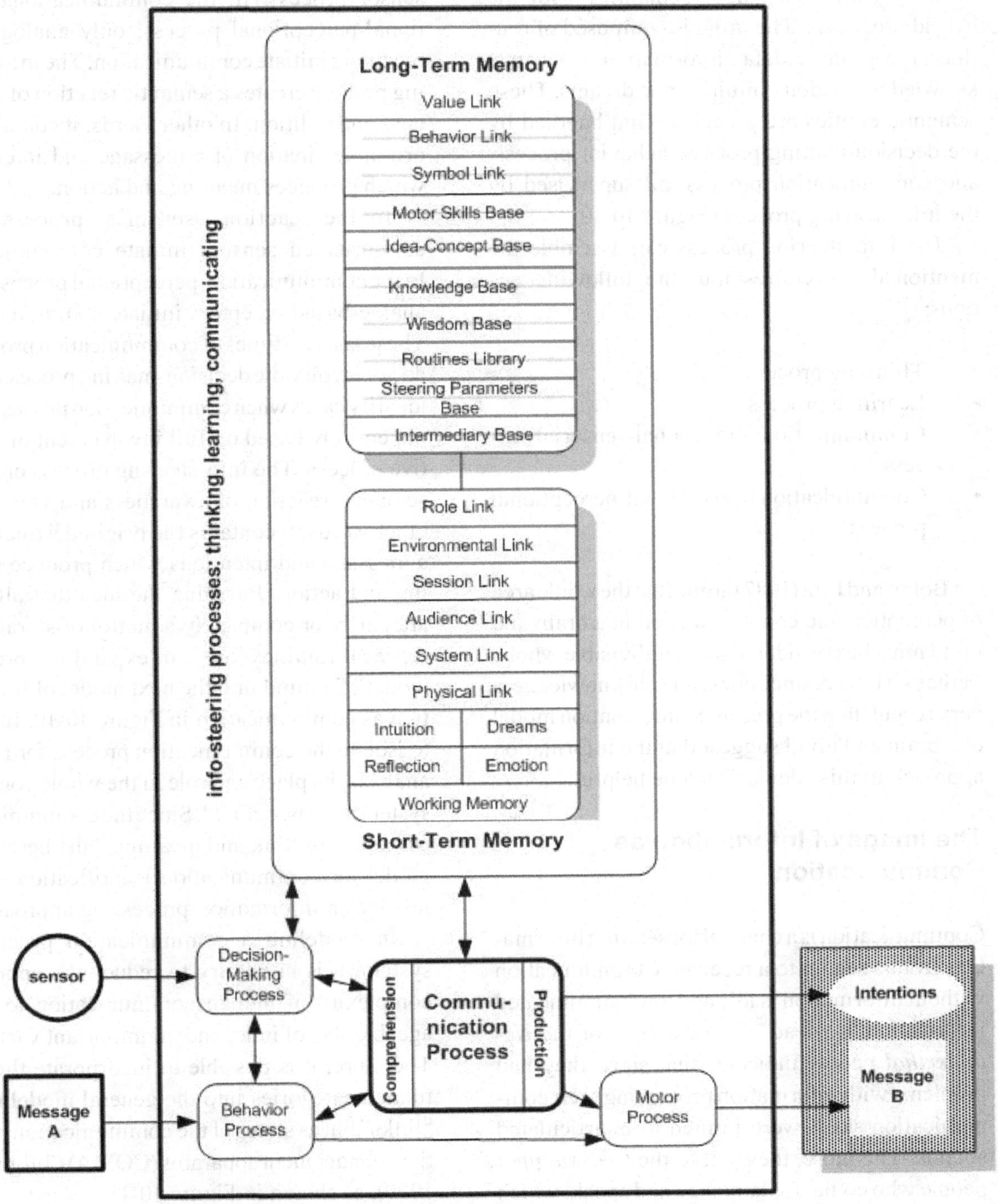

info-steering processes: thinking, learning, communicating

Long-Term Memory

- Value Link
- Behavior Link
- Symbol Link
- Motor Skills Base
- Idea-Concept Base
- Knowledge Base
- Wisdom Base
- Routines Library
- Steering Parameters Base
- Intermediary Base

- Role Link
- Environmental Link
- Session Link
- Audience Link
- System Link
- Physical Link

Intuition	Dreams
Reflection	Emotion

- Working Memory

Short-Term Memory

sensor → Decision-Making Process

Message A → Behavior Process

Comprehension — **Communication Process** — Production

Motor Process

Intentions

Message B

processes. The contents of a brain constitute a mind, which exchanges semantics with the hybrid processes. The mind is composed of routines (programs), data, information, concepts, knowledge, wisdom, intuition and dreams. These semantic entities are processed and handled by the decision-making process, behavior process, and communication process, all supervised by the info-steering process (Figure 10-10).

The info-steering process can assemble the mentioned procedures into the following actions:

- Thinking process
- Learning process
- Communicational-reactional-sensorial process
- Communicational- reactional-perceptional process

Bohm and Peat (1987) argue that the whole area of perception and communication in a brain and mind must be considered as an indivisible whole. Perhaps it is true, since our scientific knowledge is very recent, that the presented information model of a brain and mind suggest that the information approach to this "device" can be helpful.

The Image of Information as Communication

Communication is a channel for sending information from a sender to a receiver. Communication without information is idle and uncommunicated information is "dead." The example of the *Neanderthal* people indicates that since they had problems with information processing their communication skills were limited to unarticulated sounds. Therefore, they lost to the *Cro-Magnon* people who could use language and speak, which let them be better socially organized.

Continuing analysis of the information-communication-oriented brain, let us take a look again at the model in Figure 10-9, where symbol-oriented

sensors trigger the communicational-reactional-sensor process. In the communicational-reactional-perceptional process, only analog-based receptors initiate communication. The info-steering process creates a semantic reaction of awareness and volition. In other words, it contains the origin/destination of a message and intentions, which produces meaning and action.

In the reactional-sensorial process, only data-oriented sensors initiate communication. In the communication-perceptional process, only analog-based receptors initiate communication. These last two types of communication processes do not involve the decision-making process. They identify cases when communication processes are not entirely based on full involvement of cognitive process. The info-steering process creates a semantic reaction of awareness and volition. In other words, it contains the origin/destination of a message and intentions which produce meaning and action. Pursuing the idea that all links are partly or completely a matter of storage and retrieval routines, one can expand the previous model of a mind into the next model of information as communication in Figure 10-10. In order to isolate the communication process for further analysis, its place and role in the whole cognitive system must be defined. Since the communication paradigm is "link and meaning," the best-suited model for communication identification should involve an information-processing approach.

In modeling a communication process or system, it is necessary to reduce the enormous complexity of human communication to manageable sets of independent important variables. Therefore, it is possible to incorporate the postulated categories into the general model not as "links" but as states of the communication operation management apparatus (COMA) (Targowski, 1990), as shown in Figure 10-11.

The new set of communication process variables combines the operational states (interest, desire, emotion, knowledge) of a communicator with the strategic levels of his/her value link, be-

Figure 10-11. The architecture of communication operation management apparatus (COMA) (The Targowski-van Hoorde Model)

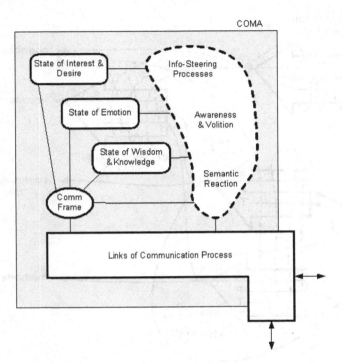

havior link, and tactical level of storage retrieval link that filters a given communication process (Targowski & Bowman, 1988).

The Image of Information as Synchronism

The concept of an info-steering process can be applied in almost every facet of the Information Wave. Let us examine the dynamics of a management process as it is defined in Figure 10-12. This process produces the following outcomes:

- Means (resources allocation)
- Cognition (data, information, concepts, knowledge, wisdom)
- Communication (message and intention)
- Methods ("tools")

These outcomes are possible, since the info-steering process coordinates other managerial processes, such as life process (a person who manages), human-organization behavior process, and the decision-making process. As Chajtman (1973) defined in his production theory, each of these processes takes place because a substance, performers, and tools exist. The synchronized role of the info-steering process is explicitly shown in Figure 10-12.

The life process of a real person's substance is his/her behavior. A performer is that person, and his/her tools are food and other necessities for sustenance. This process provides support for performers of other managerial processes.

The organization process generates methods that are appropriate for another related process in a given time period. For example, it can be a

Figure 10-12 The information-oriented architecture of management process: S-Substance, P-Performers, T-Tools (The Chajtman-Targowski Model)

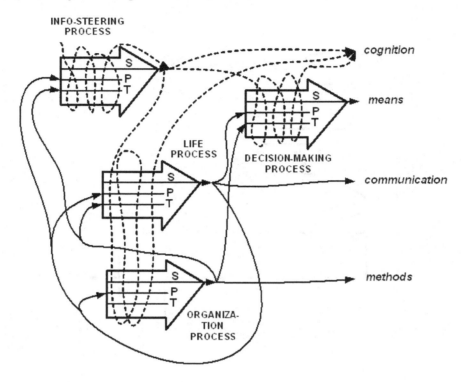

computer information system, a management by objectives (MBO), e-mail, mobile communication, or so forth.

The decision-making process operates on means (money, manpower, material, machines, time, information, etc.) and allocates them under a form of a chosen decision. A performer/decision-maker applies decisional tools (information systems, optimization techniques, services, infrastructure, etc.) in making decisions.

The info-steering process produces informed synchronization of all other processes' components. It also produces units of cognition; data, information, concepts, knowledge, and wisdom.

The image of information as a synchronizing process of the managerial processes enters into Bohm and Peat's (1987) vision of matter and mind. The information synchronism is in fact a

force of a manager's (politician's, sociologist's, historian's as well) sensitivity to harmony and the invisibility of consciousness, humanity, and technology. The fragmentation of the management theory (as well as the social theory) is not able to explain the major issues and their nuances that face individuals, organizations, nations, and the world without looking at them from the information-oriented synchronism point of view.

The Image of Information as a Superhighway

Today, *information* is the wellspring of great fortunes, much as land was a century ago. Nowadays, *information* of any kind—words, images, voice, video—can race along electronic "*information superhighways*" or "highways of minds" at the speed of light. The big telephone companies are allies in building the new fiber-optic infrastructure around the globe. In the 1990s, the biggest story in the world has been the creation of an integrated telecommunication industry—a convergence of telephones, television, computers, and an array of data banks, including newspapers, libraries, and even Hollywood studios. That convergence means that traditional categories are losing their boundaries. Telephone companies are going into the cable business, cable companies provide telephone services, and very soon it will be impossible to make a distinction between the two.

Albert Gore (1991) writes that a network of *"information superhighways"* will help turn the mounting load of unused data into knowledge for problem solving. He created a new word "ex-formation," information that exists outside the conscious awareness of any living being, but that exists in such enormous quantities that it sloshes around and changes the context and the weight of any problem one addresses. The goal of the *"information superhighway"* is to convert "ex-formation" into *information* and then to convert it into shared-communicated concepts, knowledge, and wisdom.

Tomorrow that kind of system will send data millions of times faster than can be done today. One fiber-optic cable is capable of transmitting the entire Library of Congress—all 110 million volumes—in less than five minutes. That is more than we want to read most evenings. But it is an example of what the "national information

Figure 10-13. Information as a superhighway

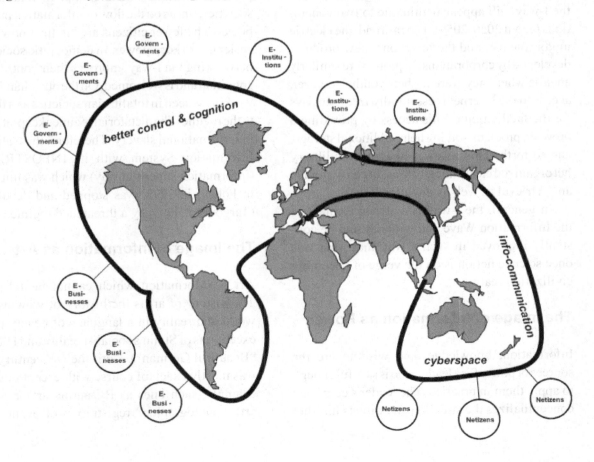

superhighway" may one day make available in nearly every home.

The *"information superhighway"* connecting schools, universities, hospitals, businesses, governments, and net-citizens will help create high-quality education in the smallest and most remote schools, or start a society-wide revolution as important as the invention of printing in 1454. Conversely, if access to the I-way is restricted to those who already have money, power, and information, then this highway becomes nothing more than a classic case of economic imperialism, taxation without communication, that one critic has dubbed "toll roads between castles" (Karraker, 1991).

As a model of the "information superhighway" shows in Figure 10-13, it covers mostly developed countries or about 1 billion people with a password, while the remaining 5 billion people are kept in information darkness. Perhaps the great payoff of the I-way will appear within one to two generations (about 2020-2050). The railroad, the electric motor, the car, and the telephone, new products developed by corporations for profit were similarly anemic when they were in their youth. However, access to the Internet is essentially free; one pays for the facilitation of this access by providing a browser, problem-solving help, additional storage, and so forth. This I-way is like a public library but organized electronically to assure easy storage and retrieval as well as downloading.

In general, the I-way is a strong element of the Information Wave and will stay and be constantly improved in such a way that what was once science fiction is on the verge of becoming civilization reality.

The Image of Information as Power

Information, knowledge, and wisdom are the sources of power for a leader who is skillful enough to apply them in practice. The leader's cognition conceptualizes the situation and directs him/her

toward defensive or active power. The former is the capability to prevent unwanted change and the latter is the capability to produce wanted change (Boulder, 1989).

Access to and the art of using information are two of the most important factors of power. Relevant information and access to it on time may trigger correct decisions about incoming change. The prevention or reinforcement of this change is a sign of strong power. Power based on understanding is very often more significant than power based on economic or military might. It is power of conscience, since, for example, Jesus, Muhammad, and the Buddha, gained long-term influence over their followers than did Caesar, Napoleon, Hitler, and Stalin, or even the Morgans, Rockefellers, Carnegie, and Gates in business.

Information may play two roles in maintaining power. In democracy, free flow of information prevents unwanted dictatorship. In totalitarian societies, limits on the flow of information protect power. The fewer citizens are "in the know," the easier it is to keep power. In democratic societies, networking via I-way improves their control and cognition and is welcomed. On the other hand, networking is seen in totalitarian societies as a threat to the regime. The dictatorial regimes keep citizens in informational slavery. Therefore, the National Information System with its INFOSTRADA (information superhighway) which was initiated in Poland in 1972, was stopped and destroyed (Targowski, 1991) by a threatened regime.

The Image of Information as Art

Art is information which cannot be falsified. The history of art is the history of viewing the world and reality in a language of beauty (with exceptions of Stalin's socialist reality and Hitler's "Beautiful German"). Until the 18th century, art was mostly exact (of course with exceptions, for example, such ones as Byzantine art or Asian art), "photographic" registration of events and

Figure 10-14. National information system (CAS-Computer Aided Service, CAD-Computer-Aided Design, CAM-Computer-Aided Manufacturing) (The Targowski Model 1972)

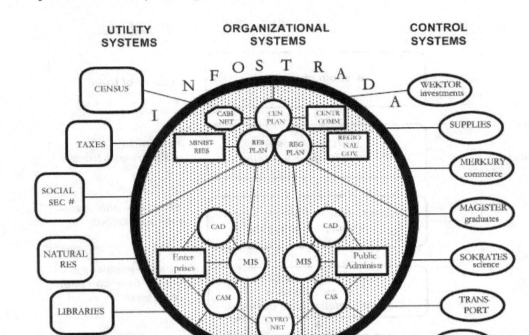

figures playing important roles in the society. It was a time of Leonardo da Vinci's academicism, emphasizing symmetry and perspective (*data processing*). Art, was in those times, a rhetoric of power. Its mission was to glorify a ruler and his court.

After the French Revolution, artists abandoned their sponsors; they become poorer, but free to do what they wanted to do. In the 19th century, romanticism in music and literature, as well impressionism in painting, liberated artists. They left their studios and entered the real world of the beauty of nature. Van Gogh, Matisse, and Gauguin went to the countryside and painted sun, flowers,

and good mood, supported by good company and good wine. Ever since, artists have tried to define their own concepts of reality, and they often saw it as a processed actuality, with a message for change: "We are free and can paint as we wish" (*information processing*) (Figure 10-15).

Academicism in art, based on Leonardo da Vinci's (and Piero Della) rules of symmetry and perspective, was replaced in the 20th century by an anarchy making anything possible in art. It was the manifesto of post-impressionism, which Paul Gauguin proclaimed in 1901. The artists broke with any strategy of *how* to paint, and looked for a new strategy of *what* to paint. Now art and sci-

Figure 10-15. Information as art

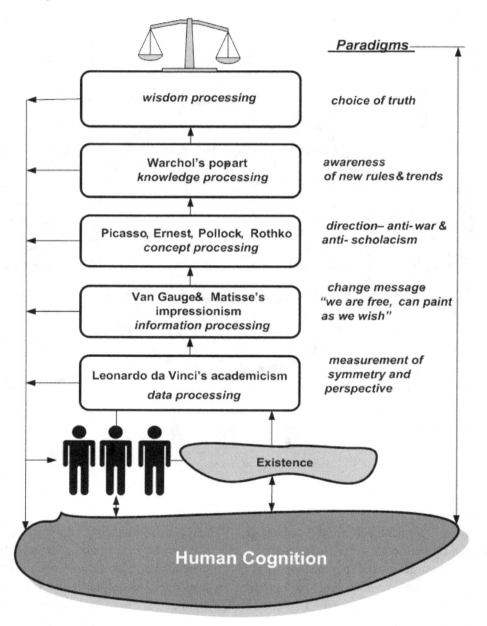

ence seek the same clue, which is *truth*. The 20ᵗʰ century in art is a century of permanent search by the avant-garde for a perception and synthesis of times (*concept processing*).

Pollock's action painting is an art without beginning and end. It is a reflection of reality in life, science, and politics. Art wants to optimize our perception and feelings. First Picasso's cubism, then futurism, the Bauhaus's holism, Dada, Dali's surrealism—these art schools are manifestos of change and engagement in a social process, which can be illustrated by Picasso's *Guernica* (1937), *Pigeon of Peace* (1948), and *Massacre in Korea* (1951). He is followed by Pollock and Rothko in New York and by others in Europe (*concept processing*), by Andy Warhol's pop-art, New York's happenings, Italian transavangard, and superrealism. All these schools quest for a message through new rules and patterns. Marshall McLuhan even proclaimed "the medium is the message." Information "converts itself" into energy and matter, a secret of life and its chance of survival (*knowledge processing*).

Whether art will reach a level of wisdom processing is a question. Jean Dubuffet, who is considered by many equal to Picasso, says: "The wise art? What a crazy question! Art is nothing more than a product of happiness and craziness. A man without bread dies; without art, the man dies from boredom." It is one artist's opinion.

The Polish artist Stanislaw Witkiewicz said in 1919: "Art is such a discipline where a lie never leads to positive results." The Witkiewicz rule can be tested in the Soviet Union and Nazi Germany. In the former, after the Bolshevik Revolution in 1917, the new order accepted only socialist realism in art. The artists could only glorify work in the fields and on the shop-floors. Such artists as the great poet Osip Mandelstam, who did not follow this directive, were sent to the general administration of the camps, (Gulag) or convicted as parasites. Joseph Brodsky, a future Nobel laureate, did not obtain a government license to be a poet! Vladimir Mayakovskiy, a poet of the Revolution,

committed suicide in protest against this official cultural policy. Boris Pasternak, who received the Nobel Prize for *Doctor Zhivago*, could not accept the prize because the Soviet first secretary of the Communist Party, Nikita Khrushchev, did not like the book. At the beginning of the 1980s under the Brezhnev regime, the avant-garde exhibition in Moscow was demolished by government bulldozers. Needless to say, in those 70 years, Soviet official art lied. However, it lost control of its artists in 1991 when the Soviet Union was dissolved.

In the period between the two World Wars, Berlin became the capital of decadence. The play and movie "Cabaret" illustrates this period in German culture. In 1933 when Hitler came to power, the deconstruction of German culture began on a wide and premeditated scale. Police closed the famous Bauhaus school. About 25 directors of museums were fired; leading artists fled the country. Minister of Propaganda Joseph Goebbels ordered books to be burned which were not in line with national propaganda. It took place in the same country where a century before Heinrich Heine had said: "where books burn there minds flare up." All avant-garde painters were condemned. The Fuhrer asked "what artist is that who paints sky in green and grass in blue?" He called the avant-garde a sick people who should be sent to psychiatric hospitals. Only a new school of "the beautiful German" could be practiced. It was nothing more than a repetition of Soviet socialist realism.

Both Communism and Nazism are histories of censored and falsified information. Their goal was to keep people under strong control through fear and tension. Both "new civilizations" "overwhelmed the minds" of citizens and did not allow independent, critical, active thinking. One civilization was eliminated by force, the other by the idea of freedom.

Today, a free man applies art, literature, and music as a thermometer of life's rush and a compass which indicates the world's state of mind. These

Table 10-2. Information matrix, perspectives vs images in 2000th

PERSPEC-TIVES OF INFOR-MATION	INFORMATION & IMAGE AS								
	Re-source	System	Mind	Commu-nication	SySynchro-nism	Super-Highway	Power	Art	TOTAL
Quantitative	COM	COM	COM	COM	COM	COM	COM	COM	8 8 COM
Qualitative	CTR	CTR	CTR	CTR	CTR	CTR	CTR	CTR COG	8 8 CTR 1 1 COG
Cognitive	CTR	CTR	COG	COG	CTR	COG COM	CTR	COG	4 4 CTR 4 4 COG 1 1 COM
Computer	CTR	CTR	COG	CTR COG COM	CTR	CTR COM COG	CTR	COM	6 6 CTR 3 3 COG 3 3 COM
Decision-Making	CTR	CCTR	COG	COM	CTR	CTR COM COG	CTR	COG COM CTR	6 6 CTR 3 3 COG 3 3 COM
Managerial	CTR	CCTR	COG	CTR COG COM	CTR	CTR COM COG	CTR	CTR	7 7 CTR 3 3 COG 2 2 COM
TOTAL	5 CTR 1COM	5CTR 1 COM	4COG 1COM 1CTR	4COG 4COM 3CTR	5CTR 1COM	5COM 4CTR 4COG	5CTR 1COM	3COG 3COM 3CTR	3 31 CTR 1 17 COM 1 14 COG

Source: The author's estimation

instruments are metaphors, since art's calling is to provide a perception of reality in a language of beauty. Nevertheless, art, to be important, must look for truth. This quest is undertaken nowadays by artist-photographers who travel around the world and document tragic and unwise human stories, which can be called *wisdom processing*, as an alert to be more informed and wise about these causes and results.

THE INFORMATION MATRIX

The use of information perspectives and images depends on a kind of application. Table 10-2 il-

lustrates a combination of possible inclusions of either information perspectives or images to each other, taking into account such goals as control (CTR), cognition (COG), and communication (COM). For example, if a decision-making processual perspective is designed thus, it would be recommended to include six CONTROL-indicated information images to optimize that goal, three COGNITION-indicated information images to optimize that goal, and three COMMUNICA-TION-indicated information images to optimize that goal. Vice versa, if a resource image of information is planned thus, it would be recommended to include five CONTROL-indicated information perspectives to optimize that goal and one COMMUNICATION-indicated information perspective to optimize that goal.

Table 10-2 helps in defining the following conclusions that:

1. The most popular aim of information is control (CTR).
2. Aims of information images as communication (COM) and cognition (COG) goals are only half as popular than CRT.

It would perhaps be wise to advise that, to avoid unnecessary conflicts at all levels of humanity, goals of improving cognition and communication should be supported strongly and more widely than nowadays. Even saying that, the more we know, the less we need to be controlled or to be engaged in controlling. Of course, communication should also be improved, since it is a tool to share cognition.

THE INFORMATED ARCHITECTURE OF AN ORGANIZATION

The Information Wave impacts the architecture of an organization, which becomes more information-systems-intensive, as is shown in Figure 10-16. Every facet of an organization is nowadays supported by computerized information systems (CIS) which interact through computer networks. The architecture shown is an ideal one, which identifies popular CIS, applicable in business and institutional organizations. Of course, it is still too soon to identify any organization which applies all those systems in a very orderly manner.

A process of reaching a level of "perfect" systematization of an entity passes through the following organization configurations, classified by the technology criterion (Targowski, 2003):

1. *Off-line organization* – is a typical solution for the kind of industrial enterprise which operated in the 1950s and 1960s. Several applications, such as payroll, stock control, production control, and customer orders, are processed independently, and their data is provided in batches.
2. *Networked organization* – is based on computer networks such as Local Area Network (LAN), Metropolitan Area Network (MAN), Wide Area Network (WAN), Global Area Network (GAN), and the Internet. Applications are interconnected electronically, which leads toward a so-called extended organization, or in business, an *extended enterprise*, in which suppliers are connected with producers via a supply chain management (SCM) system to support just-in-time manufacturing.
3. *Integrated organization* – once an organization is connected into computer networks, the next step in its evolution is the integration of applications around a common database. In business, this integration is done presently by enterprise resource planning (ERP) software.
4. *Informated organization* – when an organization is networked and integrated, organizations look for the added value that CIS can bring to management. So far, the CIS(s) have been organized around a formula of *planned versus actual* performance, and systems are of the OLTP (online transaction processing) kind. In the *informated* configuration, systems are driven by OLAP (online analytical processing), which leads toward the application of a knowledge management system (KMS). This system's main component is data mining, which generates new patterns and rules of a given organization's stakeholders' behavior. This is de facto knowledge processing, increasing awareness of decision-makers about issues, which up till then were beyond their grasp.
5. *Communicated organization* – when the content of information is at the optimal level (connected and integrated), it is necessary

Figure 10-16. The info-communication system architecture of an organization (ICS-Info-Communication System, CAD-Computer-aided Design, CAA-Computer-aided Advertising, CAM-Computer-aided Manufacturing, CAP-Computer-aided Publishing, CAS-Computer-aided Service, DBMS-Database Management System, DMS-Document Management System, RMS-Records Management System, TPS-Transaction Procession System)

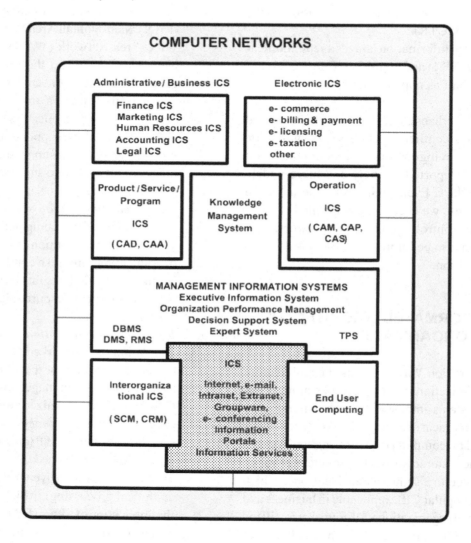

to communicate it to all stakeholders of an organization through: groupware (such collaborative software as Lotus Notes), intranet, extranet (the Internet, which, together with e-mail, can be installed at any level of organization configuration), e-conferencing, information portals, and information services (news and published content of journals, books, music, etc.).

6. *Agile organization* – is a business solution for mass customization of products and services through computer integrated manufacturing (CIM), which integrates computer-aided design (CAD), computer-aided manufacturing (CAM), and management information systems (MIS). This programmable technology may deliver 100 to 1,000 different products from the same production facility, because it reduces setup and changeover times and lowers run size and the cost of customization.

7. *Mobile organization* – electronically and usually wirelessly connects field workers with central applications and office workers via handheld personal computers (HPC) and personal digital assistants (PDA) to increase the velocity of operations, very often via workflow systems (WFS) to access SCM, CRM, and ERP systems via Web technology.

8. *Electronic organization* – is the electronic implementation of previously mentioned systems, particularly through Web technology, e-document management systems (e-DMS), WFS, information portals, and so forth. Its goal is to implement a paperless organization.

Figure 10-17. Virtual enterprise at the beginning of the 21ˢᵗ century (dotted lines -- Outsourced functions)

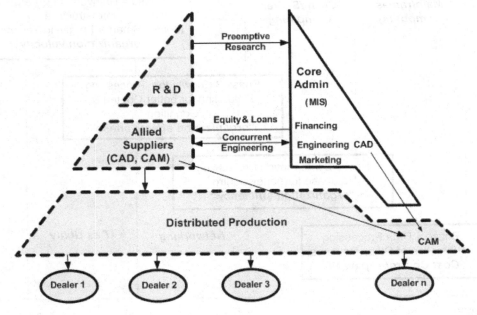

9. *Virtual organization* – is formed dynamically in response to customer demand and dissolved as soon as it becomes economically unviable. Its processes are partially outsourced and sub-contractors are treated as partners who are involved in a common process of accomplishing a task, for example, a designer's spring fashion collection. This organization partially or entirely operates without a real building, mostly via the cyberspace of the virtual organization. The architecture of a virtual enterprise is shown in Figure 10-17.

The organization ecosystem of the 21st century will be characterized by a blurring of once distinct boundaries: between public and private, foreign and domestic, insider and outsider, friend and foe. The effect will be invigorating in many ways. Corporations will be freer to pursue an opportunity wherever in the world they find it, and exploit it according to the changing requirements of circumstances. Outsourcing will become ever more ubiquitous, transforming many corporations into super-efficient organizations. The growing flexibility of vital relationships will require constant attention and inventiveness by all engaged.

Figure 10-18. The stages of IT impact on organization performance

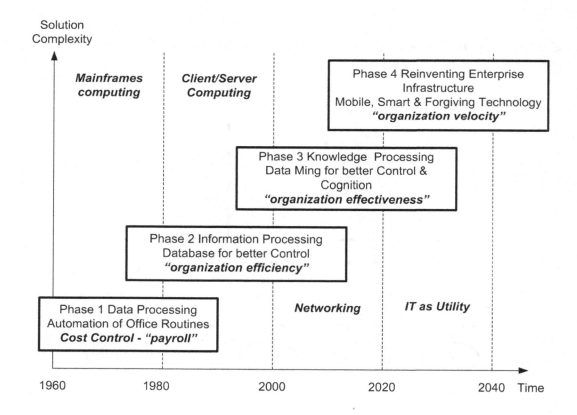

Figure 10-18 illustrates the impact of IT on organization performance in selected technology solutions. This model indicates that modern computing is still very young. At the beginning it is involved in automation of simple office routines; later it shows an ambition to impact an organization's efficiency, effectiveness, and velocity. Will it be enough to slow down civilization's drainage of resources or, instead, will it lead to faster depletion of strategic resources and put the whole civilization in limbo?

THE INFORMATED ARCHITECTURE OF MANAGEMENT

Anthony's (1965) model of planning and control consists of three categories: strategic planning, management control, and operational control[4]. This model has dominated the theory and practice of business for the last 40 years. Anthony's model reflects a closed-system concept of isolated enterprises in a formatted (machines and materials) national economy. This economy was based on the division of a specialized and massive labor force similar to the military in World War I and II with a rigid command structure. The 1980s were the last decade when this model could be successfully applied in business without major modification.

The 1990s were the decade of an emerging global and informated (computers & communication) economy in a post-industrial era, where "borderless-stateless" multinational companies and national companies compete with foreign products and services through innovation, price movements, and time controls. The competition, cooperation, and partnership among company peers, research centers, and suppliers through enterprise-wide computer information systems have shifted the management structure. It has been transformed from a tall to a flattened hierarchy of four or fewer layers with network communications subordinated to result-oriented performers

within and among ad hoc project teams. This new structure reminds one of university governance. In essence, this new multi-domestic enterprise has two rules: "Each person is his/her own boss," and "think globally, act locally."

The steep hierarchy in the Information Wave area is no longer an adequate base of power. Today's managers get work done by building a lateral network of information sharing relationships, and by developing commitment rather than compliance to a shared vision. They also find new sources of ideas and opportunities, and broker deals across internal and external corporate boundaries. Effective managers are integrators, conductors, facilitators, and "fertilizers," not watchdogs or supervisors (Nye & Owens, 1996).

A network is a recognized group of managers (seldom fewer than 25 or more than 100) assembled by senior management. Network membership solution criteria are simple, yet subtle: which selected group managers, by virtue of their business skills, personal motivation, drive, and control of resources, are uniquely positioned to shape and deliver a winning strategy? Networks, the new social architecture, are important for the change of organizational behavior; the frequency, intensity, and honesty of the dialogue among managers determines the outcomes of priority tasks. The network operates at its best when it guarantees the visibility and free exchange of information to all participating members (Harris, 1985; Kanter, 1989; Halal, 1996).

In companies such as Conrail, Dun & Bradstreet Europe, MasterCard International, General Electric, Dupont, and Royal Bank of Canada, networking plays to the participants' best interest, by achieving commitment for specific tasks. Over time, the network induces emotional energy, builds commitment, and enjoys the work (Charan, 1994).

Figure 10-19 depicts a synthesis of existing practices and postulates solutions for a new campus structure of management in a network-

Figure 10-19. Campus management apparatus-driven by the information wave

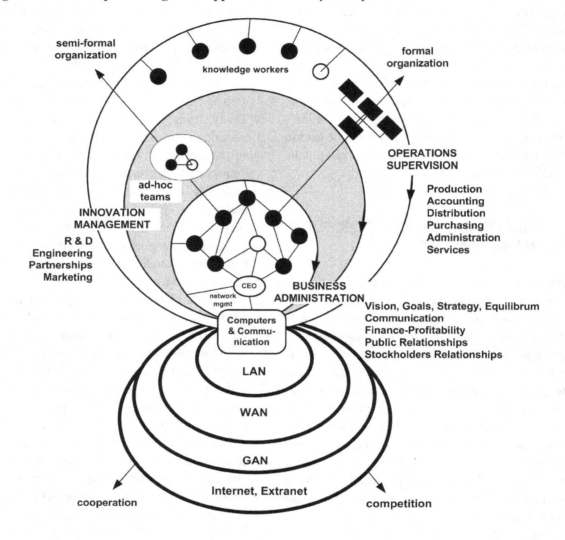

cooperative enterprise. Since knowledge becomes a strategic resource, knowledge-based firms will evolve into university-like organization structures (Davis & Botkin, 1994). As such, they will turn to this structure, which will have dual processes: a formal organization for strict procedures of production, accounting, and so forth, and a semi-formal organization for such innovation-oriented procedures as R&D, engineering, marketing and so forth. A president (CEO) is in such structure a facilitator, not a "boss," while knowledge workers ("faculty") are result-driven workers who are facing customers (students).

In the campus apparatus of management for business settings, the old steep hierarchical structure is inverted and flattened. The new apparatus is divided along three time dimensions: long-, medium-, and short-range. It is also electronically integrated by an enterprise-wide communications and computer information system. Outside of the halls of academia, this model has been fully embraced by Intel and Microsoft.

In the campus model, business administration must provide the vision, motivation, corporate culture, agenda, goals and strategy, communication, profitability, discipline and equilibrium. Business administration is a long-term management function, carried out by a CEO and executives (CFOs, COOs, CIOs, etc.) who ensure a spirit of competition and cooperation. They must also provide new opportunities and customers. The skills required are intellectual, with a global strategic conceptualization of business.

One can suggest the new rules of business in the times of the Information Wave:

1. From one stakeholder and system to many
2. Act locally, think and profit globally
3. Customers, not executives, drive a business
4. Knowledge is as important a strategic resource as capital
5. Cooperation precedes and is integrated into the competitive process
6. Lead time, innovation, quality, and utility satisfy a customer
7. Do not separate thinking from doing and ethics

8. The integration of islands of automation into an enterprise information infrastructure is a gateway to the Electronic Global Village.

These rules (and other ones offered by Kelly [1998] and Herzenberg, Alic, & Wial [1998]) may lead to more efficient, effective, and fast-moving organizations, but we cannot forget that if this can be an impressive achievement from the organization theory point of view, it can be also criticized for profound degradation of the ecosystem, which cannot last forever with such an effective "civilization machine."

THE TRANSFORMATION FROM AN INDUSTRIAL TO AN INFORMATED ENTERPRISE

The transformation of an industrial to an informated enterprise is a very complex and lengthy process. It involves shifts at all levels of an enterprise structure, for example:

*   from a business strategy of economy of scale to one of economy of scope, and therefore from mass production to mass customization

Table 10-3. The comparison of industrial and informated models of an enterprise

Criterion	Industrial Model	Informated Model	Shift Challenge
Work System	Rigid	Flexible	Computer Skills
Control System	Hierarchical	Networked	Knowledge Mgmt
Industrial Relations	"Disposable" workers	High-Trust Relations	Cooperation
Human Resources Practice	Separation of Thinking from Doing	Integration of Thinking, Doing & Ethics	Learning Organization
Business Strategy	Maximization	Optimization	Knowledge Mgmt
Business Reach	Concentrated	Dispersed	Computer Networks

Figure 10-20. The transformation from an industrial to informated enterprise at the beginning of the 21st century

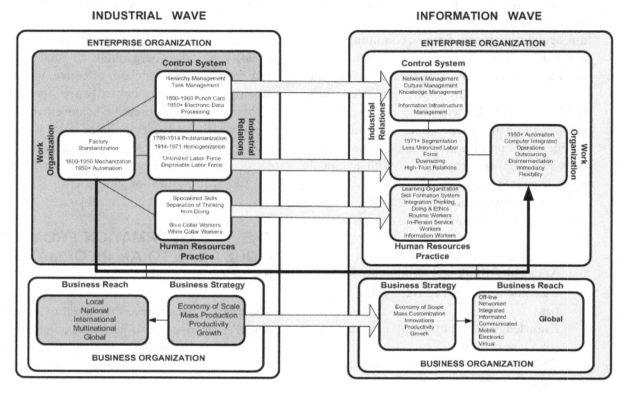

•   from enterprise reach of many levels to the global level, supported by different organization configurations driven by IT

•   from a hierarchical to a network control system of enterprise organization

•   from homogenized and disposable workers to high-trust industrial relations

•   from separated to integrated thinking and doing and ethics in human resources practice

•   from rigid to flexible production, therefore from mechanization to informated automation

The comparison of the industrial and informated model of an enterprise is provided in Table 10-3.

As Table 10-3 and Figure 10-20 indicate, challenges triggered by the Information Wave that an organization must meet are profound and not easy to implement, particularly by unreconstructed managers whose ways of thinking were established before the Information Wave.

CONCLUSION

The Information Wave impacts strongly the way humans perceive cognition and its role in an organization's transformation from the industrial to the informated model. Information itself has no single universal definition. It can be perceived in terms of perspectives or images or both, depending on circumstances. Once civilization learned how to process materials; now it learns how to process information. This leads to the transformation of hard to soft civilization, with more emphasis on informed, knowledgeable and even wiser control of events, with the desire to investigate process more and more. The latter is a good sign of human awareness that the future of civilization depends on human wisdom, which comes along with more knowledge-based and positive experiences of its applications.

On the other hand, the more informed and knowledgeable that decisions are for business, the more problems they may bring for the society, which is growing at a time when employment goes down and strategic resources are more intensively used or even used up. What does it mean for civilization? As we know more, shall we want more and be in more trouble? Can we overcome knowledge that we created?

A. Further Research Directions

- Investigate the relationships among different approaches to the definition of information and their impact on different spheres of human activities. Find out some similarities and differences in information definitions and their impact on understanding how information leads to better performance of organizations and humans.

- Investigate different enterprise configurations driven by information-communication systems and their ability to apply in business and public organizations. Find out some similarities and differences in approaches to the way enterprise configurations are planned and executed. Also examine how information leads to better performances from organizations and people.

- Investigate successful methods and techniques which should be applied in the transformation from industrial to informated organizations.

B. Research Opportunities

- The research opportunity is in investigating the relationships among civilization waves at the levels of economy, organizations, individuals, and society.

C. Additional Ideas

- The Information Wave intellectualizes the human experience, minimizes muscular effort and should lead to a wiser civilization. Investigate the reasons why this premise is not fully successful in human activities.

D. Rationale

- Information is a "substance," which is handled and processed by people and computers. However, information is just a colloquial term, which has several variations (data, concept, knowledge, wisdom), each of which plays a different role in improving humans' systemic control and cognition. This concept is information "arithmetic," which allows for developing information "calculus," needed for more complex information solutions. So far, the development and implementation of information systems unguided by lack of information "arithmetic" have led to automation islands. However, along with better knowledge about *information* these concepts are gradually transforming into information infrastructures. Many new business models enabled by IT are arising for the internal organization and functioning of business and public organizations and for their external interactions with customers/citizens/users, suppliers, and competitors. Those models have to be generalized in order to secure their standardization and cross-organizations communication. To make human and organization activities more efficient and effective, one must *informate* old (agricultural and industrial) organizations. Therefore, methods and techniques supporting this transformation should be investigated and in terms of their technological might and also their social and ethical solutions.

E.   Additional Reading

Anderson, R., Feldman, P., Gerwehr, S., Houghton, B., Mesic, R., Pinder, J., et al. (1999). *Securing the U.S. defense information infrastructure: A proposal approach.* Santa Monica, CA: RAND.

Arndt, C. (2004). *Information measures, information and its description in science and engineering.* (Springer Series: Signals and Communication Technology). New York, NY: Springer.

Ash, R. (1990). *Information theory.* New York, NY: Dover.

Bamford, J. (1983). *The puzzle palace.* New York, NY: Penguin Books.

Bayer, H. (2004). *Information. The new language of science.* Cambridge, MA: Harvard University Press.

Bekenstein, J. (2003). Information in the holographic Universe. *Scientific American.* Retrieved October 16, 2007, from http://www.referencenter.com.

Bikson, T., & Panis, C. (1999). *Citizens, computers and connectivity. A review of trends.* Santa Monica, CA: RAND.

Brillouin, L. (2004). *Science and information theory.* Mineola, NY: Dover.

Cover, T., & Thomas, J. (2006). *Elements of information theory.* New York, NY: Wiley-Interscience.

Davis, B. (1999). *Technoism: At the crossroads of society and technology.* Lulu.com

Drake, W. (1995). *The new information infrastructure.* New York, NY: The Twentieth Century Fund Press.

Eager, W. (1995). *The information payoff.* Englewood Cliffs, NJ: Prentice Hall PTR.

Floridi, L. (2005). Is information meaningful data?. *Philosophy and Phenomenological Research, 70*(2), 351-370.

Gallager, R. (1968). *Information theory and reliable communication.* New York, NY: John Wiley and Sons.

Goldman, S. (1969). *Information theory.* New York, NY: Dover.

Hartley, R. (1928). Transmission of information. *Bell System Technical Journal, 7,* 535.

Kelly, J., Jr. (1956). A new interpretation of information rate. *Bell System Technical Journal, 35,* 917-26.

Khinchin, A. (1957). *Mathematical foundations of information theory.* New York, NY: Dover.

Landauer, R. (2000). Irreversibility and heat generation in the computing process. *IBM Journal of Resource Development, 44*(1-2), 261-270.

------------------(1993). Information is physical. Workshop on Physics and Computation PhysComp'92. Los Alamos. *IEEE Comp. Science Press,* (pp. 1-4).

Leff, H., & Rex, A. (Eds.). (1990). *Maxwell's demon: Entropy, information, computing.* Princeton, NJ: Princeton University Press.

Libicki, M. (2000). *Who runs what in the global information grid?.* Santa Monica, CA: RAND.

Libicki, M., Schneider, M., Frelinger, D., & Slomovic, A. (2000). *Scaffolding the new Web.* Santa Monica, CA: RAND.

MacKay, D. 2003). *Information theory, inference, and learning algorithms.* Cambridge: Cambridge University Press.

Mansuripur, M. (1987). *Introduction to information theory.* New York, NY: Prentice Hall.

Molander, R., Wilson, P., Mussington, B., & Mesic, R. (1998). *Strategic information warfare rising.* Santa Monica, CA: RAND.

Poster, M. (1990). *The mode of information.* Chicago, IL: The University of Chicago Press.

Reza, F. (1994). *An introduction to information theory.* New York, NY: Dover.

Shannon, C. (1948). A mathematical theory of communication. *Bell System Technical Journal, 27,* 379-423; 623-656.

Shannon, C., & Weaver, W. (1949). *The mathematical theory of communication.* Urbana-Champaign, IL: University of Illinois Press.

Shapiro, C., & Varian, H. (1999). *Information rules.* Cambridge, MA: Harvard Business School Press.

Seife, C. (2006). *Decoding the universe.* New York, NY: Viking.

Siegfried, T. (2000). *The bit and the pendulum.* New York, NY: Wiley.

Slack, J., & Fejes, F. (1987). *The ideology of the information age.* Norwood, NJ: Ablex Publishing Books.

Wainfam, L., & Davis, P. (2004). *Challenges in virtual collaboration.* Santa Monica, CA: RAND.

Wang, M. (2000). *Accelerated logistics.* Santa Monica, CA: RAND.

Ware, W. (1998). *The cyber-posture of the national information infrastructure.* Santa Monica, CA. RAND.

Yeung, R. (2002). *A first course in information theory.* London: Kluwer Academic/Plenum Publishers.

REFERENCES

Ackoff, R. (1967). Management misinformation systems. *Management Science, 14,* 147-156.

_____(1978). *The art of problem solving.* New York, NY: J. Wiley.

Anthony, R. (1965). *Planning and control systems: A framework for analysis.* Boston, MA: Harvard University Press.

Beach, L., Mitchel, T., Daeton, M., & Prothero, D. (1997). Information relevance, content, and source credibility in the revision of options. *Organizational Behavior and Human Performance, 21,* 1-16.

Bohm, D., & Peat, F. (1978). *Science, order, and creativity.* New York, NY: Bantam Books.

Boulder, K. (1989). *Three faces of power.* Newbury Park, CA: Sage Publications.

Chajtman, S. (1973). *Organizacja produkcji rytmicznej (Organization of rhythmic production).* Warsaw: PWE.

Charan, R. (1991). New networks reshape organizations—for results. *Harvard Business Review, 69*(5), 104-115.

Cyert, R., & March, J. (1963). *A behavioral theory of the firm.* Englewood Cliffs, NJ: Prentice Hall.

Dewhirst, H. (1971). Influence of perceived information-sharing norms on communication channel utilization. *Academy of Management Journal, 14*(3), 305-315.

Daft, R., & Lengel, R. (1986). Organizational information requirements, media richness and structural design. *Management Science, 32*(5), 554-571.

Davis, S., & Botkin, J. (1994). The coming of knowledge-based business. *Harvard Business Review, 72*(5), 165-189.

Draft, R., & Lengel, R. (1984). *Information richness*. Greenwich, CT: JAI Press.

Galbraith, J. (1973). *Strategies of organization design*. Reading, MA: Addison-Wesley.

Gore, A. (1991). Information superhighways: The next information revolution. *The Futurist, 25*(1), 21-23.

_____(1993). *Earth in the balance*. New York, NY: A Plume Books.

Halal, W. (1996). *The new management*. San Francisco, CA: Berett-Koechler Publishers.

Harris, P. (1985). *Management in transition*. San Francisco, CA: Jossey Bass Publishers.

Herzberg, S., Alic, J., & Wial, G. (1998). *New rules for a new economy*. Ithaca, NY: ILR Press.

Kanter, R. (1989). The new managerial work. *Harvard Business Review, 67*(6), 85-92.

Karraker, R. (1991). Highways of mind, nationwide information network. *Whole Earth Review, Spring*, 4-15.

Kelly, K. (1998). *New rules for the new economy*. New York, NY: Viking

Leavitt, H. (1975). Beyond the analytical manager. *California Management Review, 17*(3), 5-12.

Mintzberg, H., Raisinghani, D., & Theoret, A. (1976). The structure of unstructured decision processes. *Administrative Science Quarterly, 21*(2), 246-275.

Monge, P., Edwards, J., & Kirstel, K. (1978). The determination of communication structure in large organizations: A review of research. In: B. Ruben (Ed.), *Communication Yearbook* (pp. 311-331). New Brunswick, NJ: Transaction Books.

Naylor, J. (1964). Accuracy and variability of information sources of determiners and source preference of decision makers. *Journal of Applied Psychology, 48*, 43-49.

Nye, J., &Owens, W. (1996). America's information age. *Foreign Affairs, 75*(2), 26-36.

O'Reilly, C. (1982). Variations in decision makers' use of information sources: The impact of quality and accessibility of information. *Academy of Management Journal, 25*(4), 756-771.

O'Reilly, C., Chatman, J., & Anderson, J. (1978). Message flow and decision making. In: F. Joblin, L. Putman, K. Roberts, & L. Porter (Eds.), *Handbook of organizational communication*. Newbury Park, CA: SAGE.

Powers, W. (1973). *Behavior: The control of perception*. Chicago, IL: Aldine Publishing Co.

Roberts, K., & O'Reilly, C. (1978). Organization as communication structures: An empirical approach. *Human Communication Research, 44*, 283-293.

Shannon, C., & Weaver, W. (1949). *The mathematical theory of communication*. Urbana, IL: University of Illinois Press.

Simon, H. (1965). *The shape of automation*. New York, NY: Harper and Row.

Starr, M. (1971). *Management: A modern approach*. New York, NY: Harcourt Brace Jovanovich, Inc.

Targowski, A. (1990a). Beyond a concept of a communication process. *The Journal of Business Communication, 27*(1), 75-86.

_____(1990b). *The strategy and architecture of enterprise-wide information management systems*. Harrisburg, PA: Idea Group Publishing.

_____(1991). Computing in a totalitarian State: Poland's way to an informed society. *Journal of Information Management, Information Executive, 4*(3), 10-16.

_____(2003). *Electronic enterprise, strategy and architecture*. Harrisburg, PA: Idea Group Publishing.

Targowski, A., & Bowman, J. (1988) The layer-based pragmatic model of the communication process. *The Journal of Business Communication, 25*(1), 5-24.

Weick, K. (1979). *The social psychology of organizing* (2nd ed.). Reading, MA: Addison-Wesley.

ENDNOTES

1   This will work only if semantic meaning is rejected not only as a subjective factor but as an objective one as well. That is, the format of a message must consciously and successfully exclude all assumed subtexts. Otherwise, subtexts can be the key to a message. Just ask any teenager how much of their communication is based on shared values that never have to be spoken. To reject semantics is to say that a message cannot be anything more than a list. This may work in business so long as it is rigorously enforced, but such enforcement programs tend to be extremely uncomfortable to the people they are enforced on. Even when it works, it creates a world as rigorously formal as a video game, and the surgery required on data may end up carving away some very inevitable side effects.

2   O'Reilly, Chatman, and Andersen (1978) indicate that decision makers are noticeably biased in their procurement of information. Instead of relying in the most accurate sources of information, they rely on more accessible sources (Naylor, 1964). O'Reilly (1982) found that although decision makers recognized information sources of high quality, they use sources that provide lower-quality information that are more accessible. He explains those results in terms of the cost involved in acquiring information from less accessible sources. The bias toward accessible information is also reflected in managers' strong preferences for oral as opposed to written information (Dewhirst, 1971), as well as information from credible sources (Beach et al., 1978).

3   On this topic, there are some interesting ideas provided by Draft and Lengel (1986) who argue that rich media are needed to process information on complex organizational topics, therefore managers will turn to face-to-face or telephone communications. Ackoff (1967) and Leavitt (1975) argue that computerized information systems for management provide data about stable, recurring, predictable events but do not provide insight into the intangible, social dimensions of an organization. Weick (1979) and Galbraith (1973) argue for the support of management hierarchy, because it reduces uncertainty of information and reduces ambiguity of communication.

4   This looks like a direct borrowing of 1930s Soviet military theory, with its division of war into strategic, operational, and tactical levels, as against everyone else's two-level (strategic and tactical) division at that time. The idea has become canonical everywhere since that time. Did R. N. Anthony know about it?

Chapter XI
Service Science and Automation Laws

INTRODUCTION

The purpose of this chapter is to define a scope of service science and service automation in service economy based on ideal generic service systems originally developed by the author. There are two goals of this study: 1) to develop generic service categories and their generic systems, and 2) to define a scope of service science based upon the presented generic models of service systems, which determine the required support from emerging system science. The research methodology is based on the architectural modeling according the paradigm of enterprise-wide systems (Targowski, 2003).

The architectural system approach is based on the philosophy of the system approach (Klir, 1985), and management cybernetics (Beer, 1981) which provide comprehensive and cohesive solutions to the problems of systems design, thus eliminating the fuziveness of the "application portfolio" and the "information archipelago" (McFarlan, 1981; Targowski, 1990). The mission of the architectural system approach is to find the ultimate synthesis of the whole system structure that involves appropriate logic, appropriate technological accommodation, operational quality, a positive user involvement, and co-existence with nature

(Targowski, 1990). In its nature, the architectural system approach is of deductive rather than inductive nature. It looks for the ideal model of a solution, which in practice is far away from its perfect level. The difference between the architectural system approach and the engineering approach is in the level of abstraction. The architectural models are more conceptual whereas engineering outcomes are more technical and specific. The architectural system approach is the response to the complexity of expected outcomes. Prior to spending a few million dollars for a new information system, one must provide its information architecture and the business and social implications associated with it (Targowski, 2003). In this sense, this study will define service systems' architectures.

Service economy can refer to one or both of two recent economic developments. First is the increased importance of the sector in industrialized economies. Services account for a higher percentage of U.S. GDP than 20 years ago, since modern-day off-shore outsourcing of manufacturing contributes to the growing service sector of the American economy. The 2006 Fortune 500 companies list contains more service companies and fewer manufacturers than in previous decades. The service sector is classified as the tertiary sector of industry (also known as the service industry) and is one of the three main industrial categories of a developed economy, the others being the secondary industry (manufacturing, construction), and primary industry (extraction such as mining, agriculture and fishing). Services are defined in conventional literature as "intangible goods" (Drucker, 1969; Rathmell, 1974; Bell, 1976; Shostack, 1977). According to Laroche (2001), it is clear that intangibility has been cited by several authors as the fundamental factor differentiating services from goods (Rust, Zahorik, & Keiningham, 1996; Breivik, Troye, & Olsson, 1998; Lovelock, 2001). All other differences emerge from this distinction (Bateson, 1979; Zeithaml & Bitner, 2000). According to evident practice, service tends to be wealth-consuming, whereas manufacturing is wealth-producing. The tertiary sector of industry involves the provision of services to businesses as well as final consumers and citizens (users of government services). Services may involve the transport, distribution and sale of goods from producer to a consumer as may happen in wholesaling and retailing, or may involve the provision of a service such as in pest control or entertainment. Goods may be transformed in the process of providing a service, as happens in the restaurant industry. However, the focus is on people interacting with people and serving the customer rather than transforming physical goods.

Since the 1960s, there has been a substantial shift from the other two industry sectors to the tertiary sector in industrialized countries. The service sector also consists of the "soft" parts of the economy such as insurance, government, tourism, banking, retail and education. In soft sector employment, people use time to deploy knowledge assets, collaboration assets, and process-engagement to create productivity (effectiveness), performance improvement potential (potential) and sustainability. Typically, the output of this time is content (information), service, attention, advice, experiences, and/or discussion ("intangible goods"). Other examples of service

sector employment include public utilities, which are often considered part of the tertiary sector as they provide services to people. Creating the utility's infrastructure is often considered part of the secondary sector even though the same business may be involved in both aspects of the operation.

Economies tend to follow a developmental progression that takes them from a heavy reliance on agriculture and mining toward the development of industry (e.g., automobiles, textiles, shipbuilding, and steel) and finally toward a more service-based structure. For example, IBM treats its business as a service business. Although it still manufactures high-end computers, it sees the physical goods as a small part of the "business solutions" industry. They have found that the price elasticity of demand for "business solutions" is much less elastic than for hardware. There has been a corresponding shift to a subscription pricing model rather than receiving a single payment for a piece of manufactured equipment. Many manufacturers are now receiving a steady stream of revenue for ongoing contracts.

Manufacturing tends to be more open to international trade and competition than services. As a result, there has been a tendency for the first economies to industrialize to come under competitive attack by those seeking to industrialize later, for example, because production, especially labor costs, are lower than in those industrializing later. The resultant shrinkage of manufacturing in the leading economies might explain their growing reliance on the service sector.

Service economy can refer to the relative importance of service in a product offering. That is, products today have a higher service component than in previous decades. In the management literature, this is referred to as the servitization of products. Virtually every product today has a service component to it. The old dichotomy between product and service has been replaced by a service-product continuum. Many products are being transformed into services.

Figure 11-1 depicts the contribution of the service sector to the U.S. gross domestic product in 2005. Since government provides mostly services to its citizens, one can state that the service sector contributes 80% to the U.S. gross domestic product. This level of contribution must turn attention of system developers, who up till now are mostly engaged in the production and commerce systems.

THE NATURE OF SERVICES

The first goal of this study will be pursued in defining first the nature of services and their categories. Later, comprehensive graphic models will be developed for generic systems, supporting major categories of service processes.

Service can be defined as follows:

Services are a diverse group of economic activities that include high-technology, knowledge-intensive sub-sectors as well as labor-intensive, low-skill areas. In many aspects, service sectors exhibit marked differences from manufacturing, although these distinctions may be blurring (OECD Report, 2000).

A good review of definitions of service is provided by Heskett (1990). Simply defined, services on demand are a diverse group of economic activities not directly associated with the manufacture of goods, mining or agriculture. They typically involve the provision of human value added in the form of labor, advice, managerial skill, entertainment, training, intermediation and the like, mostly after manufacturing or goods (such as natural resources and food) delivered to customers. They differ from other types of economic activities in a number of ways. Many, for example, cannot be inventoried and must be consumed ("customized") at the point of production. This could include trips to the doctor, enjoying a meal at a restaurant, flying from Chicago to Paris, or attending a concert.

This is in marked contrast with manufactured products, whose tangible character allows them to be stored, distributed widely, and consumed without direct interaction with the entity that produced the good.

Technological advances are, however, narrowing the differences between services and other economic activities. While it has not reached the point where someone can enjoy the ambience of a good restaurant without physically going to one, information and communication technology (ICT) now enables people to participate in a growing number of service-related activities in real or deferred time without having to be physically present. Copies of movies and most other performances can be recorded and mass-produced for future consumption like manufactured products. Software is developed and boxed like any other manufactured product and is considered, for all intents and purposes, a good—albeit with a high service-related content. In these instances, services have, in a sense, taken on the characteristics of commodities—one provider is mass-producing a common product for many people. Service providers are thus increasingly able to benefit from economies of scale. The benefits have not, however, been restricted to large enterprises as small firms can achieve similar gains through increased networking.

The relationship between service providers and consumers is also changing in other ways that may have significant implications for economies. Technology now allows providers to produce a single product which is not mass-produced but which is capable of being mass-consumed, either on a standardized or customized basis. Such is the case with online Internet access to dictionaries, encyclopedias, newspapers, museum collections, and so forth. It will also apparently be the case with key, basic operating software in the near future, as both Microsoft and Sun Microsystems have announced their intention to supplement distribution of "boxed" software with online versions (Taylor, 1999).

Technology is also affecting the relationship between providers and consumers in areas previously unthinkable such as healthcare, where the need for personal contact to diagnose and treat ailments is becoming less essential. Internet-based banking, real estate, retail and financial services provide other examples where personal or on-site contact with service providers is no longer essential for the services to be performed. In many instances, such services can, in fact, be provided far more efficiently via the Internet.

Table 11-1 characterizes services in the developed economy

Figure 11-2 illustrates the processive architecture of the U.S. national economy, which also indicates that "service" dominates the economic activities of the American Society in term of its functionality, business, and pursuit for the complete life.

A CLASSIFICATION OF SERVICES IN A DEVELOPED ECONOMY

Once the developed economies moved to service economies in the second part of the 20th century (Bell, 1973), the development of different kinds of services became almost endless. In order to grasp their realm, it is necessary to classify them. Some of the first who undertook this task were Malchup

Table 11-1. Illustrative list of services

Service	Activities Related to the:
Wholesale and retail trade	Sale of goods
Information	Gathering and dissemination of written, audio or visual information including films and records
Transportation and warehousing	Distribution of goods
Finance and insurance	Facilitation of financial transactions, including those related to risk management
Real estate, rental and leasing	Temporary transfer of property, and the temporary or definitive transfer of real estate
Professional, scientific and technical	Provision of specialized, generally "knowledge-based," expertise (e.g., legal, accountancy, and engineering)
Management of companies and enterprises	Management of holding companies
Healthcare and social assistance	Provision of healthcare and social assistance (e.g., doctors, hospitals and clinics)
Education	Provision of instruction and training (e.g., schools and specialized training centers)
Arts, entertainment and recreation	Provision of entertainment in a broad sense (e.g., museums, opera, theatre, sports and gambling establishments)
Accommodation and food services	Provision of lodging, or the provision of meals, snacks or beverages
Public administration	Governing or administration of public entities and programs
Other	Provision of personal services, repair and maintenance activities, professional societies, religious institutions, and so forth

Source: Based on US Bureau of Census, 1999

Figure 11-1. Contribution by sector to U.S. gross domestic product 2005

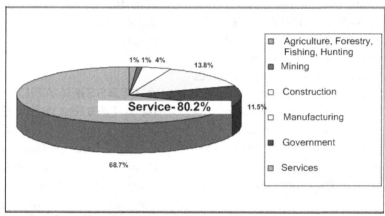

Source: Bureau of Economic Analysis, Industry Table E, January 2007

(1962) and Porat (1977) who wanted to address the rise of knowledge and information-based activities in national economy. They provoked Bell (1981) to emphasize that industrial economy is being transformed into information economy, which defined four criteria of his classification schema. All these tree classifications turned public attention to new economic activities and emerging people's knowledge and skills. Eventually, business strategies intercepted the torch of service classifications. The first was Lovelock (1983), who defined classification of services from the point of view of how to gain strategic marketing internally. Later in his famous and very good textbook with Wirtz (2007), he extended this classification into the four categories of service classification.

A review of these service classifications is provided in Table 11-2.

Every listed classification in Table 11-2 was defined according to a given purpose. The economic orientation is the purpose of first seven classifications while the marketing orientation is the purpose of the last two classifications. Certainly, these purposes served well in the broad context of national economy and marketing strategies, respectively.

In this investigation, the e-service system architecture is the purpose of a new service classification. Three categories of service will

be recognized as the main schema of the classification. Another three categories of services will be differentiated by applying a criterion of service intangibility, defined by Laroche (2001). In the post-industrial economy, more and more physically intangible products exist in our society, often called "information products" (Freiden et al., 1998), which are almost totally intangible. Laroche (2001) characterizes tangibility as more typical for "traditional" products and services. In a new service classification, services of six categories will be recognized either as "tangible" (traditional and "touchable") or as "intangible" (idea-information-oriented).

Figure 11-3 defines six categories of services applying the following criteria:

1. Society served:

•   Services directed at citizens and communities (tangible service)
•   Services directed at the nation (intangible service)

2. People served:

•   Services directed at a person (tangible service)

Table 11-2. A review of most popular classifications of service activities

Author	Purpose	Perspective of	Classification Schema	Classification Sub-schema
Smith (1776)	To facilitate economic analysis	Economist	1.Productive activities (creating tangible product) 2.Nonproductive activities (creating intangible services)	
Clark (1940)	To analyze the transition of economy	Economist	1.Primary sector (extracting) 2.Secondary sector (manufacturing) 3.Tertiary sector (services)	
Gersuny and Rosengren (1973)	To analyze the economic activities	Economist	Tertiary sector	Quasi-domestic services (food and lodging) Business services "quinary" group including recreation, healthcare, and education
Machlup (1962)	To emphasize the importance of knowledge production and distribution	Economist	1. Education 2. R & D 3. Communication media 4. Information machines 5. Information services	Expenditures made by: Government Business Consumers
Porat (1977)	To define what economic activities can be attributed to information activities	Economist	1.Markets for information	Media and educational institutions
			2.Information in markets	Advertising, insurance, finance, brokerages
			3.Information infrastructure	Printing, data processing, telecommunications, information goods
			4. Wholesale and retail trade in information goods	Bookstores, computer stores, theaters, and so on
			5.Support facilities for information activities	Buildings used by information industries, office furnishing, and so on
Bureau of Economic Analysis (2008)	To calculate GDP	Economist	1.Finance, insurance, Real estate 2.Retail trade 3.Wholesale Trade 4.Transportation and Public Utilities 5.Communications 6.Other services 7.Government and government enterprises	

continued on following page

Table 11-2. continued

Bell (1981)	To indicating the transfer from Industrial to Information Economy	Sociologist and Economist	1.	Knowledge	Education, R &D, Libraries, Lawyers, Doctors, Accountants
			2.	Entertainment	Motion Picture Television, Music
			3.	Economic Transactions and Records	Banking, Insurance, Brokerage
			4.	Infrastructure Services	Telecommunications, Computers, and Programs
Lovelock (1983)	To gain strategic marketing inside	Business marketing strategist	1.Basic demand characteristics		Object served (persons vs. property), Extend of demand/supply imbalances, Discrete vs. continuous relationships between customers and providers,
			2. Service content and benefits		Extent of physical goods content, Extent of personal service content, Single service vs. bundle of service, Timing and duration of benefits
			3.Service delivery procedures		Multisite vs. single site delivery, Allocation of capacity (reservation vs. first come, first served
Bowen (1990a)	To integrate marketing with organizational behavior	Business marketing strategist	1. Service production 2. Service delivery 3. Service consumption		Focusing on service as a face-to-face game between persons.

- Services directed at a people's awareness (intangible service)

3. Possession served (criterion applied by Lovelock and Wirtz 2007):

- Services directed at property (tangible service)

- Services directed at information-communication handling (intangible service)

This classification is, to a certain degree, extending Lovelock and Wirtz's classification (2007) which is business-oriented. Their classification of service categories contains *four* major categories, such as tangible actions of people, tangible actions of possessions, intangible actions of people, and

Figure 11-2. The progressive architecture of the U.S. national economy

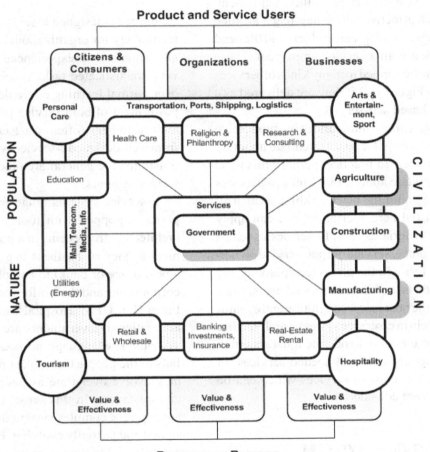

intangible actions of possessions. The presented classification in Figure 11-3 differentiates *six* major categories and differs in some titles of these categories and their content. For example, two new categories were added to reflect the whole national economy, and not just business such as society served at the levels of citizens and communities and the nation; this includes 20 new kinds of services. Some titles in the presented classification look perhaps similar but are more precise. For example, "information processing" is recognized as "info-communication handling," which incorporates many telecommunication-oriented services typical for the Information Age

(1998+). In comparison, the older classification of "data processing" is more characteristic for the Computer Age (1980+) when technology-based services emerged as the main trend in the economy, but certainly not as e-services. The old classification's "mental stimulus processing" services sounds too Freudelian. The new classification offers "services directed at people's awareness."

The new service classifications presented can be applied to modeling of the same type of services' systems. The service modeling approach by Dabholkar (1996) is mostly limited to technology-based self-service and testing customer attitude in the scope of cognitive attributes (e.g., speed of delivery, ease of use, reliability, enjoyment, control) and affective attributes (e.g., attitude toward using technological products and the need for interaction with a service employee). These attributes can be applied to many kinds of services classified in Figure 11-3 if they are delivered as a technology-based self-service.

Applying three main and six supportive criteria, it was possible to differentiate about 82 kinds of services. In practice, perhaps this table can accommodate about 1,000 kinds of services (e.g., copying, tanning, blacksmithing) which all cannot be listed here. Certainly, one can apply many other criteria to classify services such as service substance, service output, service ownership, and so forth. In the presented approach, the main criterion is the kind of serviced users, since this leads to the processes recognition and eventually should help in e-service systems' architecture planning. On the other hand, one must state that e-service may not cover all needed services. In this approach a scope of services which can be globalized is not considered.

THE E-SERVICE SYSTEM REQUIREMENTS

E-service system (e-SS) is a mission-goal-strategy-driven configuration of technology, organizational processes and networks designed to deliver services that satisfy the needs, wants, or aspirations of customers, citizens, and users. Marketing, operations, and global environment considerations have significant implications for the design of an e-service system. Four criteria can impact e-service systems architecture:

- service business model
- customer contact and level of involvement (service user interface),
- service provider's enterprise complexity (enterprise systems and networks)

- scope of goods involved in service

Properly designed e-service systems employ technology for organizational networks that can allow relatively inexperienced people to perform very sophisticated tasks quickly, vaulting them over normal learning curve delays. Ideally, empowerment of both service provider employees and customers (often via tself-service) results from well-designed e-service systems. Figure 11-4 illustrates the general architecture of IT-driven service systems.

E-service systems range from an individual person equipped with tools of the trade (e.g., architect, entrepreneur) to a portion of a government agency or business (e.g., branch office of a post office or bank) to complete multinational corporations and their information systems (e.g., Pizza Hut, UPS). Hospitals, universities, cities, and national governments are designed service systems. The language, norms, attitudes, and beliefs of the people that make up a service system may evolve over time as people adjust to new circumstances. In this sense, e-service systems are a type of complex system that is partially designed and partially evolving. E-service systems are designed to *deliver* or *provision* services but they often consume services as well.

The e-service system is both a service provider and a customer of multiple types of services. Because service systems are designed both in how they provision and consume services, services systems are often linked into a complex service value chain or value network where each link is a value proposition. Service systems may be nested inside of service systems, for example, a staff and operating room unit inside a hospital that is part of a nationwide healthcare provider network.

E-service system developers and architects often seek to exploit economic complementarities or network effect to rapidly grow and scale up the service. For example, credit card usage is part of a service system in which the more people and businesses that use and accept the credit cards, the more value the credit cards system can eventually

Figure 11-3. Six categories of services

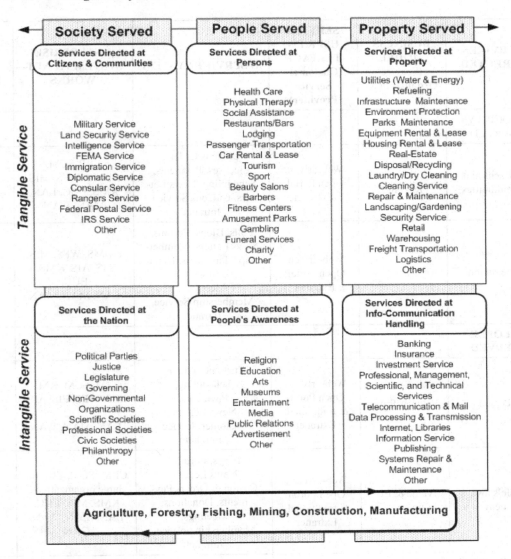

offer to the provider and all stakeholders in the e-service system. E-service system innovation often requires integrating technology innovation, business model (or value proposition) innovation, social-organizational innovation, and demand (new customer wants, needs, aspirations) innovation. For example, a national e-service system may be designed with policies that enable more citizens (the customers of the governments) to become an entrepreneur, and thereby create more innovation and wealth for the nation. E-service systems may include payment mechanisms for selecting a level of service to be provided (up-front or one-time payment) or payment based on downstream value sharing or taxation derived from customers who received the benefit of the service (downstream or ongoing payment). Payments may also be in the form of or other types of intangible value.

Table 11-3. Application requirements for e-service and enterprise systems

SERVICES DIRECTED at	BUSINESS MODEL (Service Organization)	SERVICE USER INTERFACE (Customer-Service Provider)	E-SERVICE SYSTEM	ENTERPRISE SYSTEMS & NETWORKS	GOODS INVOLVED
SOCIETY SERVED					
Citizens and communities	Efficiency & Value	Web-driven, Open Portal, Extranet	Citizens Orders, Licenses, Payments, Scheduling, News Letters, Citizens Service, Intranet	ERP, SCM, e-DMS, WFS, MIS, KMS, EUC, LAN, MAN, WAN	Highly
The nation	Value	Web-driven, Open Portal, Extranet	Polls, Blogs, Forums, News Letters, Memberships, Payments, Donations, Meetings, Membership Service, Intranet	e-DMS, WFS, MIS, FIS, AIS, KMS, EUC, LAN, MAN, WAN	Minimal
PEOPLE SERVED					
Person	Value & Profit	Web-driven , Open Portal & traditional, Extranet	Customer Orders, Scheduling, Payments, News Letters, Customer Service, Intranet	CRM, SCM, KMS, MIS, WFS, FIS, AIS, EUC LAN, MAN, WAN	Significantly
People's awareness	Value & Efficiency	Web-driven , Open Portal & traditional, Extranet	Blogs, Forums, News Letters, Customer Orders Payments, Donations, Meetings, Membership Service, Intranet	CRM, SCM, ERP for large organizations KMS, MIS, EUC, LAN, MAN, WAN, GAN	Significantly
POSSESSION SERVED					
Property	Effectiveness	Web-driven, Open Portal & traditional Extranet	Customer/Citizens Orders, Payments, Scheduling, Forums, News Letters, Customer/Citizens Services, Intranet	CRM, SCM, ERP for large organizations KMS, MIS, WFS, EUC, LAN, MAN, WAN	Highly
Info-communication handling	Value & Effectiveness	Web-driven, Open Portal & traditional Extranet	Customer Orders, Payments, Scheduling, News Letters, Customer Service, Intranet	CRM, SCM, ERP for large organizations and KMS, WFS, MIS, FIS, AIS, EUC, LAN, MAN, WAN	Depends

Figure 11-4. The general architecture of service-driven IT systems

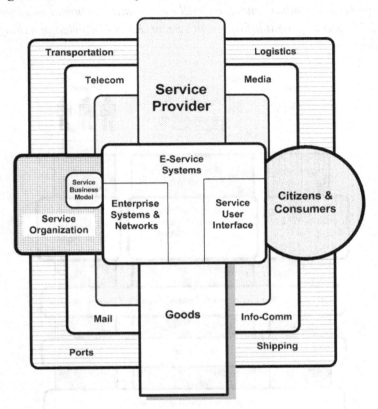

Table 11-3 provides application requirements for each of the six e-services systems categories. It is important to notice that in majority cases, the e-service system is the transition layer between service user interface and enterprise systems and networks.

The architectures of Web-driven services are well developed and widely described in the professional literature of the emerging 21st century (Erl, 2004; Felipe, 2005; Rosenfeld & Morvil, 2006; and others). In this study, the main point is that the Web-based service architectures should be an extension of enterprise-wide computing, of course, if the nature of e-service is based on relatively complex enterprise computing, which is called the "mortar and click" solution. If a solution is based on the modest "click and click" approach, then the enterprise-wide computing may be of limited application.

The following components are included in the e-service and enterprise systems requirements (Targowski, 2003):

- ERP as a set of service demand planning (SDP), service resources planning (SRP), financial information system (FIS), accounting information system (AIS), and others
- SCM – supply chain management
- CRM – customer relations management
- WFS – work flow system
- E-DMS – electronic document management system
- KMS – knowledge management system, composed of data warehouse and data mining

Figure 11-5. The architecture of a citizens and community e-service system (ERP - enterprise resource planning, SCM - supply chain management, e-DMS - electronic document management system, WFS - work flow system, MIS - management information system, KMS - knowledge management system, EUC - end user comupting)

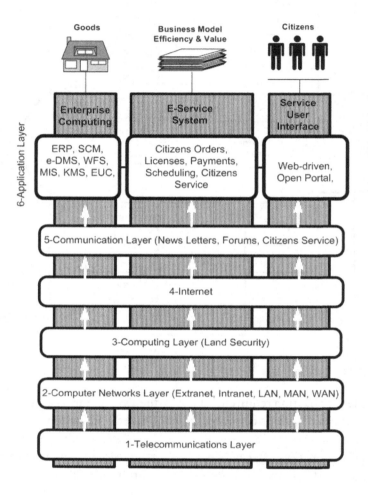

- MIS–management information system, composed of transactions processing system (TPS), enterprise data base management system (EDBMS), enterprise performance management system (EPMS), and executive information system (EIS)
- EUC-end-user computing
- LAN-Local Area Network
- MAN-Metropolitan Network
- WAN-Wide Area Network
- GAN-Global Area Network
- Other

THE GENERIC ARCHITECTURES OF E-SERVICE SYSTEMS (E-SS)

Based on the application requirements provided in Table 11-2, two generic architectures are defined for the citizen and community e-service system

Figure 11-6. The architecture of a personal e-service system (FIS - financial information system, AIS - accounting information systems)

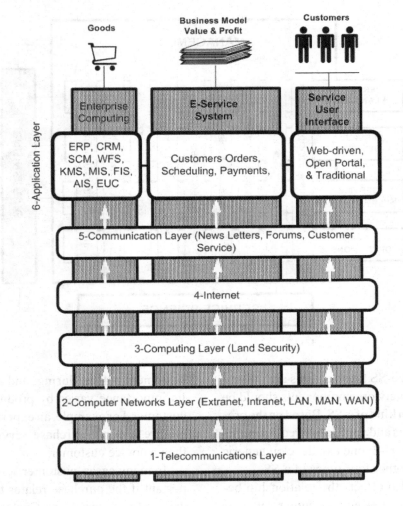

(Figure 11-5) and for the person e-service system (Figure 6). This is assumed that the enterprise system and end-user-computing are included in the e-SS.

Figure 11-5 illustrates the architecture of the citizens and community e-service system category. It indicates that the e-service system and service user interface vertical segments are new additions to the enterprise computing vertical segment. Furthermore, these segments are built from six horizontal layers: telecommunication, computer networks, computing, Internet, communication, and applications. These six horizontal layers are typical for enterprise computing. It indicates that if possible, a successful e-service system should be based on the previously developed enterprise computing.

Figure 11-6 illustrates the architecture of a person e-service system category. It also indicates the same regularities in the layer complexity as it was shown in Figure 11-5, reflecting a different e-service system category. However, the major difference between these two e-service system categories is in their application layers, where different kinds of services are provided in online processing.

Figure 11-7. The relationships among service science, management and engineering (SSME) approaches within the context of developmental and operational service stages

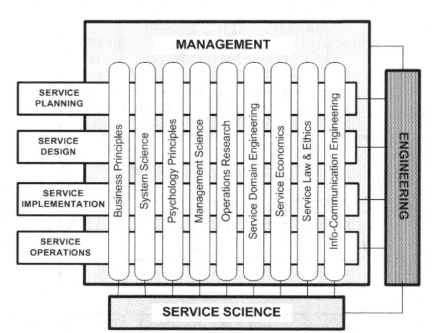

The presented e-SS architectures are generic and their system/network components should be tailored for a given kind of e-SS. Based on the provided architectures and application requirements provided in Table 11-2, one can develop generic architectures for other four types of e-SS.

Technology also affects the relationship between service providers and consumers in areas previously unthinkable, such as healthcare, where the need for personal contact to diagnose and treat ailments is becoming less essential. Internet-based banking, real estate, retail and financial services provide other examples where personal or on-site contact with service providers is no longer essential for the services to be performed. In many instances, such services can, in fact, be provided far more efficiently via the Internet or through other remote communication modes.

One of the most critical components of the e-SS in customer service is the provision of service to customers before, during, and after a purchase. Its importance varies by product, industry and customer. For example, an expert customer might require less pre-purchase service (i.e., advice) than a novice customer.

In many cases, customer service is more important if the purchase relates to a "service" as opposed to a "product." Customer service may be provided by a person (e.g., sales and service representative) or by automated means called self-service. Examples of self service are Internet sites. Customer service is normally an integral part of a company's business model. An example of a service delivery system for the Best Buy chain is shown in Figure 11-7 (the application layer of previous models is expanded). This model indicates that if enterprise systems are well developed then e-service system is a natural addition to them. The most critical systems for e-service are: portal, e-catalog, e-customer orders, supply chain management (SCM), customer relations management (CRM) and document management system (DMS). Such sub-systems of CRM not shown in Figure 11-7 are: e-customer service (Web-driven), call center, e-customer support (Web-driven), e-store, e-payment, e-field service, contact management, Internet relationships management, telemarketing, and so forth.

TOWARD THE SERVICE SCIENCE SCOPE

The second goal of this study is to define a scope of service science based upon the generic service systems offered in the previous sections.

The key to defining service science is the understanding of the nature of service. Nowadays, *service* is a complex system which is characterized by the following attributes:

1. It is aimed to satisfy a customer/citizen/society
2. It is a system composed of customer/citizens, service providers, service-oriented technology, and control-oriented technology (IT)
3. It is driven by value, time, cost, and profit
4. It is a "product," which is planned, designed, implemented ("produced"), operated, and managed

Based upon these attributes, one can define a matrix of developmental, operational, and management activities within a framework established by the IBM discipline named SSME (Glushko, 2008). Supporting the IBM framework are theoretical disciplines which include a set of theories and approaches integrated and called service science (Figure 11-7).

Table 11-4 defines key outcomes of service science areas within the framework of service stages.

The discipline of *service science* is the systematic study of the theoretical foundations of service development, operations, and management. These foundations are perceived as complex systems which are service-technology-oriented and service managing technology-driven for the benefits of a society, person, and property in the scope of tangible and intangible services.

A *mission* of service science is to pursue the interdisciplinary theory (verified in practice) based on selected rules of business, system science, psychology, management science, operations research, service domain engineering, service economics, service law and ethics with information-communication science (ICS) in order to apply them in service, planning, design, implementation, operations, and management.

As such, service science's *aim* is to integrate these particular disciplines into a *coherent whole*. In fact, IBM relabeled its initiative in this area as "service sciences, management, and engineering" to highlight the interdisciplinary nature of the effort. Furthermore, HP created a center for service and systems science for the same reason. Universities have also begun to act on the need or service science (SSME) as well. For instance, UC Berkeley has created an SSME program. North Carolina State University created an MBA track for service and a computer engineering degree for services well. In both cases, the schools recognize the interdisciplinary character of the field and incorporate content from a variety of disciplines. Other schools with interdisciplinary interests in SSME include the University of Maryland, Arizona State University, Northern Illinois University, UC Santa Cruz, MIT, RPI, and others.

Academic publications in SSME are also starting to appear. For instance, one can recommend the special issue of the *Communications of the ACM* (July 2006) focused entirely on service science. *The International Journal of Services Operations and Informatics* issued its first volume in 2006. One can expect that the mentioned strong supporters and universities' faculty will pursue the interesting and inspiring task of supporting the

Table 11-4. Key outcomes of service science

SERVICE SCIENCE AREAS	SERVICE STAGES				
	SERVICE PLANNING	SERVICE DESIGN	SERVICE IMPLEMENTA-TION	SERVICE OPERATIONS	SERVICE MANAGE-MENT
Business Principles	Business Model	Business Model Revised	Business Model Implemented	Business Model Practiced	Service Project Defined
System Science	Service Model	Service Model Tested	Service Model Prototyped, Pilot-ed, Implemented	Service Model Maintained & Improved	System Project Management
Psychology Principles	Customer Behavior Expected	Customer Behavior Updated	Customer Behavior Tested	Customer Behavior Updated	Customer Behavior Analyzed
Management Science	Decision Optimization Criteria	Decisions Optimized	Decisions Structured	Optimal Deci-sions Applied	CPM Applied
Operations Research	Service Optimization Criteria	Service Flow Optimized	Service Flow Established	Service Flow Operated	Service Flow Simulated
Service Domain Engineering	Service Processes Scopes	Service Processes Designed	Service Processes Implemented	Service Processes Main-tained & Improved	Service Engineering Project Management
Service Economics	Expected Economic Impact	Economic Impact Verified	Economic Impact Tested	Economic Impact Updated	Local, National, Global Impact Managed
Service Law & Ethics	Ethics & Compliance	Ethics & Compli-ance Assured	Ethics & Compliance Observed	Ethics & Compliance Revised	Ethics & Compli-ance Controlled
Information-Communica-tion Engineering	Architecture of CIS	CIS Tested	CIS Prototyped, Piloted, Imple-mented	CIS in Operations	CIS Project Management

U.S. service economy by theory-based service science.

THE SERVICE SCIENCE STARTEGY FOR INNOVATIONS

Perhaps the lack of academic involvement in systematization and innovation in the service economy put it in crisis. Gutek and Welsh (2000) write that "we are not thrilled with the quality of customer service today. Dissatisfaction with service has reached epidemic proportions in America—a sad state of affairs for a so-called 'service economy.'" According to authors Barbara Gutek and Theresa Welsh, this is because service businesses are not adapting to the changing nature of service delivery. Instead, they are trying to

Figure 11-8. The paradigms of service evolution

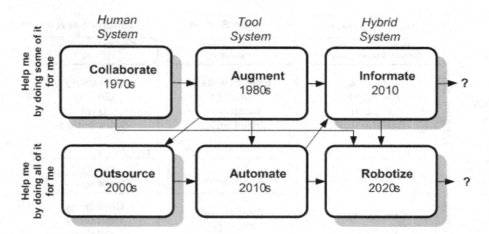

impose traditional aspects of customer service on completely new breeds of service. These tactics simply do not work and result in feelings of alienation, resentment, and cynicism in both customers and providers.

A role of universities in service innovation is to research the evolution of service delivery and teach students how to assure social and corporate responsibility in planning, developing, operating, and managing service systems. Figure 11-9 depicts a model[1] of service evolution by six stages and their paradigms.

The *Collaborate Model* (1970s) is staffed with experts who can troubleshoot and easily explain to the service users all the problems with service since they created that particular service. Even today this is the case for start-up companies whose developers provide first-hand help to service recipients in areas such as software.

The *augment* model (1980s) applies service communication tools answering to the service users the most frequently asked questions (FAQ). The first FAQ system was initiated by phone and later was applied to Web sites. A service user must still find out by how to use a service by him/her.

The *outsource* model (2000s) delegates servicing to a third party located on-shore or most frequently off-shore (e.g., India). This model was triggered by the strategy of restructuring and cost-cutting by allocating manufacturing to China and IT projects and customer service to India as both countries provide low-cost labor. This model leads to the decline of middle class in developed nations and as far as customer service is concerned, is not embraced by the American customers because the level of help and expertise provided is rather low, perhaps due to the physical distance from the places of action.

The *automate* model (2010s) is supported by high-tech companies which need to engage their available (idle?) resources in the next wave of technology development. This model eliminates humans from service processes and generates market demand for advanced technology. This is a very controversial strategy first, in terms of a right technical solution and second, in terms of the right social solution. As far as the former is concerned, automation of *complex* service systems cannot be a reliable solution since many factors are not known for designers. For example, the FAA does not allow pilots to use an auto-pilot system in bad weather. If we look at the control

Figure 11-9. The developmental paradigms of six categories of services

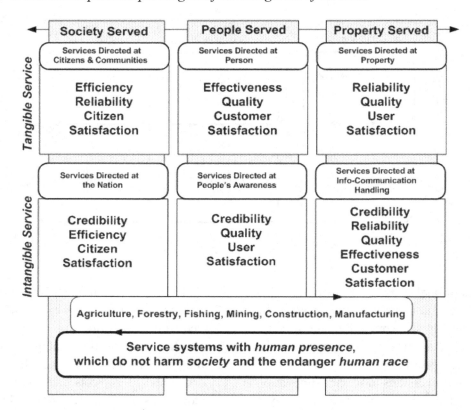

rooms of many process installations, we see a lot of instrumentation, but we also wee operators who do nothing since the process control has been automated. In the case of an emergency, these operators very often do not know what to do because they are without practice of how to handle crisis situations. As far as the latter is concerned, service automation should not lead to the drastic decline of employment as it has occurred in agriculture and manufacturing. People should have something to do and have the necessary income to support their lives and the society (including the demand creation for high-tech companies), even with the cost inefficiencies! Particularly if the population is constantly growing! Technology, particularly computers, may merely further automate blue- and white-collar jobs, achieving unprecedented speed and consistency, robbing

workers of whatever skill and gratification they may retain, and increasing the impersonality and remoteness of management.

The *informate* model (2010) empowers ordinary working people with overall knowledge of service processes, making them capable of critical and collaborative judgment about service. This model assumes some sort of automated information-communication infrastructure. However, it is operated and supervised by humans supported by e-information which leaves room for the human to conceptualize status (change) and required decisions filtered by human knowledge (very often under the form of given business knowledge, coming from data mining) leading to wise decisions finally made ultimately by humans. This model is particularly appropriate for semi-ill and ill-structured decisions under uncertainty.

This model to a certain extent co-exists with the automate model. A pilot who lands a plane by hand in a bad weather and a policeman who directs traffic when traffic lights fail (but is still in wireless communication with the command center) are good examples of this model.

The *robotize* model (2020) is a combination of the collaborate, automate, and informate models, particularly in a case of Japan. In some countries, there is a shortage in the supply of labor for industrial work, which drives up investment in robotics. With the present demographic trends, this shortage will be even more pronounced in years to come, which will further stimulate robotics investment in repetitive lifts involved in handling materials such as parts, beverage crates, and so forth. The number of robots is constantly increasing in manufacturing industry: Japan 280 per 10,000 people; Singapore 148; Rep. of Korea 116; Germany 102; Sweden 69; Italy 67; Finland 51; Benelux 49; United States 48; France 48; Switzerland 46; Austria 44; Spain 41 Australia 25; Denmark 24; United Kingdom 23; Norway 16 (UN/ECE NEWS, 2000). It is interesting that in Japan a robot does not replace a worker; rather the worker serves as its "master," taking care of it.

"Organizations that take steps toward exclusively automating strategy can set a course that is not easily reversed. They are likely to find themselves crippled by antagonism from the workforce and the depletion of knowledge that would be needed in value-adding activities. The absence of a self-conscious strategy to exploit the informating capacity of the new technology has tended to mean that managerial action flows along the path of least resistance—a path that, at least superficially, appears to serve only the interest of managerial hegemony" (Zuboff, 1988, p. 391).

The automation strategy of service creates the environment of jobbers, who are also required to act "automatically," leading in its conclusion again to deadliest, most sterile passivity history, which has been known since the fall of the Roman Empire (476 A.D.). This strategy will push humans into the bifurcation stage when complex systems designers will be very sophisticated people and the users of this systems will be very simple people. It has occurred in the history of the human race, when language-speaking *Cro Magnions* replaced the *Neanderthals*, who could only "bark" about 40,000 years ago in Europe.

The current role of universities is to launch service-oriented programs, whose systemic components to certain degrees are available and technologically are in the reach of the faculty and students. However, the most important role of the university is to research and teach the social, corporate, and personal responsibility in developing and managing ethical complex service systems!

In order to fulfill this noble task, the three laws of service systems cannot be violated by their developers and operators. These laws are similar to Isaac Asimov's approach to robotization but directed towards service automation and should be a subject of broader discussions among specialists in ethics, law, and other appropriate disciplines:

Law I - Do not develop service systems without human presence.

Law II - Do not develop service systems which harm society.

Law III - Do not develop service systems which endanger human race.

Law I protects people against passivity. Law II protects society against structured unemployment. Law III protects the human race against the bifurcation into two kinds of species. It would be necessary for governments, scientific, professional, trade and industrial associations to sign the service systems agreement based on these laws to be sure that service systems are developed and managed in a responsible manner.

Figure 11-10 depicts a model of six service categories and their developmental paradigms.

The role of service science is to constantly update these paradigms and implement into research, reaching, and consulting.

CONCLUSION

1. Service economy is a fact, which has not been yet noticed by IT developers and operators, which is still involved in enterprise systems, supporting steadily disappearing manufacturing systems, which are being outsourced off-shore.
2. The e-SS does not replace an enterprise system. Rather, it is the next layer above the layer of the enterprise system, and both layers are entered through the service user interface which is Web-driven and can be open or entered by the rxtranet.
3. Web technology is key solution for the e-SS, which has become an online-interactive information-communication tool for service users (citizens and customers).
4. Service science must support practical e-SS projects, which due to their complexity require a strong theoretical foundation.
5. The state of the art service systems' components are advanced which allows for the development of relatively complex service systems.
6. The development of service systems must comply with the three laws and with social, corporate, and personal responsibility.
7. To secure the right development of complex service systems, the *service systems agreement* should be signed by appropriate stakeholders.
8. The future trends in e-service development will probably oscillate between fully automated and automated with human touch. The latter should be the preferred trend.
9. Further research may focus on how the implemented e-service systems are com-

plying with the ideal architecture-based solutions, sketched in this chapter.

REFERENCES

Bateson, J. (1979). Why we need service marketing. In O. Ferrell, S. Brown, & C. Lamb (Eds.), *Conceptual and theoretical developments in marketing* (pp. 131-146). Chicago, IL: American Marketing Association.

Bell, D. (1976). *The coming of post-industrial society.* New York, NY: Basic Books.

Bell, D. (1981). The social framework of the information society. In: T. Forester (Ed.), *The microelectronics revolution* (pp. 500-549).

. Cambridge, MA: The MIT Press.

Beer, S. (1981). *Brain of the firm.* Chichester: John Wiley & Sons.

Bowen, D. (1990a). Interdisciplinary study of service: Some progress, some prospects. *Journal of Business Research, 20*(1), 71-79.

Bowen, D., Chase, R., Cummings, T., & Associates (Eds.). (1990). *Service management effectiveness, balancing strategy, organization and human resources, operations, and marketing.* San Francisco, CA: Jossey-Bass Publishers.

Breivik, E., Troye, S., & Olsson, U. (1998). *Dimensions of intangibility and their impact on product evaluation.* Working paper presented at the annual conference (October) of the Association for Consumer Research. Montreal, Canada.

Bureau of Economic Analysis. (2008). Retrieved April 28, 2008, from http//www.bea.gov/national.

Clark, C. (1940). *The conditions of economic progress.* London: Macmillan.

Dabholkar, P. (1994). Technology-based service delivery, a classification scheme for developing marketing strategies. *Advances in Service Marketing and Management, 3,* 241-271.Greenwich, CT: JAI Press.

Dabholkar, P. (1996). Consumer evaluation of new technology-based self-service options: An investigation of alternative models of service quality. *International Journal of Research Marketing, 13*(1), 29-51.

Drucker, P. (1969). *The age of discontinuity.* New York, NY: Harper & Row.

Erl, T, (2004). *Service-oriented architecture: A field guide to integrating XML and Web services.* Upper Saddle River, NJ: Prentice Hall.

Felipe, L. (2005). *Web services architecture and its specifications: Essential for understanding WS (Pro-Developer).* Redwood, WA: Microsoft Press.

Freiden, J., Goldsmith, R., Takacs, S., & Hofacker, C. (1998). Information as a product: Not goods, not services. *Marketing Intelligence and Planning, 16*(Fall), 210-220.

Gadrey, J., & Gallouj, F. (2002). *Productivity, innovation and knowledge in services, new economic and socio-economic approaches.* Cheltenham, UK: Edward Elgar.

Gersuny, C., & Rosengren, W. (1973). *The service society.* Cambridge, MA: Schenkman.

Glushko, R. (2008). Design a service science discipline with disciple. *IBM Systems Journal, 47*(1), 15-27.

Gutek, B., & Welsh, T. (2000). *The brave new service strategy.* New York, NY: AMA.

Hall, G. (1999). Presentation at the OECD Business and Industry Policy Forum on *Realizing the Potential of the Service Economy,* 28 September.

Heskett, J. (1990). Rethinking strategy for service management. In: D. Bowen, R. Chase, T. Cummings, and Associates (Eds.), *Service management effectiveness, balancing strategy, organization and human resources, operations, and marketing* (pp. 17-40). San Francisco, CA: Jossey-Bass Publishers.

Hsu, C. (Ed.). (2007). _____*Service Enterprise Integration: An Enterprise Engineering Perspective.* Springer Science.

Klir, J. (1985). *Architect of system problem solving.* New York, NY: Plenum Press.

McFarlan, F. (1981). Portfolio approach to information systems. *Harvard Business Review, September-October,* 142-150.

Laroche, M., Bergerson, J., & Goutaland, C. (2001). A three-dimensional scale of intangibility. *Journal of Service Research, 4*(1), 26-38.

Lovelock, C. (1983). Classifying services to gain strategic marketing insights. *Journal of Marketing, 47*(Summer), 9-20.

Lovelock, C. (2001). *Services marketing: People, technology, strategy.* Upper Saddle River, NJ: Prentice Hall.

Lovelock, C., & Wirtz, J. (2007). *Service marketing, people, technology, strategy.* Upper Saddle River, NJ: Pearson-Prentice Hall.

OECD. (2000). *The service economy.* Paris: OECD.

Rathmell, J. (1974). *Marketing in the service sector.* Cambridge, MA: Winthrop.

Rosenfeld, L., & Morvile, P. (2006). *Information architecture for the World Wide Web: Designing large-scale Web sites.* Sebastopol, CA: O'Reilly Media, Inc.

Rust, R., Zahorik, A., Keiningham, T. (1996). *Service marketing.* New York, NY: HarperCollins.

Sampson, S. (2001). *Understanding service businesses.* New York, NY: John Wiley.

___ (2006, June). *ORMS Today.*

Shostack, G. (1977). Breaking free from product marketing. *Journal of Marketing, 41*(April), 73.

Smith, A. (1776). *The wealth of nations.* New York, NY: Dutton.

Targowski, A. (1990). *The architecture and planning of enterprise-wide information management systems.* Harrisburg, PA: Idea group Publishing.

Targowski, A. (2003). *Electronic enterprise.* Harrisburg, PA: The IRM Press.

Taylor, R. (1999, September 30). Microsoft to rent software on the Internet. *WSJ Interactive.*

Teboul, J. (2006). *Service is front stage.* INSEAD. Business Press.

Trends in Services Sciences in Japan and Abroad. (2006). *Science and Technology Trends Quarterly Review*, April.

U.S. Bureau of The Census. (1999). *North American Industry Classification*

System, http://www.census.gov/epcd/ www/na-ics.html.52.

U.S. Council of Economic Advisers and the U.S. Department of Labor. (1999). *20 Million Jobs: January 1993-November 1999*

World Services Congress 99. (1999). Recommendations of the global Services Network and Business Policy Forums for Services 2000 Trade Negotiations. Retrieved November, 20, 2008, from http://www.worldservicescongress. com/home.cfm.

Zeithaml, V., & Bitner, M. (2000). *Services marketing: Integrating customer focus across the firms.* New York, NY: McGraw-Hill.

ENDNOTE

[1]	This 6 stages model is the author's improvement of the 4 stages model developed by J. Spohrer and P. P. Maglio, from the IBM Almaden Research Center.

Chapter XII
Information Laws

INTRODUCTION

The purpose of this chapter is to define information laws which control the development of the global and universal civilizations as well as individual autonomous civilizations.

Mankind progresses in proportion to its wisdom, which has roots in practice, acquired skills, available data, and information, concepts and knowledge. To be wise, humankind needs to be both informed and knowledgeable, otherwise it will not survive its own failures. Progress in knowledge was painfully slow as long as the spatial memory was transmitted only by oral tradition. With the inventions of writing and books, the process of knowledge discovery and dissemination was accelerated. Today, computers and their networks speed up that process far beyond our imagination. In the 21st century, the Information Wave significantly controls the Agricultural and Industrial Waves through millions of computers. IT supports decision-making based on knowledge-oriented systems such as "data mining" that, for example, discover knowledge about customers and organization dynamics to achieve competitive advantage.

Information and knowledge have become the strategic resource that *engineering science* was in the Industrial Wave. However, the discovery of human cognition potential must be guided by *knowledge science*, which is just emerging. One of the signs of any science is its set of data, universal rules, laws, and systems of rules and laws. Hence, this chapter offers the first attempt to develop main laws of information that should increase our awareness about the Information Wave, the new stage of civilization dynamics that is taking place at the beginning of the third millennium. The chapter also provides the framework for the analysis of human capital from an information perspective. These considerations reflect a still emerging approach which I call *macro-information ecology*.

MACRO-INFORMATION ECOLOGY

Macro-information ecology is based on the premise that the growth rate of discovery of new information (knowledge) is the key determinant of macroeconomic activities in the service-industrial-global economy (so-called the "*new economy*").

This new emerging school of macroeconomics may be called *knowledgism*.

Macro-information ecology is the study of information (cognition) as a whole. It is concerned with *aggregates* across nations and markets. Macro-information ecology studies the behaviors of societies and economies (nationally and globally) measuring:

- the value of human capital
- the potential efficiency of human capital
- knowledge output
- Economic output driven by knowledge in a given period, and so forth

It also studies measures derived from many individual nations:

- markets such as the price of human capital
- the total structure of employed workers by such categories as production workers in-person service workers, and information workers

Another interesting facet of this emerging discipline is the qualitative analysis of civilization paradigm shifts and the application of civilization tools as a result of increased cognition about us.

To control national output with the development of a global economy, *knowledgists* stress the need to control the growth of new knowledge discovery. Given the long and variable lags of knowledge and information policies behind events and the difficulty in forecasting future economic events (such as recessions), *knowledgists* question the ability of industrial or service-oriented macroeconomics to implement even "correct" economic policy.

The knowledge approach suggests that direct government intervention within the economic system should be guided by the "predicted *history of the futures.*" Knowledge *policy* is the key to this intervention. In this sense, knowledge policy is closer in economic theory to the Keynesian interventionists than to "conservative" monetarists.

The supply and demand of information (knowledge) is the most basic subject of *information ecology* (IE). However, before presenting this model, we must examine the stages of development of the *information reservoir*. Figure 12-1 illustrates this process.

Based on the information reservoir's (IR) dynamics, the general information laws will be defined in the following section.

GENERAL INFORMATION LAWS

At the present stage of knowledge discovery, the information reservoir (IR) can only minimize or try to "control" chaos. Every increase in new information also increases the level of complexity of understanding. Based on the analysis of knowledge dynamics provided by Wojciechowski (1989), one can define the following laws of information:

Law I: The complexity of the ecosystem (man, material, cognition, and nature) is growing proportionately to the level of the existing information reservoir.

This complexity is the state of a system whose components and relationships co-evolve through an enormous number of interconnections, creating dynamic structures either chaotic or orderly. The more information we have at our disposal, the more complex the ecosystem is perceived to be. In the old saw, the more we know, the less we understand. The founders of the Santa Fe Institute, which explores the new science of complexity, investigates such questions as why ancient ecosystems often remained stable for millions of years, only to vanish in a geological instant—and what such events have to do with the sudden collapse of Soviet Communism in the late 1980s.

Figure 12-1. Stages of information reservoir development

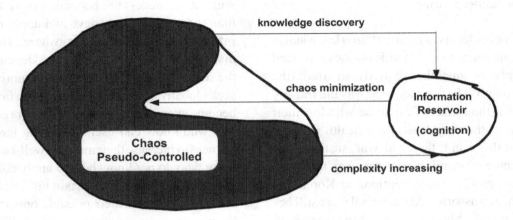

Stage I: Knowledge Discovery

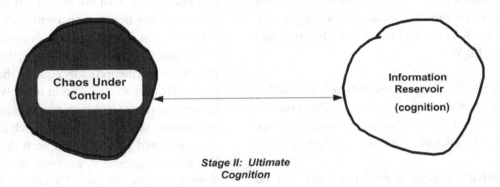

Stage II: Ultimate Cognition

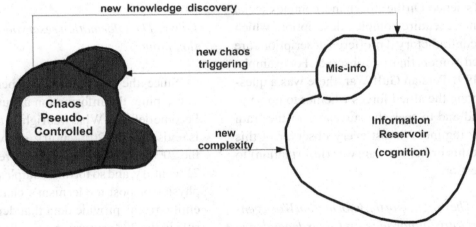

Stage III: New Chaos and Complexity

Law II: Information generates consequences which it cannot foresee.

One of the forms of information is knowledge, such as atomic physics. Atomic physics produced rules and techniques that allowed man to build the atomic bomb. The consequence was the tragedy that befell thousands of Japanese who lost their lives or, at the very least, their health in 1945. On the other hand, the Cold War, sustained by the balance of atomic weaponry, was relatively bloodless (with some exceptions to Korea and Vietnam and assorted African civil wars still being unraveled). Should science stop research on atomic physics or gene engineering because their consequences may get out of control? Or, being under control, can said research produce positive results, such as the Cold War, which foreclosed another Hot War?

Law III: Precision and certainty of information grow in proportion with the simplicity of the described object or process or, inversely, decline with the complexity of the object or process.

Relatively simple material objects can be described by relatively simple information in natural science. On the other hand, complex social phenomena require complex description, which can be contradictory if proffered descriptions are provided by more than one observer. For example, in the 1991 Persian Gulf War, there was a question among the allied forces whether to go on to Baghdad and to seek the surrender of the Iraqi military regime. Almost every observer of this war had his or her own answer (information) to this question.

Law IV: The progress of the Information Wave generates relative ignorance and interdependence among individuals and globalizes humanity.

The advancement of mediated information requires information skills to access information infrastructure, systems, and services. People without this access are becoming more ignorant than those who can retrieve and apply required information anytime and anywhere. The information poor are becoming more dependent on the information rich; the latter are motivated to seek globally more useful information in order to become even richer. College professors or graduates who know end-user computing have more chances to increase their material well-being than those who do not know how to apply computers to gather and process important information and are ignorant about their possible opportunities. Even an experienced business person, if ignorant about information technology, may lose business resources, or at least not increase them, if he/she does not know how to transform his/her business from *brick 'n mortar* to *brick 'n click*.

At Stage II, ultimate cognition, the amount of information is theoretically equal to the amount of chaos. From mankind's point of view, this equilibrium in macro-ecology never happens, since the amount of time needed for such equilibrium to be attained is infinite. In such disciplines as business management, perhaps one can achieve short-term equilibrium. Therefore, a fifth law can be defined:

Law V: The information reservoir has no saturation point.

Since the ecosystem is imperfect and still developing, the information about it has not yet become definite. What was right in the 19th century is revised in the 20th century, and what is right in the 20th century will perhaps be redefined in the 21st century, and so forth. Examples of Newtonian physics or post-modernism's challenge of "scientific truth" provide data that demonstrate this rule in the 20th century. A new discovery usually decreases the chaos; and, *eo ips* requires more information to improve understanding.

Stage III -- If the capacity of the information reservoir should exceed the capacity ("quantity") of chaos, then new chaos and complexity are created by misinformation, which begins to penetrate the IR. But this is only an assumption since, according to Law V, such a situation should not happen.

THE INFORMATION MACRO-ECOLOGY MODEL

The macro-ecology of the information equilibrium model (Figure 12-2) indicates that civilization, most of the time, operates in darkness. The mathematical model of the information reservoir is as follows:

Stage I: $I < E$

where:

I = Information Reservoir capacity
E = Entropy, a measure of chaos
D = Darkness (or net entropy E-I)

The macro-ecology goal is $D_t = 0$ and the task is to determine the elasticity of the increased entropy or information and how a user or organization responds to changes (+, -) caused either by the increase of information reservoir or by its "enemy"—entropy.

Figure 12-2. Information macro-ecology model (I-Information, E-Entropy)

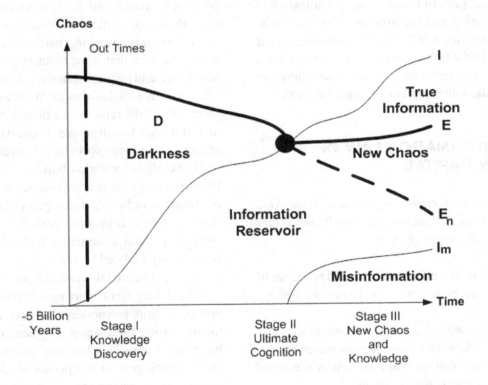

$D(E_t) = f(I_{Mt}, C_t)$ or $D(I_t) = f(E_t, C_t)$

where: I_M = Misinformation [1]
C = Complexity
 t = time

The elasticity of *information* is a measure of the sensitivity or responsiveness of the information value demanded to create changes in price, revenue, unemployment, and in other factors of the Information Wave. Information elasticity will be one of the major indexes of the emerging Information Wave.

Macro-information ecology is also interested in the creation of *human capital* as a medium of knowledge generation and application. Particularly, a relation between human capital and economic development is a strategic inquiry of IE.

The mechanism of material civilization in modern capitalistic theory was built on the rule that market growth triggers the specialization of human capital and the growth of its income as well as of its level of living ("net satisfaction per capita"). In the Information Wave, the situation is different. The new motor forces of economy can express the following law of human capital.

THE INFORMATION LAW OF HUMAN CAPITAL

Law VI: Human capital's growth in knowledge generates specialization and productivity and sustains the growth of income.

As Kevin Murphy[2] noticed the old sequence in economic development in the Industrial Wave:

- (old) material sequence: *market growth - specialization - more income* transforms in the Information Wave into a new sequence in economic development
- (new) early information sequence: *knowledge growth - specialization - more income*

The new sequence is true as long as the specialization of human capital sustains the increase of productivity in the material sector or in the information sector. The necessary co-ordination of specialists, particularly those in the information sector, may consume the new "speed" of knowledge and not only contribute to the economic growth, but misguide it.

The most important question, however, is whether or not we should apply new knowledge to promote economic development by growth or whether we should just apply that knowledge's message, when that message says that zero growth is wiser and is the only appropriate policy to achieve a sustainable society and economy.

A ruthless trend occurred in the American human capital system in the 1990s. It is implemented in the name of restructuring and trimming corporate "fat" as a "surplus" of human capital. American human capital is being downsized and atomized; as the Scottish farmers were torn away from their soil, millions of Americans are being evicted from the working worlds that sustained them, the jobs that gave them not only wages, healthcare, and pensions, but also a context, a sense of self-worth, a kind of identity. Work was the tribe: there were IBM reps, Sera's men, GM workers, and Anheuser-Busch people. Those still are there, of course, but their world has changed.

The early Information Wave, controlled only by corporate profit, deconstructed the work force of America and other developed countries. In a time of surreal transition, America is working without a social contract or with one that has been deeply violated.

In the industrial civilization, Americans practiced long-term marriage, careers through apprenticeship, promotions, success, and retirement. Getting fired was a disgrace. That epoch has passed. America has now entered the age of the contingent or temporary worker, of the consultant or subcontractor, of just-in-time human capital—fluid, flexible, and, worst of all, disposable. Is this really the future?

If the Information Wave is to work without knowledge and information policies, the work force of the future will constantly have to sell its skills and invent new relationships with employers, who must themselves change and adapt constantly in order to survive in a ruthless global market.

This is the new metaphysics of work. Companies are portable, workers are throwaway. The rise of the Information Wave means a shift, in less than 20 years, from the overbuilt systems of large, slow-moving economic units to an array of small, widely-dispersed networked economic centers. In the early stages of the Information Wave, highways are becoming electronic: even "Wall Street" has no reason to be in Manhattan anymore. Companies become virtual, based on a networked concept and their dematerialization, and strangely conscienceless. In 1988, contingent workers were about a quarter of the labor force; by 2008, they are expected to make up half of it.

The Industrial Revolution was inevitable even as the Luddites howled and broke the machines. There are solid economic reasons for a current restructuring of the American work force (e.g., low productivity due to overstaffed companies), but the human capital costs are enormous.

The uncontrolled development of the Information Wave may lead to another economic sequence:

- further information sequence: *knowledge growth - specialization - collapse of economy (?)*

This sequence produces an economy that is too specialized and productive, requiring a small workforce without the means to create a demand for economic output. In current practice, robots and computers do not pay taxes.

Information ecology has to include a human dimension of the Information Wave in its inquiry. Better knowledge should provide a better level of living, not inspire self-destruction and limit progress to technology alone. Technology is not neutral; the new knowledge should define *telematic* technology as a tool of honorable and sustainable living. This is possible if we consider the Electronic Global Village as a tool of information and knowledge creation and distribution (bottom-up and top-down), and as a globally interconnected aware tribe.

The steered Information Wave should offer the following sequence of events:

- expected information sequence: *knowledge growth - solutions - sustainable economy*

If "human capital" becomes wise enough, this sequence should probably be implemented in the 21st century. Otherwise, the population and ecological bombs (around 2050) will return us to the beginning stages of the history of mankind (Paleolithic).

HUMAN CAPITAL DEVELOPMENT

Human capital in the 21st century will become the most important economic resource. This is a medium which generates and applies knowledge. Its architecture of "organs" is depicted on Figure 12-3.

In post-modern notation the architecture contains left brain and right brain attributes, which in combination determine the value of human capital. This capital develops in three stages:

Stage I: Elementary Human Capital: Knowledge, Skills, Cases (Experience), Attitude

Stage II: Advanced Human Capital: Info-Utility Access, Professionalism and Artistry, Motivation

Stage III: Mature Human Capital: Wisdom, Cross-culture Communication, Change, Leadership

Figure 12-3. Human capital on development stages

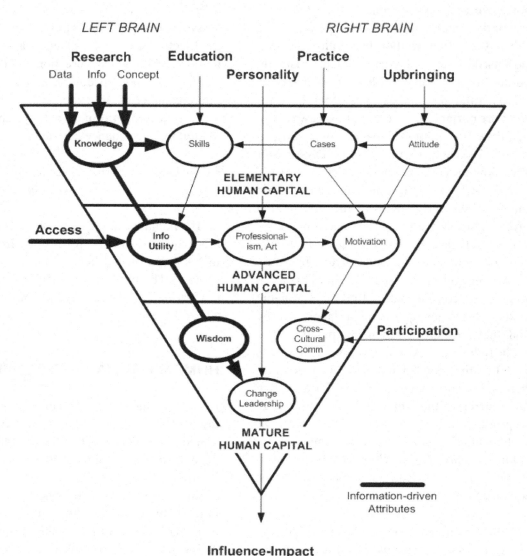

Only four attributes are information-driven: knowledge, skills, information utility access, and wisdom. This means that the development of human capital cannot be limited only to issues of information. The process of socialization into a society plays a very important role in the development of human capital values, and this process is culture-driven.

The measurement of human capital value can be done through the estimation of the value space of a work force (macro-ecology) or through a given person (micro-ecology). Figure 12-4 illustrates the value space of human capital.

Each attribute (A) can be measured on a five-point scale. The sum total of all attribute points provides a value of given human capital (V). This

Figure 12-4. The value space of human capital

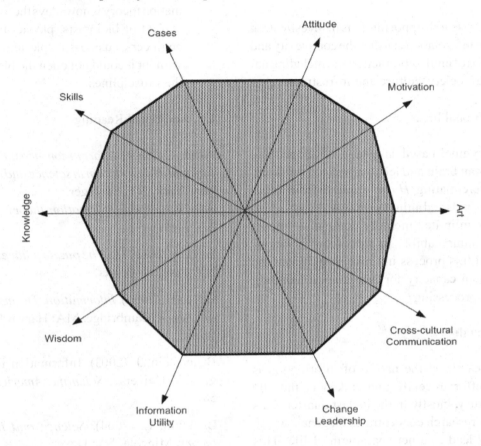

is a comparative unit of human capital value. It can be applied in comparisons of economies, organizations, or persons. It can also be applied in the analysis of human capital efficiency potential.

CONCLUSION

Macro-information ecology is just emerging, along with the development of Information Wave practices. Researchers should turn their attention both to the application of the information laws and also to their further discovery and corrections in the analysis and design of values and tools of the Information Wave and civilization in general.

A. Further Research Directions

- Develop more information laws and investigate their impact on human existence in macro-information ecology.
- Investigate information laws, rules, and observations and their impact on human existence in the micro-information ecology.
- Investigate the value space of human capital in different spheres of civilization.

B.   Research Opportunities

- The research opportunity is in investigating how information clarifies the complexity and chaos of civilization activities (including nature, society, culture and infrastructure).

C.   Additional Ideas

- A symbol-based language developed the human brain and led to advanced thinking, differentiating *Homo sapiens* from other hominids and animals. How will high-speed and unlimited-memory computers impact the human ability to process information? Will this process improve or diminish the human capacity for information handling and processing?

D.   Rationale

- Research on the nature of information is an effort recently undertaken in the 20th century, mostly in the its last quarter. This new research concentrates on genes, which may lead to a new paradigm of life. This research first focused on the concept of DNA, which is like a molecule (or atom if two molecules are considered) of human biology. Recent medical research has been aiming at the concept and role of RNA, which is in charge of bio-communication among DNA molecules. It looks like information is *Decoding the Universe* (Seife, 2006). Seife claims that whether information is packed into a bar code, encrypted in a secret wartime message, or sucked into a black hole (St. Howking, the author of the black hole theory, thinks this way), reaches the galaxy, it is everywhere, and it is not just an abstract concept. Information is a concrete property of matter and energy that is every bit as real as the weight of a chunk of lead, something that is inside every living cell and is inscribed upon every cosmic phenomenon. The information theory is nowadays the main research subject of biologists, physicists, chemists, engineers, businesspeople, and others, who without it could not open the black boxes of their disciplines.

E.   Additional Reading

Arndt, C. (2004). *Information measures, information and its description in science and engineering* New York, NY: Springer.

Ash, R. (1990). *Information theory.* New York, NY: Dover.

Bamford, J. (1983). *The puzzle palace.* New York, NY: Penguin Books.

Bayer, H. (2004). *Information. The new language of science.* Cambridge, MA: Harvard University Press.

Bekenstein, J. (2003). Information in the holographic Universe. *Scientific American, 289*(2), 58.

Brillouin, L. (2004). *Science and information theory.* Mineola, NY: Dover.

Cover, T., & Thomas, J. (2006). *Elements of information theory.* New York, NY: Wiley-Interscience.

Eager, W. (1995). *The information payoff.* Englewood Cliffs, NJ: Prentice Hall PTR.

Floridi, L. (2005). Is information meaningful data?. *Philosophy and Phenomenological Research, 70*(2), 351-370.

Gallagher, R. (1968). *Information theory and reliable communication.* New York, NY: John Wiley and Sons.

Goldman. S. (1969). *Information theory.* New York, NY: Dover.

Hartley, R. (1928). Transmission of information. *Bell System Technical Journal, 7,* 535.

Kelly, J., Jr. (1956). A new interpretation of information rate. *Bell System Technical Journal, 35,* 917-926.

Khinchin, A. (1957). *Mathematical foundations of information theory.* New York, NY: Dover.

Landauer, R. (2000). Irreversibility and heat generation in the computing process. *IBM Journal of Resource Development, 44*(1-2), 261-270.

_____(1993). Information is physical. *Proceedings of the Workshop on Physics and Computation PhysComp'92* (pp. 1-4). Los Alamos: IEEE Comp. Sci.Press:

Leff, H., & Rex, A. (Eds.). (1990). *Maxwell's demon: Entropy, information, computing.* Princeton, NJ: Princeton University Press.

Libicki, M. (2000). *Who runs what in the global information grid?* Santa Monica, CA: RAND

MacKay, D. (2003). *Information theory, inference, and learning algorithms.* Cambridge: Cambridge University Press.

Mansuripur, M. (1987). *Introduction to information theory.* New York, NY: Prentice Hall.

Poster, M. (1990). *The mode of information.* Chicago, IL: The University of Chicago Press.

Reza. F. (1994). *An introduction to information theory.* New York, NY: Dover.

Shannon, C. (1948). A mathematical theory of communication. *Bell System Technical Journal, 27,* 379-423; 623-656.

Shannon, C., & Weaver, W. (1949). *The mathematical theory of communication.* Urbana-Champaign, IL: University of Illinois Press.

Seife, C. (2006). *Decoding the Universe.* New York, NY: Viking.

Siegfried, T. (2000). *The bit and the pendulum.* New York, NY: Wiley.

Slack, J., & Fejes, F. (1987). *The ideology of the information age.* Norwood, NJ: Ablex Publishing Books.

Yeung, R. (2002). *A first course in information theory.* London: Kluwer Academic/Plenum Publishers.

REFERENCES

Badaracco, J., Jr. (1991). *The knowledge link.* Boston, MA: Harvard Business School Press.

Beach, L., Mitchell, T., Daeton, M., & Prothero, J. (1997). Information relevance, content, and source credibility in the revision of opinions. *Organizational Behavior and Human Performance, 21,* 1-16.

Bohm, D., & Peat, F. (1978). *Science, order and creativity.* New York, NY: Bantam Books.

Bell, D. (1973). *The coming of the post-information society: A venture in social forecasting.* New York, NY: Basic Books.

Blumenthal, A. (1977). *The process of cognition.* Englewood Cliffs, NJ: Prentice-Hall, Inc.

Drucker, P. (1988). The coming of the new organization. *Harvard Business Review, 88*(1), 45-53.

_____(1993). *Post-capitalist society.* New York, NY: HarperBusiness.

Ekecrantz, J. (1987). The sociological order of the new information society. In: J. Slack & F. Fejes (Eds.), *The ideology of the information age.* Norwood, NJ: Ablex Publishing Corp.

Gore, A. (1991). Information superhighways: The next information revolution. *The Futurist, 1,* 21-23.

Karraker, R. (1988). Highways of minds. *Whole Earth Review, Spring,* 4-15.

Laszlo, E. (1972). *Introduction to systems philosophy.* New York, NY: Harper and Row.

McWhirter, B. (1993, March 29). Disposable workers of America. *Time,* pp. 41-43.

Nowell, A., Perils, A., & Simon, H. (1987). What is computer science?. *Science, 235*(4794), 1373-1374.

Parker, E. (1976). Social implications of computer/telecoms systems. *Telecommunications Policy, 1,* 3-20.

Porat, M. (1977). *The information economy.* Washington, D.C.: U.S.Office of Telecommunications.

Poster, M. (1990). *The mode of information.* Chicago, IL: The University of Chicago Press.

Pricher, W. (1987). Tours through the back-country of imperfectly informed society. In. J. Slack & F. Fejes (Eds.), *The ideology of the information age.* Norwood, NJ: Ablex Publishing Corp.

Sakaiya, T. (1991). *The knowledge-value revolution.* New York, NY: Kodansha International.

Shannon, C. (1948). A mathematical theory of communication. *Bell System Technical Journal, 27,* 379-423; 623-656.

Targowski, A. (1999). *Enterprise information infrastructure.* Harrisburg, PA: Idea Publishing Group.

Toffler, A. (1980). *The third wave.* New York, NY: Bantam Books.

Wojciechowski, J. (1989). Progress of knowledge and right-left dichotomy: Are existing ideologies adequate?. *Man & Development, XI*(1).

Van Doren, C. (1991). *A history of knowledge.* New York, NY: Ballantine Books.

ENDNOTES

[1] Misinformation means that an explanation of an object or process is incorrectly provided, whether purposely or accidentally.

[2] During his public lecture at Western Michigan University (December 13, 1992).

Chapter XIII
The Electronic Global Village

INTRODUCTION

The purpose of this chapter is to define the architecture of information-communication systems which play key roles in the development of the *Electronic Global Village (EGV)* as the metaphoric mechanism for the implementation of the Information Wave.

THE BIRTH OF THE ELECTRONIC GLOBAL VILLAGE

During the Communications Age (since the 1950s), the activities of business, organization, and everyday life begin with social action that is defined by communication-mediated choices. A generation ago, Marshall McLuhan proclaimed the advent of a "global village," a sort of borderless world in which communication media would transcend the boundaries of nations (McLuhan, 1968). "Time" has ceased; "space" has vanished. We now live in a simultaneous happening. The globe is linked by media and visual, icon-like messages. The messages spread out and cause instantaneous, proactive responses. Ever since, history has been driven by a "compressed" capsule of time. One of the mini bangs (the birth of humankind) expands through the communication

of ideas. Logistics becomes secondary to symbols. Human minds and cognition are placed in charge of that mini bang's consequences.

The Global Economic Age (since the 1980s) is a product of liberal democracy and free-trade policy. Market participants are encouraged to compete globally. From these circumstances, we are experiencing a flexible movement of people and goods with less regard for national boundaries. A car made in America by Honda and Toyota is classified as a domestic product. It does not matter that "British" sneakers by Reebok were made in Korea, or that a French ski by Rossignol is made in Spain. What a consumer cares about is the product's quality, price, design, value, and appeal.

Figure 13-1 illustrates the process of the birth of the *Electronic Global Village (EGV)* (Targowski, 1990). The result of *EGV* is an *electronic global citizen (EGC)*, as well as tele-cities, tele-nations, and information infrastructure and services. They may lead toward the healthy human family utopia. This utopia can be perceived as a technique to manage the growing, educated, and aware populations of conflict-less nations.

In 1989 (the rise of Solidarity in Poland) and 1991 (the Soviet Union's collapse), the world experienced a bifurcation into two paths:

Figure 13-1. The birth of the electronic global village

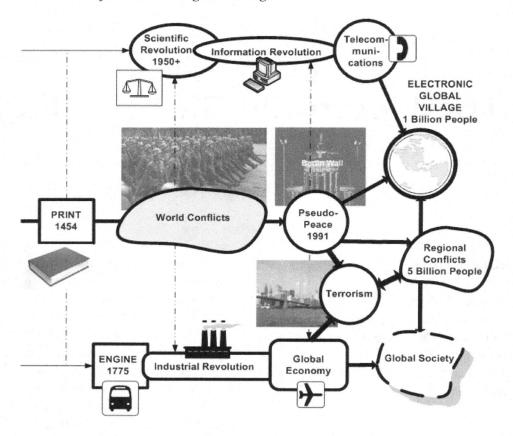

- A global path of peaceful development of the *EGV*, in which 1 billion people have a computer password
- A tribal path of national, racist, and religious conflicts, in which about 5.6 billion people do not have a computer password

The international perspective of the information civilization may be stressed by a metaphor: "Jihad versus McWorld" (Barber, 1992). According to Barber, there are two possible futures: tribalism and globalism. The former is a retribalization of large swaths of humankind by war and bloodshed, a threatened Lebanonization of national states in which culture is pitted against culture, people against people, and tribe against tribe.

The latter is being borne in on us by the onrush of economic and ecological forces that demand integration and uniformity and that mesmerize the world of fast music, fast computers, and fast food—MTV; Macintosh, and MacDonald's—pressing nations into one commercially homogenous global network: one McWorld tied together by technology, ecology, communications, and commerce.

The globe is falling precipitously apart and coming reluctantly together at the very same moment. The forces of Jihad and McWorld operate with equal strength in opposite directions, one driven by parochial hatreds, the other by global markets.

THE GENERAL ARCHITECTURE OF EGV

The emerging *Global Digital Consciousness (GDC)*, the symbiosis of humans and machines, provides cognition and external memory systems that support the global civilization and vice versa. The GDC is composed of (Figure 13-2):

- Infosphere (computerized information-communication systems composed of databases, applications, and networks)
- Cyberspace (the Internet and Web technology)
- Mediasphere (radio, TV, cable)
- Mindsphere (global ideas generated by previous global spheres).

Figure 13-2. The general architecture of the electraonic global village

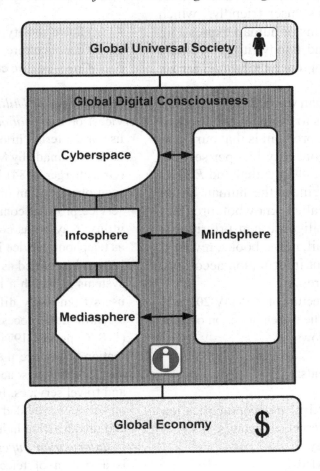

THE DEFINITION OF EGV

The EGV is the hybridization of facsimile, VCRs, answering machines, compact discs, cellular phones, video games, computers, telecommunications networks, and high-definition television (Targowski, 1990; Koelsch, 1995). Like most revolutions, this one has roots in economics. The alliance between computing and telecommunications technologies has been and is currently driving the service sector. Nearly 75% of U.S. workers in 1990 were employed in service, up from 55% in 1948 (Reich, 1992). In such an economy, most wealth is generated by information.

This type of wealth generation is a movement from "things to thinking." Information technology becomes "user friendly," which exploits natural forms of human expression: speech, gesture, and handwriting. Workers at Apple call this approach the *whole-person* paradigm.

Marshall McLuhan warned that "the more information one has to evaluate, the less one knows." The major problem is that our brain can only absorb about fifty bits per second. Technology will not change that and *EGV* is not going to re-engineer the human brain. However, the so-called knowbot program using artificial intelligence can prioritize a user's electronic mail, news, books, reviews, and selected relevant information according to each user's preference.

The system architecture of the EGV-2007+ is shown in Fig. 12-3. The systematization of *EGV* components is as follows:

1. Common elements:

    *   Information utility (telecommunication services, the Internet, computers, TV)
    *   Electronic money
    *   Electronic knowledge
    *   Information systems
    *   Information services
    *   Information-communication systems (e.g., e-commerce)
    *   Information policy
    *   Cyberspace

2. Electronic organizations, such as

    *   Virtual school and university
    *   Virtual enterprise
    *   Online government
    *   Electronic global citizens

3. Electronic social structures

    *   Tele-cities
    *   Tele-nations

4. Global society
5. Global culture
6. Cross-culture communications

Information Utility (telecommunication services) or *Information Superhighway.* The first use of the term "information utility" appears to have been made by Martin Greenberger in 1964 (Greenberger, 1984). He stated, "Barring unforeseen obstacles, an on-line interactive computer service, provided commercially by an information utility, may be as commonplace by 2000 A.D. as telephone service is today." Information utility can be defined as a class of online real-time systems in which a large number of individual users from many different organizations share a central data processing and memory complex (U.S. Congress, 1974). Some examples of information utility are the post office, libraries, tax services, savings accounts, stock brokerages, and travel services. Information utility is based on services provided by the telecommunication and broadcasting industries.

Information Superhighway (*INFOSTRADA*) is a system of telecommunications pathways and connections that transmits and receives voice, video, and data. The pathways consist

Figure 13-3. The system architecture of the electronic global village 21ˢᵗ century

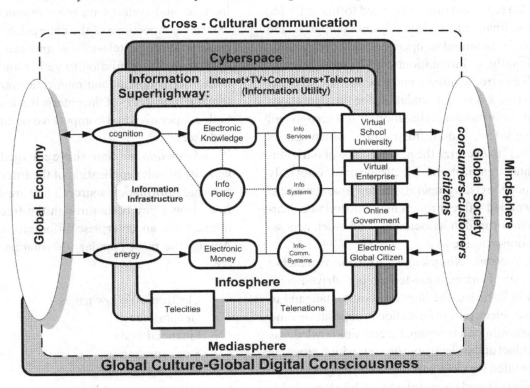

of copper wire, fiber-optic cable, coaxial cable, microwave line-of-sight signals, and satellite linkages. Individuals connect to these highways through hardware such as telephones, computers, and audio/video receivers. The United States currently possesses a basic information highway that provides virtual links for every individual through telephone and television. An information superhighway consists of broadband (high-capacity) telecommunications circuits, increasingly based on fiber-optic technology, which can carry much greater amounts of digitized information, such as high-resolution video, at faster speeds (Targowski, 1996).

The Internet is a globe-spanning public system of computer networks communicating through such protocols as the transmission control protocol (TCP) and the Internet protocol (IP). The most popular service of the Internet is based on the World Wide Web (WWW), which applies home pages programmed in hypertext markup language (HTML). This service allows for communication through hyperlinks among Web sites of organizations and people.

Electronic Money. This is a payment system applying, for example, *CyberCash* or the electronic fund transfer system (EFTS), in which the processing and communications necessary to effect economic exchanges for the production and distribution of services incidental or related to economic exchanges are dependent wholly or in large part on the use of electronics (U.S. Congress, 1974). The EFTS can be described as a growing array of financial services. Among these services are wire transfer of funds, direct deposit of income checks, periodic or authorized payments, check verification, and credit card authorizations. Point-of-sale (POS) systems, automated teller machines (ATM), and automated clearing houses (ACH) represent more advanced forms of EFTS. These financial services rely on computers and have the potential to operate locally, regionally, nationally, or internationally. The emergence of both electronic money and a new financial order provides a strong foundation for the operations of an information civilization. It is a component of the information infrastructure, which acts as a "fuel" to energize the performance of individuals and organizations. Electronic money not only supports existing operations but also generates new added value through new information (particularly through associations and quick access) and opportunities.

Electronic Knowledge. With the increasing number of information-technology-driven projects in libraries, the impetus to automate and to include electronic information in depositories and to disseminate it is strong. Electronic knowledge is a product of the *electronic library*, which provides automated services and electronic easy access to holdings stored electronically. While these holdings may be stored locally, it will be more probable that more holdings will be stored elsewhere. A library gateway will transmit patrons' requests through LANs, MANs, WANs, and GANs to other electronic libraries. The *electronic library* will become a place in which a certain specialized type of information or service is available, perhaps locally oriented.

Information systems. Information systems have been developed in business, government, and institutions along with the applications of punched-card machines and computers since the beginning of the twentieth century. The state of the art of these systems includes enterprise-wide information management complexes of management information systems, product information systems, operations information systems, inter-organizational information systems, international information systems, and end-user computing. Information systems mostly are involved in internal data/information processing and ac-

cessing; however, the inter-organizational and international systems are more oriented toward external connections of the enterprise. They are passing through tele-cities' and tele-nations' cyberspaces in a mission to gather and provide more information and communications among different remote parts of the enterprise, and service both cooperative and competitive organizations and users.

Information services – have emerged together with the broader application of the Internet as an external information source. They are delivered free or on a pay basis through the Internet and intranet (as an enterprise information portal). Among the most popular information services are:

- Electronic Yellow pages
- General news
- Financial news
- Stock quotations
- Foreign exchange data
- U.S. government bond data
- Maps
- Search/navigation

Info-communication systems – are the Internet-driven systems which combine information content and communication capability. For example, e-commerce is an information-communication system.

Cyberspace is an infinite world in which humans navigate in information-based space, and it is the ultimate computer-human interface to nonmaterial reality and virtual reality triggering science fiction ideas (Gibson, 1984; Benedikt, 1993). Also, it can be defined as a prime location around the information superhighway highway.

Telecity is a set of community computers, MANs, teleports (a dish to communicate with satellites), information kiosks, video-conferencing facilities, tele-work centers, and specialized networks to allow for the delivery of integrated and shared local, national, and global information on healthcare, education, business, government, and so forth. It is a miniature of the EGV; reduced to the local dimension and at the same time with an exit to the *telenation* and the EGV (Targowski, 1996).

Tele-nation is a set of tele-ities, national information superhighways allowing for the delivery of national information and telecommunication services and information and information-communication systems (Grossman, 1995). A *telenation* such as those in North America supports the following:

- The development of jobs, growth, and U.S. technological leadership
- The reduction of healthcare costs
- The delivery of higher-quality, lower-cost government services
- The preparation of our children for the fast-paced workplace of the twenty-first century
- The building of a more open and participatory democracy at all levels of government and the society

Information policy. Information policy is a set of rules, standards, and accepted practices that regulate the users' and service providers' behavior in cyberspace. Information infrastructure as a physical system provides the base for the delivery of consumer and business-oriented services over and derived from telecommunications networks. These allow for the access to such information resources as electronic money and electronic knowledge.

INFORMATIVE ORGANIZATIONS

Virtual schools and universities are telematic-oriented learning environments such as a distance learning school, a telematic school, a teacher-parent link, an electronic global university, a global lecture hall, even an electronic university. A distance learning school is the provision of education and training opportunities from one site to multiple sites simultaneously, or any educational experience in which the learner and the educator are interacting across space. Technology links can be chosen from among the following solutions: fiber optics, satellite, instructional television fixed service (IFFS), microwave, and coaxial cable. A telematic super-school is a set of applications such as administrative offices, distance learning classrooms, home learning centers, library/learning resource centers, and advanced-studies centers. The pipelines of communication technology are expanding the walls of the traditional classroom, taking children across the country. In a telematic super-school, for example, students use this pipeline to:

- Take a computer voyage through the chambers of a dog's heart
- Create a thunderstorm in a computer-generated weather lab
- Share a face-to-face language lesson with students in Montreal, and much, much more

By 1996 or shortly thereafter, with the spread of "smart phones," which are already becoming available in the corporate environment, parents will be able to dial up assignments, class schedules, school menus, notices of meetings, and other information displayed onscreen. More widespread use of voice messaging services will also support voicemail conversations, which can allow parents and teachers to communicate without the usual difficulties of arranging "live" conversation during working hours. The *electronic global university's* (*EGU*) purpose is to:

- Provide affordable education in those countries and national locations that are far away from academic centers (Becker, 1989)
- Provide telematic access to advanced, competitive education in those countries and

national locations that are looking for such solutions

- Offer to many people the chance of updating their education with refresher courses that could be taken without having to drop out of the workforce

The global lecture hall is a pilot project initiated in 1972 by Takeshi Utsumi, chairman of Global Systems Analysis and Simulation Association (GLOSAS). If effect, GLOSAS developed a concept of the global lecture hall and implemented several global teleconferences. The demonstrations encompassed more than two dozen universities linked together, from the East Coast of North America to Japan, the Republic of Korea, Spain, Guam, Alaska, Venezuela, and Australia, to Western and Eastern Europe, and to Mediterranean countries. These demonstrations helped GLOSAS discover and compensate for the technical, regulatory, economic, and marketing impediments to the creation of an electronic global university. The *EGU* is conceived as a worldwide educational network and a permanent organization of international education exchange via various telematic media. Its goals are:

- To globalize educational opportunities
- To support research in the scope of global problems
- To use global-scale tools to simulate and meet on problems of an interdependent world

The electronic university is referred to as the campus of the future, in which there will be TV consoles that could beam up taped lectures by any professor on campus or even let students monitor courses from other schools. Built-in computer terminals will tap into the card catalogs of most of the college libraries in the country, call up encyclopedia articles, or scan daily papers. During the great expansion that took place after World War II, American colleges and universities sought to be all things to all people. In the new age of austerity (the 1990s and beyond), schools are being forced to rethink their mission, decide what they can do best, and—in a form of academic triage—abandon certain fields of learning to other institutions. As a result of this strategy, a *virtual university* emerges. The virtual university is a temporary network of independent education centers/courses, providers, students, instructors, even erstwhile rivals, linked by information and telecommunication technology to share knowledge, skills, laboratories, costs, and access to other programs. It will have neither a central office nor an organization chart. It will have no hierarchy and no vertical integration.

Virtual enterprise is based on enterprise-wide computing, which is the ability to link different facilities at different locations around the world through information systems and communications networks to facilitate cooperative research and development with other firms, concurrent engineering by trusted and organized alliances of suppliers and manufacturers, or the distribution of manufacturing to far locations. These enterprise functions are integrated by such information systems as computer-aided design (CAD), computer-aided process planning (CAPP), computer-aided manufacturing (CAM), office automation systems, and management information system (MIS), as well as communications networking such as LANs, WANs, and GANs. If the information architecture leads only to information transport, it is computer networking; however, if that network is based on a multimedia communications architecture to support the integration of enterprise-wide systems, including telepower applications (such as telepresence in the virtual mode) throughout the enterprise, then it is enterprise-wide computing. The information and communications architectures determine the corporate electronic infrastructure as an evolving solution, an intermediate solution (corporate network computing), or an ultimate solution (enterprise networking). A key success factor to enterprise-wide computing is the architectural planning of telematic technology components as tools supporting a business strategy. Architectures of information and communications across multiple tiers of the enterprise are vital. These architectures should provide information and communication across the enterprise, much as a utility provides electricity.

Online government is the empowerment of citizens in participatory governing of public affairs. A strong internetworking among citizens and electronic public records is based on a graphic user interface (GUI), which supports a menu-driven, user-friendly interactive access. Government workers and officials have to learn and exercise power sharing in order to democratize equal access to power and seek service satisfaction by customers. Electronic town meetings can be one example of online government; this is an introduction of customer online scope-feedback into the governmental modus operandi. In this type of government, the citizens have easy, interactive, online access to governmental units and services. The supportive information systems are in electronic format. The electronic global citizen is a person who has telematic skills to work in/with virtual enterprise, online government, and virtual schools/universities. This person may telecommute to work or school and still be a productive worker or student. People are EGCs when as consumers they have mediated access to information about goods, services, and processes (e.g., working, learning, governing) from around the world.

All those organizations and systems are supported by information infrastructures.

INFORMATION INFRASTRUCTURE

The information infrastructure is the second-generation civilization infrastructure. The first generation of the civilization infrastructure is the set of core, foundational and integrational infrastructures as it is shown in Figure 13-4. As the latter deteriorates through the processes of the material civilization, the soft information infrastructure compensates for the losses of the urban, rural, and transportation infrastructures.

The basic components of civilization information infrastructure are being developed in the following layers (Figure 13-4):

1. Telecommunication Layer – provides services in the scope of:

   - Access and transmission technology via telephony, cable TV, satellites, and wireless
   - Switching and networking technology via local (LATA) and long-distance transmissions (IXC, e.g., ATT, Sprint, WorldCom) as narrow or broad-band service sending information through packet- or circuit-switching networks

2. Computer Networks Layer – contains end-users and organizational networks such as HAN (Home Area Network), LAN (Local Area Network), MAN (Metropolitan Area Network), RAN (Rural Area Network), WAN (Wide Area Network), GAN (Global Area Network), which are implemented on the telecommunication networks, with the exceptions of HAN and LAN

3. Internet Layer – provides global services of information-communication systems

4. Computing Layer – contains computer servers, computer terminals, operating systems, utility software, database management software, programming languages, computer-aided software engineering (CASE), and so forth

5. Communication Layer – secures such services as e-mail, EDI (electronic data interexchange) e-conferencing, teleconferencing, telecommuting, groupware for team

Figure 13-4. Civilization information infrastructure architecture

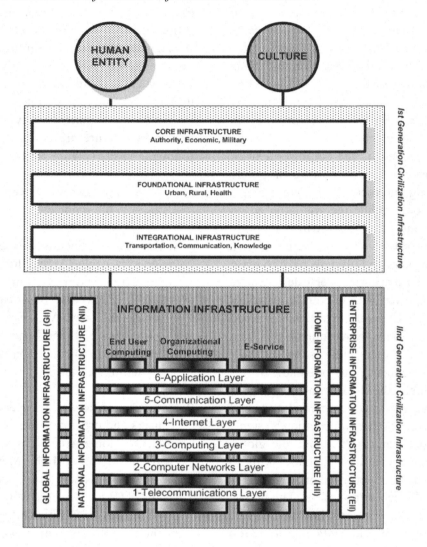

collaboration, and so forth

6. Application Layer – provides software for such applications as Office Automation (word processing, spreadsheet, micro-database, presentation, Web-navigation, automated calendaring, etc.), enterprise information systems, e-business.

The civilization information infrastructure can be divided into the following major categories:

- Enterprise Information Infrastructure (EII), (Targowski, 2001) shown in Figure 13-5
- National Information Infrastructure (NII), (Huth & Gould, 1993; Targowski, 1996) shown in Figure 13-6
- Local Information Infrastructure (LII), (Targowski, 1996) shown in Figure 13-7
- Global Information Infrastructure (GII), (Targowski, 1996) shown in Figure 13-8
- Home Information Infrastructure (HII), (Targowski, 1990) shown in Figure 13-9

Figure 13-5. Enterprise information infrastructure architecture (MIS-Management Information System, CRM-Customer Relations Manager, SCM-Supply Chain Management, EPM-Enterprise Performance Management, CAD-Computer-aided Design, CAM-Computer-aided Manufacturing, EIP-Enterprise Information Portal)

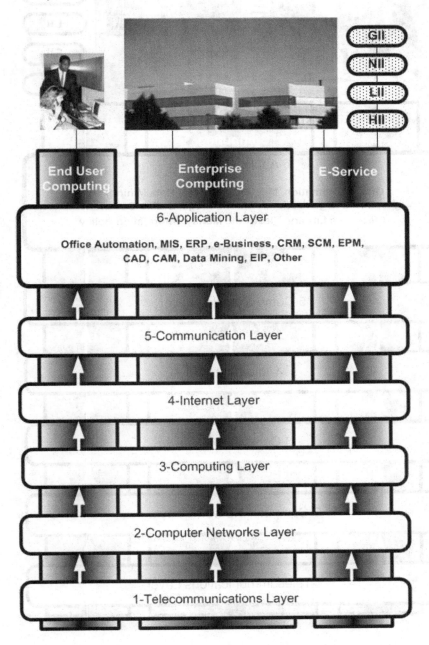

Figure 13-6. National information infrastructure architecture (MIS-Management Information System, OIP-Organization Information Portal)

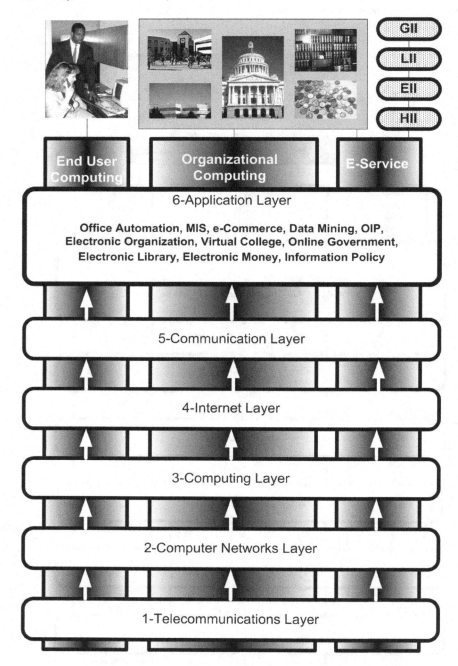

Figure 13-7. Local information infrastructure architecture (MIS-Management Information System, OIP-Organization Information Portal)

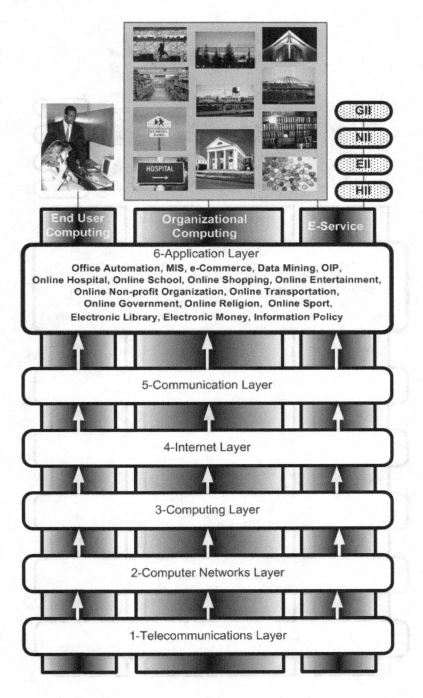

Figure 13-8. Global information infrastructure architecture (MIS-Management Information System, EIP-Enterprise Information Portal)

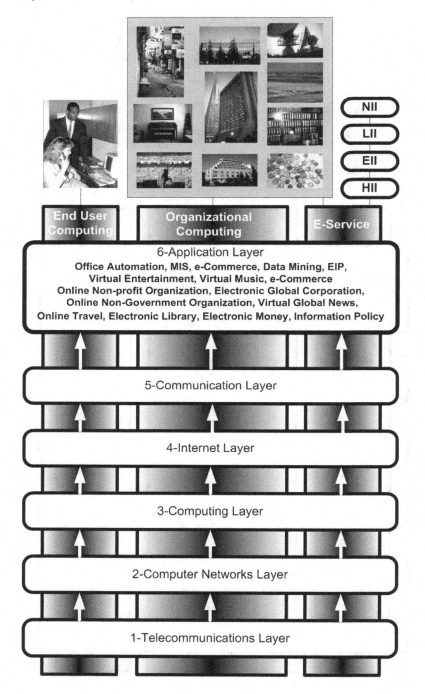

Figure 13-9. Home information infrastructure architecture (IS-Information System, HIP-Home Information Portal)

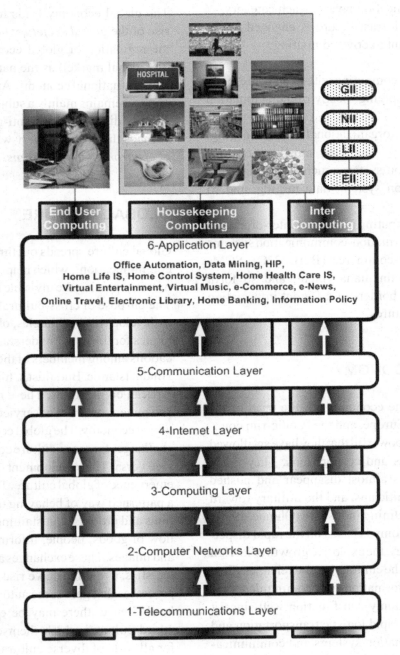

Each of these infrastructures comprise components that are specific for them and are differentiated in the application layer of each category.

Also, each infrastructure is engaged in the three types of interactive computing:

- End-user computing either at home or at work – applying mostly office automation software
- Enterprise (organizational or housekeeping) computing – applying mostly enterprise information systems such as management information system, data mining, and so forth
- Inter-Computing in cases of inter-organizational information-communication systems such as e-commerce (B2B, B2C), SCM-supply chain management, and so forth that cross borders of different information infrastructures.

GLOBAL ECONOMY

In the 1990s, the economies of the triad of the United States, Europe, and the Pacific-rim countries became so powerful that they have swallowed most consumers and corporations. They made national borders almost disappear and pushed bureaucrats, politicians, and the military toward the status of declining industries (Ohmae, 1990). The global economy is based on the rapid dispersion of technology, the explosive growth of foreign exchanges, and the cumulative and relentless flow of mediated information and communications. The global economy can function well since it is supported by rapid logistic transportation and powerful information systems and communications networks. These latter telematic technologies make "distance" an obsolete term. The global economy accelerates the progress of technology, and technology advances the proficiency of the global economy[1].

GLOBAL SOCIETY

The global economy leads towards the gradual rise of the *global society*, whose mission will be the regulation of global economic transactions (the global market) as the national society regulates the national economy. At present, the *global society* remains mainly a subject of academic and political discussions and anti-globalism activities. Perhaps the *global society* will be a community of *electronic global citizens*.

GLOBAL CULTURE

Global culture spreads out through cross-culture communication[2], which helps in understanding a message passing the invisible borders of the EGV. The purpose of cross-cultural communication is to develop rules, strategies, objectives, and techniques for the better understanding of communications among members of the Western, Eastern, Hindu, Islamic, Buddhist, Chinese, Japanese, and African civilizations. These members are either consumers or product/services providers in the global economy. The global economy creates new challenges for cross-culture communications and vice versa. The development of EGV leads to the emergence of global culture. The global culture is a patterned way of behaving under global conditions and processes, sustaining the exchange and flow of goods, people, information, knowledge, and images. These exchanges and flows of people, logistics, and minds give rise to communication processes that gain some autonomy on the global level. Hence, there may be emerging sets of a "third culture" which themselves are conduits for all sorts of diverse cultural flows that cannot be merely understood as the product of bilateral exchanges between nation-states (Featherstone, 1990). Trade, travel, and television lay the groundwork for the global culture. In 1990, 1 billion passengers flew the world's airways. By the year

2010, it will be 2+ billion passengers. In food, fashion, and fun, one can afford to be open to all sorts of foreign influences. In Times Square, on the Ginza, and on the Champs-Elysees sushi bars, croissant shops, and McDonald's compete for the same customers and expensive real estate (Nashbitt & Aburdene, 1990).

ELECTRONIC CULTURE

The term "electronic culture" means the *electronization* of the "information culture" which has been rapidly developing since the invention of print in 1454. In the last 500 years, information culture was developed by such media as print, telegraph, telephone, telecommunications, recorded sound (wire, tapes, records and CDs), movies, radio, television, and so forth. In the last 50 years, new media such as computers (software) and the Internet have electronized information culture.

In general, information culture has been under development ever since people could communicate symbols, but this accelerated when books could be printed in the 15th century and information could be communicated over "wires" in the 19th century. The 21st century is the century of information machines, which increased our desire for better control and cognition. This, however, differs among particular civilizations and also among different levels of people's income. A more open flow of information and its better use lead toward more open and democratic societies, as is indicated by the fall of the Soviet Union in 1991, after a policy of "openness" was introduced by M. Gorbachev. The readership of underground publications exceeded the readership of official news in Poland in the 1980s, which led to the rise of the free union solidarity and fall of the Berlin Wall in 1989.

Electronic information culture is not only about electric transmission of words and images or pushing down messages via mass media ("mass communication"); it also invites "to enlarge the human conversation by comprehending what others are saying" (Carey, 1992). Carey noticed also that "citizens now suffer in many areas from overloads of communication and overdoses of participation." Therefore, in the new electronic world, we should be able to focus on meaningful communication and important issues. Otherwise, the newly created information chaos will make us deaf, blind, and insensitive.

The electronic information process triggered new values such as: connected-expected feedback, rhythm, productivity, velocity, impatience, techno-ism, cyber-ethics, informated optimization, big picture versus small picture, global awareness, self-consciousness, and so forth. The physical world is being affected by new ways of computer-aided development and creation/implementation of such technologies as e-communication, distance learning, e-office, telecommuting, e-knowledge, artificial intelligence, e-capital, e-commerce, precision farming, mass customization, precision targeting, information warfare, net entertainment, e-art, cyber-dating, and cyber-crime. Of course, such a huge infusion of new e-technologies also generates among people (net-citizens) new "electronic behavior" identified by such attributes as a net-centric anytime, anywhere approach, the "death of distance," direct (no middleman) contacts, more intense curiosity and discovery, cyber-elitism, the digital divide, information wealth, poverty of attention, and so forth. These attributes create so-called *digital capital*, which according to Tapscott, Ticoll, and Lowy (2000) is a set of new rules of engagement in the new economy.

Electronic culture defines an e-mindsphere, e-global consciousness, and eventually the global-universal society, which acts in its e-borderless world, mostly in a cyberspace but by the nature of *"click and brick"* in the physical world, too. Figure 13-10 illustrates components and relationships of electronic culture.

Figure 13-10. Electronic culture architecture

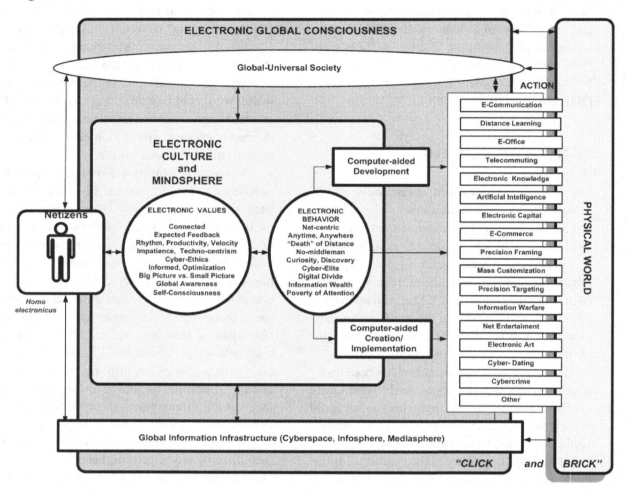

Figure 13-11. The relationship between digital and physical cultures

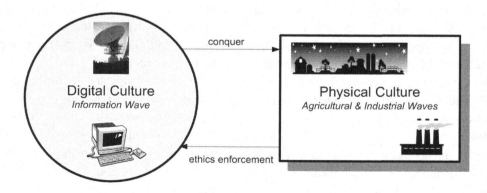

Electronic culture shapes or rather conquers the development and operations of information culture, which in consequence shapes the Agricultural and Industrial Waves of civilization, as is depicted in Figure 13-11.

These latter waves defend themselves by enforcing e-culture to comply with old-fashioned social ethics tested though centuries in society. Electronic culture is a culture which likes velocity, accessibility, and non-stop novelty. It is a culture which likes control and cognition and promotes democracy through free speech and net-driven equality.

ELECTRONIC GLOBAL CITIZEN (EGC)

At the beginning of the 21st century, e-culture remains a culture of white-middle class males with corporate backgrounds who can navigate electronically or physically around the globe in a search for better opportunities and solutions for an increasingly frictionless capitalism. However, the high school kids, the twenties or in general, the younger generation is also net-centered. This kind of person is a net-citizen with e-global consciousness who can skillfully apply tools of the global information infrastructure. In effect, the *electronic global citizen* is a citizen of the *Electronic Global Village*, who is certainly an enlightened person, ready for dialogue and to share his vision and opportunities with others, respecting their diversity, seeing the planet from above as one world, one civilization and wanting to learn about it to protect it as long as possible. Perhaps the *EGC* is ready to accept the universal values within a framework of diversity. As a result of it, perhaps the *EGC* will minimize the *digital divide* and make e-globe accessible for all who want to be on it.

Of course this "rosy" picture is full of unexpected negative motives and actions triggered by computer hackers, criminals, and anti-social agents. The new e-world has the same or even more intensified crimes as the physical world; therefore, it is not yet a paradise or utopia. Rather, it is some hope for a better, hopefully wiser control and cognition, applied by humans in their quest for the survival in the present settings of the universe.

CONCLUSION

The development of the *EGV* can help unleash a social revolution that will change forever the way people live, work, and interact with each other.

- People could live almost anywhere they wish, without foregoing opportunities for useful and fulfilling employment, by "telecommuting" to their offices through an information highway.
- The best schools, teachers, and courses would be available to all students, without regard to geography, distance, resources, or disability.
- Services that improve a nation's healthcare system and respond to other important social needs could be available online, without waiting in line, when and where you need them.
- Freedom and better quality of life will be more popular in the world.
- Application of control and cognition will be wiser and eventually leading to longer lasting civilization.

Also, the *EGV* creates information highways that require rules of the road. These rules are being created along with these practical applications. The *EGV* supports globalism and at the same time it supports regionalism, which organizes local resources to survive and flourish in global cooperation and competition.

A. Further Research Directions

- Investigate the relationships among the *global universal society*, *global digital consciousness*, and global economy in the 21st century and in the future.
- Investigate the relationships within the *global digital consciousness* among such components as cyberspace, infosphere, mindsphere, and mediasphere.
- Investigate the development of the enterprise information infrastructure in the scope of relationships among end user, enterprise, and service computing, particularly these last two pillars of enterprise infrastructure, which will define the emerging trend of the 21st century.

B. Research Opportunities

- The research opportunity is in investigating emerging electronic culture, which leads towards the emergence of electronic global citizenships.

C. Additional Ideas

- The emergence of electronic culture and citizenships will perhaps lead to a new bifurcation of human race.

D. Rationale

- Global village is a term coined by Wyndham Lewis in his book *America and Cosmic Man* (1948). However, Herbert Marshall McLuhan also wrote about this term in his book *The Gutenberg Galaxy: The Making of Typographic Man* (1962). His book describes how electronic mass media collapse space and time barriers in human communication, enabling people to interact and live on a global scale. In this sense, the globe has been turned into a village by the electronic mass media. Today, the term *Electronic Global Village* is mostly used as a metaphor to describe the Internet and World Wide Web. This new reality has implications for forming new sociological structures within the context of civilization. The Gutenberg Galaxy phase of Western civilization is being replaced by computer networks and electronic information-communication, leading to "electronic interdependence." In this phase, electronic media replace the visual culture of the Gutenberg phase, producing cognitive shifts and new social organizations based on digital media technologies. As a result of this shift in technology and media, humankind is moving from the individualism and fragmentation that characterized the Gutenberg Galaxy to a collective identity, with a "tribal base" within the *Electronic Global Village*. Instead of tending towards a vast Alexandrian library, the world has become an electronic brain, with the *global digital consciousness* and ability to pursue problem-solving through a world-wide forum, creating a new concept of digital world community acting in a planetary cyberspace. Therefore, it is important to investigate electronic/digital components of that new "brain," "consciousness," "culture," and "civilization." Perhaps we are facing a new civilization bifurcation of mankind.

E. Additional Reading

Barnet, R., & Cavanagh, J. (1994). *Imperial corporations and the new world order*. New York, NY: Simon & Schuster.

Bell, D. (1980). *Sociological journeys: Essays 1960-1980*. London: Heinemann.

Bernal, J. (1989). *The social function of science*. Berlin: Academie-Verlag.

Bradley, S., Hausman, J., & Nolan, R. (1993). *Globalization, technology and competition*. Boston,

MA: Harvard Business School.

Brzezinski, Z. (1976). *Between two ages: America in the technetronic era.* New York, NY: Penguin

Cairncross, F. (1997). *The death of distance. How the communications revolution will change our lives.* Boston, MA: Harvard Business School Press.

Clark, C. (1940). *Conditions of economic progress.* London: McMillan and Co.

Gilder, G. (1989). *Microcosmos.* New York, NY: Simon & Schuster.

Grossman, L. (1995). *The electronic republic.* New York, NY: Viking.

Harman, W. (1988). *Global mind challenge.* Sausalito, CA: Werner Books.

Hiltz, S., & Turoff, M. (1993). *The network nation.* Cambridge, MA: The MIT Press.

Hitt, W. (1998). *The global citizen.* Columbus, OH: Battelle Press.

Hundley, R., Anderson, R., Bikson, T., & Neu, C. (2003). *The global course of the information revolution. Recurring themes and regional variations.* Santa Monica, CA: RAND

King, A., & Schneider, B. (1991). *The first global revolution.* New York, NY: Pantheon Books.

Lewis, W. (1948). *America and cosmic man.* London: Nicholson & Watson.

Mann, C. (2006). *Accelerating the globalization of America. The role of information technology.* Washington, D.C.: Institute for International Economics.

McLuhan, M. (1962). *The Gutenberg galaxy: The making of typographic man.* Toronto: University of Toronto Press.

_____ (1964). *Understanding media: The extension of man.* New York, NY: A Signet Book

_____ (1967). *The medium is the message.* New York, NY: Bantam Books.

_____ (1968). *War and peace.* New York, NY: Bantam Books.

Moran, R., & Riesenberger, J. (1994). *The global challenge, building the new worldwide enterprise.* Berkshire, UK: McGraw-Hill International.

Ostry, S., & Nelson, R. (1995). *Techno-nationalism and techno-globalism.* Washington, D.C.: The Brookings Institute.

Porat, M-U. (1976). *The information economy.* Doctoral dissertation. University of Stanford.

Rushkoff, D. (1994). *Cyberia. Life in the trenches of hyperspace.* New York, NY: HarperCollins.

Ricardo, D. (1978). *The principles of political economy and taxation.* London: Dent.

Richta, R. (Ed.). (1969). *Civilization at the crossroads.* New York, NY: M.E. Sharp.

Shaffer, C., & Anundsen, K. (1993). *Creating community anywhere.* New York, NY: Jeremy P. Tarcher/Perigee

Shannon, C., & Weaver, W. (1949). *The mathematical theory of communication.* Urbana, IL: University of Illinois Press.

Silberglitt, R., Howell, D., & Wong, A. (2006). *The global technology revolution 2020.* Santa Monica, CA: RAND.

Veneris, Y. (1984). *The informational revolution, cybernetics and urban modeling.* Doctoral thesis, University of Newcastle upon Tyne, UK.

_____ (1990). Modeling the transition from the industrial to the informational revolution. *Environment and Planning, 22*(3), 399-416.

Wiener, N. (1948) *Cybernetics*. Cambridge, MA: MIT Press.

REFERENCES

Carey, J. (1992). *Communication as culture*. New York, NY: Routledge.

Barber, B. (1992). Jihad vs. McWorld. *Atlantic Monthly, March,* 53-63.

Becker, J. (1989). The concept of a university of the world. *Information Society, 6*(3), 83-92.

Benedikt, M. (1993). *Cyberspace first steps*. Cambridge, MA: MIT Press.

Bequai, A. (1981). *The cashless society: EFTS at the crossroads*. New York, NY: John Wiley.

Featherstone, M. (1990). *Global culture*. Newbury Park, CA: SAGE Publications.

Gibson, W. (1984). *Neuromancer*. New York, NY: Ace Books.

Greenberger, M. (1984). The computers of tomorrow. *Atlantic Monthly, May,* 63-67.

Grossman, L. (1995). *The electronic republic*. New York, NY: Viking.

Huth, V., & Gould, S. (1993). *The national information infrastructure: The federal role*. Congressional Research Service, Washington, D.C.: The Library of Congress.

Koelsch, F. (1995). *The Infomedia revolution*. Toronto: McGraw-Hill Ryerson.

McLuhan, M. (1968). *War and peace in the global village*. New York, NY: Bantam Books.

Nashbitt, J., & Aburdene, P. (1990). *Megatrends 2000*. New York, NY: William Morrow and Company.

Ohmae, K. (1990). *The borderless world*. New York, NY: Harper Perennial.

Reich, R. (1992). *The work of nations*. New York, NY: Vintage Books.

Soros, G. (1998). *The crisis of global capitalism*. New York, NY: Public Affairs.

Tapscoe, D., Ticoll, D., & Lowy, A. (2000). *Digital capital. Harnessing the power of business webs*. Cambridge, MA: Harvard Business School Press.

Targowski, A. (1990). Strategies and architecture of the electronic global village. *Information Society, 7*(3), 187-202.

_____(1990b). *The architecture of enterprise-wide ims*. Harrisburg, PA: Idea Group Publishing.

_____(1996). *Global information infrastructure*. Harrisburg, PA: Idea Group Publishing.

_____(2001). *Enterprise information infrastructure*. Boston, MA: Pearson.

U.S. Congress. (1974). A definition offered by the National Commission on Electronic Fund Transfer (NCEFT). *Public Law,* 93-495.

ENDNOTES

[1] More on global economy is provided in Chapter VII.

[2] More on cross-culture is provided in Chapter XV.

Chapter XIV
Information Societies

INTRODUCTION

The purpose of this chapter is to define the evolution and key indicators of the information society that is being triggered by the Information Wave of the last 25 years. Several types of the information society from the point of view of information-communication technology (ICT) will be reviewed and their developmental paths will be defined.

The fast development of the global economy based on information-communication technology (ICT) is supported by the information society, because without this technology it would be rather impossible to perceive information society. Depending on the different levels of a given country's development, the information society has different levels of complexity and influence on the global economy and vice versa. Hence, it is important to recognize the information society's different trends of development and their solutions and internal and external consequences. A question appears whether the information society is a new tool of thought or a new way of life. The answer to this question is provided in this chapter.

THE FORCES OF CHANGE

The "information society" is a fuzzy concept. It is considered the answer to the problems created by the postindustrial *modus operandi*. In a modern economy, growth is owed to advances in information-communication technology. By the beginning of the 21st century, the need for information handling and processing in world societies is being shaped by the following trends:

1. Politics in the post-Cold War Era. A new world order may lead to the formation of 1,000 countries and a highly decentralized "international society." This physical trend of disintegration will require tools to integrate such entities informationally. Eventually, this new system of nations will be based on a new information-communication infrastructure, which needs new information-communication systems and services.

2. Democratization and peacemaking. Societies would like to be better informed; therefore, they need more communication based on free speech and solutions like the Internet.

3. Globalizing information. This is caused by the proliferation of ICT and is a major

driving force in the trans-nationalization of the world economy. Eastabrooks (1988) predicts that programmed capitalism in a computer-mediated society will integrate all national markets and create one international market.

4. The globalizing economy. A network of 50 global corporations now "rules the world," because they apply the global information infrastructure. ICT is at the core of the current process of economic globalization (Madon, 1997).

5. Population growth and health threats. In 2025 there will be about 8-9 billion people, who will generate at least twice as many transactions as are currently processed today. This means more needs for ICT capacity.

6. Global environmental threats. If these threats are considered seriously, then there is a need for planetary management and ecology. This new management and ecology will require monitoring information-communication systems and services.

7. A new path for development. Since the gap between rich and poor nations continues to widen, a world focused on people is being created. This undertaking requires new concepts of human security, new models of sustainable human development, new partnerships between state and market, new patterns of national and global governance, and new forms of international corporations (Boutros-Ghali, 1994). This trend requires more education and research, which will necessitate the formation of "knowledge" and "learning" societies (Marien, 1995).

As society, particularly the information society, becomes more interconnected, we face a loss of boundaries, throwing into question the basic conceptual distinctions we use to make sense of the world. As society becomes more complex and takes on more variety and differentiated configurations, the capacity of existing regula-

tory (governance) systems is being overwhelmed. A group of 14 Canadian public servants offered the following new focus how to govern in the information society (Rossel, 1992):

*   Information-based ways of organizing to include more players to innovate and learn
*   Forging consensus
*   Strategic use of information to provide leadership in the continuing process of learning

For example, the Japanese information society's purpose is the transformation of *Homo sapiens* into *Homo intelligens* in the spirit of globalism through transparent networks and an open educational system. This purpose portends that anyone, anywhere, at anytime in Japan should be able to get any information easily, quickly, and inexpensively. We see that these premises treat the information society as a "computopia" and as a rebirth of technological synergism (Masuda, 1971). Perhaps we expect too much from the information society, which can provide "computopian" platforms for information-communications but does not necessarily require that people use them.

As ICT makes information society a reality, its analysis is undertaken by many researchers from many disciplines. Frank Webster (1995; 2004) provides a very useful review of different approaches towards the information society concept. Table 1 presents another summary of the different approaches to the understanding of information society.

Based on this review of major developmental trends of information society, a matrix of these trends is defined in Figure 14-1. This model allows for the following observations:

*   ICT is not *neutral*, it can be of developmental or regressive characters
*   ICT-triggered *surveillance* and *digital divide* are regressive and strong trends

Table 14-1. Different approaches towards information society

PERIOD	SYMPTOMS	PARADIGM	REASON	IDEA PIONEERS
Transformations due to ICT growing applications				
1970s	Political Transformation	Informed Society	To intellectualize the Japanese Society To break censorship in Poland 1971-74	Masuda (1971) Targowski (1971; 1980; 1991)
1970s	Economic Transformation	Post-Industrial Society		Bell (1973), Porat (1977)
1990s	Job Transformation	Information Society	Intensive Computerization	Reich (1992)
1990s	Work place transformation (from local to global, migrating for a job)	Mobile Society	To open boarders after the fall of Communism	Urry (1995)
1990s	Solutions Transformation (from simple to complex)	Knowledge Society	Competition at the level of innovations	Mulchap (1962) Stehr (1994)
1990s	Landscape Transformation (from physical to virtual)	Virtual Society	Growth of cyberspace	Balsamo (1995)
Networking due to computer-telecom networks & Internet wide applications				
1980s		Information Wave		Toefler (1980)
1980s	From Global to Electronic Global Village integration	Electronic Global Village	Growth of computer-telecom networks	Targowski (1990)
2000s	Connecting people	Network Nation Electronic Republic Network Society Digital Nation	Wide spread of netcitizens	Hiltz and Turoff (1993) Grossman (1995) Castell (1996) Wilhelm (2004)
Digital Divide due to too high cost of ICT for underprivileged				
1990s	From truth to greed	Uninfomed Society	Manipulation of data on purpose	Schiller (1996)
2000s	Deepening inequality	Disconnected Society	The gap between those with an access and those without an access to the Internet	Norris (2001) Van Dijk (2005)
Surveillance due to desire for better control & efficiency				
1940s 1970s 1980s 1990s 2000s	Utopian quest for better efficiency	Big Brother Prisoned Society Dossier Society Informated Society Automated Society	Total control A cell for every one A file for everyone Every worker informated Automated Service	Orwell (1949) Foucault (1979) Laudon (1886) Zuboff (1988) Targowski (2008, Chapter XI)

continued on following page

Table 14-1. continued

Democracy due to better informed citizens				
1970s	Applying technology by government to control society	Controlled Society	Scientific government	Westin (1971)
1970s	Applying fair game in discussion	Liberal Public Sphere	Growth of public media	Habermas (1974)
1980s	Preserving freedom	Free-speaking Society	To apply technologies of freedom	De Sola Pool (1983)
1980s	Searching for better democracy	Teledemocracy	Technology as protecting democracy	Arterton (1987)
1990s	Searching for democratic politics of technology	Democratic Technology	Political-social criteria is more important than economic criteria in technology assessment	Scolve (1995)
2000s	Fragmentation of "virtual sphere"	Flaming and Unresolved Conflicts	To search for equal access opportunity	Papacharissi (2002)
Virtualities due to growing presence in cyberspace				
1990s	Growth of cyberspace-oriented life	Virtual Society	Quest for a culture of the future	Michaels (1994)
1990s	Growth of women participation in IT profession	Powered women	Future has no place for "historical man"	Plant (1996)

Source: (1) the Author and (2) the categorization of five kinds of techno-social trends by Webster (2004).

- ICT-triggered democracy may be preserved, since the citizens are better informed

Of course all six ICT-driven societal trends require very active and responsible social actions and regulations. But information-oriented social action is per se positive, since it leads to better awareness of strength and weaknesses of social and technological issues and their solutions.

On the other hand, information society is not the *panacea* of every social problem. Even May (2002) argues that while there have been some major and important changes prompted by the information technology revolution, these are often changes only in the forms of activity and not their substance. The Information Age according to May supports previous social practices rather than overthrows all that has been practiced before. Perhaps it is too skeptical a view, since a better informed person is more knowledgeable and wiser; this is a great progress of civilization.

In the following sections of this chapter, the information society will be synthesized from the ICT point of view since without this technology there is no information society.

THE INFORMATION SOCIETY: A NEW TOOL OF THOUGHT OR A NEW WAY OF LIFE?

The impact of information-communication technology on individuals and organizations has

Figure 14-1. A matrix of ICT and politics-driven trends of the information society development

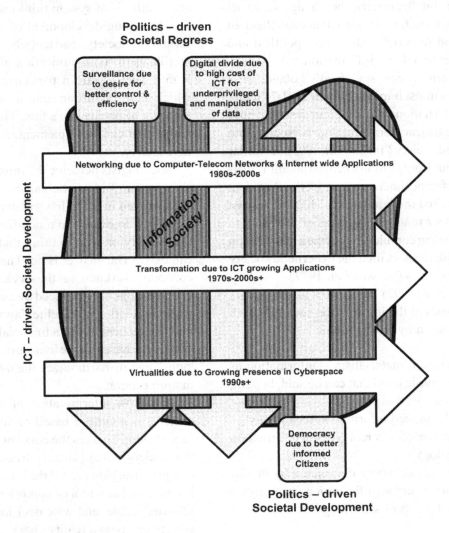

been analyzed under the rubric of the information society since the beginning of the computer revolution in the 1960s (Masuda, 1971; Bell, 1973). It is a socio-economic view of the impact of computers on society in general. The increasing role of computer and network applications affects almost every facet of human life. Sociologists and computer pioneers have tried to rationalize the computer's role in society.

The term "information society" was applied for the first time by Koyama in 1968 and subse-quently by his compatriot Masuda in 1971 in his master plan for building the Japanese information society. The "information society" evolved from such slogans in the 1960s and 1970s as computer-serviced society (Sackman, 1967), Age of Cybernetics, Information Era (McLuhan, 1968), knowledge society (Drucker, 1970), technotronic society (Brzezinski, 1971), computer revolution, wired society (Martin, 1978), telematic society (Martin, 1981), post-industrial society (Bell, 1973), and Gutenberg Two (Godfred & Parkhil,

1979). The term "information society" was coined in order to intellectualize the change in social behavior which transformed the capitalism of "capital and material" into a new political and social order based on "information."

In Eastern Europe, specifically Poland, these ideas were almost implemented in 1971-74 under the form of a national information system whose purpose was to transform a totalitarian society into an informed society (Targowski, 1991). A similar project, though only a tool of central planning, was a subject of experimentation in Chile. President Allende invited the famous British cyberneticist Stanford Beer to apply his ideas of feedback to reduce planning complexity, but the assassination of the president also killed the cybernetic society in South America (Schwember, 1977).

Pawlowska (1992) offers the following six characteristics of the information society, which are agreed upon by most authors:

1. Information materialism – information as an economic good that can be sold, bought, and possessed
2. Widely applied information technology
3. Integration of different types of information technology
4. A national economy dominated by the information sector (information economy)
5. Special status of knowledge

The information society with its information economy occurred as a result of industrial evolution rather than resulting from the information revolution. Although it is the same capitalistic society with the same values, the focus on information increases human cognition and changes the future of mankind and its environment, particularly its infrastructures, and perhaps brings along with that a change in societal values. The information society requires that the human process of cognition is no longer limited to reductionism, mechanism, and analysis. The process in this new society can be more open, more expansive in generating ideas

and solutions channeled by a better focus (aims) and synthesis of system thinking.

The strong development of media in the information society, particularly interactive ICT, facilitates the communication of one's message. It may lead toward a participatory democracy which should assure an equal access to power and the right to decide one's fate. These are the new values that can be implemented in the information society.

Sociologists perceive the information society as a dream of idealistic values and clean hands not involved in the "dirty" material economy. Is it realistic to expect so much from the information society or even to think that such a society can exist? The answer is no. The post-industrial economy, also known as the service or information economy, has been reduced by Daniel Bell (1973) to an association of the elite (lawyers, financiers, and researchers). Such a financial system cannot sustain the nation in the long term, since it exports "jobs" and disharmonizes the development of a mature economy.

A narrow interpretation of the information society, as a culture based on information as a "commodity" makes the concept of the information society more of an unfulfilled, even misleading, premise. However, if the information society is conceived as a tool of making more informed, knowledgeable, and wise decisions, then such a society can pass a reality check and its development should be supported. Such a society has the chance of becoming the "conscious society" on the way to developing into the "wise society," driven not only by information and knowledge, but also by the wisdom of how to survive and be satisfied.

If the information society applies electronic mail, telecommuting, electronic commerce and/or distance learning on a wide scale, then these technologies lead to new ways of human behavior in civilization.

The politics of information should also be as important as "computer literacy." We pay a lot of attention to applying computer tools, but do we scrutinize the application systems design and operations of the information society? This lack of application design checks may lead to the abuse of social activities, and ICT may become unwanted technology.

THE ESSENCE OF THE INFORMATION SOCIETY

The social framework of the information society defined by Bell (1979) is a new integrated computer-telecomunication infrastructure which transmits structured facts, ideas, judgments and experimental results. Bell's view that technology is the main agent of change has been questioned by several authors, who argue, that the new technology is not the main cause of change in our society today. On the other hand, Bell may be thinking the same way when referring to Machlup's (1962) and Porat's (1979) thesis that the information society is defined by the proportion of information/knowledge activities to material ones. If the latter activities are more important than the former, then the information sector becomes the primary one (information products and services), with two deviated information sectors (public and private bureaucracies). The three remaining sectors are the private productive (producing goods), public productive (building roads, dams, and so on), and household sectors.

Beniger (1986) hypothesizes that the information society is the answer to the control crisis caused by the industrial revolution. Hence, he concludes that "control" is the engine of the information society.

Where are the real roots of the information society? They are in the concept of "information" rather than in that of "material control." Information is a process of forming a new idea, concept, event, material, energy, product, service and so on. By forming some idea or description, we inform it. Peters (1987) argues that with the decline of scholasticism and the rise of empiricism around the seventeenth century (the rise of the natural sciences), "information" gradually came to refer to "the information of the senses" (such formulations are found in Bacon, Locke, Berkeley, and others). Where once "information" referred to the defining of universals, nowadays it also describes the processing of particulars (data, information, concept, knowledge, wisdom).

Instead of defining the information society by its dominant product, information, the author perceives perceive the information society through its general structure of social and economic relations.

An investigation of the general structure of social and economic relations must lead to the analysis of civilization. Civilization is an info-material structure developed by humans to effectively cope with themselves, nature and their creator. The mission of civilization is to improve human existence. The civilization model (Figure 14-2) has the following components:

- Human entity – organized humans
- Culture – a value-driven and symbols-driven processes of developing patterns of human behavior
- Infrastructure – technology-driven additive process of acquiring and applying material means

A human entity in the political sense is a family, tribe, ethnos, people, proto-nation, nation, international community, global society, and so forth. A society is an organized human entity on the same territory in order (more on this topic in Chapter I):

- to support their own existence through the exchange of specialized services and goods via infrastructures
- to develop the human race by the development of culture and infrastructures

Figure 14-2. A model of civilization

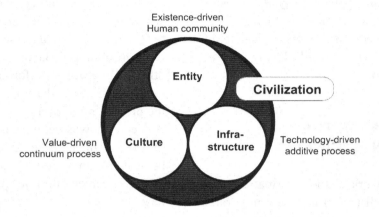

The role of a society in a civilization context must take into account the stage of civilization development. The first civilizations (Mesopotamian, Egyptian, Minoan, Indic) were societal civilizations: they organized society. Based on these, the next civilizations (Hellenic, Roman, Sinic, Japanese, Buddhist, Islamic, Eastern, Western, Sub-Saharan, and Carthaginian/Punic [Maghrebian nowadays] in B.C. times) were organized around cultural issues. Hence, we can call them cultural civilizations. The third generation of civilizations (Japanese, Buddhist, Sinic, Hindu, Islamic, Eastern, Western, and African in our times) are organized around the issues of developing infrastructures; therefore (Chapter I), we will name them the infrastructural civilizations.

Among civilization infrastructures one can recognize the following configurations:

1.   Core infrastructure (authority I, economic I, military I)
2.   Foundational infrastructures (urban I, rural I, health I)

3.   Integrational infrastructures (transportation I, knowledge I, communication I, Information I)

Does the level of development in a society depend on the era in which the civilization existed? Although all eight civilizations developed infrastructures, each put a different emphasis on a particular category of infrastructure. Most literature describes the societal development in Western civilization. In fact, the current Western emphasis is on the integrational infrastructure, which is being developed for the purpose of pursuing the culture of management, media, education, and entertainment as well as strengthening the economic, military, and health infrastructures. Of course, societies from other civilizations have different priorities. Western societies develop the integrational infrastructure not for the sake of infrastructure but for the purpose of developing the aforementioned cultures. In other words, an information society emerges when a society's purpose and primary means of solving problems are focused on information handling and processing.

For example, the levels of ICT advancement in both the United States and Singapore are high. However, the proportion of information to material activities in the U.S. is much higher than in Singapore, although that city is still involved in manufacturing American goods. Does this mean that there is no information society in Singapore? Singapore is an automated state-city with some solutions that are not conceivable in the U.S. Are both states at the level of an information society? At this moment, we may say that the U.S. has entered the "informed" society level while Singapore is at the level of the "informative" society. (See below for elaboration of these and related technical terms.)

Alvin Toffler (1980) offered a very elegant concept of civilization development through three waves of agriculture, industry, and information. Later, Alvin and Heidi Toffler (1994) became advocates of the "new civilization," because they perceived the information wave as replacing the agricultural and industrial waves. Is bread being replaced by "Windows XP" or a car by the Internet? That will not happen. The next wave includes the previous ones as illustrated in Figure 14-3. The quality of any information society depends on the quality of the previous societies. In other words, the information society is not exclusive but inclusive. The relationships among these societies determine the quality of life in the information society.

TYPES OF THE INFORMATION SOCIETY

The term "the information society" was sufficiently descriptive in itself when it was first described 30 years ago. Nowadays, the information society is being developed in several mutations. Some types of the information society are:

Figure 14-3. The inclusiveness of civilization waves

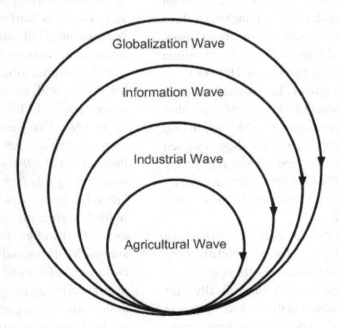

The Data (Dossier) Society: A Big Brother Control

The industrial revolution made it possible to "process" materials, such as coal, metal, and cloth, at unprecedented volumes and speeds. Such acceleration of material processing increased the demand for "control" of industrial operations. For instance, the many problems of scheduling and coordinating in the early days of the railroads resulted in missed connections or accidents, leading initially to such coordinating mechanisms as the invention of standardized time zones. According to Beniger (1986), the control revolution is a watershed transformation in capacities of "information processing," as the industrial revolution was in material processing.

The control revolution created punch-card machines in the 19th century and computers in the 20th century. Almost the first 100 years of mediated information handling was involved in data processing for the purpose of accounting and management. As the industrial revolution marked the discontinuity of coupling energy, data processing played the same role by exploiting business data/information. The emergence of information processing equipment, whether punched cards or computers, led first to the development of transaction processing and later in the 1970s to online transaction processing applications (OLTP).

With computers quickly becoming the modus operandi of government and business, a number of questions have developed. How do they fit into the political landscape? How are they designed and implemented? How are ethical and policy judgments made? The Dossier society defined by Laudon (1986) places computers in the context of the Constitution.

The genius of American politics is its balance more in favor of individual freedom and diversity than of organizational demands for control and efficiency. Contemporary ICT can radically alter the organization of power in the United States and with it our traditional conceptions and experiences of individual freedom, security, and privacy. The other side of the data society is a "dossier society." According to Kenneth Laudon, from a technical point of view, the dossier society is the integration of distinct files serving unique programs and policies into a more or less permanent national database. It may lead to an aggregation of power in the federal, state and local governments without precedent in peacetime America. The dossier (data) society can expose the life of an individual to governmental screening and composite analysis that can be analytically "right," but is not reflective of the reality of the individual's life. Even if the analytical screening is right, may the government penetrate the privacy of the individual? Do we not have the right to shadow some of our citizens' lives? The Bush administration in 2000 had problems with the foreign intelligence surveillance act, which tried to give the Government too much power in this process, which was later watered by Congress.

Most Americans want a society where criminals are effectively brought to justice. Most Americans also want a society where government programs are effectively and efficiently administered using, where necessary, advanced ICT. Power is limited by segmental authority, segregation of information flows, creation of multiple checkpoints, and encouragement of lengthy and slow deliberation. These practical principles are at odds with the capabilities and premises of contemporary ICT applications.

In 1984, Congress signaled a virtual retreat from the Privacy Act by passing the Deficit Reduction Act of 1984, which contained provisions establishing a de facto national data center capability. Congress required all states to participate in file merging, matching, and linking programs to verify the eligibility of beneficiaries in food stamps, Medicare, aid to families with dependent children (AFDC), and a host of other "needs" and insurance-based programs. Involved here is the systematic merging and linking of social security, medical, and personal data with Internal Revenue and private employer data. These "matching" and "linking" programs are "limited" to about 50 million Americans (Laudon, 1986). There are no technical barriers to extend them to corporations like Ford, CitiBank, Coca-Cola, Kellogg, or the American Medical Association and other professional interest groups. Then the dossier society will become a reality as it was in East Germany (Stasi-1950s-1991) and still is in Russia, where the top politicians, including the president come from the secret police (KGB).

The Computer Society: A New Social Tool

In the 1960s, the evolution of computer applications progressed from mathematical computation to information processing and even to real-time control. Computers increasingly catalyze the growth of scientific information and human control through computer-aided system development. By the end of the 1960s, with the development of online terminals, computer access had been broadening along with the idea of the computer-serviced society. The emergence of the computer society was a result of social information systems. The trend of these applications may be charted through three stages: human information systems (libraries), industrialized man-machine systems (factories), and man-machine digital systems (online banking). The first stage corresponds to primitive and underdeveloped societies, the second to the advent of machines operated through controlled power, prominent through the first industrial revolution, and the third to the progressive computerization of advanced industrialized societies since World War II. The computer society was then projected as a possible new utopia, destined for oblivion or success in proportion to man's capability to chart and control his own evolution (Sackman, 1967).

From today's point of view, the computer society is mostly preoccupied with the issue of how to apply computers. This issue became particularly popular in the United States in the 1980s with the advent of personal computers. The issue is still popular in developing and less developed nations which are at an early stage of computer literacy.

The Informative Society: A Way of Processing Information

A combination of features from the data-dossier society, industrial society, and computer society creates the informative society. The informative society transforms the way business, government, and citizens work. It is helping organizations get leaner, smarter, and closer to the customer. Those who seize the opportunities inherent in this revolution are capturing important competitive advantages. Those who lag behind are forced to scramble breathlessly to catch up, or to go out of business.

The informative society is the result of the merged data and computer societies based upon advanced software such as online analytical processing (OLAP). OLAP software, such as data warehousing and mining, transforms OLTP into value-added information. In the mid 1990s, data warehousing became one of the buzzwords of the ICT industry. However, it was invented by real companies to make use of vast volumes of databases. During 1965-1999, almost every aspect of data processing was automated in the name of efficiency. With the increased power of ICT, more complex systems could be implemented. For example, from simple bookkeeping applications, the banking industry moved to ubiquitous automated teller machines (ATM), which can provide a good base for customer behavior analysis and further the development of customer-based relation banking.

In the 1990s, IBM evaluated how to move from a computer- (hardware in mind) based business to managing a business based on information (software in mind). This led to the concept of data mining in order to extract a new value of information in the business context. The solution to this quest is data-warehousing software, in which a single, complete, and consistent store of data from internal and external sources is delivered to end users who can process data into information in the business context (Devlin, 1997).

"Informative systems" were defined in the U.S. by Zuboff (1988) in her popular book *In the Age of the Smart Machine*. "The Smart Machine" is applied to transform the nature of work and can provide negative (alienation) and positive (empowerment) results. However, that same technology may "informate," empowering ordinary working people with a broad knowledge of the production/service process, making them capable of critical judgment about production/service. The author argues that systems should be informated rather than automated.

The informative society is a community of developers and users who understand which data/information to process in order to achieve added value in decision making both at the personal and the organizational level. This elite community, which is no longer in the computer society, struggles with the issue of how to apply "Windows XP or a scanner." Members of the informative society are better informed than members of the previous societies, since they use meaningful information in a given context instead of merely applying data to decision-making.

The Networked Society: A New Social Super-Connectivity

In the networked society, home computers are as common as the telephone. These electronic appliances link people to people, shrinking time and distance barriers among them, and nearly eliminating barriers between people and information. In its simplest form the networked society is a place where thoughts are exchanged easily and democratically and intellect affords more personal power than a pleasing appearance does. In *The Network Nation*, Hiltz and Turoff (1993) write:

'The Network Nation or Society' is a collection of communities with overlapping networks for actual and potential communication and exchange. We will become the Network Nation, exchanging vast amounts of both information and social communications with colleagues, friends, and 'strangers' who are spread out all over the nation and share similar interests. ... Ultimately, as communication satellites and international packet-switching networks reach out to other cities and villages around the world, these social networks, facilitated by computer-mediated communications, will become international; we will become a 'global village' whose boundaries are demarcated only by the political decisions of those governments that choose not to become part of an international communication.

The networked infrastructure can be utilized to substitute for the use of limited physical resources. In the 21st century, we will probably see:

- Increased scale and distinction of community-oriented networks for academia, government, business, politics, social aspects and other purposes
- A variety of virtual educational institutions
- "Networked" organizations, with flatter, more consolidated and better connected structures of firms, and changes in the nature of work ("End of Job")
- The integration of ICT resulting in "super-connectivity" for all those users with an access to networks

The networked society applies ICT to produce a culture and systems supporting the service-material base. Analyzing the potential for conflict among new information and communications opportunities, one can identify five major areas in which public policy issues are likely to arise[1]:

1. Equitable access to information and communications opportunities

2. Security and the survivability of the network infrastructure
3. Interoperability of the network infrastructure
4. Modernization and technological development of the network infrastructure
5. Jurisdiction in formulating and implementing national information policy

The network society operates in cyberspace, which is a new social space that shapes networks into "networlds," the global matrix of minds, stimulated by interconnected computer networks. Komito (1998) perceives the following categories of the networked society: moral, normative, and proximate communities. These communities are generated by the networked society, which becomes a foraging (constantly searching for "something") society of flexible communities.

Network diffusion modifies the operation and outcomes of trade (*e-commerce*), production (*computer-integrated manufacturing*), experience (*end-user computing*), power (e-republic), and culture (*icons*). Castells (1996) argues that the presence or absence in the networked society and the dynamics of each network vis-a-vis others are critical sources of domination and change in our society; a society that is characterized by the preeminence of social structure over social action. In other words, the power of flows (constant searching and switching scopes of interest) takes precedence over the flows of power.

The Mass Media Society: Provided Consciousness

The term "mass media" means communication by such media as television, radio, newspapers, and books. The most distinguishing characteristic of mass media communication is that it is mostly one-way. To attract as large an audience as possible, the media are addressed to the largest number of people, very often at the lowest common denominator.

Since the advent of television, mass media have created the mass media society, which is stimulated by the media as informers, interpreters, persuaders, entertainers. The mass media democratic society is strongly influenced by the media that become the fourth estate ("a quasi-fourth branch of government"), after the executive, legislative, and judicial branches.

Today, in developed nations, electronic voting and opinion-registering technologies make a two-way flow of what was once a one-way pipeline, with information no longer going just from the top down, from lawmakers to people, but now also from the bottom up, from the people back to the lawmakers. A new political system is emerging, as the mass media society is entering the status of electronic republic (Grossman, 1995).

America is turning into an electronic republic, a democratic system that is vastly increasing the people's day-to-day influence on the decisions of state. This transformation is triggered by the remarkable convergence of television, telephone, satellites, cable, and personal computers. The electronic mass society is heading from representative democracy toward direct democracy, a form that originated in the first millennium B.C. in small, self-contained Greece. At the beginning of the 21st century, in democratic nations, the electronic mass media society is transforming the isolated citizen into an electronic citizen, who feels that his/her vote may have some meaning in pursuing the common good.

The Virtual Society: Anyone, Anywhere, Anytime

The virtual society is a community which operates in cyberspace, generated by computer networks, software, e-files, and interactive dialogues among the participants. The virtual society's members interact among themselves without physical presence and interact with organizations that are digital. Virtual corporations, communities (e.g., WELL in San Francisco), shops, schools, and agencies broaden and intensify the social and business interactions of the virtual society. Agres, Edberg, and Igbaria (1998) argue that the "virtual" empowers individuals who can easily interact within the digital environment. The individual can be electronically present in more digital places than he/she could manage to be in the same range of physical localities. The virtual society's members are better communicated and informed. Virtual cyberspace may enhance job performance and training, improve product design, assist surgeons, and create interactive forms of entertainment. But it will be years before that becomes a reality, if it ever happens at all.

The Communicated Society: Familiarity of Events and Facts

The application and dissemination of omnipotent ICT may transform the United States, Western Europe, and Japan into a "technopoly," which has sovereignty over social institutions and national life, and becomes self-justifying, self-perpetuating, and omnipresent. Postmen (1992) traces the historical movement of technology from being a support system for a culture's traditions into being an agency competing with them, and finally, to creating a totalitarian order with no use for tradition at all. However, if it includes a strong insistence on the value of free speech, ICT may make citizens better informed. Of course, to do so, the communicated society should pass the stages of mass media, networks, and virtual societies.

The Informed Society: Awarded Members

The informed society is created when the informative and communicated societies achieve the status of mature entities. The informed society's members are characterized by a good level of awareness and sense of what is going on in the society and the economy. The members of such society can make wise decisions based on their

own judgment, which is supported by data-mining technologies, as well as networked and enterprise-wide systems and services. This society is a computerized society at the level of social sophistication and finesse.

The Robotized Society: Automated Judgment

The robotized society is composed of robots, even thinking robots. These robots' behavior is based on the rules of artificial intelligence. Robots may not be the best of musicians, but they can be used for testing instruments as if they were manufacturers. If we are to use robots on a large scale, and if technological advances toward the "thinking" computer continue, it will become necessary to lay down guidelines governing where and how they are used. Isaac Asimov (1950; 1985) proposed Three Laws of Robotics:

1. A robot may not injure a human being, or through inaction, allow a human being to come to harm.
2. A robot must obey the orders given to it by human beings except where such orders would conflict with the first law.
3. A robot must protect its own existence as long as such protection does not conflict with the first or second law.

Robots in the real world do not look a bit like most examples we have grown used to in films and stories. But they are still extraordinary devices and far more clever than machines of earlier times (Asimov, 1985). Their ability to accomplish simple, repetitive tasks in a broad range of applications may cause unemployment and a demand for highly skillful workers. On the other hand, if they are applied in very complex systems and prove to be highly reliable, then their applications can be useful and recommended.

The Knowledge Society: Understanding Members

In *Post-Capitalistic Society,* Peter Drucker (1993) describes how every few hundred years a sharp transformation has taken place and greatly affected society—its world view, its basic values, its business and economics, and its social and political structure. According to Drucker, we are right in the middle of another time of radical change, from the Age of Capitalism and the nation-state to a knowledge society and a society of organizations. The primary resource in the post-capitalistic society will be knowledge, and the leading social groups will be "knowledge workers." The industries that moved into the center of the economy in 1958-1998 have as their business the production and distribution of knowledge and information rather than the production and distribution of things. Microsoft's market value exceeds the market value of three big car makers, General Motors, Ford, and Chrysler. Why? Microsoft employs only 50,000 workers but they produce $400,000 per capita per year. Their knowledge is costly.

The super-rich of the old capitalism were the 19th-century steel barons like Andrew Carnegie, robber barons like Jay Gould, oil barons like John Rockefeller, and transportation barons like Cornelius Vanderbilt. The super-rich of the knowledge society are computer makers (Steve Wozniak, Steve Jobs), software makers (Bill Gates), and systems developers (Ross Perot). Knowledge becomes an economic resource and a tool of genuine innovations that provide a competitive advantage in business. Knowledge is a set of rules, laws and their systems that communicate by information handling and processing. The major drivers of the development of a knowledge society are the demand for innovations in the marketplace and a lifelong learning process which requires permanently improving work conditions and creates higher productivity and effectiveness.

The knowledge society applies tools needed for problem solving. Among these tools one can mention high-speed computers, information retrieval services, and networks of talent groups.

The Learning Society: Developing Members

The development of the knowledge society requires constant discovery, assimilation, and organization of knowledge. These processes constitute learning activities, which at the beginning of the 21st century require skillfully swimming in the ocean of information, artfully using information-rich sources, and using a supporting learning environment to self-pace and self-structure the user's own programs of learning. The learning society gets its major input from higher education and provides its output to employers (MacFarlane, 1998).

The learning society is created not only by higher education institutions but also by "learning organizations" in business, industry, government, and non-profit units. "Learning organizations" overcome learning disabilities to understand threats clearly and recognize new opportunities. Not only is the learning organization a new source of competitive advantage, it also offers a marvelously empowering approach to work, one which promises that as Archimedes put it, "with a lever long enough...single-handed I can move the world" (Senge, 1990).

The paradigm of the learning society is understanding and its purpose is to strengthen human planning and behavior in complex environments, such as the modern global economy.

The e-Global-Universal Society: Justice and Peace for a Whole Planet

As a result of learning, people and their governments who promote a global economy may try to create a formal, global, universal society. The global economy is based on free movement of goods, services, capital, and ideas. The globalization of financial markets means that the movement of exchange rates, interest rates, and stock prices in various countries are intimately interconnected. Global integration has brought the benefits of the international division of labor, economies of scale, and the rapid spread of innovations from one country to another. However, the global economy is the global capitalistic system, which is not without problems, as Soros (1998) writes in his quest for the global open society.

The organization of the global-universal society is needed because such a society must regulate deficiencies in the global capitalistic system. Among these deficiencies, Soros lists the uneven distribution of benefits, the instability of the financial system, the threat of global monopolies and oligopolies, the ambiguous role of the state, and the question of values and social cohesion. Since global markets reduce everything to commodities, we can have a market economy but we cannot have a market society. Globalization increases the demands on the state to provide social nets while reducing its ability to do so. This creates the seeds of social conflict. This may lead to a new wave of protectionism and the breakdown of the capitalistic system, as happened in the 1930s.

To prevent the next breakdown of the capitalistic system, one must organize the global open society, which is governed by the rule of law: respect for human rights, respect for diversity, respect for minorities and minority opinions, division of power; and a market economy in the electronic environment. Of course, the e-global-universal society is organized around information and by networks and around common-complementary values of universal-complementary civilization[1]. This society requires many alliances (including virtual) that will establish a code for international patterns of expected behavior. Such alliances will apply information, computerized networks to disseminate and enforce these standards. Some

such alliances are The World Trade Organization, NATO, and the World Tribunal. Unfortunately, the United Nations is an organization designed only for peacekeeping, not for other concerns. This global society should be open and communicated, which means that it will be effective if it works as an e-global-universal society. This means that it should be based on democratic principles and global justice for all inhabitants and their natural surroundings.

The Self-Sustainable Society: Surviving Members

The death triangle of mankind, composed of the expected bombs in population (2050), ecology (2050), and resource depletion (2300), is two generations away from the generation of 2000 *anno domini*. The next 42 years (2000-2050) are crucial for the survival of mankind. If we look back at the last 50 years, we see that this period passed so quickly and produced positive results never before known in world history. It also created the threat "to be or not to be" for humans on Earth. The next 50 years are just a period of two generations. If we miss these generations, we also will miss the opportunity to educate them and we will be overwhelmed by the complexity of the coming crisis and probable failure of human civilization. Although people, cultures, and nations have done this for centuries, the death triangle of mankind has never before been so close.

A new society with new politics should be defined in the first part of the 21st century and implemented in 2025-2050. Otherwise mankind may disappear from the Earth. The targets for the 21st century can be defined as follows:

1. To achieve sustainable and diversified culture
2. To achieve mass consumption of green products from regenerative food and fiber systems through biodiversity (Dahlhberg, 1993)

To achieve these targets, the way goes through the development of the non-material society (value-driven) and self-sustainable society (survival-oriented).

The modern scourges of Western civilization, such as youth suicide, drug abuse, and crime are usually explained in personal, social, and economic terms: unemployment, poverty, child abuse, family breakdown, and so on. However, the author suggests that these trends are to a certain degree independent of such factors. These curses are rather caused by a failure to provide a sense of meaning, belonging, and purpose in our lives, as well as a framework of values. A person needs to have something to believe in and live for, to feel he is a part of a community, a valued member of society, and to have a sense of spiritual fulfillment—that is, a sense of relatedness and connectedness to the world and the universe in which people exist.

The self-sustainable society should be the next step in social development. It should provide an orientation on values (e.g., family), norms and attitudes and the spiritual life. In other words, we have to reinvent culture in such a way that it will be sustainable. Moller (1993) argues for the need to emphasize inputs from different cultures in order to amalgamate a single concept for all of us. This transformation can be achieved if the learning and global open societies are to form a mature mankind.

The Monitoring Society: Limited Communication

If we do not secure feeding and caring for the 10 billion people who are likely to be alive within a couple of generations, then we have to secure the minimal means of social communication. It can be organized through the application of satellites or by primitive monitoring by the sound of African tum-tum drums. Such an environment will be managed by the monitoring society, which will be very limited in technology and other resources. It may be the beginning of the end of mankind.

THE PARADIGMS AND MEASUREMENTS

The issue of how to measure the information society preoccupies the research of several authors. Measurements of the information economy were offered by the previously mentioned authors, Machlup (1962) and Porat (1979). Hudson and Leung (1988) applied Porat's method to measure the information society of Texas. The Jahoda Index (Ito, 1981, p. 674), applied by Japan's Research Institute of Telecommunications and Economics (RITE), has ten components and does not even include such words as "computers," "software," or "networks." This index is almost 20 years old and does not reflect the ICT and IM solutions that are fruits of the Information Age and Telecommunications Age. About five years later, the Japanese Information Processing and Development Center offered the JIPIDEC Index. This index includes such categories as "hardware," "software," and "transmission."

Do these measurements define the information society (Dordick & Wang, 1993). To answer this question, a new set of measuring indexes has been offered in Table 14-2. These measurements are from the citizen's (user's) point of view, and explore how ICT penetrates the population and what type of paradigm, purpose, and main solutions are provided by each type of information society.

Of course, the information society can be perceived at different levels of the population. The most popular level is the nation; however, one can analyze the information society at the level of a region or city as well as at the level of an organization. In other words, in the same nation, as well as in the same large organization,

Table 14-2. *The paradigms and measurements of information societies*

IS Type	Paradigm	Purpose	Main Information Solution	Measures Per 1,000 population
Data (Dossier)	Measurement	Reduction	Mechanization and Automation, Off-line systems	Number of data entry personnel
Computer	Measurement	Reduction	Automation and How to compute? Off-line systems	Number of computers
Mass Media	News	Dissemination	Printing	Number of newspapers, and Number of TV sets
Networked	Connection	Exchange	Internet, Intranet, Networked enterprise	Number of Internet Users, Number of Intranet servers
Virtual	Electronic presence	Exchange and Opinion	Internet, Intranet Virtual enterprise systems	Number of bulletin board systems (national and organizational)
Informative	Optimization	Decision-making	What to process? Data mining, Online systems, Application Portfolio	Number of OLAP software per organization, % of GDP spent on IM, % of I-workers in the labor force
Communicated	Familiarity	Planning	Networking, Online systems, Networked enterprise	Number of Internet users, Number of telephones, Number of TV sets and Number of newspapers, % of GDP spent on telecomm.
Knowledge	Rules	Understan-ding	Research, education Information retrieval	Number of scientists, Number of professors, Number of students
Robotized	Rules	Decision-making	Automation of judgment	Number of expert systems
Informed	Awareness	Decision-making	Data mining, Networking, Enterprise-wide systems	Number of OLAP software, and Mass Media and Network Indexes, Free press
Learning	Understan-ding	Planning and acting	Computer-aided instruction, Information retrieval, Digital library	Number of published books, Number of digital books and scientific documents
e-Global	Justice	Operations	Virtual government e-Global systems	Number of applied virtual global agencies
Self-sustainable	Optimization	Survival	Green economy Ecological systems	Amount of energy from renewable sources
Monitoring	Warning	Survival	Satellites or tom-tom drums	Number of served people

there can operate different types of information societies.

THE DEVELOPMENTAL PATHS OF INFORMATION SOCIETIES: FUTURE TRENDS

The developmental paths of information societies are presented in Figure 14-4. The model is self-explanatory with the exception of the expert society. The main idea of the model is based on the prerequisites required in order to move to the next developmental stage. For example, the informed society can launch its operations if its members pass through the stage of the informative and communicated societies. The application of artificial intelligence may help in many areas of civilization; however, it requires advanced knowledge among developers and only limited skills among operators of expert systems. Therefore, too many applications of robot systems may lead backwards to the computer society, where the main challenge is how to apply the system. On the other hand, some limited applications of expert systems in technological environments that are too complex may help the informative and learning societies in their operations and developments.

A CASE OF THE POLISH INFORMATION SOCIETY (2008-2013)

Poland, since the fall of communism in 1989, continues to approach a comprehensive strategy of developing ICT, particularly in respect to the Polish information society (PIS). The first time this kind of approach was attempted occurred in 1971-74 when the concept of the National Information System, driven by INFOSTRADA, had been tried and some its elements had been implemented (Targowski, 1980; 1991, Figure 10-14).

The following is a sketch, developed by the Author, of the strategy of the development of PIS for 2008-2013. This strategy, submitted on behalf of Ernst & Young, won an international competition hosted by the Polish government in May 2008.

The Polish information society is composed of the following members:

Figure 14-4. The paths of the informative society's development

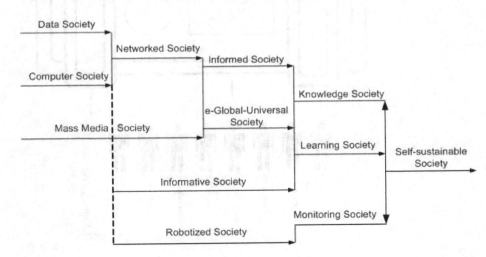

- e-Citizen
- e-Worker
- e-Consumer
- e-Pupil/Student
- e-Patient
- e-Unemployed
- e-Retiree
- e-Foreigner

A model of the PIS is depicted in Figure 14-5 and is composed of:

- Business private networks LAN, RAN, MAN, WAN, GAN, VAN
- Government private network INFOSTRADA
- Public network – the Internet
- Information systems for sectors of the economy
- E-systems for business, government, education, health, civic organizations

Figure 14-5. The architecture of the Polish Information Society (The Targowski Model 2008)

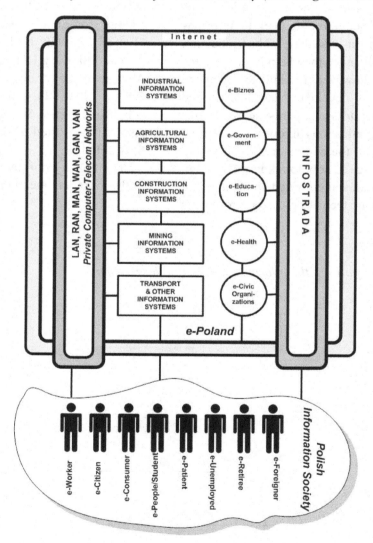

All these networks and systems are components of PIS and are being developed with the following aims:

- **Credo**: Polish information society is a key to knowledge and prosperity
- **Mission**: To wisely steer agricultural, industrial, information, global, knowledge, nano-tech, and bio-tech societies in order to make Poland a modern, prosperous and citizen-friendly state where decisions are made on advanced information and knowledge.
- **Goal**: To optimize the development and operations of all stages of society in such a way to minimize the use of strategic resources and increase the options for more life choices for people and their quality of life, based on full employment.
- **Strategy 1**: To develop 12 main e-services for people and eight e-services for businesses (defined by the European Union and e-Voting) as well as e-HELP (monitoring crises & catastrophes) and CYBERSHIELD (to defend the Polish cyberspace) functioning through the INFOSTRADA, a government network (Figure 14-6)
- **Strategy 2**: To develop tele-cities as a local information infrastructure, provided an access to global, national, and local systems from home, work, and public points of Internet access (PPIA) via business private networks (MAN/RAN), governmental INFOSTRADA, and wireless fidelity municipal area network (Wi Fi MAN) (Figure 14-7).
- **Strategy 3**: The development, implementation, and operations of PIS require a wise and flexible coordination at all governmental levels by appropriate CIO and PIS operators, as it is explained in a model in Figure 14-19.

The e-government's services should be developed according the stages defined in Table 14-3.

The transformation of a Polish local citizen into a global citizen's purposes are as follows:

1. To develop a positive role for a Pole in global employment or business

Table 14-3. Stages of e-government's services

STAGE	RESULT OF e-SERVICE	A WAY OF DELIVERING e-SERVICE
0	Off-line	There is no service in the Internet
I	INFORMATION	e-Access to information of how to handle e-Service
II	DOCUMENT	e-Printing a document
III	INTERACTION	e-Printing, filling out and legally signing an e-Document
IV	SINGLE TRANSACTION	Complete handling of the whole transaction, including e-Payment
V	MULTIPLE TRANSACTIONS	Complete handling of multiple transactions, including e-Payment from a single access point
VI	CLIENT'S INTENTION	Application of the CRM approach towards a citizen as a welcomed client who, if satisfied, should return to the agency

Figure 14-6. The architecure of Polish e-government (The Targowski Model 2008)

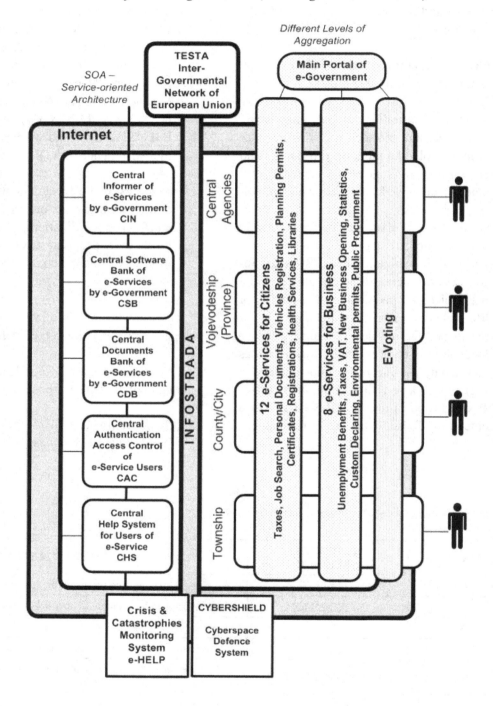

2. To make a Pole more active in participation in the emerging global civil society, which should have some regulatory role in operations of the global economy

The number of international NGOs (non-governmental organizations) has grown from 1,000 in the 1950s to 20,000 in 1999. In the scope of transnational social movement organizations (TSMO), the growth in the same period is tenfold, from 100 to 1,000. For example, the French citizens are the most active; they belong to 553 TSMO and 3,551 INGOs. At the second end, the scale there are such countries as Afghanistan, Northern Korea, and Oman (Yearbook of International Associations [Union of International Associations]; 2004).

Poland is among 25 nations most active in INGOs and TSMOs, which include the most developed nations.

If globalization is unstoppable, then the global civil society should regulate globalization soon by the increased activism and awareness of issues and their solutions.

A model of a Polish inhabitant functioning concurrently in the three civilizational spaces is shown in Figure 14-7. A Pole does not have to leave his/her local space to be active in national and global spaces. The Polish information society should allow him/her to do so. His two "virtual spaces" are tested in his/her physical local space according to the rule "act locally, think globally."

The presented architectures of the Polish information society do not explain issues triggered by it, such as *digital divide, surveillance* and *democracy's improvements*. However, e-voting helps in solving the last issue since the Poles do not participate in votes in large percentage. At this moment in time, the Polish information society should help Poland in all of its transformations.

Figure 4-7. A citizen as an inhabitant of three civilizational spaces concurently (The Targowski Model 2008)

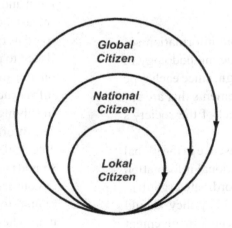

Figure 14-8. The architecture of a teleCITY (PPIA-Public Points of Interest Access, MAN-Metropolitan Area Network

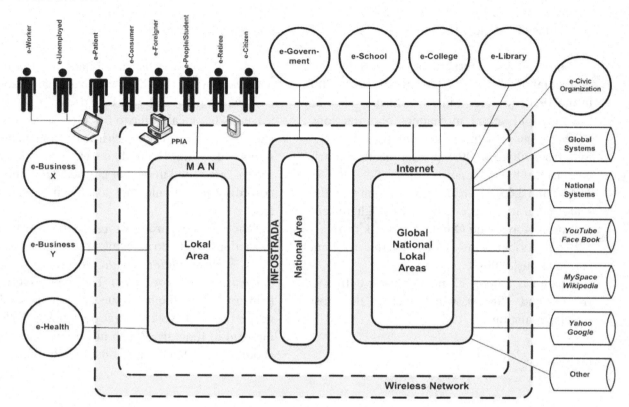

CONCLUSION

1. The study of types of the information society should influence the methodology of application systems design, since each type will have its own requirements that are appropriate for a given level of the society's information maturity.

2. As nations build their presence in the global economy, they need a national information policy to allocate and coordinate organizational responsibilities. This policy should include direct governmental involvement in developing an information infrastructure similar to urban and rural infrastructures. Some indirect incentives for the develop-

ment and modernization of the information infrastructure should be provided too. A regulatory environment should be established to provide more conducive decisions on the modernization of the information infrastructure. A case of Poland can help in solving this issue.

3. The information societies should emerge as a neutral tool of social development. They should not support any politics either liberal or conservative. They should close the loop of man-to-information and information-to-man. Their mission is the present and future of humankind equipped with the ability and tools of information and communication processing and handling. This may lead to more aware social decisions and actions.

Figure 14-9. A chart of steering of the development of the Polish Information Society (PIS) in 2008-2013 (The Targowski Model 2008)

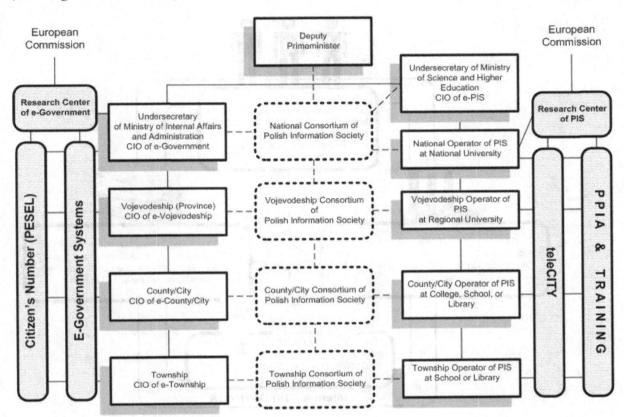

Nowadays, knowledge, learning and consciousness are at the mercy of ICT tools that may control the development of civilization either well or poorly. This civilization's current mood is based on the importance of a sense of being.

A. Further Research Directions

•   Investigate relationships among levels of economic and information society developments and their impact on society in the 21st century.

•   Investigate the challenges of the global economy for different kinds of information societies in the 21st century.

•   Investigate how e-mobile systems impact the development and operations of information societies in the 21st century.

B. Research Opportunities

•   The research opportunity is in going beyond the concept of a knowledge society and investigating the concept of a wise society and its impact on civilization.

C. Additional Ideas

•   The information society may have some problems in operating in non-agricultural and non-industrial economies, since *infor-*

Figure 14-10. The generalized goals of the Polish Information Society in 2008-2013 (The Targowski Model 2008)

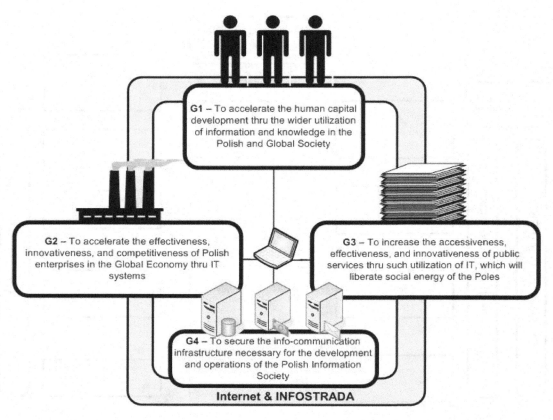

mation is always about something "else," like agriculture and industrial products-processes-systems-consumers-users.

D. Rationale

•   An information society is a society in which the creation, distribution, diffusion, use, and manipulation of information are significant economic, political, and cultural activities. The knowledge economy is its economic counterpart, whereby wealth is created through the economic exploitation of understanding. There is currently no universally accepted concept of what exactly can be called "information society" and what should not be so termed. Most theoreticians agree that we see a transformation which started somewhere between the 1970s and today and is fundamentally changing the way societies work. Information technology includes more than the Internet, and there are discussions regarding the actual influence of specific media or specific modes of production. One of the most popular kinds of information society is knowledge society, which inspires knowledgeable people to cooperate. The knowledge society emphasizes the importance of knowledge and also the importance of proper knowledge distribution, sharing, and building for social development. However, wisdom, not knowledge, is the ultimate cognition which decides societal successes. Therefore, the wisdom society is the ultimate, almost utopian target of social development. Is it possible for mankind to expect that one day we can attain that kind of a society? What stages must the information society pass through in order to reach this ultimate level of social organization?

E.   Additional Reading

Abbate, J. (1999) *Inventing the Internet.* Cambridge, MA: MIT Press.

Agre, P. (1997). Beyond the mirror world: Privacy and the representational practices of computing. In P. Agre, & M. Rotenberg (Eds.), *Technology and privacy: The new landscape.* Cambridge, MA: MIT Press.

Agre, P. (1999). The distances of education. *Academe, 85*(5), 37-41.

Barlow, J. (1996). *A declaration of the independence of cyberspace.* Retrieved September 20, 2007, from http://www.eff.org/~barlow/Declaration-Final.html.

Barney, D. (2003). *The network society.* Cambridge, MA: Polity.

Bates, M. (1996). The Getty end-user online searching project in the humanities, Report No. 6: Overview and conclusions. *College and Research Libraries, 57,* 514-523.

Bell, D. (1976). *The coming of post-industrial society.* New York, NY: Basic Books.

Borgman, C. (2000). *From Gutenberg to the global information infrastructure: Access to information in the networked world.* Cambridge, MA: MIT Press.

Brown, T. (1998). *Empower the people: A 7-step plan to overthrow the conspiracy that is stealing your money and freedom.* New York, NY: Morrow.

Cairncross, F. (1997). *The Death of distance: How the communications revolution will change our lives.* Boston, MA: Harvard Business School Press.

Chapman, G. (1995). Wired. *New Republic, 212*(2-3), 19-21.

Chapman, G. (1999, January 4). The future lies beyond the box. *Los Angeles Times,* C4.

Casson, M. (1997). *Information and organization: A new perspective on the theory of the firm.* New York, NY: Clarendon Press.

Castells, M. (2000). *The rise of the network society. The information age: Economy, society and culture* (2nd ed., vol.1). Malden: Blackwell.

Commons, J. (1970). *The economics of collective action.* Madison, WI: University of Wisconsin Press.

Dawson, M., & Foster, J. (1998). Virtual capitalism. In: R. McChesney, M. Wood, & J. Foster (Eds.), *Capitalism and the information age* (pp. 51-67). New York, NY: Monthly Review Press.

Deutsch, K. (1983). Soziale und politische aspekte der informationsgesellschaft. (Social and political aspect of information relations). In: P. Sonntag (Ed.), *Die zukunft der informationsgesellschaft* (Future of information relations). Frankfurt/Main: Haag & Herchen.

Dolence, M., & Norris, D. (1995). *Transforming higher education: A vision for learning in the 21st century.* Ann Arbor, MI: Society for College and University Planning.

Drucker, P. (1969). *The age of discontinuity.* London: Heinemann.

Dutton, W. (1999). *Society on the line: Information politics in the digital age.* Oxford: Oxford University Press.

Dyson, E., Gilder, G., Keyworth, J., & Toffler, A. (1994). A magna carta for the knowledge age. *New Perspectives Quarterly, 11*(4), 26-37.

Edwards, P. (1996). *The closed world: Computers and the politics of discourse in cold war America.* Cambridge, MA: MIT Press.

Farrell, K. (1998). *Post-traumatic culture: Injury and interpretation in the nineties.* Baltimore, MD: Johns Hopkins University Press.

Fitzpatrick, T. (2002). Critical theory, information society and surveillance technologies. *Information, Communication and Society, 5*(3), 357-378.

Friedman, A. (1989). *Computer systems development: History, organization and implementation.* Chichester, UK: Wiley.

Fukuyama, F. (1999, June 12). Death of the hierarchy. *Financial Times,* I.

Fuchs, C. (2005). *Emanzipation! technik und politik bei Herbert Marcuse.* (Emancipation! technique, and politics of Herbert Marcuse). Aachen: Shaker.

_____(2007). Transnational space and the network society. *21st Century Society, 2*(1), 1-30.

Garnham, N. (2004). Information society theory as ideology. In: F. Webster (Ed.), *The information society reader.* London: Routledge.

Gates, B. (1995). *The road ahead.* New York, NY: Viking.

Gershenfeld, N. (1999). *When things start to think.* New York, NY: Holt.

Gibson, J. (1986). *The perfect war: Technowar in Vietnam.* Boston, MA: Atlantic Monthly Press.

Gibson, J. (1994). *Warrior dreams: Paramilitary culture in post-Vietnam America.* New York, NY: Hill and Wang.

Gibson, W. (1984). *Neuromancer.* New York, NY: Ace Books.

Gilder, G. (1992). *Life after television.* New York, NY: Norton.

Goodin, R. (Ed.). (1996). *The theory of institutional design.* Cambridge: Cambridge University Press.

Greene, J. (1993). *The intellectual construction of America.* Chapel Hill, NC: University of North Carolina Press.

Hafner, K., & Lyon, M. (1996). *Where wizards stay up late: The origins of the internet.* New York, NY: Simon and Schuster.

Hakken, D. (1999). *Cyborgs@cyberspace? An ethnographer looks to the future.* New York, NY: Routledge.

Hardt, M., & Negri, A. (2001). *Empire.* Cambridge, MA: Harvard University Press.

Hardt, M., & Negri, A. (2005) *Multitude. War and democracy in the age of the empire.* New York, NY: Hamish Hamilton.

Harvey, D. (1989). *The condition of post-modernity.* London: Blackwell.

Haug, W. (2003). *High-tech-kapitalismus.* Hamburg: Argument.

Healy, D. (1997). Cyberspace and place: The Internet as middle landscape on the electronic frontier. In: D. Porter (Ed.), *Internet culture.* New York, NY: Routledge.

Hirschfield, R. (Ed.). (1997). *Financial cryptography: First international conference.* Berlin: Springer.

Johnson, D., & Post, D. (1996). Law and borders: The rise of law in cyberspace. *Stanford Law Review, 48*(5), 1367-1402.

Kling, R., & Iacono, S. (1988). The mobilization of support for computerization: The role of computerization movements. *Social Problems, 35*(3), 226-243.

Kling, R. (Ed.). (1996). *Computerization and controversy: Value conflicts and social choices* (2nd ed.). San Diego, CA: Academic Press.

Kling, R., & Lamb, R. (1998). Bits of cities: How utopian visions structure social power in physical space and cyberspace. In: E. Eveno (Ed.), *Urban powers and utopias in the world*. Toulouse: Presses Universitaires du Mirail.

Lyotard, J. (1984). *The post-modern condition*. Manchester: Manchester University Press.

Machlup, F. (1962). *The production and distribution of knowledge in the United States*. Princeton, NJ: Princeton University Press.

March, J., & Olsen, J. (1989). *Rediscovering institutions: The organizational basis of politics*. New York, NY: Free Press.

Marx, L. (1964). *The machine in the garden: Technology and the pastoral ideal in America*. New York, NY: Oxford University Press.

Melody, W. (1987). Information: An emerging dimension of institutional analysis. *Journal of Economic Issues, 21*(3), 1313-1339.

Mitchell, W. (1995). *City of bits: Space, place, and the infobahn*. Cambridge, MA: MIT Press.

Mitchell, W. (2000). Designing the digital city. In: T. Ishida, & K. Isbister (Eds.), *Digital cities: Technologies, experiences, and future perspectives*. Berlin: Springer.

Noble, D. (1997). *The religion of technology: The divinity of man and the spirit of invention*. New York, NY: Knopf.

Norman, D. (1998). *The Invisible computer: Why good products can fail, the personal computer is so complex, and information appliances are the solution*. Cambridge, MA: MIT Press.

North, D. (1990). *Institutions, institutional change, and economic performance*. Cambridge: Cambridge University Press.

OECD. (1981). *Information activities, electronics and telecommunications technologies: Impact on employment, growth and trade*. Paris: OECD.

OECD. (1986). *Trends in the information economy*. Paris: OECD.

Offe, C. (1996). Designing institutions in East European transitions. In: R. Goodin (Ed.), *The theory of institutional design*. Cambridge: Cambridge University Press.

Ovitt, G., Jr. (1987). *The restoration of perfection: Labor and technology in medieval culture*. New Brunswick, NJ: Rutgers University Press.

Pfaffenberger, B. (1988). The social meaning of the personal computer: Or, why the personal computer revolution was no revolution. *Anthropological Quarterly, 61*(1): 39-47.

Porat, M. (1977). *The information economy*. Washington, D.C.: U.S. Department of Commerce.

Powell, W., & DiMaggio, P. (Eds.). (1991). *The new institutionalism in organizational analysis*. Chicago, IL: University of Chicago Press.

Ravetz (Eds.). (1996). *Cyberfutures: Culture and politics on the information superhighway*. New York, NY: New York University Press.

Richta, R. (1977). The scientific and technological revolution and the prospects of social development. In: R. Dahrendorf (Ed.), *Scientific-technological revolution. Social aspects*. London: Sage.

Shapiro, C., & Varian, H. (1998) *Information rules: A strategic guide to the network economy*. Boston, MA: Harvard Business School Press.

Sobchack, V. (1996). Democratic franchise and the electronic frontier. In: Z. Sardar, & J. Ravetz (Eds.), *Cyberfutures: Culture and politics on the information superhighway*. New York, NY: New York University Press.

Shain, B. (1996). *The myth of American individualism*. Princeton, NJ: Princeton University Press.

Spulber, D. (1996). Market microstructure and intermediation. *Journal of Economic Perspectives, 10*(3), 135-152.

Schmiede, R. (2006a). Knowledge, work and subject in informational capitalism. In: J. Berleur, M. Nurminen, & J. Impagliazzo (Eds.), *Social informatics: An information society for all?*. New York, NY: Springer.

Stehr, N. (2002a). *A world made of knowledge.* Lecture at the Conference "New knowledge and new consciousness in the era of the knowledge society", Budapest, January 31, 2002.

_____ (2002b). *Knowledge & economic conduct.* Toronto: University of Toronto Press.

Thomas, D., & Loader, B. (Eds.). (2000). Cybercrime: Law enforcement, security and surveillance in the information age. London: Routledge.

Touraine, A. (1988). *Return of the actor.* Minneapolis, MN: University of Minnesota Press.

Van Dijk, J. (2006). *The network society* (2nd ed.). London: Sage.

Webster, F. (2002a). The information society revisited. In: L. Lievrouw, & S. Livingstone (Eds.), *Handbook of new media.* London: Sage.

_____(2002b). *Theories of the information society.* London: Routledge.

Weiser, M. (1993) Ubiquitous computing. *Computer, 26*(10), 71-72.

REFERENCES

Arterton, F. (1987). *Teledemocracy.* Newbury Park, CA: Sage Publications

Asimov, I. (1950). I, Robot. Gnom Press.

Asimov, I. (1985). *Your world 2000: Technology.* New York, NY: Facts on File Publications.

Agres, C., Edberg, D., & Igbaria, M. (1998). Transformation to virtual societies: Forces and issues. *The Information Society, 14*(2), 71-82.

Bates, B. (1984). *Conceptualizing the information society: The search for a definition of social attributes.* Paper presented to The International Communication Association. San Francisco, CA.

Bell, D. (1976). *The coming of the post-industrial society: A venture in social forecasting.* New York, NY: Basic Books.

_____(1979). The social framework of the information society. In: M. Dertouzos, & J. Moses (Eds.), *The computer age: A twenty-year view.* Cambridge, MA: MIT Press.

Beniger, J. (1986). *The control revolution.* Cambridge, MA: Harvard University Press.

Boutros-Ghali, B. (1994). *An agenda for development.* New York, NY: United Nations.

Brzezinski, Z. (1971). Moving into a technotronic society. In: A. Westin, (Ed.), *Information technology in democracy.* Cambridge, MA: Harvard University Press.

Balsamo, A. (1995). Forms of technological embodiment. In: M. Featherstone, & R. Burrows (Eds.), *Cyberspace, cyberbodies, cyberpunk* (pp. 215-237). London: Sage.

Castells, M. (1996). *The rise of the network society.* Malden, MA: Blackwell Publishers.

Dahlhberg, K. (1993). *Transition from agriculture to regenerative food systems.* A paper for the panel: Key Elements of Sustainability, World Future Society General Assembly, Washington, D.C. June 27-July 1.

Devlin, B. (1997). *Data warehouse.* Reading, MA: Addison-Wesley.

von Dijk, J. (2005). *The deepening divide.* London: Sage.

Dizard, W. (1984). *The coming information age.* New York, NY: Longman.

Dordick, H., & Wang, G. (1993). *The information society.* Newbury Park, CA: SAGE Publications.

Drucker, P. (1970). *Technology, management and society.* New York, NY: HarperCollins.

_____(1993). *Post-capitalistic society.* New York, NY: HarperBusiness.

Eastabrooks, M. (1988). *Programmed capitalism: A computer-mediated global society.* Armonk, NY: M. E. Sharpe.

Faucault, M. (1997). *Discipline and punish: The birth of the prison.* London: Vintage Books Edition.

Godfred, D., & Parkhil, D. (Eds). (1979). *Gutenberg two.* Toronto: Press Porcepic Ltd.

Goban-Klas, T., & Sienkiewicz, P. (1999). *Społeczeństwo informacyjne: Szanse, zagrożenia, wyzwania. (Information society, chances, threats, and challenges).* Kraków: Wyd. Fundacji Postępu Telekomunikacji.

Grossman, L. (1995). *The electronic republic.* New York, NY: Viking.

Habermas, J. (1974). The public sphere. *New German Critique, 3*(Fall).

Hiltz, S., & Turroff, M. (1993). *The network nation.* Cambridge, MA: MIT Press.

Hudson, H., & Leung, L. (1988). The growth of the information sector. In: F. Williams (Ed.), *Measuring the information society.* Newbury Park, CA: SAGE Publications.

Ito, Y. (1981). The "Jahoda Shakai" approach to the study of communication in Japan. In: G. Wilhoit & H. de Bock (Eds.), *Mass communication review yearbook.* Newbury, CA: SAGE Publications, Inc.

Laudon, K. (1986). *Dossier society.* New York, NY: Columbia University Press.

Kling, R. (1991). Social controversies about computerization. In: R. Kling (Ed.), *Computerization and controversy.* San Diego, CA: Academic Press.

Komito, L. (1998). The net as a foraging society: Flexible communities. *The Information Journal, 14*(2), 97-106.

MacFarlane, A. (1998). Information, knowledge and learning. *Higher Education Quarterly, 52*(1), 77-92.

Machlup, F. (1962). *The production and distribution of knowledge in the United States.* Princeton, NJ: Princeton University Press.

Madon, S. (1997). Information-based global economy and socioeconomic development: The case of Bangalore. *The Information Society, 13*(2), 227-243.

Marien, M. (1995). *World futures and the United Nations.* Bethesda, MD: World Future Society.

Martin, J. (1978). *Wired society.* Englewood Cliffs, NJ: Prentice-Hall, Inc.

_____(1981). *Telematic society.* Englewood Cliffs, NJ: Prentice-Hall, Inc.

_____(1984). *Viewdata and the information society.* Englewood Cliffs, NJ: Prentice Hall, Inc.

Masuda, Y. (1971). *The plan for information society: A national goal toward the year 2000.* Tokyo: Japanese Computer Usage Development Institute.

_____(1981). *The information society as post-industrial society.* Bethesda, MD: World Future Society.

McLuhan, M. (1968). *War and peace in the global village.* New York, NY: Bantam Books.

Michaels, E. (1994). For a cultural future. In: H. Newcomb (Ed.), *Television: The critical view* (5th ed., pp. 616-30). Oxford: Oxford University Press.

Moller, J. (1993). Europe. The coming of the 'non-material' society. *The Futurist, 27*(6), 23-27.

May, C. (2002). *The information society, a skeptical view.* Cambridge, UK: Polity.

Nora, S., & Minc, A. (1980). *Computerization and society.* Boston, MA: MIT Press.

Norris, P. (2001). *Digital divide.* New York, NY: Cambridge University Press.

Orwell, G. (1949). *Nineteen eighty-four.* London: Secker & Warburg.

Papacharissi, Z. (2002). The virtual sphere, the internet as a public sphere. *New Media and Society, 4*(1), 9-27.

Parker, E. (1981). Information services and economic growth. *The Information Society, 1*(1), 71-78.

Pawlowska, A. (1992). Conditions of preserving the universal values in information society. In: L. Zacher (Ed.), *Spoleczenstwo informacyjne.* Lublin-Warszawa: Warszgraf.

Peters, T. (1987). *Thriving on chaos.* New York, NY: Random House.

Plant, S. (1996). The future looms, weaving woman and cybernetics. In: M. Featherstone, & R. Burrows (Eds.), *Cyberspace, cyberbodies, cyberpunk* (pp. 45-64). London: Sage.

Pol, I.(1983). Tracking the flow of information. *Science, 221,* 609-613.

_____ (1983). *Technologies of freedom.* Cambridge, MA: The Belknap Press of Harvard University Press.

Porat, M. (1977). *The information economy: Definition and measurements.* Washington,

D.C.: U.S. Department of Commerce, Office of Telecommunications.

_____(1978). Global implications of an information society. *Journal of Communication, 28*(1), 70-80.

Postman, N. (1992). *Technopoly.* New York, NY: Alfred A. Knopf.

Reich, R. (1992). *The work of nations: Preparing ourselves for the 21st century capitalism.* New York, NY: Vintage, pp. 171-84.

Rossel, S. (1992). *Governing in an information society.* Montreal: Institute for Research and Public Policy.

Sackman, H. (1967). *Computers, system science, and evolving society: The challenge of man-machine digital systems.* New York, NY: John Wiley.

Salvaggio, J. (1983). The social problems of information societies. *Telecommunications Policy, 7*(3), 228-242.

_____(1989). *The information society, economic, social, & structural issues.* Hillsdale, NJ: Lawrence Erlbaum Associates, Publishers.

Schiller, D. (2000). *Digital capitalism.* Cambridge, MA: MIT Press.

Scolve, R. (1995). *Democracy and technology.* New York, NY: The Guilford Press.

Schiller, H. (1996). *Information inequality* (pp. 43-57). New York, NY: Routledge.

Shapiro, A. (1999). *The control revolution.* New York, NY: A Century Foundation Book.

Schwember, H. (1977). Cybernetics in government: Experiment in Chile 1971-1973. In h. Bassel (Ed.), *Concepts and tools of computer-assisted policy analysis.* Stuttgart: Birkhauser Verlag.

Senge, P. (1990). *The fifth discipline.* New York, NY: Doubleday Currency.

Soros, G. (1998). The economy: Toward a global open society. *The Atlantic Monthly, 28*(1), 20-33.

Stehr, N. (1994). *Knowledge societies* (pp. 121-159). London: Sage.

Targowski, A. (1971*). Informatyka klucz do dobrobytu* (*Informatics a Key to Prosperity*). Warsaw: PIW.

Targowski, A. (1980). *Informatyka; modele systemów i rozwoju.* (*Informatics; Models of Systems and Development*). Warsaw: PWE.

Targowski, A. (1990). Strategies and architecture of the electronic global village. *The Information Society, 7*(3), 187-202.

Targowski, A. (1991). Computing in totalitarian states: Poland's way to an informed society. *Information Executive, The Journal of Information Systems Management, 4*(3), 10-16.

Toffler, A. (1980). *The third wave*. New York, NY: Batman Books.

Toffler, A., & Toffler, H. (1995). *Creating a new civilization*. Atlanta, GA: Turner Publishing, Inc.

Tonn, B. (1985). Information technology and society: Prospects and problems. *The Information Society, 2*(3), 241-260.

Urry, J. (1995). Mobile society. *British Journal of Sociology, 51*(1), 185-203

Urry, J. (2000). *Sociology beyond society*. London: Sage.

Webster, F. (1995). *Theories of the information society*. London: Routledge

Webster, F. (2004). *The information society reader*. London: Routledge

Westin, A. (1971). *Information technology in a democracy*. Cambridge, MA: Harvard University Press.

Wilhelm, A. (2004). *Digital nation*. Cambridge, MA: The MIT Press.

Zacher, L. (Ed.). (1999). *Społeczeństwo informacyjne*. (Information society). Warsaw: Lublin-Warszawa: Warszgraf.

Zubboff, S. (1988). *In the age of the smart machine*. New York, NY: Basic Books.

ENDNOTES

[1] More on universal-complementary civilization in Chapter VII.

[2] Adapted from U.S. Congress, Office of Technology Assessment, Critical Connections: Communication for the Future, OTA-CIT-407, Washington, D.C.: Government Printing Office, January 1990.

A part of this chapter was published in Yi-chen Lan (Ed.). (2005). Global information society (pp. 1-26). Hershey, PA: Idea Group Publishing.

Section IV
Modeling of Civilization

Chapter XV
Asymmetric Communication

Andrew Targowski and Ali Metwalli

INTRODUCTION

This chapter defines a framework for the cross-cultural communication process, including efficiency and cost. The framework provides some directions for dialogue among civilizations, which is one of the main routes toward creation of the universal civilization. A developed architectural design of the cross-cultural communication process is based on a universal system approach that not only considers the complexities of the various cultural hierarchies and their corresponding communication climates, but also compares and quantifies the cultural-specific attributes with the intention of increasing efficiency levels in cross-cultural communication. The attributes for two selected cultures (Western-West and Egyptian) are estimated in a normative way using expert opinions, measuring on a scale from 1 to 5 with 5 as the best value.

Quantifying cultural richness (R), cultural efficiency (η), modified cultural differences (D_{MC}, and cultural ability (B) reflects how a given culture's strength can overcome cultural differences and enhance its competitive advantage (V). Two components of the culture factor cost, explicit (C_E) and implicit (C_I), are defined, examined and quantified for the purposes not only of control-

ling the cost of doing business across cultures, but also to determine the amount of investment needed to overcome cultural differences in a global economy.

In this new millennium, global organizations will increasingly focus on the critical value of the cross-cultural communication process, its efficiency, its competence, its cost of doing business. In order to successfully communicate cross-culturally, knowledge and understanding of such cultural factors as values, attitudes, beliefs and behaviors should be acquired. Because culture is a powerful force that strongly influences communication behavior, culture and communication are inseparably linked.

Worldwide, in the last 20 years, countries have experienced a phenomenal growth in international trade and foreign direct investment. Similarly, they have discovered the importance of cross-cultural communication. As a result, practitioners and scholars are paying attention to the fact that cultural dimensions influence management practices (Hofstede, 1980; Child, 1981; Triandis, 1982; Adler, 1983; Laurent, 1983; Maruyama, 1984). In recent years, empirical work in the cross-cultural arena has focused on the role of culture on employee behavior in communicating within business organizations (Tayeb, 1988). But current work on cross-cultural business communication has paid little attention to either (a) how to adapt these seminal works on general communication to the needs of intercultural business or (b) how to create new models more relevant to cross-cultural business exchanges (Limaye & Victor, 1991, p. 283). There are many focused empirical studies on cross-cultural communication between two specific cultures (e.g., Wong & Hildebrandt, 1983; Halpern, 1983; Victor, 1987; Eiler & Victor, 1988; Varner, 1988; Victor & Danak, 1990), but such results must be arguable when extrapolated across multiple cultures. The prevailing western classical linear and process models of communication (Shannon & Weaver, 1949; Berlo, 1960) neglect the complexity of cross-cultural communication. Targowski and Bowman (1988) developed a layer-based pragmatic communication process model which covered more variables than any previous model and indirectly addressed the role of cultural factors among their layer-based variables. In a similar manner, the channel ratio model for intercultural communication developed by Haworth and Savage (1989) has also failed to account completely for the multiple communication variables in cross-cultural environments. So far, there is no adequate model that can explain the cross-cultural communication process and efficiency, let alone estimate the cost of doing business with other cultures worldwide.

The purpose of this research is to define the framework for a cross-cultural communication process, efficiency and cost of doing business in a global economy. This task is very important for the promotion of global peace through trade, since it aims at understanding how to communicate successfully among different cultures from different civilizations. This understanding should minimize conflicts, increase international trade and investment, and facilitate the development of the global economy. The research method is based on the architectural design of a cross-cultural communication process and system and their quantitative analysis. Their attributes are

estimated in a normative way on a scale from 1 to 5, when 5 is the best value. The attributes for two selected cultures (Western-West and Egyptian) are estimated by expert opinions.

The developed framework based on the architectural design of a cross-cultural communication process adopts a systems approach (of which the traditional linear process and the nonlinear approach are only parts) that can be applied to managing communication between western and non-western cultures. The designed system and its quantitative analysis (based on operations research and information systems) is broad enough not only to include but to go beyond Fisher's (1988) non-linear approach to general communication (with a focus on international political negotiation). The design considers the complexities of the various cultural hierarchies and their corresponding communication climates as they influence behavioral differences and filter communication messages and intentions between business partners in different cultures. Moreover, the design offers a way to compare and quantify attributes that are culture-specific. The intention is not only to reduce the miscommunication between global business partners but also to increase the level of efficiency in cross-cultural business communication between western and non-western countries. Many countries in Asia, the Middle East, and parts of Latin America have recently become successful in world trade. This has forced upon western business organizations a new reality of non-linear culture patterns of communication processes, behavior and practices. The universal approach in our architectural design will accurately delineate the non-western reality that exists in other cultures around the globe. This also will raise awareness and encourage research to improve cross-cultural communication processes, efficiency and practices.

A conceptual framework is introduced to evaluate and estimate the implicit and explicit cost of cultural-specific differences in entering new foreign markets. Such valuation is undoubtedly an important addition to the study of cross-cultural communication processes and efficiency in the global economy. It enables global organizations to estimate the cost of overcoming cultural differences and allows them to achieve not only efficiency but also effectiveness in communicating and operating across cultures.

A CONCEPT OF CULTURE

Culture is a value- and symbol-guided continuous process of developing patterned human behaviors, feelings, and reactions, based upon symbols, learning from it and being a product of it. Cultures do not satisfy needs; rather, they demand values and define symbols. In turn, values in their broadest sense define for the citizen of each culture the nature of any culture's need for rationality, meaningfulness in emotional experience, richness of imagination and depth of faith (Laszlo, 1972). Human communication, therefore, is on the one hand a vehicle for cultural dissemination, while on the other hand is itself culture-driven.

Cultures are the components of a civilization that guide their behavioral patterns. For example, Western civilization currently is composed of the following cultures:

- The Western-West, containing Western Europe and Northern America
- The Western-Central, embracing Poland, the Czech Republic, Slovakia, Hungary, Estonia, Latvia, Lithuania, Croatia, and Slovenia
- The Western-Jewish
- The Western-Latin, composed of Latin America's states

There is some opinion that, after the end of the Cold War in 1989-1991, world politics is entering a new phase. Intellectuals have not hesitated to proliferate visions of what it will be—the end of history (Fukuyama, 1992) or the clash of civili-zations (Huntington, 1996). Huntington (1996) predicts that the fundamental source of conflict in this new world will not be primarily ideological or primarily economic. He perceives that the great divisions among humankind and their dominating source of conflict will be cultural (values- and symbols-driven)

The consequences of the clash of civilizations and cultures have already been seen in business undertakings, particularly after the Asian crisis in 1997-99, when Islamic Malaysia said that the West speculates too much in the Asian market and that Asian countries are not going to pursue the policy of westernization. In general these clashes take place around the following issues: security, westernization, modernization, trade, globalization, freedom, intellectual property, population control, and ecology.

The clashes of civilizations and cultures make a strong impact on the costs of pursuing business in international settings. There are only a few cases of businesses and countries that are making a profit in the global economy (Rodrik, 2003). Most businesses and countries, however, support the development of the global economy, first because it is difficult to stop, and second, because perhaps one day this economy may bring some positive solutions to global problems. One of the factors that can contribute to the positive outcome of the global economy is understanding the cross-cultural process, including efficiency and cost in the global business environment.

THE CROSS-CULTURAL COMMUNICATION PROCESS

We assume that doing business in the global economy depends mostly on the partners' ability to communicate successfully in a cross-cultural environment. People pursue and communicate many common aims, including the values of pure biological survival, social collaboration, creative expression, organizational adaptability and business undertakings. From such common values one can form a hierarchy of human cultural layers:

1. Biological culture layer
2. Personal culture layer
3. Group culture layer
4. Organization culture layer (e.g., business enterprise)
5. Regional culture layer
6. National culture layer
7. Global culture layer (including supra-national, regional ones)

Those layers of cultures and the communication climates associated with them filter messages and intentions of business partners and determine the success of business undertakings. A model of the cross-cultural communication process is shown in Figure 15-1 (Targowski & Bowman, 1988).

The model of the cross-cultural communication process applies at least between two partners who, in order to communicate, must send both a message and their intentions through several layers of cultures. For example, to communicate in the global economy between two different cultures each partner filters a message and intentions through seven layers of cultures (biological, personal, group, organization, regional, national, and global). Of course, to be successful, such cross-cultural communication must be based upon a good understanding of the rules and practices that govern each layer of culture.

Let us define components of the cross-cultural communication process in the global economy.

Figure 15-1. The culture layers and communication climates in the cross-cultural communication process (CC-Communication Climate, GCC-Global CC, NCC-National CC, RCC-Regional CC, OCC-Organization CC, GCC-Grpoup CC, PCC-Personal CC)

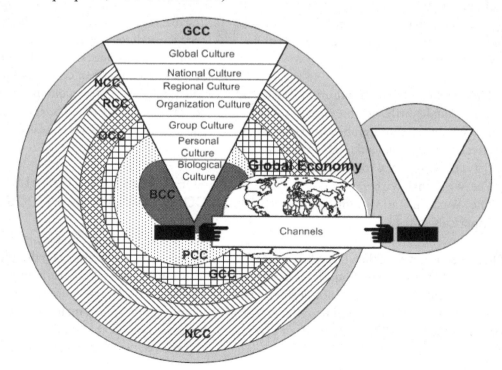

Global Economy

The global economy is largely understood in terms of world-wide economic and political convergence around liberal market principles and the increasing real-time integration of business, technological and financial systems (World Bank, 1997). Based on an expansion and deepening of market conditions, globalization is synonymous with an irresistible process of economic, political and cultural change that is sweeping all national boundaries and protectionist tendencies before it. This pervasive neo-liberal assumption has been dubbed "hyperglobalization" (Held et al., 1997).

"Globalization" is not yet truly global; it has yet to touch a large chunk of the world's economy. Roughly half of the developing world's people have been left out of the much-discussed rise in the volume of international trade and capital flow since the early 1980s. Governments' hesitance to open up to the world economy is partly understandable. Joining the global economy, like devolving power from the center, carries risks as well as opportunities. For example, it can make countries more vulnerable to external price shocks or to large, destabilizing shifts in capital flows. But the difficulties should not be exaggerated, particularly when laid against the risks of being left out of the globalization process (World Bank, 1997, p.12).

Global economic integration gives rise to international threats such as wars, terrorism, global warming, instability and conflict. Economic, cultural and other differences between countries, civilizations and cultures can make cooperation difficult—at times, even impossible. This is why the understanding and practice of good cross-cultural communication is so important.

The globalization process is supported by electronic communication that makes geography, borders, and time zones irrelevant to the way we conduct our business and personal lives. The "death of distance" will be the single most important economic force shaping all of society over the next half century (Cairncross, 1997). Friends, colleagues, and customers could easily be anywhere—around the corner or around the world—and new ways of communicating will effectively wipe out distance as a cost factor, indeed as a perceptible concept from our lives.

The growth of the global economy triggers the growth of a global information infrastructure (GII) which improves connections among organizations and individuals. Most people on earth will eventually have access to computer networks that are switched, interactive, and broadband, with capacity to receive TV-quality motion pictures. While the Internet will continue to exist in its present form, it is also be integrated into other services, such as telephone and television (Targowski, 1996).

Although the communication revolution has increased connections among partners through technology, it simultaneously requires a better understanding of rules and practices of cross-cultural communication, regardless of the media being applied.

Culture Layers

The biological culture layer is the basic stratum of human background which provides common reactions, based on the similarity of physical needs that results from a common biological makeup. This layer is common for humankind in all civilizations and cultures.

The personal culture layer is the means by which the individual survives, operates and develops within the group, organization, region, nation, and globe. The essence of an individual's personal culture is the acceptance of underlying assumptions or "theories-in-use" (Argyris & Schon, 1974; Argyris, 1976). These assumptions are, for the individual, an inarguable understanding of reality, time and space (Schein, 1985). Consequently, since personal culture differentiates between all individuals, all communication between two or more parties must be seen as intercultural to that degree. Besides personal culture, each individual is additionally a member of various groups and organizations, as well as regional, national, and global cultures.

The group culture layer is a manager's or an employee's tool to accomplish an organizational task or to protect the interest of group members (formal or informal). A *group* may be here defined as any collection of individuals united by a common relationship (i.e., work, profession or family). Group culture is the organizational equivalent of regional culture within the setting of national culture.

The organization culture layer is a management tool which uses professional communication to influence organizational performance (Sypher et al., 1985) and which is created (or destroyed) by its leaders (Schein, 1985). A derivative of organization culture is a corporate culture, which is a set of broad, tacitly understood rules (policies) informing employees how to behave under a variety of circumstances. Cultural rules have economic efficiency; they allow firms to administer effectively contracts or terms of employment with employees. Because employees and firms cannot anticipate all of the contingencies in their work relationships, broad cultural rules created by the firm act as a substitute in unanticipated situations for deciding appropriate courses of action (Camerer & Vepsalainen, 1988).

The regional culture layer contains commonalities based on the values of variables which individuals bear within a given region of a nation. Regional variables derive from two sources: 1) environmental influences (Farmerer & Richman, 1966; Terpstra & David, 1985; Borisoff & Victor, 1989) which have particular historical, political, economic, and social characteristics; and 2) traditions whose participants have similar ways of viewing space, time, things, and people (Schein, 1985; Weiss, 1988).

Regional culture may extend beyond national boundaries. In such cases, regional culture is *supranational*. For example, European culture encompasses dozens of nations with some shared values. Supranational culture can also be global (Featherstone, 1990). Regional culture may act as a subset of a particular national culture. In such cases, regional culture is *sub-national*. For example, Brittany has a distinct regional culture within France but remains a part of French national culture. Finally, regional culture may overlap with national culture. For example, Australian culture is at the same time both the culture of a nation state and that of a region (when compared to European or Latin American regions) which happens to be coterminous with the nation state.

The national culture layer is a set of common understandings, traditions, and ways of thinking, feeling, behaving, and communication, based on the same judgments about variables which influence communication throughout the nation. National culture is a learned behavior of its members' historical experience. For example, one can recognize an American culture, a Chinese culture, an Egyptian culture, a Polish culture, and so forth.

The global culture layer is the new emerging layer, triggered by the developments of the global economy. At this layer, partners from different cultures and civilizations deliberately apply the same patterns of behavior in order to achieve successful communication in business (political, social, and so forth) endeavors. These patterns may not come all from their own national cultures, but they are applied in order to create a level playing field among all partners or participants. For example, partners may speak in English, which is being recognized as the global business language, or they may use the dollar or euro as a currency in business transactions.

Figure 15-2 provides the basic structure of a culture layer.

Figure 15-2. The basic structure of a culture layer

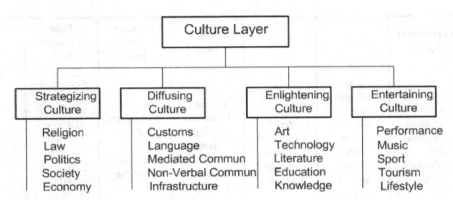

Communication Climates

Communication climate (or "atmosphere") can be defined as a set of conditions which transforms cultural behavior and information into desired (or undesired) states of a given entity (person, group, organization, region, nation, the globe) through the communication process. Communication climate refers to the prevailing condition which exists within a specific entity. An entity's communication climate affects the degree of openness with which people communicate (Perkins & Stout, 1987). For example, within China there are at least three communication climates. The most open communication climate exists in Hong Kong, a less open one is allowed in special economic zones such as in Shenzhen, and a closed communication climate operates in the remaining parts of China, albeit one that is being loosened by the spreading Internet.

Communication climate consists of seven components: space (territory), style, time, desire for interaction (or relationship), frequency (participation), tone (receptivity or friendliness), and quality. Table 15-1 provides weighted attributes of communication climates for all layers of culture except the biological, which is more or less the same for all cultures.

Because the process of cross-cultural communication in the global economy is dynamic, its success depends upon the communication climate among communicating parties. For example, the business communication climate between the U.S. and China at the beginning of 1999 was very good; however, after the accidental bombardment of the Chinese Embassy in Belgrade in May of that year, the communication climate between both countries was briefly at a very low level.

Communication Channels

A communication channel is the vehicle or medium in which a message travels. Thus, channels range from light waves for non-verbal cues to radio or computers as modes for transmitting sound and visual messages. For example, the effective operation of a highly complex weapon system may hinge on adherence to formal channels of communication, while effective performance in investment banking may rely on informal as well

Table 15-1. The weighted attributes (A) of communication climates

CC Layer	(Territory) Space	Style	Time	Relation-ship	Frequency (Participa-tion)	Tone (Friendli-ness)	Quality
Global CC	5-Personal 4-Semi-formal 3-Formal 2-Informal 1-Imper-sonal	5-Open 4-Semi-open 3-Semi-con-trolled 2-Con-trolled 1-Closed	5-Fixed 4-Semi-fixed 3-Inflexible 2-Semi-flexible 1-Flexible	5-Very Friendly 4-Friendly 3-Semi-friendly 2. Un-friendly 1. Hostile	5-High 4-Moderate 3-Low 2-Infre-quent 1-Ad-hoc	5-Support-ing 4-Guiding 3-Com-mand-ing 2-Manipu-lating 1.Critiquing	5-Transcom-munication 4-Pseudocom-munication 3-Paracom-munication 2-Miscommuni-cation 1-Metacom-munication
National CC	5-Personal 4-Semi-formal 3-Formal 2-Informal 1-Imper-sonal	5-Demo-cratic 4-Authori-tarian 3-Dictato-rial 2-Totalitar-ian 1-Chaotic	5-Fixed 4-Semi-fixed 3-Inflexible 2-Semi-flexible 1-Flexible	5-Very Friendly 4-Friendly 3-Semi-friendly 2. Un-friendly 1. Hostile	5-High 4-Moderate 3-Low 2-Infre-quent 1-Ad hoc	5-Support-ing 4-Guiding 3-Com-mand-ing 2-Manipu-lating 1.Critiquing	5-Transcommu-nication -Paracommuni-cation -Pseudocom-munication -Metacommu-nication -Miscommuni-cation
Regional CC	5-Personal 4-Semi-formal 3-Formal 2-Informal 1-Imper-sonal	5-Laisser-faire 4-Coordi-nated 3-Partner-ship 2-Domi-nance 1-Hegemo-nic	5-Fixed 4-Semi-fixed 3-Inflexible 2-Semi-flexible 1-Flexible	5-Very Friendly 4-Friendly 3-Semi-friendly 2. Un-friendly 1. Hostile	5-High 4-Moderate 3-Low 2-Infre-quent 1-Ad hoc	5-Support-ing 4-Guiding 3-Com-mand-ing 2-Manipu-lating 1.Critiquing	5-Transcommu-nication 4-Pseudocom-munication 3-Paracommuni-cation 2-Miscommuni-cation 1-Metacommu-nication
Organi-za-tion CC	5-Networks 4-System structure 3-Matrix structure 2-Flat hierarchy 1-Tall hierarchy	5-Merito-cratic 4-Pluto-cratic 3-Techno-cratic 2-Bureau-cratic 1-Chaotic	5-Fixed 4-Semi-fixed 3-Inflexible 2-Semi-flexible 1-Flexible	5-Very Friendly 4-Friendly 3-Semi-friendly 2. Un-friendly 1. Hostile	5-High 4-Moderate 3-Low 2-Infre-quent 1-Ad hoc	5-Support-ing 4-Guiding 3-Com-mand-ing 2-Manipu-lating 1.Critiquing	5-Transcommu-nication 4-Pseudocom-munication 3-Paracommu-nication 2-Miscom-munication 1-Metacom-munication

continued on following page

Table 15-1. continued

Group CC	5-Sub-networks 4-Networks 3-informal 2-Semi-Formal 1-Formal	5-Merito-cratic 4-Pluto-cratic 3-Techno-cratic 2-Bureau-cratic 1-Chaotic	5-Fixed 4-Semi-fixed 3-Inflexible 2-Semi-flexible 1-Flexible	5-Very Friendly 4-Friendly 3-Semi-friendly 2. Un-friendly 1. Hostile	5-High 4-Moderate 3-Low 2-Infre-quent 1-Ad hoc	5-Support-ing 4-Guiding 3-Com-mand-ing 2-Manipu-lating 1.Critiquing	5-Transcom-munication 4-Pseudocom-munication 3-Paracom-munication 2-Miscom-munication 1-Metacom-munication
Personal CC	5-Home 4-Social 3-Semi-so-cial 2-Anti-so-cial 1-Work	5-Merito-cratic 4-Pluto-cratic 3-Techno-cratic 2-Bureau-cratic 1-Chaotic	5-Fixed 4-Semi-fixed 3-In-flexible 2-Semi-flexible 1-Flexible	5-Very Friendly 4-Friendly 3-Semi-friendly 2. Un-friendly 1. Hostile	5-High 4-Moderate 3-Low 2-Infre-quent 1-Ad hoc	5-Support-ing 4-Guiding 3-Com-mand-ing 2-Manipu-lating 1.Critiquing	5-Transcom-munication 4-Pseudocom-munication 3-Paracommu-nication 2-Miscom-munication 1-Metacom-munication

as formal communication channels. The formal channels of communication help create and maintain authority as well as give authenticity to messages, but they also inhibit communication; indeed, they alienate users. In the global economy, informal channels such as the Internet prevail. They create a horizontal society which exchanges messages that otherwise would not have been created.

The fact that electronic media create new inter-organizational and interpersonal networks raises concerns about the individuals and groups excluded either intentionally through organizational policy and politics or accidentally through inadequate access to networking resources.

THE EFFICIENCY OF CROSS-CULTURAL COMMUNICATION

Applying these attributes in cross-cultural communication, let us take an example of communication in the global economy between the Western-West and Egyptian cultures. To assess the influence of each attribute in the communication process, apply weights on the scale from 1 to 5, where 5 is the highest value of the attribute. Table 15-2 compares those attributes of two cultures, based on the authors' expertise within both cultures.

The cultural difference (Dc) in attribute weights of Western-West culture richness (RWW) and Egyptian culture richness (RE) is:

$$D_c = R_{WW} - R_E = 91\text{-}75 = 16 \text{ points} \qquad [1]$$

in favor of the Western-West culture. This means that the two cultures are not at the same developmental level; but to succeed in communication among both partners in the global economy, both partners must invest in their own abilities to cross-communicate successfully. We shall see how to evaluate the cost of such investments.

The efficiency of Western-West culture in the global economy is $\eta = 91\%$. This means that only 9 times out of 100 is a Western-West business

Table 15-2. The comparison of richness of western-west and Egyptian cultures

Culture Components	Western – West Culture	Islamic (Egyptian) Culture
STRATEGIZING SUB-CULTURE 25	21	20
Religion	3	5
Law	5	5
Political	4	3
Society	4	4
Economy	5	3
DIFFUSING SUB-CULTURE 25	22	21
Customs	4	5
Language	5	5
Mediated Communication	5	3
Non-verbal communication	3	5
Infrastructure	5	3
ENLIGHTENING SUB-CULTURE 25	24	16
Art	4	4
Technology	5	2
Literature	5	4
Education	5	3
Knowledge	5	3
ENTERTAINING SUB-CULTURE 25	24	18
Performance	4	4
Music	5	4
Sport	5	3
Tourism	5	4
Life style	5	3
CULTURE RICHNESS (R) $R_{max} = 100$	$R_{WW} = 91$	$R_E = 75$
CULTURE EFFICIENCY (η)	$\eta = 91 \%$	$\eta = 75 \%$

person likely to have errors in communication because of a lack of cultural understanding of or by a business partner. On the other hand, the Egyptian culture's efficiency in the global economy is $\eta = 75\%$, which means that an Egyptian business person may have faulty communication 25 times out of 100. Almost every fourth transac-tion (with Western-West business person) will be communicated erroneously because of a failure to account for cultural differences.

The role of the communication climate in cross-cultural communication is to facilitate that communication. For example, let us examine a case of communication between the Western-West and Egyptian cultures. Table 15-3 illustrates that comparison.

The communication climate difference (D_{CC}) between both cultures is:

$$D_{CC} = A_{WW} - A_E = 29\text{-}27 = 2 \text{ points} \qquad [2]$$

in favor of the Western-West culture. This means that a Western-West business person entering into a transaction with an Egyptian partner should decrease the cultural difference (D_C) = 14 points by D_{CC}=2, calculated above. The modified culture difference of Western-West culture ($D_{MC/WW}$) after the adjustment by the communication climate difference is:

$$D_{MC/WW} = D_C - D_{CC} = 16 - 2 = 14 \text{ points} \quad [3]$$

On the other hand, the Egyptian partner has to increase the Egyptian culture difference ($D_{MC/E}$) by the same coefficient:

$$D_{MC/E} = D_C - D_{CC} = 16 + 2 = 18 \text{ points} \quad [4]$$

After the adjustments, the modified culture difference (D_{MC}) between Western-West culture and Egyptian culture has increased for Egyptian culture ($D_{MC/E}$) from 14 points to 16 points and for Western-West culture ($D_{MC/WW}$) it has decreased from 14 to 12 points. The communication climate favors Western-West culture, while it disfavors the Egyptian culture. In other words, a business person from a Western-West culture has a communication advantage in the global economy, while a business person from the Egyptian culture has to work harder at the communication effort in order to succeed in the global economy.

The ability of a Western-West culture's business person (B_{WW}) to deal with a business partner from Egyptian culture is:

$$B_{WW} = R_{WW} : D_{MC/WW} = 91 : 14 = 6.5 \qquad [5]$$

The ability of the Egyptian culture's business partner (B_E) to deal with a business partner from Western-West culture is:

$$B_E = R_E : D_{MC/E} = 75 : 18 = 4.2 \qquad [6]$$

The culture's ability reflects how a given culture's strength can overcome cultural differences. The comparison of both cultures' abilities reflects a partner's cultural strength at the business table.

Table 15-3. The comparison of communication climate attributes (A) of western-west (A_{WW}) and Egyptian cultures (A_E) in global economy settings

Global Comm. Climate	Western-West Culture	Egyptian Culture
Territory (Space)	3-Formal	5-Personal
Style	5-Open	4-Semi-open
Time	5-Fixed	2-Semi-flexible
Relationship	4-Friendly	5-Very Friendly
Frequency (Participation)	5-High	3-High
Tone (Friendliness)	4-Guiding	2-Commanding
Quality	3-Paracommunication	4-Paracommunication
TOTAL POINTS	A_{WW} = 29	A_E = 27

It also reflects his/her competitive advantage (V). The competitive advantage of a Western-West partner over an Egyptian partner can be computed in the following manner:

$$V_{WW} = B_{WW} : B_E = 6.5 : 4.2 = 1.6 \text{ or } 160\% \quad [7]$$

In our example, B_{WW} is 1.6 (160%) times stronger than B_E. In common language, this comparison means that in a global economy of bilateral relationships, an American business person has almost twice the strength in overcoming cultural differences (dealing with an Egyptian) as the Egyptian partner. If such knowledge is known to either partner, it can bring competitive advantage to him/her.

THE CULTURE COST FACTOR IN THE GLOBAL ECONOMY

A business entering the global economy is aware that it has to improve the understanding of foreign markets' dynamics and practices. Usually, new entry to a foreign market is associated with two types of cost:

- The explicit cost (C_E) can be anticipated, planned and quantified (transportation, building purchase or rental, interpreter's salary and all other overhead costs) in terms of its financial impact on doing business in a specific culture.
- The implicit cost (C_I) of cultural differences is intuitively understandable, but it is usually very difficult to predict or evaluate its structure and range. So, to guarantee success, it is very critical for a global firm to identify, examine and project the implicit costs associated with entering a foreign market.

The following conceptual framework of the implicit cost of the culture factor (C_I) will provide a definition and range of that type of cost:

$$C_I = f(GNP_C, R_C, D_{MC}, N_D, N_W) \quad [8]$$

Where:

GNP – Gross national product per capita of a given culture in terms of purchasing power parity (*ppp*);
R_C - Richness of a given culture
D_{MC} - Adjusted modified culture difference between involved cultures
N_D - Number of working days in another culture
N_W - Number of workers in another culture

Based on the variables' relationships in formula [8], one can define a formula for the culture factor cost of the culture which has a positive culture difference ($+D_{MC}$):

$$C_{I(+D)} = [(\$GNP_{C(+D)} - \$GNP_{C(-D)}) : (R_{C(+D)} + D_{MC})] \times (N_D \times N_W) \quad [9]$$

In the case of the richer culture (formula [9]), the culture difference (D_{MC}) is in favor of that culture ($R_{C(+D)}$); therefore, both variables are added to decrease the cost of overcoming the culture difference.

This formula provides a balance between economic means, expressed in GNP level and culture richness (R). In other words, low-richness cultures (measured by a low R) with high GNPs will not communicate in the global economy at the low cost. By analogy, persons from such cultures may remind their associates of the behavior of a *nouveau riche*, whose manners sometimes appear assumed and uninformed to the point of indicating exploitability, "greenness." New millionaires from countries that are being transformed from a central planning to a market economy sometimes invade the French Riviera and behave there like an elephant in a china shop. Due to a limited practice in the market economy and old attitudes, very often those *nouveaux riches* prefer quick deals rather than long-term business collaboration. They are aware that their low-richness culture does not generate enough confidence in partners from a rich culture to establish long-term business relations. An additional factor also plays a role. A fresh business culture in some of those countries, very often driven by mafias, does not motivate those business persons to long-term commitments. As a result of it, they prefer to invest abroad rather than in their own countries. In effect, their business cultures do not develop.

In the case of the less rich culture (formula [10], the culture difference (D_{MC}) is not in favor of that culture ($R_{C(-D)}$); therefore, D_{MC} is subtracted from $R_{C(+D)}$ to increase the cost of overcoming the culture difference.

$$C_{I(-D)} = [(\$GNP_{C(-D)} - \$GNP_{C(-D)}) : (R_{C(-D)} - D_{MC})] \times (N_D \times N_W) \qquad [10]$$

The application of these formulas to the example of cross-cultural communication between a person of Western-West culture [9] and one of Egyptian culture [10] for the business duration = 30 days and the involvement of 1 worker, provides the following results (GNP according to World Bank, 1998-99):

$$C_{WW} = [(\$28,740 - \$2,940) : (91 + 14)] \times [30 \times 1] = \$7,400 \qquad [11]$$

$$C_E = [(\$28,740 - \$2,940) : (75 - 18)] \times [30 \times 1] = \$13,600 \qquad [12]$$

The richer culture (Western-West), in order to successfully communicate a business plan to the Egyptian culture, must invest only $7,400 to overcome culture differences. However, the less rich culture should spend 1.8 times more than the rich culture to overcome culture differences in 20

culture components (Table 2) and seven culture communication climate attributes (Table 3).

This example only confirms the old truth, that the comprehensive development of a rich culture takes a long time and requires many means. The paradox of this example is that the culture of Egypt is about 6,000 years old, while the Western-West culture is only 1,200 years old, but has developed more comprehensively with much, much bigger means. This is reflected in the GNPs per capita of both cultures. Apparently 1+ millennium is enough time to enrich the culture of Western civilization.

The cost of overcoming culture differences should focus on learning through education, training, and practice in all culture categories that are disadvantageous. To see the scope of such an effort one must analyze a comparison of the two cultures, as is provided in Table 15-2 and Table 15-3.

CONCLUSION

This study has outlined and defined a framework for a cross-cultural communication process, its efficiency, and the cost of doing business in the global economy. A universal system design was developed not only to compare and quantify cultural efficiency and the attributes of communication climates through seven cultural layers (biological, personal, group, organization, regional, national and global), but also to explain the cross-cultural communication process and quantify the cultural cost in the global economy. This culture-specific design will help reduce miscommunication between partners across cultures and raise the awareness of differences in the levels of efficiency and cost in the communication process, behavior and practices between Western and non-Western cultural patterns.

Based on the presented framework, one can state that in order to be successful in cross-cultural communication in the global economy, engaged parties should be aware of the following five efficiency and cost rules:

- *Culture Richness Rule I: A party from a less-rich culture (lower R) will more frequently communicate erroneously with a party from a richer culture (higher R) (Formula 1).*
- *Communication Climate Rule II: A party from a "warmer" communication climate (higher A) will be in the advantageous position over a party from a "cooler" communication climate (lower A) (Formulas 3 and 4).*
- *Communication Ability Rule III: When large differences exist between cultures, the person from the richer culture has the best chance to communicate his own message (higher R) (Formulas 5 and 6).*
- *Communication Competitive Advantage Rule IV: The difference in communication ability gives a measurable competitive advantage to the more skillful communicator (Formula 7).*
- *Communication Cost Rule V: A party with a higher GNP and a richer culture communicates in the cross-cultural setting at lower costs than a party with the opposite attributes (Formulas 8, 9, and 10).*

The presented framework of cross-cultural communication in the global economy provides pragmatic tools for how to define a communication strategy, train representatives and conduct business talks in order to achieve success.

It is obvious that each business acts in the broader context of a given civilization's culture; therefore, in order to pursue the best communication practice by a given company, it has to be supported by national policies promoting the development of harmonious culture.

This framework should motivate researchers and practitioners to increase production and distribution of knowledge and skills in the area of cross-cultural communication.

A. Further Research Directions

- Investigate dynamics of asymmetric communication between different kinds of civilizations in the 21st century by applying key indicators defined in this book.
- Investigate different key indicators which can impact asymmetric communication among civilizations.
- Investigate more rules and laws governing asymmetric communication.

B. Research Opportunities

- The research opportunity is in defining a communication space in a civilization and subsequently comparing cross-civilization communications.

C. Additional Ideas

- Asymmetric communication is most often used mode of communication which can be investigated (beyond a civilization level) at all levels of human activities, such as marriage, parenthood, teacher-hood, business-hood, and so forth.

D. Rationale

- Asymmetric communication is *de facto* about cross-cultural communication, which is a field of study that looks at how people from differing cultures (civilizations also) communicate. Since different cultures/civilizations have different patterns of behavior, roots, education, and economics, usually one of the communicating sides has an advantage over the other one. If one can know laws, rules, and principles governing such communication then one can be better prepared for such processes and predict their outcomes. These regularities of communication define cultural competence, which defines the ability of people of one culture to understand (via communication) and feel comfortable with the cultures of other people. This kind of ability is crucial for people who want to be successful in the global civilization, which horizontally integrates several religion-oriented civilizations. One of the main factors supporting this integration is the ability of people to minimize asymmetric communication. Improvements in communication and transportation technology have made it possible for previously stable cultures to meet in unstructured situations; for example, the Internet opens lines of communication without mediation, while budget airlines transplant ordinary citizens into unfamiliar milieus. Experience proves that merely crossing cultural boundaries can be considered threatening, while positive attempts to interact may provoke defensive responses. Some groups believe that the phenomenon of globalization has reduced cultural diversity and so reduced the opportunity for misunderstandings, but characterizing people as a homogeneous market is overly simplistic. If we cannot expect that people will be homogeneously communicating, at least they should be aware of the principles of asymmetric communication principles in order to avoid drastic errors.

E.   Additional Reading

Anderson, B. (1983). *Imagined communities.* London: Verso.

Andrea, W. (1994). Resolving conflict in a multicultural environment. *MCS Conciliation Quarterly, Summer*(2), 2-6.

Boulding, E. (1991). The challenge of imagining peace in wartime. *Conflict Resolution Notes, 8*(4), 34-36.

Brockman, J. (1996). *The third culture.* New York: Simon & Schuster.

Brown, S. (1995). The impact of electronic mail usage on the influence processes in geographically dispersed decision-making groups. *Dissertation abstracts international, section a: Humanities and social science, 56*(6-A), 2421.

Carey, J. (1989). *Communication as culture.* New York: Routledge.

Castells, M. (1996). *The rise of the network society.* Malden, MA: Blackwell Publishers, Inc.

Drezner, D. (2007). The new world order. *Foreign Affairs, 86*(2), 34-46.

DuPraw, M., & Axner, M. (2007). Working on common cross-cultural communication challenges. Retrieved February 12, 2007, from http://www.wwcd.org/action/ampu/crosscult.html.

Featherstone, M. (1990). *Global culture, nationalism, globalization and modernity.* Newbury Park, CA: Sage Publications.

Friedman, T. (2006). *The world is flat.* New York: Farrar, Strauss and Giroux.

Gudykunst, W., & Kim, Y. (1995). Communicating with strangers: An approach to intercultural communication. In: J. Stewart (Ed.), *Bridges not walls* (6th ed., pp. 429-442). New York: McGraw-Hill.

Harrison, L., & Huntington, S. (2000). *Culture matters: How values shape human progress.* New York: Basic Books.

Hiltz, S., & Turoff, M. (1978). *The network nation: Human communication via computer.* Reading, MA: Addison-Wesley.

Lessing, L. (2001). *The future of ideas: The fate of the commons in a connected world.* New York: Random House.

Luhmann, N. (1982). The world society as a social system. *International Journal of General Systems, 8,* 131-138.

Maznevski, M., & Chudoba, K. (2000). Bridging space over time: global virtual team dynamics and effectiveness. *Organization Science, 11*(5), 473-492.

Moore, W. (1966). Global sociology. The world as a singular system. *American Journal of Sociology, 71,* 475-482.

O'Hara-Devereaux, M., & Wilbur, S. (1994). *Global work: Bridging distance, culture, and time.* San Francisco, CA: Jossey-Bass.

Olson, G., & Olson, J. (2000). Distance matters. *Human-Computer Interaction, 15,* 139-178.

Robertson, R. (1990). Globality, global culture and images of world order. In: H. Haferkamp, & N. Smesler (Eds.), *Social change and modernity.* Berkeley, CA: University of California Press.

Salacuse, J. (1991). Making deals in strange places: A beginner's guide to international business negotiations. In: W. Breslin, & J. Rubin (Eds.), *Negotiation theory and practice* (pp. 251-260). Cambridge, MA: The program on negotiation at Harvard Law School.

Shenk, D. (1999). *The end of patience.* Bloomington, IN: Indiana University Press.

Trompenaars, F. (1994). *Riding the waves of culture.* Chicago, IL. Irwin.

Wainfan, L., & Davis, P. (2004). *Challenges in virtual collaboration.* Santa Monica, CA: RAND

REFERENCES

Adler, N. (1983). Cross-culture management research: The ostrich and the trend. *Academy of Management Review, 8,* 226-232.

Argyris, C. (1976). *Increasing leadership effectiveness.* New York: Wiley-Interscience.

Argyris, C., & Schon, D. (1974). *Theory in practice: Increasing professional effectiveness.* San Francisco, CA: Jossey-Bass.

Beamer, L. (1992). Learning intercultural communication competence. *Journal of Business Communication, 29*(3), 285-303.

Berlo, D. (1960). *The process of communication.* New York: Holt, Rinehart & Winston.

Borisoff, D., & Victor, D. (1989). *Conflict management: A communication skills approach.* Englewood Cliffs, NJ: Prentice-Hall, Inc.

Cairncross, F. (1997). *The death of distance.* Boston, MA: Harvard Business School Press.

Camerer, C., & Vepsalainen, A. (1988). The economic efficiency of corporate culture. *Journal of Business Communication, 24*(4), 21-34.

Chaney, L., & Martin, J. (1995). *Intercultural business communication.* Englewood Cliffs, NJ: Prentice-Hall, Inc.

Charlten, A. (1992). Breaking cultural barriers. *Quality Progress, 25*(9), 47-49.

Child, J. (1981). Culture, contingency and capitalism in the cross-national study of organizations. *Research in Organizational Behavior, 3,* 303-356.

Eiler, M., & Victor, D. (1988). Genre and Function in the Italian and U.S. Business Letter. *Proceedings of the Sixth Annual Conference on Languages and Communications for World Business and the Professions.* Ann Arbor, MI: University of Michigan.

Farmerer, R., & Richman, B. (1966). *International business: An operational theory.* Homewood, IL: Richard D. Irwin.

Featherstone, M. (1990). *Global culture, nationalism, globalization and modernity.* Newbury Park, CA: Sage Publications, Ltd.

Fisher, G. (1988). *Mindsets: The role of culture and perception in international relations.* Yarmouth, ME: Intercultural Press.

Fukuyama, F. (1992). *The end of history*. New York: Free Press.

Granner, B. (1980). Cross-culture adaptation in international business. *Journal of Contemporary Business, 9*(3), 101-108.

Halpern, J. (1983). Business communication in china: A second perspective. *The Journal of Business Communication, 20,* 43-55.

Haworth, D., & Savage, G. (1989). A channel-ratio model of intercultural communication. *The Journal of Business Communication, 26,* 231-254.

Held, D., Goldblatt, D., McGrew, A., & Perraton, J. (1997). The globalization of economic activity. *New Political Economy, 2,* 257-277.

Hofstede, G. (1980). *Culture's consequences: International differences in work-related values.* Newbury Park, CA: Sage.

Howard, E. (1998). Can business cross the cultural divide?. *Communication World, 15*(9), 1-7.

Huntington, S. (1996). *The clash of civilizations and the remaking of world order*. New York: Simon & Schuster.

Johnson, C. (1995). Cultural sensitivity adds up to good business sense. *HR Magazine, 4,* 82-85.

Laszlo, E. (1972). *The system view of the world.* New York: George Braziller.

Laurent, A. (1983). The culture diversity of western conceptions of management. *International Studies of Management and Organization, 13*(1-2), 75-96.

Limaye, M., & Victor, D. (1991). Cross-culture business communication research: State of the art and hypotheses for the 1990s. *Journal of Business Communication, 28*(3), 277-299.

Lindsley, S. (1999). A layered model of problematic intercultural communication in U.S.-owned aquiladoras in Mexico. *Communication Monographs, 66*(2), 145-167.

Maruyama, M. (1984). Alternative concepts of management: Insights from Asia and Africa. *Asia Pacific Journal of Management, 1*(2), 100-111.

Moran, R., & Richard, D. (1991). Preparing technical professionals for cross-cultural interactions. *Journal of European Industrial Training, 15*(3), 17-21.

Richard, L. (1990). *How do you develop pan-European communication?* 7, (8), 1-6.

Rodrik, D. (2003). Free trade optimism. *Foreign Policy, 82*(3), 135

Schein, E. (1985). *Organizational culture and leadership*. San Francisco, CA: Jossey-Bass.

Scott, J. (1999). Developing cultural fluency: The goal of international business communication instruction in the 21st century. *Journal of Education for Business, 74*(3), 140-143.

Sussman, L., & Johnson, D. (1993). The interpreted executive: Theory, models, and implications, *Journal of Business Communication, 30*(4), 415-434.

Sypher, B., Applegate, J., & Sypher, H. (1985). Culture and communication in organizational context. In: W. Gudykunst, L. Stewart, & S. Ting-Toomey (Eds.), *Communication, culture, and organizational process*. Newbury Park, CA: SAGE Publications.

Targowski, A. (1996). *Global information infrastructure*. Harrisburg, PA: Idea Group Publishing.

_____(2007). The civilization index. *Comparative Civilizations Review, 57*(Fall), 92-112.

Targowski, A., & Bowman, J. (1988). The layer-based pragmatic model of the communication process. *Journal of Business Communication, 25*(1), 5-24.

Tayeb, M. (1988). *Organizations and national culture: A comparative analysis*. London, Newbury Park, CA: Sage.

Terpstra, V., & David, K. (1985). *The cultural environment of business* (2nd ed.). Cincinnati, OH: South-Western Publishing Company.

Triandis, H. (1982). Dimensions of cultural variations as parameters of organizational theories. *International Studies of Management and Organization, 12*(4), 139-169.

Varner, I., & Beamer, L. (1995). *Intercultural communication in the global workplace.* Chicago, IL: Irwin.

Varner, I. (1988). A comparison of American and French business communication. *The Journal of Business Communication, 25*(4), 55-65.

Victor, D. (1987). Franco-American business communication practices: A survey. *World Communication, 16*(2), 158-175.

Victor, D. (1992). *International business communication.* New York: Harper Collins Press.

Victor, D., & Danak, J. (1990). *Genre and function in the U.S. and Indian English-language Business Letter: A Survey.* Paper presented at the Conference on Language and Communication for World Business and the Professions, Ypsilanti, Michigan, Eastern Michigan University.

Weiss, J. (1988). *Regional cultures, managerial behavior and entrepreneurship: An international perspective.* Westport, CT: Greenwood Press.

Williams, M. (1991). Will diversity = equality for multicultural communicators?. *Communicational World, 8*(3), 27-30.

Wong, B., & Hildebrandt, H. (1983). Business communication in the People's Republic of China. *The Journal of Business Communication, 20,* 25-33.

World Bank. (1997). *The state in a changing world: The world development report.* Washington, D.C.: World Bank.

World Bank. (1998/99). *Knowledge for development: The world development report.* Washington, D.C.: World Bank.

This chapter originally was published in E. Szewczak and C. Snodgrass (Eds.). (2002). Managing the human side of information technology (pp. 291-310). Hershey, PA: Idea Group Publishing.

Chapter XVI
Civilization Market Integration

INTRODUCTION

The purpose of this chapter is to define the dynamics of the economic infrastructure, which supports any civilization and defines the *modus operandi* of the world civilization in the 21st century and third millennium.

This chapter especially addresses the economic roles of two countries/civilizations: Will the Chinese economy, as many suggest, continue its strong economic advance under its system of "authoritarian capitalism" and surpass in size that of the United States and its economically integrated partners (currently NAFTA), or will China convulse and stagnate? This chapter explores the scenario that the United States will see its destiny at the heart of a free trade area of the Atlantic with an economy significantly greater than China's and with an even larger population. China will remain the dominant Asian economy, but it will do so independently, not as part of a regional economic union.

The future of capitalism is also addressed. What kind of capitalism or other economic system must be applied in order to keep the world population within the threshold of the Ecosystem? The answer to this question will determine the future of civilization.

THE EVOLUTION OF CIVILIZATION MARKETS

Why are some nations rich and others poor? Why are the poorest countries failing and what can be done about it? Why can the poor countries not apply the rich countries' strategies to achieve the same level of living? There are many possible approaches to answer these questions, many exclusive of each other. In this study, the civilizational conditioning of economic development will be synthesized.

In 2005, the average income per capita of residents of the United States was $41,950 (in *purchasing power parity* (ppp) = common basket prices). In Switzerland, the most prosperous European country, it amounted to $37,080 (ppp). For the European Union this income reaches $28,915 (ppp). For China, this income was at the level of $6,600 (ppp), while in Hong Kong it was $34,670; in also Chinese-oriented Singapore, it was $27,780. But in African Malawi, it was only $650. (World Bank, 2007, pp. 14-16) Why?

As of the beginning of the 21st century, there are about 50 economically-failing states, which pose the central challenge of the developing world. The standard solutions cannot overcome problems with civil wars, a dependence on the extraction and export of natural resources, and bad governance (Collier, 2007). Perhaps these problems are conditioned by each civilization's history.

The focus of this part of the study will be on a few civilizations only, those which are the most eager to dominate economic development in the 21st century and beyond. Figure 16-1 illustrates these civilizations' development paths, which lead to the competition of the Western and Chinese civilizations in the 21st century.

Classical economics defines as determinants of economic development the factors of production, such as land, labor, and capital, economic structure (relationships among various sectors of the economy), production systems, and pro-

ductivity. In this study more attention will paid to such factors as information-communication and knowledge, since it is these mind-driven factors that mostly determine the complexity and productivity of production systems.

Economic development in pre-civilized times was based mostly on recurring rounds of feast and famine, depending on natural variations in climate and on skill and luck in hunting. Life was certainly difficult, rough, and short. Average life spans were not more than about 20 years; few people could survive over the age of 50 (Leakey, 1996).

Due to improved climate after the end of the Ice Age, since 9,000 B.C. people have transformed from nomads dependent on hunting and gathering

Figure 16-1. The basic evolution of civilizations which are the foci of this study of the market development until after 2000+ (many other civilizations are not shown in this model)

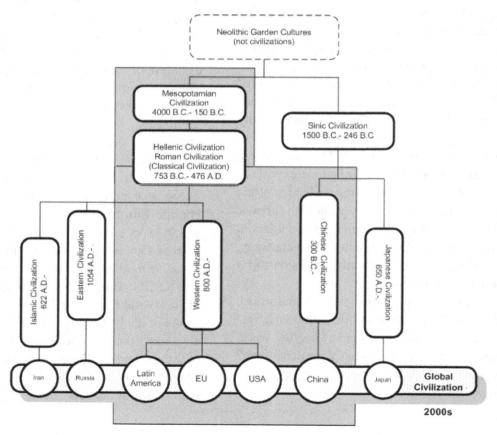

to settlers developing agriculture and domesticating animals. These inventions allow people to store material goods and wealth. People became more productive and innovative, which led to the development of irrigation systems and division of labor as well as to a necessity to protect wealth. The last factor eventually led to the emergence of the first cities, city-states, and empires, to civilization with its rules, elite, administration and military.

As the first civilization, the Mesopotamian civilization (in the Tigris and Euphrates Valley, nowadays Iraq) had key characteristics that are shown in Figure 16-2.

The Mesopotamian civilization could be more successful and better organized than "Neolithic garden cultures" (Quigley, 1979) because its elite could communicate through a written language. Writing developed into an efficient tool to stabilize and implement law and organize expeditions, whether for trade or conquest.

Agricultural and labor specialization was the Mesopotamian civilization's major contribution to economic development. This lasted for thousands of years and eventually gave birth to the next, more advanced, Hellenic civilization. This was very rich in new ideas, which lasted almost until now.

Figure 16-2. The Mesopotamian civilization system (key characteristics)

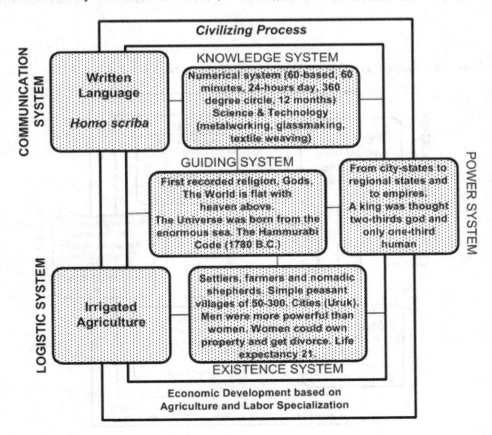

The relationship between communication and logistic systems was not critical in directly supporting economic development of the Mesopotamian civilization. Its influence was indirect through the power system, which was first developed to protect wealth creators, who triggered the development of irrigation systems in order to increase the productivity of cultivated land.

The Mesopotamian civilization led to the development of several short-lived civilizations. Eventually, this process triggered the rise of Hellenic civilization, with contributions that are still valid. The key characteristics of this civilization are shown in Figure 16-3.

From the point of view of economic development, the shores of the Mediterranean Sea, occupied by the Greeks and later by the Romans, were convenient for the expansion of highly developed trade networks, opening new markets for this civilization's products and services. Population growth was also creating demand for more goods and was supporting trade networks to provide them, which eventually led to the invention of coined money.

The relation between the communication and logistic systems began to play an important role from this time. Land- and sea-oriented transportation roads and systems thereof were developed to support growing trade with all corners of the Roman Empire in Europe, the Middle East, and Africa. The power system was driving economic development by expanding new markets for Roman traders.

Growing use of slaves and servants, who were the most productive workers of the times, led to a passiveness of the elite and in consequence to the lack of technological creativity, despite the brilliant development of arts and literature. The elite were concentrating on war, government, arts, and, famously, on *la dolce vita*. This kind

Figure 16-3. The classical civilization system (key characteristics)

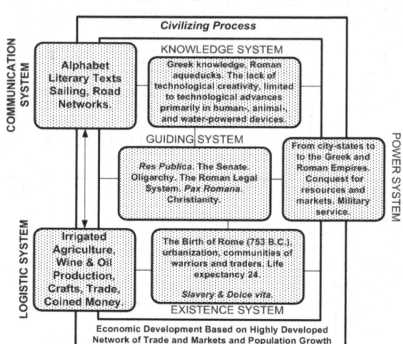

366

of society could not produce sustained economic development. By the year 200 A.D. the Roman Empire's military was unable to keep extending new markets and providing new supplies of slaves. The craftsmen began leaving towns and returning to the countryside, where a strategy of self-sufficiency was applied by the landlord class. A long economic depression began and the government's actions were directed increasingly toward enlargement of the bureaucracy and increasing tax collection. Trade consequently began to decrease sharply and Rome's balance of trade became unfavorable. The civilian landed class was gradually replaced by military anarchy; violence, grasping materialism, and ignorance were prevailing. At the bottom of the society it led to dark superstitions and exalted spirituality, which was steadily replacing the classical ideas. As Quigley stated (1979, p. 328): "without its ideology no culture can survive."

The fall of the Roman Empire in the west, conventionally dated 476 A.D., was the death of Roman civilization and coincided with an influx of barbarian peoples from northern into southern Europe. The next 300 "dark" years (500-800) served as a kind of buffer zone in which three new civilizations were forming, eventually becoming the Islamic (622 A.D.), Western (800 A.D.), and Eastern (1054 A.D.). Other civilizations appeared in the coming centuries and have lasted to now.

Let us further focus on Western civilization's impact on world economic development.

In terms of economic development, the Western civilization has lingered through two millennia. According to the monumental statistical work of Maddison (2001, p. 17), in the past (second) millennium, the world population rose 22-fold, per capita income increased 13-fold, and world GDP nearly 300-fold. From the year 1000 to 1820 the advance in per capita income was slow; the world average rose only 50%. Most of the growth went to accommodate a fourfold increase in population. Since 1820, world development has been much more dynamic. Per capita income

rose more than eight-fold, population more than five-fold. Life expectancy has risen 3.3-fold, from 24 years (1000) to 80 years (2005) (World Bank, 2007, pp. 28-30).

The economic development of Western civilization in its 1200+ years of existence was based on the following factors (Maddison, 2001, p. 18):

(1) Conquest and settlement of relatively empty lands
(2) International trade and capital movement
(3) Technological and institutional innovations

The year 1820 was cited by Angus Maddison as the year of accelerated change in the world's economic development and is associated with the rising importance of the industrializing United Kingdom, then the leader of the Industrial Revolution. Shortly afterward, the British adopted a policy of free trade, and their willingness to import a large part of their food had positive effects on the world economy and the diffusion of technical progress.

The civilizational approach herein employed recognizes not two (as defined by A. Maddison) but three phases of Western civilization, driven by different ideas of economic development:

- Phase I – driven by the feudal system and merchant capitalism (800-1820)
- Phase II – driven by commercial capitalism (1820-1990s), although, particularly in the U.S., such forms as *"robber baron capitalism, regulated capitalism* (after 1910), *managed capitalism* (New Deal), and *liberal capitalism* were impacting *commercial capitalism*
- Phase III – driven by *managerial, global, and super capitalisms*, is motivated by the globalization of world markets, which was made possible by the expansion of the Internet in the 1990s

Figure 16-4. The Western civilization system in the 1990s (key characteristics)

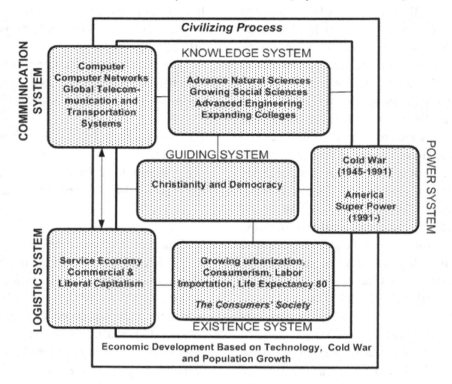

The key characteristics of the Western civilization in its second developmental phase (1820-1990s) are depicted in Figure 16-4. From the civilizational point of view, the economic success of Western civilization in these times was due to the three factors defined by Angus Maddison and also to three other factors:

(4) Christianity and its wing Protestantism, which glorifies a cult of hard work

(5) Democracy, which liberates individuals from the "collective" and gives them freedom in economic decisions, guided by an *invisible hand* in the marketplace

(6) The Cold War (1945-1991), which through the confrontation of *democracy* with *communism* enhanced the well-being of Western civilization

In comparison to the Hellenic and Roman civilizations (also known as classic civilization), the Western civilization transformed regional transportation systems into the global transportation system. Handmade products have been replaced by machine-made products. Furthermore, information processing was mechanized first by punched-card machines, later by computers and their networks. All these improvements increased dramatically humans' economic productivity. These technological gains based on machine, computer, and networking provided a very strong foundation for the development of the third phase of Western civilization, driven by globalization, which is accelerated by the use of the global Internet. This phase "flattens" the world and triggers the rise of a new system which we call global civilization (see Chapter I).

THE WORLD IS "FLATTENING"

Electronic mail supported by the Internet has made distance "dead" and allowed India and China, and many other countries with cheap labor, to become part of the global supply chain for services and manufacturing. It created an explosion of wealth in the middle classes of the world's two most populous nations and gave them a huge new stake in the success of globalization and a special role in the global civilization. The key characteristics of the Western civilization in its third, globalizing phase (1990s-) are depicted in Figure 16-5.

The global civilization System shown in Figure 16-5 is mostly driven by the global communication system and by *managerial* and *global*

*capitalism*s, which at this time are guided by the greed of global investors and fat bonuses given to CEOs for their decisions to move factories to countries with cheap labor. The politicians are reluctant to regulate illegal immigration to the U.S., since imported workers work almost like slaves, bringing good profits to employers. The middle class is destabilized and shrinking, not much aware what is going on, since the government is constantly saying that globalization is good for America. In fact it brings about $500 billions/year in gains, but most of this is taken by 0.6% of the labor force (Scheve & Slaughter, 2007).

Thomas Friedman noticed in his best-selling book *The World is Flat* (2005), that along with the transfer of services and manufacturing from the developed to developing nations, there also

Figure 16-5. The global civilization system in the 2000s (key characteristics)

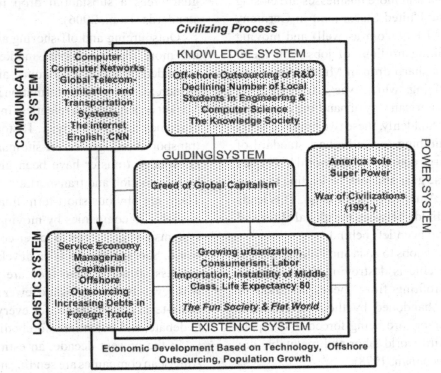

takes place a transfer of wealth. As a result of it, the world is becoming economically "flat." It is interesting to notice that the main tool of this flattening process is the Internet, which was not developed because it was financed by wise capital, as is true in many other technologies. In fact, the Internet was developed by the military and scientific communities. The latter have played an even more important role in implementing "World Wide Web" technology and very user-friendly browsers (Mosaic and Netscape). But business immediately recognized its great potential for global instant communication and feasibility for off-shore outsourcing of services and manufacturing and even R&D, since the distant locations could be communicated to in just a few seconds and materiel could be delivered by the global transportation system and business transactions could be handled by the global finance system very effectively.

With the new feasibility of outsourcing jobs off-shore and the free trade policy of the global economy, more and more businesses are closing up shop in the United States (and in Germany and the United Kingdom as well) and moving elsewhere, taking millions of jobs with them. The result is a sharp drop in Middle America's standard of living, which was a fruit of 200+ years of the American way of handling economic development. Suddenly, these two hundred years of steadily climbing to the highest standard of living (by a large country) in the world have been put into reverse gear and may be leading to a big crunch of the American middle class. This leads to a national divide between the global elites and those who have been left behind.

By exporting jobs to Asia and Latin America, the corporate elite is destroying the American dream and profiting from the exploitation of sweatshops. Abandoned by their government, American workers are being forced to compete with cheap third world labor and inevitably are losing out (Buchanan, 1998).

Faux (2006) even argues that the politics of the new world market is dominated by a virtual "Party of Davos," the globe-trotting network of corporate investors and CEOs, politicians and journalists who work on their behalf. He also shows that NAFTA, the WTO, and similar "free trade" agreements are really deals among the global elite to rip up the social contract that used to allow the benefits of *commercial capitalism* to be broadly shared. Commercial capitalism is transforming into *managerial* and *global capitalisms* and the WTO is elaborating the Bill of Rights to protect "one citizen," who is the large stateless corporation.

Global and stateless corporations are profitable, but the competitiveness of the people, business, and communities rooted in the U.S. economy is relentlessly deteriorating. American (and to a certain degree English and German as well) workers, from the unskilled to highly educated engineers and research scientists, have been set adrift in a sea of dog-eat-dog competition that guarantees a substantial drop in their living standards (Faux, 2006).

Outsourcing and off-shoring are really nothing more than traditional market competition expanded in a global economy, and enabled by an increasingly robust information infrastructure. Market economies are relentless in their drive for efficiency and productivity. Historic barriers of transportation logistics, off-site management, and knowledge transfer have been greatly reduced by information and transportation technologies. There are obvious short-term financial benefits available to companies by moving well-defined systems and processes to lower-cost areas of the world. Short-term effects on developed societies are less attractive than they are to companies with fewer available jobs and fewer opportunities. Long-term consequences for everyone are open to debate, and potentially foreboding.

In the present decade, an estimated 12% of American companies are sending manufacturing jobs to foreign countries. About 3 million direct manufacturing jobs have been lost in the United States with 4-5 million support jobs disappearing with them (ACCRA, 2004). Many U. S.-based airlines are linked via computers and telephone lines with reservation clerks in Ireland where labor costs are lower than in the U.S. and education level is high. Many American computer firms have technological support in India. There is less current demand for engineers, IT students and MBAs in the United States. The middle class is shrinking even as healthcare and energy costs are rising rapidly. Greed appears to run rampant in corporate executive suites as dislocated workers struggle with unemployment and severe financial pressure. Annual trade deficits in the U. S. grew to about $791 billion by the end of 2005 (World Bank, 2007, p. 248).

Forrester Research estimated in 2004 that American companies will move 3.4 million jobs off-shore by 2015. About a third of those jobs pay $46,000 per year or higher (Atkinson, 2004). The labor organization AFL-CIO estimates that the United States lost about 2.7 million manufacturing jobs between January 2001 and August 2004 (AFL-CIO, 2007). The U. S. Government Accounting Office indicates that services associated with off-shoring grew from $21.2 billion in 1997 to about $37.5 billion in 2002, an increase of more than 76%. But exports from the U. S. of those same types of services also increased by over 48% (Hughes, 2002).

Now that the China price is impacting both the low-tech and high-tech sectors, politicians and U. S. workers are asking what industries will produce jobs for American workers to replace the ones vanishing to other parts of the globe. Innovation is frequently mentioned as the way out of the China price dilemma, but innovation is not something that can be delivered on a strict timetable. How much time do we have to shore up the American economy?

Can it be that the United States is pricing itself out of the global economy? Education is often proposed as a solution to the American economic quandary. In his description of the growth of health services in India, Colvin (2004) states that U.S. physicians will not lose business due to some supposed inferiority in education. In fact, they are the best educated medical practitioners in the world. Their problem is that they are overpriced. Is this a race to the bottom, with continually declining wages and continually declining standards of living for most of the U. S. population? If American salvation lies in biotechnology and nanotechnology, we will be waiting a long time for its impact. But American workers must pay the rent or mortgage every month and eat every day.

Figure 16-6 describes the long-term effects of continued job losses from off-shoring. Short-term profits for U.S. companies improve from lower costs. But long-term effects of a less complex economy, resulting from the loss of the country's manufacturing base, the proliferation of low-paying service jobs, a shrinking middle class, and large trade deficits produce a new world economic order in which the United States will play a much less prominent role. In this scenario, the country that experiences a lower national level of personal security becomes a follower rather than a leader in technology and education, experiences a decline in standard of living for its citizenry, and has to contend with a much more radicalized political structure.

Some other issues generated by off-shore outsourcing are as follows:

- The outsourcing and off-shoring that the U.S. is experiencing today are akin to what happened at the turn of the 20th century when the U.S. ceased being an agricultural economy and became an industrial one.

    o The role of agriculture was not ended merely because productivity was increased.
    o Downgrading manufacturing means that potential intelligence and com-

Figure 16-6. A model of the consequences of offshore outsourcing for the U.S.

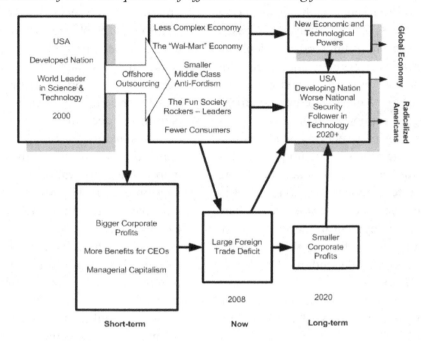

plexity in engineering and information technology are leaving as well.

o Americans are maintaining lifestyle by selling "reputation," for example, treasury bonds sold to foreign creditors. As "industrialists" the Americans used to pay in goods. Now they pay by debts. How long can that continue?

• The global economy is about free trade, and outsourcing/off-shoring is the 21st century face of free trade

o Free trade is about exporting/importing goods at low tariffs, but is it also about exporting millions of jobs?

• Americans should just learn new jobs.

o What jobs are available? The China price affects both low-tech and high-tech industries. Perhaps nanotechnology and biotechnology are an answer, but how many jobs will these emerging indus-

tries produce and how long will it take to develop them? They are still about 20 to 100 years away.

• Americans should move to more complex jobs.

o Which more complex jobs? Before you can run, you need to learn how to walk. One cannot teach classical music if the symphony orchestra is in another country.

The following conclusions on off-shore outsourcing can be offered:

1. Outsourcing needs sophisticated management that balances short-term profit with long-term investment in competitive positions. *The sky is no longer without limits.*

2. Off-shore outsourcing of manufacturing and information technology is a potential

strategic threat for the American economy and society.

3. Off-shore outsourcing is driven by "Lenin's rope." He observed as a lesson that capitalists will compete to sell their own hanging rope to their executioners.

A typical argument for globalization and off-shore outsourcing is that the American economy is transforming from industrial to service and the Americans have no other options but to learn new knowledge and skills and adapt to new challenges. Those who argue this way forget that the Americans never replaced agriculture by another industry; they only improved its productivity. Also, manufacturing cannot be replaced by life-science-oriented industry or by information technology. In fact, IT has no purpose if agriculture and industry are liquidated, since IT processes data/information about something "else." If this "else" does not exist, IT will follow.

If American wages continue falling, then protectionism will rise, which is a bad solution. Inequality in the U.S. is greater in the 2000s than at any other time in the last 70 years. To save globalization, policymakers must spread its gain widely. The best way to do that is by redistributing income through new formulas of taxation (Scheve & Slaughter, 2007).

Is it possible to redistribute income in the U.S.? Perhaps not. Saul (2005) thinks that we are seeing the collapse of globalism. Like many other geopolitical ideologies, it is dead, according to him. This is despite the near-religious conviction that nation-states are heading toward irrelevance, that economics, not politics or arms, will determine the course of human events, that growth in international trade will foster prosperous societies that will in turn abolish poverty and change dictatorships into democracies. Instead of surrendering or sharing sovereignty, governments and citizens are reasserting their national interests. This Canadian author argues that the United States appears determined to ignore its in-

ternational critics. Europe is faced with problems of immigration, racism, terrorism, and renewed internal nationalism. Elsewhere, the world looks for answers to African debt, the AIDS epidemic, the return of fundamentalism and terrorism, all of which were supposed to disappear because the rising global prosperity will eliminate them.

To make globalization work, one must democratize international institutions, argues the Nobel laureate Joseph E. Stiglitz (2007). His list of necessary changes is good but very long, but it is possible if done through a coordinated international political process. However, as is very well known, such a process is very hard to imagine in the immediate future.

From the international point of view, the fact that the Americans are worse off due to globalization is not a problem. There is an opinion that this situation may be only the correction of historic exploitation of poor nations by the Americans. If this is true, is it possible in long-term perspective that the world will be better off if Americans are worse off?

How long can the Americans pay their foreign trade debt by "credit cards?" In 2006, its accumulated value (from 1985) reached $6.6 trillion, which is 55% of GDP. The U.S.'s annual international trade deficit is 35% larger than social security spending, 50% larger than all defense spending, and 2.5 times larger than Medicare (http://mwhodges.home.att.net/reserves.htm). Can this debt ever be paid off? Is it not true that the U.S. has helped and does help other nations whenever it can? Is it not true that the U.S. used to lead the world mostly by the ideas of freedom, democracy and prosperity?

But it is also true that after the victory over communism and the terrorist attack on New York in 1991, and unsuccessful wars in Afghanistan and Iraq, the U.S. lost its "magic" touch and needs to restore America's right place in the world. From the civilizational perspective, the U.S. reminds one of the case of the Roman Empire, which collapsed due to losing control of its borders,

Table 16-1. Comparison of the Roman empire and the U.S. in times of crisis

Criteria	The Roman Empire 5th Century A.D.	The United States The 2000s
Rulers	Insensitive	Arrogant
Politicians	Irrelevant	Self-serving
Elite	Passive	Detached
Military	Dispersed	Stretched-out
Work done by	Slaves & Servants	Computers Illegal immigrants-working like slaves Off-shore cheap labor
Ideas	Lack of ideas	Lack of ideas
Purpose of life	Dolce vita	The fun society
Mindset	Return to country-side and autarchy	Protectionist and besieged
Confidence by others	Falling & attacked and beaten by weaker forces	Falling; attacked by terrorists against whom we cannot win

giving work to slaves and servants, and finding "happiness" in *la dolce vita*. Table 16-1 compares both "Romes."

This comparison of Rome I and "Rome III" gives the impression that the state of the global civilization is not good. It is unstable. To improve its well-being, the fixing of economic problems will be not enough. Certainly, the civilizational logistic system must first of all be controlled by the civilizational guiding systems. A proposal for a solution in this area is provided in Chapter VII.

THE CHINA FACTOR

The China factor in the 2000s is not new in world history. The Chinese civilization (one of the oldest) had more advanced technology than Europeans in the first 1.5 millennia A.D. They invented the magnetic compass and the art of making paper, which reached Europe with the help of Arabic merchants. They also introduced new crops, such as rice (double cropping), sugar cane,

cotton, citrus fruit, the watermelon, and many other fruits and vegetables. The manufacturing of silk cloth was originated in China at a very early date. Porcelain ("*china*") was also invented by the Chinese. They used paper money before the Europeans. China's ships were superior in technology to those of the Portuguese in the 15th century, more seaworthy and more comfortable, with watertight compartments, many more cabins, and a capacity to navigate over large distances to Africa, Southern Asia, the Indian Ocean, the Persian Gulf, and Indonesia. The Chinese reached a higher level of technological solutions well in advance of the Western Europeans.

The Mongol invasion of China in the 13th century affected Chinese progress. In 1433, the Emperor Xuande stopped long-distance voyages, ordered the destruction of ocean-going ships, and prohibited his subjects from traveling abroad. When the Great Wall (4,700 miles long and guarded by 1 million men) was rebuilt in the 15th century to protect against the next Mongol attacks from the north, it also put the Chinese civilization into isolation from the rest of the world and its economy. In those times, the Portuguese, Spanish, and Dutch were at the peak of their geographical discoveries and colonizing missions, which soon gave them superiority over Chinese marine technology.

Until the 19th century, China was a much bigger and more powerful state than any other in Europe and Asia. Its skilled bureaucracy secured higher levels of income per capita than existed in Western Europe during 400 to 1,300 A.D. (Maddison, 2001, p. 42). After the middle of the 15th century, China was without naval defenses and its elite had no interest in European technological solutions and education presented to them by some foreign visitors. (They had no interest in European technology as a life-changing means of development, but they had plenty of interest in it for curiosity's sake, witnessing the activities of the Jesuits). In the 19th century, China was defeated by the British, French, and Japanese. Eventually, China had to accept low-tariff treaties with many European countries and the U.S., in a situation that may be called *free-trade imperialism*. In 1931, Japan again invaded China (Manchuria), and the fighting became additionally complicated by a civil war between Kuomintang and communist forces from 1937 to 1949. Consequently, the People's Republic of China was created under the control of the Communist Party of China and its chairman Mao Zedong. Until 1978, the Chinese economy was under state ownership and control, in a situation generally called *state capitalism*. After 1978, autarkic self-reliance was abandoned, special free-trade zones were established, and market forces emerged. After the fall of the Soviet Union in 1991, China, wanting to avoid such chaos of political transition from communism to capitalism as happened in Russia, introduced new economic policies, which in practice created *authoritarian capitalism*. China has since become a very competitive player in the global economy again, as it used to be about 1000+ years ago. The Chinese civilization is strong and should handle wisely its "second coming."

The Chinese civilization's key characteristics are shown in Figure 16-7. The party apparatus does not believe that *democracy* in the Western sense of the word guarantees economic efficiency. They are only afraid that *central planning*, which formerly created a passiveness in the labor force, may now lead to workers' unrest and counter-revolution as happened in the Soviet Block in 1989-1991. Therefore, they would like to loosen up economic relationships at the bottom and still keep power at the top. In such a manner, *authoritarian capitalism* does secure central power and controls the "free" market and trade (e.g., controlled currency exchange and management nominations).

In contrast to the situation in the Western civilization, the Chinese communication system is controlled directly by the state, which is exemplified by the censored Internet and Google search engine system.

A very strong influence is the Chinese guiding system, which is a mixture of religion (Buddhism and Taoism) and such civil values as Confucianism and communism. Their composite value is the respect for authority and obedience. These values combined with Chinese patience and a middle-of-the-road attitude make the Chinese a very effective people, particularly if they are allowed to open their eyes and see what is going on around them. Then their devotion to the family life and nation can make "miracles."

In the following sections China's chances in the global economy will be projected.

THE WORLD'S LARGEST MARKET IN 2010

Table 16-2 illustrates that the projected rankings of the world's largest markets have remained unchanged since the end of the 20th century. In 2010, NAFTA will remain the world's largest market followed by the EU. The Chinese economy will grow

Figure 16-7. The Chinese civilization system in the 2000s (key characteristics)

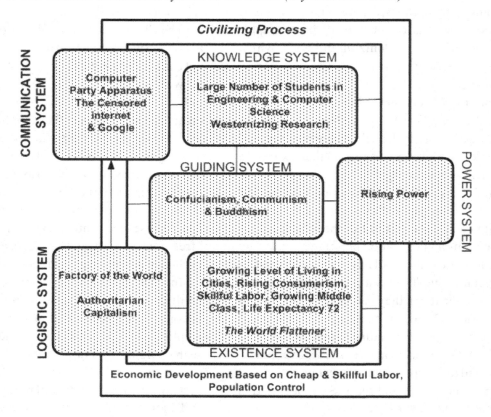

more than 100%. It will have sharply increased its lead over Japan as the world's largest single-nation economy (two and a half times as large) and will approach the size of the European Union. Moreover, in respect to market share, only China will increase its world share—from 11% in 1988 to 17% in 2010 (Targowski & Korth, 2003).

THE WORLD'S LARGEST MARKET IN 2020

The momentum upon which the projections for 2010 are based is well developed. Of course, disruptions may well occur. However, even a major regional disruption, such as the Asian financial crisis of 1997-99, had only a moderate impact on China. There is an excellent chance that the

economic projections through 2010 will occur. What happens after 2010 is much more difficult to foresee. An economic forecast of the world market's dynamics in 2010-2020 is illustrated in Table 16-3.

The prediction for the world's largest market in 2020 is based upon the following assumptions (Targowski & Korth, 2003):

- NAFTA will likely expand its reach to most of Latin America after 2010, if not sooner. Signs of this can be perceived even today: Mexico already has a free-trade agreement with Chile and the United States has an agreement with the countries of Costa Rica, El Salvador, Guatemala, Honduras, Nicaragua, and the Dominican Republic under the form of a Central American Free

Table 16-2. The world's largest market in 2010 (1998 US$; purchasing power parity)

MARKETS	(1) POPULA-TION (MILLIONS; (2010)	(2) GNP MEASU-RED AT PPP/ COUN-TRY IN $ BILLIONS; (1998)	(3) GNP ANNUAL GROWTH (% 1998-2010; VS. 1990-1998)	(4) GNP MEA-SURED AT PPP/ COUNTRY IN $ BIL-LIONS (2010)	(5) MARKET\ SHARE (2010, %; VS. 1998)
NAFTA	444	$9,000	3.0% (2.5%)	$12,800	23% (26%)
European Union	519	$8,000	2.5% (1.6%)	$10,700	19% (22%)
China (Scenario A)	1,335	$4,000	6.3% (11.1%)	$8,300	17% (11%)
Japan	125	$2,900	1% (1.1%)	$3,300	6% (8%)
Rest of World (187 countries)	4,265	$12,100	3.7% (3.3%)	$18,700	35% (33%)
World (210 countries)	6,688	$36,500	3.3% (2.4%)	$53,800	100%

Source: columns 1, 2, 3 adapted from: Global Economic Prospects and the Developing Countries, Washington, DC: The World Bank, 1997, p. 92., and Entering the 21st Century, World Development Report 1999/2000, Washington, DC: The World Bank, 1999, p. 250, and other computations by the authors. Figures are in 1998 dollars. (Targowski & Korth, 2003).

Trade Agreement—DR/CAFTA—which was created in 2004. However, if the United States persists in excluding the rest of Latin America from the benefits of participation in regional trade blocs, the region will turn elsewhere in its own self-interest.

Mexico has already signed a free-trade agreement with the EU. And MERCOSUR, the free-trade area of the "southern cone" of South America, has accepted a European Union invitation to explore a free-trade area. Despite the opposition in Congress, the U.S. has signed a protocol and is giving at least verbal support to the creation of a Free-Trade Area of the Americas (FTAA). The FTAA would clearly be dominated by the massive U.S. economy, with its moderate rate of economic growth. Nevertheless, a growth rate of 4% per year for the entire group would be plausible and conservative:

(1) Experience has shown that the opening up of regulated markets leads to accelerated economic growth. Integration would likely stimulate much more rapid economic growth among the Latin members, such as has already been seen in Chile and Mexico in recent years.

(2) Most of Latin America would be rebounding from very slow recent growth.

(3) The principal reason why such countries as Japan, Korea, China and Chile have been

Table 16-3. The world's largest market in 2020 (purchasing power parity; 1998 U.S.$)

MARKETS	(1) POPULATION IN MILLIONS (2020)	(2) GNP MEASURED AT PPP/ COUNTRY IN $ BILLIONS (2010)	(3) GNP ANNUAL GROWTH (2010-25)	(4) GNP MEASURED AT PPP/ COUNT-RY ($ BILLIONS; 2020)	(5) MARKET SHARE (2020 VS. 2010)
FTAA -NAFTA -15 others	1,004	$16,500 $12,800 $ 3,700	4.0%	$24,400	32% (23%)
Europe -EU 18 -10 others	519	$11,300 $10,700 $600	2.0%	$13,800	18% (19%)
China (Scenario A)	1,413	$8,300	3.5%	$11,700	16% (17%)
Japan	124	$3,300	1.4%	$3,800	5% (6%)
Rest of World (162 countries)	4,543	$14,300	3.9%	$21,000	29% (35%)
World (210 countries)	7,600	$53,800	3.3%	$74,700	100%

Sources: the population: The Wall Street Journal Almanac (1998, pp. 501-503), Column 2: Table 16-2.
(Targowski & Korth, 2003).

able to grow at such high rates is that they are playing catch-up—rapidly absorbing the technology and techniques of the industrialized countries.

(4) There is likely to continue to be a very significant inflow of foreign direct investment, such as has been seen in telecommunications. Of course, this projection assumes that the U.S. economy will return to a dynamic period of growth after the post-2000 world recession. Under such stimuli, a growth rate of 4% is very feasible.

• The European Union embraced most European states in 2007. However, the expansion of the EU is likely to be more awkward and less economically dynamic than that in Latin America. The current members are older and wealthier and, very significantly, most of the new members are weighed down by the legacy of communism. The process of integrating them into the style of the Western-West democratic capitalist societies will encounter problems, similar to the problems of integrating East Germany with West Germany. Therefore, an economic growth rate of 2% annually may be all the region can realistically expect.

• Perhaps Japan's economy will enter a phase of very modest recovery. However, even an optimistic projection sees Japan growing at no more than 1.5% annually after 2010. As was seen above, some very responsible Japanese estimates place the growth much lower than that. Even the Japanese government's Ministry of International Trade and Industry (MITI) estimates the maximum potential economic growth through 2010 to be no more than 1.8% and only 0.8% thereafter (Hartcher, 1998).

- China's economy is not likely to grow at the rate of more than 3.5% annually, even under the most favorable scenario in the 2010-2020 decade, due to over-exploitation of extensive reserves in the previous periods.
- The rest of the world will grow faster than in the first decade of the new century. Due to the expansions of NAFTA and the EU, as many as 40-50 countries will join either FTAA or the EU. The remaining 140-150 countries will be heavily stimulated by the four larger markets. There will also be benefits as more and more of these countries open their economies to world markets and capitalism. Therefore, economic growth of close to 4% per year is reasonable. And there are some potentially very strong countries in that group: in addition to the "tigers and dragons," India, South Africa, Australia and the oil producers. All have favorable potential. India may very well compete with China as the most dynamic of all of the major developing countries. Also, the possible success of other integrated regional markets, such as ASEAN or any group involving India, should be considered.

During 2010-2020, the anticipated dynamics of world markets suggest that FTAA's share should increase from NAFTA's 23% in 2010 to 32% in 2020. FTAA would be the largest market on the planet. Despite the slowdown of the Chinese economy and the enlargement of the EU, China will close the gap between the two. The Japanese economy will continue to lose market share. The rest of the world, despite solid growth, will also yield market share due to the loss of about 25 countries to either FTAA or the expanded EU.

The projection of China's advance into the second position depends upon a continuation of *authoritarian capitalism* after 2010. If not, then China's economy will likely decline, due to new uncertainty.

BEYOND 2020: THE TRIUMPH OF GLOBALIZATION

It has been said that "economics controls politics." The successful integration of the rapidly-growing American market and simultaneous slow growth of the European market may lead toward the further integration of the all components of Western civilization (Western-West, Western-Central, Western-Latin, and Western-Jewish). As a result, the Americas may integrate with Europe into the *FTA* of *the Atlantic* (FTAAT), with at least fifty Western civilization countries forming the world's largest market.

Several factors will propel Europeans in that direction. Both areas already trade much more with each other than with Asia. Furthermore, Great Britain trades twice as much with NAFTA as it does with its EU partners and would prefer to have its own currency and political identity as a member of FTAAT rather than become a member of a political union (Black, 1999). Also, Italy and Central Europe have strong ethnic ties with the United States as a result of massive migration from Europe to the U.S. These are only some of the influences that may lead to the emergence of FTAAT Targowski & Korth, 2003).

FTAAT could have half of the world's market and 1.5 billion consumers – more than in China. Table 16-4 illustrates this new division of the world market. Assuming a continuation of the *authoritarian capitalism* scenario for China, the most optimistic scenario, by 2020 China will ap-

Table 16-4. The world market after the integration of the western economies 2020+ (1998 U.S.$)

MARKET	(1) POPULATION MILLIONS (2020)	(2) GNP MEASURED AT PPP/ COUNTRY BILLIONS (2020)	(3) MARKET SHARE In % (2020+)	(4) GNP MEASURED AT PPP/CAPITA (2020+)
FTAAT (FTAA + Europe)	1,523	$38,200	51%	$25,000
China	1,413	$11,700	16%	$8,200
Japan	124	$3,800	5%	$30,600
Rest of World	4,543	$21,000	29%	$4,600
Total	7,600	$74,700	100%	$9,800

Source: Targowski and Korth (2003)

proach a GNP level of $10,000 per capita. It will be another of China's "Great Leaps"; within 22 years its citizens' GNP per capita will have almost tripled. However, by 2020, China may be at its economic peak. Figure 16-8 illustrates the shares of the world marketplace by major civilizations (Targowski & Korth, 2003).

THE MYTHS AND THE REALITIES OF THE WORLD MARKET

There is no question that NAFTA will be the world's largest market in 2010. And FTAA, if it develops as suggested here, will have the same position in 2020. If a free-trade area of the Atlantic evolved, it would emphasize this trend even further. Indeed, beyond 2020, FTAAT would even have the most consumers.

China will not be the largest economy, as many predicted at the end of 20th century. It is very possible that after 2020 or even earlier, China will enter a period of chaos, either pursuing

military expansion or transforming to *democratic capitalism.*

Japan will remain among the richest countries in the world but its economy will grow slowly while its population not only ages but shrinks.

The globalization strategy will be better accepted in 2010-2020 and beyond, since it works very well for poor economies. Emotional attacks upon the World Trade Organization, the International Monetary Fund and the World Bank cannot obscure the fact that freer trade raises standards of living. And it is the poorest countries that have the most to gain from freer trade! The strong economies have no choice but to seek more markets for their high-performing economic engines. The wealthier countries will continue to grow, but the developing countries will have the opportunity to grow much faster as they adopt the economic model of the industrialized world. Not only China but Japan, Turkey, Chile, the Asian tigers and others have shown how poor countries can develop at rates far beyond what the traditional industrial countries were ever able

Figure 16-8. The integration of civilization markets

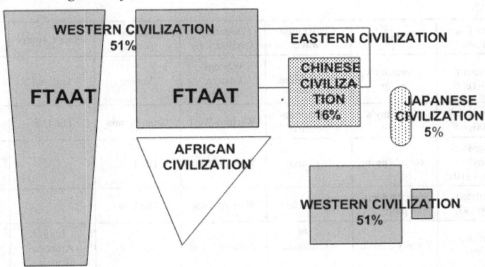

to accomplish. It is a long-term positive outlook which offers hope to the world's masses.

The world market in 2020 will not be saturated. The 162 countries comprising the "rest of the world" will be markets for FTAA and FTAAT, China, and Japan. The economic prospects for the world look good. In the next 20 years, the world economy will grow 100% and GNP per capita will also grow rapidly, especially in the developing countries.

However, there are potential "flies in the ointment." These predictions assume a world without major wars (either between countries or between ideologies) or economic disasters. But strong economic performance, coupled with continued increase in the world population (an increase of 1.7 billion—almost 30%!), will cause continued deterioration of the environment. And the development of the global economy will pass through crises such as the one experienced in East Asia in the late 1990s, or even worse.

The proliferation of Internet access will open intriguing scenarios. On the one hand, windows of opportunity will be offered for developing markets (e.g., India and Brazil already have booming software-development industries). Also, ready access to the communication and information opportunities provided by the Internet may help stimulate education, improve health, and encourage entrepreneurs—thereby improving living standards and stimulating the economies. On the other hand, the dissemination of information, together with the ready access to free worldwide communication, can abet terrorist groups such as al Qaeda. Also, as widespread cyber-attacks have shown, the Internet is open to abuse—from anywhere in the world (Targowski & Korth, 2003).

THE CIVILIZATIONAL PATTERNS OF ECONOMIC DEVELOPMENT

Civilization has developed so quickly and impressively in the last 500 years because it was guided by the ideology of *capitalism*. The first 5,500 years of civilization's history had very slow progress, but an acceleration took place in the following

Table 16-5. Characteristics of kinds of capitalism in 1500-2000+

Kind of Capitalism	Purpose	Civilization Wave	Dominant Civilizations	Pioneer Country	Other Country	Other
Merchant 1500-1800	Merchant's profit	Agricultural	Western, Eastern, Islamic	Venice	Holland	
Commercial 1600s+	Company's profit	Agricultural Industrial	Western-West	Great Britain	The U.S.	
Robber Barons' 1840s-1910s	Baron's profit	Industrial	Western-West	The U.S.		
Regulated 1910s-1933	Stake Holders' profit	Industrial	Western-West	The U.S.		
Family 1900s+	Family's profit	Agriculture	Western-Latin	Mexico	Latin America Russia	
Managed 1933-1943	Individual's income	Industrial	Western-West	The U.S.	Germany	
Social 1945-1990s	Business' Profit and Labor's Better off	Industrial Information	Western-West	The U.S		Post-war Western Europe
State 1917-1991	State's gain	Agricultural Industrial	Eastern Chinese Western-Central	Soviet Union China	North Korea	
Crony 1989+	Politicians' and Tycoons' profit	Industrial Information	Western-Central	Poland	Russia	Transformation from state to liberal capita-lism
Authorita-rian 1991+	Business-men's profit	Industrial Information	Eastern, Chinese	China Russia	Singapore	
Managerial 1990s+	CEOs' Profit, No Social Consider-ations	Industrial Information	Western-West	The U.S.		
Global 1900s+	Investors' & CEOs' profit	Industrial Information	Western-West	The U.S.	UK Germany Sweden	
Super 2000+	Capitalism wins over democracy	Industrial Information	Western-West	The U.S.		More concern for efficiency than equity

500 years, when clever individuals learned how to profit from production, commerce, and trade. But first of all, they had to develop certain kinds of economic activities, and it took some time.

Table 16-5 indicates that one can recognize at least 13 kinds of capitalism. Two kinds are now extinct, "Robber Barons'" and Crony. But the other 11 kinds played or still play a strong role in economic development. Even State Capitalism (centrally planned), which was ineffective in practice, provided a sort of laboratory experiment, albeit one that if possible should be avoided. The latter's 74 years of experimentation are like a minute in human civilization's history.

Social Capitalism (1945-90) was developed in the West during the Cold War in response to the "workers"-oriented economy in the Soviet Block. Social capitalism divides the concept of economy into two tiers: A participatory group of society working functionally in an upper economy (tier one) and an underlying economy of dependent poor communities and criminal elements (tier two). Tier one generally comprises upper and middle classes while tier two represents many low-wage workers, impoverished persons, mentally ill individuals, and criminals. Social capitalism posits that providing tier two with the means to participate in the market would discourage tier two from completely dropping out of the system, hence, causing major disruptions to the market. A larger and more inclusive market is a more efficient and more stable market. Social capitalism practiced is capitalism with a social conscience. The positive messages sent from a business will only increase profits as consumers and investors see the actions and take it into account when purchasing goods from the company. One of the greatest achievements of the twentieth century was a social contract that provided far more economic security and prosperity for working Americans than had existed in any previous period.

Managerial Capitalism (1990s+) is characterized as an enormous transfer of wealth from public investors to the hands of CEOs regardless of their performance. (In fact, it could be argued that in many cases, payouts are inverse to success since many have been occasioned by the firing of the recipients.) Some critics contend that managers have received a disproportionate share of the fruits of corporate success, leaving too little for workers or owners (Bogle, 2005). The "golden parachutes" given to top management reveal that America's business leaders can pursue their own personal goals through the securities markets, designed for *owners' capitalism*. Managerial capitalism replaced "relationships" among people by faceless "transactions" with management. These transactions are intensified by automation (bar code readers, unmanned customer service, etc.), which in addition eliminates routine human skills. Inequality in society increases in managerial capitalism. The winner-takes-all strategy lowers or even eliminates institutional loyalty, diminishes informal trust among workers, and weakens institutional knowledge, which are the key attributes of social capital. In such a manner, the social has been diminished; capitalism remains (Sennett, 2006). The permanent quest for better performance of capitalism increases the application of technology, which needs rather new skills than old ones. The "old" veteran workers were formerly a key source of competency; vice versa, many view these individuals as the obstacle to it. This new kind of economy based on managerial capitalism operates "flexible" (programmed) production/service, which has tremendous personal consequences of work. Eventually, it leads to the corrosion of character because it triggers the loss of anchorage and self-understanding of the employee (Sennett, 1998).

Global Capitalism (1990s+) In the past decade, globalization—meaning the rise of market capitalism around the world—has undeniably contributed to America's new economy boom. It has created millions of jobs from Malaysia to Mexico and a cornucopia of affordable goods for Western consumers. It has brought phone service to some 300 million households in developing nations and a transfer of nearly $2 trillion from rich countries to poor through equity, bond investments, and commercial loans. It has helped to topple dictators by making information available in once sheltered societies. The Internet is now poised to narrow the gulf that separates rich nations from the poor even further in the decade to come (Business Week, 2000). Globalization has brought huge overall benefits, but earnings for most U.S. workers—even those with college

Figure 16-9. A tree of capitalism's evolution as the driving force of civililzational dynamics

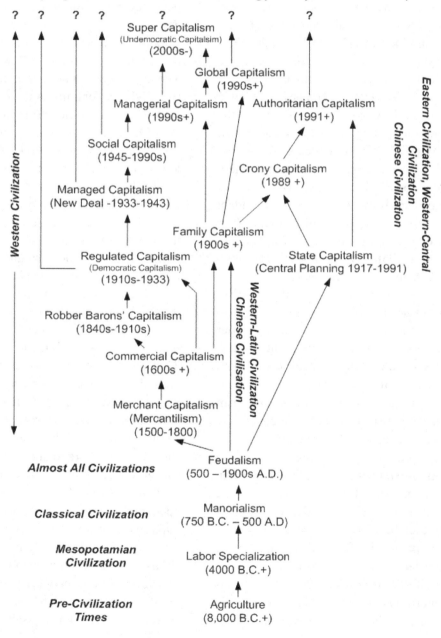

degrees—have been falling recently; inequality is greater now than at any other time in the last 70 years. Whatever the cause, the result has been a surge in protectionism. According to Scheve and Slaughter (2007), to save globalization, policy-makers must spread its gains more widely. The best way to do this is by redistributing income. Instead of implementing that kind of policy, the beneficiaries of *global capitalism* are converting it to *super capitalism.*

The newer concept of super capitalism (particularly in the U.S.) is emerging from managerial and global capitalisms and is intervening into every facet of democracy, exemplified by the dominance of corporate lobbyists, lawyers, and public relations professionals over the entire political process, pouring in the corporate money that engulfs the system on a day-to-day basis, making it almost impossible for citizens' voices to be heard (Reich, 2007, p. 211).

The tree of capitalism's idea evolution is presented in Figure 16-9. It shows relationships among those 13 kinds of capitalism and, most importantly, it allows thinking about the future of capitalism.

If capitalism was driving the economic development of civilization in the last 500 years, can it drive civilization forever? It proved to be very effective in creating a rising standard of living, but not necessarily in increasing human happiness. In fact, it can be a source of human unhappiness, particularly for the weak and the people unprotected by resources.

According to Maddison (2001), world economic performance was very much better in the second millennium of our era than in the first. Between 1000 and 1998, the world population rose 22-fold and per capita income 13-fold. In the previous millennium, the population rose by a sixth and per capita GDP fell slightly. The sec-

Table 16-6. World population (millions) and rates of growth (0-3000 A.D.)

	0	1000	Growth Rate 0-1000	2000	Growth Rate 1000-2000	3000 Projec-tion	Assumed Growth Rate 2000-3000	Economic System for 2000-3000
World	231	268	1.16	6,000	22	8,000	1.3	Ecologism (Self-sustainable Economy)
World						12,000	2	Authoritarian Capitalism
World						18,000	3	?
World						30,000	5	?
World						60,000	10	?
World						132,000	22	Unregulated Capitalism
World						180,000	30	Unregulated Capitalism

Source: For years of 0-2000 based on Maddison (2001), p. 241. Years beyond 2000, projected by the Author.

Figure 16-10. The power of modern capitalism

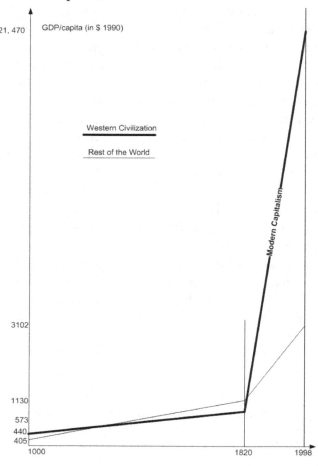

ond millennium comprised two distinct periods. From 1000 to 1820, the upward movement in per capita was slow; for the world as a whole the rise was about 50%. Growth was largely "extensive" in character. Most of it went to accommodate a four-fold increase in population. Since 1820 (the Industrial Revolution), world development has been much more dynamic and more "intensive." Per capita income rose faster than the population. By 1998, it was 8.5 times as high as in 1820 and the population rose 5.6-fold. However, if one looks at the Western civilization (Western Europe, USA, Canada, Australia and New Zealand) and Japan, their average per capita income grew nearly four times as fast as the average of the rest of the world. The differential continued between 1820 (the In-

dustrial Wave) and 1998 (the Information Wave) when per capita income of the first group rose 19-fold and 5.4- fold for the second. This means that *commercial capitalism* and *Robber Baron's capitalism,* as well as *regulated capitalism* and *social capitalism,* partially even *managerial capitalism* or in general *modern capitalism,* has been very effective (Figure 16-10).

Every kind of capitalism acted or acts within given civilizational constraints, and is rather more focused than it is universal. Perhaps two of its kinds; *regulated, social* and *global,* can be considered as universal. However, at this moment (2008) *global and super capitalisms* need to be regulated; otherwise, it will be rejected by a mood of *protectionism* among people who cannot share globalization's gains.

What kinds of regulations are needed to protect civilization's population in the third millennium? As table 16-6 illustrates, in the first millennium, when *capitalism* was absent, the population growth was almost stagnant (there are some exception of course such as China). In the second millennium, when *capitalism* was active, the population grew 22-fold.

If *capitalism* continues its spectacular performance, the world's population in the third millennium may reach anywhere between 8 and 180 billion people. However, the former level will probably be reached in the middle of the 21st century. Other projected population levels by the end of the current millennium would have inconceivable effects. For example, if the rate growth of the second millennium remains the same in the third millennium, then the population will reach 132 billion. But due to "progress," if this rate is even bigger in the present millennium than in the last one, the world's population will be 180 billion. As is analyzed in Chapter XVII, the ecosystem can support only 8 to 9 billion people. This means that current kinds of *capitalism* must be rejected if we think to continue humanity's confinement to Earth, a small planet with limited strategic resources. Only a new economic system—*ecologism* can support a *self-sustainable economy*, which would be possible if the world's population increases only 1.3-fold by the end of the third millennium, we *must* return to the *pre-capitalistic* period of civilization!

The presented characteristics and evolution of *capitalism* allow for the following observations:

1. The present kinds of *capitalism* are not optimal to protect civilization's population, which will grow in the third millennium beyond Earth's supply of strategic resources (see Chapter XVII).

2. Perhaps *global and super capitalisms* should be re-oriented into *authoritarian capitalism*, which will control the optimal distribution of strategic resources among population, still in religion-oriented civilizations. At the current level of agreement among world populations, this solution looks like utopia. Also, *authoritarian capitalism* has a tendency to become *crony capitalism*, since people in power abuse it for personal benefits. Furthermore, with the exceptions of the Chinese, Buddhist civilizations, other cultures reject *authoritarian* control of society.

3. The future of civilization is in the following implemented solutions:

a. Birth control accepted by religions and people

b. Strategic resources replaced by man-made ones

c. Universal-complementary civilization is implemented (Chapter VII)

d. Other planets are searched for possible colonization and supply of strategic resources. (However, it is unlikely we will use other planets for this; they have gravity wells, which make exports prohibitively expensive. More likely we would use ships with hydrogen-oxygen engines, powered by water from the carbonaceous chondrite asteroids, to mine the metallic asteroids in the belt. They are closer and have no gravity wells to speak of. Even then, the initial investment in such a project would be staggering).

Can these strategies be implemented? They should, but it will not happen soon or perhaps even ever. This would mean that the future of civilization is in wars, epidemic attacks, and catastrophes, which will "automatically" control the world's population into small growth or even expected decline. Should this statement not be written and published, because is too pessimistic? But the scientific approach cannot be based on optimism or pessimism, only on the truth.

CONCLUSION

The coming generation will be a period of great change—political as well as economic. The evolution toward multi-country economic integration will continue—especially in the Atlantic region. Today's economic powers will continue to dominate the coming years. China may well become the world's largest individual economy. However, the United States, which is very likely to integrate with larger groups of countries into a massive free-trade area, will continue to be the dominant world economic force.

As China's wealth grows, it will become a more diverse economy. It will eventually become the massive consumer market of which western marketers have long dreamed. Its entry into the World Trade Organization and advancement up the economic-development scale will greatly increase its role in international trade and investment. As this development progresses, China will also become an important competitor in world markets to NAFTA, Europe, and Japan. The present China is more complementary to these markets than competitive; its success is primarily that of a supplier. However, it is already learning rapidly and advancing technologically. More and more, it is copying modern products and methods. In coming years, as Japan did so successfully before it, China will begin innovating. Then civilization relationship will be competitive rather than complementary.

China will evolve into an industrial power. Its economic strength will give it the potential for much greater political influence in the world. But the extent to which these developments occur will depend upon whether China will apply *authoritarian* or *democratic capitalism*. In any event, China will continue to grow as an economic force. In coming years, it will likely develop very strong heavy industries and strong automotive and electronic industries. Given its size, its impact may be much greater than was even Japan's in its heyday.

The future of *capitalism* depends on how humans will "slow down" its performance, which supports a too-fast population growth, which exceeds the ecosystem's capacity. A new economic system is needed—*ecologism*—which would control a *self-sustainable economy*. In order to develop and implement this system, humans must be more knowledgeable, socially wise and skillful in applying information technology, which offers many optimalization-providing solutions.

A. Further Research Directions

- Investigate how civilizations in the 21st century impact international relations.
- Investigate how civilizations in the 21st century impact foreign trade and the integration of markets under the form of free-trade zones.
- Investigate rules and laws of intra- and inter-civilization political and commercial relations.

B. Research Opportunities

- The research opportunity is in applying a civilization concept in analyzing foreign political and commercial relations and predicting their potential for success or failure.

C. Additional Ideas

- The tendency of world politics for "integrational" movements in the 21st century goes beyond the boundaries of regions and nations. A new tendency is to protect "borders of a civilization" within a region, city, or nation. It evolves from so-called ethnic communities and has a global reach. It develops new kinds of loyalty and patterns of behavior.

D. Rationale

- Mass production of goods and profits requires a strategy of permanent growth. Nowadays, a real global economic growth of 3% a year sets the global economy at the level of $45 trillion in 2005 (World Bank, 2007, p. 16). If this pace is sustained, the economy will reach $75 trillion in 2030. This vast expansion of output will have major consequences for production and consumption, particularly of food, water, and energy, and will stress the environment even more drastically. As a result of the growth strategy, businesses need larger markets, going beyond national boundaries. Therefore, such alliances of so-called free-trade zones, large-scale complexes like NAFTA, or CAFTA, and the EU have been created in the second part of the 20th century. At the beginning of the 21st century, there are 26 FTAs and five more are planned (Inter-American, Inter-Atlantic-TAFTA, Inter-Asian, and others). If one looks more carefully at these zones, they look like the civilization criterion (a civilization as a competitive unit) is integrating their members. Therefore, the nation criterion, which has been working since the French Revolution, is being replaced in the 21st century by the civilization criterion. It is important to be aware of this and be prepared for inter-civilization trade principles and tendencies.

E. Additional Reading

Anderson, K., & Martin, W. (Eds.). (2006). *Agricultural trade reform and the Doha development agenda.* Washington, D.C.: Palgrave Macmillan and the World Bank.

Baird, A., & Valentine, V. (2006). Port privatization in the United Kingdom. *China Development Zones.* Retrieved January 17, 2006, from http://www.cadz.org.cn/en/kfq/hidz.asp.

Bhargava, V. (2006). *Global issues for global citizens: An introduction to key development challenges.* Washington, D.C.: World Bank.

Blinder, A. (2006). Off-shoring: The next industrial revolution?. *Foreign Affairs, 85*(2), 113-128.

Croxton, K., Garcia-Dastogue, S., Lambert, D., & Rogens, D. (2001). The supply chain management processes, the organizational concepts. *The International Journal of Logistics Management, 12*(2), 14.

Dervis, K. (2005). *A better globalization: Legitimacy, governance and reform.* Washington, D.C.: Center for Global Development.

Dimaran, B., Ianchovichina, E., & Martin, W. (2006). Competing with giants: Who wins, who loses?. In: A. Winters, & S. Yusuf (Eds.), *Dancing with giants: China, India, and the global economy.* Washington, D.C. and Singapore: World Bank.

Farell, D. (2004, July 4). How Germany can win from off-shoring. *The McKinsey Quarterly.*

Friedman, M. (1997). The case for free trade. *Hoover Digest, Fall,* 4.

Friedman, T. (2005). *The world is flat: A brief history of the 21st century.* New York: Farrar, Straus and Giroux.

Fuller, D., & Geide-Stevenson, D. (2003). Consensus among economists: revisited. *Journal of Economic Review, 34*(4), 369-387.

Lewison, M. (2006). *The box: How the shipping container made the world smaller and the world economy bigger.* Princeton, NJ: Princeton University Press.

Kusago, T., & Tzannatos, Z. (1998). *Export processing zones: A review in need of an update.* SP Discussion Paper No. 9802. The World Bank.

Maddison, A. (2001). *The world economy: A millennial perspective.* Paris: Development Centre Studies, OECD.

Mishkin, F. (2006). *The next great civilization.* Princeton, NJ: Princeton University Press.

Norman, J., & Shen, L. (2005). *Trade, Doha, and development: A window into the issues.* Washington, D.C.: World Bank.

Stiglitz, J. (2007). *Making globalization work.* New York: Norton.

UNCTAD. (2004). The shift toward services. *World Investment Report 2004* (pp. 169-174).

Wade, N. (2006). *Before the dawn: Recovering the lost history of our ancestors.* New York: Penguin.

WEPZA. (1997). *International directory of export processing zones and free trade zones.* Arizona: Flagstaff Institute.

Whaples, R. (2006). Do economists agree on anything? Yes. *The Economists' Voice, 3*(9), 1.

World Bank. (2007). *Global economic prospects.* Washington, D.C.: World Bank.

WTO. (2004). International trade statistics, Geneva: WTO. Retrieved January 17, 2006, from http://www.wto.org/english/res_e/statis_e/its2004_e/its2004_e.pdf.

REFERENCES

ACCRA. (2004). *How is off-shoring impacting the American economy?.* Retrieved January 22, 2005, from http://www.accra.org/newsletter/off-shoring.htm.

AFL-CIO. (2007). Retrieved November 20, 2007, from http://www.aflcio.org/issues/jobseconomy/exportingamerica/).

Asian Development Bank. (1997). *Asian development outlook, 1996 and 1997.* New York: Oxford University Press.

Atkinson, R. (2004). *Understanding the off-shoring challenge.* Retrieved January 22, 2005, from http://www.accra.org/newsletter/PPIoff-shoring.pdf.

Black, C. (1999). Britain's Atlantic option. *The National Interest, Spring*(55), 15-24.

Bogle, J. (2005). *The battle for the soul of capitalism.* New Haven, CT: Yale University Press.

Bramall, C. (2000). *Sources of Chinese economic growth, 1978-1996.* New York: Oxford University Press.

Brodsgaard, K., Strand, E., & Strand, D. (1998). *Reconstructing twentieth-century China. State control, civil society, and national identity.* New York: Oxford University Press.

Buchanan, P. (1998). *The great betrayal.* Boston, MA: Little, Brown and Company.

Buchanan, P. (2006). *State of reckoning.* New York: Thomas Dunne Books.

Buchanan, P. (2007). *Day of emergency.* New York: Thomas Dunne Books.

Brzezinski, Z. (2004). *The choice, global domination or global leadership.* New York: Basic Books.

Clover, C. (1999). Dreams of the Eurasian heartland. *Foreign Affairs, 78*(2), 9-13.

Collier, P. (2007). *The bottom billion.* New York: Oxford University Press.

Colvin, G. (2004, December 13). Think your job can't be sent to India? Just watch. *Fortune, 150,* 80.

Dickson, B. (1997). Unsettled succession. *The National Interest, 49,* 64-72.

_____ (1998). *Democratization in China and Taiwan.* New York: Oxford University Press.

Dobbs, L. (2007). *War on middle class.* New York: Penguin Books.

Edmonds, R. (2000). *The People's Republic of China after 50 years.* New York: Oxford University Press.

Faux, J. (2006). *The global class war.* New York: John Wiley & Sons, Inc.

Finance and Economics. (1999). China's private surprise. *The Economist, 8124,* 69-70.

Foy, C., & Maddison, A. (1999). China: A world economic leader? *OECD Observer, 215,* 39-42.

Frank, A. (1998). *Global economy in the Asian Age.* Berkeley, CA: University of California Press.

Friedman, T. (2005). *The world is flat.* New York: Farrar, Straus, and Giroux.

Gilboy, G., & Heginbotham, E. (2001). China's coming transformation. *Foreign Affairs, 80*(4), 2639.

Gilley, B. (1998). *Tiger on the brink: Jiang Zemin and China's new elite.* Berkeley, CA: University of California Press.

Gladstone, J. (1995). The coming Chinese collapse. *Foreign Policy, 99,* 35-53.

Gore, L. (1999). *Market communism: The institutional foundation of China's post-Mao hypergrowth.* New York: Oxford University Press.

Hartcher, P. (1998). Can Japan come back?. *The National Interest, Winter*(54), 32-39.

Hay, D., Morris, G., & Liu, S. (1994). *Economic reform and state-owned enterprises in China, 1979-87.* New York: Oxford University Press.

Henderson, C. (1999). *China on the brink.* New York: McGraw-Hill.

Hines, A. (1997). The coming Chinese century: Big, rich, and a force to be reckoned with. *The Futurist, 31*(5), 8-9.

Hughes, N. (2002). *China's economic challenge: Smashing the iron rice bowl.* Armonk, NY: M. E. Sharpe

Hutchings, G. (2001). *Modern China: A guide to a century of change.* Cambridge, MA: Harvard University Press.

Jue, F. (1998). A program for democratic reform. *Journal of Democracy, 9*(4), 9-19.

Kwan, D. (1999, April 15). Students wanted democracy, says Zhu. *South China Morning Post.*

Kueh, Y., Chai, J., & Fau, G. (1999). *Industrial reform and macroeconomic instability in China.* New York: Oxford University Press.

Lardy, N. (2002*). Integrating China into the global economy.* Washington, D.C.: Brookings Institute Press.

Leakey, R. (1996). *The origin of humankind.* New York: HarperCollins Publishers.

Lilley, J., & Ford, C. (1999). China's military: A second opinion. *The National Interest, 57,* 71-77.

Lin, Z., & Robinson, T. (1994). *The Chinese and their future. Beijing, Taipei and Hong Kong.* Washington, D.C.: The American Enterprise Institute Press.

Linge, G. (1998). *China's new spatial economy, heading towards 2020.* New York: Oxford University Press.

Mazzar, M. (1999). *Global trends 2005: An owner's manual for the next decade.* New York: St. Martin's Press.

Moore, T. (2002). *China in the world market: Chinese industry and international sources of reform in the post-Mao era.* New York: Cambridge University Press.

Moser, J., & Zee, W. (Eds.). (1999). *China tax guide.* Hong Kong: Oxford University Press.

Nathan, J., & Gilley, B. (2002). China's new rulers: What they want. *New York Review of Books, 49*(15), 28.

Nolan, P. (2001). *China and the global economy: National champions, industrial policy, and the big business revolution.* New York: Palgrave Macmillan.

Pei, M. (2002). China's governance crisis. *Foreign Affairs, 81*(5), 96.

Pomerantz, K. (2001). *The great divergence: China, Europe, and the making of the modern world economy.* Princeton, NJ: Princeton University Press.

Przeworski, A. (1991). *Democracy and the market: Political and economic reform in Eastern Europe and Latin America.* New York: Cambridge University Press.

Quigley, C. (1979). *The evolution of civilizations.* Indianapolis, IN: Liberty Fund.

Reich, R. (2007). *Supercapitalism. The transformation of business, democracy, and everyday life.* New York: Alfred A. Knopf.

Robinson, T. (1994). *Post-Cold War security in the Asia-Pacific region.* In: Z. Lin, & T. Robinson (Eds.), *The Chinese and their future. Beijing, Taipei and Hong Kong* (pp. 386-417). Washington, D.C.: The AEI Press.

Saul, J. (2005). *The collapse of globalism.* New York: The Overlook Press.

Scheve, K., & Slaugther, M. (2007). A new deal for globalization. *Foreign Affairs, 86*(4), 34-48. Segal, G. (1999). The China question, does it matter? *Current, 417,* 19.

Sennett, R. (1998). *The corrosion of character.* New York: W. W. Norton & Company.

Sennett, R. (2006). *The culture of the new capitalism.* New Haven, CT: Yale University Press.

Shambaugh, D. (2001). Facing reality in China policy. *Foreign Affairs, 80*(1), 50-64.

Shaw, V. (1996). *Social control in China.* Westport, CT: Praeger.

Sheff, D. (2002). *China down: The story of a technology and business revolution.* New York: HarperBusiness.

Soros, G. (2006). *The age of fallibility.* New York: PublicAffairs.

Stanley Foundation. (1993). An Asian colossus awakens. *World Press Review, 40*(4), 14-16.

Stiglitz, J. (2007). *Making globalization work.* New York: W. W. Norton & Company.

Studewell, J. (2002). *The Chinese dream: The quest for the last great market on earth.* New York: Atlantic Monthly Press.

Targowski, A., & Korth, C. (2003). China or NAFTA: The world's largest market in the 21st century?. *Advances in Competitiveness Research, 11*(1), 87-115.

Walder, A. (1996). *China's transitional economy.* New York: Oxford University Press.

Wong, R. (2000). *China transformed: Historical change and limits of European Experience.* Ithaca, NY: Cornell University Press.

Wong, Y., Maher, T., Jenner, R., Appel, A., &.Herbert, L. (1999). Are joint ventures losing their appeal in China?. *SAM Advanced Management Journal, 64*(1), 4-12.

Woodside, A., & Pitts, R. (1996). *Creating and managing international joint ventures.* Westport, CT: Quorum Books.

World Bank. (1999). *Entering the 21st century, world development report 1999/2000.* Washington, D.C.: World Bank.

World Bank. (2007). *World development indicators.* Washington, D.C.: World Bank.

Yao, C. (1998). *Stock market and futures market in the people's republic of China.* New York: Oxford University Press.

Zweig, D. (1999). Undemocratic capitalism. *The National Interest, Summer*(56), 63-72.

Section V
The Future of Civilization

Chapter XVII
The Future of Civilization

INTRODUCTION

The purpose of this chapter is the investigation whether human civilization has much of a future on the Earth. This investigation is partially based upon research by members of the Polish Academy of Arts and Sciences (Krakow), conducted in 1998-2002.

The discoveries and applications of technology which led to our civilization are impressive. Archaeology and history teach us about it. However, in the Age of information-communication technology, it is apparent that technology may no longer merely support civilization but conquer it. In the past, civilization's progress was slow. Centuries elapsed with no events meaningful to modern questions. Nowadays, civilization faces an impact from technology so tremendous as to disturb the fragile equilibrium between humans and the ecosystem.

This raises many questions in respect of the future of civilization and its ability to survive despite many threats. Therefore, it is worthy to reflect on its future and duration. Can or even must it vanish due to the inevitable end of the solar system?

In the short run, let us look at current problems of civilization, a very complex system composed of three components (Figure 17-1):

- Human entities
- Culture
- Infrastructure

The development of human civilization, as defined in this study[1], has been proceeding as long as humans have lived in organized societies in favorable environments. According to accepted estimates, hominids began to live in the Earth about 6-5 million years ago. The development of more skillful mankind began about 200,000-150,000 years ago, when modern man, *Homo sapiens*, was living in South-Eastern Africa[2]. From this location, *Homo sapiens* began to move to: South-Western Asia (50,000 years ago), Australia (50,000), Europe (40,000), New Guinea (40,000), Siberia (25,000), and North America (12,000) (Burenhult, 2003a). Modern men began to be more social first as hunter-gatherers, then when the Ice Age ended (-10,000) as farmers and town-dwellers (-9,000). Recorded historic civilization is about 6,000 years old (Burenhult, 2003b) and is associated with the rise of Mesopotamian civilization (includes Sumerian and Semitic people) (4,000 B.C.), followed by Egyptian (3,100 B.C.), Indus (2,500 B.C.), and Sinic (1,500 B.C.), and so forth.

At the beginning of the 21st century, humans (applying electronic information-communication tools based on unlimited memories and on

Figure 17-1. Civilization system

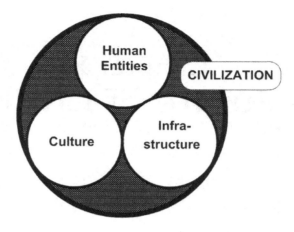

friendly graphic user interfaces that require huge memories and processing speed) improve their symbols processing capability as humans were 60,000 years ago, when language was formed and decided about human socialization and organization through the rapid development of brain/mind as *Homo verbalis*[2]. The next leap took place in about 4,000 B.C. when *Homo scriba* applied INFOCO-2 (*manuscripts*). Nowadays, we deal with the information-communication revolution or INFOCO revolution (*Homo electronicus*), which is the next challenge for civilization. It leads to the faster development of knowledge and wisdom; on the other hand, it may support projects which may first conquer and later destroy civilization.

Does civilization, as a short cosmologic instance, have any chance of survival? Let us reflect on this possibility in the next sections.

CIVILIZATION THREATS

The synthesis of civilization threats will be presented according to the classification of civilization elements and will begin with those ones which are the least depended on human action.

Natural Threats: Cosmic[3]

End of the Universe

The universe began about 13-14 billion years ago, after the Big Bang (t=0). According to Edwin Hubble, the universe is expanding as galaxies moving away from one another. When in the 1970s we could collect hard data about conditions after the Big Bang, it became apparent that the bulk of the universe is made of dark energy, about which we know virtually nothing. The nature of dark energy is important for the fate of the universe. If dark energy is stable, the universe will continue to expand and accelerate forever. If dark energy is unstable, the universe could ultimately come apart. Dubbed the "Big Rip," this doomsday scenario has the universe accelerating to speeds that rip apart the fabric of space-time to a point where even atoms are torn apart (Wilson, 2007). On the flip side, if dark energy is dynamic, it could gradually decelerate and turn over to become an attractive force that contracts the universe into a "big crunch" implosion. If this is true, the event could be 50-60 billion years away.

End of the Milky Way Galaxy

Our civilization is in the Milky Way Galaxy. It is one of billions of galaxies. According to some cosmologists, the Milky Way will collide with the Andromeda M31 Galaxy within 5 billion years. Moreover, some dwarf galaxy in the Orion star system is currently penetrating our galaxy and the eventual collision (so far absorptions happen) with it perhaps would be fatal for our civilization. The explosion of a supernova in the Milky Way Galaxy may generate radiation 10^9 to 10^{10} times bigger than that of the Sun, which if oriented in our direction would burn the Earth. (However, this will not happen in the foreseeable future. The only pending supernova within the distance at which calculations are trustworthy is Eta Carinae, and its axis of spin is pointing in the wrong direction. If we do not count effects from a polar gamma ray burst, the star would have to be within a few dozen light years for a supernova to affect us, and there are no stars large enough to go supernova within that distance now or within any predicted future.) Hypothetically speaking, this type of explosion can send a "fireball" of radiation to the Earth at any time or every few million years.

If such cosmic threats are only "probable," the death of the Sun within 4 to 5 billion years could be possible. This means that with probability p=1 human civilization will be dead if we cannot escape to another star out of the solar system.

Collisions with Other Astronomical Objects

The Earth can be hit by asteroids and comets, called sometimes "blue objects," because their orbits cross the Earth's orbit. In the past, the Earth was hit by the Tunguska Meteorite (1908) in Siberia, a meteorite in Arizona (-50,000), and a planetoid in Yucatan (-65 million). About 250 million years ago, such an impact may have been responsible for the end-Permian extinction event that killed 90% of all sea creatures and was roughly equally catastrophic to land dwellers. (Another theory argues that these creatures were killed by volcanic eruptions.) Moreover, the collisions among "blue objects" and also peripheral collisions with the solar system can eventually (but not necessarily) generate gravitational disturbances that would redirect other "blue objects" towards the Earth, destroying civilization.

Natural Threats: Climate

Climate changes are typical for Earth. Civilization emerged when the Ice Age ended about 10,000 years ago. In the Middle Ages, between 1,000 and 1,400 A.D., a relatively warm period occurred, succeeded by a Little Ice Age from 1,400 to 1,800 A.D. (Gribbin, 2005). Nowadays, there is an opinion that climate changes are being caused by a too- aggressive civilization process (Hunter, 2000). It was found that each 10% increment of population is associated with a 7.5%-8% increment of CO_2 (Sitch, Smith, Prentice, Arneth, Bondeau, Cramer et al., 2003). As a result, a greenhouse effect takes place. The CO_2 absorbs solar radiation, warms up the Earth's atmosphere and increases surface temperature. In 1980 and 1990, the average global temperatures were respectively 0.26 and 0.40 degree above the normal level (Brown, 2003). This may lead to:

1. Rising ocean levels, submerging the most populated seashores (the 1990 data indicate that the sea level is rising by 0.32 millimeter a year, which means that the sea level may rise by 0.88 meters in the 21st century [Brown, 2003]). "A UN study (made in 2007) said that by the end of the century the global sea level was likely to rise between 18 and 59 centimeters – a prediction made with the important rider that it did not include 'processes related to ice flow,' in other words, the possibly disastrous effects of chunks of Greenland and Antarctica sliding into the sea at a quickening pace" (*The Economist*,

2007). Reduced land use for agriculture. Cars (de facto, cities and suburbs) compete with crops for land and the world grain area has shrunk from 732 hectares in 1981 to 647 million hectares in 2002 (Brown, 2003).

2. Increased land desertification and deforestation.
3. Increased geographic ranges of tropical and sub-tropical diseases.
4. Decreased volume of drinking water. (In some areas farmers are now pumping water from 4,000-foot-deep wells. In general, water shortages are emerging Brown, 2003]).

Kolenda (2000) treats these predictions as speculative, since the data and mathematical models applied are not reliable and are characterized by large computing errors if different methods are compared. Kolenda even argues that the increased volume of carbon dioxide in the atmosphere is positive for photosynthesis, which controls vegetation growth. Warmer winters should be better for those who suffer circulatory diseases. Two things are sure: These problems must be investigated further and gas emissions should be better controlled.

Natural Threats – Extreme[4]

As a result of civilization's development, sometimes the ecosystem is in a state of shaken equilibrium, leading toward unusually frequent and widespread occurrence of such extreme phenomena as heavy rainfalls, floods, droughts, winds, hard frost, heat waves, and fires. Many of these disasters are caused by natural forces, but some are caused by humans. Deterioration of water-treatment installations, misuse of water, and construction of too many dams can be avoided. People should move out from territories where the risk of earthquakes, floods, and volcanic eruptions is high. These solutions require huge investments, better spatial planning, better monitoring of nature, and better post-crisis help.

Natural Threats: Energy[5]

If strategic resources are depleted, civilization will enter a stage of crisis and may return to the Stone Age. The well-being of Earth will be decided by the known and potential reserves of strategic resources. As the known reserves are shrinking, the potential reserves should last till the year 5,000+. This means that modern resource-consuming civilization may endure another 3,000 years, which is only 50% of the whole past age of civilization (6,000). In other words, people will be able to live comfortably for only 9,000 years. What will happen after the year 5000? Hrynkiewicz (1998) looks more optimistically and argues that nuclear energy is the future of civilization. However, Ney (1998) warns that uranium reserves, which are used by nuclear power stations, may last only 45 years, till 2050. Also new technologies as a breeder reactor, which makes new atomic fuel, may be civilization's hope. Of course, one thing that no one seems to mention about atomic power is that in the end all energy degrades to heat, which would just add to the heat input to the planet.

Natural Threats: Resources[6]

Civilization cannot function without strategic resources, which is rather obvious. The forecast in this respect is not good for civilization. For example, oil reserves should last about 40 years, gas – 51 (Chapter VII), coal – 200 (*Rottenberg, 2003), uranium, iron, lead, copper, and zinc – 30 to 70 years (different estimates). Therefore, humanity's* task is to replace these non-renewable resources with ones that are either man-made (e.g., ethanol) or not subject to depletion (e.g., solar energy). Otherwise, civilization will stop.

Human Biological Threats

Population Growth Threat

In 2050, about 9 billion people will be in the Earth, assuming two children in a family (UN, 2003). However, if the level of reproduction in developing countries does not change, then population in 2150 will grow to 24.4 billion and decline in 2300 to 13.4 billion. Even if an average family has only 0.25 children more, the population will reach 36.4 billion in 2300. One can estimate that it is very probable that the population will grow from 6 billion in 2004 to 9 billion in 2050, because nothing shows that people have changed their lifestyle in developing countries. The quoted UN Report predicts there will be 8-9 billion people in 2050. Hence, one can assume that in 2050, the population bomb will be triggered, since the ecosystem can sustain only 9 to 12 billion people. However, the prognoses for Europe, Japan, and Canada, assuming 1-4 children per family, predict that their populations will decline by a factor of four.

Biological Diversity Destruction Threat[7]

The present level of biological diversity may include 30 million species of multi-cellular plants and animals living in the Earth, and they are vanishing faster than scientists can describe them. Most of this is a result of human action, despite the fact that the biological equilibrium depends on biological diversity.

It is a recognized fact that the efficiency of intercepting solar energy depends on biodiversity. Biological diversity eventually led to the formation of *Homo sapiens* and its civilization. On the other hand, current losses in biological diversity are not a strong threat for civilization, which can feed itself adequately from only five crops (rice, wheat, corn, soybeans, and potatoes); however, biologists and dieticians may argue with this statement, despite the fact that the number of

noxious insects and other competitors for these crops is very large.

We can produce many medications and biological materials synthetically that used to come from the ecosystem. However, we cannot produce all required bio-components by ourselves. It is obvious that declining biological diversity leads towards unification and such is usually a cause of stagnation. Hence, declining biological diversity is a threat to civilization development, particularly in the area of culture, where diversity triggers social progress.

Cloning Threat[8]

Human cloning of embryos triggers a lot of ethical issues. On the other hand, animal cloning for medical therapies for humans is worthy of support. If human cloning is accepted, then it could lead to the bifurcation of humans into stronger and weaker breeding lines/individuals. Today, we do not know whether this would happen via evolution or bloody wars. A similar case took place 30,000-40,000 years ago, when speaking Cro-Magnon men "eliminated" simple communication of Neanderthals, who had bigger brains than Cro-Magnons and had already settled in Europe 30,000 years before, because Cro-Magnons were living in a better organized society.

Intensive Selection Threat[9]

The genetic enhancement of animals has led in several countries to doubling the production of meat, milk, and derivative products. However, this process stopped the natural selection among those animals which had optimized their adaptation to their home environments. As a result of it, the smaller genetic diversity is a source of many illnesses among animals and people (e.g., the case of the Irish potato famine of 1848 and after. The potatoes were all of one variety and all succumbed to the same fungus). For example, fast increase of meat mass in animals may sometimes lead to same effect among people who eat that meat. Some countries are reluctant to import meat from the U.S. for that reason.

Infectious Diseases Threat[10]

New infectious diseases, such as AIDS, have become one of the most dangerous threats to civilization. This kind of threat becomes more dangerous because the effectiveness of antibiotics is declining and new more focused medications have more side effects.

Lead-Oriented Industrial Poisons Threat[10]

Lead and its compounds are toxic. Lead can be found in industrial and urban environments, particularly where leaded gasoline and certain kinds of paint are stored and distributed. Lead is harmful for human health, since it generates aggression, leading to more conflicts at different levels of human society. Lead is harmful because it destroys neural connections and possibly some other ones.

Culture Threats

Ignorance and Superstition Threat[11]

Ignorance is mental darkness concerning basic issues; superstition is fear-driven misconception. People who possess these traits try to develop a model of reality despite a lack of knowledge and rational understanding of occurrences. Ignorance and superstition obscure humanity's relationship with nature, most obviously in history in health treatments and environment protection when science was at the beginning of its advanced development. Today, they trivialize science in an effort to explain complex problems in simplistic language. This kind of approach is full of errors, which encourage fear and the escape to superstition even further.

Even the modern liberalized education can be harmful, through its rejection of the natural sciences in favor of a loosely comparative methodology of the humanities whereby different interpretations of literary and art works are encouraged. Teachers, journalists and publicists accordingly bias public opinion, often in a false manner, for example, by beginning with a statement "on this issue opinions are divided." But in fact, in the natural sciences, the usual saying is, "a beautiful theory, slain by an ugly fact."

If democracy leads to "politically correct" positions sanctioning such statements as "the truth is in the center," then it can be a threat to the future development of civilization, resulting in scientific illiteracy, which swindles scientific research.

This kind of illiteracy takes place even when after a half-century (in the 20th century) of unparalleled economic and social development, there are worldwide still 875 million adults who are illiterate and 115+ million children who do not attend schools. About 60% of them are women with large families who live in poverty. These people are "students" of superstition and ignorance. Without literacy, it is difficult to apply democracy (Brown, 2003).

Moral Crisis Threat[12]

The atrophy of moral relationships, the crisis of confidence, loyalty and solidarity, and the dissemination of a culture of cynicism, manipulation and indifference are all crucial in determining important threats for contemporary civilization. Although people opposed to this threat organize themselves in real and virtual (Internet) organizations, the threat is developing faster than its remedy.

Truth Relativity Threat[13]

Post-modern ideology tries to equate the credibility of astronomy with that of astrology and of scientific experiment with magic. It wants to shape the public mind to assume that it has a monopoly for deciding what is truth and what is untruth. This can mean the dawn of the "tyranny" of science and intellectuals, unless they are post-modernists. Post-modernism doubts whether it is possible to achieve universal knowledge in any domain. On the assumption that sociology, not physics, should be the model for a universal approach in science, even the theories of physics need social interpretations similar to those in sociology. Perhaps as a result of this assumption, politicians have a disrespectful attitude toward science and scientists, which may lead to ignorance and superstition, hostile to the knowledgeable civilization development.

Current Physics State of the Art Threat[14]

The current state of the art in theoretical physics has no integrated view of the world. This indicates indirectly that science faces a new degree of complexity in investigating the universe. Modern science began in the 16th century, when Nicolaus Copernicus (1473-1543) negated the old dogma that the Earth is the center of the universe and argued that the Earth circles around the Sun. Consequently in the 17th century, Johannes Kepler (1571-1630) discovered laws of planetary movement[15] described in mathematics. In 1687, Isaac Newton further investigated the law of planetary motions and discovered the equations of motion of objects[16], which were also defined in mathematics. Both sets of laws provided then a coherent view of the physical world. However, physics was still a badly fragmented field of study.

At the beginning of the 20th century, Max Planck (1900) discovered that light, heat, and other forms of radiation existed in tiny bundles which he called quanta. In 1905, Albert Einstein found that objects cannot travel faster than light and updated Newton's law to apply to the world of subatomic particles. Ever since, in the last 100 years, physicists have struggled with the challenge of defining the unified field theory of everything. The lack of success to date in this project is the source of scientific frustration and limits our understanding of the universe and civilization (Staruszkiewicz, 2001).

Values Crisis Threat[17]

The crisis of experiencing values in contemporary civilization leads to a loss of sensitivity for values and their applications. The truth becomes relative, beauty becomes ugliness. Goodness, and particularly public goodness, becomes subject to laughter. The values which should steer human actions are unperceived, so men fail to adopt them. The reaction of the elites to this threat is the development of new values, such as human, civil, and consumer rights, which in the past were inapplicable or unknown. The dispute about values triggered the clash of civilizations in September 11, 2001, which threatens the well-being of civilization.

Culture Commercialization Threat[18]

The commercialization of the arts in the world leads to publication mostly of sensational best-sellers, promotion of music for the tastes of youngsters, collection of art by banks instead of museums, performance of mostly comic and sex-driven plays, and violent and unrealistic movies, which have nothing in common with the life's real issues. This state of culture vulgarizes and desensitizes societies for more sublime living. It does not lead to the effective development of civilization, which is reduced only to provision of fun. Such "civilization" becomes a target for itself, unaware of real civilization challenges.

Anti-Democracy Threat

Democracy based on the will of the majority of people and equal rights of all is a very young political system in the history of civilization. Despite the fact that it has roots in ancient Athens (Solon [638-558 B.C.]); just the English (1640-60), American (1775-83) and French (1789-99) Revolutions gave meaning to democracy in practice. In North America, it has been practiced ever since; in Europe it has been practiced as of the 20th century. At the beginning of the 21st century, about 30% of countries are democratic, while the majority of the world's population lives under undemocratic, authoritarian and totalitarian political systems. Many so-called democratic regimes are characterized by election corruption and swindles. These kinds of regimes hinder the development of knowledge, free flow of information, and opposing views, as well as intercepting income from national resources for personal needs. They are agents of internal and international conflicts, including those between civilizations. They also have tendencies to use resources ineffectively, which usually leads to a lack of resource equality among populations.

Threat by Fundamentalism

Fundamentalism is the fossilized approach to religion, economics and other aspects of human life. Fundamentalism does not accept any modifications of views and beliefs that do not comply with dogmas of a given domain. Very often, fundamentalism in religion wants to turn back history, even at the price of murders and bloody wars. For example, Christianity applied fundamentalism over a long period of inquisitions from the 13th to the 19th century (the last rule of the Inquisition was removed in the 20th century). At the end of the 20th century, Islamic fundamentalism began its reign in Iran and Afghanistan (Taliban), precipitating the war of civilizations (Targowski, 2003a) by attacking the United States on September 11, 2001. Actually, fundamentalism is restorationist only in theory. In practice, it needs very little time before starting to extrapolate its own fresh hypotheses.

Likewise, economic fundamentalism is based on old dogma, which accepts only the role of the "invisible hand of the marketplace." The modern economy is regulated by many factors, such as taxes, customs, and credit rates, which decisively influence demand and supply. The strict application of fundamentalism can nevertheless be a threat to human-friendly civilization, particularly in those countries that have been transformed from a planned economy to a market economy (the former Soviet Bloc countries in 1989-91). Too often, this leads in this former block to a reduced, handicraft scale of production, dependence on such extractive industries as mining, banks controlled by the politicians for political effect, and equally political control of science and technology institutions.

Threat by Terrorism[19]

Terrorism is a form of fighting that is applied by some religions. It is popular in militarily weak countries, which use terrorism against militarily stronger countries. The victims of terrorism are citizens, because in such a manner, the whole society is threatened. The most dangerous weapon of terrorism is the weapon of mass destruction (WMD); chemical and biological. Some even say that the Internet also belongs to this category.

The biological weapon is easy and inexpensive to produce and transport and very difficult to detect. Smart use of these weapons can destroy a whole city or country. The cost of killing most of people in 1 km^2 by a conventional weapon is about $800, but by a biological one, about $1. The possible biological arsenal consists of anthrax, smallpox, bubonic plague, tularemia, botulism, filoviruses (e.g., Ebola, Marburg), arenaviruses (e.g., Lassa, Janin). No country is well-protected against a biological attack, because the kind of weapon is unknown to those it is used against. Consequently, there is not enough vaccine, which may not even exist. This means that there is no defense against biological weapons, which are a great threat for the most important civilization centers.

Globalization Threat

At the end of the 20th century, the world economy has been steered by the globalization of a free flow of information, capital, products, services, as well as by people who support this policy. Due to global systems of transportation and electronic information-communication (Internet and telecommunication), people and business can instantly communicate and exchange information and goods between advanced countries and countries with a less-expensive labor force. In such a manner, China becomes the *world's factory* and India becomes the *world's laboratory.*

One can notice a transfer of jobs from developed to developing countries, which is raising the standard of living in the latter, but lowering it in the former by the diminishing size of the middle class and thereby consumers. This process leads to a decided increase in the civilization's asymmetry between rich and poor, a redistribution of income so that it becomes increasingly concentrated among the rich (*managerial capitalism*).

On the other hand, nobody is satisfied by this state of society; because there is a strong conviction that globalization is mostly good for corporations (mostly their CEOs), not for the common man and even not for stockholders.

The developing countries, in spite of financial gains, deteriorate their environments and sanction work by adolescents and young children in unsafe conditions. These countries feel that the developed countries take advantage of them. In the end, citizens of developed countries feel that they lose too many jobs, and to compete with less-expensive labor abroad they have to give up that dream about the potential of the middle class which was the source of their success. For example, in the U.S., electrical engineers are asked to accept less demanding but less profitable positions. In such a manner, globalization becomes a source of social and political conflict, which is reflected in the anti-globalization movement.

According to George Soros (1998), the global economy should be regulated by the global society, which does not yet exist. Hence, the unregulated development of globalization is a threat to the smooth improvement of civilization (Soros, 2003; Targowski & Korth, 2003).

Infrastructural Threats

Rain Forest Removal Threat

Rain forests are the lungs of the Earth. Every year, 31,000 square miles (80,000 km^2) of forest are being removed, which is equivalent to the size of nations such as Austria (Conkin, 2007). About 3 billion people use wood for heating and to build houses (Conkin, 2007). The loss of forests reduces vegetation cover in general, because it transforms agricultural soil into deserts. The production of food in those areas declines, as well as the number of animal farms, which means that a smaller number of people get enough nutritionally balanced food. The growth of deserts also causes the decline of rainfall, which also influences climate change (Middleton, 1989).

Urbanization Threat

The high degree of urbanization is the measure of a country's advancement. The developed countries have about 70%-80% of their population living in cities (Hunter, 2000). The agriculture processes are mechanized and even automated, such that so-called precision farming is guided by satellites to optimize the distribution of fertilizers according to the soil's consistency. In the less developed countries, the purpose of migration to cities is to find jobs. As a result of it, cities transform into Moloch agglomerations, such as Mexico City with 30 million habitants, which provides 44% of GNP, 52% of production, and 54% of services of the whole country. Every day, about 1,000 new inhabitants settle in this city, without a serious hope for a better life. The environmental contamination in Mexico City is so great that it is equal to 40 cigarettes smoked every day by each inhabitant (Hunter, 2000).

Similar living conditions exist in Sao Paulo (20 million), Calcutta (13), Buenos Aries (12), Shanghai (11), and Manila (10). Even in developed countries, such cities as Tokyo (17), New York (15), Los Angeles (10), and London (10) have characteristically high rates of crime and alienation of citizens, which worsen quality of life. Consequently, one can state that high urbanization is a threat for human-friendly civilization (Hunter, 2000).

Technology and Computer Threat

The rapid growth of mechanization dates from James Watt's invention of the steam engine in 1769. In the 19th century mechanization cut back muscle work and so led to more time spent on education and engineering. Thus, it led to automation, informatization, and robotization of industrial and mental processes in the 20th century. In the 21st century, informatization and robotization are the main factors of productivity growth at the annual rate of 5%. But it triggers the growth of the economy without the growth of new jobs (jobless economy). If this trend reaches the whole world, it may provoke global unemployment in times when population growth already surpasses the number of available jobs. This strong but chaotic productivity development may not be good for civilization (Targowski, 2003b).

THE "DEATH TRIANGLE" OF CIVILIZATION I

This interaction of threats illustrates a model[20] of "The Death Triangle of Civilization I," shown in Figure 17-2 (Targowski, 1999). This event is driven by the population bomb (bomb P), ecological bomb (bomb E), and resources bomb (bomb R). The most dangerous is the bomb P, which initiates the others. The bomb P's activities are strengthened by ten biological and cultural threats.

Figure 17-2. The death triangle of civilization

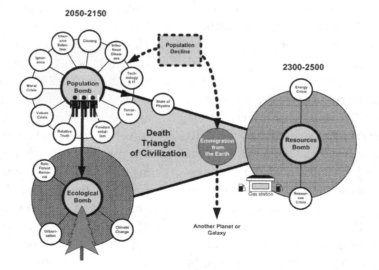

Although the danger of each threat is not by itself critical for civilization, a combination of all ten threats and the bomb P may put civilization in a deep crisis.

The year 2050 is the assumed beginning of bomb P activities, since about that time world population will reach 9 billion. This number falls into the lower limit of the ecosystem's capacity, which is about 9 to 12 billion people[21]. Even 36.4 billion people in 2300, assuming smaller reproduction per family, will exceed three times the capacity of the ecosystem.

Such a big population on the Earth will trigger the blast of the bomb E, which even nowadays is perceived in the less-developed countries. Its impact is strengthened by the removal of the rain forest, climate change, aggressive urbanization, land desertification, and other human actions against environment quality.

More productive industry will produce more goods for the growing population, causing depletion of strategic resources in 2300-2500. It is worth noticing that the high quality of life in developed countries now is possible because 80% of global population does not participate in such a resource-rich way of life. For this reason, 20% of global population may enjoy easy access to natural resources. Of course, man is capable of substituting some man-made resources for natural ones. However, humans will not be able in any foreseeable future to provide artificial substitutes for all natural resources.

The presented model indicates that civilization I can be saved if population declines or if part of society is transported off the Earth. The first solution is feasible if the United Nations and church agree on the solution to population control, and people follow their recommendations. The second solution requires huge funds and new discoveries, which would allow for travel faster than the speed of light. If the first solution is possible, the second one is less probable at this time.

Table 17-1. The cosmic threats to civilization

CIVILIZA-TION THREATS	SYMP-TOMS	STATE OF THREAT	SOLUTION	RESPONSIBLE	PROBABILITY OF SOLUTION SUCCESS	IMPLE-MENTATION TIME IN YEARS
End of the Solar System	Sun extinction	Ultimate	People out the Solar System	Science must discover how to travel faster than light	Very low, more metaphysical than real	2 billion
End of Milky Way Galaxy	Collision with other galaxy or supernova	Ultimate	People out of the Solar System	Science must discover how to travel faster than light	Very low, more metaphysical than real	5 billion
Collision with Blue Objects	Anytime	Highest	Resteering of Blue Objects	Scence and NASA (USA)	Low	Several decades

Table 17-2. The natural threats to civilization

CIVILIZA-TION THREATS	SYMP-TOMS	STATE OF THREAT	SOLUTION	RESPONSIBLE	PROBABILITY OF SO-LUTION SUCCESS	IMPLE-MENTATION TIME IN YEARS
Climatic	Greenhouse Effect	Depends on views	More research, fewer gas emissions	Science, governments, UN	Moderate	100
Extreme	Floods Drought, etc.	Moderate	Better planning and monitoring, more investments, relocations	Governments	Moderate	50
Energetic	Shrink-ing reserves	High	Nuclear energy and forms [[OF WHAT? SOLAR ENERGY?]]	Scence, technology, governments	Good	20
Resources	Shrink-ing reserves	Highest	Man-made Substitutions	Science, technology, governments	Good	15

MEANS OF REMOVING CIVILIZATION THREATS[22]

The characteristics of each civilization threat are provided in the following tables, including the degree of each threat and its possible removal. The cosmic threats are characterized in Table 17-1. It looks like the Earth has 2 billion years to support life; after that the solar system will be not useful for humans, and life will disappear. There are other possible cosmic catastrophes against which there is no good protection yet.

The natural threats to civilization are listed in Table 17-2.

The biological threats to civilization are shown in Table 17-3. The most critical threat is the uncontrollable growth of population. This threat triggers others. The cloning of humans

seems to be a very dangerous threat, since it can open a Pandora's box of intra-species conflicts over planetary dominance, with consequences which are very difficult to predict. For example, cloning may initiate the creation of new kind of humans and destruction of *Homo sapiens*. The threat of infectious diseases, particularly from AIDS, can destroy the whole population of Africa, if the lifestyle there does not change. The present anti-AIDS medications are so complex in their applications that it is almost impossible to count on their success. If the lifestyle in developing countries cannot be changed, then population can decrease to 3.9 billion in 2150 and to 2.3 in 2300 (UN, 2003).

The characteristics of cultural threats are shown in Table 17-4. The most critical is a threat of terrorism, which if not contained in time can

Table 17-3. The biological threats to civilization[23]

CIVILIZA-TION THREATS	SYMP-TOMS	STATE OF THREAT	SOLUTION	RESPONSIBLE	PROBABILITY OF SO-LUTION SUCCESS	IMPLE-MENTATION TIME IN YEARS
Population Growth	Overpop-ulated cities and trans-port	Critical	Birth Control	UN, States and Church	Good	5-15
Destruction of biological diversity	Disappear-ance of species	Small	Environ-mental protection	State	Good	5-15
Human cloning	Intra-species conflict	High	Regulated research	UN, States and Church	Good	3-10
Intensive selection	Animal diseases	High	Regulated selection	State	Good	5-15
Infectious diseases	Incurable Diseases	High	More research	State and WHO	Good	5-15
Lead Poisoning	Human Aggres-siveness	Low	Envi-ronmental protection	State	High	5-15

have unpredictable negative consequences. The remaining threats are dangerous for civilization but will mostly only worsen the quality of life. The push toward consumerism and the constant increase of material possessions causes negligence of higher-order values, which leads to truth relativism, which falsifies reality. This approach threatens further progress in science and in wise civilization development based on self-sustainability.

The characteristics of the infrastructural threats to civilization are provided in Table 17-5. The most critical threats are the gradual removal of the rain forest and an overly aggressive application of technology and informatics. These lead to more and more productive work, but eventually the population will grow too big and there will not be enough jobs for new workers.

According to data provided in the above tables, it looks like civilization I is entering into a crisis stage which could lead to its fall in the third millennium. The tables provide means of removing or minimizing those threats, if indicated organizations and individuals take the necessary steps to making this a possibility.

In summary, one can state that the most critical task is the elimination of the population growth threat. However, eventual success in this project also depends on the removal of cultural threats which influence the population issue.

The processes of removing or minimizing cultural and population threats should take place concurrently. Their positive elimination will provide the foundation for positive solutions in respect to the next threats of the bomb E and bomb R.

Table 17-4. The cultural threats to civilization

CIVILIZATION THREATS	SYMP-TOMS	STATE OF THREAT	SOLUTION	RESPONSIBLE	PROBABILITY OF SOLUTION SUCCESS	IMPLE-MENTATION TIME IN YEARS
Ignorance and Super-stition	Scientific illiteracy	Middle	Critical position of scientific as-sociations	Sincere leaders and intellectuals	Middle	Instant
Crisis of moral rela-tions	Cynicism and mani-pulation	Middle	Anti-consume-rism actions	Chuch and fami-ly associations	Middle	Instant
Truth relati-vism	Fuzzi-ness of truth and responsi-bility	Middle	Critical position of scientific as-sociations	Sincere leaders and intellectuals	Middle	Instant
State of theoretical physics	Science stagna-tion	High	Science	Sincere leaders and intellectuals	Middle	Instant
Value crisis	Loss of sensitiv-ity toward values	Middle	Education	Chuch and schools	Middle	Instant
Culture comercia-lization	Loss of taste	Low	Education	State	High	Instant
Anti-demo-cracy	Mind cap-tiva-tion	Middle	Open Society	Social and poli-tical leaders	High	Instant
Funda-mentalism	Mind cap-tiva-tion	High	Open Society	Social and poli-tical leaders	Low	Instant
Terrorism	Innocent victims	High	Open Society	International Cooperation	Middle	Instant
Globali-za-tion	Corporate greed	Middle	Global Society and Universal Civilization	International Cooperation	Middle	Instant

The model of hierarchical removal of civilization threats is shown in Figure 17-3.

THE FUTURE OF CIVILIZATION

Civilization is about 6,000 years old and reached its peak in the 20th century. But due to its spectacular development in the last 100 years, this civilization is now under stress and in trouble (Brown, 2003). Civilization takes place on the Earth, which is a relatively small planet, an "island" in the universe. This "island" has limited resources, which are being depleted in an increasingly rapid manner[24]. This is the major problem of the civilization. If humans will not adapt a self-sustainable strategy for their existence, they will face the following crises (Figure 17-4):

1. Short-term crisis – "the Death Triangle of Civilization" in years 2050-2500

2. Mid-term crisis – depletion of potential reserves of resources in years 5000+ and a new Ice Age within 15,000-50,000 years (different estimates).

3. Long-term crisis – the solar expansion within 2 billion years (Figure 17-5).

The mid-term crisis is very obvious, since the Earth has a limited volume of natural resources. Hence civilization can last only 9,000 years or 3,000 years more, only 50% of its actual existence so far (6,000 years). There is not much time left for all of us. The solution can come from the implementation of the universal civilization I, which should transform from the present restricted civilization I (see Preface) A set of world values of that civilization should be based upon such grand values as wisdom, goodness, self-sustainability, and dialogue as well as upon a set of chosen values of global and autonomous civilizations (Kuczynski, 1986; Targowski, 2004b). If humans

Table 17-5. The infrastructural threats to civilization

CIVILIZ-ATION THREATS	SYMP-TOMS	STATE OF THREAT	SOLUTION	RESPONSIBLE	PROBABI-LITY OF SO-LUTION SUCCESS	IMPLE-MENTATION TIME IN YEARS
Loss of forests	Climate and habitat change	High	Environment Protection	State and international organizations	Middle	Instant
Urbani-zation	Diseases and crime	Middle	Spatial Policy	State	Middle	Instant
Technology and informatics	Loss of privacy and jobs	High	Privacy Protection and job security	State	High	Instant

Figure 17-3. The model of hierarchical removal of civilization threats

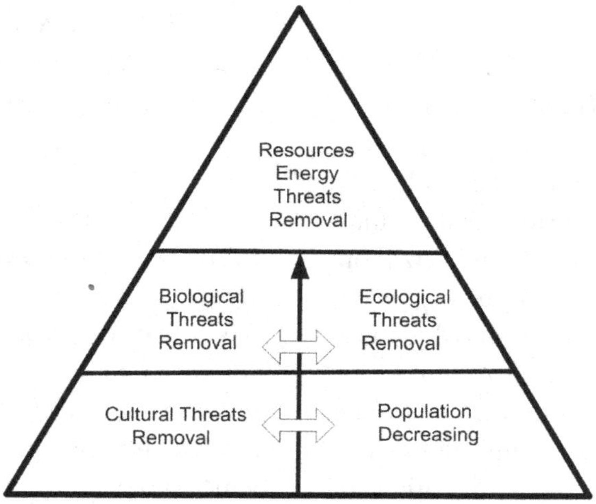

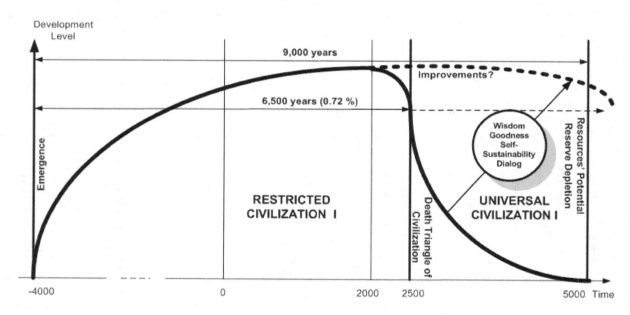

Figure 17-4. The short and mid-term crises of civilization

Figure 17-5. The fate of of civilization (shown periods are not to scale)

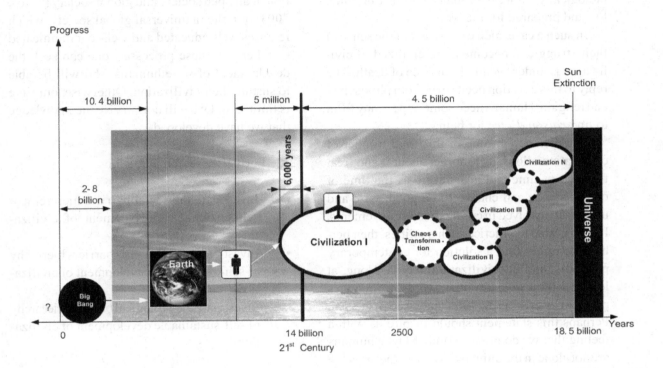

are successful (rising to their greatness) in the implementation of the universal civilization I, they may eliminate the threat of the death triangle and mid-term crisis of civilization I. The game is about saving more years ("buying time") for civilization I. How many years more do we have? A few hundred or a few thousand or more?

The long-term future of civilization depends on its internal processes and the physical permanence of the Earth. The Earth remains a larger-scale *"Titanic,"* since it will be a cemetery after 2 billion years.

Some other data indicate that the Earth is getting darker. Between 1960 and 1990, some scientists believe, the amount of solar radiation reaching Earth's surface may have declined or is filtered by air pollution as much as 10%; in some places, Hong Kong, for example, more than 35%[25]. The fate of civilization is illustrated by a model in Figure 17-5. It shows that the end of civilization I does not mean the death of human-

kind; rather, the end may be disorganized, with a return to the Stone Age, beginning civilization again from square one. Hence, one can imagine such a developmental scenario of civilization, that its consecutive phases can be separated by phases of chaos and inter-civilization transformations. (On the other hand, we have already used up all the mineral resources that are easy to get at; future redevelopments would not be able to repeat our industrialization, or even our bronze and iron ages. Well, maybe they could mine the ruined cities.)

Up till now, 181 generations[26] of mankind have been participating in civilization. There is a chance that another (about or less) 60,600,000 generations may live on the Earth, unless it becomes "an empty refrigerator" without sufficient "food" in it within 2 billion years (when life conditions will be worsening).

The finiteness of civilization explains why man is mortal in the universe. If the "invisible hand" of the universe decided that the Earth is biologically finite, then mankind must be finite too and prepared for the worst.

In such a case, men can ask about the sense of their struggle to become more civilized, if civilization is under eventual sentence of death. The reply to this question needs help from philosophy and religion. Humans need some hope in any form to find *raison d'être* for being.

The distance in time of this final frontier of civilization allows us to forget about it and treat the present time and near future as the time of our existence and chance to be good, wise and universal, involved in civilization improvements. If man is able to practice such qualities, then perhaps he might find a solution for contemporary problems, and his civilization may last long, at least 2 billion years. In other words, from man's point of view, civilization may seem eternal. Perhaps this statement should inspire us with a feeling that we do not lose time. Maybe humans are not alone in the universe. Maybe "the invisible hand" controls us in the universe.

CONCLUSION

Accurate prognoses rarely prove themselves, since people treat them seriously and try to avoid their doomsday predictions. Let us hope that this will be the case with the predictions for civilization provided in this study.

Presently, the critical task is to contain the growth of population and cultural threats, which influence the bomb P. To achieve this, civilization should transform from the restricted autonomous and global civilizations into universal civilization, based on dialogue and universal values (Kuczynski, 1986; Targowski, 2004b) acceptable by all contemporary religion-oriented (restricted) civilizations, such as Western, Eastern, Chinese, Japanese, Buddhist, Islamic, Hindu, and African.

Leading this transformation can be the promotion of an open society and global society (Soros, 2003) or rather a universal global society, which requires well-educated and well- communicated members. In these processes, one can seek the development of wise humans who will be able to sustain their civilization. Otherwise, our time is limited and we will not survive the knowledge that we have developed.

A. Further Research Directions

•   Investigate the social barriers hierarchy of self-sustainable development of civilization.
•   Investigate the economic barriers hierarchy of self-sustainable development of civilization.
•   Investigate the ecological barriers hierarchy of self-sustainable development of civilization.

B. Research Opportunities

•   The research opportunity is in "connecting dots" among major barriers of civilization development and motivating decision-makers for wiser decisions about humans' well-being.

C. Additional Ideas

•   The future of civilization is bleak and cannot be corrected by political action, since political action is driven by a very short-term horizon. The solution is in defining a new solution (beyond a political one). How do we manage civilization's existence? Perhaps by forming the civilization council?

D. Rationale

•   Many studies provide a very sad prognosis for the future of our world. The pace of human progress accelerated profoundly in the 20th century, spawning revolutionary advances in medicine, agriculture, and industry. Between 1900 and 2000, the world's population quadrupled, and production and consumption of goods increased by a factor of twelve. These activities have begun to deplete critical resources such as soil nutrients and fresh water, leading to potentially widespread shortages in the world's poorest regions. Fossil fuel emissions have assured a rapid increase in greenhouse gases and contributed to rising surface and ocean temperature, a warning that is almost certain to continue throughout the twenty-first century. The complex interactions between pollution, warming, and resource depletion certainly threaten the planet's biodiversity and endanger innumerable species. If one connects the dots of population growth, ecological devastation, and strategic resources depletion, then arrival of the death triangle of mankind will be perceived very soon, about 2050! Hence humans have not much time to think and act wisely to protect civilization against extinction or very drastic decline. This kind of research and political agenda should be humans' first priority in working on civilization betterment.

E. Additional Reading

Appleyard, B. (2007). *The future of civilization.* Retrieved November 11, 2007, from http://crnano.typepad.com/crnblog/2005/10/the_future_of_c.html.

Corey, S. (2000). Twenty ways the world could end suddenly. *Discover Magazine, 10,* 1-5.

Crenshaw, J. (2007). *The future of civilization.* Retrieved January 24, 2007, from http://www.renewamerica.us/columns/crenshaw/030301.

Diamond, J. (2005). *Collapse: How societies choose to fail or succeed.* New York: Viking.

Dickman, S. (1998). *The future of civilization.* Retrieved January 7, 2007, from http://www.humanistsofutah.org/1998/mainjan98.html.

Future of Civilization. Retrieved January 10, 2007, from http://biglizards.net/blog/archives/futurism/future_of_civilization/.

Gore, A. (1993). *Earth in the balance.* New York: A Plume Book.

Herzfeld, J. (2007). *Bright future of civilization?.* Retrieved January 10, 2007, from http://query.nytimes.com/gst/fullpage.html?res=9905E3D7133FF935A35751C0A9619C8B63.

Holt, J. (2004). How will the universe end?. *Slate.* Retrieved January 15, 2007, from http://www.humanistsofutah.org/1998/mainjan98.html.

Jensen, D. (2006). *Endgame.* New York: Seven Stories Press.

Kunstler, J. (1994). *Geography of nowhere: The rise and decline of America's man-made landscape.* New York: Touchstone.

_____(2005). *The long emergency: Surviving the converging catastrophes of the twenty-first century.* Boston: Grove/Atlantic Monthly Press.

Leslie, J. (1996). *The end of the world.* London: Routledge.

McFaul, T. (2006). *The future of peace and justice in the global village: The role of the world religions in the 21st century.* New York: Praeger Publisher.

Peterson, J. (1997). *Out of the blue: How to anticipate big future surprises.* New York: Madison Books.

Possible future global catastrophes. Retrieved February 12, 2007, from http://humanknowledge.net/SocialScience/Futurology/Catastrophes.html.

Rees, M. (2004). *Our final hour: A scientist's warning: How terror, error, and environmental disaster* threaten humankind's future in this century—on earth and beyond. New York: Basic Books.

Rischard, J. (2003). *High noon, 20 global problems, 20 years to solve them.* New York: Basic Books.

Rockwell, L., Jr. (2005). *Academic freedom and the future of civilization.* Retrieved March 5, 2007, from http://www.lewrockwell.com/rockwell/academic-freedom.html.

Saint-Andre, P. (2001). *Islam and the future of civilization.* Retrieved March 14, 2007, from http://www.saint-andre.com/thoughts/islam.html.

Sarkar, S. (1999). *The future of civilization.* Retrieved March 10, 2007, from http://www.proutworld.org/features/futsci.htm.

Some patterns in world history and how they can be used to predict the future. Retrieved March 10, 2007, from http://www.worldhistorysite.com/prediction.html.

Stein, M. (2006). *Stain on the future of civilization.* Retrieved March 10, 2007, from http://www.estatevaults.com/bol/archives/2006/08/17/steyn_on_the_fu.html.

Volsung, B. (2003). *Engineering the future of civilization.* North Charleston, SC: GreatUNpublished.com.

Wilson, E. (2003). *The future of life.* Grand Rapids, MI: Abacus.

REFERENCES

Braudel, F. (1993). *A history of civilizations.* New York: Penguin Books.

Brown, L. (2003). *Plan B, rescuing a planet under stress and a civilization in trouble.* New York: Norton & Co.

Burenhult, G. (2003a). *People of the past.* San Francisco, CA: Fog City Press.

_____ (2003b). *Great civilizations.* San Francisco, CA: Fog City Press.

Cakiewicz, W. (2001). Kapital a strefy zagrozenia kultury (Capital and civilization threats). *Zagrozenia Cywilizacyjne (Civilization Threats), 4,* 43-50. Krakow: Polska Akademia Umiejetnosci (Polish Academy of Arts and Sciences).

Cohen, J. (1995). *How many people can the earth support?.* New York: W.W. Norton & Co.

Conkin, P. (2007). *The state of earth.* Lexington, KY: The University Press of Kentucky.

Ding, Y., Chi, H., Grady, D., Morishima, A., Kidd, J., Kidd, K., et al. (2002). Evidence of positive selection acting at the human dopamine receptor D4 gene locus. *Proceedings of the National Academy of Sciences, 99,* 309-314.

The Economist. (2007). The icy road to Bali. *The Economist, 385*(8553), 73-75.

Erlich, A. (1998). *Looking for the ceiling: Estimates of earth's carrying capacity.* Retrieved November 11, 2007, from http//lists.isb.sdnpk.org//pipermail/eco-list-old.

Gribbin, J., & Gribbin, M. (2002). *Ice age.* New York: Barnes & Noble, Inc.

Grotowski, K. (1999). Zagroenia kosmiczne. Rozwazania o koncu swiata (Cosmic threats. thoughts on the end of the universe). *Zagrozenia Cywilizacyjne. (Civilization Threats), 2,* 245-58. Krakow: Polska Akademia Umiejetnosci (Polish Academy of Arts and Sciences).

Heczko, P., & Jawie, M. (2002). Bron biologiczna (Biological weapon). *Zagrozenia Cywilizacyjne (Civilization Threats), 5,* 97-116. Krakow: Polska Akademia Umiejetnosci (Polish Academy of Arts and Sciences).

Hoffmann, H. (2000). Way too many of us. *Cornell University Alumni News*. October.

Hryniewicz, A. (1998). Dwa oblicza energii jadrowej (Two faces of atomic energy). *Zagrozenia Cywilizacyjne (Civilization Threats), 1*, 69-86. Krakow: Polska Akademia Umiejetnosci (Polish Academy of Arts and Sciences).

Hryniewicz, W. (2004). Hope seeks understanding. *Dialogue and Universalism, XIV*(1-2), 67-76

Hunter, L. (2000). *The environmental implications of population dynamics*. Santa Monica, CA: RAND.

Huntington, S. (1996). *The clash of civilizations and remaking of world order*. New York: Simon & Schuster.

Janik, J. (2000). Relatywizm prawdy? (Relativism of truth?). *Zagrozenia Cywilizacyjne (Civilization Threats), 3*, 35-42. Krakow: Polska Akademia Umiejetnosci (Polish Academy of Arts and Sciences).

_____ (1999). Postmodernizm kontra fizyce (Postmodernism versus physics). *Zagrozenia Cywilizacyjne (Civilization Threats), 2*, 37-44. Krakow: Polska Akademia Umiejetnosci (Polish Academy of Arts and Sciences).

Jeljaszewicz, J. (1999). Zakazenia i choroby zakazne—zagrozenia cywilizacyjne (Infections and infectious deases). *Zagrozenia Cywilizacyjne (Civilization Threats), 3*, 7-14. Krakow: Polska Akademia Umiejetnosci (Polish Academy of Arts and Sciences).

Kolenda, Z. (2000). Kontrowersje wokol ocieplenia klimatu (Controversies of climate warming). *Zagrozenia Cywilizacyjne (Civilization Threats), 3*, 125-148. Krakow: Polska Akademia Umiejetnosci (Polish Academy of Arts and Sciences).

Koneczny, F. (1962). *On the plurality of civilizations*. London: Wydawnictwa Towarzystwa im. Romana Dmowskiego (Publications of the Roman Dmowski Association).

Korohoda, W. (2002). Inzynieria komórkowa i tkankowa na pocztku XXI wieku—nowe nadzieje i nowe zagrozenia (Cell and tissue engineering – new hope and new threats). *Zagrozenia Cywilizacyjne (Civilization Threats), 5*, 123-137. Krakow: Polska Akademia Umiejetnosci (Polish Academy of Arts and Sciences).

Krzanowska, H. (1998). Problemy klonowania organizmów (Problems of organisms' cloning). *Zagrozenia Cywilizacyjne (Civilization Threats), 1*, 11-20. Krakow: Polska Akademia Umiejetnosci (Polish Academy of Arts and Sciences).

Kuczynski, J. (1986). Universalism as the meaning of recent history. *Dialectics and Humanism, XIII*(1), 101-118.

Middleton, N. (1989). *Atlas of world and environmental issues*. New York: Facts on File, Inc.

Millennium Ecosystem Assessment. (2003). *Ecosystems and human well-being. A framework for assessment*. Washington, D.C.: Island Press.

Nash, M. (2004, May 24). Is earth getting darker?. *Time, 60*.

Ney, R. (1998). Czy swiatu grozi brak surowców mineralnych? (Is there a threat that the world will be without mineral resources?). *Zagrozenia Cywilizacyjne (Civilization Threats), 1*, 33-44. Krakow: Polska Akademia Umiejetnosci (Polish Academy of Arts and Sciences).

Pampuch, R. (1998). Podtrzymujcy sie rozwój i struktura stosowanych badan materialowych (Self-sustainable development and the structure of applied research of materials). *Zagrozenia Cywilizacyjne (Civilization Threats), 1*, 63-68. Krakow: Polska Akademia Umiejetnosci (Polish Academy of Arts and Sciences).

Przestalski, S. (2000). Wplyw zakazen olowiem na zywe organizmy (The impact of lead-driven infections upon live organisms). *Zagrozenia Cywilizacyjne (Civilization Threats), 3*, 19-34.

Krakow: Polska Akademia Umiejetnosci. (Polish Academy of Arts and Sciences).

Rees, W., & Wackernagel, M. (1995). *Our ecological footprint*. Gabriela Island, BC, Canada: New Society Publications.

Rottenberg, D. (2003). In the kingdom of coal: An American family and the rock that changed the world. London: Routledge.

Siemek, J. (1999). Bezpieczenstwo energetyczne panstw (The energy-oriented security of states). *Zagrozenia Cywilizacyjne (Civilization Threats), 2,* 59-80. Krakow: Polska Akademia Umiejetnosci (Polish Academy of Arts and Sciences).

Sitch, S., Smith, B., Prentice, I., Arneth, A., Bondeau, A., & Cramer, W. (2003). Evaluation of ecosystem dynamics, plant geography and terrestrial carbon cycling in the LPJ dynamic global vegetation model. *Global Change Biology, 9,* 161-185.

Soros, G. (1998). *The crisis of global capitalism.* New York: Public Affairs.

_____(2003). *The bubble of American supremacy.* New York: Public Affairs.

Stableford, B., & Langford, D. (1985). *The third millennium.* New York: Alfred A. Knopf, Inc.

Starkel, L. (1999). Ulewy, powodzie i inne zdarzenia ekstremalne (Rains, floods and other extreme events). *Zagrozenia Cywilizacyjne (Civilization Threats), 3,* 81-96. Krakow: Polska Akademia Umiejetnosci (Polish Academy of Arts and Sciences).

Staruszkiewicz, A. (2001). Wspólczesny stan fizyki teoretycznej powaznym zagrozeniem cywilizacyjnym (The contemporary state of physics as a serious threat for civilization). *Zagrozenia Cywilizacyjne (Civilization Threats), 4,* 59-62. Krakow: Polska Akademia Umiejetnosci (Polish Academy of Arts and Sciences).

Strózewski, W. (2000). Filozofia i kryzys wartosci (Philosophy and values crisis). *Zagrozenia Cywilizacyjne (Civilization Threats), 3,* 43-56. Krakow: Polska Akademia Umiejetnosci (Polish Academy of Arts and Sciences).

Sztompka, P. (1999). Czy kryzys wiezi moralnej w swiecie wsplóczesnym? (Is it a crisis of moral relations in the contemporary world?). *Zagrozenia Cywilizacyjne (Civilization Threats), 2,* 15-22. Krakow: Polska Akademia Umiejetnosci (Polish Academy of Arts and Sciences).

Targowski, A. (1999). *Enterprise information infrastructure.* Boston: Pearson.

_____(2003a). The civilization war. *Zeszyty Naukowe (Scientific Notes), 50*(1), 15-39. Warsaw: Academy of National Defense.

_____(2003b). *Electronic enterprise, strategy and architecture.* Harrisburg, PA: Idea Group Publishing.

_____(2004a). A grand model of civilization. *Comparative Civilizations Review, 53,* 81-106.

_____(2004b). From global to universal civilization. *Dialogue and Universalism, XV*(3-4), 121-142.

Targowski, A., & Korth, C. (2003). China or NAFTA: The world's largest market in the 21st century. *Advances in Competitiveness Research, 11*(1), 87-115.

Tischner, M. (1998). Nowe metody biotechnologii rozrodu bydla i zagrozenia intensywnej selekcji. (New biotechnological methods of cattles reproduction and threats of intensiv selection). *Zagrozenia Cywilizacyjne (Civilization Threats), 2,* 21-32. Krakow: Polska Akademia Umiejetnosci (Polish Academy of Arts and Sciences).

Toynbee, A. (1995). *A study of history.* New York: Barnes & Noble.

United Nations. (2003). *World population in 2300*. New York: UN: ESA/WP.187

Wackernagel, M. (2002). *Ecological footprints of nations*. Costa Rica: The Earth Council.

Wackernagel, M., & Onisto, L. (1997). *The ecological footprints of nations report*. Xalapa, Mexico: The Centro de Estudios para la Sustentabilidad at the Universidad Anahuac de Xalapa. Retrieved October 15, 2006, from http://www.ecouncil.ac.cr/rio/focus/report/english.

Weiner, J. (1999). Ciemnota i zabobon jako zagrozenia cywilizacyjne (Ignorance and superstition as civilization threats). *CywilizacyjneZagrozen (Civilization Threats), 2*, 7-20. Krakow: Polska Akademia Umiejetnosci (Polish Academy of Arts and Sciences).

_____(2001). Czy niszczenie rónorodnosci biologicznej stanowi zagrozenie cywilizacyjne? (Whether destruction of biological diversity is the threat for civilization?). *Zagrozenia Cywilizacyjne (Civilization Threats), 4*, 7-20. Krakow: Polska Akademia Umiejetnosci (Polish Academy of Arts and Sciences).

Wilson, R. (2007). The universe, detecting the signature of the Big Bang. In: L. Glover, A. Chalkin, P. Daniels, A. Gianopoulos, & J. Malay (Eds.), *National geographic encyclopedia of space*. Washington, D.C.: National Geographic.

World Bank. (1999). *World bank atlas, the world development indicators*. Washington, D.C.: World Bank.

ENDNOTES

[1] See Chapter I for a discussion of the proposed nature of civilization.

[2] There is a theory that about 40,000 years ago humans passed a genetic mutation with the gene DRD4, which influences human intelligence by encoding a neuron-receptor-dopamine (Ding et al., 2000).

[3] Based on Kazimierz Grotowski (1999).

[4] Based on Leszek Starkel (1999).

[5] Based on Jakub Siemek (1999) and Andrzej Z. Hryniewicz (1998).

[6] Based on Roman Ney (1998) and Roman Pampuch (1998)

[7] Based on Halina Krzanowska (1998) and Wlodzimierz Korohoda (2002).

[8] Based on Marian Tischner (1998).

[9] Based on Janusz Jeljaszewicz (1999).

[10] Based on Stanisław Przestalski (2000).

[11] Based on January Weiner (1999).

[12] Based on Piotr Sztompka (1999).

[13] Based on Jerzy A. Janik (1999) and Jerzy A. Janik (2000).

[14] Based on Andrzej Staruszkiewicz (2001).

[15] (1) Planets move in elliptic orbits around the Sun, (2) An imaginary straight line joining a planet to the Sun sweeps out equal areas of the ellipse in space in equal intervals of time, (3) the square of the period of revolution of a planet is in direct proportion to the cube of the semi-major axis of its orbit.

[16] Newton's Law of Inertia, Law of Constant Acceleration and Law of Conservation of Momentum.

[17] Based on Wladyslaw Strozewski (2000).

[18] Based on Witold Ceckiewicz (2001).

[19] Based on Piotr Heczko and Miroslaw Jawien (2002).

[20] A name of the model is provided in quotes because it reflects indirectly the importance and urgency of the issue.

[21] People are the integral part of the ecosystem. The ecosystem is a collection of the environment, plants, animals, microorganisms, and dead matter, which co-habitat as a functional system. The ecosystem secures for animals and people food and water, regulates floods, droughts, land degradation, and plagues, and supports soil formation, food recycling, recreation, spiritual instances, religion, and so forth.

22   This is the response to Plan A—Business as Usual, accelerating environmental decline, spreading hunger, growing unrest and political conflicts, increasing streams of refugees, growing population, being overwhelmed by problems (Brown, 2003).

23   More profound analysis of this topic is provided in millennium ecosystem assessment (2003).

24   For example, the awakening of China and India as economic powers in the 21st century will deplete natural resources faster than one can predict. China with 20% of the world's population used to apply only 6% of the world's annual mining of natural resources, whereas it may consume several times more when it produces 50%+ of world goods.

25   It appears that increased air pollution over Asia during those 30 years increased cloudiness, which exerted a cooling influence (Nash, 2004).

26   One generation has 33 years for present purposes.

Chapter XVIII
The Information Architecture of the Universe

INTRODUCTION

For years, the construction of the universe has occupied the best minds of theologians and scientists. The first modern breakthrough was made by Copernicus about 500 years ago. Later, in the 20th century, contributions were made with the bold theories developed by Albert Einstein, Edwin Hubble, Roger Penrose, Stephen Hawking, and others. Science continues to discover the great mystery of the universe and life. But the more we know about this subject, the worse our outlook may be on the fate of humankind. The magnitude of the universe and our own smallness are in such contrast that it seems we are in a hopeless situation, even if you take into account only life's perspective on the earth. However, the study of the universe may bring some unexpected surprises and humankind may after all have a future, particularly if we decipher the mystery by whom and how the universe was developed.

This study has assumed the position of considering intelligent design in the origin of the universe, but with the addition of proposing that any existence of intelligent design would suggest corollary problems that must be scientifically testable.

INFORMATION CONTROL IN LIFE ORIGIN

Since the late 1950s, advances in molecular biology and biochemistry have radically improved our understanding of the mechanisms of the biological cell. The cell, the basic building block of life, possesses the ability to store, process, and transmit information. Furthermore, it can use information to steer the most fundamental metabolic processes. Cells are in fact complex information processing systems that support activities.

Information (on what and how to produce proteins) transfer within a cell takes place from DNA (deoxyribonucleic acid) to a set of 20 different kinds of amino acid molecules to assemble into each given type of protein. Protein molecules may be thought of as the workhorses of life. Some proteins act as *enzymes* with such jobs as catalyzing digestion of the proteins we eat. Other proteins, such as *hemoglobin* in blood, help carry *oxygen* from the lungs to the rest of the body. Still, others form connective and supportive tissue. Proteins constitute a large portion of the mass of every life form and are necessary in the diets of all animals. DNA is the chemical substance found in all living organisms which directs the production of proteins. DNA contains genetic information passed on to new cells and new organisms. DNA stores millions of specifically arranged chemicals called *nucleotides* or bases within the DNA's structure. The sequence of nucleotides (represented by A - Adenine, C - Cytosine, G - Guanine, and T - Thymine, horizontally linked by hydrogen bonds) in the DNA molecule convey (through the sugar-phosphate backbone) precise biochemical information that direct protein synthesis within the cell[1].

The chief function of all living cells is assembling protein molecules according to instructions (information) coded in DNA molecules. DNA is like the "operating system" of a cell, which contains coded (in different configurations of A, C, G, T) instructions of how to handle proteins. Different segments of DNA create (according to these coded instructions) *genes* that are organized in *chromosomes*, each of which has a specific function. (There are also *epigenetics*, individual genes, which can be turned on or off). All these components of a cell are information-driven. The nucleus of a cell, containing the chromosomes, is a "library" containing life's instructions. The chromosomes would be the "bookshelves" inside the library; the DNA would be "individual books" on each shelf; genes would be the "chapters" in each book; and the nucleotide bases making the strands of DNA would be the "words" (A, C, G, T) on the pages of the individual books. The information-communication messenger of DNA is RNA, which transfers "DNA-heredity patterns" between a cell's components (mostly proteins) in order to facilitate their replication and to maintain the organism.

The coded sequence of bases contains a unique pattern setting forth the chemical specifications for a living creature. These sequences of DNA pairs are, by definition, genes (special messages), which govern the chemistry of life and determine all inborn characteristics, from blood type to eye color. A human has 100,000 genes packed into 23 pairs of chromosomes (Brennan, 1992).

Writing down the DNA sequence of one human genome demands approximately 3,000 volumes of data each the size of the Bible (containing 1 million letters, punctuation marks, and spaces as estimated by Ayala [1992]).

Rupert Sheldrake (Briggs & Peat, 1984) reasoned that since every cell in an organism has exactly the same DNA code, it is difficult to see how this identical DNA configuration of each cell could be distinguished from one cell in the brain tissue and another cell in the muscle tissue. Sheldrake developed a hypothesis that there exists a state in which DNA and the forming processes of an organism are mediated. This mediator is a complex set of *hidden fields* that direct all stages of morphogenesis and acts to establish the final form that things take, including behavior. He calls this the "hypothesis of formative causation."

Yale biologist Harold Saxton Burr (1982) discovered *L-fields*, which are results of different patterns of electricity for different types of organisms—trees, slime molds, human beings—and found that each type of organism has a similar pattern. Changes in the L-field reflect a change in one's mood or a stage of an illness or his/her movements in the environment. Burr speculated that the L-fields are not a cause of evolutionary changes but that they direct the changes[2].

Figure 18-1 illustrates the information-communication model of a living cell. The information at T=0 and t=0 reflect the hidden fields of regulating formation of an underlying cell, where T=0 is the first time of the universe and t=0 is the first time of a given cell. Other components of a cell, such as DNA-ases, reverse transcriptases, and non-peptide cellular components (*steroids, flavins, GTP, GDP, ATP, lipids, sphingolipids, cholesterol, inositols*, etc., are not shown in the model. The proteins exposed in the model reflect the aggregated concept of all kinds of proteins encoded by DNA (*peptides, hormones, enzymes, cytokines, chemokines, skeletal proteins, accessory proteins, receptors, allosteric modulators*, etc.).

Figure 18-1. Info-communication model of a living cell where T = 0 is the first time of the universe and 0 is the first time of a given cell

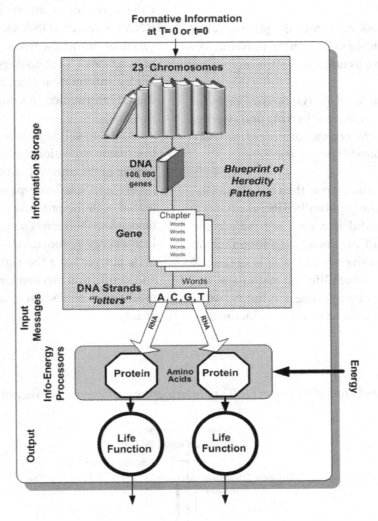

The informational properties of living systems suggest that "no materialism" can suffice to explain the degree of complexity of origin of life. The progress made in molecular biology and the information sciences have revolutionized our understanding of the complexity of life, they have also made it progressively more difficult to conceive how life might have arisen by purely mechanistic means (Meyer, 2007).

The discovery of the role of information in life's processes took place in the second part of the 20th century and is in strong contradiction with the 19th-century theories of life, which stated that life was built of cells which were in themselves no more complex than a blob of gelatin. The more we know about life's microstructures, the more the role of information in life's functioning is emphasized. Could the same be said about the role of information in the processes of matter?

HYPOTHESIS OF THE INFORMATED UNIVERSE

This study is conducted from the point of view that humankind has a chance in the universe. As a result of this, we assume the following:

Hypothesis 1: Our local life system is a hierarchical info-energy system, in which the first steering information came from either outside of the Milky Way Galaxy or outside of our universe.

If this hypothesis is true, then the physicists' effort in defining the grand unified theories (GUT)[3] cannot be successful if it does not include the integrating role of information-communication processes in the universe. This role is suggested in Figure 18-2, in which life and matter are presented as one info-energy process. A link between DNA and the rest of the universe is maintained by the human information-communication process. This is a digital process now being continually enhanced which converts internal, analog DNA/RNA processes. (DNA seems to consist of a long series of on-off switches, if it is a digital chain of reactions.) This conversion reflects a flow of analog information from/to a brain and to/from digital information in a mind and the role of hidden fields[4].

A key to solving the mechanism of information-communication synchronization of life and matter in the universe is the ability to define the nature and relationships of super-quantum potential with the processes of eventual intelligent design and their relationships with the remaining info-energy systems. At this time, our knowledge does not yet have the right tools to investigate and define this mechanism. At the moment this mechanism may seem to us as of a supernatural character.

Figure 18-2. Grand unified theories (GUT) of information and energy interactions

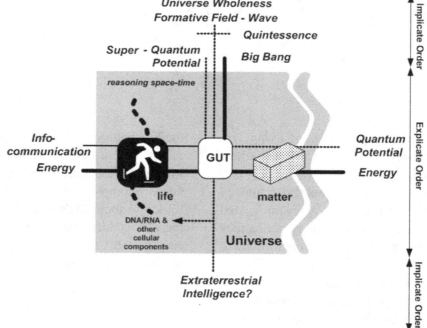

The impossibility[5] of defining the GUT by the physicists results from the fact that they do not include the information, "intelligent design," ET, quantum potential and quintessence force factors in their assumptions and calculations. The present level of our knowledge cannot define that type of information empirically. However, we should be aware that this information may come from beyond our physical reality and that this may be the key to solving the logic of the universe.

The survival of human civilization in space-time may be better understood if we first investigate the influence of intelligent or other eventual design on the expansion or contraction of the universe. This task can be associated with the issue: what is the universe?

Albert Einstein approached this task from the gravity point of view and he elaborated on the gravity equation[6] (also calling it God's equation), in which the shape of the universe depends upon its mass and the cosmological constant λ. According to this equation, the larger the mass of the universe within a given confined space, the more curved is its space, since greater gravity strongly curves space around its mass. The latest research of the universe's shape confirms that it is expanding while remaining flat within our limits of measurement.

Physicists and astronomers are fascinated by the task of defining the universe's geometry. The geometry of the universe is determined by cosmology, which attempts to define how the three-dimensional universe evolved through time:

- A spherically-shaped universe starts to expand (at an increasing rate) and then starts to collapse back on itself ($\Omega < 1$)
- A cycloidally-shaped universe ($\Omega > 1$)
- A flat universe ($\Omega = 1$) will expand at a decreasing rate

Here Ω (omega) denotes the cosmological ratio of the actual density of the universe to its critical density in the Einstein gravity equation. Figure 18-3 illustrates the universe's shape defined by the cosmological constant.

Figure 18-3. The universe's shape defined by the cosmological constant Ω (M. Kermanshani-http//www. toevault.com/articles/20/1/Shape-of-Universe/Page1.html Retrieved November 26, 2007)

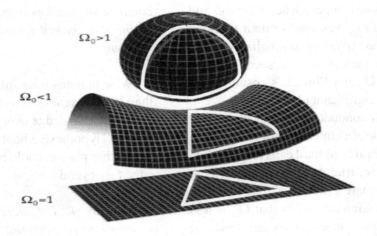

But what happens if the intelligent or other design of the universe takes place from within the same universe, which then might affect its own expansion, geometry, and destiny? If there is some "funny energy" out in space, something that we cannot see, feel, or detect but which acts on the very fabric of space-time, making it expand faster than it would otherwise, then matter and the gravitational force it produces would not be alone (Aczel, 1999). Both dark matter and dark energy are very recent hypotheses, not even thought of until a few years ago, and now they are thought to comprise 94%-96% of the effective mass of the universe.

Having in mind something unexpected, cosmologists decided to allow a portion of the total Ω to reflect the part due to matter (Ω_M), and a remaining part to identify the "unexpected energy" (Ω_Δ) (something which resembles Einstein's old cosmological constant λ). A new parameter determining the geometry of the universe is:

$$\Omega = \Omega_M + \Omega_\Delta$$

This equation means that regardless of the Ω_M, the Ω_Δ can be enough by itself to push the universe in the expansion mode forever.

In 1988, Saul Perlmutter from Lawrence Berkeley National Laboratory and his colleagues began the Supernova Cosmology Project to estimate the values of the omega parameters by studying the light curves of type I_a supernovae. They did find that the value of Ω_M was smaller than anybody had expected. The exploding stars halfway across the cosmos were pushed by an unseen force and the co-efficient Ω_Δ and Einstein's cosmological constant λ were significant (Aczel, 1999).

This research conducted by Saul Perlmutter confirmed the role of an intelligent or other design in the universe. Paul Steinhard calls this invisible force *quintessence*, after Aristotle's fifth element of nature to designate a presently unknown fifth physical force. Steinhard insists that Ω_M is less than 1 (the universe continues to expand) and that

Ω_Δ has some fundamental meaning for physics (Aczel, 1999).

To understand the mechanisms of intelligent or other design, super-quantum potential and *quintessence*, it is necessary to define the architecture of the universe, which so far has been investigated mostly by physicists as "civil engineers of the universe." The architecture of the universe is shown in Figure 18-4. Its main hypotheses are:

Hypothesis 2: Among more than billions of solar-like systems in the universe, some should have the right conditions for the existence of life, because in such an enormous set of planets, statistically the Earth should not be the only life-friendly environment.

This hypothesis can be shown highly probable with statistics, although it cannot be proved empirically by science at this time. (Each statement in this case is just an educated guess.) Polish astronomer Aleksander Wolszczan discovered the first planet outside of our solar system at the end of the 20th century, which indicated that the universe may have conditions able to support life outside of our own planet (Eduscript, 2007).

Hypothesis 3: Life in the universe may have been present long before it existed on the Earth (at most 9.4 B years after the Big Bang) and therefore could have developed its own more advanced scientific-technical knowledge and civilization wisdom.

Wise humans have inhabited earth for more than 200,000 years, but we have applied scientific-technical knowledge over just the last 500 years or so. If Hypothesis 3 holds true, living creatures from other planets could have developed knowledge far beyond ours.

Hypothesis 4: Extraterrestrial intelligence[7], super-quantum potential and the quintessence

Figure 18-4. The universe architecture

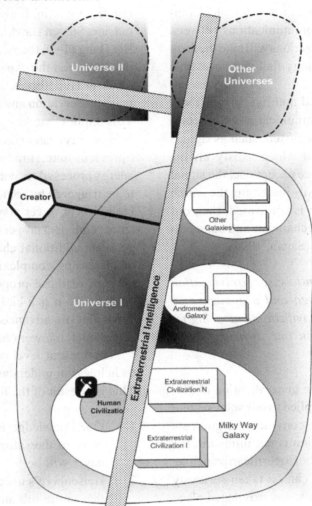

forces reach other solar systems (including the Earth's) from other civilizations or from other universes which are at a much higher developmental level than that of our own.

Carl Sagan (2000), one of the most prominent American astronomers, stated that there are many manifestations of extraterrestrial intelligence, which contemporary astronomy does not understand, for example, quasars' natural or

very high- intensity gravitational waves that are coming from the center of our galaxy remain a puzzle. He estimated that there are at least a million other stars and planets on which today there are advanced civilizations. Also, there is at least a fair probability that there are many civilizations beaming signals our way. However, because of the vast distances between stars, there will be no cosmic dialogues by radio transmission. (One conversation in a round-trip communication may take 600 of our years). Our civilization does not have enough time and money for such communications. Perhaps communications between two very advanced civilizations will take the form of a science and technology that is inaccessible to us now.

So far, we have found nothing certain about extraterrestrial (ET) communications. Some tantalizing "events" have occurred, such as signals that have been recorded which satisfy all the criteria for ET intelligence except one: the signal never repeats. We have only just begun the search for ET intelligence. If it is confirmed, then our view of the universe's mechanisms and ourselves will be forever changed (Sagan, 1997).

Hypothesis 5: The sequential rise of a civilization requires intelligent design and a quintessence force, coming from a civilization at a higher developmental level than our own or from a creator.

This hypothesis is the generalization of Hypothesis 4, which was applied to our solar system only. However, there are convincing arguments that the human civilization is not unique in the universe[8]. According to the Copernican principle, no cosmological theory can be taken seriously that puts our own galaxy at any privileged place in the universe. Which means that a civilization cannot be created by itself; it requires "bylaws" from outside.

Hypothesis 6: The triggering of the Big Bang requires the existence of the primeval atom or info-energy process (first signals) that must have come from a higher civilization. However, at the moment of the appearance of the first universe, this signal could only have come from its "creator," which can be god or nature.

This hypothesis is the generalization of Hypothesis 5, except that it applies to more than just our universe, whose Big Bang signals we can register. It also confirms that any universe cannot rise from within. It also requires "bylaws" from outside. Steven Hawking assumes that before the Big Bang (T=0) there had to be a primeval atom[9] that triggered the explosion.

Both Hypotheses 5 and 6 accept the laws of mass preservation and information preservation. This implies that the consecutive formation of an info-energy system is only a transformation from a previous state. However, information as an info-energy process does not rise from "nothing;" it has to be triggered by something or somebody. (The biologists however may question this statement, since "emergent properties", whereby systems can generate additional characteristics as a product of increasing complexity, even when there was no sign of those properties at lower orders of complexity. It is a biological process, involving capacities in advanced animals that have no precedents in lower ones.)

The present level of our knowledge renders us helpless in understanding the universe's size. This is a result of the following:

1. Our knowledge is not complete nor even close to the saturation point, and perhaps never will be[10]
2. Heisenberg's uncertainty principle implies that in the sub-atomic world there are certain kinds of information that cannot be learned in specific detail, because the act of measuring changes what we are trying to measure
3. Perhaps a "creator" does not want us to know his/her system of ruling the universe[11]

On the other hand, whether the universe is stable or unstable, open or closed, contracting or expanding, flat or spiral, has no practical meaning for humans, because these processes take place in very long periods, measured in millions and billions of years. Whether or not the universe will last 50-60 billion years does not have practical meaning for humans. But this does not mean that it is not necessary to conduct research on the universe, because some solutions may have an influence upon our short lives.

Recent observations by the Hubble Space Telescope and the Wilkinson Microwave Anisotropy Probe (WMAP) have found that the bulk of the universe is made of dark energy, which acts through dark force (the author's assumption). Current estimates of the mass/energy budget place dark energy (dark force) at roughly 70% of the universe, while visible matter and dark matter make up less than 30%. Most of the universe is made of something we know nothing about (Wilson, 2007). This observation allows for the following hypothesis:

Hypothesis 7: At the moment of the Big Bang, dark energy interacted with the united four normal forces, composed of the strong force (binding atomic nuclei), electromagnetic force (holding atoms together), weak force (controlling radioactive decay), and gravity. This interaction perhaps was triggered by the external force, coming from some external environment (universe).

As of the moment the physicists think that the four basic forces were originally united by the density and temperature of the original blob. Gravity separated out first, then the strong force, leaving the "electroweak" force which split only sometime later. (One can occasionally wonder if there is another split sometime in our future.) If there were initially only two forces (united and dark) active during the Big Bang (and up until a certain span of time over which the united force separated into the four normal forces), this idea may lead to the assumption that in fact the united force and dark force are also coming from a common force, which was perhaps the external force, coming from—T (?). If this is true, the source of the external force could be the external universe. The proposed role of the external force in this process of forming and operating our (internal) universe is illustrated in Figure 18-5.

The "controlling" function of the external force, if it does exist, should be involved in all cross-roads of the seven basic forces which rule the universes, as illustrated in Figure 18-6. This controlling function is perhaps based on a kind of quantum-potential signal and other ones, which we do not know at this moment and which are the subject of searches by several centers, including the SETI.

This study suggests that further research on the universe should include the role of information-communication processes, ET intelligence, and supernatural processes (intelligent design). Space research brings solutions in technology and medicine that can be applied in our civilization.

Up till now physicists, astronomers, and cosmologists have made good progress in deciphering the universe's construction and its development, but mostly at the level of matter and even self-contained matter. Taking into account the role of humans and the amount of external steering necessary, we need to take a look at the universe as a system (U_s), which can be defined by the following equations:

The Contents Equation of the Universe System[12]:

$$U_s = I_d \cup I_e \cup Q_{sqp} \cup Q_{ss} \cup [(H, R_h), (L, R_l), (M, V_e, R_m, R_{qp}, R_{ot})$$

where:

I_d – Intelligent design information
I_e – Extraterrestrial information
Q_{sqp} – Super-quantum potential
Q_{ss} – Quintessence (external) force
H – set of humans
R_h – set of structure-forming relationships among humans and their environment, including information-communication processes, DNA, cyberspace processes
L – set of living organisms of lower order than humans

Figure 18-5. External force as the source of other forces

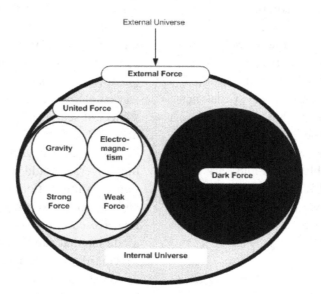

Figure 18-6. Steering role of info-communication processes in the dynamics of the seven grand forces of the universe

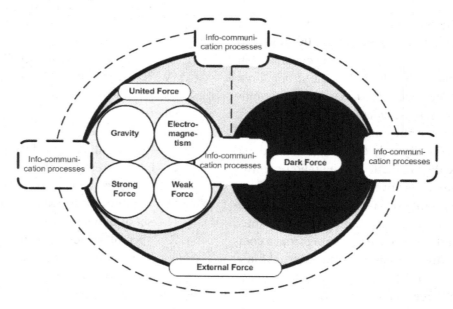

R_l – set of structure-forming relationships among living organisms

M – set of energy-matter

V_e – Vacuum energy (energy for the oscillating creation-destruction of virtual particles)

R_m – set of structure-forming forces

R_{qp} – set of structure-forming quantum potential

R_{ot} – set of other structures

To define such a dynamic character as the universe, one must escape Einstein's 4-dimensional space-time continuum (4-D). By including the role of information-communication processes and other forces, we will deal with a 10-dimensional (10-D) space-time of the universe (at least in this study, though it may not be necessary otherwise, reality can be even more complex). The new 6 dimensions are: information-communication human processes, their cyberspace, ET (extraterrestrial intelligence), eventual intelligent design (supernatural information), quantum potential, and super-quantum potential.

The task of defining the final theory of everything is unfeasible at our present level of knowledge[13]. The range of difficulties was exemplified by a mathematician from Oxford, H. Aldersley-Williams (1996), who analyzed a topology of 4-D space-time and apparently discovered a strange relationship between 4-D space-time surfaces and "exotic" physical phenomena, unique for 4-D space-time. Four-dimensional geometry is pathologically "badly behaved." One of the best specialists in 4-D space-time was the Russian mathematician Lew Pontriagin (1908-1988), who may have been able to understand that space because he was blind; his mind was not confined to the normal arrangement. One can imagine how complex 10-D space-time is, particularly if in the synthesis of the mechanism of the 10-D universe one must go beyond the quantum theory, the string theory and include the theories of entropy, fuzzy sets, imaginary numbers and perhaps others, as for example, the currently popular cutting-edge

theory, which is called "brane theory," shortened from "membrane theory," which suggests that the determining factors of the universe are a collection of approaching-but-not-intersecting planes of peculiar geometry. Gravity, for example, is so weak because it leaks between branes.

CONCLUSION

Steven Weinberg (1993), who, with collaborators, defined a part of the GUT, is optimistic and states that this task reminds him of geographical discoveries in the 19th century, when pioneers were moving towards the North Pole and gradually were discovering new territories, mountains, rivers and so forth, until there was nothing left to discover[14].

Perhaps during this century and millennium we will discover more and pursue this task of defining the final theory, or perhaps it is too soon and we will need another, let us say 10 million years, to do it. Maybe there is no such theory. Or perhaps there is a "creator" that does not want us to know it?

A. Further Research Directions

- Investigate how information-communication processes and systems impact the physical processes and systems of the Earth, and what is the impact of this interdependence on civilization.
- Investigate the grand unified theory in a more complex framework than the physicists do, in order to find interdependence between living organisms and "dead" matter, which can lead to better understanding how humans can survive in a very competitive nature.
- Investigate the possibility of life on other planets and how it can benefit humans, even in a long-term horizon.
- Investigate what kinds of technologies must be developed in order to use other planets by humans.

B.   Research Opportunities

*   The research opportunity is in analyzing the nature of the Earth and universe in the information-communication—"dead" matter framework. So far, physicists analyze the universe in terms of four forces, which do not take into account a dynamic force such as information-communication.

C.   Additional Ideas

*   If the Earth and universe are products of randomness, what is the chance that humans could have appeared? What kinds of strategies should humans develop and apply in order to be knowledgably aware of their chances? Do we have a long-term future? If not, what should be our short-term strategy? If there is hope, what should be our long-term strategy?

D.   Rationale

*   The key to the answer how to act in order to be successful in the long term, that is, not go extinct, is a research strategy which can only come from further and more profound research on the universe's dynamics. Nowadays, the 21st century is adding information-communication issues to 20th-century physics, which up till now have been only matter-oriented. Perhaps in the coming centuries, science may add to our knowledge other universe-oriented processes which are black boxes at this time. To open this kind of a black box of universe, one must understand how its complexity is a product of confrontation between order and chaos. We want to know what kind of information-communication impulses turned a primordial soup of simple molecules into the first living cell—and what the origin of life some four billion years ago can tell us

about technological innovation today. Are they a product of randomness or a distance control? Particularly very interesting is how the random process of Darwinian natural selection managed to produce such complex system as humans? Is there a sort of information-communication spark involvement? Certainly, it is a dynamic process and cannot be driven by "dead" matter's transformations only. What controls that transformation? If we apply a term "control" it implies "signal" flow and so also, information-communication dynamics. Needless to say, that kind of process will lead to a new paradigm of the universe's architecture in the coming centuries.

E. Additional Reading

Boslough, J. *Stephen Hawking's universe*. New York: Avon Books.

Britt, R. (2003). *Age of universe revised, again*. Retrieved October 12, 2006, from http://www.space.com.

Burr, H. (1982). *Blueprint for immortality: The electric patterns of live*. London: Neville Spearman.

Capra, F., & Steindl-Rast, D. (1991). *Belonging to the universe*. San Francisco: Harpers.

Capra, F. (1988). *The turning point*. New York: Bantam Books.

Einstein, A. (1934). *The world as I see it*. New York: Covici Friede Publishers.

_____ (2001). *Relativity: The special and the general theory*. London: Routledge.

Gore, A. (1993). *Earth in the balance*. New York: A Plume Book.

Harwit, M. (2003). Chemical composition of the early universe. *The Astrophysical Journal, 589*(1), 53-57.

Hawking, S. (1988). *A history of time*. New York: Bantam Books.

Hawley, J., & Holcomb, K. (1998). *Foundations of modern cosmology*. Oxford, UK: Oxford University Press.

Hinshaw, G. (2005). *Tests of the big bang: The CMB*. Retrieved October 8, 2006, from http://www.NASA WMA.org.

_____ (2006a). *New three year results on the oldest light in the universe*. Retrieved October 8, 2006, from http://www.NASA WMA.org.

_____ (2006b). *What is the universe made of?*. Retrieved October 8, 2006, from http://www.NASA WMA.org.

Kobulnicky, E., & Skillman, D. (1997). Chemical composition of the early universe. *Bulletin of the American Astronomical Society, 29,* 1329.

Lineweaver, C., & Davis, T. (2005). Misconceptions about the big bang. *Scientific American, 292*(3), 36.

Luminet, J. & Roukema, B. (1998). Topology of the universe: Theory and observations. *Proceedings of the Cosmology School*. Cargese, Corsica, August.

Mandolesi, N., Calzolari, P., Cortiglioni, S., Delpino, F., & Sironi, G. (1986). Large-scale homogeneity of the universe measured by the microwave background. *Letters to Nature 319,* 751-753.

Neil, J., Spergel, C., Starkman, G., & Komatsu, E. (2004). Constraining the topology of the universe. *Physical Review Letters*. 92 Retrieved March 10, 2007, from http://arxiv.org/abs/astro-ph/0310233.

Penrose, R. (2005). *The road to reality*. New York: Alfred A. Knopf.

Poundstone, W. (1985). *The recursive universe. cosmic complexity and the limits of scientific knowledge*. Chicago: Contemporary Books.

Sagan, C. (1994). *A vision of the human future in space. Pale blue dot*. New York: Random House.

_____ (1997). *Billions & billions*. New York: Ballantine Books.

_____ (2000). *Cosmic connection*. Cambridge, UK: Cambridge University Press.

Wright, E. (2004). *Big bang nucleosynthesis*. Berkeley, CA: UC.

_____ (2005). *Age of the universe*. Berkeley, CA: UC.

REFERENCES

Aczel, A. (1999). *God's equation*. New York: Delta.

Aldersley-Williams, H. (1996). May the force be with us?. *The Independent, December*(2), 20.

Ayala, J. (1992). *Origin of species*. Whitsett, NC: Carolina Biological Supply.

Behe, M. (1998). Intelligent design theory as a tool for analyzing biochemical systems. In: W. Dembski (Ed.), *Mere creatio*. Downers Grove, IL: InterVarsity Press.

Bode, E. (1970). *The first eastern morning*. Rome: Biblical Institute Press.

Bohm, D., & Hiley, B. (1993). *Undivided universe: An ontological interpretation of quantum theory*. London: Routledge.

Bohm, D., & Peat, F. (1987). *Science, order and creativity*. New York: Bantman Books.

Borel, E. (1962). *Probabilities of life*. New York: Dover Publications.

Boyer, P. (2001). *Religion explained*. New York: Basic Books.

Brennan, R. (1992). *Dictionary of scientific literacy.* New York: John Wiley & Sons, Inc.

Briggs, J., & Peat, F.(1984). *Looking glass universe. The emerging science of wholeness.* New York: Simon & Schuster.

Brown, L. (1996). *State of the world. A worldwatch institute report on progress toward a sustainable society.* New York: W. W. Norton & Co.

Deevey, E. (1960). The human population. *Scientific American, 203*(3), 194.

Dembski, W. (1998). *Redesigning science.* In: W. Dembski (Ed.), *Mere creation.* Downers Grove, IL: InterVarsity Press.

Iberall, A. (1972). *Toward a general science of viable systems.* New York: McGraw-Hill Book Co.

Louria, D. (2002). Second thoughts on extending life-spans. *The Futurist, 36*(1), 44-48.

Nielsen, K. (1993). No! A defense of atheism. In: J. Moreland & K. Nielsen (Eds.), *Does a god exist?.* Amherst, NY: Prometheus Books. S. 48.

Meyer, S. (2007). *DNA by design. An inference to the best explanation for the origin of biological information.* Retrieved November 26, 2007, from http://www.macrodevelopment.org/library/meyer.html.

Overman, D. (1997). *A case against accident and self-organization.* Lanham, MD: Rowman & Littlefield Publishers, Inc.

Peat, F. (1988). *Synchronicity. The bridge between matter and mind.* New York: Bantman Books.

Sagan, C. (1997). *Billions & billions.* New York: Ballantine Books.

_____ (2000). *Cosmic connection. An extraterrestrial perspective.* Cambridge, UK: Cambridge University Press

Struve, O. (1962). *The universe.* Cambridge, MA: The MIT Press.

Teilhard de Chardin, P. (1994). *The phenomenon of humanity.* Portland, OR: Sussex Academic Press.

Weinberg, S. (1993). *Dreams of a final theory.* New York: Vintage Books.

Wilson, R. (2007). The universe, detecting the signature of the big bang. In: L. Glover, A. Chalkin, P. Daniels, A. Gianopoulos, & J. Malay (Eds.), *National geographic encyclopedia of space.* Washington, D.C.: National Geographic.

Eduscript. (2007). Retrieved November 26, 2007, from http://www.eduskrypt.pl/polish_astronomers_have_discovered_an_extrasolar_planet-info-6706.html.

ENDNOTES

[1] The amount of DNA in a cell varies roughly with the complexity of the organism. Bacteria have several million nucleotides of DNA, fungi have several tens of millions, flowering plants may have several hundred billion and humans come in at around three billion nucleotides.

[2] Despite Burr's rigorous adherence to acceptable scientific methods, his hypothesis did not receive much attention.

[3] Sometimes this is also called TOE—theory of everything.

[4] Hidden fields mentioned by Rupert Sheldrake.

[5] Theoretical physicists continue to search for a "theory of everything" (TOE). The most promising candidates are "string theories," which propose that sub-atomic particles are point-like but are strings so tiny that they appear to us as points. It is thought that these strings vibrate at different frequencies, like

a violin string playing different notes, and each different vibration is seen in our world as a different particle. Some theories predict the existence of new particles, which have not yet been detected. They should be associated with information-communication processes and super-quantum potential and quintessence force. A mysterious 'fifth element'—in addition to air, earth, fire and water—which held the moon and stars in place. Quintessence, some cosmologists say, is an exotic kind of energy field that pushes particles away from each other, overpowering gravity and the other fundamental forces.

[6] $R_{\mu\nu} - 1/2 g_{\mu\nu} R - \lambda g_{\mu\nu} = -8\pi G T_{\mu\nu}$ where $R_{\mu\nu}$ is the Ricci tensor, R is its trace, λ is the cosmological constant, $g_{\mu\nu}$ is the measure of distance—the metric tensor of the geometry of space, G is Newton's gravitational constant, $T_{\mu\nu}$ is the tensor capturing the properties of energy, momentum and matter.

[7] The search for other beings in the universe has been a common theme for the last two centuries. Science fiction writers, including Jules Verne, Ray Bradbury, Arthur Clarke, Isaac Asimov and Stanislaw Lem, as well as such popular entertainment as *Star Trek*, have been fascinated by the possible existence of extraterrestrials. In 1960, Frank Drake sent signals to Epsilon Eridani and Tau Ceti from Green Bank Radio Astronomy Observatory, in Project Ozma. This was the first real attempt to contact extraterrestrial species. A search for extraterrestrial intelligence (SETI) program was initiated by NASA in 1992 and canceled in 1993. Since then, the SETI Institute in Mountain View California has initiated a privately-founded project in Phoenix. Another SETI program is privately funded—Megachannel Extraterrestrial Assay (META), sponsored by the Planetary Society. The major problem with SETI is the distances involved to receive a signal and figuring out what language to use. What are the chances of hearing from another intelligence? No one really knows. We may be receiving signals from other beings right now, but are not yet able to interpret their way of communication. It is interesting to note that we have not had any contact that we know of with other civilizations, either because they have disappeared or they contacted us in systems that we do not know. Perhaps we may still receive such contacts or perhaps there are no such civilizations. Another hypothesis, well known among sci-fi buffs, argues that earth is a "nature preserve," deliberately left alone until we meet some qualifying status.

[8] There is an opinion that it was a fireball at a diameter of 100,000,000 miles and temperature $10^{10}\,^{\circ}K$ (Iberall, 1972).

[9] "When the number of factors coming into play in a phenomenological complex is too large, scientific method in most cases fails us" (Albert Einstein).

[10] This idea was developed in genesis, with the tree of the fruit of knowledge.

[11] One can define the universe system as a hierarchical one.

[12] The string theory at least combines quantum mechanics and gravity in a way that explains how the gravitational force is carried, but if a string represents a gravity quantum, it can be treated also as a information-communication quantum (similarly to a guitar string under tension, which generates different musical notes).

[13] The task of defining the final theory is according to Karl Popper not possible, because "every explanation may be further explained by a theory or conjecture of a higher degree of universality."

434

About the Contributors

Prof. Dr. Andrew Targowski was engaged in the development of social computing in totalitarian Poland (*INFOSTRADA and Social Security # for 38 million citizens-PESEL,* 1972) and received political asylum in the U.S. during the crackdown on solidarity in 1981. He has been a professor of business information systems at Western Michigan University since 1980. He published 21 books on information technology, history, and political science (*Red Fascism,* 1982) in English and Polish. During the 1990s, he was a director of the TeleCITY of Kalamazoo Project, one of the first digital cities in the U.S. He investigates the role of information-communication in enterprise, economy, and civilization. He is a president of the International Society for the Comparative Study of Civilizations and a former chairman of the Advisory Council of the Information Resources Management Association (1995-2003).

Dr. Ali. M. Metwalli was born in Egypt and received his bachelor's degree in commerce from Cairo University. He has a MBA from Siena Collage in New York State and he earned his PhD in business administration from St. Louis University in Missouri. He has served in the healthcare industry in various executive, research, and consulting positions since 1965. He moved to Grand Rapids in 1980 to teach for Western Michigan University and served as director of the MBA program in Grand Rapids campus from 1985 until the end of 1999. He continues to teach at WMU, conduct research, and consult independently. He is a co-founder of MW Stone Importers, LTD. Dr. Metwalli has served as a chairman of the Board (Shora Committee) of the Islamic Mosque and Religious Institute in Grand Rapids for the last two years. He served for six years as a member of the board of directors of the West Central Michigan American Red Cross. He also served on the advisory council for the American College of Healthcare Executives, and is active in numerous other civic and university activities. He has a long list of publications in a number of academic journals focusing on global business and finance. His last publication in 2006 is a book in international finance that focuses on mergers and acquisitions in Asia.

Index